MON NATIONALISM AND CIVIL WAR IN BURMA

A major contribution to the literature of Burmese history and politics, this book traces the rich and tragic history of the Mon people of Burma and Thailand, from the pre-colonial era to the present day. This vivid account of ethnic politics and civil war situates the story of Mon nationalism within the 'big picture' of developments in Burma, Thailand and the region. Primarily an empirical study, it also addresses issues of identity and anticipates Burmese politics in the new millennium. A particular feature of the book is its first-hand descriptions of insurgency and displacement, drawn from the author's experiences as an aid worker in the war zone.

Ashley South is an independent consultant, specialising in ethnic politics, displacement and humanitarian issues in Burma. He has lived and worked in Burma and Thailand for seven years, first as a teacher and later as a co-ordinator of a major international relief operation. He has visited Burma more than 50 times, and observed the conflict at close quarters, working with Burmese ethnic minority refugees and many key insurgent leaders.

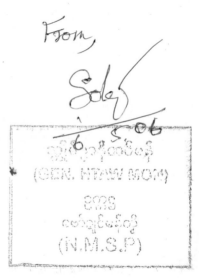
MON NATIONALISM AND CIVIL WAR IN BURMA

The Golden Sheldrake

Ashley South

Routledge
Taylor & Francis Group

LONDON AND NEW YORK

First published in hardback 2003
Reprinted 2005
First published in paperback 2005
by Routledge
2 Park Square, Milton Park, Abingdon, Oxfordshire OX14 4RN

Simultaneously published in the USA and Canada
by Routledge
270 Madison Ave, New York, NY 10016, USA

Routledge is an imprint of the Taylor & Francis Group

© 2003, 2005 Ashley South

Originally typeset in Sabon by Laserscript Ltd
Printed and bound in India by Replika Press Pvt. Ltd

British Library Cataloguing in Publication Data
A catalogue record for this book is available from the British Library

Library of Congress Cataloging in Publication Data
A catalog record for this book has been requested

ISBN 0–7007–1609–2 (hbk)
ISBN 0–415–37411–1(Taylor & Francis Asia Pacific paperback edition)

Contents

Contents

List of Maps and Tables

Maps

Tables

Note Regarding Names and Titles

1. **Burma or Myanmar?** In June 1989 the State Law and Order Restoration Council (SLORC) re-named the state *Myanmar Naing-Ngan*. At the same time, a number of other place names were changed – e.g. Rangoon became *Yangon*, Pegu became *Bago*, Moulmein became *Mawlamyine*. In some cases, these changes represented a 'Burmanisation' of indigenous names; in others, the new word more closely resembled local pronunciation than had the old colonial-era romanisation. This book will follow the majority of commentators in retaining 'Burma'.

2. **Burmese, Burman and *Bama*.** 'Burmese' refers to the language and the country as a whole, 'Burman' to the *Bama* majority ethnic group.

3. **Personal Titles.** 'U' is the respectful title for an adult Burman male (e.g. U Nu), 'Daw' for a woman (e.g. Daw Aung San Suu Kyi). In Mon, the title for an adult male who has spent some time in the monkhood is 'Nai'; a male who has not entered the *sangha* is known as 'Mehm'; the honorific for a Mon woman is 'Mi'.

Acronyms and Abbreviations

Mon Organisations

In Burma:

NMSP – New Mon State Party. Principal Mon insurgent organisation, which agreed a ceasefire with the government in 1995; established 1958.
NMSP Departments: **MNEC/MNHC** – Mon National Education/Health Committee; **MWO** – Mon Women's Organisation.
MNLA – Mon National Liberation Army. Armed wing of the NMSP; established 1971.

MAMD – Mon Army Mergui District. Breakaway MNLA faction; established 1996.

RRA – Ramanya Restoration Army (or Monland Return Army). MAMD faction; established 1997.

MIO – Monland Independence Organisation. RRA political wing; established 2000.

HRP – Hongsawatoi Restoration Party; established 2001.

MRA – Monland Restoration Army (incorporating Mon National Defence Army). Breakaway MNLA faction; armed wing of HRP

ARMA – All Ramanya Mon Association. Cultural association; established 1939.
MLCC – Mon Literature and Culture Committee. ARMA-affiliated cultural association.
MYO – Mon Youth Organisation. Established 1941.

MNDF – Mon National Democratic Front. Political party; established 1988; outlawed in 1992.

In Thailand:

Burmese Mon groups: OMYMU – Overseas Mon Young Monks Union; **MYMDAG** – Mon Young Monks Democracy Action Group; **OMNSO** –

Overseas Mon National Students Organisation (branches in North America and Australia); **MIS** – Mon Information Service; **HRFM** – Human Rights Foundation of Monland; **IMNA** – Independent Mon News Agency; **MCL** – Mon Culture and Literature Survival Project; **MWHRG** – Mon Women's Human Rights Group; **MAA** – Mon Alliance Association; **OMNNDF** – Overseas Mon National Democratic Front; **MYLO** – Mon Youth Liberty Organisation; **MYPO** – Mon Youth Progressive Organisation.

Thai Mon groups: TRA – Thai Ramon Association; **MYC** – Mon Youth Community; **MLPO** – Mon Literature Promotion Organisation; **CRMCH** – Committee for Revitalisation of Mon Cultural Heritage; **MNU** – Mon National University.

MUL – Mon Unity League. Mon nationalist 'umbrella front' (incorporating the United Mon Patriotic Forces [Overseas] – UMPF[O]); established 1996.

Overseas Mon Organisations:

AMA – Australia Mon Association; **AMNSU** – All Mon National Students Union (Australia); **MRC** – Monland Restoration Council (USA); **MCC** – Mon Community of Canada (incorporating Mon Canadian Association – **MCA**); **MCS** – Mon Cultural Society (Canada); **MIN** – Mon Information Network (Canada); **OMA [NZ]** – Overseas Mon Association [New Zealand]; **OMNDF** – Overseas Mon National Democratic Front (Thailand, Australia and Malaysia); **OMO [D]** – Overseas Mon Organisation [Denmark]; **OMWO** – Overseas Mon Workers' Organisation/Union (Thailand, Malaysia, Singapore and Japan); **OMYO** – Overseas Mon Youth Organisation (Japan); **MBSASL** – Mon Buddhist Students' Association of Sri Lanka; **MIO** – Mon Information Office (Finland); **UMPF [O]** – United Mon Patriotic Forces [Overseas].

Refugee Relief and Development:

MNRC – Mon National Relief Committee; established 1984, re-organised in 2000 as: **MRDC** – Mon Relief and Development Committee.
RHRC – Ramanya Human Rights Committee. Associated with Ramanya Restoration Army; established 1997.

Burmese Opposition Grcups

NLD – National League for Democracy. Political party; established 1988; NLD [Liberated Area] (**NLD[LA]**) established on the Thailand-Burma border in 1990, after the failure of the SLORC regime to recognise the NLD's victory in the general election that year.

KIO – Kachin Independence Organisation. Principal Kachin insurgent organisation, which agreed a ceasefire with the government in 1994; established 1961.

KNU – Karen National Union. Principal Karen ethnic insurgent organisation; established 1948.

MDUF – Mergui-Davoy United Front (or Mergui-Tavoy United Front). Ethnic Tavoyan insurgent organisation; established 1995; previously Communist Party of Burma (CPB), Southern Command.

ABSDF – All Burma Students Democratic Front. Burmese students' organisation; established 1988.

Opposition Alliances:

NDF – National Democratic Front. Ethnic nationalist insurgent alliance (members include NMSP, KIO and KNU); established 1976.

DAB – Democratic Alliance of Burma. Opposition alliance (NDF members, plus ABSDF and other groups); established 1988.

NCUB – National Council of the Union of Burma. Opposition alliance (NDF, NLD [LA], DAB and exiled members of parliament); established 1990 (as Democratic Front of Burma).

UNLD – United Nationalities League for Democracy. Alliance of legal ethnic political parties; established in 1989 to fight 1990 general election; UNLD [Liberated Area] (UNLD[LA]) established on the Thailand-Burma border in 1998.

ENSCC – Ethnic Nationalities Solidarity and Co-operation Committee. Ethnic nationalist alliance; established 2001.

Burmese Government

SLORC – State Law and Order Restoration Council; established 1988, succeeded by: **SPDC** – State Peace and Development Council; established 1997.

Inter-Government Organisations

ASEAN – Association of Southeast Asian Nations. Regional grouping; established 1967 (Burma and Laos granted membership in 1997).

UNHCR – United Nations High Commissioner for Refugees; established by international convention and protocol, 1951 and 1967.

International Non-Goverment Organisations (NGOs)

BBC – Burmese Border Consortium. Refugee relief agency; established 1984.

MSF (France) – Medecins Sans Frontieres ('Doctors Without Borders'). Medical relief agency; established 1971.

Preface and
Acknowledgements

Bellay Htoo and I arrived at Heathrow Airport early on the morning of 17th June 1997. This was the first time my wife had been outside of Southeast Asia. It was a cold and windy morning, the first of many that summer. One week later, I started work on this book.

Bellay and I had been married in Thailand, a little less than three months previously. We had hoped to marry in Htee Hta, my wife's home village in Burma, but the Burma Army had put an end to that plan when, in early 1997, they occupied the last strongholds of the Karen insurgency, forcing Bellay's parents to become refugees in Thailand. My wife had been a school teacher in the Karen revolution; now she was starting a new life as a student in England.

◆◆◆

By June 1997 I had lived and worked on the Thailand-Burma border for six-and-a-half years. I had been based mostly in Thailand, but had made nearly a hundred visits to the rebel-held 'liberated zones' of Burma.

Having previously taught English to refugees on both sides of the border, from 1994–97 I worked for the Burmese Border Consortium (BBC), an international refugee relief organisation, with its headquarters in Bangkok. I was based in Sangkhlaburi, a small town half-way up the border, near the Three Pagodas Pass. The BBC job involved co-ordinating the supply of humanitarian assistance to ethnic minority refugees along the 875 Km southern section of the border, from Thailand's Tak and Kanchanaburi Provinces in the north to Chumpon Province in the south. Unlike the other Karen and Karenni refugee settlements further to the north, which were all located in Thai territory, the four Mon and six Karen refugee camps along this stretch of the border were all either in insurgent-controlled Burma, or right on the ill-defined frontier.

Until the mid-1990s, these bamboo and thatch villages, deep in the inaccessible borderland forests, enjoyed a degree of autonomy and partial self-reliance unusual in refugee situations. The camps were administered by refugee committees, which of necessity enjoyed a close relationship with the insurgents. Therefore, as part of the job, I came into frequent contact with members of the New Mon State Party (NMSP), the Karen National Union (KNU) and the wider Mon and Karen nationalist movements.

In June 1995, following a campaign of political and military pressure orchestrated by the Royal Thai and Burma Armies, the NMSP reluctantly agreed a ceasefire with the Burmese military government. The KNU held 'talks about talks' with Rangoon, but these broke down, and the Karen's fifty year armed struggle for independence entered a desperate new stage. The subsequent 1997 Burma Army offensives against the KNU marked the end of an era. With the loss of their last remaining territory inside Burma, the Karen rebels were forced to abandon fixed positions and adopt mobile guerrilla tactics.

Following the Mon ceasefire, in 1996 the Thai authorities had repatriated the last of the Mon refugees to Burma, where today they continue to live in NMSP-controlled zones along the border. In contrast, by mid-1997 the Karen refugees had fled further east, into Thailand proper. By the end of the year, conditions in many of the camps were similar to those familiar from TV scenes of refugee crises the world over, with victims huddled under temporary shelter, wholly dependent on humanitarian aid. For me though, there was one terrible difference: some of these people were my colleagues, friends and family.

◄◆►

I have many intense and vivid memories of my years along the border. I visited places that were way, way off the track for most Western visitors – many of which have since been reclaimed by the forest, or occupied by the Burma Army. It was sometimes difficult not to romanticise a situation which for my travelling companions, and the people we met along the way, was often a matter of life and death. In what follows, I have tried as much as possible to keep myself out of the picture: this is not the story of a white boy in Burma. First though, a few impressions to set the scene.

What I remember most happily is travelling through the Burmese countryside, either in the BBC's battered, white Toyota four-wheel-drive truck – which was twice written-off, and then re-built – or on foot, with my Mon or Karen friends and colleagues (it was only very rarely that I travelled with both groups at the same time). In the rainy season we walked down jungle tracks, along which we had driven in the dry season. Whether in a cloud of dust or, at the start of the rains, in a slow, muddy series of winch-assisted episodes, driving along and across the border was always an adventure – for me, at least.

When walking, we encountered hoards of leeches and mosquitoes; I contracted malaria more than a dozen times. There were bigger animals too: one morning we woke to find tiger tracks yards from our temporary campsite. On another occasion, walking ahead of the main group, I came across a herd of wild boar and had to be dissuaded by my rapidly advancing Mon friends from getting any closer, as they might charge if spooked. I was usually pretty gung-ho about such things, but one creature I would not have dreamt of approaching was the more than six foot long, jet black king cobra that we came across whilst driving through the forest down in Chumpon, sunning itself on the red dirt road. At least on this occasion we didn't wait to see in which direction the snake would cross our path, and thus determine whether the omens for our continued journey were good.

◄◆◆►

The most inaccessible of the two dozen-or-so refugee settlements along the Thailand-Burma border was the Mon camp at Bee Ree, in the Ye River watershed. During the dry season, Bee Ree was a five-to-eight hour drive, up – and then back down – some of the steepest hills on the border. The six and ten-wheel drive vehicles that we used to transport rice to the other camps could not manage these roads, and in the forest half way to Bee Ree supplies had to be transferred to four-wheel-drive trucks – or even carried the rest of the way by the refugees. Watching at nightfall from the banks of the Ye River, the taillights of trucks departing up the steep border range for Sangkhlaburi looked liked aeroplanes taking-off.

Walking in to Bee Ree was a serious proposition. The round trip, including time in and around the two refugee settlements on the Ye River and meeting with the Mon authorities, took not less than five days, and often a week or more. The first part of the journey consisted of an hour-and-a-half's 'long-tail' boat ride, across the lake from Sangkhlaburi, to the site of the abandoned refugee camp at Loh Loe. This was a fine way to travel, providing that the sun was out, but damn chilly at five o'clock on a misty December morning. At Loh Loe we shouldered our packs and headed west. This part of the journey consisted of a ten-to-twelve hour walk, or longer if one had the rare – and surprisingly comfortable – luxury of elephant transport. If I had my way, we would break our journey with an overnight stay in the forest.

An hour or so west of Loh Loe, the path started to zigzag up into the hills, and as we neared the border the forest became gradually more substantial, until we were walking under the canopy of giant hardwood trees. Although the last rhinoceros in these parts had disappeared some time in the early 1990s, the area was still home to tigers, wild boar, monkeys and huge eagles. In the nesting season, hornbills flew between the treetops, their wings booming overhead.

And then there was the golden sheldrake – the mythical *hamsa*, or *hongsa* – ancient symbol of the Mon people. The NMSP flag featured a sheldrake, flying beneath a blue pole star, against a blood-red background.

Lashed to a bamboo flagpole at an insurgent checkpoint on an isolated hill-top, the sheldrake flag marked the border between Thailand and Monland, the NMSP's 'liberated zone'.

━◄◆►━

On my return to the UK, I set out to discover more about the Mon. I found that, while a good deal is known regarding their significant role in precolonial Southeast Asia, little has been published regarding the Mon in the modern period. Indeed, some of the literature suggested that Mon was a dying language, and the people and their culture in irreversible decline. I hope to demonstrate that this is far from the case.

The one million-plus Mon people today living in Burma and Thailand are inheritors of a nearly two thousand year-old culture. This book is the result of my attempts to trace this heritage, and relate it to contemporary developments. At a time when Mon studies appear to be undergoing something of a revival, it is useful to consider Mon political history in the context of events in Burma, Thailand and the region as a whole. In recent years, Mon authors have begun to record and analyse the history of the nationalist movement in Burma, and partial accounts have appeared in English, Mon, Thai and Burmese. However, no comprehensive treatment of this subject has previously been attempted.

With one or two exceptions, Westerners writing about contemporary Burmese politics have tended to neglect the Mon and other ethnic minority groups, and down-play the significance of the ceasefire process in Burma. At the risk of over-emphasising the role of the former, and without necessarily endorsing the latter, this book is an attempt to redress the balance.

━◄◆►━

I could not have written this book without the support and assistance of my wife, Naw Bellay Htoo. Thanks also to my parents, who patiently awaited the outcome of a project that at times seemed never-ending.

I am greatly indebted to Martin Smith for encouragement and advice, for providing detailed comments on the text, and allowing me access to his vast store of knowledge regarding insurgency and the politics of ethnicity in Burma. Thanks also to Jonathan Price of RoutledgeCurzon.

When I started out, I had something quite different in mind to the book that eventually emerged. In order to understand Mon nationalism, I have had to venture into fields more properly the domain of the specialist academic. In particular, I have borrowed from the work of Emmanuel Guillon, on the historical Mon civilisation, and from Mikael Gravers' work on nationalism and ethnicity in Burma. Thanks also to Justin Watkins, for insights into the Mon and Burmese languages, and to Benedicte Brac de la Perriere, for clarifying some points regarding 'La Bufflesse de Pegou'. My apologies to these scholars for any blunders I have made with their work.

My old boss, Jack Dunford, carefully scrutinised sections of the text. I hope he will forgive any errors of interpretation which remain. Thanks also to Sally Thompson, Alan Smith, Glen Hill, Donna Guest; to Gavin Clarke, for technical and moral support; to Deborah January; and to David Wyatt, for copy-editing the revised text, and a hundred-and-one other things. Thanks to Vicky Bamforth, for producing the maps, and Maria Raudva, for the *hamsa* illustration.

Obviously, many of those from Burma who have contributed to this project must remain anonymous. I would though, like to acknowledge the invaluable support received from members of the New Mon State Party, and in particular from Nai Shwe Kyin, Nai Taw Mon, Nai Hongsa, Nai B-L- and Nai M-N-. Thanks also to the Mon National Education Committee, and of course to members of the Mon Relief and Development Committee, past and present. I owe a special debt to Nai Sunthorn Sriparngern of the Mon Unity League, who helped me enormously with my research. Thanks also to the Overseas Mon Young Monks Union and the monks of Wat Prok. Of the other overseas Mon groups, I am particularly grateful to Nai Pon Nya Mon and the Monland Restoration Council, to Nai Cham Toik and the Mon Community of Canada, and to the Australia Mon Association. I would also like to thank Nai Pisarn Boonpook of Koh Kret, for a fascinating introduction to the Mon community in Thailand, and Dr Chamlong Thongdee of the Mon National University.

Thanks also to Karen friends, including P'doh Kweh Htoo, Daw Daisy, 'Uncle', Bo M- and Kyaw K-L-; to Poo C- and Uncle G-; and to the inspiring example of Thramu Olivia and the Christian community at Huay M'lai.

The Sir Heinz Koeppler Trust and the Burma Project of the Open Society Institute provided financial support when it was most needed, and without which I would have ground to a halt.

◄◆►

Each chapter of the book begins with a summary of the material covered therein. The Endnotes contain additional material, as well as bibliographic references.

The first chapter in Part One defines some key terms, before going on to describe Burma's chief physical characteristics, and outline recent events in Burmese and Mon history. This preliminary section is followed by accounts of Mon demographics, language, culture and religion, and the tricky but crucial subject of ethnic identity. Part One concludes with an examination of Mon nationalism in contemporary Thailand and Burma.

Part Two surveys the precolonial Mon civilisation and the colonial period, from the shadowy realm of pre-history, through the rise and fall of the Mon kingdoms, to the Burman – and later British – ascendancy. Parts Three, Four and Five contain a history of Mon nationalism from 1945–2000, in the context of developments in Burma, Thailand and the region. Part Five concludes with a discussion of policy issues and of Burma's place in the international community. Part Six brings the story up to date, before re-examining some key themes.

A good deal of the text is based on published accounts. I have also made use of 'grey literature' – i.e. unpublished, or limited circulation materials, including government and non-government organisation (NGO) reports. Wherever possible, I have used the work of Mon and other people native to Burma and Thailand. Especially in the field of human rights, I have referred to the Mon Information Service, the Human Rights Foundation of Monland and the Mon refugee authorities, rather than international organisations, such as Amnesty International and Human Rights Watch. The latter are quoted in order to establish credibility, but in most cases information regarding civil and human rights has been taken from those working on the ground, who often risk their lives in their work..

To their credit, these groups concentrate not only on the plight of Mon villagers, but also on the Karen and other ethnic groups. The author has had the opportunity to observe the activities and corroborate the findings of each of the above-named organisations, and can vouch for the reliability of their reports.

Map One: The Historical Mon Civilisation
Adapted from Emmanuel Guillon (1999)

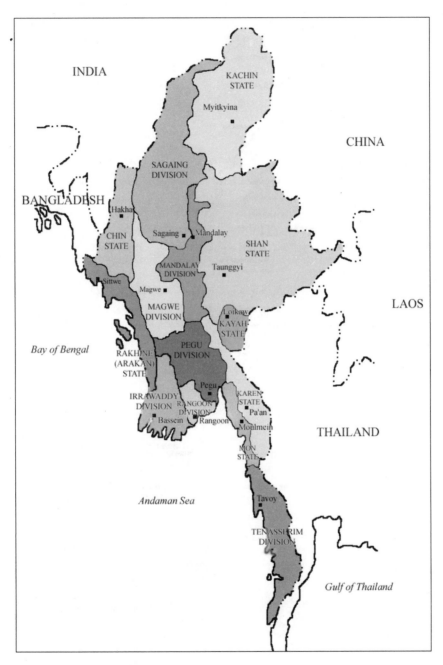

Map Two: Modern Burma

Map Three: Thailand-Burma Border

Tables

Table One: Armed Ceasefire and Insurgent Groups

Main Ceasefire Organisations	Leader	Year
Myanmar National Democratic Alliance Army	Pheung Kya-shin	1989
United Wa State Army/Party	Pauk Yo Chang	1989
National Democratic Alliance Army	Lin Ming Xian	1989
Shan State Army/Shan State Progress Party*	Sai Nawng	1989
New Democratic Army	Ting Ying	1989
Kachin Defence Army	Mahtu Naw	1991
Pa-O National Organisation*	Aung Kham Hti	1991
Palaung State Liberation Party*	Aik Mone	1991
Kayan National Guard	Htay Ko	1992
Kachin Independence Organisation*	Lamung Tu Jai	1994
Karenni State Nationalities Liberation Front (or Karenni State Nationalities People's Liberation Force)	Tun Kyaw	1994
Kayan New Land Party*	Shwe Aye	1994
Shan State Nationalities Liberation Organisation	Tha Kalei	1994
New Mon State Party*	Nai Shwe Kyin	1995

Other Ceasefire Groups[1]		
Democratic Karen Buddhist Army/Organisation	U Thuzana	1995
Mongko Region Defence Army	Mong Hsala	1995
Shan State National Army (front-line status unclear)	Gun Yawd	1995
Mong Tai Army	Khun Sa	1996
Karenni National Defence Army	Lee Rey	1996
Karen Peace Force (ex-KNU 16th Battalion)	Thu Mu Hei	1997
Communist Party of Burma (Arakan Province)	Saw Tun Oo	1997
Mon Army Mergui District (NMSP splinter group)	Ong Suik Heang	1997
KNU Special Region Group (Toungoo)	Fareh Moe	1997

Main Non-Ceasefire Armed Groups[2]	
Arakan Liberation Party*	Khine Ye Khine
Chin National Front*	Thomas Thangnou
Karen National Union*	Bo Mya
Karenni National Progressive Party* (1995 ceasefire broke down)	The Buphe
Lahu National Organisation*	Pya Ja Oo
Mergui-Davoy United Front (ex-CPB, mainly ethnic Tavoyan)	Saw Han
National Socialist Council of Nagaland	
NSCN (East)	Khaplang
NSCN (main faction)	Isaac/Muivah
National Unity Party of Arakan	Shwe Tha
Hongsawatoi Restoration Party	Pan Nyunt
Rohingya National Alliance	
Arakan Rohingya Islamic Front	Nurul Islam
Rohingya Solidarity Organisation	Dr Yunus
Shan Unity Revolutionary Army (reformed after 1996 MTA surrender)	Yord Serk
Wa National Organisation*	Maha San

Former or current member of National Democractic Front.
Adapted from Martin Smith (1999)

Table Two: Burmese Refugee Caseload – 1984–2001

Year	Refugee population	Total NGO assistance (Millions Baht)[3]	Mon refugees assisted by BBC[4]	Number of Mon Camps (total Burmese camps)
1984	9,502	10	0	(9)
1985	16,144	19	0	(8)
1986	18,428	21	0	(9)
1987	19,675	26	0	(9)
1988	19,636	33	0	(9)
1989	22,751	35	0	(13)
1990	43,500	48	8,657	5 (21)
1991	55,700	82	12,004	7 (25)
1992	65.900	101	10,170	4 (30)
1993	72,366	126	10,346	3 (30)
1994	77,107	169	8,910	4 (32)
1995	92,505	313	10,852	4 (28)
1996	101,425	299	11,452	4 (26)
1997	116,264	419	8,987	3 (24)
1998	111,813	592	9,895	3 (16)
1999	116,047	647	10,622	3 (15)
2000	122,914	720	10,622	3 (15)
2001	138,117	800	12,999	3 (13)

Adapted from Burmese Border Consortium (December 2001)

PART ONE

THE MON IN BURMA (AND THAILAND)

"In sculpture, literature, law, religion, and social organisation alike, the Mons have known periods of the greatest brilliance, and others marked by destruction, exile, silence."

Emmanuel Guillon[1]

CHAPTER ONE

Introduction

The one million-plus Mon people today living in Burma and neighbouring Thailand constitute an ethnic minority. However, this has not always been the case.

From early in the first millennium, for a period of more than a thousand years, Mon and Khmer kings ruled over much of mainland Southeast Asia. Across northern and central Thailand until six or seven hundred years ago, and in central and lower Burma for another three hundred years, the bulk of the population were ethnic Mons. The classical period of Mon history came to an end in 1757, when the great Burman warrior-king Alaungphaya defeated the last Mon ruler of Pegu. Thousands of his followers were driven into exile in Ayuthaiya (Thailand), where they settled in the border areas adjoining Burma. At times over the two-and-a-half centuries since the fall of Pegu, it has been supposed that Mon was a dying language and the people in the twilight of their history. The Mons' very success has threatened to be their undoing.

Mon civilisation was among the most distinctive and influential in precolonial Southeast Asia. Significant aspects of the language, art and architecture, political and legal arrangements, and above all the religion of the great Thai and Burman civilisations were derived from the earlier Mon society, which acted as a vector in the transmission of Theravada Buddhism and Indianised political culture to the region. This civilising role helps to explain the enduring prestige attached to the Mon heritage across mainland Southeast Asia.

Mon nationalists have looked back to the classical era as a golden age – a source of inspiration and legitimacy. They have struggled to defend the historical Mon identity from assimilation into that of the Burman and Thai majorities.

Like the Burmans and Thais, the Mon are a lowland people. However, over the centuries, many have fled or been displaced within their traditional homelands. Thus recent Mon history has much in common with that of the

Karen and other persecuted 'hilltribe' groups. (In some respects, the destiny of the Mon also recalls that of the dwindling Cham minority in Cambodia and Vietnam, whose ancestors once ruled the Mekong Delta, but who now exist on the periphery of these states.)

Elites among the Mon, Karen and Burma's more than one hundred other ethnic minority groups have long sought to define themselves in opposition to the Burman majority, which has dominated the central government in Rangoon since independence. Perhaps inevitably, political and cultural struggle has led to armed conflict. The result has been a series of insurrections which still constitute a major factor in Burma's highly unstable security situation, as well as a pretext for the continuing and well-documented abuses of the present military regime.

The Mon and Karen nationalists first took up arms against Rangoon shortly after independence in 1948. By the 1960s, they and the communists had been joined in rebellion by the Kachin and other ethnic groups. Today, the civil war constitutes the longest-running such conflict in the world. The complex history of the war has been influenced by numerous factors, among the most important of which have been the roles of Burma's neighbours to the north and east – communist China and capitalist Thailand. The gradual shift from a Cold War regional environment of political polarisation, to one of economic competition and co-operation in Southeast Asia, has had significant consequences for the conflict in Burma. In the case of the Mon, by 1995 the commercial and geo-strategic realignments of the post-Cold War era, and in particular the withdrawal of support by their erstwhile backers in the Thai military, had generated pressures which left the New Mon State Party (NMSP) with little choice but to agree a ceasefire with Rangoon. As had the Kachin Independence Organisation (KIO) and fourteen other armed ethnic groups before them, the NMSP 'returned to the legal fold' (to use the regime's preferred expression). By the late 1990s, the greatly weakened Karen National Union (KNU) was the only major insurgent group in Burma not to have agreed a ceasefire.

Although, under the 1995 agreement, the Mon National Liberation Army (MNLA) retained its arms, some in Burmese opposition circles, and within the wider Mon nationalist community, accused the NMSP of 'selling out' to Rangoon. However, the military regime has recently criticised Mon politicians for their support of the Burmese democracy movement, led by the Nobel prize-winner, Daw Aung San Suu Kyi.

Meanwhile, Mon, Kachin and other ethnic nationalist leaders in Burma are attempting to map out a new politics – one which avoids both the dead-end of armed insurgency and the corrupting influence of the military dictatorship. New strategies will inevitably result in compromises, which some observers – more used to the certainties of a long and divisive civil war – may find unpalatable. However, if ethnic minority leaders are able to achieve a working relationship with the urban, predominantly Burman political class, the new millennium may yet prove a watershed in Burmese history.[2]

The ceasefires represent a major gamble on the part of the erstwhile insurgents. Although they had long ceased to pose a substantial military threat to Rangoon, having 'returned to the legal fold', the ceasefire groups no longer represent even token armed resistance to the government. Their symbolic role as proponents of military solutions to Burma's 'ethnic question' having been relinquished, the onus is on these groups to deliver on another front. The ex-insurgents must prove to their ethnic constituencies and assorted Burma-watchers that they remain relevant, and that the ceasefires have resulted in concrete achievements in the fields of social, economic and/or political development. If the ceasefire groups are not to become marginalised, new paradigms are required. However, it is by no means clear whether NMSP or KIO leaders have the vision or ability to transform their parties into popular, post-insurgent organisations.

Some within the nationalist community have refused to accept the 1995 NMSP-SLORC ceasefire. Motivated by a combination of principle and self-interest, at least five armed, anti-ceasefire Mon groups have emerged since 1995. Whilst only two of these factions – the Mon Army Mergui District (MAMD) and Nai Pan Nyunt's Hangsawatoi Restoration Party (HRP) – have had a significant impact, the others, including the Hongsa Command and the Ramanya Restoration Army (RRA), have also engaged the *Tatmadaw* (and sometimes also the MNLA) for control of key resources.

However, these armed groups are not the only Mon players on the Burmese political stage. Since 1988, the Mon National Democratic Front (MNDF), a successful political party – until it was banned by the government – has emerged to challenge the NMSP for leadership of the nationalist camp. Sometimes regarded as the political wing of the NMSP, the MNDF is in fact an independent, urban-based organisation, with a clear agenda and history of its own. One result of the NMSP ceasefire was that, for a few years at least, the MNDF had more room within which to manoeuvre in the dangerous and restricted field of Burmese politics.

Meanwhile in Thailand, since 1995 a number of small Mon groups have remained active in opposition circles, as have Mon exiles in North America and Australia. Finally, the *sangha* (monkhood), repository of the ancient culture, retains a prestige which extends to all strata of Mon society. Indeed, a distinct Mon identity has survived in large part because of its inter-connection with Buddhism.[3]

Religion and history are central to the preservation and revival of the Mon language and culture. Thus, since the 1930s, educated elites in Burma and Thailand have implemented a variety of educational programmes, intended to foster a national spirit and remind the people of their true identity.[4]

'Mon Nationalism'

The *Collins English Dictionary* defines 'nationalism' as "a sentiment based on common cultural characteristics that binds a population and often produces a policy of national independence or separatism." For centuries, Mon politicians have elaborated and exploited an ethnic and national identity which was already well-established before the arrival in Southeast Asia of the first Europeans (although see Lieberman's caveats – below).

Concepts of nationality are notoriously problematic. The defining criteria of ethnicity (itself a complex idea), language use, history, culture etc. are all more-or-less controversial. This study eschews such debates, making no claims to theoretical rigor. Another disclaimer: this is primarily an account of elite politics. As Eric Hobsbawm notes, "we know too little about what . . . goes on, in the minds of most relatively inarticulate men and women, to speak with any confidence about their thoughts and feelings towards the nationalities and nation-states which claim their loyalties."[5] The manner in which 'ordinary' Mon people have responded to the nationalist agenda is often unclear. The great majority are poor rice farmers, and day-to-day survival is the prime consideration. Nevertheless, surveys of the refugee population, and impressions of the Mon community 'inside'[6] Burma, indicate that very large numbers of people do subscribe to a distinct Mon identity.

The term 'Mon (or Karen or Kachin) nationalism' will be used to indicate a movement or ideology which aims to achieve certain goals on behalf of the ethnic constituency in question. Groups or individuals acting out of ethnic nationalist sentiments may endorse a variety of political programmes, with different objectives and employing sometimes very different strategies and tactics. The main point is that they are motivated primarily by an 'ethnic agenda'.

At some time over the past fifty years, representatives of nearly every ethnic group in Burma have taken up arms against the government. Inasmuch as they have acted in the name of a particular ethnicity, this wide variety of insurgent organisations may be regarded as fundamentally similar in type.[7] However, to some Mon activists, this superficial similarity masks a profound difference between themselves and other allied ethnic groups. The Mon have not merely sought to protect their rights and *establish* a Mon nation; they have been fighting to *re-establish* Monland and preserve a culture that, unlike those of the so-called 'hilltribes', was dominant for centuries across much of Burma and Thailand. Although, to younger and more cosmopolitan nationalists, this distinction has generally been less important than for the generation that initiated the armed struggle, it is nevertheless crucial to an understanding of Mon national identity.

In contrast to the ethnic nationalists, organisations as diverse as the Communist Party of Burma (CPB), the National League for Democracy

(NLD) and the All Burma Students Democratic Front (ABSDF) may be characterised as 'political'. In principal, these groups draw support from all ethnic constituencies, and seek to achieve national goals for the country *as a whole*. Although they may sympathise with ethnic minority aspirations, these supposedly pan-Burmese groups have in practice often been dominated by members of the Burman political class.

Burma – Political and Physical Geography

Burma has been called 'the golden land'.[8] A country of still-abundant natural resources, possessing a rich and complex history and culture, it is a land of contradictions – of profound beauty and intense suffering.

With a land area of approximately 678,500 square Km, Burma had an estimated population in 2000 of between forty-seven and fifty million people, two thirds of whom worked in the agricultural sector. The British census-takers of 1872 were of the opinion that "there is probably no country in the world whose inhabitants are more varied in race, custom, and language than those of Burma."[9] Of these diverse peoples, at least sixty per cent are ethnic Burmans and related Rakhines and Tavoyans. There are also sizeable Indian (Bengali) and Chinese minorities, concentrated mostly in urban centres. The one hundred-plus languages found in the country[10] include thirteen more-or-less mutually unintelligible Karen dialects, in southern and eastern Burma, as well as the Tai language of the Shan people of the northeastern plateau.[11] The various Karen groups, including the Karenni, constitute perhaps seven-to-ten per cent of the population, as do the Shan. Other ethnic groups with populations of more than one million include the Muslim *Rohingya* people on the western border with Bangladesh, the Chin and Kachin peoples of north and northwest Burma, the Palaung and Wa of the northeast,[12] and the Mon.

The existence of such complexity makes it useful to consider Burma according to the British colonial division (adopted from the precolonial state) between 'Burma Proper' and the 'Frontier Areas'. The majority of Burmans live in Burma Proper, in the central plains between Mandalay and Rangoon, and (together with substantial Mon and Karen populations), in the Irrawaddy Delta in the southwest, and along the coast of Mon State and Tenasserim Division in the southeast.

Present day Mon State was established in 1974. It covers an area of 12,000 square Km, extending from the Gulf of Martaban to the Thailand border. The second smallest ethnic state in Burma, it is also the most densely populated, with an estimated 181.6 people per square Km (compared with 44.4 per sq. Km in neighbouring Karen State).[13] In the north, Mon State is located opposite Pegu Division, on the east bank of the Sittaung River. The state extends southwards past Ye town to the marshy land above the Heinze Channel. Northern Mon State shares a similar geography to adjacent areas of Pegu Division (flat farmland) and Karen State (hilly). South of Kyaikto and Bilin however, it becomes more tropical in character. The coastal landscape, west of the pagoda-dotted Tenghyo mountain range, is noted for its lush rice farming villages and coconut groves. From the small town of Thaton – ancient capital of the Mon[14] – south past the modern state capital of Moulmein (Burma's third city, with a population of about 300,000), the local economy is based on rice farming, fishing and rubber plantations.[15] To the east, beyond the wooded hills which run north-south down the length of Mon State, is the southern part of the larger and more rural Karen State; in the far southeast are the Thailand-Burma frontier and the historic Three Pagodas Pass.

The planes, valleys and low hills of Mon State and the rest of Burma Proper are surrounded by a horse-shoe of steeper hills and mountains. Projections of the Himalayas, these ranges constitute natural boundaries between Burma and the neighbouring countries of Bangladesh and India to the west, China (and Tibet) to the north, Laos to the northeast, and the 2,096 Km long border with Thailand, to the east.[16] These 'Frontier Areas' are less densely populated than the lowlands, and the climate is more temperate. Despite heavy and often indiscriminate logging activities in recent years, large areas are still densely forested. These beautiful and inaccessible regions are the homelands of Burma's ethnic minorities, including the Chin, Kachin, Karen, Karenni, Wa and Palaung. Unlike the lowland peoples, most of whom are irrigated rice farmers, these groups have traditionally practised 'slash and burn' (swidden) rice cultivation.

Three major rivers run north-south through the country: the Chindwin in the northwest, the great Irrawaddy which flows through the heart of Burma to its vast delta, and the Salween, which originates in China and flows down through the Shan, Kayah (Karenni) and Karen States to Moulmein, on the Gulf of Martaban. Except for the central and lower Irrawaddy, these rivers are not readily navigable over long distances. Together with the mountain ranges on the periphery, they have constituted natural defences against invasion by neighbouring states.

Burma – 1945–2000: An Overview

Although Burma has little reason to fear direct military aggression from its neighbours, it is one of the most heavily militarised states in the world. This phenomena is more easily explained by recourse to the country's history, than to geography. The Burma Army (*Tatmadaw*) was forged in the struggle for independence from the British colonial power, and thus has a proud history. Sadly though, in the modern period it has been used primarily to crush internal dissent.

When Burma gained independence from Britain on 4th January 1948 it did not join the Commonwealth, but rather attempted to steer a non-aligned course through the stormy international waters of the Cold War era. As a result of increasingly isolationist policies pursued by successive governments, by the late 1980s Burma had become one of the most insular countries in Asia.

Both opponents and supporters of the military government have likened Burma to the former Yugoslavia: age-old ethnic antipathies have threatened to tear the country apart, and forms of 'ethnic cleansing' have for some thirty years been a fact of life in many ethnic minority areas. Mikael Gravers observes that "the initial explanation of Burma's present situation must be sought in the legacy of the colonial era, or rather in the nationalistic paranoia ... linking fear of the disintegration of both union and state with the foreign take-over of power and the disappearance of Burmese culture."[17] The *Tatmadaw's* attempts to 'preserve the union', and at the same time the political, economic and cultural domination of an elite within the Burman majority, have led to destruction and suffering on a massive scale.

One event, above all others during the hectic pre-independence period, prefigures the violence and devastation of modern Burmese history. On 19th July 1947 General Aung San, the charismatic young leader of the independence movement and prime minister-designate, was assassinated in Rangoon, together with half his cabinet. Although some details remain obscure, and the possibility of a more wide-ranging conspiracy cannot be dismissed, the principal author of this disaster seems to have been a rival Burma politician, U Saw, who was executed for his role in the plot. From the outset then, modern Burmese politics has been violent and bitterly contested.

After the Second World War the Mon, Karen, Rakhine and other ethnic groups lobbied unsuccessfully for a degree of autonomy – if not outright independence – from Rangoon. At the same time the Communist Party of Burma (CPB) was becoming increasingly active and by March 1948, three months after independence, took up arms against the government of Aung San's successor, Burma's first prime minister, U Nu. Soon afterwards, a number of key *Tatmadaw* units rebelled, and in August the Mon nationalists went underground, together with the more numerous and better-armed Karen forces. After a series of early successes, during which they briefly occupied Moulmein and other urban centres in lower Burma, the Mon and Karen insurgents were forced to abandon the armed struggle in the towns and cities. Like the communists and other insurgents in the north and west, they took to the countryside, where resistance to the central government continues to this day.

Following a decade of military setbacks, in 1958 the bulk of the Mon insurgents agreed a ceasefire with Rangoon, as did several other armed groups. However, the CPB and most of the Karen rebel forces fought on. It seemed for a while in 1958–60 that the Mon nationalists' demands might be met and that the government would create a Mon state. However,

General Ne Win's military coups of 1958 and 1962 extinguished such hopes, ushering-in an era of repressive, centralised one-party rule.

Meanwhile, Nai Shwe Kyin and a small group of followers had rejected the 1958 ceasefire and established the New Mon State Party (NMSP), which was in the vanguard of the struggle for Monland for the next forty years. According to its founder, the NMSP aimed "to establish an independent sovereign state unless the Burmese government is willing to permit a confederation of free nationalities exercising the full right of self-determination inclusive of right of secession."[18]

In the late 1940s various communist and ethnic insurgent organisations had controlled more than half the country, but by the 1960s the Mon and other groups had been driven back to a series of bases in the border regions. By this time attitudes had polarised on both sides. After 1962, the process of militarisation and authoritarian rule in Burma accelerated rapidly and the *Tatmadaw* came to dominate affairs of state. General Ne Win's 'Burmese Way to Socialism' was characterised by economic and political stagnation and the widespread abuse of human rights. Throughout the 1960s and '70s there were occasional urban demonstrations against the regime, including major disturbances in December 1974, centred on the funeral of U Thant, the Burmese Secretary-General of the United Nations (1962–71). Nevertheless, the major security issue of the Ne Win era was the insurgency in the countryside, where a variety of political and nationalist organisations, of various ideological persuasions, controlled extensive swathes of territory.

These 'liberated zones' did not necessarily enjoy a more liberal administration than that exercised by Rangoon. However, with the exception of those controlled by the CPB in northern Burma, they were largely free of Burman domination. Although unrecognised by the international community, the rebel administrations manifested many of the characteristics of the state: exclusive control over territory, the raising of taxes and in some cases the establishment of relatively sophisticated government structures. The ethnic revolutions were financed by taxation of the black market trade between Burma and neighbouring countries, and later by the proceeds of the logging business. In some cases, well-equipped insurgent armies were built up by exploiting the drugs trade, or in the case of the Kachin, the jade mines of northern Burma. Furthermore, various military and security agencies in China, India and Thailand supported the rebels in their struggle against the historically belligerent Burmese state.

The different parties to the civil war increasingly defined themselves in opposition to each other. The *Tatmadaw* and the government in Rangoon justified their policies by pointing to the threat to the union posed by the rebel groups: only a strong state and army, they argued, could hope to save the country from disintegration. For the insurgents, identity and the claim to legitimacy came to reside in the act of rebellion itself: the ethnic insurgencies became institutionalised and in many cases the revolutionaries began to resemble warlords. Meanwhile, on the ideological front, the rebels were split between the CPB and its allies' Marxist-Maoist rhetoric, and the specifically ethno-nationalistic concept of liberation espoused by many of the more conservative armed groups.

The government and the disparate opposition forces were locked into a hugely destructive spiral of conflict, each side justifying its position in terms of the real and perceived iniquities of the other. This was though, a 'low intensity' war and despite the cumulative damage to the lives, property and culture of millions of people, the conflict did not attract significant international attention.

It was not until the momentous and bloody events of 1988 that opposition to the military regime in Burma began to feature in the foreign media. In September 1987 the Ne Win government had ordered an eccentric and hugely unpopular demonitisation, which wiped out the savings of families across the country overnight. One year later, following a summer of massive and unprecedented protests by students, monks and hundreds of thousands of ordinary citizens, Burma's towns and cities were in the throes of revolt.

The 1988 democracy uprising started in March, with street protests in downtown Rangoon. Organised by groups of students, the demonstrations quickly began to attract support from less traditionally radical groups. In a sign of things to come, by the end of the month more than one hundred protestors had been killed by government troops. Then, following a series of anti-government demonstrations across the country, on 23rd July 1988 General Ne Win surprised the nation by resigning as Burma Socialist Programme Party (BSPP) Chairman, bringing to an end the disastrous Burmese Way to Socialism. Unfortunately, at this historic juncture the Mon and Karen insurgent 'allies' were engaged in a short and nasty little war at Three Pagodas Pass, over what was basically a financial dispute – a poignant illustration of the persistent factionalism of Burmese opposition politics.

Meanwhile, despite the killing of more protestors by the *Tatmadaw*, and the declaration of martial law on 3rd August, on the morning of 8th August 1988 (8-8-88 – a highly auspicious date) further mass demonstrations broke out in Rangoon. On the same day, 100,000 people took to the streets in Moulmein,[19] and over the next few weeks protestors seized control of scores of towns and cities across Burma. More than a hundred students and others were killed or injured, as riot police and units of the *Tatmadaw* attempted to reassert control. Despite the army's heavy-handed response however, it seemed for a few weeks that 'people's power' might prevail in Burma, as it had two years previously in the Philippines.

Also in August, another major factor entered the Burmese political equation, recalling the emergence of Corazon Aquino as key player in

Philippine politics. Daw Aung San Suu Kyi, the daughter of Burma's martyred independence hero, returned from the UK, where she had been living with her British husband, a noted academic. On 26th August, in her first public appearance in her homeland, Aung San Suu Kyi addressed an estimated half a million people at the Shwedagon Pagoda in Rangoon, Burma's holiest Buddhist temple. She called for democracy and restoration of the rule of law, in what she termed Burma's "second struggle for independence."[20]

The three weeks following Daw Aung San Suu Kyi's speech in downtown Rangoon saw almost daily mass demonstrations against the regime, which in quick succession was headed by two Ne Win cronies: Brigadier Sein Lwin and Dr Maung Maung. For a while it seemed that the military, sections of which had joined the demonstrators, together with civil servants, policemen and representatives of every sector of society, might return to barracks. However, on the afternoon of 18th September the *Tatmadaw*, under its Commander-in-Chief, General Saw Maung, unleashed a massive attack on the fledgling democracy movement. Over the next few days and weeks, some 3,000 unarmed civilians were killed across Burma, while thousands more were arrested. Sein Lwin was dubbed 'the butcher of Rangoon' for his role in co-ordinating the March and September massacres.[21] As a result of the crack-down, thousands of young democracy activists fled to the insurgent-controlled liberated zones.

On the first day of the crack-down, the military established a new junta, the State Law and Order Restoration Council (SLORC); six days later Daw Aung San Suu Kyi and her colleagues founded the NLD, which for the next decade was to lead the urban struggle against the SLORC and its successor, the State Peace and Development Council (SPDC). According to Burton Levin, US Ambassador to Burma from 1987–90, Aung San Suu Kyi initially owed her status to being "the daughter of the nation's founding father ... but it was her courage, charisma and the force and eloquence of her message that earned her the adulation, bordering on worship, of virtually the entire population and elevated her to the leadership of the anti-regime movement. The Burmese people felt that at long last someone was standing up for their rights."[22]

However, NLD supporters were to pay a high price for their defiance. Since 1988 courts and military tribunals have handed down thousands of harsh prison terms to opposition figures, and many have died in prison from torture and neglect. On 20th July 1989 the confrontation between the SLORC and the NLD claimed two more victims, when the league's Chairman, ex-General Tin Oo, and its most popular leader, Aung San Suu Kyi, were each placed under house arrest. Despite being awarded the Nobel Peace Prize in 1991, Aung San Suu Kyi was to remain in detention for six years.

The year after her arrest, General Saw Maung's SLORC confounded observers by holding elections in Burma (or 'Myanmar', as the country was re-named in 1989). In part at least, the 1990 elections were conducted in order to placate international opinion. Governments in the West, if not among Burma's Southeast Asian neighbours, were united in their condemnation of the latest and most brutal incarnation of Burmese military rule. Since 1988, the United States, Japan and most European nations had embargoed all aid to the SLORC and various UN agencies had called on the regime to reform its appalling record. The generals calculated that holding an election would mute international criticism, whilst serving to flush out any remaining centres of resistance. Presumably, the SLORC calculated that the results could be manipulated. This was a major self-deception, perhaps engendered by a quarter century of authoritarian rule.

More than seventy per cent of the electorate voted in the May 1990 poll. Although Daw Aung San Suu Kyi remained under house arrest, and was thus barred from campaigning or standing for election, the NLD won sixty per cent of the popular vote and 392 of the 485 seats. Sixty-five representatives of ethnic parties were also elected, including five members of the Mon National Democratic Front (MNDF). Jubilation among the opposition was short-lived however, as the following month the SLORC ruled out any transfer of power to the elected MPs, instigating a new wave of repression and political terror. The MNDF was subsequently outlawed in 1992 and several members thrown into jail.

Meanwhile, in the border areas controlled by the Mon, Karen, Karenni and Kachin insurgents, students and other refugees from the 1988 democracy uprising had begun to organise. The All Burma Students Democratic Front (ABSDF) was formed on 5th November 1988, with units along the Thailand and China borders. Later the same month, the ABSDF, NMSP, KNU and twenty other anti-SLORC groups formed the Democratic Alliance of Burma (DAB), a broad-based, joint ethnic minority-Burman opposition front.

Between 1988–90 some 10,000 students and other activists fled to the Thailand-Burma border. They established a series of camps, spread out between the Karenni National Progressive Party (KNPP) liberated zone in the north and the KNU's Fourth Brigade area in Tenasserim Division, more than a thousand Km to the south. There were some 3,000 would-be 'student soldiers' in the KNU's Sixth Brigade alone, of whom several hundred were based at Three Pagodas Pass, which following the fratricidal conflict of 1988 was jointly administered by the NMSP and the KNU.

Although only a small proportion of the ABSDF 'Students Army' were ever armed and trained by the insurgents, the political significance of these new arrivals to the revolution was considerable. The events of 1988–90 had focused international attention on the situation in Burma and it seemed at last that a degree of unity had emerged between the ethnic insurgents and the previously largely urban, Burman-dominated 'political' opposition. The new alliance represented a real threat to the legitimacy of the SLORC.

In the DAB liberated zones, the early 1990s witnessed a degree of optimism absent from the ethnic insurgencies for more than a decade. However, the armed opposition was probably weaker militarily than at any time since independence, due in part to the withdrawal of Chinese, and later Thai, support. This situation was compounded in 1989 by the collapse of the CPB, and the disintegration of its People's Army into a number of narco-trafficking ethnic militia, with which the SLORC proceeded to negotiate a series of ceasefire agreements. In 1993 the KIO followed the ex-communist groups, and three smaller ex-DAB member organisations, into 'the legal fold' (the KIO ceasefire was finalised in February 1994). These ceasefires in northern Burma allowed the *Tatmadaw* to concentrate its fire on the new and potentially powerful alliance based in Mon and Karen-controlled territory along the Thailand-Burma border.

Under this renewed onslaught, the NMSP, the KNU and their allies suffered a series of military setbacks and defections. With most of their territory overrun by the *Tatmadaw*, the insurgents were forced up to, and then across the border into Thailand. Previously, the Thai security and military establishments had covertly aided the Burmese rebels. However, from the early 1990s this support was withdrawn, in favour of a policy of 'constructive engagement' with Rangoon. No longer in control of significant amounts of territory inside Burma, the armed groups along the border found themselves increasingly marginalised. Meanwhile, the international community, though willing to condemn Burma in the UN General Assembly and other fora, was unwilling to lend substantial material support to the insurgents, other than by feeding the growing number of refugees.

Meanwhile inside Burma, although the NLD continued to oppose the government, following the 1988 democracy uprising and the 1990 election, national politics stagnated and the situation for ordinary people and activists alike continued to deteriorate. In an effort to break the stalemate, in the second half of 1998 the NLD, together with a number of ethnic minority parties, including the MNDF, attempted to re-form the 'political-ethnic' alliance and unilaterally convene the '1990 parliament'. This significant development was supported by a number of ceasefire groups, including the NMSP.

Unsurprisingly, the military reacted to this perceived threat with a major clampdown and another round of arrests, which succeeded in breaking-up the emergent opposition front and – for the time being at least – frightening the NMSP back into the government fold. Nevertheless, the enduring potential of an alliance between the democracy movement and progressive ethnic nationalist politicians had been demonstrated. Observers were therefore heartened when, in early 2001, the NMSP and other ceasefire groups reacted positively to news that the NLD and SPDC had entered into apparently substantial political negotiations.

The Struggle for Monland:
The Mon Refugees and the New Mon State Party

Like other ethnic groups in Burma, the Mon people have suffered under the *Tatmadaw's* notorious 'Four Cuts' counter-insurgency campaign. Since the 1960s, the Burma Army has taken the civil war to the rural civilian population, whom it has accused – often with a degree of justification – of being rebel sympathisers. In an attempt to undermine support for the insurgents, thousands of villages across Burma have been forcibly relocated, and entire communities subjected to an appalling and well-documented litany of human rights abuses, including forced labour, looting and arbitrary taxation, rape, torture and murder.

As the security situation in rural Burma deteriorated in the 1970s and '80s, increasingly large numbers of people became displaced. Many fled to Thailand, where they sought work in the kingdom's expanding black economy. Others settled in the refugee camps – either in Thailand, or just across the border in insurgent-held territory. The presence of these displaced populations in or adjacent to the rebels' 'liberated zones' tended to reinforce the *Tatmadaw's* perception of refugees as the enemy, rather than victims of the war.

The first semi-permanent Mon refugee camps in Thailand were established in 1990, after the fall of the insurgent base at Three Pagodas Pass. By this time, there were already more than 30,000 Karen and Karenni refugees in the kingdom, living in temporary settlements along the northern stretch of the border, between Mae Sot and Mae Hong Son. The Royal Thai Government refused to grant these people refugee status, referring to them instead as 'temporarily displaced persons', and denying them all but the most cursory access to the United Nations High Commissioner for Refugees (UNHCR). The refugees' food, shelter and medical needs were attended to by Western NGOs. At the request of the Thai authorities, these charitable groups kept their presence on the ground to a minimum.

The refugee settlements were largely self-governing, which helped to keep 'aid dependency' to a minimum. Naturally, the refugees and their leaders maintained close links with parent insurgent organisations in Burma, which often used the camps as rear bases in the war to liberate their homelands. Although hardly unprecedented internationally, there was from the beginning a controversial relationship between the insurgents, the refugees, the NGOs and UNHCR.

As ever more people fled to the border areas, the Mon and Karen rebellions became dangerously dependent on Thailand. The kingdom proved an unreliable ally: in co-ordination with the *Tatmadaw*, between 1992–95 the Thai military gradually moved the Mon refugees back across the border, to the NMSP-controlled zones in Burma. At the same time, the

15

authorities began to restrict the activities in Thailand of NMSP and KNU personnel, who hitherto had enjoyed liberal freedom of movement.

Although the Thai military and security establishment's continued influence over the Mon resistance along the border was still a useful tool in Bangkok's relations with Rangoon, the 'good old days' were coming to an end. For decades, insurgent organisations – which in many cases represented ethnic groups which had traditionally been clients of the Thai state – had been employed as proxy armies in the American-backed war against communism in Southeast Asia. Thailand's unofficial policy towards its neighbours had been to sponsor insurgency, thus undermining state security in Burma, and blocking the advance of communism in Laos and Cambodia. However, by the mid-1990s, the disparate – and increasingly desperate – rebel groups still holding-out against Rangoon had been reduced to bit players, and their utility to the shadowy agents of Thai national security was coming to an end. In fact, the Thai generals and politicians, and their counterparts in the *Tatmadaw*, stood to make money out of 'development projects' and natural resource extraction in the ethnic peoples' lands, if these areas could be 'pacified'. As the Thai prime minister (and retired general) Chatchai Choonhaven put it, the new policy focussed on 'turning battlefields into marketplaces.'

The changing Thai policy environment is partly explained by the growing importance of the Association of Southeast Asian Nations (ASEAN) regional grouping, and the economic incentives to 'Constructive Engagement' with Rangoon (as the new approach was called). In the 1990s, the Southeast Asian nations became increasingly wary of the growing power of China, which they hoped to counter by drawing Burma into their sphere of influence. This business and security-driven post-Cold War agenda resulted in the Mon, Karen, Karenni, Shan and other insurgent groups in Burma becoming identified as obstacles to development and diplomacy, rather than freedom fighters and useful clients.

Therefore, in the early 1990s the Thai military and security establishment applied growing pressure on the NMSP, KNU and other insurgent organisations to renounce the armed conflict. Eventually, in June 1995 the NMSP became the fifteenth group to agree a ceasefire with the SLORC. Meanwhile, in the forests of southeast Burma, the KNU fought on.

By 1996, the last of the 10,000 Mon refugees had been repatriated to Burma. By the end of 2001, the NMSP still controlled territory along the border, where the majority of the Mon returnees continued to live in settlements similar to their old camps in Thailand, receiving limited cross-border assistance from the same NGOs that supplied the Karen and Karenni refugees. Due to a well-founded fear of persecution, these people could not return to their home villages. It was debatable however, whether they should be categorised as refugees or Internally Displaced Persons (IDPs).

Meanwhile, the situation 'inside' Burma remained dire. Although in the 1990s the government had initiated some infrastructure development projects in the Mon and other ethnic minority areas, it was questionable whether these had benefited local people. In many areas the fighting had stopped, but despite some marginal improvements, villagers' basic rights continued to be routinely abused by the military and government.

CHAPTER TWO

Demographics, Language and Ethnic Identity

At the height of their power, the number and geographical spread of the Mon population was much greater than today. The conquest of the Mon lands by the Burmans, and later the British, together with the earlier – and somewhat less violent – rise of the Thai states of Sukhothai, Ayuthaiya and Bangkok, had a major impact on the cultural and linguistic orientation of the populations of lower Burma and Thailand. In time, large numbers of Mon speakers came to adopt the language of the new elite. In Thailand at least, Mon language use seemed destined to oblivion – the fate of minority languages across the world in the twentieth century.

Language use is not the sole criterion of ethnic identification. However, the restricted use in modern times of the ancient Mon tongue has had an important effect on the number of people identifying themselves as 'Mon', of whom there are perhaps one-and-a-half million, five per cent of whom live in Thailand. This figure corresponds roughly with the number of Mon speakers, but does not include the very large number of people of Mon decent who do not speak the language.

Ethnic minority identity in contemporary Southeast Asia is under assault from a number of directions. Thailand is home to approximately 750,000 'hilltribe' people (not including Mon, Lao, Khmer, Malay or other lowland groups).[23] The authorities have set out to win the 'hearts and minds' of these often isolated communities, among which the Communist Party of Thailand (CPT) insurgency was active in the 1970s and early '80s. This has meant drawing ethnic minority populations into the orbit of the state, through Thai language education and rural development projects patronised by His Majesty the King. This relatively benign pressure to assimilate has been reinforced by the necessity of adopting a Thai identity in order to acquire, for example, a driving licence or bank account. C.F. Keyes and others have demonstrated that minority people in Thailand often possess multiple ethnic identities, being 'Karen' (or Lawa, or Lao etc.) in some contexts, and 'Thai' in others.[24]

Since 1962, the Burmese military government has adopted less sophisticated assimilationist policies. The Mon nationalists' struggle to preserve the integrity of their lands, language and culture in the face of an orchestrated policy of 'Burmanisation' is a central theme of this book. Before examining the subject in detail however, it is necessary to briefly sketch the historical distribution of the Mon people and survey contemporary Mon demographics.

Population and Location – Past and Present

Subscriptions and ascriptions of ethnic identity rely on a number of factors. Among the most important are geographic location, language use and the related issue of population size.

Evidence of 'Dvaravati style' Mon settlements in the area today known as central Thailand dates from at least the sixth century AD.[25] In the following century Mon communities were established in northeast Thailand and Laos, as well as in the south, at Nakhon Sri Thammarat and Chaiya. However, by the end of the first millennium, these most far-flung principalities were already in decline, or had been conquered, as by 1100 had those at Lopburi, Nakhon Pathom and Ratchaburi. The Mon at Suphanburi – together with those at Sukhothai, which was established around 1000 AD – remained independent until the thirteenth century, as did the northern Mon kingdom of Haripunjaya, centred around modern-day Lamphun, and founded in the eighth century. However, by the end of the thirteenth century, the eastern Mon principalities had all expired, either falling under the influence of the Malay states to the south, of the still-expanding Khmer empire in the east, or of Tai princelings from the north.

Inscriptions and archaeological evidence reveal that further to the west, by the seventh century, Mon settlements had been established in the Tenasserim region, and in the Irrawaddy, Sittaung and Salween River deltas. The latter were to survive for a thousand years, although in the early decades of the second millennium the Mon principalities of Thaton and Pegu (known collectively as Ramanyadesa) succumbed to the Burman kings, whom the Mon themselves helped to establish at Pagan. Never-theless, the Mon cities of 'Burma' rose again some two hundred years later and were to maintain their independence on-and-off until the eighteenth century.[26]

Turning to the present, the majority of the 'Thai Mon' population are descendants of several waves of refugees, who fled Burma during the seventeenth-nineteenth centuries.[27] These 'Peguans' settled under royal patronage in traditionally Mon areas, where they helped defend Siam against the mutual Burman enemy. Over the following centuries, these immigrants became assimilated into Thai society where, unlike the Karen and other 'hilltribe' groups, they were not considered culturally alien.

Indeed, it is only in the very recent past that the 'Thai Mon' have been legally recognised as a 'minority community'.[28]

In an important essay on 'Language and Ethnicity: the Mon in Burma and Thailand', Christian Bauer warns that "most reports about the size of the Mon populations in both Burma and Thailand present conflicting figures."[29] Estimates of the contemporary Mon population in Thailand range between 60,000–200,000 people, depending in part on whether language use is considered a key criterion. Bauer calculates that the number of Mon speakers is unlikely to exceed 60–80,000.

In central Thailand alone, there are some two hundred monasteries possessing Mon manuscripts. Most of these temples were founded in the eighteenth and nineteenth centuries, although a few of the manuscripts are older. However, less than half of these monasteries have Mon-speaking monks.

Although one respected Thai Mon community leader has suggested to the author that some two million people in Thailand are of direct Mon descent, only a small proportion of these speak the language. The contemporary Thai Mon community is widely dispersed. Scattered communities are reported at the old Siamese capital of Ayuthaiya,[30] in Nonthaburi (in Pak Kret District, and particularly on Koh Kret, a small artificial island on the Chao Phya River, just north of Bangkok), in Pathum Thani,[31] Uthai Thani and Lopburi in the Chao Phya River valley north of Bangkok, and at Phra Padaeng[32] in Samut Prakorn Province to the south.

There are also Thai Mon communities – and many Burmese Mon migrant labourers – in Samut Sakorn,[33] Samut Songkram[34] and Nakhon Pathom,[35] and in the border provinces opposite Burma's Mon State and Tenasserim Division: Kanchanaburi, Phetburi,[36] Prachuab Kiri Kahn, and Ratchaburi – where the villages along the Mae Klong River (in Baan Pong and Photharam Districts) are home to the second largest concentration of Mon speakers in Thailand (after the Chao Phya settlements). There are reportedly also Mon settlements further to the south, in Nakhon Sri Thammarat and the Tha Sae District of Chumpon Province,[37] and in Malaysia and Singapore.[38]

In addition, the Mon population in Thailand includes remnants of an earlier strata of settlement. Some 2,000 Nya Kur (or Chao Bon) people, speaking a language apparently derived from Dvaravati-Mon ancestors who flourished in central Thailand a thousand years ago, live in Korat Province in northeast Thailand.[39] These people were only identified with Dvaravati in the 1980s, by Gerard Diffloth. As the Mon scholar, Nai Pan Hla, puts it, they "are a lost nation rediscovered by scientific linguistic studies."[40] However, the small Mon speaking population around Lamphun and Lampang – site of the northern Mon kingdom of Haripunjaya – are the descendants of more recent migrants from Burma.[41]

Today, the Mon population in Thailand is small, and probably declining (see below). However, that in Burma is more robust, although exactly who counts as 'Mon' is no less problematic. Christian Bauer points out that approximately thirty per cent of the contemporary population of Mon State are not ethnic Mons, but rather Burmans, Tavoyans (*Dawei*), Pwo and S'ghaw Karen,[42] and Bengali Muslims, who arrived in Burma during the period of colonial rule.[43] He further notes that in 1985, of 214 monasteries in Burma where Mon writing was taught, twenty per cent were located outside Mon State. Sizeable Mon populations live in adjoining areas of Karen State (Kawkareik, Kya-In Seik-Kyi and Pa'an Townships) and to a lesser extent also in Pegu Division, capital of Hongsawaddy, the last Mon kingdom. In addition, the 1983 government census found 668 Mon living further to the north, in Karenni State – probably in the vicinity of the tin mines at Mawchi, developed by the British.[44]

Following British annexation, the rich soil of lower Burma was intensely cultivated and large numbers of Burman and other peoples moved into the area. Likewise, in a little over a decade during the mid-nineteenth century, the population of Pegu more than doubled, and in many areas Mon communities were overwhelmed by newcomers.[45] Nevertheless, until the early years of the twentieth century, there were still significant Mon populations in Pegu and the Irrawaddy Delta.[46]

According to the last colonial census, by 1931 all but three per cent of the Mon population of Burma was confined to Amherst District and what is today central Mon State.[47] The descendants of the Rangoon and delta Mon were already largely indistinguishable from those of the Burman, Rakhine, Karen and Bengali Muslim populations. Today, few if any Mon-speakers remain in the Irrawaddy Delta, and most of the Mon living in Bahan Township in Rangoon, and in Mandalay, were born elsewhere.[48]

Some commentators have denied the existence of Mon populations south of the current Mon State boundaries. However, this author's fieldwork confirms Christian Bauer's contention that Mon villages are to be found at least as far south as the port of Tavoy. Further south, the population is composed of Karen, who live in the inaccessible river valleys along the border with Thailand, and of Burmans and Tavoyans, as well as small numbers of Mon, Thais, Bengali Muslims and, in the islands of the Mergui archipelago, Moken (or Salon) 'sea gypsies'.[49]

In both Thailand and Burma, surveys and censuses have tended to classify ethnic groups according to religion and language use, rather than self-ascribed 'ethnonym'. Thus, for example, a great many Burmese speaking, Buddhist Karen in the Irrawaddy Delta have been classified as ethnic Burmans.[50] In Burma in particular, successive governments have consistently underestimated the size of ethnic minority populations, and underemphasised the issue of ethnic identity. As Martin Smith states "quite consciously there has been no attempt to take an accurate ethnic survey since the last British census in 1931, which itself contained many errors."[51] Many ethnic minority citizens of Burma would agree with the Human Rights Foundation of Monland, that "successive military governments in Burma since 1962, have adopted racist assimilationist policies against the non-Burman ethnic nationalities."[52]

Unfortunately therefore, the contemporary Mon population of Burma can only be estimated, based on various more-or-less inadequate surveys. The potentially divisive task of implementing a proper census will be one of the more controversial duties to befall a future, more enlightened Burmese government.

Extrapolation from the 1931 colonial census led Bauer to estimate the Mon population in Burma in 1996 at about 800,000 people, and certainly not more than one million.[53] In April 1983 the government calculated the population of Mon State at 1,682,157 people (4.76 per cent of the national total), of whom 38.8 per cent were recorded as Mon (652,677 people), 37.2 per cent Burman and 15.7 per cent Karen.[54] This data must be regarded as incomplete, as the survey team did not penetrate the still extensive war and liberated zones. Nevertheless, based on the 1983 census, and on a 1992 UN Fertility survey, which calculated the population of Mon State at 2.2 million people,[55] there may be between one-and-a-quarter and one-and-a-half million Mon people in Mon State, and as many as two million in all of Burma.[56] However, nationalist leaders have claimed a Mon population in Burma of four million people, plus as many as three million in Thailand.[57]

The considerable differences between these estimates are due in part to the politics of demography in Burma, where ethnic nationalists have been keen to 'talk up' their numbers, while the government has attempted to down-play the size of minority populations, and thus the importance of the groups concerned. Further difficulties arise in distinguishing between the 'Mon proper' and those who have adopted the Burmese language, and to a greater or lesser degree been assimilated into the Burman majority. For example, the 1921 colonial census gave 324,000 Mons "by race", but only 189,000 "speakers of Mon."[58] Presumably, the descendants of the non-Mon speaking group would today be classified as ethnic Burmans.[59] Certainly, if the higher range of estimates for the Mon population of Burma is accepted, then this must be understood to include very large numbers of people who are Mon by ancestry, but do not speak the language.[60]

A 'guestimate' of the total Mon population in Burma today might be one-and-a-half million people. However, the population of the NMSP-controlled liberated zones is only a fraction of this: about 25–30,000 people – including several thousand Karen and about 8,000 repatriated Mon refugees – live under the party's direct jurisdiction.

This raises questions regarding the credibility of the insurgent and ex-insurgent groups. Ultimately of course, the NMSP claims to represent *all*

Mon people and posits a (somewhat ill-defined) ethnic nationalist agenda as an alternative to Burman-dominated military rule. To a degree though, the party's importance and legitimacy derive from the number of people and extent of territory under its control. Therefore, the NMSP can only be seen as one element in the complex picture of Mon ethnic politics.

Ethnonym and Exonym, Religion and Culture

'Mon' – or in the classical literature, 'Raman' – is the only name by which the people refer to themselves, i.e. the only true ethnonym.[61] The term, previously mentioned in sixth-to-tenth century Khmer slave lists, first appears in the Mon language in Kyanzittha's early twelfth century 'new palace inscriptions' at Pagan. (Mon language inscriptions have been discovered dating from the seventh century.)[62]

Two main exonyms have been applied to the Mon. *Talaing*, which was adopted by the British, and used historically by the Burmans, but never by the Mon, is considered derogatory: in the Mon language it means 'bastard' or 'the downtrodden', and perhaps refers to the disinherited status of the Mon after the fall of Pegu.[63] Alternatively, it may derive from the Mons' supposed origins in the Telingana region of southeast India.[64] In 1930, and again in 1947, Mon community leaders petitioned the British authorities against the use of *Talaing*, claiming that it caused offence.[65] The other term that occurs in British colonial records is *Peguan*, a geographical-historical name derived from Pegu, the ancient Mon capital.

Mon nationalist aspirations are grounded in a conception of ethnic self-identity. According to NMSP President Nai Shwe Kyin, the Mon "base our right of self-determination on ethnic history, territory and culture."[66] To be Mon is to identify with a certain territory, with a distinct civilisation and culture nearly two thousand years old, and with the Theravada Buddhist religion.

Bauer agrees with the Mon leader's assessment that at least ninety-five per cent of his people are Buddhist, and a recent survey confirms this figure for the Mon refugee population.[67] Although the Mon monkhood has for centuries been formally incorporated into the Burmese *sangha*, many of the great monasteries of southeast Burma retain a distinct Mon identity. Something of a sleeping giant, and often neglected by commentators, the Mon *sangha* retains a strong influence among the lay community, as is indicated by the widespread patronage of monks and monasteries.[68]

The few Mons who are not Buddhists, are Christians. While there are Mon Catholics and Anglicans, the majority are Baptists (as is the case in Karen and Kachin Christian communities). Church sources have calculated the total number of Mon Baptists in Burma at about 2,000 people,[69] distributed among thirteen churches[70] organised under the Mon chapter of the Myanmar Baptist Convention (of which the Mon, Nai Ba Shin, was from 1962–66 Associate General Secretary). Based on these figures, it would seem that the Buddhist Mon population in Burma constitutes as much as ninety-nine per cent of the total.

In rural villages in particular, orthodox Buddhist belief co-exists with a deep and abiding adherence to the animist pantheon. In many respects similar to the Burman *Nat*, the Mon *Kalok* is manifest in various forms, including the house or other local 'spirit of place', clan or totem spirit, or ghost. The *Kalok* is invoked by means of the spirit dance and other shamanistic practices, which to this day characterise many rural Mon communities, serving to distinguish them from adjacent Burman, Karen and Thai villages (which have their own animist traditions).[71]

Many such customs were first described by Robert Halliday, the 'father of Mon studies' and author of an important 1917 work on Mon culture and society.[72] These include the Mons' unique funeral practices,[73] traditional dancing and music (often associated in Thailand with funerary rites[74]), medical practices[75] and a set of taboos and rituals which, according to Michael Smithies, are "completely distinctive."[76]

Among the most striking traditions are those relating to totem animals. Although few Mon communities today take seriously the complicated injunctions regarding the capture and cooking of tortoises, most are aware that such taboos exist.[77] Furthermore, although only a minority of the author's Mon friends could name their family's totem animal,[78] most are aware that taboo-based clans once played an important part in Mon society, and that each clan traditionally observed a particular animal taboo.[79] Such impressions accord with Brian Foster's research in the 1970s.[80]

The contemporary remnants of such practices contain echoes of the ancient Mon court culture.[81] In a 1999 lecture to the Siam Society, Emmanuel Guillon noted that "if we compare those ceremonies (from early Pagan) with the rituals of the construction of a family house in a traditional Mon village of our days, we can see that the tradition of those royal rituals was still alive thirty years ago."[82]

As might be expected from the demographics, exogamy (and especially marriage to Karens or Burmans) is not uncommon among the Mon in Burma.[83] As for the contemporary Thai Mon, according to Smithies "intermarriage with Thais is quite common, but very rare with nearby Muslims."[84] There is some uncertainty among anthropologists as to whether Mon marriages were traditionally 'arranged' or not.[85]

In concluding this section, it may be noted that the Mon tend to have wavier hair, and be taller and darker skinned, than most other ethnic groups in lower Burma or Thailand; consequently, they are sometimes considered somewhat 'Indian' in appearance.[86] Robert Halliday, the Baptist missionary who lived for many years among the Mon was "often forced to exclaim, 'what a fine-looking man!'"[87] However, he did not think it possible to distinguish by physical appearance alone between Thai, Burman or Mon.[88] (Regarding temperament, although famed primarily for their skills in the arts of civilisation, the Mon are nevertheless a proud people, and have sometimes been accused of arrogance.[89])

The Mon Language

There are three major language families in Burma and western Thailand: Tai-Kadai, Tibeto-Burman and Mon-Khmer. Mon and Khmer are related to Vietnamese – through the Viet-Muong branch of the Mon-Khmer family – as well as to more than one hundred other Austro-Asiatic languages spoken in Burma, Cambodia, China, India, Laos, Thailand, Vietnam and the Malay peninsula. Most of these have no written form.

Scholars have traditionally sub-divided the language into three broad historical categories: Old Mon, Middle Mon and Modern Mon – the latter dating from the fall of Pegu, in the mid-eighteenth century. However, as H.L. Shorto notes (regarding Old and Middle Mon), "we owe these terms to an accident of history, in that the inscriptions in Burma, which were the first to be studied, include two large groups ... from the turn of the twelfth century and the late fifteenth" (i.e. from the periods of Pagan and Peguan ascendancy).[90] Shorto recommended that term 'classical Mon' be adopted for these two periods. However, Emmanuel Guillon suggests a fourfold historical division: Proto-Mon, a reconstructed language "which seems to have separated from the other languages of the (Mon-Khmer) group towards about the fourth century of this era; Old Mon, from about the sixth century to the end of the twelfth; Middle Mon, from the thirteenth century to the eighteenth; and Modern Mon."[91]

The Mon script is modelled on the Grantha and Pallava writing systems of southern India. Mon also contains a substantial corpus of vocabulary borrowed from Sanskrit, and later from Pali, many elements of which are found in other languages in the region.[92] The contemporary Mon, Burmese, Karen and Thai languages have a number of words in common, most of which derive from the Mon. According to a recent study, nearly seven hundred Thai words in current use are of Mon origin,[93] most of which were borrowed during the latter half of the first millennium.[94] Nearly two hundred more Thai words have been borrowed from Mon via Khmer, its 'linguistic cousin'.[95] (Khmer possesses a distinctive Mon-like 'quack', and the similarities between the two languages have in recent years encouraged large numbers of young Mon men to seek their fortunes in the ruby mines of Cambodia).

Mon has been a literary language since at least the sixth century – i.e. well before the ancestors of the Thais or Burmans reached modern-day Thailand or Burma. Some of the oldest inscriptions in the region are written in Mon-Khmer characters and, with the exception of the long-departed

Pyu, the Mon was the first literate culture in Burma.[96] Furthermore, the Burmese script is derived from the Mon, as are some aspects of the Thai.[97]

A non-tonal language, contemporary Mon in Burma has three main dialects: Martaban-Moulmein ('Central Mon' or *Mon Te*), Pegu ('Northern Mon' or *Mon Tang*) and the Ye dialect ('Southern Mon' or *Mon Nya*). These variations may be vestiges of the three ancient 'Mon races' referred to in some legends.[98] All three dialects are mutually intelligible, with only minor differences in pronunciation and idiom. Each is more-or-less comprehensible to 'Thai Mon' speakers,[99] whose own minor dialectical variations are attributed to their descent from different waves of 'Burmese Mon' migrants.[100]

As noted above, Mon demographics are complicated by the fact that many people of Mon ancestry are unfamiliar with the language, although they may still identify with the ethnonym. An NMSP document published in 1985 stated that sixty per cent of Mon people in Burma, and eighty per cent of those in Thailand, were literate, but that – crucially – not all were literate in Mon.[101] This helps to explain why Nai Shwe Kyin's declaration (quoted above) does not mention language use an element in ethnic identity: to do so would restrict the range of those classified as Mon. The NMSP leader is following a line established in the late 1930s by the All Ramanya Mon Association (ARMA), the first Mon nationalist organisation of modern times, which held that a person was Mon by descent, regardless of language use.[102] Although, as long ago as 1891, the British census-takers stated that "the process of (Mon linguistic) decay ... has ... advanced too far to be checked by any transient revival of national feeling",[103] Nai Shwe Kyin remains convinced that, should the NMSP ever gain real power in Burma, large numbers of assimilated Mon will reclaim their 'original' identity.[104]

The Baptist missionary, Haswell,[105] and the British scholars, Blagden and Shorto, supposed that Mon is – or soon will be – obsolete. However, Halliday and others have disagreed.[106] According to Bauer, "publications in Mon ... are numerous and are likely to represent the largest number of books and magazines after Burmese."[107] Furthermore, both old and new styles of Mon music, and Mon traditional theatre and stage acts, remain very popular in Burma.[108]

Clearly, Mon is not a dying tongue. Although, since the early 1960s, the government has restricted the teaching and official use of Mon and other minority languages, there are still many villages in middle and lower Mon State where Mon is the only language spoken and a large proportion of villagers are literate in the ancient tongue. In fact, Mon is the first language of many communities on the periphery of the state. No reliable modern survey exists (other than for the refugee population; see below). The author has though, met children in Thanbyuzayat – which by Burmese standards is hardly off the beaten track – who speak Mon first, and Burmese only second, and often imperfectly. Bauer, for one, is certain that "Mon will continue to be a major regional language."[109]

This contention is born out by the findings of a 1995 survey of Mon refugees on the Thailand-Burma border. All but a very few of the refugees interviewed spoke, and identified themselves as, Mon (the exceptions being a few hundred ethnic Karen and Burmans). More than sixty per cent of males were literate, of whom forty-seven per cent were literate in both Mon and Burmese, thirty per cent in Mon only and twenty per cent in Burmese only. However, less than fifty per cent of all females were literate in any language, of whom forty-one per cent were literate in Mon and Burmese, thirty-nine per cent in Burmese only and seventeen per cent in Mon exclusively.[110] This bias among women towards the Burmese language probably reflects the fact that, until recently – its use having been banned in schools – Mon has been taught only in the monasteries, to which girls have traditionally had limited access. On a positive note – which attests to the effectiveness of the NMSP school system – literacy levels were higher among younger age groups than older, especially for women.

Minority peoples everywhere tend towards bi-lingualism. The great majority of the author's Mon and Karen friends speak their own ethnic language, plus Burmese (or Thai), and often one or more other languages (including English).[111] In many cases, Burmese is the first language and the person's ethnic language ability has been developed only *after* coming out to the Thailand-Burma border, either in order to join the revolution, or to escape persecution in Burma.

The opposite is also sometimes the case: those who have grown up in the isolated 'liberated zones' of Burma tend to speak an ethnic language first, and Burmese second, and often imperfectly. This had led to concern, in the NMSP and KNU education departments, that a generation of children is growing up unable to properly handle the Burmese language. Given the deplorable condition to which the government has allowed the Burmese state education system to decline, and the limited resources available to the insurgents' school systems, it is not surprising that those parents able to do so often educate their children in Thailand.

For the majority of Mon people, who have remained under Burmese state hegemony, access to Mon language education has been circumscribed both by government and social factors. As Nai Pan Hla recounts:

(As a child) I did go to stay in the Buddhist monastery in my village when I was under ten years old. But my father, Headman of the village asked the Abbot monk to teach me only Myanmar and English languages. My father said, 'Mon is no use.' He knew only Mon and he was very difficult to deal with the official matters. When I grew up, I studied Mon by my own will. I have found that Mon parents in modern society, ask their children to study Myanmar and English like my father because they want their offspring to become officers. It is a great problem to prevent the younger generation of the Mon people not to drop off their mother tongue.[112]

The process of assimilation is influenced by physical, as well as social and political factors. The ethnic Mon scholar, Dr S-M-, notes that "many of the ethnic groups of Myanmar, particularly the Chins and Kachins enjoy the protection of geographic location and difficult access so that they are relatively unaffected by the assimilative process. The Mons, living in the fertile plains of lower Myanmar, do not enjoy that seclusion."[113]

Meanwhile in Thailand, since the 1920s all schooling has been conducted in Thai, and minority languages have been largely banished from the classroom. With the Thai Mon community spread more thinly than in Burma, and given Thailand's rapid development over the past half-century, it is not surprising that Mon language use in the kingdom is in decline. The Mon island of Koh Kret which, because of its thriving potteries and proximity to Bangkok, has in recent years attracted the attention of scholars and journalists, provides a good example. Although approximately eighty per cent of the residents of the island's seven villages are of Mon ancestry, only the elderly and some monks regularly use the language; many young people are said to understand Mon, but most rarely speak it. However, the Mon of Koh Kret still keep up many of their distinctive traditions, such as ceramics production, and celebration of the *Kalok* spirit festival, held a week after the end of *songkran* (new year). Furthermore, as Donald Wilson reports and the present author can confirm, despite being part of the ever-expanding metropolitan Bangkok, Koh Kret "still retains a distinctly Mon flavour" and worshippers at Wat Pramai Yikawat still talk of *Muang Mon* (or Monland) across the border in Burma.[114]

In a 1973 essay on the Mon in Thailand, Foster suggested that the forces of modernisation would inevitably undermine this dispersed community's distinct ethnic identity. Foster assumed that "the difference between being really Mon and not Mon depends on language" and that "as a written language Mon is virtually dead in Thailand."[115] He stated that in most cases 'Mon' identity in modern Thailand consists of not much more than "a knowledge of some Mon ancestry . . . some superficial awareness of the Mon historical tradition . . . (and) of the influence of Mon Buddhism" in Thailand, together with a few words of Mon.[116] The 'Thai Mon' were said to be "homogenous neither socially, culturally, nor in their own or other's view of them."[117] Foster concluded that "the possibilities for the further retention of Mon ethnicity are not favourable. Thai society is rapidly closing in on the villages which have remained Mon simply through isolation, and the number of children born now whose primary ethnic identity will be Mon will be small indeed."[118]

However, just one year previously Michael Smithies had come to a different conclusion.[119] He found that at Laadgrabang, "so near to Bangkok ... Mon customs and language still survive."[120] Regarding the persistence of distinct traditions among the Thai Mon, Smithies noted that "what makes these practices still more interesting is that most people have been assuming ... (that) the Mons were totally absorbed and no loner existed as an individual ethnic community." However, according to Smithies, such assumptions were not justified, even for the younger generation.[121]

After another quarter-century of rapid social and economic change in Thailand, the Mon villages in Laadgrabang, Pak Kret and Photharam still contain significant numbers of Mon speakers, as do many of the more recently-arrived Mon communities in the border provinces.[122] Furthermore, due to their geographical isolation, the Nya Kur people – the descendants of ancient Dvaravati, whose name in Mon means 'highland people'[123] – have also preserved their language (which diverges considerably from modern Thai or Burmese Mon).[124] Nevertheless, these pockets of Mon identity are under considerable pressure from the forces of modernisation, and Mon language use is certainly in decline in Thailand. This does not mean that Mon identity is inevitably doomed, though: Mon culture still retains its cachet.

As a recent study of funerary music in Bangkok reports, a distinct Thai Mon identity persists.[125] Indeed, to be Mon in Thailand is considered rather high class. A number of nationally prominent figures are of Mon ancestry, including Thailand's widely-respected former UN ambassador and prime minister, Anand Panyarachun.[126] For many years, the presence of Mon sympathisers among the Thai military elite ensured the insurgents along the border a degree of protection and patronage.[127] However, when NMSP leaders meet with the Thai military, the *lingua franca* is Thai, or occasionally English.

Identity, Control and Assimilation

If the name 'Mon' is restricted to those who share the language, or consciously identify with the cultural heritage – categories which the nationalists have been keen to consolidate and expand – then Mon identity is less problematic than that of many other minority groups. Robert Taylor and others have suggested that modern forms of ethnic nationalism in Burma are derived from the misguided racial theories and ascriptions of the colonial period.[128] As with other minority groups in Southeast Asia, Karen ethnic identity has been labelled an artificial construction, based on speculative missionary ethnography and politically expedient colonial classification.[129]

However, it is a mistake to assume that, before the arrival of the British, non-Burman ethnic and political identities did not exist. Baptist missionaries and colonial administrators no doubt played a significant role in shaping the modern form of Karen identity, and it is true that there are considerable differences of language, religion and culture between different Karen sub-groups. Nevertheless, the similarities clearly outweigh the differences.[130] Certainly, in the modern era Karen nationalists have had no hesitation in positing a common, pan-Karen ethnic and national identity. Although this 'imagined' identity may be constructed from disparate elements, it is nonetheless authentic for that.[131] The fifty year struggle for the free Karen state of Kaw Thoo Lei is testimony to the enduring appeal of the Karen national idea.[132]

The population of Burma is nearly fifty million people. The five-seven million strong Karen community is always going to be large enough to influence the political scene. By contrast, in the modern period the Mon, with perhaps two per cent of Burma's population, have sometimes been perceived as too few in number to play a significant role on the national stage. This has not always been the case.

During the golden age of Pegu, Mon culture was dominant over most of lower Burma (or Ramanyadesa). Of course, this does not mean that the Mon ethnic group was a monolithic entity, sharing the same clan and dynastic loyalties. Victor Lieberman suggests that the 'Mon' kingdoms were in fact expressions of something more complex, and that "the correlation between cultural, i.e. ethnic, identity and political loyalty was necessarily very imperfect, because groups enjoying the same language and culture were fragmented by regional ties."[133]

Lieberman point out that ethnicity was only one factor among several (including religion, culture, region and position in the tributary status hierarchy) constituting personal and regime identity in precolonial times. As authority was vested in the person of the monarch, it was he that commanded primary loyalty, rather than any abstract idea of ethnic community. A Burman king could be the patron of Mon princely clients, and vice-versa.

Lieberman concedes that the edicts of the warrior-king Alaungphaya made a clear ethnic distinction between his own (Burman) followers and those of the "Talaing renegades."[134] Indeed, according to this reading, the ethnic polarisation of Burma accelerated rapidly under Alaungphaya, who played the 'race card' to his advantage.[135] Since no later than the mid-eighteenth century therefore, individuals and communities have chosen – or been forced – to represent themselves as either 'Mon' or 'Burman', depending on the political situation. Mon and Burman leaders, be they kings or modern politicians, have used ethnic labels to create and control power bases, which since the colonial period have tended to become ossified as ethnic communities.

Michael Aung-Thwin has also examined episodes in Burmese history, previously read as instances of ethnic conflict, and concluded that these events were not necessarily perceived as such by the participants. He demonstrates that the Mon-Burman wars of the eleventh-eighteenth centuries were understood by the elites of lower and upper Burma primarily in terms of religious, economic and geo-political struggle. "However, in the twentieth century, when the prospect of Burma as an independent entity composed of several ethnic groups ... became a real possibility", ethnicity came to dominate the historiography of Burma.[136]

In particular, Aung-Thwin argues that the supposition of ethnicity as a *cause* of historical events is the creation of (primarily Western) historians. The frameworks imposed by these scholars have had a profound influence on the interpretation of Burmese history and politics. This legacy has perhaps led to an over-emphasis on themes of ethnicity.[137] Nevertheless – and notwithstanding Aung-Thwin's recent work, questioning 'the Mon paradigm' – a distinct Mon identity clearly *did* exist in precolonial Southeast Asia. More troublesome to nationalists is the suggestion that this distinct Mon identity has been – or is being – erased.

According to Robert Taylor, the upheavals of seventeenth and eighteenth century Burma led to a "gradual transformation of the residents' ethnic affinities" in which "the permanency and power of the state, and its identity with monarchs who were considered to be ethnically and culturally Burman, led communities and individuals to accept the state's definition of their cultural orientation ... The distinctive identity of being a Mon which had marked the south in earlier eras was disappearing."[138] In fact, this identity had been under threat since the beginning of the second millennium, when the Burman kings of Pagan first adopted the Mons' Theravada religion, together with aspects of their language and political culture. The Mon have been fighting a rearguard action against assimilation ever since.[139]

As the expansionist Burman kings adopted the Mons' culture, so they came to appropriate their history and territory. As Dr S-M- observes, across lower Burma "only the names of Mon villages, creeks or pagodas ... bear testimony to the fact that these places were once inhabited by the Mons."[140] Mon place names themselves have also been distorted – e.g. Moulmein (or Mawlamyine) was originally known as *Mot Mae Reum* ('one eye destroyed' – a reference to the Mon legend wherein the crafty Burmans tricked and maimed a three-eyed Mon king).

Another example is provided by the very symbol of the Burmese state – the Shwedagon (Golden Dagon) Pagoda. Built by Mon monarchs no later than the fourteenth century, on the site of a much older cult centre,[141] the Shwedagon was originally known in Mon as the *Kyaik Dagon* (or *Kyaik Lagon*[142]). According to Guillon, this is "*the* sacred place" of the Mons.[143] Its religious centrality to the Burmans, since the eighteenth century, illustrate the degree to which Mon culture has been adopted and reproduced as Burmese 'national culture'. Similarly, the great Shwemawdaw Pagoda in Pegu[144] has the Mon title, *Kyaik Mawdaw*.[145]

31

As the Burmans came to dominate the land, the vestiges of Mon history were colonised. The process of assimilation continued under British colonial rule. The 1872 census noted that "intermarriage between Burmese and Talaings is more frequent now than formerly and among the Talaing of Pegu and Martaban the admixture of Burman blood is apparent."[146] Although, since the British occupation, "any oppression of the Talaings ... has, of course, disappeared.... another process – that of absorption by the more powerful race – is effecting the obliteration of the Talaing."[147]

The "obliteration of the Talaing" and other minority groups has continued into the post-independence era. In a rare public justification of 'Burmanisation', shortly after seizing power in 1962, General Ne Win made a speech in which he denied the need for a separate Mon culture and ethnicity. According to Ne Win (who claimed himself to be of mixed Mon ancestry[148]), the Mon tradition had been incorporated into Burmese 'national' culture. In August 1991 the then-SLORC Chairman, General Saw Maung, made a similar speech, in which he denied the need for a separate Mon identity.[149]

Such propositions are obviously political: in denying the existence of a separate Mon identity, the military government undermines the nationalists' calls for self-determination, and rejects the limited cultural and political rights extended to the Mon under U Nu's civilian government in the late 1950s and early '60s. Rather, Ne Win and Saw Maung proposed that the Mon devote their energies to the *Tatmadaw's* self-appointed task of building a modern 'Burmese' nation. Such a perspective fails to acknowledge the extent to which the state has been captured by members of the Burman ethnic group.[150]

The conception of Mon-Burman relations outlined above is illustrated by an incident that reportedly occurred at a United Nations conference on minorities in New York, in 1970. U Thant, the Burmese UN Secretary-General, declared that, as the Mons had long ago been absorbed into the Burman majority, "the last Mon is dead." However, in a fine piece of diplomatic theatre, Thailand's ambassador to the UN, the Thai Mon, Anand Panyarachun, publicly refuted U Thant's claim and, in Nai Shwe Kyin's words, "put him to shame."[151]

However, this incident must be understood in context. As a representative of the Irrawaddy Delta aristocracy, U Thant – whose mother was in fact half-Mon – would have identified strongly with lower Burma and the Mon heritage, without realising that this was still a living tradition. A product of his social class and times, U Thant would have viewed the Mon from a purely historical perspective. Indeed, his grandson (the scholar and diplomat, U Thant Myint U) has told the author of the surprise with which members of the family later greeted the discovery that Mon speakers were still to be found in lower Burma: the last Mon had not yet disappeared!

However, since 1962, the authorities have suppressed all but the most anodyne expression of non-Burman identity, and the Mon population of lower Burma has come under increasing pressure to assimilate. The government's campaign of 'Burmanisation' has been particularly marked since the advent of the SLORC in 1988.

In his study of 'Mental Culture in Burmese Crisis Politics', Gustaaf Houtman describes how the SLORC has attempted to divert attention from its civil and human rights record, by means of appeals to a 'Myanmar national culture', and by emphasising the present regime's supposed continuity with the precolonial monarchy.[152] He calls Burma a 'culture state', bent on consolidating the 'Myanmafication' of culture and history. Mikael Gravers refers to this process as "cultural corporatism", in which an "imagined Myanmar has one singular cultural essence which is embodied in all individual citizens."[153]

In its appeal to a monolithic national identity, 'Myanmafication' displays aspects of fascist ideology. Furthermore, the emphasis on Burmese (read Burman) purity, and the denial of minority cultures, has led to a characteristically totalitarian re-writing of history. As Houtman notes, since the early 1990s, the government has sponsored construction of a series of new national museums across the country, which are intended to institutionalise and reproduce 'Myanmar national culture'.

Few of the Mon artefacts in the new National Museum in Rangoon,[154] which opened in 1996, are credited to the Mon.[155] Rather, the emphasis is on the glory of the Myanmar-Burman heritage, while the 'Showroom for the Cultures of National Races' is relegated to a little-visited room on the fourth floor. Similarly, although it contains some interesting exhibits, the shabby state of the Mon Cultural Museum in Moulmein testifies to a lack of official interest.[156]

A particularly striking example of the 'Myanmafication' of history is the reconstruction of the Kambawzathadi Palace at Pegu, on the supposed site of the mid-sixteenth century capital of the Burman king, Tabinshwehti, and his successor, Bayinnaung. Since 1990, the royal apartments and audience hall have been excavated and rebuilt, in concrete. As historians have little idea what the original palace looked like, the new buildings are modelled on nineteenth century palace designs from Mandalay.[157] In addition to this historical inaccuracy, and despite the discovery of a number of inscribed foundation posts in the area, it is by no means certain that this is actually the site of Tabinshwehti and Bayinnaungs' palace, rather than that of later rulers.[158]

Nevertheless, the Kambawzathadi Palace project received a major boost in September 1999, when it was visited by Lt-General Khin Nyunt – an event which made the front page of the state-controlled *New Light of Myanmar*.[159] The clear purpose here was to glorify the achievements of Bayinnaungs' expansive 'second Myanmar dynasty', and by association,

Burma's current leaders, who are said to fancy themselves as princes of a 'fourth Myanmar dynasty'.[160] However, what the government-sponsored literature on Kambawzathadi mentions only in passing is that the new palace was in fact built upon the much older remains of the Mon capital of Pegu.

In fact, parts of the largely un-excavated Mon site are today still visible as a series of grassy mounds and depressions, between the foot of the great Shwemawdaw Pagoda and the newly-'rebuilt' royal chambers. The existence of these remains, which disappear beneath the new concrete 'throne hall', are indicated by a some crudely-painted wooden signposts. If properly examined, this archaeological site might yield important information regarding the development of mainland Southeast Asian polity and religion in the fourteenth-sixteenth centuries. As it is however, the neglected remains of Hongsawaddy are a symbolic reminder of the balance of power in modern Burma: it is the victors who write history. Needless to say, few of the artefacts in the nearby museum are attributed to Mon kings or craftsmen.

In contrast to the care and considerable funds that have been dedicated to the (re-)construction of 'Myanmar' (i.e. Burman) history, that of Burma's other ethnic groups has been marginalised and neglected. The Karen and other minority peoples' languages have been suppressed, and their culture and history relegated to the status of regional 'handicrafts' and 'folktales'.[161] Although it has been relatively more difficult for the architects of 'Burmanisation' to sweep nearly two thousand years of Mon civilisation under the carpet, the claim that Mon history should be relegated to a dead past, and subsumed under that of 'Myanmar', amounts to a denial of Mon identity in the present. As a recent verse published by Mon monks in Thailand laments:

Our history is rich
Our future is bright
We gave Southeast Asia Buddhism
Here we were the first peoples to write
The Thais and the Burmans
were our pupils
How do they treat their teacher now?[162]

CHAPTER THREE

Mon Nationalism in Burma (and Thailand)

For nearly a thousand years, the Mon heritage has been under threat from a 'Burmanisation' of culture and history. However, the Mon have not always been passive victims in this process. Identity is plastic, and can be effected by long-term historical processes, as well as by the more immediate actions of politicians and generals. This truth has inspired generations of Mon activists, who have campaigned to conserve and resurrect the Mon language, history and culture – the foundations of Mon identity. Some have gone further, and sought to re-establish Monland as a more-or-less independent political entity.

Since the 1920s, various Burmese political leaders have pursued a variety of nationalist, anti-colonial policies. However, the distinction between 'Burmese' and 'Burman' nationalism has not always been clear, and the former has often been indistinguishable from the latter. According to D.R. SarDesai and other historians, nationalism in Southeast Asia "has been in most cases a response to imperialism and the political and economic exploitation of the governed. In a certain sense, nationalist revolutions were the creation of Western colonial powers themselves."[163] This has also been true of ethnic nationalism in independent Burma, vis-à-vis the Burman-dominated central government, which in ethnic minority areas has often behaved like, and been perceived as, a colonial regime.

SarDesai defines nationalism as "conscious sentiment of kinship ... fostered by common characteristics like language, territory, religion, race, and heritage. Beyond this, sociologists have stressed common cultural and psychological traits or the group consciousness engendered by literature, arts, and institutions."[164] Notwithstanding Eric Hobsbawm's warning that "nations do not make nationalisms but rather the other way round",[165] it seems clear that the Mon *do* possess a distinct cultural and historical identity. Mon nationalist movements in the modern era have used this identity as the basis for claims to an independent, or at least autonomous, Monland.[166] As Michael Gravers puts it "identity thus becomes the

35

foundation of political rights." Gravers calls this process "*ethnicicism ...* the separation or seclusion of ethnic groups from nation states in the name of ethnic freedom ... where cultural differences are classified as primordial and antagonistic."[167]

Given the fact of Mon national identity, a number of fundamental questions present themselves: is the quest to (re-)establish Monland either practicable, or in the best interests of the Mon people as a whole? Do the nationalists propose a coherent programme? Is the struggle for Mon rights best served by confrontation, or by compromise with other interest groups, such as the military government or democratic opposition? Is the struggle for ethnic rights and self-determination the same as that for human rights and democracy? If so, to what extent are these concerns reflected in the ethnic nationalists' strategy and practice?

Turning to the NMSP, what is its relevance today, given that the party has never controlled more than a small portion of the Mon people's ancestral lands, and is no longer at war with Rangoon? What is the relationship between the insurgents and the people they aim to liberate – including the refugees, whose plight is at least in part a consequence of the rebels' actions? Finally, what is, or should be, the role in this complex scenario of the international community – the media, NGOs, foreign governments and regional and international bodies?

Mon National Sentiment in the Modern Era

Although, during the late 1950s and early '60s, U Nu's elected civilian administrations allowed the Mon a degree of cultural and political freedom, since 1962, Mon identity has been under direct assault from the military government. Mon language teaching has been banned from state schools and all but the most apolitical cultural celebrations have been repressed.[168]

An exception to the general rule has been the authorities' limited toleration of Mon language studies. Although ignored by the state school system and bureaucracy since the mid-1960s, the Mon language has been investigated by scholars, both within and outside Burma. The former include the Mon linguist and historian, Dr Nai Pan Hla, lately of the Burmese Epigraphic Survey and Tokyo University of Foreign Studies.[169] It is encouraging to note that, since the 1995 NMSP-SLORC ceasefire, a few postgraduate students at Rangoon and Moulmein Universities have taken up studies of the Mon inscriptions. Despite such developments in the study of Classical Mon, Shorto's *A Dictionary of Modern Spoken Mon*[170] and Nai Tun Way's Mon-Burmese and Mon-English dictionaries[171] are among the few comprehensive descriptions of the language in its contemporary form.

The NMSP's failure, since 1995, to win concessions from the government over the teaching of Mon in state schools has been a major disappointment to the nationalist community. Nevertheless, the party's

36

school system has expanded since the mid-90s: by 2001, the NMSP Education Department was running 148 Mon National Schools and 217 'mixed schools' (government schools, in which Mon was taught after school hours, and usually unofficially), teaching some 51,000 children and employing 917 teachers.[172] By the late 1990s, there were more NMSP schools in government-controlled Burma than in the 'liberated zones'. This expansion of education services constituted one of the most positive developments of the post-ceasefire era. Furthermore, the ceasefire created the political space within which to promote Mon language teaching 'inside' Burma, beyond the NMSP school system's catchment areas.

Since 1995, groups such as the Mon Literature and Culture Committee (MLCC) and the Association for Summer Mon Literature and Buddhist Teachings Training have been at the forefront of a drive to expand and consolidate the Mon language skills, and thereby the cultural and historical awareness, of the Mon community in Burma. A successor to the ARMA and other cultural and youth groups of the 1930s and '40s, the MLCC pioneered Mon literacy training in the 1950s. Although it was largely dormant during the repressive Ne Win era, monasteries across lower Burma continued to teach Mon throughout 1960s–80s.[173] Since 1996, the MLCC has re-emerged as a leading player in this field, participating in a series of successful Mon Language Literacy Training Courses (or Summer Language Trainings), organised by Mon educationalists and the *sangha*.

With the Karen and other Literature and Culture Committees, the MLCC is among the handful of specifically 'ethnic' organisations tolerated by the military regime. It maintains branches in Rangoon and at Moulmein University, and in village monasteries across Mon State and in Pegu and Tenasserim Divisions. The success of the Summer Language Trainings, which in 2001 attracted more than 45,000 (mostly primary) school students, is testimony to the continued relevance to families across lower Burma of a distinctly Mon education.[174]

The impact of the literacy campaign has in part been due to its association with the prestigious Mon *sangha*. A related characteristic is the way in which the literacy drives have galvanised local communities. As Dr S-M- states, "no matter how strong the external forces pushing for the decline of the Mon language are, it is the internal forces within the community – its spirit and determination ... that is crucial for stemming the decline." Unless local people are involved with the preservation and propagation of their language and culture, these will slide "steadily towards final obliteration." Fortunately, Dr S-M- regards the recent literacy drives as "signs of revival (meriting) further encouragement."[175]

The revival of Mon national sentiment in Burma over the past decade is related to the great democracy uprising of 1988, the foundation that year of the Mon National Democratic Front (MNDF), and the success of Mon candidates in the 1990 election. Among the generation of young Mon nationalists that emerged in 1988–90, a number first became radicalised through their association with the MLCC. Indeed, it was often only upon attending Moulmein University that many of these elite students attained literacy in Mon. Many also took Mon names at the same time (ethnic minority citizens are obliged to adopt a Burman name, if they wish to 'get on').

As noted above, between 1988–90 large numbers of university and other students came out to the Thailand-Burma border, where many joined the insurgents in the jungle. Among these were several hundred Mon activists. It is significant that most of these did not join the Burman-led All Burma Students Democratic Front (ABSDF), but rather made common cause with the NMSP and other specifically Mon organisations.[176] These educated young people obviously identified at least as much with an 'ethnic' agenda as with a purely 'political' one. The Mon insurgency thus gained an infusion of fresh idealism, and new ideas regarding the nature of democracy and the importance of human rights. The young activists in turn learned some tough lessons in the realities of jungle life. Those who remained for any length of time along the border gradually absorbed the insurgents' history and culture, manifest in the various holidays celebrated in the liberated zones.

Since 1974, Mon State Day celebrations have been held in government-controlled Burma every March 19th. These commemorate the 1974 constitution, under which the BSPP regime established Mon and Rakhine (Arakan) States. However, ethnic nationalists charge that these entities have only ever existed on paper. Mon State Day has not therefore, achieved the popularity of Mon *National* Day, in February, which since its inception in 1947 has become a symbol of Mon independence, celebrating as it does the mythic foundation of Pegu.

Many of Burma's other minority peoples have their own national days, which in most cases are not recognised by the state. Karen National Day, on 11th February, commemorates the 1948 demonstrations that crystallised Karen aspirations for equality and self-determination in newly-independent Burma. However, it is Karen New Year that most closely approximates the significance of Mon National Day. Although the dates of both festivals are determined by the traditional lunar calendar, neither is of ancient origin, having been established during the final days of the colonial period as expressions of, and encouragements, to ethnic nationalist sentiment.[177]

As well as among the nationalist community in Burma and Thailand, Mon National Day has been celebrated since the 1990s by exiles in North America and Australia. Furthermore, in recent years, under the leadership of the Mon Unity League (MUL) and Thai Ramon Association (TRA), the holiday has been adopted by members of the 'Thai Mon' community in greater Bangkok, and in the Mon provinces of southwest Thailand.

In Burma, Mon National Day is still an occasion for the display of Mon strength and unity, and a stimulus to linguistic and cultural revival. Every year, National Day celebrations are held at NMSP headquarters (or 'Central'), and in each of the districts into which the party divides its territory. The leadership uses such occasions to demonstrate the party's continued relevance and potency in the post-ceasefire period.

Since 1995, major events have also been organised further 'inside' Burma. In 1999, the largest of these were held in Pegu and Moulmein,[178] with smaller celebrations staged in Tavoy and other towns across lower Burma. Each was attended by representatives of the NMSP or MNLA, as well as by monks and other members of the wider Mon community. Although celebration of the 2000 and 2001 Mon National Days was suppressed by the authorities in Rangoon and elsewhere, the NMSP still held large-scale celebrations throughout the liberated zones.[179]

The political significance of Mon National Day is illustrated by the case of an armed, anti-ceasefire Mon faction active in NMSP Tavoy district in the late 1990s. The NMSP denied any legitimacy to the 'Mon Armed Group', referring to it as a *dacoit* (bandit) gang. However, the group clearly had political aspirations, and in February 2000 chose to highlight its nationalist credentials by holding a National Day celebration at Paupingwin village, in Yebyu township. The wave of *Tatmadaw* repression which followed this defiant gesture caused several thousand local people to flee their villages, thus indirectly reinforcing the symbolic importance of such nationalist anniversaries.[180]

In February 1998 the Mon National Day Celebration Committee, an overseas Mon association, issued a statement marking the 51st anniversary of National Day:

> Traditionally we Mon have celebrated the founding of our Nation on the first Waning of Mide, a Mon lunar date, which happens to fall this year on 12th February.

> Mon National Day commemorates the inception of the Mon kingdom, Hongsawadee, founded in 825 AD by two brothers, Samala and Vimala, in what is now called Pegu, in Lower Burma. On this auspicious day may all Mon people be blessed with physical and mental health ...

> The fall of Mon Kingdom to the Burmans in 1757 not only marked the end of the once flourishing Mon kingdom but of all administrative and political powers as well. Thus a nation of great significance in Southeast Asian history was reduced to an ethnic minority and has tended to have been forgotten by the modern world.

> Mon political forces joined hand in hand with Burmans and other ethnic groups in gaining independence from the British in 1948. But after the independence the Mon were denied their political rights with the excuse that there were no particular differences between the Mon

39

and the Burmans. As the result of this, the Mons continued to endure suppression of their rights and their country . . .

We Mon people are still severely oppressed under the ruling of dictatorship, SPDC and had been deprived of our fundamental rights, the rights of self- determination.

In this auspicious occasion, Mon National Day, let all Mon people commit ourselves to be united as . . . one family and to struggle for freedom of our homeland where we Mon could exercise the rights of self-determination and where we could enjoy a peaceful life.[181]

Since the fall of the last Mon kingdom, both royals and revolutionaries have sought to re-gain Monland by force of arms. Another key date in the nationalist calendar is thus Mon Revolution (or Resistance) Day, which falls on the full moon of *Khadoisoi* (August[182]), and marks the day in 1947 when Mon insurgents first took up arms.[183] Unsurprisingly, observance of Revolution Day is not encouraged in government-controlled areas, and its celebration is confined to the NMSP-controlled liberated zones. Other important nationalist holidays are NMSP Day, celebrated on 20th July – the day that Nai Shwe Kyin founded the party – and MNLA Day on 29th August, marking the formation in 1971 of the Mon National Liberation Army.[184] These historic dates are recorded on the iconic calendars issued every year by the NMSP and other ethnic nationalist movements in Burma (and by many other institutions, from monasteries to government departments).

Of course, the majority of Mon people may not necessarily share sentiments articulated by a small, educated elite. However, the success of Mon politicians in the 1990 election, and the enthusiastic response of 'ordinary villagers' to Mon National Day celebrations, do seem to indicate the existence of a strong Mon nationalist spirit in Burma.

In general however, only committed nationalists, and those who have been educated in the upper levels of the NMSP school system, together with members of the *sangha*, possess a detailed knowledge of Mon history and politics. For more than two centuries since the fall of Pegu, the key sources of monks' and educated lay people's understanding of their history have been the Mon chronicles, and in particular the *Rajadhiraj*, a narrative of fourteenth and fifteenth century Pegu,[185] and the *History of Kings*, by the venerable monk of Acwo (or Athwo).[186]

The traditional cultural-religious festivals remain more popular than any state or ethnic nationalist-sponsored event. Of these, the most important is *songkran*, the new year celebration, held in mid-April. Today in Thailand and much of Burma, this occasion has become vulgarised as a sometimes riotous 'water festival'. However, among the Mon communities of both countries, the holiday still retains much of its original good-humoured dignity, as younger people pay respects to their elders, by offering special food, and pouring lustrative waters over the hands of parents, teachers and monks.[187]

As noted above, such festivities indicate the persistence of a definite community spirit among the Mon in Thailand. The number of Mon speakers may still be in decline, but in recent years there has been something of a 'Mon revival' in the kingdom – although one less politicised than that across the border in Burma. Groups such as the Thai Ramon Association (TRA) and Mon Youth Community (MYC) have co-operated with monks and schoolteachers to produce Mon language textbooks, and have conducted literacy trainings on Koh Kret, at Phra Padaeng and in the Mon villages of Ratchaburi, as well as among the Burmese Mon population of Sangkhlaburi.

Further evidence for a revival of interest in Mon culture is provided by the opening of the Wat Muang Folk Museum in August 1992. A collection of Mon artefacts dedicated to Her Majesty Queen Sirikit, the museum is situated in a *Maha Yen* sect monastery in the heart of the Ratchaburi Mon community, on the banks of the Mae Klong River. The Wat Muang Folk Museum attests to a continued respect for the Mon heritage in Thailand, as does the smaller but beautifully-presented Mon museum at Wat Kong Kahrom (also in Ratchaburi), which possesses an important collection of palm leaf manuscripts in Mon and Pali.

Significantly however, this appreciation is based on an historical perspective, which views the Mon culture's contemporary manifestations as anachronistic. Another noteworthy aspect of the Mon tradition in Thailand is its relationship with the royal family, as indicated by Her Majesty's patronage of the Mon Muang Folk Museum.[188]

Mon National Day on the Thailand-Burma Border

In February 1996 the author attended Mon National Day celebrations at Halochanee refugee camp, just inside Burma and a few Km from NMSP Moulmein District headquarters. Two hours' walk from the *Tatmadaw* garrison at Three Pagodas Pass, and in the dry season less than an hour's drive from Sangkhlaburi, Halochanee was the most accessible of the Mon refugee camps.

This accessibility offered both advantages and disadvantages to the 4,000-odd refugees who had been moved here by the Thai authorities in 1994: access to Thai goods and the kingdom's labour market was easier than from the other two Mon refugee camps, but Halochanee was also more vulnerable to attack. In fact, in July 1994, Baleh Donephai, the westernmost section of the camp (furthest inside Burma) had been overrun and burnt down by the *Tatmadaw*.[189] Since then, about one hundred families had returned to Baleh Donephai, while the majority of the refugees still lived in the main section of camp, in a narrow valley at the foot of a hillock marking the border.

I would normally visit Halochanee about once a month, together with one or two members of the Mon National Relief Committee (MNRC). On this occasion, we arrived earlier than usual, at about seven in the morning. It was decidedly chilly, with patches of cool season mist still un-dispersed by the sun. Nevertheless, people were on the move – walking down the valley to where the camp opened out onto a large parade ground-cum-playing field.

Nai B-L- and I stopped first to inspect the main rice store and for a quick chat with the camp leader. Then we were off again, driving slowly past the Medecins Sans Frontieres (MSF)-sponsored hospital, the school and dozens of improvised stalls selling *mohinga* noodles, cakes and candy, and bundles of giant Burmese cheroots. We stopped to buy ourselves a few quids of betel nut, then parked the truck – a procedure complicated by the simultaneous disembarkment of twenty-odd people who had clambered up onto the back of the vehicle as we drove along, cramming themselves in for the free ride down to the festival site.

After stopping to talk briefly with a couple of Mon teachers, we set off to find the NMSP Joint General Secretary, Nai Hongsa. We spotted him on the veranda of a small bamboo house across from the parade ground, drinking tea together with the local MNLA battalion commander and half-a-dozen other dignitaries. They had already changed into Mon national costume: white Burmese-style cotton jackets and red Mon *longyis* with a delicate white check.[190] While Nai B-L- changed out of his fatigues and t-shirt, we sat and discussed the qualities of fish paste, and the chances of last year's ceasefire holding.

At about nine o'clock, the party men (and they were all men) set off in a little procession towards a temporary stage that had been erected on the far side of the parade ground. Nai B-L- went with them, while I waited for a few minutes before trying to take an inconspicuous place among the bustling crowd. It seemed that the whole camp had turned out, as well as Mon from further inside Burma and from Sangkhlaburi and beyond.

My efforts to remain inconspicuous were not successful. As the only Westerner present, I was ushered to the VIP seats right in front of the stage, where I sat alongside twenty or so monks and a handful of NMSP worthies. For the next hour-and-a-half I twisted to the left and right, unsuccessfully trying to avoid a dozen cameras – amongst which I knew would be those of Mon, Thai and Burmese intelligence. I speak hardly any Mon, so I couldn't follow the lengthy speeches. I was though, impressed to note that Nai B-L- would make an address, on the subject of 'democracy and duty'. Here was a representative of the up-and-coming young generation of activists who had joined the movement since 1988, taking his place among the upper-middle ranks of the party. I wondered if my friend's idealism could survive the

42

many compromises he would need to make in order to succeed in his career as a nationalist politician.

The previous night there had been a stage show, with tumblers and actors, dancing and singing. However, this morning was an altogether more serious affair. The speeches were followed by a parade by the local MNLA battalion. Although their drill was impressive enough, it was somewhat undermined by the small number of soldiers taking part – perhaps forty in all. No doubt their comrades were not far off, guarding against a surprise *Tatmadaw* incursion: the ceasefire was only seven months old and the Burma Army often choose ethnic nationalist holidays to launch attacks on minority communities.

The MNLA parade was followed by a march-past of teachers and school children, nurses and medics, and Mon Women's Organisation (MWO) members. It was getting hot by now, so we broke for lunch, which we dignitaries would take at the camp monastery overlooking the parade ground.

The monastery at Halochanee was a large affair, built of bamboo and hardwood, with a fine new leaf-thatch roof. I enjoyed the view out over the camp and into Burma, while the NMSP officers gathered below to pay their respects to a visiting Thai military officer. I was keeping out of the way, as they plied this shady-looking character, in mirror shades and a bright silk shirt, with whisky and instant coffee. When he departed, we sat down on bamboo benches in the shade of the monastery, to a lunch of rice and vegetable curries, accompanied by traditional harp music and dancing.

By early afternoon, it was time to make the bumpy trip back to Sangkhla. After dropping-off a couple of MNRC passengers on the 'Mon side' of town, I drove back over the bridge, to my house on the other side of the lake. I wondered whether I had just returned from a refugee camp, a displaced person's settlement, an insurgent base or a trading village.

'Whither NMSP?'

The primary anomaly here is the presence of a Western aid worker: only a small minority of the victims of Burma's civil war have ever received international humanitarian assistance. Otherwise, with variations in personnel and iconography, the scenes outlined above could have been played out at any time over the past thirty years or so, in territory controlled by any one of several dozen rebel groups. What has changed in that period is the balance of power between Rangoon and the insurgents, one consequence of which has been the series of ceasefires agreed since 1989.

The nature of the ceasefire groups is not uniform. Several organisations in northern Burma are little more than narco-trafficking armies, operating in cahoots with *Tatmadaw* commanders; others, such as the NMSP and the

KIO, have considerable revolutionary pedigrees and explicitly political goals. In spite of their differences however, the ceasefire groups share a number of common characteristics, including important symbolic roles as alternative centres of power to Rangoon, the occupation of more-or-less well-defined territory, over which at least a semblance of administrative control is exercised, and the ability to deploy armed forces – the strength of which varies from a hundred-or-so troops, to 20,000-plus soldiers, in the case of the ex-CPB United Wa State Army (UWSA).

By 2002, fifteen insurgent groups had negotiated ceasefires with the government, only one of which (the 1995 KNPP-SLORC agreement) had subsequently broken down. About ten more irregular militias had also reached more-or-less informal understandings with local *Tatmadaw* commanders. Whilst the KNU and about a dozen smaller groups continued the armed struggle, it seemed that in the new millennium Burma's long-running insurgencies had entered a terminal phase.

By 1995, the NMSP had been in the vanguard of the armed struggle for Monland for thirty-seven years. However, after nearly fifty years of civil war, the position of Burma's ethnic minority groups had deteriorated considerably from that at independence, when their relative inferiority vis-à-vis the Burman majority had been a key factor in the early nationalist revolts. The civil war had clearly not resolved the 'ethnic question'. Burma's ethnic nationalists therefore required new strategies, and a new vision of relations with the central government.

The ethnic insurgents, who claimed to represent constituencies 'inside' Burma as well as in the liberated zones, had in some cases controlled large amounts of territory for decades. However, by 2002 many of these territories had fallen to government forces, and the few remaining groups still engaged in the armed struggle could offer only token resistance to the nearly 500,000-strong *Tatmadaw*. Whilst, until the early-mid 1990s, the opposition alliance based at the KNU's Mannerplaw headquarters could be represented as of real importance to the political equation in the country, by the end of the decade the situation on the Thailand-Burma border had become peripheral to the mainstream of Burmese politics. Although the issue of refugee and displaced persons' protection was still of importance, the remaining insurgent groups had become marginalised – even in relation to their own communities.

The history of the Mon insurgency had for many years paralleled that of the Karen, but the events of 1995–2000 worked out very differently for the two ethnic nationalist movements. Although little remarked upon in the Western media, the NMSP-SLORC and other ceasefires offered at least the prospect of change, and an end to the cycle of violence. However, as the NMSP Central Committee stated at the time, the truce was "merely a military ceasefire" and the "arduous task to a find satisfactory political solution (was) still in abeyance."[191] The Mon, Kachin and other ceasefire agreements quite specifically did not address the social and political issues at the heart of the civil war. Although the fighting had stopped, these were not 'peace treaties'. In fact, according to some critics, they amounted to little more than self-interested business deals.

Many within the Mon nationalist community remained highly critical of the ceasefire, including perhaps a majority of rank-and-file NMSP members. They saw little progress since 1995 on the key issues of self-determination and human rights. To these people, the ceasefire seemed merely expedient, at best. There were even wide-spread suspicions that some senior NMSP leaders had had private financial reasons for agreeing to the deal.

Many of those most strongly opposed to the ceasefire had left the party in the mid-late 1990s (by some estimates, the NMSP lost as many as half of its active members following the ceasefire). Most of those remaining within the party took a pragmatic view: although flawed, the agreement was unlikely to be broken in the short-term – at least by the Mon. However, others – including several MNLA field commanders – remained deeply critical of the ceasefire. A number of these eventually chose to quite the NMSP, either to resume the armed struggle, or retire from the military-political arena.

By late 2001, tensions between the pro- and anti-ceasefire wings of the party had reached a crisis-point. To many observers, it seemed that the Mon nationalist movement was on the verge of yet another large-scale and messy split.[192]

◄◆◆►

What then, was the role of a post-insurgent NMSP? Had the ethnic nationalists' goals changed, or was the ceasefire merely a new strategic move? Although the MNLA retained its arms, the party was no longer at war with Rangoon. What then was the basis of NMSP legitimacy and policy in the new era?

The party faced three broad options. It might resume the armed struggle and almost inevitably face overwhelming military defeat and the loss of the remaining liberated zones. This might free the MNLA from a restrictive defence of fixed positions, allowing the Mon army to engage in guerrilla warfare – a strategy that had recently been forced upon the KNU. Although such developments might please hard-liners, it was difficult to see how this option could be sustained, or what its long-term benefits might be. Fifty years of armed struggle had shown the civil war to be a dead-end.

A second alternative involved the pursuit of closer working relations with the military government. Although Nai Shwe Kyin and colleagues sometimes sent out mixed signals, between 1996–99 this was the option seemingly most favoured by the party leadership. However, this line was questioned by many cadres, and strongly criticised in opposition and wider nationalist circles.

Many on the progressive wing of the party supported a third option: alliance with Daw Aung San Suu Kyi and the Burmese democracy movement. Should the NLD ever be in a position to implement its agenda, then democratic reforms might offer a significant degree of political participation to ethnic minority peoples, as well as an improvement in the human rights situation in Burma. Furthermore, such an alliance would meet the approval of many foreign observers, and of Mon groups in Thailand and overseas. Naturally, the government could be expected to react harshly to the emergence any NMSP-NLD coalition.

Faced by such dilemmas, during the first four years of the ceasefire, the NMSP leadership generally opposed moves to back the NLD, thus alienating many previous supporters, and furthering the military regime's policy of 'divide and rule'. The NMSP position between 1995–99 might be characterised as 'wait and see'. Where possible, the party pursued business and local development projects, keeping direct co-operation with either the government or the NLD to a minimum. It maintained low-level contacts with erstwhile allies, such as the KNU, developed somewhat more open relations with the KIO and other ceasefire groups, and 'kept its powder dry'. In some respects, this policy was the most perilous of all: it invited the displeasure of many, while satisfying few.

Therefore, many NMSP supporters were relieved when in mid-1998 the party appeared to exert itself on the national political stage. Before 1995, any contact between above-ground political parties and the NMSP would have exposed the former to charges of consorting with rebels. However, following the ceasefire, those politicians who since the early 1960s had remained 'within the legal fold', such as Nai Tun Thein and Nai Ngwe Thein of the MNDF, were able to link up with old colleagues in the NMSP. Contacts were soon also renewed with the NLD, and in 1998 a fledgling alliance emerged, representing the best prospect since 1990 for a solution to the 'ethnic question'.

Although the attempt to establish a joint front with the NLD was ultimately quashed by the SPDC, the vision of such a coalition retained its power. Thus, when in late 1999 Nai Shwe Kyin reasserted his support for the democracy movement, and the NMSP again moved to distance itself from the government, it seemed that the party was at last ready to take the initiative, and might enter the new millennium poised for a new era of political struggle.

PART TWO

CLASSICAL MON CIVILISATION AND THE COLONIAL PERIOD

"The king of Pego ... had more rubies on him than the prince of a great city, and he had them on all his toes. He wore great rings of gold on his legs, decorated with the most beautiful rubies; his arms and his fingers were also covered with rubies. His ears hung down the length of your palm because of the great weight of jewels he wore in them. Thus when you look at the king by light, at night-time, he shines so brightly that you would think it were the sun shining."

Ludovico di Varthema of Bologna, who visited Pegu in 1505–06[1]

CHAPTER FOUR

The Rise of the Mon

The Mon populations of modern Burma and Thailand are descendants of a branch of the Mon-Khmer peoples who first established settlements across mainland Southeast Asia at least two thousand years ago. Emmanuel Guillon has called the Mon a "vector of civilisation... of architectural, sculptural, literary, juridical and social creations as beautiful and powerful as those which were produced in Central Thailand ... or Pagan.... Mon civilisation had the vigour to bring Buddhist thought to western Southeast Asia, adapting it to its own genius and that of its neighbours."[2] For more than a thousand years, neighbouring societies have been deeply influenced by Mon cultural, religious and political concepts. It is this phenomena that gives the Mon a special place in the history of Southeast Asia.

Although their achievements are widely acknowledged, Mon history has nevertheless received relatively less attention than that of the later Burman and Thai civilisations. This is in part a political issue, related to the lack of academic freedom in Burma since 1962.

The decline in Mon political fortunes over the last two-to-four centuries has led to a considerable reduction in the number and geographic spread of their population in both Thailand and Burma. A sophisticated, lowland culture, the ancient Mon civilisation thrived on commerce and a rich agricultural surplus. Today the people of the Mon heartland in Burma are less well-off.

In the fifty years since independence, and in particular over the past twenty years, a significant proportion of the Burmese Mon population has been forced to seek shelter in the mountains and jungle of the border regions. Those living in the small NMSP-controlled 'liberated zones' survive largely on swidden rice cultivation (as well as humanitarian aid). They occupy a habitat very different to that settled by their forefathers. Nevertheless, the residents of this far-flung corner of Monland are encouraged to remember the great Mon kingdoms of Ramanyadesa: Hongsawaddy in lower Burma, and Dvaravati and Haripunjaya across the border in present-day Thailand.

49

The Burmese state school curriculum devotes considerable attention to the heroic deeds of the great Burman warrior-kings and dynastic founders: Anawratha, Bayinnaung and Alaungphaya. Non-Burman peoples such as the Mon, at whose expense the unification of Burma often occurred and whose history and languages are not represented in the school system, have viewed these historical developments in a less positive light, as part of an on-going process of assimilation. Mon nationalists in particular have been keen to redress the balance, and see their people's rich history receive proper recognition.

Writing about nationalism in Burma, Mikael Gravers states that "historical memory is crucial to defining identity, legitimising classifications ... or rendering subjective concepts of, for example, an ethnic movement authentic."[3] The past is mediated in the present and control over the interpretation and dissemination of history has been a key goal of all party's to the 'ethnic question' in Burma. As C.F. Keyes puts it, "the past is not simply the source of modern practices: it is also actively interpreted by rulers and counterelites alike in their efforts to shape the present."[4]

According to Gravers, "editing the past in the present is an important instrument in most political struggles, particularly when nationalism is heading the political agenda."[5] The transmission of Mon history remains one of the nationalist movement's principal goals. Elite groups within the Mon community have sought to counter the perceived 'Burmanisation' of history and culture, and reinforce an idea of Mon identity based on their people's distinct historical legacy. To this end, Mon educators have produced several series of literature and history textbooks, many of which are well-regarded both among the Mon community and by Western educationalists.[6]

Milestones in Mon Studies[7]

The history of Mon studies in English begins in 1603, with the publication of a fifty-five word Peguan vocabulary.[8] The first outline English language history of the Mon appeared in 1837 and by the middle of the century various Mon vocabularies were in circulation among Christian missionaries in Burma.[9] The colonial authorities being largely unconcerned with such matters, throughout the nineteenth century the Baptist missionaries remained at the forefront of the study of Mon linguistics, and in 1874 the Rev. J.M. Haswell published his *Grammatical Notes and Vocabulary of the Peguan Language*.[10]

In 1883 Sir Arthur Phayre published the first comprehensive *History of Burma*. Following the Second Anglo-Burmese War (see below), Phayre had been the first British Commissioner for Pegu. According to J. S. Furnivall, he was "a soldier, a statesman, a scholar, and a gentleman, the greatest Englishman who has ever given his life to this outlying province of the

Indian empire."[11] Based on the Burmese chronicles and a Burmese translation of the Mon monk of Acwo's *History of Kings*, Phayre's account of the complex, multi-centred nature of precolonial power politics introduced the achievements of precolonial Mon civilisation to a non-specialist audience for the first time. However, his work has since been criticised for its rather free interpretation of the sources and for introducing an unwonted ethnic dimension into Burmese historiography.[12]

Mon studies really took off with the foundation of The Burma Research Society, which was established in Rangoon in 1910 by the Frenchman and Superintendent of the Archaeological Survey, Charles Duroiselle, and the renowned British colonial administrator, economist and historian, J.S. Furnivall. Members' research was published from 1911 in the *Journal of the Burma Research Society*, and focused particularly on Mon studies.[13]

Another pioneer of Mon studies was the Scottish Baptist missionary, Robert Halliday (1864–1933), who lived among the Mon at Ye in Burma and at Pak Kret in Siam. Halliday's (perhaps unfortunately-titled) *The Talaings* was published by the colonial government in 1917, and re-issued by rival Bangkok publishers in 1999 and 2000.[14] Until the publication of Dr Guillon's survey of Mon history in 1999, this was the only book-length study of Mon culture and society available in English. The British 'Monist', H.L. Shorto, called Halliday "the father of Mon studies."[15] According to Christian Bauer (in 1984), "with the exception of the chapters on history and language his study of the Mons (had still not been) superseded."[16] Particularly impressive is Halliday's evident respect for all aspects of the Mon culture, including the Buddhist religion and spirit worship, which one of his calling and era might be expected to have disparaged. In 1922 Halliday published *A Mon-English Dictionary*, which was re-printed by the Burmese government in 1955.

One of the first scholars to apply a rigorous, analytic approach to Mon studies was Charles Otto Blagden, a correspondent of Halliday's. Although he never visited Burma, Blagden worked with Duroiselle and U Mya on deciphering the Mon inscriptions, which were published in several volumes of the 'Epigraphia Birminica'.[17] Blagden was succeeded by Gordon H. Luce, another Briton from London University's School of Oriental and African Studies (SOAS), with whom he co-published the Peguan word list mentioned above.

Luce pioneered the study of Burmese history at Rangoon University, remaining in Burma until shortly after the 1962 military coup. He had married a Burman and intended to continue residing in the country. However, he was accused of being a CIA agent and given only days to leave Burma, having lived in the country for some forty-five years.[18] One of the last foreigners to be driven out by the xenophobic Ne Win regime, Luce eventually published his masterpiece – the three volume *Old Burma, Early Pagan* – between 1969–70. He retired to Jersey, where he died in 1979 at

the age of ninety, a few years after Ne Win's abolition of The Burma
Research Society.

In 1945 a Mon lectureship was established at SOAS, where Mon studies
reached its apotheosis under Harry L. Shorto, whose dictionary of spoken
Mon was the first modern linguistic description of the language.[19] This and
Shorto's dictionary of the classical Mon inscriptions helped to further
establish Mon studies in the academic mainstream.[20] Shorto's work was
informed by that of Blagden, Halliday and Luce, by the renowned French
orientalist George Coedes,[21] and by the Burmese professor, U Pe Maung
Tin, who was himself of Mon ancestry and whose sister had married Luce.

Among the present generation of Mon specialists are Nai Pan Hla, the
German professor, Christian Bauer, and the French historian, Emmanuel
Guillon. Unfortunately, due to the political climate and difficulty of access,
this generation of scholars has had only limited access to important Mon
archaeological sites in Burma.

The Golden Sheldrake and Myths of Origin

The image of the sheldrake is reproduced on one side of the ivory 'Chansen
comb', one of the most celebrated archaeological finds in Thailand, which
dates from about 200 AD.[22] The golden sheldrake is known in Pali and
classical Mon as the *hamsa* or *hongsa*, and in Burmese as the *hintha*. In
Hindu mythology, the *hamsa* is the sacred mount of Brahma – a symbol of
divine kingship. It is the national symbol of the Mon people, and a popular
image in traditional Burmese, Indian, Khmer and Cham art. The peacock
meanwhile is a Burmese national emblem.[23]

In modern Mon, the golden sheldrake is known as the *bophtaw*. This
mythical beast is modelled on a real creature – the Brahminy Duck, or Ruddy
Sheldrake (*Tadorna Ferraginea*).[24] A creature of "large size and goose-like
shape" with "orange chestnut" (or golden) "body plumage and buffy head",
the Ruddy Sheldrake produces a "a nasal, goose-like honking", which recalls
the distinctive sound of the Mon tongue (described by Karen informants as
resembling that of a ball falling down stairs). Although its numbers are in
decline, the Ruddy Sheldrake is still migrant in parts of Burma, Thailand,
India, China, Eurasia and East Africa; its habitats are "lakes, marshes, rivers
and flooded paddies."[25] A particular characteristic is its tendency (like the
hornbill – a Chin and Karen icon) to pair and mate for life.[26] This fact may
help to explain the sheldrake's special place in Mon culture, as exemplified in
the following legend, which is often recounted to this day, and the image of
which is reproduced numerous times across lower Burma.

At the time of Gottama Buddha, the Mon lands were still submerged
beneath the sea. Some years after his enlightenment, the Buddha and his
retinue passed overhead, on an aerial tour of the lands east of India. The
Buddha observed two sheldrakes, the female perched upon the back of the

male, settled on a pinnacle jutting out from the sea. He prophesied that a great nation would one day emerge from the seas here, and that its people would glorify Buddhism. Several centuries later, the god Indra founded the city of Hongsawaddy (or Pegu) and made it over to two brothers, Samala and Vimala, princes of Thaton.[27] A great city was built on the spot where the sheldrakes had rested, the site of which is today marked by the Hinthagone Pagoda, which offers spectacular views west over Pegu to the Maha Zedi Pagoda (built by the Burman king, Bayinnaung).[28]

In a symbol that neatly combines its pastoral role and nationalist credentials, the logo of the Mon National Relief Committee/Mon Relief and Development Committee (MNRC/RMDC) depicts a sheldrake perched upon the back, and protected by the wings of, another larger bird. An image of the golden sheldrake features on the NMSP flag, flying against a red background, together with a five-pointed blue pole-star – symbol of revolutionary truth and conviction. (The MNLA flag depicts a blue star above a crown and sword – symbols of dominion – wreathed by two stalks of paddy; the MNLA arm-patch employs a golden lion emblem.[29]) The *hintha* is also the official emblem of Mon State in government-controlled 'Myanmar'. However, there is in an important difference between the Mon nationalists' and the state's depiction of the sheldrake. The seals and flags of the NMSP, and of the Mon National Democratic Front (MNDF), feature a flying *hamsa*; the military regime and its organs invariably picture the sheldrake seated, or standing on the ground. The symbolic message is clear: Mon ascendancy ended with the fall of Hongsawaddy, and whilst the Burmese peacock rules, the *hamsa* will not fly. (Until after the 1995 NMSP-SLORC ceasefire, representations of the *hamsa* in flight were effectively banned in Burma.)

The image of the *hamsa* is ubiquitous across lower Burma – 'the golden land'; the land of the golden sheldrake. In towns and villages south and east of Pegu, the icon is emblazoned on monasteries and markets alike; on bus stops, billboards, and bookshops. As Emmanuel Guillon notes, "every book, every monument, every monastery of the present-day Mons has the Hamsa as an emblem."[30] Even the Myanmar Border Trade Department's official logo features an image of the traditional *hintha*-shaped measuring weight, recalling the Mon's age-old role as international commercial and cultural entrepreneurs.

Meanwhile in Thailand, the *hamsa* adorns Buddhist temples, from Bangkok to the southern provinces.[31] On a more worldly level, the poplar *Hong Thong* brand of rice whisky sports a distinctive golden *hongsa* logo.

The myth of the golden sheldrake, and the origin of this symbol in Brahmin-Hindu religion, clearly indicates the formative influence of Indian culture on Mon civilisation. This is confirmed in another popular Mon legend, which is recounted in the chronicles and inscriptions of both Burma and Sri Lanka, the two countries which fostered Theravada Buddhism after its decline in India.[32]

Shortly after achieving enlightenment, the Buddha received a meal of milk rice and honey cakes, proffered by two brothers, the merchants Phussa (or Ita Pu) and Bhandika (or Ita Paw), from Ukkalapa in India. These mythical ancestors of the Mon, who went on to propagate Buddhism in the east, asked for a memorial of their service, and were given eight of the Buddha's hairs, the first and most important of all Buddhist relics. The hairs were later enshrined in great splendour, together with relics of three previous Buddhas, beneath a *chedi* (pagoda) on the top of Singhuttara hill, near the ancient cult centre of Dagon. Thus originated the Shwedagon Pagoda, the most renowned in all Burma. The legend is recounted in both the Shwedagon and Kalyani Sima inscriptions (see below), and in the *History of Kings*,[33] and is memorialised in sculpture at the 'golden rock' Kyaiktiyo monastery in Mon State, near where the brothers are supposed to have landed on their arrival from India.[34]

Another important Mon legend is the cosmological myth of *Mulah Muh* – or 'Ultimate Origin' – which according to Guillon is "a kind of vast 'natural history of good and evil' ... strongly tinged with Buddhism."[35] Although it contains elements common to Khmer and other creation myths, the tale is essentially unique to the Mon, and "manuscripts of this work could be found even recently in nearly all Mon monasteries."[36]

The Emergence of the Mon and the Early Kingdoms

The primary forms of evidence regarding early Mon society are the colourful, but not always reliable, chronicles of the Mon, Thai, Burman and Chinese[37] courts, which were originally written on palm leaf manuscripts. In recent years, groups such as the Mon Culture and Literature Survival Project (MCL) and the Committee for Revitalization of Mon Cultural Heritage (CRMCH)[38] in Thailand, and the Mon Literature and Culture Committee (MLCC) in Burma, have worked to catalogue (and in some cases transcribe onto disc) the extensive Mon literary heritage. Nevertheless, the task of preserving and studying the often fragile Mon palm leaf manuscripts is still far from complete.[39]

Other important sources include the little-explored remains of the early, characteristically Mon, oval cities,[40] numerous fine examples of Buddhist sculpture and religious iconography, and of course, the great Mon inscriptions. The most well-known examples of Mon sacred architecture, such as the Shwedagon and the earlier temples at Pagan, have been fairly well explored by Western and Burmese specialists. However, since the early 1960s, the internationally important archaeological sites at Syriam, Pegu, Thaton and Martaban have been largely neglected.[41] Factors explaining the poor preservation of Burma's rich heritage include lack of funds and government indifference and obstruction, as well as the international isolation of Burmese archaeologists. Fortunately, across the border in Thailand, the Mon ruins at U-Thong, Nakhon Pathom and Lopburi (which has been more-or-less continuously inhabited since the second millennium BC) are relatively well-documented. Nevertheless, as Dr Guillon notes, "there are big holes in the puzzle" of early Mon history.[42]

The Mon-Khmer peoples have been resident in Southeast Asia for at least two thousand years. However, the possibility exists that their ancestors may have lived in the region for as long as five thousand years. In this case, one theory suggests that they originated in northern Vietnam, where the richest variety of Mon-Khmer dialects are found today. However, the more orthodox supposition is that 'proto-Mon-Khmer' settlers arrived in Southeast Asia some time around the end of the first millennium BC, either from southeast India, as Mon myths suggest, or from Mongolia, via Yunan in southern China.

If the Mon-Khmer peoples did originate in southern India, then their west-east pattern of migration into Southeast Asia would go against the more usual north-south flow of folk movement into the region. Based on linguistic evidence, Nai Pan Hla, like most other scholars, favours the China theory: the "Yangtze was the mother river of the Mon-Khmer people before the coming of the Chinese... In those days, it seems that Mon, Khmer and other akin languages might be only one people speaking one language."[43]

Whatever their distant origins, the proto-Mon seem to have arrived in 'Burma' some time after the Pyu. The earliest people to have left evidence of a substantial degree of social organisation in the country, the Pyu were probably the first Buddhists in Southeast Asia. Their origins, and many aspects of the Pyu culture, remain shrouded in mystery.

Mon settlements seem to have been founded in central and lower Burma several centuries before the arrival from the north of the first Karen and Chin migrants. Although experts are unsure exactly when the various hill peoples first settled in Burma, many were already well-established before the appearance of the Burmans, whose arrival from Tibet in large numbers in the ninth century no doubt accelerated the process whereby the Karen and other groups moved up into the hills and remote forests. Meanwhile in lower Burma, the Mon had developed a flourishing civilisation.

Legend has it that, on his return from India, one of the two merchant brothers and disciples of the Buddha mentioned above established the port of Thaton (in Sanskrit, *Sudhammavati*).[44] It seems that the early Mon inhabitants of lower Burma lived side-by-side with a substantial Indian population, whose influence was considerable.

By the end of the first millennium BC, mercantile, cultural – and perhaps even political – contacts had been established between eastern India and lower Burma. According to Indian, Mon and Burman chronicles, in the third century BC the great Indian Buddhist monarch, Asoka, sent missions across the Bay of Bengal, to the 'golden land' (*Suvannaphumi*), which has been identified with lower Burma and the Tenasserim coast (later known as Ramanyadesa). A receptive audience was found among the early Mon settlements, which were in the process of separating from the generic Mon-Khmer language family. According to the chronicles, the missionaries established an important monastic community at Kalasa, in the vicinity of Thaton.[45]

Early Buddhism in Burma was syncretic, combining elements of both the Theravada and Mahayana traditions. Analysis of the Mon legends, and of archaeological finds in the Pegu-Thaton-Martaban area,[46] indicate an Indian presence, which until about 500 AD was as much Hindu-Brahman as Buddhist in character. Both Dr Guillon and Dr Nai Pan Hla suggest that Brahman influences may have existed alongside Buddhism well into the second half of the first millennium. This is an important field for future study.

Another grey area is the relationship between the Mon, the Pyu and the supposed first human inhabitants of lower Burma, the 'Negritos'. It seems that Mon legends of baby-eating 'sea demons' along the Tenasserim coast may refer to the pre-Mongoloid Negritos, who were possibly the ancestors of the Semang people of the Malay Peninsula. Interestingly, Bilu Kyun, the name of a large Mon-populated island opposite Moulmein, means 'demon island' in Mon.[47]

If the traces of Mon-Negrito relations are difficult to discern, then those with the Pyu are not much less so. Pyu influence may have been profound: Mon Buddhism was not necessarily imported directly from India, but may also have been adopted from the Pyu, the remains of whose fifth century settlements in central Burma have so far yielded the earliest Buddhist artefacts in the region. Again, this is an an important field for further research. The early history of Thailand and Burma has yet to fully emerge from the 'holes' in history.

It seems that, by no later than the fifth century AD, the Mon had adopted a Sanskrit-based script, as well as models of cultural, social and political organisation borrowed from India. Meanwhile, in the early centuries of the first millennium, as the Mon were displacing the Pyu and Negritos in central and lower Burma, a branch of the race had already settled in modern-day Cambodia. Here, they may have mixed with an earlier wave of 'proto-Malay' settlers,[48] before establishing the first Indochinese civilisation – the kingdom (later, empire) of Funan, which flourished along the lower Mekong River until the sixth century AD.

The remains of the earliest known Mon sites in Thailand, in the Menam basin, date from around this time. However, D.G.E. Hall and others have suggested that the eastern Mon kingdom of Dvaravati may be several centuries older.[49] With major centres at Nakhon Pathom, 30 miles west of modern Bangkok, and at Lopburi and U-Thong on the Chao Phya River,

Dvaravati was part of a major political and cultural bloc. By no later than the sixth century, the eastern Mon had re-established contact with the Khmer and over the next five hundred years a great Asian civilisation developed. The Buddhist Mon and Hindu (Shaivite) Khmer monarchs established kingdoms of overlapping influence, the authority of which extended over modern-day Cambodia and Thailand, and into Laos.[50]

By the sixth century, Dvaravati culture was already established in central Thailand; by the end of the following century its influence extended as far north as Laos, and in the south as far as Nakhon Sri Thammarat. It is from this period that the earliest extant inscriptions date. These were discovered at Nakhon Pathom, Lopburi and Rangoon, and date from the late sixth and seventh centuries.[51] Although the inscriptions include records of war – of the rise, fall and resurrection of kingdoms – they are primarily catalogues of religious works and the good deeds of kings, summarised thus by Guillon: "I, Lord X..., performed this meritorious deed. Give me credit for it!"[52]

As noted above, research on the early Mon states in Thailand has been more substantial than in Burma. This fact owes as much to the politics of archaeological investigation as it does to the existence of evidence in the ground: many of the most promising sites in Burma have never been excavated, or only cursorily so. However, the discovery of the Rangoon inscriptions, and of numerous tiny, exquisite gold and silver coins, based on the classical Indian model, confirm that by the middle of the first millennium AD the Mon had established a series of prosperous settlements between Bassein, in the Irrawaddy Delta, and Tavoy in the southern Tenasserim region.

Meanwhile, by the seventh century, a new wave of Khmer migrants had overthrown Funan and established the first kingdom of Camboja. Over the following centuries, Khmer influence was to expand west into 'Thailand' and east into lower 'Vietnam' – or rather, into the kingdom of Champa. Founded in the second century AD, Champa's wealth was based on lowland, irrigated rice cultivation. Like the Mon, the Cham were also traders and their coastal towns north of the Mekong Delta were exposed to cultural influences from India and the Indonesian archipelago.[53] Also like the Mon, the Cham were pitted against powerful, expansive neighbours from the north (see below).

The records of eighth and ninth century Arab merchants indicate that during this period the Tenasserim seaboard was home to a flourishing society, based on rice cultivation and maritime trade. Meanwhile in 'Thailand', by the eighth century the great era of Dvaravati achievement was well underway.[54] Rather than regarding Dvaravati as a monolithic political entity, it is perhaps more accurate to think of it as a style of civilisation – in politics and the law, and above all in art and religion. In the Hindu 'Mahabarata', 'Dvaravati' was the city of Krishna. Dvaravati culture is best know today for its superb Buddhist sculpture, produced between the seventh and ninth centuries. As well as the characteristic 'wheels of the law' (or *dhamma*) emanating from this period, Dvaravati has bequeathed numerous exquisitely crafted standing Buddha images, which display a quite distinct artistic style. Examples of these, together with several beautifully expressive terra cotta heads and bas reliefs, can be found in the Lopburi, Nakhon Pathom, Nakhon Sri Thammarat, Songkhla and Bangkok National Museums in Thailand, and in the British Museum and the Guimet in Paris.

In an event of great importance to subsequent Mon (and Thai) history, in the late eighth or early ninth century, Princess Camadevi of Lopburi (the principal city of Dvaravati) founded the northern Mon kingdom of Haripunjaya, centred at modern-day Lamphun, 25Km south of Chiang Mai. According to legend, which dates the foundation of Haripunjaya to the mid-seventh century, the beautiful Camadevi was cursed with a striking body odour. She was afflicted with this unfortunate condition as a youth, in punishment for stepping over a lighted candle placed in front of a Buddha image. As an adult however, she more than made up for this sacrilege.

Haripunjaya was famed for its Buddhist statues, *chedi* and *sutras*, and Queen Camadevi and her fellow pioneers, including hundreds of monks, are credited with introducing Buddhism and Mon culture to the indigenous Mon-Khmer speaking Lawa hill people.[55] An important element in this saga is the early example it gives of a Mon 'march to the north', in which the more advanced Mon civilisation was transported to and propagated among less developed peoples (a theme which will be re-visited below). The foundation of Haripunjaya also indicates the growing importance, in the second half of the first millennium, of trade routes between inland Southeast Asia and ports along the coast.

Haripunjaya was the northern outpost of the Lopburi-Pegu-Thaton nexus. As such, it played a key role in the transmission of Indianised culture to the hinterland. In the late tenth and early eleventh centuries, Haripunjaya was instrumental in forming the Buddhist character of the early Tai sate of Yonok, centred around Chiang Saen, north of Lamphun.[56] Over the next few hundred years, the Mons' role as 'vector of civilisation' helped to transform the politics and culture of mainland Southeast Asia.

By the second half of the first millennium, Mon elites had attained a high degree of Buddhist culture. Among other important innovations, inscriptions from this period testify to the first emergence in Southeast Asia of the *Arannasi*, or 'forest monks', an order derived from Sinnhalese models.[57] Furthermore, one of the greatest interpreters of the Theravada tradition, the scholar-monk Buddhaghosa, taught during this period, and may have been born or resided for a time at Kalasa near Thaton.

Among the common people however, the first millennium in Southeast Asia was marked by religious heterodoxy. Popular religion was characterised by a syncretic mixture of Indian Buddhism and Brahminism, together with indigenous local cults. A uniform Theravada Buddhist culture did not emerge until the thirteenth century, and as late as the fifteenth century eight different schools of Buddhism still flourished in lower Burma.[58]

Despite this heterodoxy, by the end of the first millennium, the Mon seem to have established something akin to a 'national culture'. Architecture and the arts flourished, and over the following centuries there developed a considerable body of Mon literature, described by Guillon as prone to lyricism and flowery imagery, as well as to extremes of elision. The cannon is dominated by religious works, but also includes a number of medical texts, based on the Indian Ayurvedic system.[59]

Although Thaton may once have been under the suzerainty of Sri Jaya,[60] and Dvaravati possibly subject to Funan,[61] by the late-eighth century the Mon kingdoms had joined in a loose confederacy, known as Ramanyadesa, which flourished until at least the mid-eleventh century. However, relations with the wider world were not always cordial. The Chinese chronicles mention a series the ninth century wars between Nan-Chao in western Yunan and the Pyu (and probably also the Mon) kingdoms.[62]

It is not until the second millennium that Mon history can be traced with a degree of continuity. The first Mon kingdom in 'Burma' about which scholars have much detailed knowledge is the great city-state of Hongsawaddy ('the kingdom of the golden sheldrake'). Successor to the smaller principality of Thaton, Hongsawaddy was situated between the estuaries of three rivers: the Irrawaddy, the Sittaung and the Salween.

As noted above, the nature of surviving evidence makes it difficult to fix the exact dates of the early kingdoms.[63] Tradition has it that Pegu, the capital of Hongsawaddy, was established in 825 AD. This is around the same time that the Khmer kings were beginning construction of their spectacular capital at Angkor and the first wave of Burman migrants began arriving in upper Burma. By now, Buddhism had already been established as a cornerstone of Ramanyadesa and Mon monks were travelling regularly to the great Buddhist kingdom of Ceylon, to study or be ordained.[64] The Mon aristocracy meanwhile, accumulated wealth through the export of rice and sugar cane to the distant markets of Malacca and the East Indian coast.[65] Through the patronage of religious works, they built up stores of merit for the life to come.

The Mon *Mandala*

Suitable economic conditions must prevail before a society achieves the degree of political, religious and cultural development associated with the Mon and Khmer kingdoms on the eve of the second millennium. Upon the rich alluvial soils of central and lower Burma, and on the shores of the Tonle Sap in Cambodia, the Mon-Khmer peoples established 'hydraulic societies', based on the systematic cultivation of irrigated rice. Political power in such societies was organised along lines of patronage, which probably emerged in relation to the control of water courses and the agricultural system.

Another important factor in the emergence of literate cultures among the Mon and the Khmer (and before them, the Pyu and the Cham) was the foundation of urban centres. Although the earliest 'cities' of mainland Southeast Asia were primarily religious centres,[66] since ancient times their economic role as foci of trade had also been important: systems of writing, borrowed from Indian models, emerged in these early urban hubs as a bi-product of both religion and commerce.[67]

The earliest mass settlements in Southeast Asia were established on the edges of flood plains and rivers, where large-scale wet rice cultivation was most easily adopted, and from which ships departed for sometimes distant shores. The Mon have since time immemorial been a sea-faring people, and the cities of Ramanyadesa were all situated close to major rivers, and – with the exception of Haripunjaya – the sea. These kingdoms traded by ship with Ceylon and beyond, to the great emporia of India and the Indonesian archipelago, where Mon trading communities were established.[68] Important commodities included camphor, areca nuts, aromatic and hardwoods, tin and copper, and precious stones (especially rubies from northern Burma).[69] The famous glazed 'Martaban jars', which were in fact made in the interior, even found their way to such far-flung markets as Japan and Turkey.[70] As a result of these trade links, Mon society was exposed to diverse foreign cultural influences and traditions. The genius of Mon civilisation was that it combined these with classical Indian traditions, to create a sophisticated and original culture.

However, the different 'states' of Ramanyadesa were not unified in anything like the modern sense. As Guillon points out, "the political organisation of the Mons consisted of an alliance of sovereign little kingdoms which had the same culture but showed local variations."[71] In particular, these 'city-states' shared Indianised politico-religious concepts and similar economic systems.

Of central importance was the concept of divine kingship, derived from Brahmin models. According to Robert Taylor, to a large extent "the monarchy, and often the monarch himself, was seen as the state."[72] Gravers notes that "the individual's place in this system was ... dependent on ... *karma*",[73] which was determined by the accumulation of merit. The king's store of *karmic* attainment nurtured the people, and was itself dependant on harnessing the collective merit of the kingdom, through ritual acts such as the construction of pagodas. The king was the protector of his kingdom and, for so long as the bond of *karma* lasted, possessed a god-given right to rule.

The pious monarch embodied Buddhist teachings; the more ambitious even aspired to be recognised as an avatar of the *Boddhisatva*, the Buddha-to-be, whose mission is to lead sentient beings towards the accumulation of merit and the end of suffering. According to Theodore Stern, such rulers were "*cakkavatti*, a universal monarch.... presiding as the earthly analogue of Indra in the city of the gods."[74] The monarchy might be divinely-ordained, but pretenders to the throne could claim the status of *min luang*, the messianic prince whose store of righteousness and *karma* equipped and entitled him to seize state power, in order to purify the earth.

One expression of the merit of king or pretender was martial prowess: success in war proved the victor's legitimacy. This was reflected in his ability to populate the realm with captured slaves, who might be put to work cultivating the land, or constructing the metropolis and associated religious monuments.

This politico-religious ideology was expressed in the sacred, geometric architecture of the ancient Southeast Asian cities. The design of Angkor Wat, and of Pagan and the Mon cities of Pegu, Thaton, U-Thong and Nakhon Pathom, reflected an order perceived in the cosmos: the king sat at the heart of the holy citadel, which itself was situated in the centre of the kingdom.[75]

A contemporary account of the celebrated king, Dhammaceti of Pegu, describes him as "Lord of the White Elephant, whose colour was as the white of the holy lotus, of clusters of jasmine, of the autumn moon."[76] He was pious, learned and just. Despite the apparently static structure of such theocratic kingdoms though, these were violent times. Keyes notes that "kings and lords often did not live out their natural span, but were forcibly deposed by sons or other claimants to their offices."[77] On at least one occasion, pretenders to the Peguan throne were executed *en masse*.[78] A combination of skilful political manoeuvring and ostentatious patronage, of the faith and of the court, was necessary in order to maintain a ruler in power.

Below the monarchy and the court was a system of vassal chieftains and sometimes hereditary district and village headmen. 'Corve'(tax-in-kind) labour was organised at the village level, and the large infrastructure projects undertaken by the Mon, Khmer, Thai and Burman kings all employed what today might be called 'forced labour'. As well as their labour, the state also taxed peasants' rice production. However, in comparison to levels under the British colonial and modern Burmese governments, levels of taxation were probably not too onerous.[79]

Other centres of power reflecting the stratified political order included the Buddhist *sangha* and the shamanistic *Nat* cult indigenous to Burma. Following Shorto, Melford Spiro argues that the symbolic organisation of the Burmese animist pantheon was derived from the thirty-three *Nats* of Mon Thaton (and ultimately from Indian models). Each *Nat* represented a particular territory, reflecting the administrative division of the kingdom into townships, and helping to cement peoples' identification with a particular locality.[80]

The 'Buffalo mother of Pegu' is among the most colourful of the Burmese *Nats*. Incorporated into the pantheon in the late nineteenth century, the Buffalo mother is a Burmese representation of the history of Pegu, and as such may be considered an instance of the incorporation of Mon cultural identity into Burmese 'national culture'.[81]

According to Mikael Gravers, in traditional Burmese society "identity was determined by a) whether one was a Buddhist, and b) whether one was a member of an alliance with the ruling dynasty, that is, which place one held in the tributary hierarchy ... Identity and status within the tributary system were inseparable."[82] The key to the fulfilment of patron-client obligations was power, and the various strata of society were loosely integrated in a series of tributary relations.

The structure of the army reflected this semi-feudal principal. In addition to regular armed forces under the king, vassal lords from different principalities within the kingdom fielded their own troops, under license from the monarch. Furthermore, since the earliest times in Burma and across mainland Southeast Asia, local strong-men, often originating outside elite circles, have engaged in more-or-less commercially-inspired banditry. The charismatic 'warlord' stood in a patron-client relationship to his followers, reflecting that of the prince to his subjects.[83] Especially if he was the leader of a peasant rebellion, the strong-man may have claimed legitimacy as a *min laung* pretender.

Such dynastic arrangements within the precolonial state were reflected on the macro-level, in the structure of power relations between the Mon and other pre-modern kingdoms. The influence of a particular state would rise and fall, affecting its prince's relations with neighbouring powers and with the great metropolises at Angkor, Lopburi and Pegu. As Benedict Anderson notes, "states were defined by centres, borders were porous and indistinct, and sovereignties faded imperceptibly into one another."[84] Thongchai Winichakul describes such frontiers as natural buffers: "for Siam a *khetdaen* (the term now used to translate boundary) was not necessarily connected or joined with the Burmese ones. It was the limit within which the authorities of a country could exercise their power. . . . the areas left over became a huge corridor between the two countries. . . . The two sovereignties did not interface."[85]

The relative strength of a particular centre would influence the degree to which populations in outlying regions identified with the culture – and implicit ethnicity – of its ruling elite.[86] According to the historian of Laos, Martin Stuart-Fox, "to call such developments 'state formation' is to import European notions of administration over a defined territory that are inappropriate to describe these 'circles of power'. The term *mandala* better captures both the segmentary structure (larger power centres extracting tribute from similarly organised smaller ones), and variability of these power relationships."[87] Outlying regions stood in a hierarchical, tributary relation to the centre: the lords of smaller polities were vassals of a greater king – e.g. in the fourteenth-sixteenth centuries the principalities of Tavoy and Mergui were vassals of Martaban, which itself was for long periods a tributary of Pegu.[88] 'Feudal' inter-state alliances were often cemented by marriage, and kings and princes maintained harems of minor wives, symbolising their patronage over peripheral regions, from which concubines were often drawn.

The loosely-structured *mandala* of mainland Southeast Asia in the first millennium AD, including the Chinese-influenced tradition in Vietnam, represented a great flowering of civilisation. As indigenous religions were displaced in the plains and valleys by Indianised systems associated with more advanced forms of agriculture and economy, an important cultural and political distinction began to emerge. Taking their lead from elites occupying the centre of the 'cosmic polity', lowland peoples began to discriminate between themselves and the 'hilltribes' of the interior, on the periphery of the emergent *mandala*.[89]

According to Guillon, since time immemorial the Mon have made "a clear distinction between the people of the forest and the people of the rice-fields or plains."[90] Although Karen history before the eighteenth century is deeply obscure,[91] the ancestors of the Karen seem to have lived on the peripheries of the feuding, loosely-defined precolonial *mandala*, where the power of the centre held less strongly.

Attitudes in the emergent lowland states towards the hill peoples were often somewhat condescending. Although feared for their presumed jungle magic and proven hunting abilities, the animist Karen and others were considered inferior and viewed primarily as potential spies and porters, or as providers of forest products, which they were required to send down to the valleys in the form of tribute. Thus, from the earliest times, minority groups in the region were marginalised and exploited.[92]

Despite assertions to the contrary,[93] the Mon maintained an unequal, tributary relationship with Karen communities: according to Stern "the Mon are today remembered as haughty rulers towards the Karen in the days of their power."[94] Guillon confirms that, like most dominant groups in the precolonial era, the Mon were slave-owners. However, he cautions against adopting easy generalisation, based on limited historical knowledge regarding ethnic roles.[95]

Keyes states that "throughout most of Southeast Asia, hill peoples were incorporated into social systems dominated by the lowland peoples."[96] However, the influence of these systems on the more isolated 'tribal' societies was often minimal. Furthermore, the manner in which the Karen and other groups adopted and adapted lowland religious and social practices sometimes involved radical re-conceptualisations of the nature of kingship and priesthood, community, and centre-periphery relations. The distinction between upland and lowland cultures is not clear-cut: although they tended to live in the hills and mountain ranges that separated the lowland civilisations of Southeast Asia, large numbers of Karen also lived side-by-side with Mon and Burman villagers in the Irrawaddy Delta and elsewhere. Pwo Karen men in particular have long been educated in the Mon *sangha*, and there has been a high degree of inter-penetration between the two communities. The predominantly Buddhist Pwo have consequently sometimes been called 'Mon (or Talaing) Karen'.[97]

CHAPTER FIVE

Pegu and Pagan –
The Kingdoms of
Ramanyadesa and the
Mon-Burman Wars

D.R. SarDesai presents the standard version of a celebrated epoch in Burmese history. At the end of the first millennium:

> The Mons, cousins of the Khmer, held sway over maritime trade and enjoyed a cultural preeminence in Lower Myanmar, while the Burmans dominated the rest of the country... (until) in the eleventh century, fascinated by Theravada Buddhism, which the Mons had followed for centuries, thanks to their contacts with Ceylon, King Anawratha invaded ... Lower Myanmar and forcibly brought Buddhist scriptures as well as Mon scholars and artisans to Upper Myanmar. His unification of the country and adoption of Theravada Buddhism were to have long-term consequences for mainland Southeast Asia.[98]

These events inaugurated a millennium-long struggle for Mon national survival. According to tradition, the Burman king Anawratha (or Aniruddha), descended from the north to seize Mon cultural and religious experts, and set them to work at his capital, Pagan. However, recent scholarship has questioned the extent to which the Mon were passive victims of history, emphasising instead the considerable influence of Mon architects, craftsmen, monks and courtiers in early Pagan. Only in the mid-to-late twelfth century did their influence begin to wane.

Meanwhile, during the first centuries of the second millennium, the Mon *mandala* of Dvaravati and Haripunjaya, in central and northern Thailand, gradually succumbed to the emergent Tai states of Sukhothai and La Na. Following the demise of Pagan however, Mon power in lower Burma re-emerged under king Wareru, who ushered in a golden age of Mon rule. With its capital at Pegu, the kingdom of Hongsawaddy continued to prosper under the Wareru dynasty until the mid-sixteenth century, when it was subsumed under the 'second Myanmar dynasty'.

Hongsawaddy-Pegu was to enjoy a brief and troubled resurgence in the eighteenth century, during which for the first time Western powers became

seriously involved in Burmese politics. However, following a spectacular –
if short-lived – conquest of central Burma, the Mon forces were again
crushed by their Burman foes and thousands of refugees fled into exile in
Ayuthaia. Here they prospered, and long after Mon political power in the
region had gone into decline, Mon monks, soldiers, courtiers and artisans
continued to play important roles in the religious and secular development
of Siam.

Anawratha and Manuha, Pagan and Thaton

According to tradition, the eleventh century saw the first of a long series of
Mon-Burman wars, that have continued in one form or another to the
present day. The nineteenth century *Glass Palace Chronicle* recounts how
the capital of king Manuha, the Mon ruler of Thaton, was overrun in 1057
by his northern rival, king Anawratha of Pagan.

However, Emmanuel Guillon suggests that "many elements of his
(Anawratha's) history rather call to mind a *myth*, similar, moreover, to
other myths in neighbouring countries relating to the foundation of
dynasties."[99] Both the sack of Thaton and the very existence of Anawratha
are open to doubt. Guillon proposes an alternative theory: Mon influence at
Pagan may have originated in a great civilising mission – or 'march north' –
undertaken by king Manuha. Perhaps the Mon 'invaded' upper Burma,
rather than the Burmans conquering the southern Mon lands, with their
agricultural surplus and commercial wealth.[100] Such an episode is
prefigured in the eighth century mission to the north, and subsequent
foundation of Haripunjaya, undertaken by the Mon of Lopburi (Dvaravati).
According to this interpretation, the mythic sack of Thaton may have been
constructed to explain latter-day Burman domination.[101]

Martin Smith notes that the traditions of the Pa-O (a staunchly Buddhist
Karen people, living around Thaton-Pegu and in Shan State) claim king
Manuha as an ancestor, and date the Pa-Os' flight to Shan State from the
fall of Thaton in the eleventh century.[102] The truth may lie somewhere
between these versions of history. An earlier hypothesis by Luce suggested
that the events in question originated in Anawratha's defence of Pegu
and/or Thaton against a Khmer incursion from the east.[103] In this case, the
kingdoms of upper and lower Burma may have been allies, which would
explain the grandeur of the buildings in which king Manuha was housed
(or imprisoned) at Pagan, where he and his retinue were evidently lodged
in style.[104] Furthermore, Pegu seems to have exercised a degree of
independence during the Pagan ascendancy, its prince perhaps having
acquiesced in the Burman conquest of the rival *mandala* of Thaton.

In the eleventh and early twelfth centuries the Burmans' somewhat
decadent Mahayana Buddhist practices, acquired through contact with east
India, were superseded by a rigorous form of Sinnhalese Theravada

Buddhism, transmitted via the Mon. Prior to the campaign against Thaton, Anawratha is reputed to have been introduced to Mon Buddhism by the learned Mon monk, Shin Arhan. He was thus inspired to adopt – or abduct – king Manuha and 30,000 monks and artisans from Thaton, reputedly transporting them to Pagan together with thirty-two editions of the Pali *tripitaka* (the Theravada Buddhist cannon).[105]

Whether the Burmans forcibly annexed and assimilated the Mon, or the Mon kings consciously extended their influence over the 'barbarian' Burmans, the mid-eleventh century constitutes a watershed period in Burmese history. In the words of Emmanuel Guillon, "the least we can say, after all, is that following that civilising 'march up country' of the Mon to Pagan ... a brilliant civilisation was to burst into bloom for more than a century on the banks of the Irrawaddy, at first under the leadership of the Mons."[106]

Between about 1050 and 1165–1180, Mon craftsmen and architects helped to build some two thousand monuments at Pagan, the remains of which today rival the splendours of Angkor Wat.[107] Guillon proposes that this profusion of building may indicate that the dates of 'Mon Pagan' should be pushed back to the tenth century – i.e. to before the supposed capture of Thaton.[108]

The most important of the Mon temples at Pagan is the Ananda, constructed in the first decade of the twelfth century. At its base are a series of characteristically Mon, glazed terracotta plaques, the western portion of which depict the Army of Mara (the Buddhist deceiver), a subject later featured on a series of plaques from fifteenth and sixteenth century Pegu.[109] As well as in sculpture and architecture, 'Mon Pagan' produced significant achievements in the related fields of religion and language. In the eleventh and twelfth centuries the court adopted the Mon script, and guided by their Mon preceptors the kings of Pagan undertook the propagation of Theravada culture throughout the realm.[110]

The Mon thus again played a leading role in the transmission of Theravada Buddhism to Southeast Asia, at a time when the religion was undergoing a significant decline in India.[111] Indeed, in the eleventh century pilgrims from Pagan took the lead in restoring the Bodhgaya temple (site of the Buddha's enlightenment, in northeast India), and Indian Buddhist refugees were probably active in Pagan.[112] Another Indian cultural export to Southeast Asia via the Mon was the Code of Manu (or *Dharmasastra*). This Brahmin-Theravadin system of kingship and polity formed the basis of emergent Burman[113] – and later Thai[114] – legal concepts, and provided the monarchy with both practical support and ideological legitimacy.

The eleventh century also saw the re-organisation of *Nat* worship at Pagan, incorporating structural elements from the Mon tradition. Anawratha is credited with the elaboration of an official pantheon of thirty-seven *Nats*, images of which were later enshrined at the Shwezigon

Pagoda. As the individual *Nats* were associated with particular districts, the creation of this centralised state pantheon symbolised Pagan's unified authority over upper and lower Burma.[115] It also encouraged the population to look to Pagan (and nearby Mount Popa, home of the chief *Nats*) as the ritual and administrative centre of the kingdom – and indeed, the universe.

The eleventh and twelfth centuries saw the intermarriage of Mon and Burman elites and a substantial degree of assimilation of the former by the latter. The great Mon language 'Kyanzittha' inscriptions provide clear evidence of the respect with which Mon culture was regarded.[116] According to these, both Mon and Brahmin rites were used at the coronation in 1084 (or 1086) of king Kyanzittha, who constructed Mon-style pagodas at Pagan, and may himself have been an ethnic Mon.[117] As the price of the Mon princess' support for his reign, Kyanzittha was succeeded by his half-Mon nephew.[118]

A pattern had by now been established: as the Burmans (and later the Thais) subdued the Mon militarily and politically, so they adopted and assimilated Mon culture and religion. However, it seems that the Mon centres in the south still thirsted for independence: the earliest recorded uprising against northern overlords occurred in twelfth century Bassein.[119] It is perhaps no coincidence that, by the end of the twelfth century, Mon influence at Pagan had begun to decline.[120] Perhaps the fading memories of Mon tutelage date from this era, when a new tradition emerged, according to which the Burman kings unilaterally incorporated the Mon heritage into their own.

Meanwhile in Sri Lanka, in the mid-eleventh century a Sinhalese king had regained control from the Tamils. The Buddhist tradition had suffered many setbacks, and, in an effort to enhance their legitimacy (and store of *karma*), the island's new rulers sponsored a Theravadin restoration. A revived Theravada Buddhism was soon transmitted to the Southeast Asian mainland, via central and lower Burma, from where monks frequently sailed to Sri Lanka, returning with important texts and teachings.[121]

In the late twelfth century a group of monks, led by the famous Mon religious teacher Chapata, and including a Khmer prince of the blood, returned from Sri Lanka and began to preach a new and particularly strict and scholarly form of Buddhism. The 'new school' soon achieved the status of orthodox (Sinhalese) Theravada Buddhism. Once again religious reforms initiated by the Mon were taken up by the court at Pagan and, together with associated forms of iconography, spread across the region.[122]

Following this Theravadin reformation in the thirteenth century, the role and symbolic importance of kings began to change. From universal monarch and embodiment of *karmic* law, the ruler evolved into protector and patron of the faith. One result of this shift was the separation of church and state, as the rejuvenated monkhood began to organise itself as an independent and powerful institution, distinct from the court.[123] By the fourteenth century, Theravada Buddhism was no longer restricted to elite circles, but had been adopted by, or imposed upon, most sectors of lowland society.

Meanwhile, to the east of the Mon lands, within a few years of the fall of Thaton and the 'capture' of king Manuha, the Vietnamese had similarly abducted a Cham king and occupied part of his territory. Although during the twelfth century the rest of Champa was conquered by the Khmer, in the thirteenth century the Cham, like the Mon, regained their independence. The Cham people converted to Islam in the fourteenth century and their kingdom was to survive in an attenuated form until the late seventeenth century, when it succumbed to the southward expansion of Vietnam.[124]

Resurgence in the West, Realignments in the East

One thousand years ago, Mon princes ruled over large areas of Thailand, where their culture would continue to exert a profound influence for centuries to come. Further to the west, although Pegu may have retained a degree of independence, the Mon were subject to the kings of Pagan.

However, in 1283–84, and again in 1287, Mongol armies invaded a weakened Pagan empire, disrupting Burman society and allowing the Mon to re-establish their power in lower Burma.[125] The ascendance of the Shan princely states also dates from this period, during which Mongol policy seems to have concentrated on preventing the re-emergence of a major power bloc in upper Burma.[126]

In the vanguard of an on-going rejuvenation of Theravada Buddhism, the Mon were well-prepared to regain their independence. Infused with a new rigour and cultural confidence, by the end of the thirteenth century the Mon princes were ready to resume the leadership of lower Burma. However, King Wareru (or Wa Row), who is credited with the reformation of Mon power, was not of royal blood; he may even have been Shan. As Lieberman notes, "because authority derived from the power and charisma of the patron, and because each of his clients was tied to him by separate bonds, there was no need for a common identity among his followers."[127] Nevertheless, in time, dynastic houses and their followers came to bear the stamp of a particular ethnicity.[128] Whatever its origins, the Wareru clan came to embody a resurgent Mon identity.

Chief elephant keeper to king Rama Khamhaeng of Sukhothai, and later Captain of the palace Guards, Wareru was obviously a talented – and ruthless – individual. He married into the royal family, possibly eloping with a Thai princess, and in 1280 (or 1281) installed himself as lord of Martaban, opposite modern-day Moulmein at the mouth of the Salween River. Here he set about establishing his credentials as a Mon king, re-enacting the code of Manu and patronising the *sangha*.[129] Then, with the decline of Pagan in the last decade of the thirteenth century, he drove the Burman forces from the Mon lands and, together with a Peguan prince, Tarbya, re-established Mon control at Pegu (under the suzerainty of Martaban, and ultimately subject to Sukhothai). Wareru then had Tarbya killed, and installed himself as sole ruler.[130]

King Wareru is remembered today as a champion of Mon independence and culture. However, his achievements could not save him from a violent end. As was often the case at the turbulent courts of precolonial Southeast Asia, in 1296 the king was murdered by his successors, who were also his grandsons.[131]

Hongsawaddy continued to be a tributary of Sukhothai until 1319.[132] Despite occasional violent disruptions, the Mon were to retain sovereignty over lower Burma for another two centuries. The major epicentres of Hongsawaddy included not only the ancient cities of Pegu and Thaton, but also the ports of Martaban, Bassein and Syriam. The latter was situated a little downstream and across the river from Dagon, which itself had been an important pre-Buddhist cult centre, and the traditional fief of Mon queens.

Meanwhile further to the east, the fortunes of Dvaravati and Haripunjaya had been uneven. By the thirteenth century, the Tai peoples had been migrating west and south from Vietnam and Yunan for several hundred years. Keyes notes that this expansion "brought them into increasing contact with the civilised peoples of Southeast Asia. As happened with the barbarians of Europe at an earlier time, the contact between the Tai barbarians and the civilised peoples of Southeast Asia resulted in the Tai achieving political dominance while also adopting much of the civilisation they conquered."[133]

As had the rulers of Pagan, the Tai kings adopted prestigious Mon religious and linguistic models. However, neither the early Tai statelets nor the more ancient and loosely-structured Mon *mandala* were able to resist the power of an expansive Khmer empire. In the twelfth century Tai settlers had established a colony at Sukhothai, in the centre of modern-day Thailand. However, within a hundred years both Sukhothai and Lopburi had been annexed by the Khmer.[134]

Following its capture, Sukhothai continued to be governed by local Thai and Mon rulers, acting as vassals of Angkor. Then in the 1280s, king Rama Khamhaeng, who is reputed to have adapted a Khmer script to the Thai language, succeeded in throwing off this suzerainty. In 1350 one of his successors, king Ramidhipati, was crowned at the new capital of Dvaravati Sri Ayuthaiya. He later combined the Mon and Thai royal houses by marrying into the Mon royal family of U-Thong. Most of this king's subjects would have been ethnic Mon and Khmer.[135]

As the Tai peoples pushed further south, their chiefs began to gather more power to themselves. It was these lords, rather than the longer-established kings of Sukhothai, that went on to rule the new kingdom of Ayuthaiya. Nevertheless, the cultural influence of Dvaravati persisted: like the kings of Pagan and Sukhothai before them, the newcomers adopted elements of the older Mon civilisation, to create a synthetic, dynamic new tradition.[136]

A similar pattern emerged in the north. At the height of its power, in the eleventh and thirteenth centuries, the influence of Haripunjaya spread as far as modern-day Laos. The chronicles tell of an eleventh century exodus from Haripunjaya to Thaton, which followed various political and military adventures associated with Khmer advances, and was possibly also a response to outbreaks of cholera in the northern Mon kingdom.[137] However, in around 1050 the city was repopulated and it soon regained a pre-eminence that was to last for another two centuries.[138] In 1281 however, just a few years before king Wareru re-established Mon power in lower Burma, Haripunjaya was captured by the Tai king Mengrai, whom the chronicles accuse of using secret agents to sow discord among the Mon.[139]

Mengrai's 'new city' – Chiang Mai – became the capital of the powerful *mandala* of La Na, replacing Haripunjaya-Lamphun as the political centre of the north. Following his overthrow, the last king of Haripunjaya, Yi Ba, continued to reside at Lamphun, demonstrating the respect in which Mon royalty was held (notwithstanding an unsuccessful 1296 revolt against Chiang Mai, involving Yi Ba). In the late thirteenth century La Na established trade and religious contacts with Pegu, which no doubt reinforced Mon influence on the young Tai state.[140]

The Golden Age of Hongsawaddy

During the fourteenth and fifteenth centuries, the remaining outposts of Ramanyadesa came under renewed military pressure from the emergent kingdoms of La Na and Ayuthaiya to the north and east, and from the Burman kings, who by the mid-fourteenth century had established a new capital at Toungoo, in central-northern Burma. In 1356 the Mon king, Bannya U, successfully repulsed an invasion by Lan Na, but seven years later the strategically important port of Martaban was abandoned to Ayuthaiya. In 1369 Bannya U re-established his capital at Pegu. In effect, he seems to have beaten-off a Tai invasion, but at the cost of losing control over the Tenasserim region.

In 1393 Bannya U was succeeded by his son, king Rajadhirat, who allied Pegu with the kingdom of Arakan to the west, bordering east India (Bangladesh). According to Hall, Rajadhirat "was not only a statesman who played his cards with consummate skill; he has also a great name in Burmese and Mon traditions as an administrator."[141] The *History of Kings* sates that "there was no one who dared strive with him ... he was great in war always."[142] Of all the Mon kings, Rajadhirat is perhaps the most celebrated, an icon whose likeness has adorned countless nationalist posters, calendars and other publications in the modern era.

According to Hall, Pegu "became a great centre of commerce and the resort of foreign merchants. Its three busy ports ... carried on regular trade with India, Malacca, and the Malay Archipelago."[143] Rajadhirat's Pegu played a key role in containing the spread of Islam into Burma from the west. Indeed, the fifteenth century saw another major Theravadin revival, again based on the Sri Lankan model, in Burma, Thailand, Laos and Cambodia. King Rajadhirat famously donated his weight in gold to the Shwemawdaw Pagoda in Pegu,[144] and he and his successors made extensive additions to the great Shwedagon.[145]

The death of king Rajadhirat was followed by a series of short interregnums, during which the Peguan succession was disputed by a number of royal claimants, more than one of whom sought to enlist the aid of the Burman king at Ava. Rajadhirat was finally succeeded in 1453 by his daughter, Queen Shinsawbu (in Mon, Bannya Thaw or Mi Chao Bu). During the internecine manoeuvrings that had followed her father's death, she had briefly been married to the king of Ava. As scion of both the Mon and Burman royal families, Shinsawbu was well-versed in palace and dynastic intrigue.

An illustrious monarch, Queen Shinsawbu was able to ensure a degree of harmony between the rival kingdoms. Today she is remembered for the good-natured temper of her reign, for her extensive renovation of the Shwedagon Pagoda (to the *chedi* of which she donated her weight in gold) and for building a number of important monasteries, including the Kyaikmaraw near Moulmein.

The Mon queens, Camadevi of Haripunjaya and Shinsawbu of Pegu, are among the few women to have reigned over the major precolonial polities of Southeast Asia.[146] Guillon notes the considerable influence of queens in fourteenth-sixteenth century Hongsawaddy and suggests that Mon kings may often have ruled as regents on behalf of the 'great queen'.[147] Its seems that for some years Shinsawbu continued to reign in Dagon, while her religious preceptor, the renowned monk Dhammaceti, ruled as a vassal in Pegu. In what may have been a form of 'palace coup', Queen Shinsawbu eventually abdicated, to be succeeded by Dhammaceti, who in 1470 took the royal name Rajaddapti.[148]

According to the chronicles, the 'alchemist king' Dhammaceti-Rajaddapti was a great and learned monarch, who "reigned very justly ... replete with wisdom." He is said to have donated the combined weight in gold of his heir and queen to the Shwedagon,[149] and to have resurrected the Code of Manu.[150] He also constructed important temple complexes in the vicinity of Pegu, including the Shwegugyi Pagoda, with its distinctive glazed terracotta plaques, featuring images of Mara's army and daughters.[151]

On the religious front, the most important event in fifteenth century Southeast Asia was the Theravada Buddhist council, held at Wat Jed Yod in Chiang Mai in 1475. Following this great conclave, religious reforms were introduced throughout the region. Under the supervision of the ex-monk, king Dhammaceti, the Mon *sangha* – which had grown somewhat corrupt and lax – was re-unified and strenuously purified, with many monks being re-ordained according to Sinhalese rites.[152]   Scholars' relatively detailed knowledge of this era is derived from king Dhammaceti's famous Pali and Mon language Kalyani Sima inscriptions at Pegu. The original sandstone slabs, inscribed in 1480, are among the most important records of Theravadin history and polity, and still stand outside the reconstructed Maha Kalyani Sima (ordination hall) in Pegu.[153]

In 1435 Nicolo di Conti of Venice became the first European to visit lower Burma.[154] His four month stay at Pegu presaged a new era in Burmese history. As Woodman notes in her account of *The Making of Burma*, on numerous occasions between the sixteenth-nineteenth centuries, foreign powers were to ally themselves "to whichever seemed to be the winning side, and therefore in a position to make the most profitable business contacts."[155] Phayre (himself a colonial administrator) found it hardly surprising that "the native authorities, seeing the fluctuating conduct of the Europeans, should accuse them of treachery."[156] At first, the white-skinned foreigners could offer little to interest Southeast Asians, beyond mechanical devices such a clocks – and guns. However, they soon became deeply involved in regional trade and politics.

Possibly as part of a strategy to frustrate the spread of Islam, in 1511 three hundred Mon merchants living in the strategically important port of Malacca assisted the Portuguese in taking power from the local Muslim sultan. The following year, the Portuguese sent a mission to Hongsawaddy, and in 1519 the two powers agreed a treaty under which the Portuguese established a base at Martaban, where they were to maintain a presence for the next hundred years.[157]

In general, between the late thirteenth and mid-sixteenth centuries, Hongsawaddy prospered. During most of this period, the Mon rulers of lower Burma managed to contain their numerically superior but faction-ridden Burman rivals in the north. However, in 1535 the forces of king Tabinshwehti, under the command of his brother-in-law and general, Bayinnaung, launched a devastating attack on lower Burma. The northern army overran the Irrawaddy Delta and in 1539, after a four year siege during which Portuguese mercenaries fought on both sides, captured Pegu. The *History of Kings* attributes Tabinshwehti's success in part to the decadence of the Peguan king, Dhammaceti's heir.[158]

With the fall of Hongsawaddy, large numbers of refugees fled to Ayuthaiya, where the Peguan aristocracy joined the court and exercised considerable influence. Meanwhile back in Burma, the fall of Martaban in

1541 was accompanied by massacre and pillage on a large scale, as was the capture of the old Pyu capital of Prome the following year.[159] For the first time since before the Mongul invasions, most of lower and central Burma was under the control of a Burman monarch. King Tabinshwehti, founder of the new Toungoo dynasty, celebrated by decorating the Shwedagon and other pagodas with huge amounts of plundered gold.

In 1542 Tabinshwehti established his capital at Pegu, building a new palace on the site of the old Mon city. According to Phayre (who was always alert to nuances of ethnicity), "while endeavouring to secure the attachment of the Talaing people, he always put prominently forward his claim to Burmese nationality and sovereignty."[160] However, in comparison with later Toungoo kings, who persecuted the Mon (or 'Talaing') and outlawed their language, Tabinshwehti may be considered a relatively enlightened despot. In 1546 he was coronated using both Mon and Burman rites. Tabinshwehti even sported a Mon-style haircut and recognised a number of Mon princelings who had previously been loyal to Hongsawaddy.[161] These elements of Mon rule and identity were presumably adopted in order to win over his new subjects, thus demonstrating the plasticity of precolonial ethnic and feudal loyalties.[162]

In the year of Tabinshwehti's coronation, Ayuthaiya launched the first of a series of raids on lower Burma and succeeded in capturing the small port of Tavoy.[163] In 1550 the death of the increasingly dissolute king Tabinshwehti was apparently engineered by Mon courtiers, who were emboldened by another defeat of the Burman army that year by the forces of Ayuthaiya. With the Toungoo dynasty in disarray, the Mon renewed their bid for independence.

Forces under the legendary Mon rebel, the *Smin Daw* (a royal title and *nom de guerre*), succeeded in capturing the ancient settlement of Dagon and went on to drive the Burmans from Pegu. However, a series of intra-Mon disputes allowed Tabinshwehti's general, Bayinnaung, to re-take the city, again with the assistance of Portuguese mercenaries. Having defeated the *Smin Daw* in single combat, but spared his life, Bayinnaung oversaw the massacre of Pegu.

Not for the first or last time, the northern forces dealt harshly with the 'upstart Mon'. The *Smin Daw* however, escaped with his life, and over the next few years was to conduct a daring guerrilla campaign across the Irrawaddy Delta, during which he often out-manoeuvred and out-fought the occupying forces. The *Smin Daw's* skill and defiance quickly became the stuff of legend. Mon rebels and pretenders in centuries to come adopted the title *Smin Daw*, and to this day he remains a popular nationalist hero.

Eventually the *Smin Daw* was captured and executed by king Bayinnaung, bringing the Wareru dynasty to an end.[164] However, as Guillon notes, the fall of Hongsawaddy did not mean "the extinction of Mon culture, although thenceforth it was to be discontinuous."[165]

According to Nai Tun Thein, Bayinnaung "let Mon people rule in authority over townships and villages, and accepted Mon into the military.... Yet Bayinnaung did not grant the right of national self-determination, and thus the Mon became subservient to Myanmar."[166] Significant Mon uprisings occurred in 1551, and again in 1564, during which the royal palace at Pegu was destroyed.

In addition to the ongoing Mon-Burman power struggle in the sixteenth century, the region also saw incessant war between the Burma and the Tai states. Having seemingly dealt with the Mon, Bayinnaung turned his attention to the north and east, where he launched a series of campaign against the Tai. He quickly succeeded in conquering the Shan plateau, before moving on to capture Chiang Mai, capital of Lan Na (the territory of old Haripunjaya), in 1558.[167] Eventually, after some protracted military and political manoeuvring, on 8th August 1569 Bayinnaung's army took the capital of Ayuthaiya, whereupon the Thai king was abducted and replaced with a compliant vassal monarch, king Thammaracha.[168] King Bayinnaung thus extended Burman control over a larger territory than had any of his predecessors. With Pegu conquered, Ayuthaiya, La Na and the Shan states enlisted as tributary *mandalas*, and Burman troops garrisoned on the Bengali borders, 'Greater Burma' was never again to cover so large an area.

The Burmans occupied Ayuthaiya for one-and-a-half decades, until the death of Bayinnaung, following which the empire was again threatened by a Mon uprising in the west. By this time, king Thammaracha had been succeeded by his son, the great Thai hero, king Naresuan. As crown prince, Naresuan had for eight years (1564–71) been held by Bayinnaung as a hostage in Pegu,[169] during which period he is said to have developed a great respect for Mon political and religious culture. In 1581–82 Naresuan returned to Pegu, to attend the coronation rites of Bayinnaung's successor. On his return, Naresuan launched his campaign for independence. This was finally achieved following the great battle of Nong Sarai (near Suphanburi) in 1593, during which the Burman ruler was slain by Naresuan in single, elephant-back combat.[170]

Over the next decade, king Naresuan drew large numbers of Mon rebels to his cause and even threatened an assault on Pegu, which was still the capital of Burma. Mon refugees were welcomed in newly-independent Ayuthaiya: following the late sixteenth century wars, manpower was at a premium and the Mon were still widely respected as cultural preceptors. In the following century, two brothers, the descendants of the exiled Mon followers of king Naresuan, were appointed to the influential positions of minister for foreign affairs and ambassador to France.[171] Their descendants settled on the Chao Phya River north of Ayuthaiya and were still prominent in Thai royal circles in the nineteenth century.

The late sixteenth and seventeenth centuries were less propitious times for the Mon in Burma. The English adventurer, Ralph Ficht, visited Pegu in

1586, a half-century after the fall of Hongsawaddy. His journal indicates that the population was still largely Mon-speaking. However, the next decade was to be one of devastation and destruction. Another Mon exodus to the east occurred in 1595 and by 1599 vast stretches of old Hongsawaddy had been laid waste, following an invasion by Arakan. The Burman overlords conscripted tens of thousands of Mon troops, many of whom died from the effects of war and famine.

Pegu was reduced to ruins. A Jesuit priest who witnessed the aftermath of the slaughter described the Pegu River as "so covered with masses or heaps of dead bodies, half burnt planks and timber of every description, that it was with great difficulty the ships sailing the river could force their way through."[172] It is hardly surprising, given the devastation of Mon institutions in the early 1600s, that the first English-Mon vocabulary list, drawn up in 1601, shows the growing influence of Burmese on the Mon language.[173]

During this period of confusion, with the Burman empire in disarray following the Arakanese invasion, Western actors became further involved in the violent and complex world of Burmese politics. In exchange for protection from the ravages of the Burman and Arakanese armies, the Mon chiefs offered their allegiance to a representative of the Portuguese mission at Goa. Bannya Dala of Martaban, who was technically a vassal of Ayuthaiya, took the lead in negotiations with the merchant-adventurer, Philip de Brito y Nicote.

According to Guillon, in the early seventeenth century the Portuguese in lower Burma were "a law unto themselves."[174] The French ecclesiastical historian, Paul Ambroise Bigandet, describing de Brito two-and-a-half centuries after his death, called him "a true adventurer, that knew not to set bounds to his ambition ... But he soon found out his mistake, and paid dearly for his haughty behaviour and insolent proceedings."[175]

De Brito was allowed to retain a trading base at Syriam, in which he had been established by the Arakanese invaders. He proceeded to set himself up as 'king of the Mons' and, in alliance with Bannya Dala, began to tax local shipping and trade. In 1610 their forces launched a major attack on Ava, following which the Portuguese withdrew to Syriam. Here, de Brito had established a profitable fiefdom, not dissimilar in character to those of the indigenous princelings and warlords of the era.[176] Later, when de Brito began to plunder pagodas and became involved in a campaign to convert the people of lower Burma to Catholicism, the relationship with Bannya Dala turned sour.[177]

In 1613 the Burman king, Anaukpetlun, counter-attacked. With the help of Mon levies, he took de Brito's stronghold at Syriam, capturing the Portuguese adventurer in the process. As punishment for his heresy and for assisting the Mon rebels, de Brito was impaled upon a stake. Due either to foolishness, stubbornness or ignorance, he refused to adopt the recommended position, which would have ensured that the stake passed through his vital organs, guaranteeing a quick death; instead, he took two days to die.

Within a few years, Anaukpetlun had re-taken the last of the Mon lands. He re-established his capital at Pegu, following which a new wave of refugees fled to Ayuthaiya. Again, they were settled in the under-populated border provinces, from where for several decades the Mon princes launched occasional raids against outposts in Burma,[178] establishing a pattern of cross-border insurgency which in certain respects remains unchanged to this day.

Anaukpetlun was killed during another uprising, in 1629, and in 1635 the capital was moved back north, to Ava.[179] Due to lack of regular maintenance, the Pegu River soon began to silt up. The traditional heart of Hongsawaddy lost its viability as capital of lower Burma and prospects for the Mon in Burma looked bleak. Hall notes that, in the seventeenth century, the Burman rulers "treated the Mons as a subject race", rather than with the respect of previous eras.[180] A further unsuccessful Mon uprising occurred at Martaban in 1661 (or 1662), following which the Burman armies pursued fleeing Mon refugees into Ayuthaiya, via the Three Pagodas Pass.[181]

As Ava consolidated its position in the second half of the seventeenth century, the British East India Company negotiated a series of trade agreements with the court, whilst maintaining discreet contacts with restive Mon chiefs in the south. During this period, British merchants developed an interest in trading with China, via Burma.[182] The stage was set for the great military, political and economic upheavals of the eighteenth and nineteenth centuries.

The Last Mon Kings

Although the Burman kings had gained a decisive upper hand, Hall notes that "the Mons never lost their desire for independence and were bound one day to make another bid at restoring the kingdom of Pegu."[183] The opportunity arose in the early-mid eighteenth century, when Arakan and the Indian kingdom of Manipur launched a series of attacks on Ava.

The last of the great Mon uprisings was led by the *Smin Daw* Buddhaketi, whose doomed attempt to resurrect Hongsawaddy has been immortalised in literature, fables and popular song. This charismatic leader may be considered a *min laung* pretender – a claimant to the throne of pious universal ruler, whose role in the Buddhist millennial tradition is to purify the earth in preparation for the arrival of Ariyah Metteya, the future incarnate Buddha. In a pattern often repeated in Burmese history, the *min laung* uprisings of precolonial and colonial Burma combined attempts at the usurpation of political power with a religious justification.[184]

The *Smin Daw* Buddhaketi's forces emerged from the Karenni hills in 1740. They soon captured Pegu, with the help of Portuguese mercenaries,

Mon levies, disaffected Avan troops and the mysterious 'Gwe' Karen.[185] The rebels killed the local governor (who had initiated the uprising) and installed the *Smin Daw* Buddhaketi on the throne.[186] Significantly, given the 'multi-national' composure of his army, the *Smin Daw* included Burman and Karen ministers in his cabinet,[187] which according to the Mon chronicles, ruled more righteously than had his rapacious predecessor.[188]

As noted in Part One, modern readings of Burmese history tend to emphasise the exclusive ethnic identity of the different kingdoms that contested for power down the turbulent centuries of the precolonial era. In fact, affinities were mutable and the ethnic determination of different factions was not always clear. Identities reflected the changing pattern of political alignment. For example, Lieberman points out that throughout the period 1740–57 significant numbers of Mon subjects "remained faithful to the northern (Avan) court, because of personal ties or local loyalties. They constituted a sort of mirror image of the Burmese supporters of Pegu."[189] Indeed, in 1743 the *Smin Daw* placed a Burman from Pegu, rather than a local Mon, in charge of the restive port of Martaban.[190]

In a counter-offensive launched in 1743, the forces of Ava re-took Syriam, destroying the Armenian, French and Portuguese missions and churches there.[191] However, they did not touch those of the British – which were later burnt down by the returning Mon forces, in retaliation for Britain's failure to assist them against Ava.[192] Also in 1743–44, a Catholic mission to lower Burma became embroiled in various political and military intrigues, resulting in its massacre.[193] This episode coincided with a Buddhist revival, accompanying the resurrection of Mon power in the south, during which a number of important Theravadin texts were produced. The most notable religious figure of the time was the 'Master of Waw', a Mon monk from the small town of that name, thirty Km northeast of Pegu.[194]

By the mid-1740s, Pegu still controlled most of the towns and cities of lower Burma. However, the king of Ayuthaiya refused to give his daughter in marriage to the *Smin Daw*, perhaps sensing that the new Mon dynasty was not sustainable.[195] Furthermore, David Wyatt suggests that Ayuthaiya may have viewed the re-emergence of Pegu as a threat to the loyalty of its Mon subjects, many of whom retained memories of Hongsawaddy and might be expected to identify with the resurgent Mon kingdom.[196] Indeed, whilst secretly encouraging the Mon rebels, throughout the eighteenth century the Thais continued to court the stronger Burman dynasty.

The *Smin Daw* was an ineffective ruler. In 1747 he was overthrown in a palace coup and replaced by his military commander (and father-in-law), the Lord of Dala. Like king Wareru, Bannya Dala may have been a Shan. However, he too is revered as a hero of the Mon resistance.

Following his ouster, the *Smin Daw's* travels took him to Ayuthaiya, where he was briefly detained, and to China and the northern Thai kingdom of La Na.[197] Here, the small band of Mon exiles were given a sympathetic reception, but only limited support. Eventually, the *Smin Daw* died in Toungoo in 1754.

By this time, foreign powers had again become involved in Burmese politics. Since 1729, the French Company had been operating a productive shipyard at Syriam, de Brito's old haunt near Dagon. To the intense suspicion of the British, in 1751 the French agent, de Bruno, had agreed a treaty with king Bannya Dala, allowing French arms to be supplied to the Mon, in exchange for certain trading rights. East India Company attempts to expand into Syriam being thus confounded by de Bruno, in April 1753 the British seized Negrais Island, in the mouth of the Bassein River, in the Irrawaddy Delta. Situated across the Bay of Bengal from India, Negrais seemed to offer the British a number of strategic options for expansion into Burma.[198]

In the meantime, the Mon army had proceeded to invade upper Burma. However, Bannya Dala had not yet consolidated his position in the south and his forces were soon dangerously over-extended. According to Guillon, the Mon "jumped into a war of revenge and subjugation in which they had everything to loose."[199] The new offensive again made use of Portuguese mercenaries and Burman troops, and was also aided by the French, who supplied six cannon and four hundred muskets.[200] In 1752 the Mon army, under the command of the legendary general, Talaban, captured Ava and abducted the Burman king, who was later killed, ending the Toungoo Dynasty and briefly extending Mon control over all of lower and central Burma.

However, one village headman from Shwebo refused to swear allegiance to Pegu. He soon managed to re-unite the northern Burman forces and the Mon invaders were forced on to the defensive. The following year, in 1753, the emergent warrior-king and *min luang*, Alaungphaya, succeeded in liberating Ava, despite fierce resistance on the part of the Gwe and Mon defenders, who were eventually forced to flee the city in the dead of night.[201] It was only now, after the fall of Ava, that king Bannya Dala was roused to send the bulk of his army north, by which time it was too late to relieve Talaban's over-stretched expeditionary force.

This ill-conceived and disastrous military adventure was to cost the Mon dearly. By 1754, Bannya Dala's forces had been forced to retreat in disarray to Prome, following which the Burman population in the Irrawaddy Delta rose up and drove out their Mon rulers. As a result, Lieberman notes that "the frightened Peguan court ... came to doubt the loyalty of many of its Burmese subjects" and following the discovery of a Burman conspiracy among deportees brought from Ava, in October 1754 "executed over a thousand leading deportees implicated in the plot."[202]

By 1755, Alaungphaya controlled most of the delta, including the village of Dagon. This ancient religious centre was renamed Rangoon, which in Burmese can mean either 'end of strife' or 'annihilation of the enemy'.

However, the Mon were still in control of Pegu and parts of the Tenasserim region. They also continued to receive some assistance from the French at Syriam.[203] Meanwhile, both the French and the British attempted to open relations with Alaungphaya, who in 1755 was preoccupied with a Shan revolt in the north of his new kingdom. In 1757 he recognised the British position at Negrais. However, this distant station of the empire was never developed, and the East India Company withdrew following the massacre of 1759, during which Burman troops killed ten British men, women and children, whom they suspected of aiding the Mon forces.[204]

Following an ineffective Mon offensive the previous year, in 1756 Alaungphaya's army laid siege to Syriam. The French lent the Mon some limited assistance, but this was not sufficient to prevent the Burman army taking the commercially vital port. De Bruno, who had been imprisoned by the Mon after attempting to switch sides, was killed by the Burmans. First though, he was forced to lure two French ships, bearing weapons intended for the Mon, into the clutches of the northern forces. These events were followed by the introduction of a 'scorched earth' policy in lower Burma, during which Alaungphaya concentrated his forces against Pegu.[205]

Phayre's sources report that the "Talaings ... still fought with the courage of men of spirit, who struggle for national independence in its last place of refuge."[206] However, they were outnumbered and outflanked. The final blow came in May 1757 when, perhaps due to divisions in the defenders' ranks, king Alaungphaya re-took Pegu.[207]

This famous (or infamous) victory effectively unified Burma for the third time under a single king. The new Konbaung dynasty was to reign for more than a hundred years, until its unceremonious overthrow by the British in 1885. Mon folk memory, and the chronicles, recall that the fall of Pegu-Hongsawaddy was marked by the destruction of manuscripts, and that as many as 3,000 Mon monks were murdered or expelled by the conquering Burmans. According to the *History of Kings*, "the monks' robes were scattered all over land and water."[208] Guillon says that the moats of Pegu "ran red with gore."[209]

According to the Mon nationalist historian, Nai Tun Thein, "the racial oppression practised by Alaungphaya was worse than that of previous kings. He ended the cultural autonomy adopted by the former Myanmar rulers of the Pagan era, and by kings Tabinshwehti and Bayinnaung, and colonised the Mon state."[210] Lieberman and Thant Myint-Us' studies suggest that Alaungphaya was the first Burman king to consciously manipulate ethnic identity as a means to military and political domination.[211] Lieberman states that, after 1757 "many bi-lingual southerners who had hitherto identified themselves as 'Mons' may suddenly have found it politic to become 'Burmese'."[212] Nevertheless, a number of identifiably Mon headmen and princes continued to serve under the new Burman king and his successors. Although the Mon language was suppressed, lower Burma retained a distinct identity and continued to exert a cultural and religious influence across the region.

However, over the following century, the Mon, and the Arakanese to the west, were gradually assimilated into and displaced by the resurgent Burman population. By 1811, a decade prior to the First Anglo-Burmese War, when Ava banned the distinctive, Mon-style short haircut (such as had been adopted by king Tabinshwehti in the mid-sixteenth century),[213] the process of 'Burmanisation' was already well underway.

Meanwhile, thousands of Peguan survivors had fled to neighbouring Ayuthaiya. Here they were settled in the sparsely populated lands between the border and the capital, as well as further to the north, in the still semi-independent realm of La Na. With the struggle for power in lower Burma seemingly resolved, the East India Company was able to repair its relationship with Ava, and compete with the expanding French presence to the east, in Indochina.

The years 1758–59 and 1760 were marked by further unsuccessful Mon rebellions in lower Burma,[214] following which king Alaungphaya renewed the Thai-Burman feud. By launching an attack on his neighbour to the east in 1760, he hoped to capture and deport a portion of the Mon population in Ayuthaiya, and repopulate the parts of his kingdom devastated during the Mon wars, while punishing those who had fled after the fall of Pegu. Not surprisingly therefore, the overthrown Mon leadership sided with the Thais in the defence of Ayuthaiya (although there had apparently been outbreaks of rebellion among the 'Thai Mon' in 1750–55 and 1760).[215]

The Burman army pushed far to the east, eventually laying siege to Ayuthaiya itself. However, at this critical juncture, king Alaungphaya was fatally injured "in the hidden parts"[216] and the invaders were forced to withdraw. Soon afterwards, on his way back home to Shwebo, Alaungphaya died, and was buried near the Salween River.[217]

Following an abortive Mon revolt in Tavoy in 1767, which had been supported by the Thais, Ayuthaiya was finally overrun by Alaungphaya's son, king Hsinbyushin.[218] However, within a few months Thai sovereignty had been re-established by king Taksin, at the new capital of Thonburi. His successor, Rama I, the founder of the Chakri dynasty, moved the capital across the Chao Phya River to Bangkok. Despite such continuities, the sacking of Ayuthaiya is still remembered as one of the most shocking episodes in Thai history, which for two-and-a-half centuries has coloured popular perceptions of the kingdom's relations with Burma.

The Mon Diaspora

Since the great Mon-Burman wars of the sixteenth century, groups of displaced Mon people had been entering Ayuthaiya-Siam, either to settle permanently or take temporary shelter in the kingdom. Historically, these refugees were welcomed, both because of their role as Buddhist emissaries and because the Mon forces on the western frontier served a useful purpose in checking the advances of an aggressive neighbour.

In the second half of the eighteenth century, the resurgent Burman kings drove a further wave of Mon refugees into exile, as they pushed rebellious groups into the hill country east of the Salween River and south into the Tenasserim jungles.[219] During these turbulent years, large numbers of Karen were also on the move. Their leaders established vassal relations with Siam and many groups took up residence in the kingdom's Great Western Forest, which for some two thousand years effectively constituted the Thailand-Burma border.[220]

In 1773 another Mon uprising occurred in Rangoon, during which the town was burnt to the ground. Again, Ava brutally repressed the perpetrators, pursuing fleeing Mon refugees into Siamese territory beyond the Three Pagodas Pass. According to D.F. Raikes, "it is with the 1773 group of immigrants that we can still establish a direct, unbroken, line of succession right up to the present."[221] While earlier waves of Mon migrants had, by the twentieth century, been more-or-less completely assimilated into Thai society, many of the descendants of those arriving since the latter half of the eighteenth century still possess recognisably Mon characteristics.

In retaliation for the 1773 uprising, the deposed Mon king, Bannya Dala, who had been captured in 1757, was executed in 1777, thus ending the royal line of Hongsawaddy.[222] Nevertheless, further Mon revolts took place in 1782[223] and again in 1783. During the latter rebellion, Rangoon was briefly occupied by Mon forces from the Irrawaddy Delta, who killed the Burman governor and several other Avan officials. However, the Mon were undone by a treacherous detachment of Burman troops, who had pretended to side with the insurgents. Some three hundred rebels were subsequently massacred.[224]

In 1793 king Rama I briefly occupied Tavoy, in concert with local Mon chiefs. However, the invaders were unable to hold the port in the face of a Burman counter-offensive and had to return to Siam, taking large numbers of Mon captives with them.[225] Another Mon insurrection occurred at Martaban in 1814 (or 1815), a decade before the First Anglo-Burmese War. Following this failed rebellion, yet another wave of Mon refugees fled to Siam, where they were met in the border provinces by the future monarch, prince Mongkut.[226] The migrants were encouraged to settle along the lower reaches of the Burmese border, and at Pak Kret and Phra Padaeng on the Chao Phya River.

Once again, Mon forces were incorporated into the Siamese army.[227] Significantly, the Mon regiments were garrisoned and organised separately to ethnic Thai units, and were commanded by Mon officers (Vietnamese and Khmer sections of the army were similarly organised).[228] Stationed under the command of their traditional princes, until the eve of the Second

World War the 'Thai Mon' were still officially subjects of the 'Mon Chakri' (Lord) of Thailand.[229]

According to Guillon, by 1833 the population of Ratchaburi Province was almost entirely Mon.[230] These immigrants had brought palm leaf manuscripts and copper plates with them, which today constitute some of the most important records of Mon civilisation in Burma.[231] During this period, a number of Mon monasteries were established in Thailand, several of which became depositories of important artefacts from Hongsawaddy. To this day, many retain a distinctly Mon character.

As Donald Wilson remarks, "the Siamese regarded the Mons as allies in their continuing wars with the Burmese, and entrusted them with positions of authority and special rank. The Mon men were respected as warriors, and were permitted to wear their hair long and carry arms."[232] The Mon princes re-built their communities in exile and waited for the day when they might liberate Hongsawaddy. Meanwhile, members of the Mon elite achieved positions of influence in Siam. Halliday quotes a Spanish source, regarding a late nineteenth century Mon aristocrat: during a period of momentous diplomatic manoeuvres vis-à-vis France and Britain, this individual was "one of the most popular and successful Siamese ministers, at the court of St. James's."[233]

In 1855, in a newspaper article written in response to a request by the British Governor of Hong Kong, king Mongkut (Rama IV) acknowledged the Thai royal house's links with the Mon. King Mongkut's account outlined the history of the Chakri dynasty, including king Naresuan's relationship with Pegu and the high office held by his Mon followers and their successors.[234]

During the nineteenth century, there was again considerable inter-marriage between the Siamese and Mon royal families, and a number of Mon customs were incorporated into the Thai tradition. King Rama III had taken a Mon wife into his harem and their son, Prince Siriwong, also married a Mon princess, with whom he had seven children. Two of Prince Siriwong's daughters became wives of king Mongkut.[235] The elder daughter was in turn mother of the next king, Chulalongkorn (Rama V).

His mother died when he was a boy, and the young prince Chulalongkorn was raised by his Mon grandmother. He later had Wat Pramai Yikawat built in her honour, on the 'Mon island' of Koh Kret. Situated above Bangkok in the Chao Phya River, Koh Kret had since the mid-eighteenth century been an important centre of the Thai Mon community.[236] It was here that Robert Halliday helped to establish a Mon press in 1905, which published a number of important historical documents.[237] The Mon-style monastery built by king Chulalongkorn, which is modelled on the Shwedagon, today holds a number of important artefacts, including records of royal patronage and a Mon language copy of the *Tripitaka*.

King Chulalongkorn also oversaw a major renovation of the famous pagoda at Nakhon Pathom, built after a Sinnhalese model during the early Dvaravati period. The Phra Pathom pagoda was re-built by Mon craftsmen from Burma and covered with the distinctive yellow, Chinese-style glazed tiles, which in Nai Pan Hla's words "added so much to its beauty in attracting the awe and admiration of the pilgrims."[238]

During this period of renewed Mon influence, a number of Mon religious practices were adopted in Siam. In the 1850s and '60s king Mongkut (Rama IV) continued the work which he had begun during his twenty-seven years in the monkhood. He oversaw a major restructuring of the *sangha*, based largely on principles adopted from the Mon sects, which were regarded as being more disciplined and spiritually advanced than their Thai counterparts.[239]

In the 1870s the influential *Maha Yen* (or *Thamayut Thanikka*) sect was established in its modern form and in 1875 a 'Thai Mon' monk introduced the sect to Burma. The principle *Maha Yen* temple is today located opposite the east gate of the Shwedagon pagoda in Rangoon. Regarded as a major force in both Thai and Burmese Buddhism, the *Maha Yen* also has links to the *sangha* in Sri Lanka.

Here, in the cradle of Theravada Buddhism, Mon influence underwent a further revival in 1864, when the *Ramanna Nikaya* sect was established. The sect was named in honour of the Mon monkhood in Burma, which had maintained the strict discipline and practices of orthodox Theravada. The *Ramanna Nikaya* expanded dramatically in the late nineteenth century and remains to this day one of the most important sects in Sri Lanka.[240]

Thailand also benefited from the Mon refugees in more worldly ways. Not only aristocrats and warrior-princes, monks and religious preceptors settled in Siam. Mon people of every class made the kingdom their home, including peasants and artisans, who naturally constituted the largest sector of the Mon population. According to Wilson, by the nineteenth century "the Mon settlers ... had already begun their transformation from combatants to craftsmen."[241] Mon communities became well-known for their small, red 'Mon bricks', and later for the production of high quality, unglazed ceramics.[242]

In the twentieth century, as Thai society has experienced ever-greater modernisation, it has seemed to some observers that the distinctive traditions of Mon craftsmanship might die out.[243] However, as noted in Part One, this has not always been the case. Production at the Mon potteries on Koh Kret increased dramatically in the 1990s, as Thai tourists discovered the island and it became a bastion of Mon cultural revival. In 1995 Nai Pisarn Boonpook, a community leader from Koh Kret, mounted an exhibition of Mon pottery production at the Smithsonian Museum in Washington, demonstrating the continued vitality of the Mon heritage. Together with the island's lychee and durian orchards, the pottery industry today makes a significant contribution to the prosperous local economy.

Elsewhere in Thailand, the Mon have prospered also. As well as their role as artisans, they have sometimes competed with the Chinese as entrepreneurs and middle-men[244]; more than one twentieth century Thai fortune derives from the trading skills of nineteenth century Mon refugees from Burma. Another area in which the Thai Mon have thrived is as boatmen on the Chao Phya and other rivers. According to Brian Foster, in the 1970s "a large proportion of the construction materials used in Bangkok (arrived) in Mon barges."[245]

CHAPTER SIX

The British Period and the
Second World War

Since the mid-eighteenth century, the only real political autonomy enjoyed by the Mon has been of a very limited, insecure and circumscribed kind, won on the battlefields of southeast Burma. By the eve of Britain's annexation of Burma, the Mon had already become a subject people. Their ancient culture and language persisted, but the era of Mon political dominion was at an end. Although the advent of British rule in Burma was to remove the immediate fact of Burman domination, this was replaced by another, in many ways more insidious regime.

While Burman nationalist history represents foreign colonisation as an unmitigated disaster, for the Mon and other minority peoples, the arrival in force of the British in the nineteenth century was not necessarily an unwelcome development. After decades of oppression by the Burman majority, the advent of British rule at least offered a change of overlords. However, the benign neglect with which the colonial administration treated the Mon was ultimately to prove equally corrosive of their ancient culture.

The British presence in Burma was not at first intended to be permanent. However, commercial and strategic considerations, including the protection of rice and timber exports, and competition with France over control of the illusive China trade, led to a gradual extension of British control. Other factors in the conquest of Burma included the haughty responses of British officials to the sometimes aggressively independent actions of the last Burman kings, and the ambitious and self-interested manoeuvrings of colonial agents on the ground.

Under British rule, Burmese demographics underwent a significant shift, as large numbers of ethnic Burmans moved south into lower Burma, to take advantage of new opportunities in agriculture and business. The Mon and other minority groups also changed their patterns of residence, livelihood and education – and in some cases their religion too.

By the second quarter of the twentieth century, Mon politicians had assumed active roles in Burmese politics. On the eve of the Second World

War they established the All Ramanya Mon Association (ARMA), the first Mon nationalist organisation of modern times. However, so great was the erosion of Mon culture and language under the British, that by the time the colonialists finally departed there were few Mon living in the Irrawaddy Delta or in Pegu, the ancient capital of Hongsawaddy.

The Anglo-Burmese Wars

By the beginning of the nineteenth century, East India Company and independent British merchants had been active in parts of southern and western Burma for nearly two hundred years. An important trading route linked Madras, in India, to Mergui, on the Tenasserim seaboard. From here, goods were moved by boat up the Tenasserim River and then along jungle tracks to the pass at Maw Daung, and beyond to Ayuthaiya. Cutting across the Isthmus of Kra, this axis of the India-South China Seas trade avoided a much longer sea passage, via the pirate-infested straits of Malacca. The route had been pioneered by Indian and Mon merchants, and was later used by the Thais, Portuguese, Dutch and British.[246]

It was partly a desire to foster and protect this trade that led the British in India to expand eastwards into Burma. The conquest of Burma was completed over a period of sixty-one years (1824–85), and three wars. Only in the First Anglo-Burmese War of 1824–26 did much sustained fighting occur.[247] Following the British victory, two territories were brought under imperial control: Arakan in the southwest, adjacent to British India, and Tenasserim in the south, bordering the Isthmus of Kra. From the mid-sixteenth century, until they were annexed by the Burmese empire in 1792, Mergui, Tavoy and the mountains and rivers of Tenasserim were subject to Ayuthaiya; before this, they had been part of the Mon *mandala* of Martaban.

Historians have generally ascribed to the Mon and Karen in lower Burma a role in assisting British forces during the war, which originated in border clashes between two occupying armies: the Burman in Arakan and the British in Bengal. Woodman, for example, credits the Mon with being "an important strategic asset." She quotes a famous British proclamation of 1825, in which the Mon were reminded of their slave-like position under the Burmans and urged to rebel in support of the British forces, whose Commander-in-Chief, Sir Archibald Campbell, told them to "choose among yourselves a chief, and I will acknowledge him!"[248]

More than a century-and-a-half later, Mon nationalists still remember this unfulfilled pledge, which anticipates assurances given to the Karen during the Second World War.[249] In both instances, the pressing needs of war led British officers to make promises to their native allies, which the post-war government proved unable or unwilling to fulfil.[250] However, during this formative period of British rule, the colonial administration did at least briefly consider supporting Mon claims against the Burmans. Among other things, this could have meant adopting Mon, rather than Burmese, as the language of colonial administration.

In 1825–26 Captain Henry Burney of the East India Company was sent to conduct treaty negotiations with Siam. He also sought out the descendants of king Bannya Dala, who had been executed nearly fifty years before.[251] These included Phraya Choei, commander of the 'Army of Dvaravati', Siam's frontier force along the Burmese border.[252] Phraya Choei's ancestors had migrated to Ayuthaiya in 1755, together with some ten thousand of their countrymen.[253] The British anticipated that the Mon elite in Thailand would be keen to re-claim their patrimony. However, moves to re-establish a Mon court in lower Burma and undermine the authority of the Konbaung dynasty were soon abandoned. The Mon princes, including Phraya Choei, did not relish the prospect of relinquishing their privileged positions in Thai society, to pursue yet another bloody campaign against the Burmans. Although, following the outbreak of the First Anglo-Burmese War, the 'Army of Dvaravati' briefly engaged the Burmese, the Mon troops were soon recalled to Siam.[254]

Meanwhile back in Burma, Mon allegiances were similarly uncertain. Exhausted by centuries of conflict, and fearing possible Burman reprisals, Mon communities were not of particular assistance to the British during the First Anglo-Burmese War. Robert Taylor cites an 1858 anti-British rebellion, led by the ousted Mon and Burman vassal lords of Pegu, as evidence of the divided loyalties of minority groups during the early colonial period.[255] Nevertheless, a year after the war ended, the Mon chiefs of Dala and Syriam openly sided with the British, leading a revolt against the Burman king.

Maung Thaw Lay and Nai Maung Zat (or *Smin* Baru) were local commanders under the Burman governor of Rangoon. Both were born in Pegu, the latter being of Mon royal blood. In 1827 troops under Nai Maung Zat, the chief officer at Syriam, together with large numbers of Karen, launched an attack on Rangoon. Although they were soon joined by a larger force under Maung Thaw Lay, the rebels were beaten back by Burman reinforcements from the north, and were forced to retreat to the British lines at Moulmein.[256]

According to Taylor, British rule in Tenasserim "evoked little violent opposition", as the isthmus had not "been well integrated administratively or ethnically into the precolonial order."[257] The Mon inhabitants of lower Burma, including the 30,000 followers of Maung Thaw Lay and Nai Maung Zat, were among the first 'Burmese' to live under British rule. Nai Pan Hla writes that the defeated forces of Maung Zat "settled in a village in Moulmein called Min-Ywe, meaning king village, because of his royal descent. The well known Mon leaders who accompanied Maung Thaw Lay included Maung Tar Yar, Maung Po Saw and Maung Ngan, and the places where these leaders settled were accordingly named after their respective founders, and remain so up to the present day."[258] According to contemporary reports, the ratio of Mons to Burmans in early nineteenth century Moulmein was twenty-to-one.[259]

From November 1827, Maung Zat received a pension of 250 Rupees, which was paid until his death in October 1830.[260] His nephew, Maung Moo, later joined the new Talaing Corps, a local militia organised by the British in order to dispense patronage and defend their newly-acquired provinces, at minimum cost.[261] In 1835 the Commissioner for Tenasserim, E.A. Blundell, noted that "the attachment of the Talaings to us and their enmity to Burma may be implicitly relied on."[262]

As noted above, only ten years previously, the British had contemplated resurrecting the Mon court. In raising a Mon levy, they were sending a message to the Burman king, to the effect that "the whole youth of Pegu in case of hostilities with Ava ... would rejoice at the opportunity of revenging themselves on their conquerors."[263] However, uniforms and munitions were at first in short supply, and as the Mon troops were paid less than those brought over from Madras, recruitment to the Talaing Corps progressed slowly.[264] Numbers only reached something like full strength in 1839, by which time a Talaing Officer Corps had also been sanctioned.[265] In the same year, although discipline was in general said to be much improved, one Maung Ban of the Talaing Corps was "reduced for disgraceful conduct."[266] Within a few years, the corps had been disbanded, due to lack of enthusiasm on the parts of both the local Mon population and the authorities in India.[267]

Mon leaders nevertheless continued to take advantage of the British presence in their struggles against Burman overlords. Ten years after the Maung Thaw Lay-Nai Maung Zat rebellion, between 1838–40, the Mon princeling and *min laung* pretender, Maung Setkya of Pegu, led another uprising in Rangoon.[268] In contrast, a joint Mon-Karen anti-British revolt broke out in 1843, led by another aspirant *min laung*, Nga Pyan.[269]

In December 1852, following the Second Anglo-Burmese War, Pegu was formally annexed as a province of British Burma.[270] The Mon heartland was integrated into an empire far greater than that of even the most ambitious precolonial kings. Over the next century, the ethnic, political, economic and cultural characteristics of lower Burma were to undergo dramatic changes.

From the middle of the nineteenth century, large numbers of ethnic Burmans began to migrate south, from the northern strongholds of the last Burman kings. The newcomers cleared the jungle and established farms in the less-densely populated – and traditionally predominantly Mon and Karen – Irrawaddy Delta and adjoining regions. The rich soils of lower Burma provided the newcomers with opportunities to dramatically expand rice production, while the British used both paid and corve labour to construct a series of roads and railways, canals and bridges across the wetlands and forest.[271] As well as encouraging rice cultivation and rationalising the management of Burma's forests, the colonial authorities also introduced extensive rubber plantations in the Tenasserim region.

In the decades following British annexation, the population of lower Burma grew rapidly, with the arrival of large numbers of ethnic Burmans from the north and several hundred thousand Muslims and Hindus from India. Between 1826–72, the population of Tenasserim rose from 70,000 to 257,404; in the seventeen years between 1855–72, the populations of Pegu Province and Martaban District more than doubled, rising from 631,640 and 87,742 to 1,662,058 and 205,913 respectively.[272]

Due to the improved security situation during the first year of British rule, rice production in Tenasserim had risen by thirty-four per cent.[273] Nevertheless, the East India Company did not regard the province as profitable and briefly considered selling it to Siam.[274] Soon though, Burma was on the way to acquiring its reputation as 'the rice-bowl of Asia'. As a result of increased land clearance and production, rice exports rose from 162,000 tons in 1855 to two million in 1905–06, and to over three million by the 1920s.[275]

The Pax Britannica

The colonial period in Burma has been characterised by Michael Aung-Thwin as one of 'order without meaning'.[276] Despite the veneer of civility and legal-rational administration, British rule in Burma was achieved and maintained by force of arms. The role of the state was greatly extended, compared to that of the pre-colonial polity, and many of its subjects experienced British rule as a violent and alien imposition.

In 1886, following the Third Anglo-Burmese War, Burma was fully incorporated into the Empire, as a province of British India. The British divided the colony into the central lowlands of 'Burma Proper', where the bulk of the Burman population live, and a horseshoe of ethnic minority-populated 'Frontier Areas', on the periphery of the state. In the former, the British governed by direct-rule, thereby ensuring the destruction of the traditional Burmese polity.[277] In the Frontier Areas, they followed the more common British colonial model of indirect rule (also adopted by the French in Laos and Cambodia), governing via local potentates.[278] Crucially, the two zones were never integrated administratively. This tended to reduce the scope of those 'colonial pilgrimages', which might have fostered a stronger pan-Burmese identity, at least within elite circles.[279] Unlike the diverse peoples of Indonesia (all of whom were ruled by the Dutch from Java, thus helping to forge the idea of a unified Indonesian nation) – but like those in Vietnam, Cambodia and Laos – the separate identities of *Bama* and non-Burmans were reinforced by the colonial experience.[280]

Thant Myint-U has described how the British empire's extended assault on the peripheries of the (once poly-ethnic) Konbaung empire reduced the latter to an ethnic Burman, "relatively homogenous core which ... made easier a stronger sense of local patriotism."[281] The traditional social, economic and political structures of Upper Burma were overthrown, and replaced by an administration geared to the needs of British India. Although the *sangha* did survive the colonial period, its traditional educational role and close identity with the state were both undermined. Thus, members of the *Bama* majority found themselves marginalised within the colonial state, with little reason to identify with its ethos or structures, but considerable reason to resent those who did.

The colonial authorities attempted to establish a 'level playing field' among the various ethnic peoples of Burma.[282] Karen and other elites developed a sense of community (and nationhood) under colonial and missionary patronage, as the British authorities recruited large numbers of minority subjects (and Indians) into the lower levels of the colonial army, police force and administration. Such developments helped to forge strong associations within and between Christianised minority elites, and the colonial state. However, British Burma failed to win the loyalty of many of its Burman subjects, who were excluded from the armed forces as a matter of policy.

The British were quite successful in ensuring equality of opportunity for the different groups in the country, and large numbers of minority people received an education, and went on to types of employment, that would not have been open to their predecessors. Colonialism in Burma therefore fostered the emergence of self-consciously distinct 'ethnic minority' groups, such as the Karen, who were encouraged to identify themselves in opposition to the Burman majority (a Karen National Association was founded in 1881).

Until the late nineteenth century, advances in education were largely achieved as a result of missionary activity. The first American Baptists had arrived in Burma in 1813 and throughout the next two decades were particularly active in the Mon and the Karen villages around Moulmein.[283] An 'Abridged Old Testament' was published in Mon as early as 1816 and the New Testament was translated in 1847. However, a complete Mon language bible was not published until 1928.[284] Despite the success of missionary activities among the Karen, and the considerable interest in Mon language and history demonstrated by churchmen such as Haswell, Stevens and Halliday, relatively few Mons were converted to Christianity.

According to a recent Mon nationalist publication, "in the British era, the Mon people attained more chance to preserve their literature."[285] Several Mon language schools were established by monks, and by 1847 the Baptists were publishing Mon tracts in Moulmein. Later, a Mon Buddhist press was set up on Bilu Kyun Island[286] and the Hanthawaddy

Press was established in Rangoon, which printed Mon language history texts, as well as a regular journal.[287]

In general however, the colonial administration neglected Mon culture and history. In 1907 the British scholar, C.O. Blagden, asked:

"How much longer is the Government of Burma going to neglect the oldest vernacular in the province, and allow its ancient historical and literary records to remain uninterpreted?" The Burmese rulers of the country did their best, by a furious course of proscription, to destroy the Mon language, spoken by thousands, some of whom know no other tongue. It has been represented to me that it would be regarded as a boon by the Mon population of those parts if their language received more official recognition . . . I cannot deny my sympathy with such modest aspirations as some members of the Mon remnant appear to cherish.[288]

The British authorities considered the Mon to have "fairly high" standards of literacy,[289] and instigated optional civil service examinations in Mon.[290] Between 1937–42, the colonial administration funded a Mon literacy and population survey, which by 1942 was administered by Nai Tun Thein. Nevertheless, the bulk of official attention focused on potentially restive 'hilltribes', such as the Karen, who were more amenable to the colonialists' self-imposed civilising mission.[291] In contrast to the British authorities' benign neglect, following their defeat in the Second Anglo-Burmese War, the kings of Mandalay had outlawed the use of Mon in those monasteries still under their jurisdiction.[292]

Perhaps the most damaging long-term consequence of British rule was the adoption of Burmese as the language of state administration, which helped to accelerate processes of 'Burmanisation' begun centuries earlier. Nevertheless, during the British period, Mon elites were again able to assert themselves through the patronage of religious works. In the 1830s and '40s the retired rebel leader, Maung Thaw Lay, was well-know for such pious endeavours, as recorded in his inscription at Kyaik Thanlan Pagoda in Moulmein.[293] Another important nineteenth century Mon religious patron was Nai Kohn (i.e. 'boss') Shwe Lay, a teak merchant who sponsored a Burmese translation of the *Tripitaka*.

During the late nineteenth century, several thousand Mon families who had settled in Thailand during the previous century returned to their homeland, drawn by accounts of improved conditions in Burma.[294] British rule was based on that in India. Its effects included the introduction of a capitalist economy, leading to a greater degree of socio-economic mobility and the breakdown of traditional social bonds.[295] The 'rationalisation' of the state involved the replacement of patron-client relations with an administration based on modern, objective definitions of the role of government agents.[296]

As Dr S-M- points out, the improved transportation and greater mobility of the British era eroded "the status of isolation which ... had helped to protect (minority) languages and cultures" in precolonial Burma.[297] Furthermore, as a consequence of the realignment of traditional structures, increasingly large numbers of people ceased to identify with a particular region or ethnicity, but rather came to regard themselves as 'Burmese' – i.e. as citizens of a new, clearly bounded entity: the colony (and potential state) of Burma. This was particularly true of the Rangoon and Irrawaddy Delta Mon populations, many of whose chiefs had been co-opted by the British in the early nineteenth century.

When, in the 1920s and '30s, colonial rule came under assault from a militant new generation of youthful and well-educated Burmese nationalists, the institutional weakness of a potentially independent state of Burma soon became apparent.[298] With the traditional polity destroyed, and the colonial state (and its reliance on 'collaborationist', non-Burman personnel) increasingly discredited, different parties put forward competing, more-or-less articulate, ideas of a future Burma. Crucially, ethnic minority politicians failed to agree a common vision or set of demands among themselves, or even within their own communities.[299] Perceptions of their role as 'lackeys of colonialism' were reinforced by Christian Karen leaders' obvious suspicion any future unitary state, which would inevitably be dominated by the resurgent Burman centre.

Until the late 1930s, Mon political activity in Burma was largely confined to a supporting role in the wider Burmese nationalist movement. In 1906 a group of Rangoon University students founded the Young Men's Buddhist Association (YMBA), Burma's first modern political organisation. The YMBA was later reformed as the General Council of Burmese Associations (GCBA), the first overtly nationalist movement in modern Burma.[300]

One of the most well-known Burmese politicians of the 1920s and '30s went on to help found the Mon nationalist movement. U Chit Hlaing was born into a wealthy business family in 1879. Between 1898–1902 he studied law in England, where he developed a taste for adversarial politics. Robert Taylor describes him "touring the country in the style of a prince and possessing independent means and contacts with both the Indian and Burmese nationalist movements."[301] Unfortunately, such activities soon consumed his fortune and "by April 1932 he was hiding in Moulmein to avoid arrest for debt."[302]

This colourful character served for several years as president of the GCBA. He seems to have possessed genuine charisma and a real attachment to the Burmese nationalist cause. However, like many of his contemporaries he became dependent on financial backing from Indian (Chettiar) money lenders. Against his own better judgement, in the mid-1930s U Chit Hlaing supported the Indian lobby, which was opposed to Burma being recognised as a separate colony, distinct from British India.[303] A compromised figure, he was never to regain the national prominence he had once enjoyed.

Another little-known Mon contribution to the history of this period is the participation of Mon students in the 1920 University Students' strike, which was inspired by the Congress party's campaign of civil disobedience in India. The impressive degree of support mobilised by the students convinced the British to introduce a partially-elected assembly in Burma Proper in 1923. Mon farmers also took part in the 'Saya San' rebellion of 1930–31.[304]

In 1937, the year Burma ceased to be a province of India, the experiment in limited 'self rule' was extended to include a cabinet-style government, responsible to a fully-elected legislature.[305] A number of parties contested the 1937 elections, but it was to be another two years before the first Mon nationalist organisation of the modern era was established.

The All Ramanya Mon Association (ARMA) was founded at a meeting held in the 'Mon Halls', near Shwedagon Pagoda, on 6th August 1939.[306] Its first Chairman was U Kyan of Pegu; other important founder-members included the ex-GCBA President, U Chit Hlaing, and party treasurer, U Chit Thaung, a University of London-educated chemical engineer, who had participated in the 1920 student protests.[307]

Although its members included Mon Christians, the ARMA was influenced by a number of powerful monks, as was the contemporary Burmese nationalist *Dohbama Asiayone* (We Burmese Association), led by Aung San and his young colleagues from Rangoon University.[308] From the mid-1930s, the *Dohbama Asiayone* and other political groups began to organise their members – who were excluded from service in the colonial army – into lightly-armed militias (or *tats*). Members of these volunteer *tats* were to play leading roles in various Burmese armed groups in the coming war years.

Unlike the *Dohbama Asiayone* though, the ARMA was specifically not a political organisation. Its official objective was the preservation of Mon language, culture and religion. The association was reluctant to play a more active political role, for fear of fragmenting the burgeoning Burmese nationalist movement.[309]

The majority of post-war Mon leaders were at one time or another members of the ARMA. The association is regarded as the forerunner of the modern nationalist movement, and in this respect its relationship to subsequent Mon organisations is comparable with that of the Karen National Association to later Karen nationalist parties.

The Second World War

Ironically, the warrior brotherhood that emerged during the war to lead Burma to independence, was founded at a monastery which was to become

– in the 1970s and '80s – an important centre of the Mon nationalist community in Thailand. On 26th December 1941 a brief ceremony was held at Wat Prok, an obscure monastery near Sathorn Road (then a canal) in Bangkok. Beneath the branches of the sacred Bodhi tree, thirty militant young idealists, recently trained by the Japanese, mixed their blood with liquor in a silver bowl, then drank and swore an oath to fight for the freedom of their country. Three days later, the newly-founded Burma Independence Army (BIA), commanded by Maj-General Aung San, followed the Japanese army across the border into Burma.[310]

Over the following half-century, these 'Thirty Comrades' were to lead both the state of Burma and many of the principal organisations bent on undermining it.[311] From the outset, the BIA symbolised the struggle for Burmese independence. The 'birth' of Burma's national army, and the crucial early leadership provided by Aung San – the army's 'father' – have become the stuff of legend. In Burma today, to criticise the *Tatmadaw* is synonymous with treason. However, until the mid-1950s, the army was only one of several players on the Burmese political scene, and in 1941 this legendary band was still largely subservient to the Japanese war machine.

The Japanese Imperial Army entered Burma during the last week of 1941, forcing the British to withdraw to India. The initial purpose of the Japanese occupation was to secure supplies (rice and oil) for the war effort and to mark the western boundary of Japanese-controlled Southeast Asia. However, it soon became clear that Burma's new masters were not inclined to allow the people any real say in how their country was governed.

Nevertheless, between 1942–45 Dr Ba Maw's wartime government co-operated with the Japanese 'liberators'. Under the 1943 Japanese-sponsored Independence Constitution, the Frontier Areas were formally brought under central state control.[312] For the first time, Burma was a 'unified' state. In practice however, in large tracts of countryside, neither the BIA militia nor the Japanese forces had much of a presence on the ground.

The ARMA seems to have been largely inactive during the war. Unlike the Karen, the Mon did not play a significant role in assisting British officers operating behind enemy lines in Burma. However, large numbers did join the BIA, and a Mon Youth Organisation (MYO) was formed in 1941, several members of which later fought with the BIA against the departing Japanese forces.[313]

Many non-Burmans were alarmed by the chauvinistic character of some BIA leaders and by the racism inherent in the wartime government's pronouncements. The Ba Maw regime outlawed the teaching of Mon and other minority languages.[314] It espoused a quasi-national socialist ideology of "one voice, one blood, one nation",[315] projecting an image of Burmese nationhood, and the role of language, strongly identified with the Burman centre. This unitary, assimilationist concept of the nation and state was to be a major feature of the culture, government – and above all, the army – of post-war Burma. In many ways, it continues to be so today.

By mid-1945, the collaborationist administration had been thoroughly discredited and Dr Ba Maw was forced to flee the country. With Japan defeated and colonialism discredited, a spirit of national independence was in the air. By the time the British returned, Burma's political elites – Burman and ethnic minority alike – had been exposed to a host of new technologies, ideologies and political strategies. As Robert Taylor observes, by the end of the war, for many people "ethnicity, religion or Communism inspired more loyalty than did the state."[316]

PART THREE

INDEPENDENCE AND CIVIL WAR

"Our aim is to reclaim the traditional and historical homeland of the Mon people which was conquered by the Burmese in 1757 and which did not receive its own rights after independence from Great Britain in 1948."

Nai Shwe Kyin, President of the New Mon State Party[1]

CHAPTER SEVEN

Burma and the Mon –
1945–1962

When the British returned in 1945, it was a question of when – not if – Burma would gain independence. During the war, Burmese nationalists had been disappointed by the false independence granted by Japan. They were eager to be rid of the British as quickly as possible and to get on with the task of building a new Burma. From the outset however, there was considerable disagreement as to the nature of this entity, and the relationship within it between the Burman leaders of the wartime nationalist movement and the various minority groups that made up about a third of the population. Although powerful interests dominated national politics, often putting their own concerns above those of the country as a whole, it seemed to many observers that independent Burma had bright prospects.

Despite the ravages of the Second World War, the British left Burma's infrastructure in reasonable shape. When the country achieved independence in January 1948, Burma had one of the strongest economies in Southeast Asia. This prosperity was based on the extraction of oil and timber and a large agricultural surplus. Burma was 'the rice-bowl of Asia', exporting millions of tons of this vital and symbolic commodity every year. There was even a small, emergent industrial sector.

In the 1940s and '50s, despite widespread insurgency in the countryside, Burma enjoyed a free – if somewhat partisan and rumbustious – press, a functioning parliamentary system, and one of the best-educated workforces in Asia. Forty years later, the country was recognised by the United Nations as a Least Developed Nation, the economy and education systems were in deep crisis, and the level of political repression in Burma was among the most severe in Asia. This is the tragedy of recent Burmese history. It is in part explained by another bequest of the colonial era: a bitterly contested and divisive political arena.

In 1999 Mikael Gravers wrote that:

the nationalism of today's Burma differs from the nationalism of the anti-colonial struggle, as well as from the nationalism of 1947 immediately before independence, when ethnicism began to determine the future. In the 1940s nationalism meant liberation from a foreign coloniser; since independence, nationalism has become a remedy for preserving a union as one unitary state. ... Within this process there is a plurality of imaginations of a nation and a national identity – identities often based on a subjectively defined ethnic core.[2]

Burma's cultural and political diversity was perhaps bound to lead to conflict. If the British had been less precipitous in leaving the country, and had ensured on their departure a more equitable representation for the different ethnic minorities, then civil war might have been avoided. However, a more tardy departure might just as soon have precipitated a violent anti-colonial struggle in Burma, similar to those mounted in Malaya and Vietnam, which would no doubt have put further strains on inter-communal relations. Perhaps also, if Burma's independence hero and prime minister designate, Aung San, had not been assassinated in 1947 then events might have transpired differently. Such imponderables have long occupied observers of the political scene in Burma. Meanwhile, in the half century since independence a protracted civil war has ravaged the country, devastating the lives and property of millions of people.

Despite the efforts of Aung San – and his less-gifted successors – to assuage the ethnic nationalists' doubts, within a few months of independence various Mon, Karen, Karenni, Rakhine and Muslim groups had gone underground, as had the powerful Communist Party of Burma (CPB). Initially, the insurgent forces enjoyed some significant military successes, and it seemed for a while that they might force Rangoon to accede to a raft of territorial and political demands. However by 1958, when a number of rebel groups – including nearly all the Mon insurgents – agreed ceasefires with the government, it was already clear that no side would achieve outright victory in the civil war, in the foreseeable future.

The newly-legal ex-insurgents groups' participation in parliamentary democracy was brought to an abrupt halt in September 1958, when the *Tatmadaw*, under General Ne Win, initiated the first of two coups D'Etat. The disastrous consequences of the army's bid for power are still felt today. Far from solving the county's problems, the military take-over plunged Burma deeper into crisis. The insurgent forces were rejuvenated, and the civil war dragged on.

Nationalists and Competing Nationalisms – 1945–47

The seeds of Burma's 'ethnic question' were sown during the colonial period, or earlier. However, the outbreak of civil war was hastened by events leading up to independence at the beginning of 1948.

100

With the return of the British at the end of the Second World War, the All Ramanya Mon Association (ARMA) was revived under the Chairmanship of U Chit Thaung. Perhaps the most influential post-war Mon leader never to have joined the insurgents, U Chit Thaung's statue today stands outside the *Dammar Yon* Mon Halls, near the southern gate of the Shwedagon Pagoda. In early 1947 he was succeeded by U Ba Thein, the pre-war ARMA leader and cabinet minister. Other prominent post-war ARMA members included U Lun Pe (Honorary Secretary), Nai Po Cho, Mon Than, Mon Tun Yin, the young scholar Nai Pan Hla, the future Mon People's Front (MPF) and Mon National Democratic Front (MNDF) leaders Nai Ngwe Thein and Nai Tun Thein (the latter, a cousin of Nai Chit Thaung),[3] and the man who would in the years to come be their rival for the leadership of the Mon nationalist movement, Nai Ba Lwin – who later changed his name to Nai Shwe Kyin.

Between 1946–58 the ARMA produced a series of Mon language textbooks, and for several years a regular journal, *The Mon Bulletin*.[4] However, the association's aims remained specifically limited to the promotion of Mon language and culture. Despite its achievements in these fields, such restrictions soon began to chafe, and in the new atmosphere of anticipated independence that characterised post-war Burma, more radical elements within the Mon political elite became restive.

On 9th November 1945 Nai Po Cho,[5] a Moulmein-born Christian and English lecturer at Rangoon University and St John's College, formed the United Mon Association (UMA),[6] the first overtly political Mon organisation of modern times. Nai Po Cho's colleagues, Mon Than and Mon Tun Yin, became leading members of the association, of which Nai Aung Htun was elected Vice-President at the first UMA Conference, held at Pa Nga village, near Thanbyuzayat, in late 1946. Among the UMA's lasting contributions to the Mon nationalist movement was the adoption of Mon National Day, celebrating the legendary foundation of Hongsawaddy.[7]

Pushing for official recognition of the Mon language and the establishment of a Mon polity within the emerging Union of Burma, the UMA positioned itself as a distinctly Mon contribution to the struggle for *Burmese* independence. The Mon nationalist movement had not yet articulated clear separatist demands. At first, the UMA co-operated closely with the Anti-Fascist People's Freedom League (AFPFL), Aung San's newly-founded political vehicle, which was dominated by Burma Independence Army (BIA) veterans who had fought alongside, and later against, the Japanese. Nai Po Cho's relations with Aung San, Ne Win and other Burman leaders were strengthened by their having been his students in the 1930s (they owed him the respect traditionally accorded a teacher in Burma). Indeed, throughout his life Nai Po Cho, who was married to a Karen and counted Buddhist monks among his advisors, won admiration both from within his own community and further afield.

Nevertheless, there was from the beginning a tendency to factionalism within the Mon ranks and, over the next half century, lack of unity was to repeatedly undermine the Mon and other ethnic nationalist movements in Burma. In the case of the UMA, conflict arose because of the clearly political nature of the new group's work, and also because of Nai Po Cho's perceived closeness to Aung San's AFPFL. At an ARMA conference held in early 1947, a majority of delegates voted to expel the UMA leadership from the association. Nai Po Cho's move into politics also obliged him to resign his university post, so he re-trained as a lawyer. Meanwhile, the ARMA was re-organised under Chairman U Ba Thein, with Nai Hla Maung and Nai Ba Lwin (Shwe Kyin) as Tenasserim Division representatives.[8]

Although a number of ARMA members continued to combine Mon cultural activities with membership of the AFPFL, others were more interested in cultivating links with representatives of other minority groups. Mon nationalist fortunes were particularly closely tied to those of the Karen. According to the Karen leader, Saw Ba U Gyi, "the Mons and Karens (were) traditionally brothers and sisters."[9] In the period leading up to independence, Saw Ba U Gyi – a wealthy and charismatic lawyer – served for a few months as Education Minister in the British Governor's Council, in which capacity he supported the ARMA leadership's bid to introduce Mon language questions into monastic examinations.[10]

In the 1920s and '30s, leadership of the Karen nationalist movement had been passed on from its late nineteenth century founders, to a new, again largely mission-educated, elite. During the Second World War, British officers had unofficially promised Karen leaders in the eastern hills that their loyalty would be recognised and rewarded by the post-war British government. The Karen had played an important role in helping the returning allies drive the Japanese from Burma and thus had reason to expect that these commitments would be honoured. However, they were to be disappointed.

In 1945 the Burman-dominated leadership of the independence movement in Rangoon, which had at first enthusiastically co-operated with the Japanese, had switched sides to the British. As the young BIA commander, General Aung San, confided to Viscount Mountbatten, Supreme Allied Commander in Southeast Asia, the Burmese nationalists had wanted to finish the war on the winning side.[11] Their reward was to be in the vanguard of Burma's move towards independence.

The BIA veterans in the AFPFL and *Tatmadaw* (into which the BIA was incorporated in 1945) insisted that Burma was a unitary state, and strongly opposed any breakaway entity, such as that proposed by the Karen nationalists. Their counsel prevailed and the dream of a Karen free state of Kaw Thoo Lei was still-born. In part, the British failed to make good on their war-time promises to the Karen because of a change of government in London: the anti-imperialist Labour party was less supportive of the 'loyal

Karens' than the Conservatives had been. Another reason for the Atlee government's lack of enthusiasm for Karen territorial demands was their over-ambitious nature (see below).

Many in the fledgling Mon nationalist community were in sympathy with the Karen nationalists, but others, including Nai Po Cho, took offence at their audacity and strident politicking. Nai Po Cho continued to court the AFPFL, but his efforts did not result in the UMA achieving any significant degree of influence within mainstream Burmese councils. Mon leaders therefore became increasingly concerned: with the British preparing to leave, the Mon and other minority groups were in danger of being further marginalised.

In London, the situation in Burma was perceived as a footnote to that in India – 'the jewel in the crown'. The British had appointed Lord Louis Mountbatten, the aristocratic war hero, as India's last Viceroy. Huge political problems and an unprecedented loss of life resulted from Mountbatten's perhaps over-hasty acceptance of the partition of India and Pakistan. It was thus not surprising that the departing colonial rulers should veto the carving-out of any independent territory from the much smaller colony of Burma. Winston Churchill might disagree, but to the new Atlee government it seemed that Burma would be safe in the hands of Aung San and his young colleagues.

In contrast to his successors, Aung San earned a reputation during his short career for fairness in dealings with the 'ethnic nationalities', and seems to have had a more keen appreciation of the hopes and fears of Burma's minority peoples than did many of his contemporaries. He would perhaps have agreed with Robert Taylor's assertion that "the state *qua* state has no ethnicity."[12] This would though, have been to ignore the disproportionate influence of Burman personnel and culture on the emerging Union of Burma.

In an attempt to address the 'ethnic question', in February 1947 Aung San agreed to attend a Conference of the Nationalities, to be convened by the Shan *saophas* (princes) at Panglong in Shan State. In exchange for their acceptance of a new Union of Burma, his government-in-waiting issued certain guarantees of autonomy to Chin, Kachin, Karenni and Shan leaders present at the gathering. However, only representatives of those peoples identified by the British as resident in the Frontier Areas were invited to the conference, which concluded on 12th February (celebrated since as Burma's Union Day). As this restriction was based on a rather simplistic identification of ethnicity with geographical location, neither the Mon nor the Arakanese-Rakhine were represented at Panglong.

By early 1947 many Mon politicians had in any case become alienated from Aung San and the AFPFL, due to their perceived lack of sympathy for ethnic minority aspirations. Instead, Mon leaders increasingly preferred to throw in their lot with the ambitious Karen leadership which, sensing that the promises to be made at Panglong would never be fulfilled, played little part in the conference. On 5th February 1947, one week before the Panglong Agreement was finalised, Mon observers attended an historic All Karen Congress in Rangoon. The congress voted to establish a Karen National Union (KNU), which under the chairmanship of Saw Ba U Gyi would campaign for an independent Karen homeland, outside of the Union of Burma.[13]

An important outcome of the manoeuvrings at Panglong was the quasi-federal constitution of 1947, which according to Taylor "delineated the federal state, but in reality provided for a centralised governmental system."[14] Although the claims of some minority groups were acknowledged, and partially accommodated through the creation of separate, ethnic Union States, these were merely administrative arms of the central government, and enjoyed little real power. The relationship to Rangoon of the Kachin, Karenni and Shan ethnic states and the Chin Special Division was "like the relationship between Scotland and the British government in London."[15]

In an unusual constitutional concession, the Karenni and Shan States, which had enjoyed varying degrees of independence during the precolonial and colonial periods, were given the right to secession from the union, after a period of ten years. However, the nature and extent of Karen State was left unresolved, to be worked-out after independence. Such makeshift constitutional arrangements, which did not even mention the rights of the Mon, Rakhine and other groups, were to fuel violent dispute in the years to come. Furthermore, although the departing colonial authorities' *Education and Reconstruction Committee Report* of 1947 proposed that the state school system introduce teaching in ethnic minority language, this recommendation that was never acted upon.[16]

Although twenty-four seats had been specially reserved for the Karen, the KNU boycotted the 9th April 1947 elections to the Constituent Assembly, as did Nai Po Cho's UMA, which had by this time become disillusioned with the lack of recognition granted to Mon claims within the AFPFL. The ARMA also rejected an AFPFL offer of twelve places in the new parliament, stating that, as a purely cultural organisation, it had no political agenda. Therefore no assembly seats were reserved for the Mon.

Before the election, the ARMA's Nai Ba Lwin had been AFPFL Chairman in Paung Township, Thaton District. However, due to frustration at the League's centralised decision making procedures and the lack of attention paid by Aung San's party to their concerns and interests, the Mon group within the AFPFL broke away shortly before the election. After discussing the situation with the UMA, six independent Mon candidates stood for seats in the Constituent Assembly.[17] This new grouping would later coalesce as the Mon Freedom League-Mon United Front (MFL-MUF).

The AFPFL won the elections handsomely, taking sixty per cent of votes cast. However, according to Nai Shwe Kyin and others, the poll was rigged and despite vigorous campaigning and strong support among their own community, the independent Mon candidates all failed to win seats.[18] However, the AFPFL's Mon Khin Maung and Nai Po Cho's ex-colleague, Mon Than (who had opposed the UMA's decision to boycott the elections), were returned as AFPFL candidates. Mon Than, together with Mon Tun Yin, went on to form the Mon Federal State Organisation (MFSO), which later amalgamated with the AFPFL (of which the MFSO Chairman, Mon Than, became Rangoon District Chairman).[19]

In a disaster with huge implications for Burma's future, on 19th July 1947 – three months after the elections, and one month before Indian independence – Aung San was assassinated, together with half of his cabinet. This national hero and master strategist was succeeded as AFPFL leader and prime minister-designate by U Nu, a devout Buddhist and canny political fixer.

In a short account of his life written in 1994, Nai Shwe Kyin states that in late 1947, because the AFPFL candidates had won the elections by such a narrow margin:

> Prime Minister U Nu invited Mon representatives for talks. A delegation of Mon representatives led by Nai Ba Lwin (Shwe Kyin), and including Nai San Thu and Nai Sein Tun, met with Prime Minister U Nu and a delegation of the AFPFL government. The Mon representatives put up a seven point demand comprising of religious, cultural and executive administrative rights to preserve the identity of the Mon. With the exception of minimal religious and cultural rights, the right of self-government over the Mon was rejected.[20]

Another consequence of the success of Burman-dominated parties in the April 1947 election was the formation in August that year of a new party dedicated to the pursuit of Mon interests, independent of the AFPFL. The Mon Freedom League (MFL) was formally launched at a three day Mon National Conference at Pa-auk village in Mudon Township. The conference "resolved unanimously that ... the Mons now demand their full birth-right for creation of a Mon State exercising full right of self-determination." The Mon nationalist movement had crossed the rubicund and was now prepared to demand full independence from Rangoon.[21] Notice was forwarded to the AFPFL and the colonial authorities.

The MFL headquarters was established in Moulmein under President Nai Ba Lwin, with Nai San Thu as General Secretary. Although he UMA and MFL tended to operate in different areas of lower Burma, there was often a good deal of confusion as to the actual situation on the ground, and who belonged to which faction. In an effort to rationalise the movement and tighten up the chain of command, a third Mon nationalist movement, the Mon Affairs Organisation (MAO), was established under the chairmanship of Nai Hla Maung, with Nai Ba Lwin as General Secretary and Nai San Thu and Nai Ngwe Thein[22] as Joint Secretaries; other senior

105

members included a rare female Mon leader, Mi Hongsa.[23] Nai Ba Lwin was put in charge of information and propaganda activities, which included editing *The Tenasserim*, a bi-weekly Burmese language newspaper previously published by the MFL.

In late 1947 the MFL and MAO were superseded by yet another group, the Mon United Front (MUF), which was again conceived of as an 'umbrella group', but which Nai Po Cho's UMA refused to join. According to Nai Shwe Kyin, this was because of Nai Po Cho's "narrow nationalism"[24]; it may also be explained by his reluctance to abandon mainstream Burmese politics by throwing in his lot with the separatists.

Another Mon National Conference was held at Pa-auk in late 1947, during which Nai Hla Maung was elected MUF Chairman, Nai Ngwe Thein General Secretary and Nai Ba Lwin Information Officer; Mi Hongsa organised the women's wing, and there were workers and peasants' sections, as well as an active youth organisation (the *Samot Mon*), many members of which went on to play leading roles in the nationalist movement.[25] In an historically significant move, the conference adopted a resolution that, should negotiation and democratic means fail, "all necessary means should be adopted in order to achieve the goal of national self-determination."[26] Armed insurrection was now among the Mon nationalists' strategic options.

Following the Pa-auk conference, a mass demonstration was organised on the streets of Moulmein. Nai Hla Maung addressed the crowds, calling for the immediate creation of a Mon State.[27] However, the country was to achieve independence without a new Mon State being granted recognition.

Burmese Independence ... and Civil War

By the time Burma gained Independence, on 4th January 1948, the 'Red Flag' communists and Rakhine-Arakanese insurgents had already taken up arms. Within a few weeks, much of central and lower Burma was at war.

In March 1948 the mainstream 'White Flag' Communist Party of Burma (CPB) took up arms, taking sections of the Burma Army with it. By the middle of the year, mutinies had broken out across most of the country, involving further *Tatmadaw* units and most of the People's Volunteer Organisation (PVO), a well-armed BIA veterans militia. At this point, most ethnic minority leaders were still prepared to give the government the benefit of doubt, and time to address their grievances. Indeed, despite a vitriolic campaign against Karen nationalists in the Burmese language press, in December Karen and Kachin units of the *Tatmadaw* quelled a CPB uprising almost at the gates of Rangoon.[28]

The first Mon armed organisation of modern times, the Mon National Defence Organisation (MNDO), was established by Nai Hla Maung and Nai San Thu in Moulmein in March 1948, as the paramilitary wing of the

106

MFL-MUF. It was modelled on the Karen National Defence Organisation (KNDO), which had been set up by Mahn Ba Zan in July the previous year, as the armed wing of the KNU.

Although some Mon and Karen leaders had been voicing demands for independence from Rangoon since late 1947, and the two militias shared a strong ethnic nationalist ethos, the KNDO and MNDO were originally conceived of primarily as organisations for the defence of Karen and Mon civilian populations. During the Second World War, the BIA and irregular Burman forces had been involved in several massacres in ethnic minority communities, which had continued sporadically ever since. The Karen in particular had been targeted, due to their perceived loyalty to the British, and the KNDO was founded to stop these abuses.

Whilst many KNDO men retained weapons issued by the British during the war, in the early days the MNDO had few arms and little ammunition. According to Nai Tun Thein, there were only two ways to get hold of weapons: "namely purchasing or looting; the MNDO decided on looting."[29]

Nai Shwe Kyin recalls that on 20th July 1948 "a group of thirty Mon youths, led by Bo Thein and Nai Pan Tha, had three machine guns looted from the police station at Zarthabyin Village, in the east of Moulmein. That was the starting point of the Mon armed forces, and marked the date as Mon National Revolutionary Day. Many weapons were bought later with money collected from the Mon people."[30] Nai Tun Thein, who was closely involved with these events, confirms Nai Shwe Kyin's narrative and adds an historic detail: for the first time in a century, Mon insurgents at Zarthabyin raised the sheldrake flag.[31]

Following their successful liberation of Zarthabyin, in which they were assisted by local Karen police, Bo Thein, Nai Pan Tha and their band of followers went on to occupy four nearby villages and hijack a small ship. They then contacted MUF-MNDO headquarters in Moulmein, for instructions. Meanwhile, the authorities were also demanding clarification from the Mon leadership. They were assured by Nai Ngwe Thein that this outbreak of rebellion was nothing to do with the mainstream nationalist movement.

Clearly, this pre-arranged deceit could not be maintained for long. A few days later, Nai Ba Lwin and Nai Hla Maung met again with the Moulmein authorities, who demanded that they surrender Bo Thein, Nai Pan Tha and the 'Mon Youth Group'. In fact, as they went through the motions of arranging to hand over a few weapons, the MFL-MUF leaders were in fact preparing to go underground.[32]

By this time, Mahn Ba Zan was ready to lead the KNDO into revolt and introduce a new dimension to the civil war. In early August the Mon nationalists under Nai Hla Maung and Nai Shwe Kyin, and the KNU under Saw B U Gyi, agreed a four point memorandum, which was ratified in

Moulmein in October.[33] This document was to serve as the basis for a series of important agreements struck over the coming decades between the Mon and Karen insurgents, helping to cement an alliance that lasted for nearly fifty years. As Nai Shwe Kyin puts it, "fate had determined the coming together of Mons and Karens as eternal allies, having lived together during Mon kingdom hey-day."[34]

The Siege of Moulmein

According to Nai Shwe Kyin, "immediately after signing the pledge, government security forces began collecting the village defence arms from Mon villages in rural Mon areas. The heavy hand of the government had come. Nai Ba Lwin together with seventeen other Mon leaders were arrested[35] ... and put under detention at Moulmein jail. True to their pledge, the Karens in collaboration with the Mons occupied Thaton and Moulmein without firing a shot and released the Mon leaders."[36] However several other prisoners, who were judged to be pro-AFPFL, were not freed.[37]

Thaton was occupied by the KNDO on the 30th August 1948 and Moulmein by a joint Mon-Karen force the following day.[38] According to Martin Smith, certain KNU leaders were keen to occupy Moulmein in order to land munitions they hoped to – but never did – receive from shadowy foreign supporters.[39] The Karen force consisted mostly of Union Military Policemen, led by U Hla Tun Aung and Saw Tha Din (who had travelled to London with Saw Ba U Gyi two years previously, in an unsuccessful attempt to persuade the British to grant Karen autonomy). The small Mon contingent was soon reinforced with weapons and men from Zarthabyin led by Nai Pan Tha, and began to receive training from the Karen policemen. Within a few days, the rebels had been joined in Moulmein by KNU President Ba U Gyi (who was probably not involved in the original plot to occupy the city).

The Mon and Karen leaders formed a provisional committee to run Moulmein, the defence of which was mostly undertaken by the more numerous and better-equipped KNDO militia.[40] By now the Mon rebels had taken Mudon, Kyaikammi (Amherst), Ye and other places south of the city, while irregular non-aligned forces occupied the small, strategically important town of Kyaikmaraw, and Karen forces occupied Thaton and parts of Kawkareik and Kya-In Seik-Kyi Townships. Nai Tun Thein recalls that "the system of administration was not very systematic."[41] Local commanders were often laws unto themselves and it is sometimes difficult to establish the exact sequence of events in the chaotic early history of the insurrections.

Following the occupation of Moulmein, the *Tatmadaw* and pro-government militias stepped-up their harassment of Mon and Karen communities across lower Burma. Scores of people were killed, and hundreds arrested – including Nai Po Cho of the UMA, who was detained for nearly three months. By the time of his release, most of his former associates – including Nai Aung Htun, Nai Chan Mon, Nai Non Lar (the *nom de guerre* of Nai Seik No, born near Mudon on 2nd April 1917), and for a while even Mon Than of the Mon Federal State Organisation (MFSO) and AFPFL – had formed a new Mon National Solidarity Movement (MNSM), and entered into an uneasy alliance with the MUF.

In early September, with the *Tatmadaw* and other pro-government forces moving to surround Moulmein, Nai Aung Htun persuaded the MFL-MUF to open negotiations with Rangoon. Around this time, the AFPFL government announced the formation of an Enquiry Commission for Regional Autonomy, "to explore the means and ways of satisfying without hindrance, all the legitimate aspirations of the Mons, Karens and Arakanese Nationals"[42] (the largest ethnic groups not to have Union States of their own). Given that half the country was by now in the hands of armed opposition forces, this was no doubt meant as a conciliatory move. In the event, the Mon sub-committee was to be controlled by the pro-government politicians Mon Tun Yin, Mon Khin Maung and Mon Than, although it did also include two committed nationalists: Nai Po Cho and Nai Hla Maung.

On 8th September 1948, a week and a day after occupying Moulmein, the joint Mon-Karen force was persuaded to withdraw – although not before they had 'withdrawn' 500,000 Kyat from the city bank. Until the final hours, pro-government militias had attempted to re-occupy the small nearby towns of Kyaikmaraw and Mudon, but had been fought off, and a number of their officers captured by the MNDO-KNDO.[43]

The returning *Tatmadaw* and state authorities divided Moulmein into Mon, Karen and government-controlled zones, indicating that for a while at least the ex-insurgents continued to have a say in running the city. During late September, discussions took place regarding the formation of a joint Mon-Karen-*Tatmadaw* military battalion, to be based at Kyaikammi. However, relations turned sour when Burman gangs began to terrorise Mon and Karen districts in and around Moulmein, and within a few weeks any concessions granted to the ethnic nationalists had evaporated.

Although, in the face of a sustained *Tatmadaw* offensive, the rebels could probably not have held onto the city for long, the retreat from Moulmein is today still viewed in some quarters as having been premature. At the time however, the KNU leadership still felt that a negotiated settlement was possible. Although Saw Ba U Gyi prevailed upon the Mon leaders to agree a truce, within a few months the MNDO and KNDO were again at war with Rangoon.

Following the retreat from Moulmein, the Mon leadership was determined to extract maximum concessions from the U Nu regime. Nai Shwe Kyin continues his narrative by describing the Mon response to the

AFPFL initiative: "Nai Hla Maung, President of the MUF and Mon U Po Cho, President of the UMA,[44] put up their representation stating in part that, 'it is the desire of the Mons ... that an independent Mon State, enjoying full sovereign status be formed, comprising the Tenasserim Division, the Pegu Division, and the Irrawaddy Division.' The areas demanded covered the whole of Lower Burma, and constituted an attempt to resurrect the old Mon kingdom."[45] Meanwhile, perhaps in a government-inspired attempt to sow confusion, the rest of the Mon sub-committee submitted a separate report, which nevertheless covered much of the same ground.[46]

It was hardly likely that U Nu would accede to these demands, which were similar in scope to those submitted by the Karen, under which sovereignty over most of lower Burma would have been divided between the two groups.[47] The Regional Autonomy Enquiry Commission established a Karen Affairs Council, to prepare for the creation of a Karen state. Having "consulted democratically with local people" (which in practice often involved seeking-out community representatives who could be relied upon not to follow the KNU line), on 19th February 1949 the Commission published an interim report. This recommended that the new Karen state should include only the Salween region and adjacent territories, specifically excluding lands in the Irrawaddy Delta, Tenasserim Division and other areas claimed by the KNU.[48] Nevertheless – and in hindsight – those territorial and other concessions which the government was willing to grant the Karen (if not necessarily the Mon) during 1948–49 were to prove more substantial than any offered since.

In December 1951 MFL President Nai Shwe Kyin issued a statement complaining that the Enquiry Commission had not offered the Mon or Rakhine-Arakanese the same arrangements as the Karen.[49] The Mon leader suspected that the government's relatively more favourable treatment of the Karen was intended to divide the ethnic opposition. When Mon representatives met with U Nu in late September 1948, he is reported to have said that the "Mon and Burman are the same; therefore separate ethnic Mon identity should not be contemplated."[50] U Nu's attitude infuriated the Mon leaders, who had only recently agreed to abandon Moulmein. Not for the first or last time, the ethnic nationalists found themselves outmanoeuvred by politicians in Rangoon.

Meanwhile, by the end of the 1948 rainy season, with communist insurgency rampant across Burma, the MUF-MFL-MNDO and southern KNU-KNDO forces had begun to re-group in the countryside.[51] Here they encouraged the local population, most of whom were farmers, to take up arms and prepare for the forthcoming rebellion. Although their numbers continued to grow, in the case of the Mon – if not the Karen – arms and ammunition were still in short supply, and had to be purchased or looted from government sources.

By this time, Nai Ba Lwin (Shwe Kyin), Nai Hla Maung and other Mon (and Karen) leaders had again been arrested. Despite such setbacks, Nai Pan Tha managed within a few weeks to organise a four hundred-strong battalion in the Kawkareik-Kya-In region; further to the south, in the Thanbyuzayat area, there were some three hundred MNDO troops under Nai Aung Htun[52]; meanwhile, Nai Tun Maung had mustered about 600 troops around Ye.[53] According to Nai Tun Thein, at the end of the country's first year of independence, "the government ruled the cities, but the villages were ruled by the Mon and the Karen."[54]

For three months after the withdrawal from Moulmein, the armed Mon and Karen nationalists continued to control substantial 'liberated zones', without technically being at war with the central government. Throughout late 1948 and early '49, *Tatmadaw* and irregular militias continued to attack Mon and Karen villagers, and ethnic minority civilians were often left with little choice but to flee to the rebel-held territories, where the basic structures of administration, law and order, health and education had often broken down completely.

Nai Shwe Kyin continues his account of this chaotic period with the fates of some Mon leaders of the time:

Nai San Thu, General Secretary of the MFL was gunned down in the middle of the day right in the centre of Moulmein by the government secret death squad in December 1948. Another second line leader Nai Ngwe Gaing was gunned down at Mudon railway station. Assassination attempts were also made against Nai Ba Lwin, whose father was kidnapped by the government backed paramilitary PVO at Martaban jetty ... Luckily he was (later) released (but) not satisfied with that action, his house at Phalat village was ransacked and robbed of all his properties. To save his life and family he had to flee to areas under the control of Mon-Karen resistance. The Burmese leadership thought that assassinations and arrests would hinder the Mon revolutionary tide, but they underestimated the Mon determination which had been hardened by bitter past history.

Since the bloodbath had been started by the government, it was hard to put an end to it. Thus, by the end of 1948 the government added its insult by declaring the MNDO and KNDO illegal organisations. Country-wide arrests were made and communal riots were incited by the government. Nai Shwe Kyin was again arrested, along with four Karen leaders.... They were flown to Mandalay in a chartered plane. When Mandalay was about to fall to the combined forces of Kachins and Karens, they were sent to Shwebo in a car. Again when Mandalay fell to government hands after four months, they were sent back there by plane because Shwebo had been harassed by other Burman armed forces and it was no longer safe to confine the Mon and Karen top leaders there.[55]

Having occupied a number of towns across central and southern Burma, the KNDO was finally outlawed on 30th January 1949.[56] With communist, PVO, ex-*Tatmadaw* and other armed groups in open rebellion across the country, the more radical Mon and Karen leaders now abandoned any hope of negotiating with Rangoon, vowing instead to achieve their goals by force.

Burma and the Mon Rebellion – 1949–58

By 31st January 1949, when the KNU-KNDO finally went underground, the government in Rangoon controlled little more than the capital and its immediate environs. The Karen insurgents occupied the town of Insein, just fifteen miles north of Rangoon, where they were joined by an MNDO detachment from Thaton. They held on under siege from government forces for one hundred and twelve days, before abandoning Insein in the face of concerted bombardment.[57] Whilst the earlier departure from Moulmein could be represented as a strategic withdrawal, the retreat from Insein clearly could not. It was a turning point in the war – the first in a series of painful reversals suffered by the KNU and allies over the coming decades.

By the end of the year however, various insurgent forces still controlled large parts of the countryside, as well as occupying a number of towns in east, central and southern Burma. Despite the loss of several key positions, it seemed to many that the rebels still held the upper hand. The CPB in particular was able to operate across almost the entire country, and threatened to overwhelm the government forces defending Rangoon.

In addition to the two different communist factions, by 1950 the Mon, Karen, Karenni and Pa-O ethnic nationalists, together with the Muslim *mujaheed* of Arakan, were also in revolt. At the start of the year, the situation was further complicated by the arrival in the north of Chinese nationalist Koumintang (KMT) forces, which entered Shan State following their expulsion from China by the People's Liberation Army (PLA).[58] However, with a few exceptions – such as the Mon-Karen alliance – the various insurgent organisations failed to co-ordinate their actions, and were often in direct competition for control of strategic positions and resources.

The military situation on the ground was extremely complex. Numerous militias patrolled the countryside, and were often only loosely-aligned with or controlled by any central leadership. The MUF armed forces, consisting mostly of MNDO irregulars, were organised into a three battalion *Kah Saw Wah* (White Elephant) Brigade.[59] The balance of power between Mon and Karen may be gauged by the fact that this formation was given a S'ghaw

Karen name (albeit one which recalled the Mon kings' past glories: the white elephant is a royal symbol of the god Indra). However, units led by Nai Aung Htun in the Kyaikammi area, which were able to expand and purchase weapons through taxation of the local salt and rubber industries, were poorly integrated into the *Kah Saw Wah* command structure.

It should not be imagined that in this environment of confusion and lawlessness the insurgents always behaved irreproachably. Kidnapping and robbery were rife. In one notorious incident, on 18th February 1950 a sixty-seven year old American Baptist missionary was kidnapped by Mon bandits near her home at Keh Mah Wet village, twenty-five miles south of Moulmein. Miss Selma Martha Maxville had worked since 1916 as a nurse at Moulmein hospital, and was highly regarded in the community. It seems that although she was literate in Mon and well-known for her work among the poor, her evangelism had singled-out Miss Maxville for attack.

It is not clear whether her captors would have released her if their demand for 20,000 Rupees in cash, plus a quantity of gold, had been met. However, both the government and the mission refused to pay the ransom, as a matter of policy.[60] Miss Maxville was held captive for ten days, before her presence was detected in the forest near Weh Tey village. On 28th February a group of local Mon villagers took it upon themselves to attempt a rescue, and actually succeeded in freeing her from four armed guards. However, on their way back to Moulmein, the party was ambushed by the kidnap gang and Miss Maxville and twelve of her rescuers (eleven Buddhists and one Muslim) were killed in a hail of automatic gunfire; three men escaped to tell the tale.

A missionary colleague noted that:

> there are a few grains of comfort in it all. Inasmuch as she was actually rescued she had the assurance that she had not been forsaken. She could not have suffered much, if at all, from her wounds, for they would have been rapidly fatal. . . .

> A constant stream of friends of all races and creeds poured into the mission compound at Moulmein (for Miss Maxville's funeral). . . . There was no counting the wreaths and floral pieces. The abundance of flowers that the coffin could not carry was distributed among the forty nurses of the hospital ... Hundreds attended the funeral. Government offices were closed and representatives from the American Embassy were present. Saya Po Sein, the Mon pastor, had charge of the service and several choirs sang." At another memorial service "offerings were made for the bereaved families of those who had tried to rescue her.[61]

Short of funds and motivated by a determination to resist foreign influence, it may be that rogue a MNDO unit was responsible for Miss Maxville's death (as claimed by one of her team of Mon Christian nurses, now in her seventies). Alternatively, Nai Shwe Kyin suggests that PVO militiamen were the culprits.[62] This sad episode highlights the lawlessness that prevailed across Burma at the time.

The phenomena of banditry and warlordism were compounded by a dearth of incisive leadership among the rebel factions. With Nai Hla Maung still in jail, the MUF appointed a new chairman, Nai Tha Hnin, who had stood in the April 1947 elections and was an ally of the jailed Nai Ba Lwin (Shwe Kyin). The volatility of the situation is demonstrated by the circumstances of Nai Tha Hnin's death, in April 1950. According to Nai Tun Thein, the MUF Chairman was "accidentally killed" during a meeting he had called to discuss the ambush and injury of Nai Ngwe Thein and other Mon leaders by irregular Karen forces, in the Myawaddy-Kawkareik area the previous month. Nai Tha Hnin was replaced as MUF Chairman by Nai Tun Sein, who had been with the nationalists since the mid-1940s.[63]

Another prominent early casualty of the war was the KNU's Saw Ba U Gyi, who was killed in a *Tatmadaw* ambush near Myawaddy on 12th August 1950, one month after presiding over an important KNU Congress at Papun.[64] A politician of broad appeal and keen insight, the Karen revolution has never really recovered from his death. (In 1995 Nai Shwe Kyin told the author that the untimely deaths of General Aung San and Saw Ba U Gyi were the two greatest disasters of modern Burmese history.)

Following the martyrdom of Saw Ba U Gyi, the Karen and Mon insurgents suffered a series of military reversals, which saw KNU and MUF battalions withdraw from Kawkareik, whilst several front-line units were cut off from the insurgents' base areas. Realising that victory would not be achieved quickly, a number of insurgents – many of whom were peasant farmers with rifles, but little training – returned to their home villages. As the momentum and idealism of the early years slowly dissipated, large areas of the countryside fell under the control of local warlords. Meanwhile, the Mon insurgent leadership attempted to re-group, take stock of the situation and seek out new allies.

In the early 1950s Mon nationalist politicians from Burma started to cultivate contacts with Mon communities in Thailand, and through these the Thai armed forces. As early as 1948, Nai Ngwe Thein had travelled to Bangkok, where the security services agreed to assist the MUF.[65] A number of Thai military personnel even volunteered to join the Mon insurgents.[66] It suited the powerful Thai military establishment to keep the kingdom's traditional neighbour weak and divided. Furthermore, the Mon and other Burmese insurgents might prove useful allies to individual Thai power-brokers, as they jostled for position in the post-war political jungle.

In 1950 Nai Ngwe Thein, who in later years was again to lead the Mon in negotiations with Burman and other ethnic groups,[67] was granted the rank of KNU Colonel, and over the next eight years acted as sometime

Karen representative in Bangkok. Meanwhile, in 1950 Nai Hla Maung was released from jail. He and Nai Po Cho were commissioned by U Nu to meet Nai Aung Htun and Nai Chan Mon of the UMA-MUF, with a brief to negotiate a ceasefire with the AFPFL government. According to Nai Tun Thein however, as U Nu was still unwilling to countenance the creation of a Mon State, the Mon insurgents likewise refused to compromise, and vowed to fight on.[68]

On 28th November 1951 Nai Ba Lwin (Shwe Kyin), the MFL founder-President, was released from Mandalay jail, just a few days after polling had closed for the seven month 1951–52 elections. These were again won by the AFPLF, one of whose candidates was the "stooge Mon Than."[69] Within a few weeks, Nai Ba Lwin had returned to politics, with the publication of a manifesto setting out the case for an autonomous Mon State within a union based on the Swiss federal model.[70]

A few months later, with Nai Ba Lwin still under close government surveillance in the capital, the insurgent leaders in the marquis formed the Mon People's Solidarity Group (MPSG), forerunner of the Mon People's Front (MPF). Nai Ngwe Thein was chairman of the new group, which was officially established on 19th February 1952, with Nai Tun Thein as General Secretary.[71]

The MPSG was intended to re-unite the disparate Mon insurgent forces, and reign-in local military commanders – an aim in which it largely succeeded. Although it continued to be handicapped by factionalism, the MPSG-MPF was the most powerful Mon insurgent force of the 'parliamentary era' (1948–62), as well as being the first to explicitly demand the creation of an "Independent Sovereign State . . . of Monland."[72]

After a year in which he was restricted by the government to the vicinity of Rangoon, on the 29th November 1952 Nai Ba Lwin slipped away "to join the resistance movement in the bush."[73] It was at this point in his career that Nai Ba Lwin adopted the *nom de guerre* 'Nai Shwe Kyin', in honour of the *Shwegyin* Buddhist sect, renowned for its strictness and discipline.[74] He immediately took a leading hand in preparing "a statement outlining the programme of the Front (which) was issued and sent to other revolutionary parties and to foreign embassies in Rangoon and Bangkok. From a hopeless stage, the Mon resistance movement took a political turn respected by the allied ethnic groups and dreaded by the enemy."[75]

In December 1952 Mon and Karenni delegates attended another KNU conference in Papun. Following the government's creation that year of a truncated Karen State (which was rejected by the KNU), Nai Ngwe Thein and other observers apparently detected a degree of chauvinism among the KNU leadership.[76] In response to the foundation of Karen State, on the 27th March 1953 the MPSG formed a 'Provisional Government of Monland', a body which aimed "to achieve (the) cherished ideal" of Mon liberation.[77]

Nai Aung Htun, probably the most influential Mon insurgent-politician of the 1950s and '60s, became MPSG Chairman, with Nai Shwe Kyin as defence minister and Nai Ngwe Thein in charge of foreign relations. The newly-reformed Mon nationalist movement continued to liaise closely with the KNU and other fraternal organisations, including for a while the KNU's new ally, the KMT.

During the 1953 dry season, Mon forces fought together with KMT troops, under Major Francis Yap, in the unsuccessful defence of Pa Nga village, Nai Aung Htun's family home near Thanbyuzayat. Despite the opposition of some left-wing cadres, it seemed at first that the MPSG would receive significant amounts of arms and money from the Chinese nationalists. However, little assistance was actually forthcoming and the relationship soon waned.[78]

Whilst the MPSG and KNU continued warily to court the KMT, a number of Karen and Mon nationalists had already started to look to the left for ideological inspiration Two government propaganda publications from 1989 claim that, in the mid-1950s, the MPF contained both pro-KMT and pro-CPB factions, and that the latter was led by Nai Shwe Kyin and Nai Pan Tha.[79] However, the conduct of insurgent affairs was still primarily dominated by realpolitik: one's enemy's enemy was one's friend. By 1954, as the last KMT forces in lower Burma withdrew to Taiwan (via Myawaddy and Mae Sot[80]), Nai Shwe Kyin and several Karen leaders were invited to secret talks by the Thai dictator, Field Marshal Phibun Songkhram (himself of Mon descent).[81] This meeting cemented the Mon and Karen insurgents' inheritance of their ancestors' historic role as agents of Thai security policy, guarding the troublesome Burmese border.

Meanwhile back in Burma, the ARMA continued to operate as the non-political face of Mon national identity.[82] In February 1954 U Nu inaugurated a Mon Affairs Group (MAG), under the ARMA Chairman, U Chit Thaung, and U Tun Maung, and in April the group opened a travelling Mon Culture Exhibition. By the mid-1950s, over one hundred Mon primary schools, seventeen middle schools and five high schools had been established under government patronage, and Mon language classes were being introduced at several universities.[83] It seemed that at last U Nu was willing to take the Mon seriously.

In response to "the AFPFL government's political and cultural offensive", in 1954 the MPSG established a Mon Cadets' Institute, near Kawkareik. Under the leadership of Nai Shwe Kyin and Nai Ngwe Thein (who must have been busy men), thirty trainees were instructed in political science and military training, with the objective of preparing a new generation of leaders for the struggle.[84]

The MPSG held a major conference near Thanbyuzayat in April 1954. In the context of the CPB's powerful presence in northern, central and parts of southern Burma, and the spread of communist influence across Southeast

Asia during the 1950s, debate centred on the appropriateness of communist strategy and ideology to the Mon insurrection.[85] As a result of decisions taken at the conference, in early 1955 the MPSG was re-organised as the Mon People's Front (MPF). Perhaps because of the leading role he had played in the heated and sometimes divisive ideological debates of 1954–55, Nai Ngwe Thein assumed the relatively lowly position of MPF Central Committee member, under Chairman Nai Aung Htun and General Secretary Nai Chan Mon (who had played a moderating role in these discussions). It seemed that the new MPF leadership would tolerate leftist elements, but was not willing to move too far into the communist camp. The front agreed a somewhat vague and non-committed policy on the issue of class struggle, a political line reflected in the fact that Nai Shwe Kyin, a prominent a left-winger who had until then taken responsibility for information and propaganda, found no place among the front's senior office-holders.[86]

In April the following year the MPF joined the KNU and United Pa-O National Organisation (UNPO) in a new alliance, the Democratic Nationalities United Front (DNUF), chaired by Mahn Ba Zan.[87] From the outset, the DNUF was in close contact with the CPB 'White Flag' communists, who had not until then been particularly sympathetic to the ethnic cause. The inaugural DNUF congress was followed by a KNU congress which adopted a number of left-wing (although not necessarily communist) policies, sponsored by the Karen National United Party (KNUP), a leftist vanguard organisation which by the mid-1950s had come to dominate the Karen nationalist movement.[88] In recognition of his high level Karen contacts, Mon participation in the new grouping was co-ordinated by Nai Tun Thein, who expressed concern at the possibility of Burman and/or CPB domination of the alliance. Prophetically, he warned of the danger of disputes arising over demarcation of territory, on which subject he underlined the Mons' historic (but demographically, rather tenuous) claim to the area around Pegu.[89]

Notwithstanding such reservations, the DNUF seemed initially to offer the MPF a number of tangible benefits. For several years, troops from the KNU's Fifth Brigade, which was only very loosely controlled by head-quarters, had been wont to harass Mon villages in the Thaton area. Following the KMT evacuation however, the renewed alliance with the KNU promised to ease such tensions. Furthermore, the DNUF helped to train Mon personnel and supplied them with battlefield communications and other equipment. New MPF base areas were established in Karen-controlled zones west of Three Pagodas Pass, and around Thanbyuzayat and Mudon.[90]

However, by the late 1950s the Mon nationalists were becoming increasingly divided ideologically, with elements among the MPF leadership led by Nai Shwe Kyin subscribing to more left-wing views than the majority. A more immediate concern was the alliance's failure to bring success on the battlefield. After a series of military set-backs, by early 1958 the MPF leadership was ready to negotiate a ceasefire with the government, which had already demonstrated its support for Mon cultural activities.

Meanwhile, in an effort to gain popularity and merit by resolving the country's outstanding security issues, prime minister U Nu was preparing to offer a conditional amnesty to the insurgents. Crucially, for the first time he also proposed the formation of two new Union States, for the Mon and Rakhine-Arakanese. Needing no further encouragement, in early July 1958 Nai Chan Mon and Nai Non Lar began ceasefire negotiations in Thanbyuzayat with local *Tatmadaw* commanders (who refused to meet Nai Ngwe Thein, whom they accused of having undermined the abortive 1950 peace overtures).[91]

Prospects for Progress? 1958–62

After a week of tense negotiations, a ceremony was held on 12th July 1958, at which the MPF handed over a number of weapons, in exchange for government recognition as a legal political party. The bulk of the Mon insurgents had 'exchanged arms for peace' and 'returned to the legal fold'. A further ceremony was held at Moulmein on 23rd July, where, following an acrimonious dispute with local *Tatmadaw* and police officers, the MPF was eventually allowed to display its flag outside the same offices it had used in the late 1940s.[92]

U Nu's 1958 amnesty offer was intended primarily to undermine the communists by encouraging large numbers of their supporters and ethnic allies to 'return to the legal fold'. In total some 5,500 insurgents accepted the package, including CPB, PVO and Rakhine fighters, plus over one thousand Mon troops and the majority of Pa-O insurgents. Inevitably, these defections precipitated the collapse of the DNUF alliance.[93]

A secondary factor in some MPF leaders' decision to quit the insurgency was their distaste for alliance with the CPB – an issue that was to provoke divisions among Burma's insurgent groups for years to come. The current (1994) NMSP constitution retains much of the Maoist rhetoric of Southeast Asia's 'national liberation' movements of the 1950s and '60s, the influence of which on Mon nationalism may be traced from formative contacts with the KNUP and CPB. The continuing influence of leftist ideology on the Mon insurgency is in part explained by the fact that many of those most opposed to communism 'returned to the legal fold' in 1958. Those few cadres who remained 'in the revolution' were now free to cultivate relations with the CPB. In some respects, the 1958 ceasefires cemented the communist bloc they were intended to undermine.[94]

U Nu's attempt to separate ethnic nationalists from communists was meant to thwart the development of a potentially powerful alliance against

Rangoon, as well as to shore-up his precarious position as head of a faction-ridden government. However, the gambit did not pay off and the prime minister's relationship with the ethnic nationalists served only to widen a damaging split within the AFPFL. As a consequence of these divisions, combined with the military's distaste for negotiation with the insurgents, within three months of the MPF ceasefire U Nu had been replaced as prime minister by General Ne Win, who supposedly assumed the post at the invitation of the civilian government.[95]

For a few months however, the mainstream Mon nationalists continued to enjoy the benefits of legality, and seemed to be on the verge of real political breakthroughs. In August 1958 Nai Aung Htun and the MPF leadership met with their old colleagues in the United Mon Association (UMA). Further meetings were conducted throughout the month with the ARMA, the Mon *sangha* and students, and U Nu's lieutenants. However, two joint MPF-UMA conferences were unable to bring about the re-unification of the Mon nationalist movement, apparently due to Nai Po Cho's reluctance to embrace the ex-insurgent MPF leaders. However, the second conference, in late August 1958, did agree to form a new Mon National Federation (MNF).[96] Reflecting the continued influence of left-wing ideology, the federation was conceived of as a specifically anti-imperialist, working class and peasant-led movement. However, the MNF's effectiveness was undermined by the limited participation of Nai Po Cho and the rump UMA.[97]

Meanwhile, one man had set about rebuilding the Mon insurgency in the bush. At the time of the MPF ceasefire, Nai Shwe Kyin was the only senior leader to oppose the truce and remain 'in the revolution'. He had spent the 1958 dry season conducting negotiations with the CPB in the Pegu Yomas, where he met his future wife, Daw Tin (a CPB member), and deepened his appreciation of communist strategy. The day after he learnt of the MPF ceasefire, Nai Shwe Kyin formed a new underground organisation – the New Mon State Party (NMSP).[98] Today in the Mon 'liberated zones', NMSP Day is still celebrated on 20th July.

With less than a hundred die-hard supporters and family members, in the early days the small NMSP faction was almost entirely dependant for security and supplies on the CPB, and to a lesser extent the KNU. A year after its formation, in May 1959, the NMSP joined the CPB-sponsored National Democratic United Front (NDUF), which included the KNUP, and later also Chin and Karenni insurgents, and eventually a Shan faction too.[99] The NMSP stayed in the NDUF until 1975, when the party joined the non-communist Federal National Democratic Front (FNDF), forerunner of the National Democratic Front (NDF – see below). With the exception of an agreement between Rakhine-Arakanese rebels and the CPB dating from 1949, the loose and shifting NDUF coalition was the first formal alliance between 'ethnic' and 'political' insurgent forces in the civil war.

Whilst the armed opposition re-grouped in the countryside, between October 1958 and April 1960 Burma was ruled by decree, under General Ne Win's military 'caretaker government'. Following the chaotic warfare of the early-mid 1950s, the army now felt able to project an idea of independent Burma, centred on a highly politicised *Tatmadaw*. Ethnic Burman officers – who had been at the heart of the anti-British (and later, anti-Japanese) resistance struggle – were influenced by memories of the divisive colonial regime, and determined to prevent the disintegration of independent Burma. When the *Tatmadaw* assumed state power, its leaders identified the interests of this – the most 'patriotic' institution in Burma – with those of the state. As the victor in the protracted struggles for power in the decade after independence, the military was able to impose a model of state-society relations that had far-reaching implications, shaping the ground rules (or culture) of Burmese politics over the following half-century.

Despite some restrictions placed on their members' activities, the UMA and MPF were able to conduct business more-or-less as usual. In November 1958 the MPF even held an assembly in Moulmein, which adopted a new post-armed struggle constitution.[100]

The 1958 coup undoubtedly provided fresh impetus to Nai Shwe Kyin's NMSP and others who had rejected the U Nu amnesty package. It seems though, that the leaders of the recently-legalised wing of Mon nationalist movement were not so outraged by the military take-over as to seriously consider going back underground. After all, the new military regime had promised to return Burma to civilian rule, and Nai Aung Htun, Nai Po Co and colleagues still hoped to exert some influence on the government. General Ne Win played skilfully on these aspirations, co-opting a number of prominent ethnic minority leaders into the interim government, including the ARMA Chairman and founder of the Mon Affairs Group (MAG), Nai Chit Thaung.

Although by temperament more a civil servant than a politician, Nai Chit Thaung served as Minister of Culture, Industry and Labour in the first Ne Win administration. (His assistant, Nai Maung Sein, went on to become Director of the Ministry of Culture under the 1974 Ne Win government.) In January 1960 Nai Chit Thaung accompanied Ne Win to Beijing, where he met Chou Enlai and Mao Zedong.

Under Nai Chit Thaung's direction, in the late 1950s several hundred poor Mon families from Moulmein and the underdeveloped Tenasserim region were encouraged to move north to Pegu, in a modest attempt at social engineering which re-introduced a Mon population at the historic capital of Hongsawaddy for the first time in half a century. This community still resides on the west side of town, and is noted for its traditional Mon weaving.[101]

During campaigning for the April 1960 general election, that briefly returned the county to civilian rule, U Nu renewed his promise to establish two new Union States in eastern and western Burma, for the Mon and the Rakhine-Arakanese, neither of whom had been represented at the historic

1947 Panglong Conference. This commitment had been demanded as a condition of their support by a coalition of Mon political, religious and cultural groups. Following the election, a Ministry of Mon Affairs was established, to decide the constitution and boundaries of the new Mon State.[102] In November the Mon camp formed a Mon State Implementation Steering Committee, under the patronage of several senior Mon monks, with Mon Da Tu (and later, Nai Hla Maung) as chairman and Nai Ngwe Thein (later, Nai Thein Maung) as secretary. The Steering Committee called for re-negotiation of the Panglong agreement, envisioning a new political settlement for Burma's minority peoples, with the return of civilian rule.[103] In 1960, amid preparations for the creation of Mon State, a building known as the Mon Halls – which soon became the centre of the Mon community in Rangoon – was constructed opposite the *Maha Yen* monastery, to the south of the Shwedagon pagoda.

The 1960–62 parliament included three independent Mon MPs: Nai Po Sein, Nai Po Cho and Nai Aung Htun. A fourth Mon politician, Nai Aung Hla Ngwe, sat in the upper house. MPF Chairman Nai Aung Htun became U Nu's Minister for Relief and Resettlement, and in early 1961 was nominated by the Mon State Implementation Steering Committee as Minister for Mon Affairs.[104]

Despite delaying tactics by factions within U Nu's party, by early 1962 the government seems to have been on the verge of establishing Mon and Arakan as Burma's sixth and seventh Union States. Mon and Rakhine-Arakanese delegates attended a government-sponsored Union States Assembly in Taunggyi, capital of Shan State, in June 1961. The assembly called for the convention of a new National Assembly of the Union of Burma – i.e. for a revision of the Panglong Conference.[105] Seemingly, the only difficulty remaining concerned exactly which territories should be included within the new states' boundaries. As some Burman politicians had begun to agitate for the exclusion of Moulmein, on 22nd February 1962 the MPF organised a mass rally in that city, during which Mon, Rakhine and Shan politicians called for the speedy implementation of legislation to establish Mon State.[106]

By this time, Mon language and literature studies had already been introduced into the school curriculum across Thaton and Moulmein Districts.[107] With the opening-up of trade routes between Ye and Mergui following the MPF ceasefire, the cultural, economic and political revival of the traditionally prosperous Mon heartland seemed well under way. However, such optimism was to be short-lived.

The 1962 Coup D'Etat

Until 1962, a negotiated settlement between Rangoon and the remaining insurgent groups had always been a possibility. Indeed, the 2nd March coup was launched on the eve of a scheduled meeting between government ministers and a number of rebel leaders. To many observers of and participants in the civil war, this Federal Seminar had seemed the best chance since the 1940s of achieving a lasting solution to Burma's outstanding political and ethnic issues.

One of the main reasons given by General Ne Win for his seizure of power was to preserve the union and prevent U Nu from using the seminar to address secessionist demands. The new dictator moved quickly to imprison – without trial – U Nu, and Nai Aung Htun and other ministers, many of whom were to remain in custody until the early 1970s. During his first Union Day speech, on 12th February 1963, General Ne Win announced that all ethnic nationalities within the union would be guaranteed equal rights and status, but that any independent political entity for these groups was inconceivable. Above all else, he argued, the integrity of the unitary state must be preserved. By this time the new Revolutionary Council had already quashed plans to establish the new Mon and Arakan States, leading a number of Mon students to join the NMSP in the jungle.

Despite his fulminations against the 1962 Federal Seminar, within a year of seizing power, Ne Win initiated his own 'peace talks'. Between June– November 1963, thirteen insurgent organisations, including both the Red and White Flag communists, held a series of talks in Rangoon, which Nai Shwe Kyin attended as a representative of the NDUF alliance. He was disappointed to discover that Ne Win would only discuss terms of surrender. Among other conditions, the Revolutionary Council demanded that the insurgents gather their troops in specified positions and stop all party organisational work.

Discussions with the NDUF, which formally commenced on 8th October, were called-off on 14th November, with Ne Win accusing the insurgents of lacking sincerity. The next day, several Mon and other opposition politicians – including Nai Aung Htun's son, Nai Tin Aung, and his senior lieutenant, Nai Non Lar, together with Nai Tun Thein and Nai Ngwe Thein – were arrested, on the grounds that they were planning to re-join the insurgency.[108] The NDUF and the communists, having rejected Ne Win's proposals, went back to the jungle and to war with Rangoon. Nai Shwe Kyin received safe passage back to the liberated zones east of Moulmein.

However, the insurgents had not wasted their time in the cities. Nai Shwe Kyin, for example, had taken the opportunity to re-establish contact with Mon networks in Rangoon and Moulmein, and had met with many of his old MPF colleagues. These included Nai Non Lar, leader of the Moulmein Peace Committee, part of a semi-official contact network that had helped facilitate the unsuccessful peace talks.[109] Nai Non Lar was to spend the next decade in jail, before assuming the mantle of his patron, Nai Aung Htun, as leader of the anti-communist wing of the Mon nationalist movement.

Other opposition figures had likewise renewed acquaintances with underground organisers and students in the cities, and within weeks of the breakdown of talks, insurgent forces were boosted by the arrival of thousands of new recruits, disaffected by Ne Win's repressive regime. With the Kachin nationalist movement taking up arms, and the outbreak of new rebellions across Shan State, the insurrections were now truly nation-wide.

Across vast areas of rural Burma, the *Tatmadaw* and various ethnic and communist armies recommenced the fight for the control of key territory and resources, and the country's political future. Soon however, the insurgent ranks were hit by a new wave of defections. Following the disappointments of 1963, and increasingly concerned by the leftward drift of the Karen nationalist movement, in 1964 most of Saw Hunter Thamwe's small, moderately right-wing Karen Revolutionary Council (KRC) agreed to lay down their arms and 'return to the legal fold', as did a remnant MPF faction. Among other consequences, these developments facilitated the domination of the Karen nationalist movement by the left-leaning KNUP.

Meanwhile, General Ne Win had launched the Burmese Way to Socialism, under the leadership of the Burma Socialist Programme Party (BSPP). The new regime outlawed all opposition, and over the next few years proceeded to nationalise industry (including foreign-owned businesses), and bring the press and most other aspects of civil society under government control. Initially devised as a 'third way', between the corrupt and chaotic capitalism of the U Nu era and the hard-line programme of the communists, the Burmese Way to Socialism soon became a by-word for inefficient central planning and inflexible, authoritarian government.

The New System of Education, introduced by the BSPP in 1964, made no allowance for ethnic minority language instruction, which was effectively banned from the state education system.[110] The All Ramanya Mon Association (ARMA) was another victim of the coup, its extensive Mon culture and educational programmes being forced to close down, or go underground.[111]

In 1965 an Academy for the Development of National Groups was established, in order to indoctrinate potential ethnic minority leaders into the Burmese Way to Socialism – or as Robert Taylor puts it, "to train individuals from border areas to appreciate the diverse culture of the country while recognising the need for the unity of the state."[112] Such developments were characteristic of the BSPP regime's denial of rights: ethnic minority citizens could only participate in the affairs of state at the cost of suppressing their ethnic identity.[113] Those organisations which sought to promote independent political and cultural activity were suppressed. Christian Bauer cites an example: the *Lik Gatap Khet*, a Mon language journal that attempted to address political issues and "strengthen the institutional infrastructure of various Mon associations", was closed down in 1977.[114]

Nai Aung Htun was released from jail in 1968. The following year, he joined Nai Po Cho on Ne Win's advisory panel, established to provide the BSPP regime with a veneer of support from co-opted minority communities. Nai Aung Htun remained a member of this committee until his death in April 1970. Having never gone underground, Nai Po Cho was not detained in 1962, but was instead granted a state pension in recognition of his contribution to the struggle for Burmese independence. He remained in contact with his old student, Ne Win, until he passed away in the late 1980s.

Most of the other Mon politicians detained in 1962–63 were not released until the 1970s. The political environment had by this time further stagnated. A decade of one party rule had undermined the energy and diversity of the parliamentary era, and it was not until the great upheavals of 1988 that legal, urban-based political parties would again play a major role on the national stage.

CHAPTER EIGHT

Insurgents on the
Thailand-Burma Border

At times during the late 1940s and early '50s, the 'Rangoon Government' had governed little more than the capital and its immediate environs. Throughout the following three decades, insurgent forces still controlled vast tracts of countryside. Indeed, until the fall of the first KNU bases along the Thailand-Burma border in the early 1980s, the only points along the entire border under firm government control were the garrison and trading towns of Tachilek and Myawaddy.

Robert Taylor has calculated that in 1985, by which time the extent of the rebel-controlled liberated zones had already been considerably reduced, between four and ten per cent of the population was still "not under the state's hegemony."[115] This figure included a hundred thousand or more citizens of Kaw Thoo Lei, the rebel Karen state which thrived in the military, social and economic chaos of Ne Win's Burma.

The nature of the *de facto* micro-states established by the insurgents differed, according to geographic, economic, cultural and political factors. In some respects, the various liberated zones resembled the tributary *mandala* of precolonial times – overlapping circles of power, within which strong leaders dispensed patronage and vied for supremacy vis-à-vis neighbouring 'princes' and the capital (be it Rangoon or Mannerplaw). Ananda Raja has suggested "that there is a Thai border and a Burmese-Karen frontier region and accordingly ... the Karen separatist movement – and perhaps even the Burmese state – may in fact be viewed as a kind of *traditional state*" – i.e. as a *mandala*-like entity, with "fluctuating territorial boundaries."[116]

Although in some respects they resembled chronically under-developed statelets, the insurgent-controlled zones were not recognised as legitimate entities by the international community. However, for a brief period in the early 1970s, the Mon and Karen insurgents did enjoy limited support from powerful US interests. This was channelled via a new armed opposition front led by Burma's deposed prime minister, U Nu, who had gone underground in 1969. In general however, through the long years since 1948, the ethnic nationalists have been on their own in the struggle for independence, and have had to raise their own funds as best they could.

The rise – and eventual fall – of the black market 'trade gate' at Three Pagodas Pass mirrored the Mon and Karen insurgents' fortunes during this fifty year period. Although in the 1980s logging concessions became an important source of income, for three decades after 1948, the rebel Mon and Karen statelets were largely financially dependent on taxation of the cross-border black market trade between capitalist Thailand and socialist Burma. During this period, the insurgents established symbiotic relationships with the Thai military and security services, from whom they purchased arms and ammunition, and on whose behalf they patrolled Thailand's long and traditionally volatile western border.

Between the mid-1960s and late '80s, the NMSP and KNU were largely content to guard the liberated zones and trade routes along the Thailand-Burma border, rather than take the war to the *Tatmadaw*. Throughout this period Mon nationalist ranks were dogged by factionalism and recurring splits, during the most serious of which (between 1981–87) Nai Shwe Kyin was ousted as NMSP leader. By 1988 though, as pent-up anti-government sentiment swept the country, the party was again re-united under its veteran leader. Meanwhile, the Karen insurrection too had undergone a number of traumatic reversals.

General Bo Mya and the KNU Model

In the half-decade following the death of Saw Ba U Gyi, the Karen nationalist movement split into left and right-wing camps, both of which continued to loose ground to the *Tatmadaw* throughout the 1950s and '60s. Although, through to 1975, the leftist KNUP, together with the CPB, continued to operate in pockets of territory further to the west, by the late 1960s the bulk of the Karen forces had been driven back to the inaccessible hill country of Burma's eastern border regions. The Karen revolution was becoming increasingly isolated and, as independent Burma entered its third decade, was no longer a decisive factor in considerations of state security.

Following the abortive 1963 ceasefire talks, a number of senior commanders and about one thousand Karen troops had defected to the government. Amid the confusion that followed, a tough young field commander, Colonel Saw Bo Mya, became KNU Eastern Division commander. Bo Mya, who had recently married and converted from animism to become a Seventh Day Adventist, took advantage of the power vacuum in eastern Kaw Thoo Lei to build up his position in the previously disorganised Karen hills. Until this point, the Thailand border region had been an insurgent backwater.

Over the following decade, Bo Mya and a corps of loyal and politically conservative officers assumed control of the Karen insurgency. In June 1968 the re-formation of the KNU was announced, and at an historic September 1974 Congress it adopted a specifically anti-communist constitution.[117] By this time, Bo Mya had assumed the rank of lieutenant-general, having succeeded in building the Karen National Liberation Army (KNLA) into the second largest insurgent force in Burma (after the CPB People's Army). In the 1970s and '80s his influence extended to cover almost the entire gamut of non-communist insurgent forces in Burma. As Martin Smith remarks, Bo Mya enjoyed "an almost mythological reputation which, depending on one's perspective, lies somewhere between a modern-day Robin Hood, Billy the Kid, Che Guevara or Abu Nidal."[118]

The reformed KNU-KNLA was financed through taxation of the emerging cross-border trade between Thailand and Burma. The small band of Mon insurgents in the south – mostly operating out of KNLA Sixth Brigade, in southern Karen State – followed suit. Thai goods began to flow through dozens of unofficial border checkpoints, headed for the huge black market that operated in the shadows of Burma's corrupt and inefficient state-socialist economy. The rebels took their cut of the trade (usually at three-to-five per cent of the value of goods) and a number of insurgent fortunes were made.

By the 1970s, Kaw Thoo Lei was the largest of more than a dozen ethnic insurgent-controlled 'liberated zones' in Burma. The similarly constituted Mon, Rakhine, Karenni, Kachin, and Shan rebel mini-states represented alternative centres of power to the military government in Rangoon, as did the CPB zones in the north. In 1972 General Bo Mya established a new headquarters at Mannerplaw (Victory Field) on the Moei River, a hundred miles north of Mae Sot. In years to come, the new stronghold would host a series of important anti-Rangoon – and anti-communist – alliances.

Whilst the Kachin Independence Organisation (KIO) and CPB received support from China, various Mon, Karen, Karenni and Shan insurgent forces came to rely on supplies from the Thai military, which provided weapons, training and access to the outside world. In the case of some Shan and other groups, the Thai generals were attracted by the substantial revenues to be obtained from opium and heroin trafficking; in the case of General Bo Mya's KNU – and to a lesser extent, his NMSP allies – it was their role as buffers against communist insurgency that was useful.

Through its covert support for the anti-communist KNU, the Thai security establishment was largely successful in choking-off access to the well-supplied CPB, by the similarly Chinese-sponsored Communist Party of Thailand (CPT) which, until the late 1970s, continued to seriously threaten Thai state security.[119] However, in the 1970s and '80s the CPB Southern Command, in the isolated Tenasserim region, was the only Burmese communist division to link up regularly with the CPT. These contacts were facilitated in part by NMSP intermediaries, co-ordinated by an ethnic Mon, the CPB's Karen and Burmese-speaking contact officer, U Tun Kyi.[120]

A concrete example of the KNU's role in anti-Communist operations in Thailand: in the 1970s and early '80s KNLA troops from General Bo Mya's 101 Battalion, at Kaw Moo Rah, were transported by the Royal Thai Army to zones in Thailand where the CPT was active, including the forests around Um-Phang, in Tak Province, opposite KNLA Sixth Brigade. However, such operations were not very effective, as the Karen from Burma had some sympathy for their Thai Karen brothers, a number of whom had joined the CPT in western Thailand. Consequently, the KNLA did not prosecute the anti-communist campaign with much vigour. (It is noteworthy that 101 Battalion troops were selected for this operation, rather than those from the supposedly more leftist Sixth Brigade, which was not under Bo Mya's direct command.)[121]

As noted above, Thai military contacts with the Burmese insurgents date from the early 1950s, and may be seen as an extension of sixteenth-to-nineteenth century security policy. In the 1960s the KNU and NMSP established permanent offices in Bangkok and developed close working relationships with senior Thai military officers, security agents and politicians. Such relationship were often cemented in more-or-less private business deals. On the ground, insurgent forces along the Thailand-Burma border co-ordinated patrols, information gathering and signals activities with the Royal Thai Army. The Burmese rebels even policed remote areas inside Thailand that were out of bounds to the Thai authorities – either because of CPT guerrilla activities, or because these areas were occupied by the Burmese insurgent forces themselves. Examples of the latter situation include the Mon and Karen-controlled areas around Three Pagodas Pass (see below), and the KNU enclaves with grew up along the east (Thai) banks of the Salween and Moei Rivers, opposite Mannerplaw.

Throughout the 1980s and '90s, insurgent groups in Burma were spending several millions of dollars a year on arms from Thailand. As well as purchasing M16 rifles and other munitions from the Royal Thai Army, Burmese rebel agents bought weapons (including Chinese AK-47s) directly from the theatre of war on Thailand's eastern borders with Laos and Cambodia. Here prices were considerably cheaper than those offered by middle-men, although it was usually still necessary to pay off the Thai authorities, in order to ship arms across the kingdom to the Burmese border.

A further source of munitions was the enemy itself. The civil war was a complex phenomena and *Tatmadaw* officers are known on occasion to have sold weapons and ammunition to the insurgents. Sooner or later, and to a greater or lesser extent, the conflict seems to have corrupted many of those who served it.

Insurgency Inc.

Throughout the 1960s and '70s, Thailand continued to be ruled by a series of right-wing military governments. It was not until after the economy took off in the early 1980s, that a functioning, if notoriously corrupt, parliamentary system was established. However, occasional military coups continued to destabilise the body politic and in the border areas – as in many other aspects of state – the Thai military was accountable to no one.

Meanwhile in Burma, the civil war ebbed and flowed with the seasons. *Tatmadaw* dry season offensives were usually followed by withdrawal, prior to the long June–November rainy season, when re-supply of isolated positions became much more difficult. Amid the confusion of war and relocation, the 'front-line' was a nebulous concept and vast areas of the Burmese countryside were effectively controlled by neither side. The civilian population was often stuck in the middle, in what were described by the Burma Army as 'brown areas' (if contested with the insurgents) or as 'black areas' (if more-or-less firmly controlled by rebel forces).

As the insurgencies dragged on during the 1960s and '70s, the liberated zones (or 'black areas') began to resemble miniature states, with cabinet-style governments comprising departments such as forestry, finance, health and education. A number of groups developed school and hospital services, and often also youth and women's wings. To support such activities, and feed and arm their troops, the insurgents needed to raise taxes. Not surprisingly, turf wars became increasingly common.

Understandably, given the vicissitudes of war, insurgent finances were sometimes less than transparent. Tax and other revenues often found their way into the pockets of local commanders, rather than insurgent treasuries. The exigencies of mobile warfare demanded that military units be largely self-supporting and, as a result, the distinction between field commanders' personal finances and those of the revolution often became blurred. A number of insurgent leaders maintained houses and business interests in China, India and Thailand, and the 1970s and '80s saw several joint business ventures between rebel commanders and their high-level contacts in the Thai military. At the same time the Mon, Karen, Karenni, Shan and Chinese nationalist armies established bases in the isolated border regions, often planning operations in Burma from Thai soil.

In general during these long years of military stalemate, the political offensive against Rangoon, and the related task of organising among the insurgents' constituencies, were neglected. The rebels did though, help to keep alive the flame of resistance, and throughout the 1970s a steady flow of disgruntled citizens from 'inside' came out to join those already 'in the revolution'. For the better educated and more politically aware among the newcomers, insurgent life could be frustrating. The decision-making process was seen as conservative, and power and access to resources often depended as much on the patronage of individual 'big men' as on objective criteria. Aspects of this 'revolutionary' culture resembled centuries-old traditions, and the structures of the insurgent *mandala* were in many cases based on tributary and/or clan loyalties, which extended across the indistinct front-line to communities in government-controlled areas. This patrimonial network became a key target of the *Tatmadaw's* counter-insurgency programme.[122]

To many observers, the decline of the ethnic insurgents' political credibility dates from this period. The larger rebel armies still had the capacity to take the war to the enemy, rather than merely react to events, but their leaders were largely content to protect their hard-won fiefdoms and the lucrative cross-border trade routes. The NMSP, KNU and other groups undertook little in the way of development initiatives in the areas they controlled, and in many respects their administrations were no more democratic or representative than that in Rangoon. Indeed, they sometimes came to resemble the only model available – that of the enemy.[123]

Discussing nationalism and ethnic liberation, Mikael Gravers notes that "culture and liberation easily become a cover for warlordism and racism."[124] The veteran Karen leader, Skaw Ler Taw, is quoted by Martin Smith to similar effect: "of all the problems the KNU faced (military, political or financial) 'warlordism' was the greatest."[125] Time and again, the ethnic opposition has split into bitterly opposed factions. A lot of bad blood was spilt, and whilst the *Tatmadaw* – with its policy of 'divide and rule' – remained united, the insurgents' fortunes declined.

Nai Shwe Kyin and the Mon Rebellion – 1960s and '70s

The history of the Karen insurrection over the past thirty years has been dominated by the personality of General Bo Mya. Since the late 1950s, the Mon insurgency has also come to be associated with one man, whose nationalist credentials go back to the years following the end of the Second World War.

Nai Ba Lwin was born at Kawhnat village, near Thaton, on 1st March 1913.[126] The son of a middle-ranking 'native' government official, Nai Ba Lwin went to a Methodist mission school before attending Rangoon University, where he developed the analytical skills and attention to detail which to distinguish him in years to come. After graduating, he briefly worked for the colonial secretariat, before "the Mon aquatic instinct" drove him to join the British Royal Naval Volunteer Reserve. By the time of the Japanese invasion, the twenty-nine year old Nai Ba Lwin had attained the rank of instructor.

He and his two brothers were active in the anti-Japanese resistance. Nai Thaung E and Nai Ba Nyunt were both captured and tortured by the feared

Kempatei secret police, and subsequently honoured by the state for their services to the anti-fascist struggle. In the case of Nai Thaung E, the medal was awarded posthumously, as he had died under interrogation. The other brother, Nai Ba Nyunt, went on to become Karen State finance minister under the 1954–58 U Nu administration. Nai Shwe Kyin however, chose a different career. Having played a key role in founding the MFL, MPF and other early Mon nationalist organisations, in July 1958 he almost single-handedly established the New Mon State Party (NMSP), which for the next forty years was in the vanguard of the armed struggle for Monland.

Nai Shwe Kyin was as a politician, rather than a strong-man. He never exercised the same degree of military-authoritarian control over the Mon nationalist movement that General Bo Mya did over the Karen. For example, it was not unusual for NMSP Central Committee members or Congress delegates to publicly challenge their president, whose positions were sometimes at variance with those of a significant portion of the membership. Such open criticism of the 'big men' of the KNU was far rarer, and its toleration within the NMSP illustrated the party's democratic spirit.

Like General Bo Mya, Nai Shwe Kyin became an iconic figure, appearing each year on the party's calendar. Unlike Bo Mya however, he never fostered a cult of personality or sponsored large-scale celebrations of his birthday. In many other respects though, the history of Nai Shwe Kyin's NMSP mirrored that of KNU.

In 1965, two years after the collapse of Ne Win's peace talks, Nai Shwe Kyin was invited by the KNU to establish his headquarters at Nam Khok, a small village about half way up the Thailand-Burma border, three Km south of the small settlement at Three Pagodas Pass, where the KNU had recently established a permanent trade 'gate'. Controlled by the KNLA's Sixth Brigade, under Bo Mya's key ally and trusted field commander, Saw Shwe Saing, Three Pagodas Pass was one of several such gates along the border.

By the mid-1960s, as the Ne Win regime's incompetent economic planning led to shortages in the production and distribution of many basic items, the black market cross-border trade with Thailand began to take-off. Within a few years, most consumer goods, fuel and medicines for sale in the Rangoon markets originated in Thailand, and Burma's ethnic insurgencies had become important players in both the Burmese and Thai economies.[127]

Nai Shwe Kyin's timing was therefore quite fortunate: he began the task of re-building the Mon nationalist movement at the start of an economic boom, under the patronage of powerful KNU allies. He acknowledges the debt: "thanks to the sympathy and friendship of the Karen leadership, the NMSP survived huge hardships and severe sufferings during the difficult times of the 1960s."[128] In December 1967 the NMSP joined the Nationalities United Front (NUF), a new ethnic insurgent alliance where the Mon were represented by the KNUP's Saw Than Aung (later KNU Vice-Chairman).[129]

Having quit the NUF the previous year, on 25th May 1970 the NMSP entered into another alliance with the KNU. This new front united the Mon and Karen insurgents with the recently-established Parliamentary Democracy Party (PDP), led by the deposed Burmese premier, U Nu. This move marked the NMSP's emergence into the insurgent mainstream. Notwithstanding a number of previous, mainly communist-led fronts, the Nationalities United Liberation Front (NULF) was the first militarily effective partnership between ethnic nationalist insurgent groups and the predominantly Burman 'political' opposition. Ironically, U Nu, the man of peace, had allied himself with the very insurgents who in the 1950s nearly succeeded in overthrowing his government.

Having been released from jail in 1966, U Nu had initially accepted a place on Ne Win's advisory board, together with Nai Aung Htun and other politicians from the 1958–62 era. However, he had soon become disillusioned and in April 1969 headed into exile abroad. U Nu and his associates formed the PDP in Bangkok that August, and by 1971 the party's armed wing, the Patriotic Liberation Army, had recruited some 3,000 well-armed troops. These were based largely in the central and southern KNLA zones, and received material, logistic and financial support from CIA-backed sources, including Western oil companies hoping for future concessions in oil-rich Burma (an early example of the oil companies taking sides in post-independence Burmese politics).[130]

For the first time, the Mon and Karen rebels were to receive substantial – if indirect – international backing: Martin Smith reports that the NMSP received two million Thai Baht from the NULF war chest. Arguments apparently broke out within the Mon ranks over the use and distribution of the money, anticipating the traumatic splits which undermined the party in the later 1970s and 1980s.[131]

Having thrown in his lot with U Nu, Martin Smith reports that Nai Shwe Kyin "abruptly broke off all contact with the CPB."[132] Like the KNU, in the 1970s the Mon nationalist movement underwent a slow and painful ideological realignment – a shift to the right that was still not complete by the 1990s. Interestingly, the NMSP-KNU-PDP pact was brokered on behalf of the Karen by the leader of the leftist KNUP returnees – Nai Shwe Kyin's old colleague from the KNDO-MNDO, Mahn Ba Zan, who had re-united with Bo Mya's more powerful, conservative wing of the Karen nationalist movement in 1967.

Initially the new alliance enjoyed a degree of military success, and in the early 1970s joint PDP-NMSP columns operated across much of Mon State. Although primarily determined by strategic factors, the bond between Mon nationalists and the erstwhile prime minister was reinforced by a shared respect for Buddhism. Mon-Burman relations had never been as badly disrupted in the 1940s as had Karen-Burman ties, and Mon leaders had not forgotten U Nu's apparently sincere attempts to establish a Mon State prior to the 1962 military coup.

Between 1971–73, the NULF radio station in Mae Sot broadcast news and propaganda in Burmese, Mon and Karen,[133] and it seemed for a while that the alliance would resurrect the fortunes of Burma's non-communist insurgent forces. Nevertheless, strains soon began to emerge within the NULF, over the thorny issue of ethnic rights. The NMSP and KNU worked within the front to adopt a specifically federalist programme and Nai Shwe Kyin, the NULF General Secretary, persuaded the alliance to campaign for the creation of a Mon state. This shift in the balance of power, away from the PDP upset many Burman politicians, including U Nu, who abandoned the PDP-NULF in early 1972.[134]

By 1971, when the NMSP held its inaugural General Congress, the party had emerged as a fully-fledged ethnic insurgent organisation, dedicated to re-establishing Monland by force of arms. Mon troop strength again topped one thousand men, reflecting a significant upsurge in support for the NMSP since the low point of the early 1960s.[135] On the international front too, things were looking up: the NULF's American backers supplied the newly-formed Mon National Liberation Army (MNLA) with arms and other supplies, which were usually routed to the insurgents through intermediaries in the Thai military. Also in the early 1970s, NMSP personnel received some training, and logistical and moral support, from Lon Nol's right-wing, nationalist Khmer Republic (1970–75). However, association with Lon Nol's short-lived attempt to revive the ancient Mon-Khmer alliance did not result in any substantial degree of international recognition for the NMSP.

The military wing of the NMSP was established in its present form at the party General Congress in August 1971. The MNLA[136] was placed under the operational command of Brig-General Nai Pan Tha, the hero of Zarthabyin, who had re-joined the insurgency the previous year (having 'surrendered' in 1958).[137] In 1971 the NMSP was joined by the Mon People's Relief Party (MPRP), led by Nai Dhumanay (who – like Nai Shwe Kyin – had remained underground following the 1958 MPF ceasefire). The following year the NMLA was further strengthened when it merged with the Mon Restoration Army (MRA), a two hundred-strong militia operating in the Ye-Thanbyuzayat area, under Nai Kyaw Aing. The MRA united with the mainstream Mon insurgents to form the MNLA's Number Three Special Battalion, or the *Banya Ta Ram* Battalion (named after the Mon hero Bannya Dala, conqueror of Ava and last king of Pegu).

In 1973 Nai Pan Tha was replaced as military commander by Nai Non Lar, who had recently re-joined the insurgency after spending a decade in jail. Although in the vicinity of Three Pagodas Pass the NMSP was still dependant for security on the KNU, in the mid-1970s, under Nai Non Lar, the MNLA developed a system of military administration under which regional troops were assigned to a particular township, while mobile guerrilla units patrolled further afield. The latter included the Number Nine Special Battalion, or *Raja Dhi Raj* Battalion (named after the great Mon king). In 1975 Nai Non Lar's rapid ascent of the Mon insurgent ranks was confirmed, when he was appointed NMSP General Secretary

Meanwhile 'inside' Burma, on 2nd March 1974 General Ne Win's Revolutionary Council had promulgated a new constitution, under which the Union was divided into seven Burman-dominated Divisions and seven ethnic minority States, roughly corresponding to the old colonial distinction between Burma Proper and the Frontier Areas. However, the new charter was even more centralist than that of 1947, and did not accord any significant degree of autonomy to the country's diverse regions and peoples. In fact, its preamble stressed the 'one nation' identity of state socialist Burma.[138] The 1974 constitution did though, demarcate Moulmein and Thaton Districts as a new, Mon State (consisting of 10 Townships, 62 Wards and 1,207 Village Tracts).[139] As this largely cosmetic change was not accompanied by any greater degree of Mon political participation, Nai Shwe Kyin and the NMSP vowed to continue the fight for an independent Monland.

Following the demonstrations which accompanied the December 1974 funeral of U Thant, the Burmese Secretary General of the UN, a new wave of disaffected city-dwellers came out to the border, to join the insurgents in the liberated zones. Ne Win's Burmese Way to Socialism was failing and people were voting with their feet. A number of today's 'second line' Mon and Karen nationalist leaders joined the insurgency during this period, which for the Mon in particular was marked by fragmentation and internal disputes.

By 1975, when Nai Taw Mon was appointed MNLA operations commander, under the overall control of Nai Non Lar, Mon troop strength had fallen to about five hundred men. Within two years, Nai Taw Mon had stood down, to tackle growing dissension within the Mon insurgent ranks. Between 1977–78 he served as MNLA Front-line Political Commissar, while Nai Shwe Kyin took over the responsibilities of army Commander-in-Chief. These developments may be interpreted as an internal coup on the part of Nai Shwe Kyin. However, the reasoning behind Nai Taw Mon's transfer points to a more complex scenario: this tough commander's new job was to persuade errant armed Mon factions to return to the NMSP fold.

In 1974 Nai Htaw Gui defected from the MNLA, together with elements of the *Banya Ta Ram* (Number 3) Battalion. Four years later, many other ex-MRA men followed suit, establishing a new base on the Ye River, under their old leader Nai Kyaw Aing. This was a serious setback for the NMSP, not least because the new rebel faction was soon joined by the widely-respected warrior, Nai Pan Tha (who was expelled from the NMSP in 1978, for "breaking the party's discipline"). Several armed clashes between the disparate Mon rebel factions followed.

Although, by the end of the decade, many members of these pocket armies had been persuaded to rejoin the NMSP, other *Banya Ta Ram* veterans chose to join the KNU, surrender to the government, or continue to operate in small independent bands from their jungle bases. (Nai Pan Tha retired to Thailand in late 1979.) Meanwhile in 1976, more restive and loosely-organised (again, mostly ex-MRA) elements had split from the NMSP. Led by Nai Lin Htun and Nai Shau, they operated in Ye Township. Nai Shau went on to rejoin the MNLA in 1977, becoming Adjutant-General in the 1990s. In the 1980s other leaders of this band moved up to the Thanbyuzayat area, where they resurrected the independent *Banya Ta Ram* Battalion and continued to operate until the middle of the decade, when Nai Taw Gwi joined Nai Non Lar's 'official' faction of the NMSP (see below).

Three Pagodas Pass; More Splits in the Mon Ranks

The settlement at Three Pagodas Pass quickly developed into a thriving community, which served as an intelligence and market facility for the surrounding villages and insurgent armies. By the mid-1970s, many of the original bamboo and thatch buildings had been replaced by breeze block structures with zinc roofing. As well as the Karen, the population of the little town included Burmans and Bengali Muslims, and an increasingly large number of Mon, who by the 1980s are said to have outnumbered the Karen by nearly four-to-one. However, the bulk of revenue from the cross-border business still went to the KNU (fifty per cent of tax revenue stayed in Sixth Brigade, fifty per cent was sent up to the KNU Finance Department at Mannerplaw).

At an estimated two million Kyat per month in the 1980s,[140] the volume of trade going through the pass was second only to that at General Bo Mya's stronghold of Kaw Moo Rah, the 101 Battalion base opposite Mae Sot. The relationship between Kaw Moo Rah and Mae Sot was similar to that between Three Pagodas Pass and Sangkhlaburi (see below). According to *Focus* news magazine, "cloth, soap, tooth-brushes, medicines, radios, cassette recorders, bicycles, and even refrigerators and brand new air conditioners" poured across the Thai border into isolated Burma; other commodities included rice and guns, for the rebel forces. The same traders who smuggled goods in also brought raw materials out, including "minerals, jade, sapphires and rubies, cattle and water buffaloes."[141] In 1988 the World Bank estimated the total value of Burma's 'black economy' at three billion dollars (forty per cent of GDP).[142] A large proportion of this sector was taxed by the ethnic insurgents. With so much money at stake, tempers were bound to fray.

Unsurprisingly, given its history of factionalism, the NMSP suffered another major split in the 1980s. The primary cause was a personality and culture clash within the party leadership, exacerbated by financial disputes. Unfortunately for the insurgents, this was neither the first nor the last time that arguments over money got in the way of prosecuting the war against Rangoon.

A number of Mon politicians who had 'returned to the legal fold' in 1958, and been imprisoned by Ne Win in 1962–63, chose on their release to re-join the insurgency. For a while things went smoothly between Nai Shwe Kyin's tight-knit old guard and the newcomers from Rangoon and Moulmein, who rejuvenated the party with an infusion of new talent. However, it was probably inevitable that tensions would arise between these later arrivals and those who had spent a decade in the jungle.

Some observers have followed the Mon leadership in interpreting their differences in the 1980s as due to ideological divisions. While there is some justification for this interpretation, the 1981–87 NMSP split was primarily the result of a struggle over patronage and the control of key resources among the leadership. As such, the factionalism of the 1980s resembled that of the 1970s, but on a somewhat larger scale and attended by more publicity. By the end of 1981, two factions had crystallised, under party President Nai Shwe Kyin, and General Secretary Nai Non Lar.

Within a year of returning to the insurgency, Nai Non Lar had assumed overall command of the MNLA. According to Nai Shwe Kyin, the emergence of a plethora of different Mon armed groups in the 1970s was due in large part to Nai Non Lar's lax military leadership, characterised by corruption and lack of discipline. In an interview with the author in August 1999, Nai Shwe Kyin complained that the real problem was Nai Non Lar's "lack of education." However, Nai Non Lar seems to have possessed genuine charisma and was certainly popular with the troops. Nai Shwe Kyin no doubt perceived a challenge to his leadership.

The crisis came to a head over the issue of relations with the CPB, which throughout the 1970s was the most powerful rebel force in Burma. As had numerous other ethnic insurgent groups, the Mon nationalists divided into pro- and anti-CPB factions. At a special NMSP Joint Departmental Conference in October 1980 (sometimes referred to as the NMSP First Congress[143]) a dispute broke out over whether the party should condemn "Soviet social-imperialism", thus aligning itself with the CPB and its Chinese sponsors. The resolution was proposed by Nai Shwe Kyin, and opposed by Nai Non Lar and the majority of other leaders.[144]

The Nai Non Lar group accused Nai Shwe Kyin and his supporters of unreconstructed Maoist tendencies. Nai Shwe Kyin in turn charged his enemies with supporting the rival Soviet bloc – a counter-accusation which was hotly denied, although there does seem to have been at least some circumstantial evidence for this unlikely-sounding claim.[145] The dispute, which by now had spilled-over into an on-going argument over MNLA restructuring, mirrored the complex and fratricidal big power politics of the Cold War era: a few years previously, at the end of the Vietnam War, the Sino-Vietnamese rift had been deepened when China unsuccessfully demanded that the Vietnam denounce 'Soviet hegemonism'.[146] To Nai Non Lar, who shared his old mentor Nai Aung Htun's distaste for Maoist rhetoric, Nai Shwe Kyin's attempts to re-align the Mon nationalist movement with the CPB were as unacceptable in the early 1980s as they had been in the 1950s.

Acting in his capacity as party President, in February 1981 Nai Shwe Kyin suspended the congress, thus cementing a bitter polarisation.[147] Nai Non Lar's 'official' NMSP (referred to by Nai Shwe Kyin as the 'Counter-Mon Freedom Movement'[148]) set about taking over the party and military organisation, by renewing its attacks on the Nai Shwe Kyin group. The latter included future party General Secretary Nai Rot Sah (previously a student activist, and a co-sponsor of the anti-Soviet resolution), and the veteran military commanders, Nai Pan Tha and his old colleague, Nai Kyaw Aing (of the *Banya Ta Ram* Battalion). However, Nai Non Lar's was the stronger faction, enjoying the support of Nai Htin and Nai Hongsa, both of whom went on to assume senior leadership positions. With the loyalty of Nai Taw Mon and the majority of MNLA troops, the 'official' NMSP enjoyed a significant military advantage.

Following a series of fractious and inconclusive meetings in mid-March, Nai Shwe Kyin proposed a fourteen point programme, under which "the two factions (would) divide and share the revolutionary task."[149] The proposal was rejected, and fighting broke out between the two factions at the end of the month. By mid-April, Nai Non Lar's men had surrounded Nai Shwe Kyin's troops and the latter was forced to flee, with about two hundred supporters, to the small Thai border town of Sangkhlaburi, twenty Km southwest of Nam Khok. Nai Shwe Kyin was accompanied by a number of party intellectuals and *sangha* members, led by the respected monk, U Oktama. During this and subsequent periods of crisis, Nai Shwe Kyin received some support from hard-pressed southern units of the CPB, of which his wife had been a member. Such contacts reinforced perceptions of Nai Shwe Kyin's communist sympathies.

Nai Non Lar's supporters soon began accusing the previous leadership of treachery and corruption – an accusation that was strongly denied, with Nai Shwe Kyin defending himself thus: "Over the thirty-three years of violent political struggle there had been no shortcoming whatsoever that could be pointed out against him. He had always given straightforward, correct and able leadership to the Mon freedom movement. That is why he is regarded with awe by the enemy."[150] Further armed clashes broke out between the two factions in June 1981. Nai Shwe Kyin vowed revenge against Nai Non Lar's group, calling for "Victory to the genuine Mon national freedom movement!"[151]

Although this was a particularly fractious period, there were some positive developments. In 1984 Dr Chamlong Thongdee, a Thai-Mon academic, author[152] and sometime politician, launched a 'Mon National

University' (MNU) which – like the Mon Cadets' Institute of the 1950s – aimed to train a new generation of political leaders.

The MNU Charter was published (in English, Thai and Mon) on August 12th 1984.[153] A 'Non-Campus University in Exile for Mons', the MNU was sponsored by Nai Shwe Kyin's faction of the NMSP and the Bangkok-based Mon Youth Community (MYC), of which Dr Chamlong was an ex-chairman. The MNU Board of Advisors, chaired by the scholar, Nai Pan Hla, featured a number of prominent Thai-Mon figures, including Lt-General Tiab Suriyasak, retired commander of the Royal Thai Third Army, and several businessmen and other "Mon National Patriots."[154] With faculty members drawn from colleges and universities in Thailand and overseas, the MNU designed distance-learning bachelor's degree courses in Political Science, International Relations, Liberal Arts and Education; a post-graduate programme was also proposed.[155] In practice however, the actual number of students enrolled was quite small, and within a few years the MNU was largely moribund.[156] Nevertheless, it did organise several political and cultural seminars in Thailand, and publish some NMSP historical documents.[157]

Ethnic Allies, Political Allies

By the 1980s, Three Pagodas Pass and the other trade gates had become foci of a new phase in the civil war. The first serious *Tatmadaw* push against insurgent positions near the pass occurred in 1977. Another, more sustained, campaign was launched during the 1980 dry season, but was repelled by the well-armed defending forces.[158] By the mid-1980s, *Tatmadaw* offensives against the pass had become an annual affair and a major 1984 attack led to the first major exoduses into Thailand of NMSP-affiliated refugees.[159] Desmond Ball mentions a period of successful MNLA-KNLA military co-operation, during a December 1986 Burma Army offensive against positions near the pass.[160] However, when the *Tatmadaw* attacked again the following year, a number of insurgent positions were overrun.

Through the mid-1980s, while Nai Non Lar's men were based around Three Pagodas Pass, Nai Shwe Kyin's smaller group took shelter in nearby Sangkhlaburi. With only a limited KNLA presence in the area, one consequence of the Mon factional fighting was an increase in banditry and general lawlessness in the vicinity of the pass.

Although Nai Shwe Kyin received some support from Colonel Shwe Saing's KNLA Sixth Brigade in the mid-1980s,[161] in general – and despite his long-standing relationship with the Karen nationalist movement – Nai Shwe Kyin's faction was less favoured by the KNU than Nai Non Lar's. General Bo Mya was suspicious of the former's communist sympathies and had not forgotten that the 1970 NMSP-KNU-PDP pact had been brokered between Nai Shwe Kyin and Mahn Ba Zan, leader of the leftist Karen nationalists and at the time a serious rival to Bo Mya's leadership of the KNU.

On 10th June 1982 Nai No Lar's 'official' NMSP became the eleventh member of National Democratic Front (NDF), a KNU-sponsored ethnic alliance established at Mannerplaw in 1976.[162] The NMSP was represented on the NDF by Nai Hongsa, who later became a secretary of the front. According to Nai Shwe Kyin, prior to the Mon split the party had resisted joining the NDF – firstly, because it was dominated by the KNU; secondly, because of its anti-communist rhetoric; and thirdly, because the alliance's 'ethnic groups only' policy was considered misguided. Nai Shwe Kyin wanted to forge a coalition with elements of the Burman opposition[163] (presumably, including the CPB) – a goal that was to be partially achieved in the late 1980s and early '90s.

Like its predecessors – the DNUF, NDUF and NULF – the NDF was at first a more impressive proposition on paper than on the ground. Within a few years though, the new alliance had begun to make progress in both the political and military spheres. In 1983 the KIO re-joined the front, following the breakdown of peace talks with the BSPP (see below), and in a major policy shift the following year the NDF changed its position from one of principled secessionism (i.e. the advocacy of outright independence from Rangoon) to a demand for substantial autonomy within a proposed Federal Union of Burma. This was an important change in emphasis: Ne Win and the *Tatmadaw* had always accused the insurgents of scheming to wreck the union. Now though, the ethnic nationalists were aiming at a democratic, federal transformation *of* the union, rather than a total repudiation of the state of Burma.

It is not clear to what extent the Mon and other NDF leaders viewed the federal issue as merely politically expedient. It seems probable that the new policy was in part devised in accordance with what the outside world was perceived as wanting to hear. Certainly, the adoption of a federal platform meant the ethnic insurgents were well-positioned to make common cause with the wave of predominantly ethnic Burman, urban-based political activists that arrived at the border in the late 1980s (see below).

One outcome of a common policy and strategy among the non-communist ethnic insurgent groups was an increase in military co-operation on the ground. By the mid-1980s, NDF battalions were active in several areas adjacent to the main KNU strongholds, and a joint Karen-Mon-Rakhine column was established in the NDF Southern Command area.[164] For a period in the mid-1980s, it even seemed that an effective alliance might be struck between the NDF and the still-powerful CPB, with its extensive liberated zones in Shan State and along the Chinese border. Although a CPB-NDF military pact was brokered by the KIO in 1986, this potentially significant left-right coalition, under which the communists for the first time acknowledged some of the ethnic nationalists' political demands, was subsequently vetoed by General Bo Mya.[165] In many respects, the situation in Burma had changed little since the early 1970s. Between 1988–90 however, the Burmese political scene was to undergo a major upheaval.

CHAPTER NINE

Burma and the Mon –
1987–1990

The re-unification of the NMSP was finally achieved in late 1987. Unfortunately, one consequence of this development was an increase in tensions between the party and its erstwhile senior partner in insurgency, the KNU. Mon-Karen relations deteriorated rapidly in 1988 and by the middle of the year the NMSP and KNU found themselves engaged in a viscous armed conflict over control of the lucrative Three Pagodas Pass trade routes.

The dispute dragged on for nearly a month, by which time it had been overshadowed by a huge groundswell of dissent against the BSPP regime 'inside' Burma. The 1988 'democracy uprising', its brutal suppression by the *Tatmadaw* and the subsequent rise of the State Law and Order Restoration Council (SLORC) marked a watershed in Burmese history. Although Burma-watchers continued to see the hand of Ne Win behind events, in 1988 a younger generation of military leaders came to power. Over the next ten years, they brought large areas of Burma under government control, many of which had never previously been subject to Rangoon.

The momentous events of 1988 had important consequences for the sometimes feuding communist and ethnic rebel groups, which had been engaged for forty years in a 'low intensity' conflict with Rangoon. Although during these long years the Thai press had run occasional stories on the fighting, and the Burmese military government kept up a steady barrage of propaganda, it was only after 1988 that the 'forgotten war' in Burma began to attract serious attention in the international media. Although by this time the insurgents no longer posed the threat to state security they once had, the flight to the border areas in the late 1980s of some ten thousand students, and other pro-democracy activists, rejuvenated the opposition in the liberated zones.

The formation in late 1988 of a new Democratic Alliance of Burma (DAB) seemed to herald a new era in relations between the 'ethnic' and 'political' opposition, recalling the hey-day of the NULF (PDP-NMSP-KNU) alliance. The following year however, a series of mutinies broke out among rank-and-file troops of the CPB. By the end of the decade, five new ex-communist groups had emerged in northern Burma and, to the surprise and alarm of the allies at Mannerplaw, had agreed ceasefires with Rangoon. The *Tatmadaw* could now concentrate its fire on the Karen, Karenni, Mon and student allies along the Thailand-Burma border.

In February 1990 government forces succeeded in overrunning the insurgent stronghold at Three Pagodas Pass and capturing the nearby NMSP headquarters. Then, in May 1990, the SLORC surprised both domestic and international observers by overseeing a relatively free and fair general election. The newly-formed National League for Democracy (NLD), led by Daw Aung San Suu Kyi, emerged clear winners, while candidates of the Mon National Democratic Front (MNDF) and other ethnic-based parties were returned in a number of constituencies. However, the regime soon returned to form, refusing to recognise the election results and moving to suppress those parties which had won the 1990 poll.

1987–1998: Mon-Karen Tension at the Pass

On several occasions during the mid-1980s, the NDF leadership at Mannerplaw had attempted to mediate between the two NMSP factions. Finally, after a series of talks beginning in April 1987, which were facilitated by Saw Maw Reh of the Karenni National Progressive Party (KNPP), on 9th December 1987 the NMSP was re-united, with Nai Shwe Kyin as President and Nai Non Lar as Vice-President, and Nai Htin (of the Nai Non Lar camp) as General Secretary. By now, the ideological heat of the early-1980s had largely dissipated, and although the party continued to be prone to factionalism, by the end of the decade the Mon insurgent forces were probably stronger and more unified than at any time since 1958. Once the leadership put its differences aside, large numbers of activists and soldiers re-joined the insurgency. In 1988 MNLA troop strength was reported at an impressive 3–4,000 men,[166] up from 1,500 or so at the time of re-unification. These figures included local NMSP militia, as well as MNLA regulars. In comparison, in the late 1980s the Karen insurgent forces numbered nearly 8,000 men, including KNDO militiamen. (KNLA Sixth Brigade in 1988 consisted of about 1,200 troops, of whom less than 500 were stationed in the vicinity of Three Pagodas Pass.)

In the late 1980s Nai Shwe Kyin began to travel overseas regularly on behalf of the NMSP and its allies. There was a new spirit of co-operation in the air. As noted above, at the outset of the civil war in 1948 the Mon and Karen leadership had endorsed a four point agreement stating the need for "common purpose". A July 1953 addendum to this document had committed the KNU and MPF to a policy of mutual aid and recognised the right to self-determination, whilst proposing to solve Mon-Karen disputes through democratic means.[167] This last point was essential: the Mon nationalists aimed to liberate the Tenasserim, Pegu and Irrawaddy Delta Divisions (the territory of ancient Hongsawaddy). Meanwhile, the Karen nationalists regarded most of the Tenasserim and Irrawaddy Divisions as their own, together with portions of Pegu Division and all of Karen State.[168] Unless they could negotiate a compromise, the Mon and Karen allies were in danger of again becoming embroiled in territorial disputes.

There are many (mostly Pwo) Karen villages in Mon State, and at least one KNU map from the 1970s shows the KNLA's Tenth Battalion and Sixth Brigade converging in the vicinity of Ye town, right in the heart of Monland (which is not marked on the map). On the other hand, the Mon nationalists have claimed territory and been active militarily around Kya-In Seik-Kyi, Thanbyuzayat and other parts of KNLA Sixth Brigade, as well as behind Thaton, in KNLA First Brigade, and in northern and central Tenasserim Division (KNLA Tenth Battalion, and from the late 1980s, Fourth Brigade).

Clearly, any settlement of the 'ethnic question' in Burma must take account of such overlapping populations, and the competing claims of different groups for self-determination. Demands for autonomy have been suppressed by the *Tatmadaw* and military government, on the grounds that such developments would constitute an unacceptable division of the union (along the lines of the former Yugoslavia). Since the 1980s, the ethnic nationalist opposition has developed a policy of democratic federalism. However, the path to mutual understanding and compromise has not always run smoothly.

1988: the Democracy Uprising and the Mon-Karen 'Civil War'

By 1988, business at the pass was booming. Although the NMSP had been collecting some limited taxes in the area since the early 1970s, the newly-confidant Mon leadership questioned why the bulk of tax revenue should still go to the KNU. With a large civilian population, and some six-to-eight hundred troops in the area, and with their Thai arms and contacts, the Mon insurgents felt they should be allowed to establish more 'trade gates' along the route into Burma. While the NMSP leadership felt belittled, KNU cadres were angered by the increasingly strident demands of the 'pushy' Mon, who not so long ago had been able to operate only with Karen patronage and assistance.

Since the early 1980s, there had been a number of incidents involving Mon and Karen forces abusing villagers from the other community in the vicinity of the pass. On several occasions, Mon troops had ambushed convoys given safe passage by the KNU, or set up rogue checkpoints along the routes between Three Pagodas Pass and Ye or Thanbyuzayat. When the KNU complained about such activities, the Mon had the perfect excuse: each of the two NMSP factions blamed the other. In particular, Nai Shwe Kyin's troops, under the command of Nai Pan Tha, gained a reputation for unruly behaviour and the sometimes arbitrary taxation of villagers. On at least one occasion, the KNLA retaliated, attacking and partially destroying a Mon village near the pass.

The KNU and NDF leaders at Mannerplaw were not particularly worried by such local conflicts, which tended to flare up from time-to-time between different alliance members. By the late 1980s, the NDF had achieved recognition as a more effective coalition than its predecessors, and the ethnic opposition seemed to offer a plausible alternative to Ne Win's chauvinist, one party state

Meanwhile in Rangoon, events were coming to a head. After a massive currency devaluation in September 1987, and months of political discontent and protest, in July 1988 Ne Win resigned. The urban population took encouragement, and to the streets. Monks, students and hundreds of thousands of ordinary citizens rose up against one of the most oppressive regimes in Asia. At first, it seemed that 'people's power' might succeed in overthrowing the tyrants. However on 18th September, after an initially confused response, the military acted with brutal efficiency. At least three thousand protesters were massacred by troops loyal to the new State Law and Order Restoration Council (SLORC), which seized power under the leadership of *Tatmadaw* Commander-in-Chief, General Saw Maung.

This was the beginning of a new era in Burmese history. The events of August and September 1988 defined a political generation and the repercussions of the great democracy uprising are felt to this day. For several weeks, the government was in even more disarray than in the late 1940s.

When a number of front-line *Tatmadaw* units were withdrawn to Rangoon, the insurgents were presented with new political and military opportunities. Unfortunately, at a time when international attention was at last drawn to Burma, two of the country's most important ethnic insurgent groups were focused on a petty local dispute – hardly a good advertisement for opposition unity or the federal idea.

The simmering Mon-Karen conflict came to a head in late June 1988, with a series of clashes between MNLA and KNLA units in Ye and Kya-In Seik-Kyi townships. An NDF 'Commission of Enquiry' was established to look into these incidents, which by mid-July had begun to escalate in seriousness, following a KNU attack on an NMSP trade gate near Kyaikmaraw.[169]

At dawn on 23rd July 1988 – the day General Ne Win resigned as BSPP Chairman in Rangoon – serious fighting erupted at Three Pagodas Pass. According to the NMSP, Karen troops were the aggressors, attacking Mon positions around the pass on the eve of scheduled peace talks.[170] Karen

143

sources counter that the Mon had had no intention of negotiating in good faith, and were themselves on the point of launching an attack. What particularly irked the Karen was that, having taken shelter with the KNU in the 1960s, the "NMSP took advantage of the situation by setting up its own administration, exploiting natural resources, levying taxes and re-settling the Mon population in KNU territory."[171]

The dispute dragged on for twenty-seven days, coinciding with the first four weeks of the uprising in Rangoon. Although fighting was largely restricted to the vicinity of the pass, skirmishes also broke out along the Ye River. The two monasteries at Three Pagodas Pass were both destroyed by shelling and at least fifty MNLA, and between thirty and one hundred KNLA troops, were killed[172] – as were scores of non-combatants.

When the fighting started, the civilian population of some 6,000 people dispersed. The handful of Thai residents fled to nearby Sangkhlaburi; the Karen went north, to the Megatha River, and the Mon south to NMSP HQ at Nam Khok, and the nearby settlements at Paluang Japan (in Burma) and Songk'lier (in Thailand). The battle reinforced previously held animosities. Worst effected were those with a foot in both camps, such as the Bengali-Muslim community. While Mon-Muslim relations had never been particularly warm, there were long-standing Muslim communities in KNLA Fourth and Sixth Brigades, where soldiers of the All Burma Muslim Union (ABMU) operated under KNLA tactical command. It was therefore natural for the Muslims to side with the Karen and flee to KNU-controlled territory for the duration of the battle. To this day, there are those among the Mon community in Sangkhlaburi and Three Pagodas Pass who resent this perceived 'treachery'. Of course, as well as relations with the Muslim community, Mon-Karen relations were also damaged by the conflict. Particularly shocking was the case of a Mon man murdered (by local Mons) because of his marriage to a Karen woman, who had worked with and for both ethnic groups at the pass (and has continued to do so since). The NMSP later formally apologised to his widow for this act of 'ethnic cleansing'.

The Mon-Karen 'Civil War' was far from inevitable, and did not result in conclusive victory for either side. The NDF leadership was appalled by the outbreak of internecine battle at such a sensitive time, and Saw Maw Reh of the KNPP and NDF was again dispatched to mediate a reconciliation. When the fighting eventually stopped, it was agreed that tax revenues from the pass would be split fifty-fifty, under a new NMSP-KNU 'Joint Administration'.

1988–1989: Allies Old and New

In the aftermath of the 1988 democracy uprising, some ten thousand students and other activists fled to the relative sanctuary of the rebel-held liberated zones along the borders with China and Thailand. Here, despite the often hostile attitudes of the Thai and Chinese authorities, they attempted to re-group. Inspired by the independence movement of the 1930s and the example of Aung San's 'Thirty Comrades', this new generation of student activists were determined to overthrow the oppressive government in Rangoon.

On 5th November 1988 the All Burma Students Democratic Front (ABSDF) was established at the KNU's Kaw Moo Rah stronghold. Although substantial numbers remained outside the ABSDF, the front (though notoriously faction-ridden) was from the outset the most influential and widely-recognised students' organisation. Later in November, the ABSDF and a dozen other new opposition groups joined with the NDF to form a new anti-Rangoon coalition – the Democratic Alliance of Burma (DAB).[173] The first DAB Chairman was KNU boss General Bo Mya, whose Mannerplaw headquarters was home to the alliance secretariat; Nai Shwe Kyin and the KIO leader, Brang Seng, were founder-Vice-Chairmen.

In opposition circles, the formation of the DAB was regarded as a highly significant development. For the first time, large numbers of urban, predominantly ethnic Burman political activists had accepted ethnic nationalist leadership. However, despite the fairly extensive coverage accorded the DAB in the foreign media, and the self-congratulation its foundation occasioned at Mannerplaw, the alliance's impact on the political scene beyond the Thailand-Burma border regions was minimal. At the time though, optimists viewed the formation of the DAB as a political breakthrough.

As had those fleeing persecution in Burma for hundreds of years, many refugees from the events of 1988 and 1990 arrived at Three Pagodas Pass. Large numbers chose to throw in their lot with the ethnic nationalists, rather than the ABSDF. According to Martin Smith, as many as 1,300 Mon activists came out to the border between 1988–90, most of them from the Moulmein area. Hundreds joined the NMSP, adding a valuable infusion of young talent to the Mon insurgency.[174] Given the tendency of Mon students to join the NMSP rather than the ABSDF, it is perhaps not surprising that the two organisations never enjoyed particularly warm relations.

Within months of the front's creation, the NMSP started to look beyond the ABSDF for allies among the Burman political class. In January 1989 a new group had been established in Mon territory south of Three Pagodas Pass. The Alliance for Democratic Solidarity, Union of Burma (ADSUB or *Da Nya Ta*) was founded by U Aung (son of ex-prime minister U Nu) and a number of PDP veterans.[175] With support from sources in the United States and the Thai military – as well as from the NMSP, KNU and KIO – the *Da Nya Ta* hatched a plot to assassinate SLORC leaders, and thereby provoke a general mutiny or counter-coup.

Although the *Da Nya Ta* managed to convince the NDF leadership of their seriousness, and to entice some Burma Army officers and U Nu era politicians to their cause, the planned uprising never occurred – in part, because the plot had been compromised by Military Intelligence *agents provocateur* within the ADSUB. The *Da Nya Ta's* NDF sponsors, many of whom had all along been wary of the group's non-federalist policies, were not impressed by this fiasco, and by the end of the following year the *Da Nya Ta* had ceased to be an important player along the border.[176]

In 1990 the ABSDF was represented at Three Pagodas Pass by Battalions 101 and 102, which together fielded between three and six hundred troops (less than half of whom were armed).[177] Other insurgent groups based near the pass included the People's Defence Force (PDF)[178] and the Democratic Patriotic Army (DPA), formed in 1989 by the mostly ethnic Tavoyan remnants of the CPB Southern Command.[179]

Among the NMSP's other associates was General Francis (or 'Mon') Yap, the Mon-speaking Koumintang (KMT) Chinese officer who had been a key advisor for many years. General Yap maintained ties with the nationalist government in Taiwan, and with remnants of the anti-communist KMT in Shan State and along the northern stretch of the Thailand-Burma border. Mon insurgent relations with the KMT, which dated from the early 1950s, were revived in the early 1980s when General Yap's relationship with the KNU began to deteriorate. General Bo Mya had received some support from Taiwan, but was wary of the KMT's drug-trafficking links. General Yap therefore began to step-up his patronage of Nai Non Lar's 'official' NMSP, and following the Mon nationalist reunification of 1987 remained close to Nai Non Lar's anti-CPB wing of the party. By 1989, when Chinese advisors conducted a well-regarded eight month military training course at Three Pagodas Pass, the KMT had once gain become a significant source of logistical support to the MNLA. The KMT also supported Nai Pagomon's National Mon Democratic Organisation (NMDO – see below), as well as the ADSUB.[180]

The NMSP-KMT bond was weakened by a sad and dramatic incident that occurred early on 8th August 1989, at the Three Pagodas Pass parade ground. Whilst making a speech commemorating the first anniversary of the democracy uprising, Nai Non Lar suffered a heart attack, and was soon afterwards pronounced dead. As well as being a shock to the ethnic nationalist community, the demise of the popular NMSP Vice-Chairman was a great blow to the students, to whom he had been something of a mentor.

Despite his loss of influence following Nai Non Lar's death, the wily General Yap continued to court various NMSP leaders from his base in Bangkok. Unsurprisingly, this on-going relationship led to rumours about the party's role in the narcotics business. However, despite the presence of KMT officers at Three Pagodas Pass, no evidence of the NMSP's direct involvement in the drugs trade has ever emerged.[181] Although individual

Mon commanders, including officers in the southern Mergui District, have engaged in relatively small-scale marijuana production, and consignments of heroin have occasionally been smuggled into Thailand via Three Pagodas Pass, the NMSP – like the KNU – has maintained a clear anti-drugs line. (In 1998 the party imprisoned the wife of a Moulmein District cadre who had been involved in heroin smuggling.)

1989: Communists and Post-Communists

By mid-1988, the mainstream White Flag CPB had been in rebellion for forty years. After some early victories, in the 1960s the communists' People's Army had suffered a series of defeats. Although, with support from China between 1968–78, it expanded the size of its Northeast Command along the Chinese border, by the early 1980s the party's fortunes were again in decline, Chinese assistance having been greatly reduced following the death of Mao Zedong. In 1981 Ne Win judged it timely to open ceasefire talks with the CPB and KIO, which received the bulk of its arms from China. However, these negotiations broke down, and northern Burma was plunged into a new round of fighting.

Although CPB strength was not what it had been, in 1988 the People's Army was still the largest rebel force in Burma. The dramatic and unforeseen events that befell the CPB the following year sent shock waves through the insurgent establishment and marked the beginning of the endgame in Burma's civil war.

Following years of neglect by their Burman political leaders, in March and April 1989 a series of mutinies broke out among the CPB's mainly ethnic minority troops. Most of the ageing CPB politburo fled into exile in China and four new armed groups emerged from the rump of the People's Army in northern Burma. The most powerful of these was the United Wa State Army (UWSA), the armed wing of the Myanmar National Solidarity Party (MNSP), which controlled some 15,000 mostly ethnic Wa soldiers.[182]

The new SLORC junta responded with speed and strategic elan. Emissaries of the powerful Military Intelligence chief and SLORC Secretary One, Brig-General Khin Nyunt, entered into negotiations with the new ethnic Wa, Kokang-Chinese and other ex-CPB organisations. Unlike the previous Burman leadership, the new commanders of the ex-communist groups were keen to end a forty year civil war, that had driven their peoples to the depths of poverty. Therefore in early 1989 the Myanmar National Democratic Army (MNDA), a Kokang faction of the old CPB, became the first insurgent group to agree a ceasefire with the SLORC. Soon afterwards, in May 1989, the UWSA negotiated a truce, which was formalised the following November.

In September the Shan State Progress Party (SSPP) and its Shan State Army (SSA) became the first NDF member-organisation to agree a ceasefire with Rangoon. By the end of the year, five groups had 'returned to the legal fold'. Although it was not clear for how long these hastily-arranged pacts would hold, the SLORC ceasefires were in fact to prove far more durable than those which Ne Win had attempted to broker in the early 1960s.

Having for many years attempted to suppress opium cultivation in areas under its control, by the mid-1970s the CPB had become implicated in the drugs trade.[183] Most of the 'ceasefire groups' therefore inherited interests in opium production and heroin refinery, and in the 1990s the Wa, Kokang and other groups in northern Burma were to deepen their involvement in this multi-million dollar trade, as well as branching-out into amphetamine-type stimulant production and the logging business. Meanwhile in lower Burma, the war was going badly for the DAB allies.

1990: the Fall of Three Pagodas Pass; Mon Forces in the South

Martin Smith dates the advent of Burmese-Thai military co-operation against the insurgents to 1989, when the *Tatmadaw* crossed into Thailand to attack the KNU base at Maw Po Kay and rebel positions at Three Pagodas Pass.[184] The following year, Thai-Burmese military collaboration was instrumental in dislodging the insurgents from the pass.

In the 1980s Mon and Karen leaders' family members, together with Thai businessmen, had established a number of saw-mills and furniture factories on both sides of the border near Three Pagodas Pass. Logging in the vicinity of the pass was rampant, and much of it was carried out by the Sia Hook logging company, controlled by Sangkhlaburi's principal Thai-Chinese tycoon. When *Sia* (boss) Hook began to include a number of apparently 'off-duty' Burmese soldiers in his workforce, local insurgent commanders were suspicious, but took no action. In retrospect, their trust in the Thai business and security establishment was naive.

On 30th January 1990 a *Tatmadaw* column from Ye launched a probing attack against MNLA positions west of Three Pagodas Pass. As Mon troops engaged these Burma Army regulars, *Sia* Hook secretly armed members of his work force, who promptly launched an attack against the insurgents' lightly-guarded rear positions. This betrayal by their erstwhile business partner left the Mon troops facing the enemy on two fronts, with their rear supply lines cut. The position was unsustainable and, after five days of heavy fighting, the defenders were forced to withdraw. On 9th February a *Tatmadaw* force of more than 1,000 men overran the small town. Fighting continued throughout the next day, by which time at least twenty Mon troops had been killed, with the KNLA and ABSDF also suffering casualties.[185]

Over the next few days, *Tatmadaw* reinforcements arrived by helicopter, and through Thailand.[186] On the 11th February they succeeded in taking further rebel positions, including MNLA-NMSP headquarters at Nam Khok. According to the government, twenty Burmese and forty rebel soldiers lost their lives during the offensive, as did two saw-mill workers. As a result of the operation, the *Tatmadaw* also seized substantial amounts of timber and logging equipment from the insurgents, together with assorted arms and battlefield communications gear.[187]

The civilian population fled into Thailand, some making it as far as Sangkhlaburi. Over the nest month, NMSP headquarters was moved to Ri Gah, near the new Mon refugee camp at Loh Loe, a day's walk south of the pass.[188] To the annoyance of the Thai authorities, this site was very much inside their territory.

Insurgent commanders had meanwhile been drawing-up plans to strike back at the SLORC. On 22nd March 1990 a joint MNLA-ABSDF force launched a major attack on Ye town. Unfortunately, the raid ended in their rout by the *Tatmadaw* and the loss of some forty soldiers, several of whom died under bombardment by the Burmese Airforce. A number of civilian casualties were also reported and, according to MNLA sources, some Mon soldiers who surrendered were later executed by bayonet in the grounds of Ye sports pavilion.

Exactly what went wrong is not clear. The students blamed Mon officers for warning family and friends in Ye of the imminent attack; certainly the *Tatmadaw* seems to have prepared an ambush. (Interestingly, an impending NMSP attack on Ye was prefigured in a news conference presented by Brig-General Khin Nyunt on 5th August 1989.)[189] Furthermore, nearby MNLA units are said to have failed to respond their comrades' pleas for assistance.

The Ye debacle marked the end of ABSDF-MNLA joint military operations, and further strained relations between the Mon nationalists and the students. It also damaged the reputation of the MNLA and its commanders, who between 1990–91 saw several hundred troops abandon the Mon cause. Among those most sorely missed was the veteran first commander of the MNLA, Nai Pan Tha.

Sensing that his demands for a thorough investigation of the previous month's fiasco would not be acted upon, on 30th April 1990 Nai Pan Tha resigned from the NMSP. After spending two years in the Mon villages of Ratchaburi, Nai Pan Tha contacted the Burmese embassy in Bangkok, and in April 1992 'returned to the legal fold'. Having been de-briefed by Military Intelligence, he fulfilled a long-standing vow to enter the monkhood.

The 'Ye incident' and the defection of Nai Pan Tha, coming so soon after the loss of Three Pagodas Pass, severely undermined the authority of the re-formed NMSP leadership. Mon sources have suggested that Nai Shwe Kyin and colleagues were relieved to learn of Nai Pan Tha's 1992 'surrender', removing as it did the possibility of a challenge to their leadership.

For a number of NMSP leaders, the events of 1990 seem to have confirmed the impossibility of ever defeating the SLORC on the battlefield.

With the loss of the Three Pagodas Pass trade routes, the NMSP was deprived of its largest source of income. Furthermore, it seemed only a matter of time before the party lost control of its remaining liberated zone in Karen State. Therefore, upon re-grouping after the 'Ye incident', an MNLA detachment was sent down to the Chaung Chee-Huay Pak area, deep in the badlands of Tenasserim Division (KNLA Fourth Brigade), opposite Bang Saphan in Thailand's Prachuab Kiri Kahn Province. This inaccessible region was not then controlled by any one group. However, it was periodically visited by KNLA patrols and their ABMU allies, as well as by the DPA.

Chaung Chee-Huay Pak was also home to the National Mon Democratic Organisation (NMDO), led by Nai Pagomon. Other NMDO leaders included Nai Aung Htin, who left the group after a financial dispute, and Nai Rong Soi (or Rain Chai), an ex-President of the Moulmein University Students' Union and grandson of the MPF MP, Nai Po Sein. A founder-member of the NMSP, Nai Rong Soi was jailed for four years in the 1970s, before coming out to the border to re-join the party, and later defecting to Nai Pagomon's NMDO, which had operated in the south since the early 1970s. It had built up an impressive arsenal, financed by the 'taxation' of fishing and trading vessels off the Andaman seacoast, via logging activities, and through the local cultivation and export of marijuana. Nai Pagomon had also been associated with the ubiquitous General Yap.

In the late 1980s NMDO troop strength stood at about 100 men – several of whom had vowed not to cut their hair until the day of final victory over the enemy.[190] Previously, this group had been loosely allied with the NMSP, and in 1990 Nai Pagomon was persuaded to merge his forces with the mainstream Mon insurgents. However, the new NMSP Mergui District was never fully brought under the control of 'Central' (party headquarters).

1988–1990: Legal and Illegal Opposition; Legal and Illegal Government

Whilst in the border regions new alliances were being struck – and sometimes dissolved – the political scene 'inside' Burma was also under-going radical changes. After a quarter-century of the Burmese Way to Socialism, during which independent actors on the political scene had been suppressed, the events of 1988 had seen the emergence of scores of new political parties and pressure groups, many of which sought to represent particular social or ethnic constituencies.

By May 1990, several of these organisations had been legally registered, to fight the general election. The more politically mature of the new ethnic-based parties, including the Mon National Democratic Front (MNDF), allied themselves in an important coalition – the United Nationalities

League for Democracy (UNLD), which in July 1990 adopted a specifically federalist political program.[191]

The MNDF was not an NMSP front organisation, although its members did share many of the insurgents' nationalist aspirations. The front was established on 17th October 1988, under the Chairmanship of Nai Tun Thein, with another veteran politician, Nai Ngwe Thein, as Vice-Chairman. Both men had been arrested in 1962, together with other prominent Mon leaders. Following their release, they had for twenty years kept relatively low profiles, sometimes working informally as teachers among the Mon community, where – together with the MNDF's senior ideologue, Nai Theim Maung – they enjoyed high regard.

In 1988 these contemporaries of Nai Shwe Kyin were inspired once again to press Mon demands in the national arena. In particular, both Nai Tun Thein and Nai Ngwe Thein wanted to avoid repeating the experiences of 1947, when Mon politicians had failed to be elected to the constituent assembly, and thus had little say over developments in the immediate post-independence period. The NLD – which had been established one month prior to the MNDF, by a coalition of ex-*Tatmadaw* officers, student activists and intellectuals, and was led by General Aung San's popular and charismatic daughter – was an obvious ally of the MNDF.

From the outset, MNDF leaders were key players in the alliance between the 'political' NLD and the 'ethnic' parties of the UNLD. Unlike the CPB (until its final years), the NLD seemed willing to acknowledge the validity of the ethnic nationalists' long struggle. Although this attempt by the Burman political class to co-opt the ethnic groups was not necessarily accompanied by any real understanding of their history, culture and aspirations, an incipient opposition alliance was in the making. Its emergence was a direct threat to the recently-installed SLORC regime, and such defiance was likely to be punished.

On 20th July 1989 Daw Aung San Suu Kyi was arrested, just four days after attending an important NLD-UNLD strategy meeting in Rangoon, where she held discussions with the MNDF's co-ordinator for external relations, Nai Ngwe Thein. Although this aspect of the NLD General Secretary's arrest was not much remarked upon at the time, the SLORC's move to prevent the emergence of an alliance between the NLD and the ethnic minority parties set the pattern for a series of such interventions over the next decade. Meanwhile, following the bloody and momentous events of 1988, the SLORC had promised to hold elections.

For the ethnic parties in the UNLD front, the consequences of Daw Aung San Suu Kyi's continued detention were frustrating. Some other NLD leaders were less enthusiastic than she about forging an alliance with the ethnic groups, and during the 1990 election campaign some dissatisfaction was expressed in Mon circles over the perceived arrogance of NLD candidates. The league is said to have canvassed in Mon State, without

151

properly consulting Mon community leaders, thus causing a potential split in the anti-SLORC vote. However, a few months after the election, in a move which reassured the ethnic minority parties, the NLD and UNLD met in Rangoon, and on 29th August issued the 'Bo Aung Kyaw Street Declaration', calling for the convening of a National Consultative Assembly, to establish the principles of a new Union constitution, which would recognise the rights of all Burma's ethnic nationalities.

Although the voice of the people had been heard in May 1990, it was not acted upon. Contrary to most expectations, the 27th May general election constituted the first free and fair poll in Burma since the 1950s. The NLD won 392 of the 485 seats contested, despite the fact that Daw Aung San Suu Kyi remained under house arrest and was unable to stand for parliament.[192] Altogether, sixty-seven 'ethnic' candidates were elected, including representatives of seventeen UNLD parties, plus the allied Shan Nationalities League for Democracy (SNLD), with twenty-three seats. The MNDF emerged as the fifth largest party in the '1990 parliament', with five of its nineteen candidates being elected: Chairman Nai Tun Thein (Thanbyuzayat, constituency number two), General Secretary Dr Min Soe Lin (Ye, constituency number one), Joint General Secretary Dr Kyi Win (Mudon, constituency number two), Central Executive Committee member Nai Khin Maung (Kyaikmaraw, constituency number two), and Central Executive Committee member Nai Thaung Shein[193] (Kawkareik, constituency number two – in Karen State).[194]

The euphoria generated by the opposition's landslide victory was short-lived: the SLORC refused to recognise the overwhelming NLD victory and the '1990 parliament' was never allowed to convene. A little less than two years later, on 2nd March 1992, the MNDF was outlawed, in part because of the leading role it had played in marshalling pressure on the government to hand over power to the legitimate representatives of the people. Nai Tun Thein and Nai Ngwe Thein were both jailed, and not released until 1994, when ceasefire negotiations between the SLORC and the NMSP were well underway.[195] Meanwhile in the Burmese countryside, the civil war had entered its fifth decade.

CHAPTER TEN

Sangkhlaburi and Three Pagodas Pass – Karen, Mon and Thai

Three hundred and forty Km northwest of Bangkok, and two hundred Km north of the hot and dry provincial capital at Kanchanaburi, Sangkhlaburi is an outpost of Thailand. It still has the feel of a Wild West town.

Although it has seen a good deal of logging activity over the years, Sangkhla remains one of the most heavily forested districts in Thailand. Until the mid-1980s, the little town was still inaccessible by road during the height of the rainy season, when it was necessary to take a boat up-river from Thong Pah Pohm, 75 Km to the south. Sangkhla was only moved to its present location in 1984, when the old settlement and the river valley it had occupied were flooded by the Electricity Generating Authority of Thailand (EGAT) to create the Kao Laem reservoir. More than twenty Karen villages were relocated.[196] It is ironic that one of the great charms of beautiful, sleepy Sangkhla is based on the wholesale destruction of natural habitat. In fact, a number of ethnic, political and economic tensions lie just below the placid surface of the town.

Sangkhlaburi – complete with primary school, local hospital and government buildings – was re-built on a fork of high ground, overlooking what was once the confluence of three tributaries of the Kwae River (Noi): the Songk'lier, Grung Gan and Grung Htee Rivers, which now flow directly into the reservoir. In the early 1980s, in anticipation of the flooding that the dam would cause, the Royal Forestry Department granted licenses to log the effected area. There was some miscalculation involved, and many more, very valuable, trees were cut down than would have been sufficient to clear the affected area. At the same time, not all of the trees actually *in* the new lake were felled. Throughout much of the reservoir, the ghostly hulks of dead trees still loom above the surface of the water, while a range of bare hills undulates north from Sangkhlaburi to the border at Three Pagodas Pass.[197]

The hour-long drive up from Thong Pah Pohm to Sangkhlaburi is, nevertheless, stunning. The road follows the eastern edge of the reservoir,

153

opposite the still heavily-forested Kao Daeng hills, one of the least-explored stretches of the border. The best time to make the trip is at sunset, when the spectacular effect of sunlight on water as revealed by each twist in the road. The steep and twisting drive, hugging the lakeside, can be treacherous: every rainy season, the hillside slides back down onto the road that runs through it. In the 1990s Sangkhla became a popular destination among weekenders from Bangkok; over the years, scores of people have lost their lives, overestimating the speed at which it is safe to take the hairpin bends.

During the dry season, like much of Thailand, Sangkhla suffers from its share of bush and forest fires; in the rainy season though, it might be the greenest town in the kingdom. To the north and east, the town abuts the Thung Yai Naresuan Wildlife Reserve, one of Thailand' three UNESCO World Heritage Sites. Together with the adjacent Um-Phang and Kao Laem National Parks, Thung Yai constitutes the largest intact forest in mainland Southeast Asia.

Sangkhlaburi and 'Mon Side'

Sangkhla proper – 'Thai side' – is where the Thai and Karen populations live. Here are the middle school, the covered market and the *Amphur* (District) office. Five minutes walk across the longest wooden bridge in Thailand is Wangka, or 'Mon side'. Although, since the 1988 'civil war', Mon-Karen relations have improved, it is still rare to see a lone Karen in Wangka, particularly after dark.

Dominating the western skyline is the golden pagoda of Wat Wangka Wiwaikarm, which bears the town's original, Mon name.[198] Although the sixty foot tall, gold-painted *chedi* is only fifteen years old, the architectural style is borrowed from the classical Indian model of Bodhgaya, site of the Buddha's enlightenment, and prototype of several important Theravadin pagoda complexes (including Dhammaceti's fifteenth century Pegu[199]). The reverend abbot – and Sangkhlaburi's most famous person – *Loong Phoor* Oktama, is known for his close relations with the Thai royal family, and for his longevity, piety and longstanding connection to the Mon nationalist movement (he accompanied Nai Shwe Kyin on his flight from Three Pagodas Pass in 1981).

The *Loong Phoor* offers patronage and some protection to the estimated five thousand Mon people living in and around the temple compound, many of whose children attend the junior high school on 'Mon side'. His birthday celebrations, at the beginning of March, constitute a major festival, which draws Thai, Chinese and Mon visitors to Sangkhlaburi from Bangkok and beyond.[200] The abbot's standing has enabled him to construct a magnificent temple complex, the role of which within the Mon community bears some comparison with that of Wat Tham Krabok among the Hmong refugees of Saraburi Province, in northeast Thailand.[201] Wat Wanka may also be compared with the Thamanya monastery near Pa'an, where – like U Oktama, but on a larger scale – U Vinaya, the Thamanya *Sayadaw*, distributes food to displaced victims of the troubles in Burma.

The crumbling roof of the old Wangka monastery can be seen protruding from the lake, not far from the foot of the new *chedi*. Nestling between the old temple and its spectacular successor, at the foot of the western embankment, are dozens of floating bamboo and leaf-thatch houses, home to the town's underclass – including scores of exiled Burmese activists. 'Long-tail' boats and dug-out canoes ply to and fro, and in the late afternoon, hundreds of people (and in the rainy season, many millions of mosquitoes) come down to the water's edge to bathe.

Amphur Sangkhlaburi

The present border is forty Km west and twenty Km north of Sangkhlaburi. There are no ethnic Thai settlements for many miles in either direction.

The three thousand-strong Thai population of Sangkhlaburi is the only community with full citizenship. In the 1970s and '80s a number of Thai-Chinese merchants were attracted to the town by the cross-border trade, and several Kanchanaburi families established a Sangkhlaburi branch. Today, the majority of Thais are engaged either as state employees (teachers, hospital personnel, local government officials, policemen, soldiers or spies), or in business (small manufacturers, traders, loggers or smugglers).

The area's earliest inhabitants are the Pwo Karen and the Mon, both of whom came to the area from 'Burma', centuries ago. Old Sangkhlaburi may have been settled by the Mon as early as the thirteenth century, or even during the Dvaravati period. In the eighteenth century the area was subject to the exiled princes of Hongsawaddy, who settled further to the south and whose forces patrolled the inaccessible border regions and passes on behalf of Ayuthaiya.[202] However, local administration mostly devolved to Karen chieftains.

Ronald Renard describes how, in the late eighteenth and early nineteenth centuries, local Karen leaders, having been recognised by Siam and enlisted in the *Krom Atamart* intelligence and security division, "attempted to control Karens throughout the Three Pagodas area, including those on the Burmese side"[203] (at that time, the frontier would have been a elastic zone of intrigue). Following the British conquest of Burma, the minorities' security role grew in importance. Siam feared the British presence in the west and made efforts to police and be seen to govern the inaccessible border regions. The Pwo Karen princelings of Sernepong[204] and Si Sawat[205] were enrolled as district chiefs under the traditional tributary system of rule, and enjoyed considerable local power.

However, in the late nineteenth century Siam's semi-autonomous outlying districts were integrated into the centralising *Thesaphiban* system of provincial administration. During the same period, the tax system was also modernised, with unfortunate consequences for the Karen, who had previously paid their tribute to Bangkok in kind (in high quality woven cloth, and silver and the jungle products for which they were famed). When this arrangement was superseded by a cash system, the Karen found themselves further marginalised,[206] although their role as border guards and 'buffer' population was to continue into the late twentieth century.

Today, the Karen population of *Amphur* Sangkhlaburi lives mostly in the outlying villages, whilst the Mon stick to the west side of the lake. Although not officially recognised as such, the majority of Mon in Sangkhla are refugees from Burma; many have relatives across the border in Mon State – in the refugee-resettlement camps, or in the revolution. The Wangka Mon tend to be merchants or small businessmen, to hire themselves as day labourers to Thai or 'Thai Mon' employers, or earn their living fishing on the lake. The Mon quarter also has something of a reputation for gangsterism and in recent years has suffered from an influx of cheap heroin and amphetamines, which have reached the town via Bangkok and Three Pagodas Pass.

Such criminal activity is enthusiastically regulated by the notorious Sangkhlaburi police, as is the labour racket.[207] The town's brothels, restaurants and shops all employ Burmese workers and Sangkhla is a major transit point into the kingdom for migrants seeking opportunities in the Thai economy. Whether these people are 'refugees' or 'economic migrants' – or some combination thereof – is a moot point.

Few Mon in Kanchanaburi, or the other border provinces, have full Thai identity papers, although several thousand people who fled to Thailand from Burma before 1976 were issued with 'pink cards', allowing them to stay indefinitely. Even second or third generation immigrants often only have a very circumscribed status in the kingdom, whilst most of the indigenous Karen have only *baat chao kao* 'hilltribe' cards (a kind of second class Thai citizenship).[208]

A small and lively Bengali Muslim community is centred around the market and the nearby Mosque. Other ethnic groups in town include Tavoyans, Rakhines and ethnic Burmans, including a large community of exiled political dissidents, most of whom fled Burma between 1988–90, and must constantly pay off the police – and play-off various Thai intelligence agencies – in order to survive.

Probably the smallest, but most visible, ethnic group in Sangkhlaburi are the *farang*. In the 1990s Sangkhla became a popular destination for the more adventurous Western tourists – or 'travellers' – who usually stayed at one of the town's two excellent guest houses. The resident Westerners fell into two related sub-groups: relief workers and missionaries.

156

The Sangkhlaburi Christian Mission was established by the Baptists in 1960. Among its founders was the Karen elder and former KNU leader, Saw Tha Din, who had been a top nationalist leader in the 1940s, including during the liberation of Moulmein in August 1948. In 1965 a mission school and the Kwai River Christian Hospital (KRCH) were opened; both still provide an outstanding service to the local community, Christian and Buddhist alike.

In the mid-1970s the missionaries had some success evangelising among the Mon, a handful of whom were converted from Buddhism, and in the mid-80s the mission was active amongst the displaced Mon of Songk'lier, near Three Pagodas Pass.[209] When Sangkhlaburi was moved to its present location in 1984, the mission was relocated to Huay M'lai, 15 Km west of *Baan Mai*. In the 1990s the KRCH came to play an important role as the main referral hospital for the refugee camps in the area. The number of expatriate missionaries during this period was usually around four or five, including visiting interns – approximately equal to the number of aid workers in Sangkhlaburi.[210]

The Death Railway, the Three Pagodas and 'the Good Old Days'

As well as to the forest and the lake, Sangkhlaburi attracts visitors to the infamous 'death railway', built under the Japanese Army between 1942–43. The track ran from Kanchanaburi, on the banks of the Kwae River, north-northwest via Three Pagodas Pass, to Thanbyuzayat in Mon State. The appalling conditions associated with forced labour on construction of the nearly 200 Km route caused the deaths of some 16,000 allied prisoners of war, and at least 100,000 Thais, Malays, Indonesians, Indians and Burmese of various extraction.

In Burmese, *Thanbyuzayat* means 'tin-roofed shelter for travellers'. Before the international market collapsed, the area was a major tin mining centre, and a tin-roofed *zyat* still stands at the town crossroads. The road south passes the impeccably maintained war cemetery, where many victims of the 'death railway' are buried. A mile to the east are the remains of the old railway tracks, and a small pagoda dedicated by Japanese veterans to their war dead. A nearby memorial depicts two men working on the railway under guard of a Japanese soldier – under conditions which, in a dark irony of Burmese history, resemble the modern *Tatmadaw's* use of forced labour on the nearby Ye-Tavoy railway.[211]

There is an isolated cavern at the lake's edge, twenty Km south of Sangkhlaburi, where Japanese guards are said to have executed prisoners of war. Legends abound – of ghosts, and of war booty stashed hastily in the thick jungle and mountain caves along the route of the Japanese Army's retreat from Burma at the end of the Second World War. In recent years, more than one adventurer has met his end searching the caves for the cursed Japanese gold,[212] mostly looted from lower Burma, and thus including a part of the Mon heritage.

The Burmese insurgents have not been immune to this 'gold fever'. In the middle of the 1995 rainy season – not long after the Mon ceasefire – the KNLA launched a mortar attack on the *Tatmadaw* garrison at Three Pagodas Pass. Civilians fled across the border into Thailand and the Royal Thai First Army (Ninth Division) promptly sealed the one access road, forcing the refugees to repatriate the same day. However, what most attracted comment in the Sangkhla market was why the Karen had fired-off such a lot of expensive ammunition, to so little effect. Some said that the KNU was sending notice to the NMSP, not to attempt any move into the area, following their 'return to the legal fold'. Others swore that it was all to do with Japanese war gold: the very heavy rains that August had caused a huge mud-slide, uncovering a hitherto buried locomotive – together with a carriage full of gold ingots. The KNLA had got word of this and had determined to liberate the booty before the *Tatmadaw* could organise evacuation of the treasure! Alas, they were unsuccessful, and the fate of the gold remains unknown.

The pass has always attracted the desperate and/or adventurous. It has been an important crossing-point between Thailand and Burma since before either the Thai or Burman peoples settled in these countries – a route taken by migrants, invaders and traders, travelling in both directions. The placing of small pagodas was a common border demarcation device, and these three have stood in the vicinity of the pass since at least the early sixteenth century.[213] Their present position was agreed between 1865–67, by British-Siamese border commissions.[214] According to local tradition, the nearby Songk'lier (or *Songkolah*) village, and the river of that name which runs out of Tung Yai forest and through the settlement to the lake, were used as a camping place by the *kolah* (i.e. British) survey party.

The three pagodas themselves are less inspiring than their romantic connotations suggest: the three stumpy, whitewashed rock and plaster *chedi*, each about one-and-a-half meters tall, stand in the middle of a patch of grass, which serves as a traffic island. On either side of the pagodas are a tourist bazaar, where until recently you could buy souvenir paperweights, made of iron spikes from the 'death railway'. Beyond the bazaar is the border checkpoint, from where the road goes through to Thanbyuzayat, and beyond to Moulmein and Rangoon.

The remains of the old railway embankment are still clearly visible just across the border, two Km south of the pass, at Palaung Japan ('Japanese Well'). The small Mon village, which once served as the civilian counterpart to the NMSP headquarters at Nam Khok, is home to a large, concrete Japanese Second World War well, which is still used as a water-source. At the pass itself, the 'death railway' crosses the border into Burma just a few meters from the three pagodas. A Burmese and English language signpost at the nearby checkpoint states that *Phya Thonsu* (Three Pagodas) was "founded by the *Tatmadaw* and the Burmese people in 1990." It goes on to exhort readers to "love the motherland" and "respect the law."

Beyond the small garrison town at the pass lie a series of rivers and steep hills running into Burma. What strikes the visitor immediately are the jagged limestone outcrops, some several hundred feet tall, that dominate the skyline to the north and east. These distinctive feature of the local geology often serve as customary border markers.

These days, the approach to the pass from Sangkhlaburi is a lot less spectacular than it once was. Unless, like the British surveyors, one stops off along the way to bathe in the Songk'lier, it is not a particularly interesting drive. However, until the early 1990s, the road to the pass was little more than a rough logging track through thick jungle, where there was always the danger of attack by bandits, tigers or mosquitoes. However, the Thai authorities were anxious to stake their claim to the strategically important pass, the only easily accessible crossing point between Thailand and Burma for hundreds of kilometres to the north or south. Therefore, in the late 1980s, the trees were cut down, a new road was built and soon the rebel base across the border had fallen to the *Tatmadaw*. Such is progress.

Today a smooth asphalt road runs north from Sangkhlaburi, before twice curving sharply, then dropping down into a little spit of land sticking out into Burma. By cartalogical freak, this is at present part of Thailand. However, Burma also has territorial claims over the slither of territory, and the two governments and armies use different maps of the area. However, until 1990 the presence of insurgent forces in the un-demarcated border areas separating the Royal Thai and Burma Armies prevented these territorial disagreements turning nasty. While the KNU and NMSP controlled the border, its position was more likely to be set during informal discussions between Mon and Karen insurgent officers and their Thai counterparts, than between the *Tatmadaw* and the Royal Thai Army, or their respective governments.

In the 1960s and '70s the Mon insurgents developed a particularly close relationship with the Thai Border Patrol Police (the modern incarnation of the *Krom Atamart*). Acting on their behalf, the NMSP collected intelligence on *Tatmadaw* movements and depositions, and policed the border. In return, the Mon insurgents received weapons and ammunition and were allowed to establish bases and carry out business on the Thai side of the border. Until as recently as the mid-1980s, it was not unusual to see uniformed MNLA guerrillas around Sangkhlaburi: Nai Shwe Kyin's faction of the NMSP was based on 'Mon side', and upon re-unification the party continued to maintain a presence in the town.

Reciprocally, Thai military personnel have also been frequent visitors to the nearby liberated zones of Burma. Martin Smith recalls an encounter, in the mid-1980s, with a visiting group of Thai soldiers, which rolled across the border at Three Pagodas Pass atop an armoured personnel carrier. On another occasion, he met a group of Thai military cadets on an end-of-term field trip to the pass, who had come to study the Mon language and gain exposure to life along the Thailand-Burma border.[215] On several occasions, the present author too has met Thai military officers and agents in the Mon and Karen liberated zones.

In 'the good old days', Three Pagodas Pass was the southern gateway to KNLA Sixth Brigade, adjacent to NMSP Headquarters and Moulmein District. Today, Sangkhlaburi is still a stopping-off point on the way to NMSP headquarters (or 'Central') and the main staging-post and base of the Mon National Relief Committee (MNRC).[216] However, while the NMSP, KNU and other groups still maintain networks in Sangkhla and other towns along the border, in recent years their ability to operate out of Thailand has been severely curtailed.[217]

PART FOUR

REVOLUTIONARIES, WARLORDS AND REFUGEES

"It depends what they mean by 'engaged'. If they were truly engaged with both sides – the democratic forces as well as the SLORC – I think it could help a great deal. But some of the countries which are said to be pushing a constructive engagement policy seem to be only engaged with one side."

Daw Aung San Suu Kyi, interviewed after her release from house arrest in 1995[1]

CHAPTER ELEVEN

Burma and the Mon
in the 1990s

The years 1988–90 were a turning-point in Burmese history. Following the 1988 democracy uprising and Daw Aung San Suu Kyi's arrest the following year, key events 'inside' Burma in 1990 included the May election, the subsequent crackdown on the NLD and other opposition parties, and the SLORC's promulgation of new economic policies. On the international front, in February 1990 the United Nations Commission on Human Rights (UNCHR) appointed a Special Envoy for Burma; following the withdrawal of Western and Japanese aid, it seemed that sustained international pressure might be brought to bear upon the SLORC regime. Meanwhile in the liberated zones, although the fall of Three Pagodas Pass and other rebel bases had further weakened the insurgents, the formation of the Democratic Alliance of Burma (DAB) had drawn large numbers of democracy activists from the towns and cities into the armed opposition camp.

Unlike previous communist-led fronts, the DAB was not dominated by a Burman elite. Rather, its military strength was based on troops of the Mon, Karen, Kachin and other ethnic armies, whose battle-hardened leadership took the lead in developing alliance policy. Given the SLORC's evident unpopularity and the opportunities that might arise out of renewed anti-government demonstrations in Rangoon and elsewhere, it seemed that the DAB might yet affect significant change in Burma. In retrospect however, although the new alliance linked-up quite effectively with 'refugee MPs' from the 1990 election, the level of optimism at the DAB's Mannerplaw headquarters was misplaced. Victory in the civil war was already beyond the insurgent forces; realistically, any breakthrough would have to come on the political front.

In fact, the 1990s brought unprecedented new difficulties for Burma's ethnic nationalist movements. The SLORC ceasefire agreements of the late 1980s were extended to more than a dozen insurgent organisations, including the Kachin Independence Organisation (KIO), a key member of the National Democratic Front (NDF) and DAB alliances. In die-hard revolutionary circles, the 1994 KIO-SLORC ceasefire was represented as a 'sell-out', as a result of which the remaining rebel groups came under increasing political and military pressure to 'return to the legal fold'. Although as recently as 1995 C.F. Keyes could still assert that "Burma has more 'ethnic rebellions' per square mile than almost any other place in the world",[2] the civil war was entering its protracted final stages.

Alliance Politics

As Robert Taylor notes, factionalism has bedevilled Burmese "liberation forces" since the days of the British conquest, when "though the extent of the opposition was great ... the lack of unity and co-operation among the rebel leaders eased the task of the British-Indian forces."[3] Likewise since independence, the armed opposition has displayed a fatal tendency to schism and disunity, in the face of a monolithic military regime.

Since the 1940s, communist influence on the ethnic insurgencies had generally been divisive, with a number of groups splitting into pro- and anti-Communist Party of Burma (CPB) factions. However, one consequence of the CPB's collapse in 1989 was the removal of ideological obstacles to genuine partnership between Burman and ethnic minority "liberation forces." The CPB had always insisted that the ethnic nationalists accept its leading role. Although many insurgent leaders proved susceptible to the party's offer of guns, logistical support and an internationally credible ideological basis to their struggle, others rejected the CPB, claiming its domination by Burman cadres made it as unresponsive to ethnic nationalist demands as the government.

Significantly, the generation of dissidents that emerged in 1988–1990 looked to the NDF for support, rather than to the crumbling CPB. Unlike previous generations of communist dissidents, the new wave of democracy activists had no overriding ideological motivation to assume a vanguard role in the revolution. In fact, soon after arriving in the liberated zones along the Thai and Chinese borders, they realised that foreign assistance would not be quickly forthcoming and that – at least in the short-to-middle term – the ethnic insurgents represented their best hope for succour and support. Most of the students came from urban, middle class and/or military-elite families. Unused to the rigours of jungle life, many came to depend on rebel groups that for some forty years had been demonised in the Rangoon press. This process led to a greater understanding by the '1988 generation' of the plight of Burma's ethnic minorities, and thus to a new solidarity among the disparate opposition forces.

The late 1980s and early '90s were a learning period for the armed opposition. In 1988 the ethnic nationalist NDF negotiated a common federalist position with the All Burma Students Democratic Front (ABSDF), leading to the formation of the DAB. In December 1990 this co-operation was extended to include an alliance with the National League for Democracy [Liberated Area] (NLD-LA), which was established that year on the Thailand-Burma border after the failure of the SLORC to recognise the NLD election victory.

The newly-formed Democratic Front of Burma (DFB) was soon allied with the National Coalition Government of the Union of Burma (NCGUB), a 'government in exile' established at Mannerplaw in December 1990, by a handful of MPs-elect. In February 1991 the DFB was re-named the Anti-Military Dictatorship National Solidarity Committee (ANSC), which in 1992 became the National Council of the Union of Burma (NCUB). With its own War Council and political secretariat, the NCUB was the sovereign body of the non-communist armed opposition.

In July 1991 Nai Shwe Kyin begun a four year term as NDF Chairman, placing the NMSP firmly at the heart of opposition politics. In 1992 he was made a Vice-Chairman of the newly re-established NCUB, and between 1991–95 he made visits to Switzerland, the United States, Germany and France, on behalf of the NMSP and the NDF, DAB and NCUB alliances.[4] However, despite the DAB and NCUBs' apparent success, Mon leaders were wary of over-committing their limited resources to the ABSDF 'Students Army'.

As noted above, the March 1990 'Ye incident' had led to a cooling of NMSP-ABSDF relations, which in the absence of Nai Non Lar – the students' closest associate among the Mon leadership – continued to deteriorate. When, in late 1990, the MNLA began to arm the newly-established People's Defence Force (PDF), some observers took this as a snub to the Students.

A well-trained guerrilla unit, composed of Burmese students and a few ex-Burma Air Force men, the PDF was led by U Sein Mya, a widely-respected and well-connected former *Tatmadaw* colonel. U Sein Mya had been in Ne Win's Interior Ministry when Mon State was created in 1974, and had 'come out to the revolution' in 1989, briefly joining forces with the *Da Nya Ta*. In 1990 he assembled the PDF, a loyal, one hundred and fifty-strong force, which soon began to receive financial support from the KIO, NMSP and other NDF members. The PDF proved to be a good investment: by the end of November a number of politicians elected that May had been spirited out to the border by PDF guerrillas, operating from a base in NMSP Tavoy District. These MPs-elect went on to form the NCGUB 'government in exile'.[5]

In practice, NMSP backing for the PDF meant a reduction in support for the ABSDF. Although expectations of the PDF proved over-optimistic, and the NMSP was to continue in a formal alliance with the Students until 1995, relations between the ABSDF and the Mon insurgents were never the same after 1990. By the end of the following year, most of the remaining student bases in the Mon area had been re-located to Mannerplaw, or south to the KNU stronghold at E-Thaung.[6]

The KIO-SLORC Ceasefire

The 1989 SLORC-Shan State Army (SSA) ceasefire had sounded an early warning to the NDF alliance. According to Martin Smith, the agreement constituted "a timely reminder of the historic lack of unity amongst what is loosely described as the 'ethnic opposition'."[7] If the collapse of the CPB coincided with a new wave of 'ethnic-Burman' co-operation among the opposition forces, it also benefited the SLORC.

Until 1989, the *Tatmadaw* had been fighting two inter-connected civil wars – one against the ethnic nationalist insurgents and another against the CPB. With the communist threat neutralised, Rangoon could concentrate its forces on the war against the ethnic rebels. The junta devised a classic 'divide and rule' strategy, under which ceasefire agreements were struck with individual insurgent groups, while the SLORC refused to negotiate with any joint front, such as the NDF or DAB. To the consternation of the embattled allies on the Thailand-Burma border, between 1989–95 ceasefire arrangements were made with a total of fifteen insurgent organisations, including Shan, Pa-O, Palaung and Kachin NDF member-groups.

Established in 1961, the KIO was – together with the KNU – the strongest organisation in the NDF. In the 1990s its armed wing, the Kachin Independence Army (KIA), had a troop strength of some 6,000 men. However, twenty years of the *Tatmadaw's* Four Cuts had worn down the tough Kachin people's will to resist. As the civil war dragged on, KIO Chairman Brang Seng and his colleagues had become convinced that the best hope for the Kachin and other ethnic groups to influence the future shape of Burmese politics was to engage with the government in the political arena, rather than the military. Although the first attempt at a KIO-BSPP ceasefire had broken down in 1981, the Kachin leadership was prepared to try again.

With the withdrawal of Chinese support in the late 1980s, and the collapse of the CPB at the end of the decade, the KIO entered the 1990s in an increasingly isolated position. In January 1991 the KIA's Fourth Brigade, which operated on the Kachin-Shan States borders, broke away from the KIO to make a separate ceasefire with Rangoon. Like other ceasefire groups, the new Kachin Defence Army (KDA) was allowed to retain its weapons and maintain control over large swathes of territory. Later in 1991, it was followed into the ceasefire process by two of the smaller NDF groups – the Pa-O National Organisation (PNO) and the Palaung State Liberation Party (PSLP).

Under increased military pressure from the *Tatmadaw*, and new political pressure from neighbouring China, in early 1993 the KIO entered into ceasefire negotiations with Khin Nyunt's powerful Military Intelligence Service. The talks continued between April–September 1993, focussing primarily on the demarcation of territory and troop positions. The ceasefire was formalised in the Kachin State capital of Myitkyina on 24th February 1994.[8] Under this agreement, the KIO-controlled sectors consisted of about twenty distinct zones, including a headquarters area along the China-Burma border, another area to the west of Bhamo, a larger zone to the north of the Kachin State capital of Myitkyina, and the largest area – a triangle of territory between the Mali Hka and Nmai Hka rivers, extending north to the China border, adjacent to ceasefire zones controlled by the ex-CPB groups; the KIO also continued to hold sway over a number of villages in northern Shan State.

Although the Kachin ceasefire was a product of discussions between two military organisations – the KIO/KIA and the SLORC – it also involved non-insurgent members of the Kachin community, whose contributions were crucial to the agreement's strength and longevity. During the important early stage of confidence building, contacts between the KIO and Military Intelligence were mediated by the respected businessman Khun Myat and his brother, the Reverend Saboi Jum, secretary of the influential Kachin Baptist Convention (KBC).[9]

For the KIO, the civil war had become a dead end. The Kachin nationalist leadership's decision to 'return to the legal fold' represented a bold new political strategy. Despite the limitations of the truces, the KIO and other ceasefire groups at least now had some limited opportunities to pursue local development initiatives and economic projects.

By 1994, more than 10,000 Kachin refugees were living in scattered camps along the Burma-China border, another 20,000-plus were "staying with relatives in China", and as many 60,000 were internally displaced within the Kachin and northern Shan Sates.[10] By the end of 1996, most of the refugees had returned to KIO and joint KIO and SLORC-controlled zones in Burma.[11] However, the *Tatmadaw* continued to enlist villagers on forced labour projects across large areas of Kachin State. The KIO-SLORC ceasefire may have marked a new beginning, but there was still a long way to go before peace and normality returned to the Kachin lands.

As had been the case during Ne Win's 1963 ceasefire talks, throughout the 1993–94 negotiations, the government refused to discuss a political settlement to the pressing issues underlying the Kachin insurgency. Since 1989, the military junta had consistently maintained that, as an interim 'caretaker government', it could only discuss military arrangements, rather than political solutions to the 'ethnic question'. Under the SLORC ceasefires, erstwhile insurgents continued to bear arms, control territory and pursue some economic and other development initiatives, while the festering political and social legacy of a forty year civil war remained largely unexamined. These were armed truces, not peace agreements.

The SLORC ceasefires did not much resemble military arrangements in other parts of the world (Columbia and Sudan are possible comparisons). Observers have though, looked at the case of ethnic minority groups in southern China.[12] Many peoples, such as the Jinghpaw and other Kachin sub-groups, live on both sides of the border, and have been granted special 'autonomous zones' by the Chinese communist government. However, conditions in the ex-insurgent-controlled 'liberated zones' of Burma and the 'autonomous zones' of China are very different: the ethnic minorities in China generally do not bear arms and have not engaged in prolonged rebellion against the state. The type of limited, local self-government enjoyed by China's ethnic minority peoples may eventually be provided for under the Burmese government's constitutional deliberations – or the more ambitious plans of the opposition.[13]

The 1989–99 'ceasefire movement' in Burma did have indigenous precedents. In many respects, it resembled the *Ka Kwe Ye* (KKY) village militia programmes, organised by Ne Win's BSPP government in the late 1960s and '70s, under which ex-insurgent forces 'returned to the legal fold', whilst continuing to provide 'security' in the areas they had previously controlled. A number of the old KKY militias had subsequently reverted to insurgent mode, and it was some time before most observers realised the lasting significance of the new round of ceasefires.

If nothing else, the SLORC ceasefires allowed some breathing space to isolated and marginalised communities caught in the middle of a viscous civil war. However, in most of the ex-insurgent liberated zones, reconstruction projects were limited to a few new bridges, roads and dams, while the majority of peasant farmers remained in chronic poverty. For the leaders of the main Kokang, Shan and Wa groups, the most significant development of the 1990s was the expansion of the narcotics trade. For the SLORC, the benefits of the ceasefires were more far-reaching: by bringing armed revolt to a halt across large areas of rural Burma, the *Tatmadaw* was better able to control the cross-border trade with China and northern Thailand, whilst concentrating its firepower on those zones where significant rebel activity still occurred.

Another consequence of the ceasefires was that the *Tatmadaw* generally began to move units right up to the front-line, establishing new well-defended positions, that previously could only have been held in the face of intense resistance. Thus, if the ceasefires broke down, the *Tatmadaw* would be poised to attack previously inaccessible rebel bases. Militarily therefore, for the insurgents, the ceasefires were something of a one-way street: a return to war might result in the loss of their often still extensive liberated zones.

In November 1993, during a tour of Mon, Kachin and Karen States, Khin Nyunt made a widely-reported speech in which he called on the remaining "armed ethnic groups" to enter into ceasefire negotiations and "return to the legal fold."[14] Significantly, the ruthless but highly intelligent

Military Intelligence chief had avoided the usual practice of calling the insurgents 'bandits'. Optimists hoped that the KIO ceasefire would herald a new dawn in government-ethnic minority relations – one marked by a new seriousness and mutual respect.

The ceasefire issue formed an important part of discussions attended by representatives of the KIO, KNU and NMSP at the Carter Centre in Atlanta, Georgia in February 1993.[15] Although Brang Seng kept his allies closely informed about developments,[16] General Bo Mya and the Mannerplaw-based DAB hard-liners were furious at the Kachins' 'treachery'. During a visit to London in October 1993, the KNU leader explicitly condemned the KIO-SLORC ceasefire.[17] Bo Mya and his advisors maintained an uncompromising position: negotiation with the SLORC would have to involve recognition of the DAB. Furthermore, the KNU insisted that talks with the military would only be possible if the SLORC called a national ceasefire and released all political prisoners, including Daw Aung San Suu Kyi. At a time when *Tatmadaw* commanders sensed the possibility of final victory in the civil war, such hard-line positions were unlikely to meet with a positive response. The continued polarisation of attitudes on both sides allowed General Bo Mya and his allies in the KNU and ABSDF to consolidate their control over the DAB, and dig in for a desperate new phase in the war.

As well as the KIO, in 1994 three other insurgent groups 'returned to the legal fold', including another NDF member, the Kayan New Land Party (KNLP). This brought the total number of ceasefire groups – or 'peace groups', as the regime preferred to call them – to thirteen. Meanwhile, on the southern stretch of Thailand-Burma border, the NMSP leadership was becoming increasingly anxious. Relatively small groups, like the Mon, were dangerously isolated, and overwhelmingly outgunned by the *Tatmadaw*. Nai Shwe Kyin and his closest advisors began to discuss the possibility of negotiating a KIO-style ceasefire with the SLORC.

Within a year, the NMSP had 'returned the legal fold'. A half-century of military, political and organisational culture now had to be re-thought.

The NMSP in the 1990s: Policy

In 1972 Nai Shwe Kyin had reconfirmed the extent of the Mon nationalists' territorial claims: "the NMSP is reclaiming part of the old Mon State ... comprising of five districts, namely, Mergui, Tavoy, Moulmein and Thaton ... and Pegu district in Pegu Division."[18] In practice, the Mon rebels have not controlled large chunks of territory over extended periods of time, in the same way as the Kachin and Karen insurgents. Rather, the fortunes of a sometimes small band of revolutionaries have fluctuated over the years.

Mon nationalist policy was often shaped by factors beyond the control of the NMSP or its predecessors. Since the 1940s, Burma's ethnic insurgents had adopted a variety of ideological positions, often in relation to trends in international politics. For half a century, much of mainland Southeast Asia was a theatre of war, and it is not surprising that events in Cambodia, Laos, Malaysia, Thailand and Vietnam had an effect on the conception, articulation and practice of insurgent strategy in Burma.

In the 1950s leaders of the Mon and other ethnic nationalist movements in Burma adopted some aspects of communist political rhetoric. However, few ethnic minority politicians were ever fully reconciled to the Maoist call for mass class struggle against feudalism, capitalism and imperialism, under the leadership of the enlightened peasantry and proletariat – i.e. under CPB tutelage. Although groups like the Mon People's Front (MPF) – and particularly the Karen National United Party (KNUP) – employed elements of communist theory and organisation, most ethnic nationalist leaders suspected that the CPB's 'united front' strategy was merely politically expedient, to be abandoned at a later stage in the revolution, in favour of a more refined version of class war, in which non-communist elements would be purged and a 'people's democracy' established under the leadership of the (Burman-dominated) CPB.[19]

When, in the late 1960s and '70s, General Bo Mya – supported by the Thai security establishment – moved the KNU into the anti-communist camp, many in the Mon, Karenni and other smaller nationalist movements took heart. However, ideological controversy was to continue to dog the Mon and other ethnic insurgents throughout the 1980s, with most groups splitting into left and right-wing factions.

Following the death in 1988 of Nai Non Lar, who had taken the NMSP into the non-communist NDF alliance, the Nai Shwe Kyin faction re-established control over the party machinery and began to re-examine the ideological basis of the Mon insurgency. In December 1994, seven years after NMSP re-unification, the party's newly-drafted *Fundamental Political Policy and Fundamental Constitution of Administration* stated that the following were the "basic enemy of the Mons: colonialism, bureaucracy policy (capitalism), dictatorship, majority Burmanisation."[20] The NMSP constitution has remained unchanged since 1994. It clearly reflects Nai Shwe Kyin and colleagues' twin commitments to Mon national liberation and leftist political analysis.

The KNU and other non-communist ethnic nationalist groups have also inherited a good deal of left-wing rhetoric. As Martin Smith notes:

'National democracy' became an objective in itself. (The debate over exactly what it means is still being waged.) ... the term 'national democracy' has been increasingly used by virtually all Burma's ethnic insurgent groups to describe what might best be described as a 'federal' parliamentary system of government that allows minorities political, economic and cultural rights as distinctive as those enjoyed

by the French or Italians in the cantons of Switzerland or the Lahu
and Kachins in the autonomous regions of China.[21]

However, while the KNU under Bo Mya still defines its goals in terms of the
first ('national democratic') stage of Mao's two-stage theory of people's
revolution, it has abandoned the second stage of 'people's democracy'.
Communist strategy has been re-interpreted to serve ethnic nationalist ends.

Like the KNU and KIO,[22] the NMSP adapted Maoist theory to its own
needs. Although many cadres undoubtedly sympathised with the communist
cause, the actual government and day-to-day experience of life in Monland
was not dissimilar to that in the supposedly more 'right-wing' KNU
liberated zones. Ultimately, the defence and maintenance of territory was
more important than the way in which it was administered.

According to Nai Shwe Kyin in 1972, the aim of the NMSP was "to
establish an independent sovereign state unless the Burmese government is
willing to permit a confederation of free nationalities exercising the full
right of self-determination inclusive of right of secession."[23] This policy was
restated and refined in the 1994 constitution, which proposes establishing a
Mon National Democratic Republic, within a larger Union of National
Democratic Republics (i.e. a new federal union of Burma). The new union
would be "based on equal rights and self-determination for all ethnic
people including the Mon National Democratic Republic Country." This
political arrangement would guarantee "a fully democratic system" and
"multi-nationality unity."[24]

The NMSP's 1994 'national democratic' constitution defines the party as
the vanguard organisation of the Mon nationalist movement, whilst
recognising the leading role to be played in the struggle for a federal Burma
by the NDF (of which Nai Shwe Kyin was at the time chairman). The
document goes on to discuss the foundation of National Democratic
Republics (or States) within the proposed new federal union, on the basis of
the equal rights of all nationalities in Burma (although neither 'nationality'
nor 'rights' are defined).

Another important article states that "in all Democratic Republics the
first official language must be the language of the majority", but that other
languages must also be allowed (but with no serious attention regarding
how to establish boundaries). Furthermore, "each Democratic Republic
must have its sovereignty", and unless this is explicitly transferred to the
union it must be free to run in its own affairs. In addition, "each
Democratic Republic must have the right to leave and divide from the union
federal state" (the right to secession).

Other key points in the NMSP programme include provision for each
Democratic Republic to maintain a standing army – which "must be a
recognised part of the army of the union federal state." Each Democratic
Republic must also have its own flag and seals and must "have the rights

directly to deal with overseas countries and governments."[25] Although federal in principal, it would seem that the type of state envisioned would retain a very large degree of autonomy within the union.

While presumably bound by the party's *Fundamental Political Policy and Fundamental Constitution of Administration*, from the early 1990s, NMSP personnel participated in a series of seminars and workshops, which in 1997 culminated in the publication of the NCUB's Constitution of the Federal Union of Burma. The Federal Constitution-drafting process helped to focus attention on several important aspects of the 'ethnic question' in Burma. These included the demarcation and administration of different ethnic states and sub-states within the union, the powers of and relationship between these states and the federal government, the role and composition of the armed forces, and the thorny issue of secession. Although it was unlikely that the NCUB charter would ever be implemented, such discussions within opposition circles went some way towards dissipating the deep-seated suspicion of Burman chauvinism held in ethnic minority quarters.[26]

The NMSP in the 1990s: Structure, Leadership and Administration

Like several other insurgent groups in Burma, the organisational structures of the NMSP and MNLA were modelled on those of the KNU and the Karen National Liberation Army (KNLA).[27] For much of the 1960s and '70s, Nai Shwe Kyin's NMSP was dependent on the KNU for logistical and material support, as well as for territorial security. At least until the outbreak of the 1988 Mon-Karen conflict, many observers considered the NMSP to be little more than a client organisation of the KNU, like the Karenni National Progressive Party (KNPP) and several other small NDF members.

Like the KNU, the NMSP is governed by a Central Committee. The twenty-seven full Central Committee members, together with five 'candidate' members-in-waiting, are elected by secret ballot at the party Congress, which in theory is attended by one representative for every four NMSP members. Although during the 1981–87 split in the NMSP both sides held separate congresses and Central Committee meetings, since re-unification these have not been recognised as official party conclaves. Therefore, since the 1971 inaugural General Congress, there have been only five full party congresses: in 1980–81 (following which the NMSP split), in 1989 (after re-unification), in 1992–93, in 1996 and in 1999.[28]

Until 1996, representatives in Congress voted directly for the NMSP President. However, in elections to the Central Committee that year, party General Secretary Nai Rot Sah polled more votes than any other candidate, including Nai Shwe Kyin (who had the previous year led the party into an unpopular ceasefire agreement with the government).[29] Although this result should technically have allowed Nai Rot Sah to assume the presidency, he asked Nai Shwe Kyin to continue in the job. The younger man's diplomacy ensured that the NMSP continued to be led by the politician most widely-known and respected among the wider Mon (and Burmese) community. Votes in subsequent elections to top leadership positions have been restricted to the wise heads of the party Central Committee. However, Congress still elects the Central Committee, and in 1999 the NMSP rank-and-file voted a number of pro-ceasefire cadres out of office.[30]

The Central Committee elects seven of its number to the Central Executive Committee, which runs the party on a day-to-day basis and constitutes the top tier of leadership. At the time of the 1995 NMSP-SLORC ceasefire, the Central Executive Committee was composed of Nai Shwe Kyin (President of the NMSP and Chairman of its Central and Central Executive Committees), Nai Htin (NMSP Vice-President), Nai Rot Sah (General Secretary), Nai Hongsa (Joint General Secretary), Nai Chan Toih and the two senior MNLA commanders – Nai Taw Mon and Nai Aung Naing.[31]

Other senior party leaders included Nai Soe Myint – the influential, one-eyed Governor of Thaton District – and Nai Tin Aung. In 1963 Nai Tin Aung had been jailed alongside his father, MPF Chairman Nai Aung Htun. In early 1987, he joined Nai Aung Htun's old colleague, Nai Non Lar, in the 'official' NMSP. Having played an important role in the reunification negotiations, he later became NMSP commissioner for refugee affairs and Chairman of the Mon National Relief Committee (MNRC). In 1994 Nai Tin Aung was appointed NMSP minister for Foreign Affairs. A strong proponent of ceasefire negotiations, Nai Tin Aung was a key player in various post-ceasefire economic and development projects, until he suffered a stroke in 1997. Security concerns preclude the naming of other lower-ranking NMSP officers, several of whom have earned reputations for dynamism and efficiency, particularly in the fields of education, refugee relief and development and women's empowerment.

In 1995 party membership stood at about 3,500 people. Ordinary NMSP members usually received some payment, although this was distributed rather irregularly and usually amounted to no more than pocket money plus a supply of rice. Since the introduction of limited foreign assistance in 1996, Mon school teachers have been slightly better-off, receiving modest salaries distributed by the party's Mon National Education Committee (MNEC).[32]

The NMSP has a three-tier organisational structure. Cadres' place in the hierarchy reflects their number the of years 'in the revolution', factional allegiance and political-military power base. The 'old guard' are mostly in their sixties-to-eighties; many have been with the insurgency since the 1960s. They form the senior level of leadership, and the bulk of Central Committee members. However, the 'big men' usually delegate day-to-day responsibilities to the second tier leadership. These Departmental Secretaries are often men in their forties or fifties, who may also be 'candidate' (alternate) Central Committee members. For example, the Ministers for Education and Health are Central Committee members, who chair the Mon National Education and Health Committees (MNEC and MNHC) respectively. In practice however, the MNEC and MNHC are run by their secretaries, with the help of the committees' chiefs-of-staff, third-tier leaders, who are usually men in their late twenties or thirties.

The NMSP Education Department was established in 1972. It consists of the Mon Textbook Committee and the MNEC, which is responsible for running the Mon National School system. Most female party members work for either the MNEC or the MNHC, and are likely also to be members of the Mon Women's Organisation (MWO). Founded by a group of Mon university students in 1988, the MWO was soon after incorporated into the Education Department. In the 1990s MWO members were in the forefront of community development initiatives in the NMSP-controlled zones, together with MNEC staff.

Despite the existence of several talented, committed and well-educated young women in the party's middle and lower ranks, by 2001 there were still no female members on either the NMSP Central Committee or the MNRC. In comparison, the KNU Central Committee had one female member – Karen Women's Organisation (KWO) chair, Mrs Bo Mya – and the Karen Refugee Committee (KRC) had two senior women officers (including its Chairperson).

The NMSP also had an active youth section, many members of which joined the party between 1988–90. However, their energy and commitment were not always well-utilised and – as in the KNU – in the 1990s many of the younger generation came to view the party's bureaucratic-gerontocratic arrangements as inflexible, undemocratic and prone to corruption. In recent years, and particularly since the 1995 ceasefire, many bright young people have left the party, either to work with other Mon organisations or to drop out of politics altogether. However, a number of young township level officers and departmental staff – some with long-term family connections to the insurgency – do still work within the system.

Between 1990–97, the NMSP divided the territory of The Mon National Democratic Republic into four districts: Mergui District in the southern Tenasserim Division (below the Maw Daung Pass and opposite Thailand's Prachuab Kiri Kahn Province[33]), Tavoy and Moulmein Districts (to the east of those two coastal towns – the former in Tenasserim Division and the latter in Mon State) and Thaton District (covering the northern part of Mon State and parts of neighbouring Karen State and Pegu Division). This territory constituted those parts of old Hongsawaddy which still retained a significant – although often not a majority – Mon population.

Following the KNU model, and the British colonial administration in India and Burma, each NMSP district was composed of three or more

174

townships. These were the key civilian administrative units, each of which was broken down into a number of village tracts. The NMSP township officers were members of their respective departments at the district level – e.g. Township Education Officers reported to their superiors at the District Education Office, who in turn took orders from the MNEC and Central (headquarters). However, in most townships, the actual situation on the ground was complicated by the existence of the Burmese state's own structures, including schools and teachers. The liberated zones overlapped with government-controlled Burma.

Robert Taylor identifies the formal posting of government officers in the field, with the fact of state control.[34] However, since the early days of the civil war, many rural areas – often controlled by the insurgents, or actively contested with the *Tatmadaw* – had been credited by the government with structures and services which did not exist on the ground. To further complicate matters, in many areas the local NMSP administration had to co-exist with that of other insurgent groups, such as the KNU.

The Mon National Liberation Army

The NMSP-controlled 'black areas' were dwarfed by the 'white' and 'grey' areas, to which the party had at best only limited access. Even in many Mon-majority townships, the NMSP could only organise a skeleton administration, and in most cases villagers were left to fend for themselves. The Mon army however, could patrol over a much wider territory than the party could govern, and many villages which were required to support the MNLA through the 'donation' of rice, money or porters received few benefits in return from the NMSP. Furthermore, at least until 1995, the remaining liberated zones were under constant threat of violent disruption by the Burma Army. Usually, the only thing protecting villagers from such incursions was the Mon army, whose structures paralleled and often overruled any NMSP administration.

The MNLA was established in 1971, at a time when Nai Shwe Kyin's NMSP was still largely dependant on the KNU and U Nu's PDP for military support. During the 1970s and early '80s, several MNLA and KNLA officers attended American-sponsored military training courses in Thailand. However, this was a period of factionalism and in-fighting among the Mon insurgents, and the MNLA gained a reputation for ill-discipline – front-line troops often being more loyal to local commanders than to Central.

By the time Nai Taw Mon assumed operational command in 1975, the size of the MNLA had fallen to some five hundred men. Over the next decade however, its size doubled, as renegade Mon units and new recruits joined up. The handsome, rugged Nai Taw Mon led troops loyal to Nai Non Lar during the split in the Mon ranks in the 1980s, but since 1988 has been considered a close ally of Nai Shwe Kyin.

175

The MNLA Chief-of-Staff and Second-in-Command, Brig-General Aung Naing, was another commander in Nai Non Lar's 'official' faction of the party. An ex-*Tatmadaw* sergeant who joined the insurgency in 1968 (via the CPB), Nai Aung Naing is the 'strong man' of today's MNLA, and has something of the tough, heavy-jowled look of a younger Bo Mya.

Since before the 1960s, when ethnic insurgents along the Thailand-Burma border began to establish regular territorial administrations, the day-to-day government of both Monland and neighbouring Kaw Thoo Lei has been dominated by military interests. Each of the districts administered by the insurgents' civilian wings is paralleled by a related military formation – e.g. the KNU's Mergui-Tavoy and Dooplyah Districts correspond to the KNLA's Fourth and Sixth Brigade areas respectively. Likewise, each of the four NMSP Districts had its corresponding local MNLA Battalion: *Ra Ta Nam Sari* (Tenasserim) Battalion in Mergui District, Number 333 Battalion in Tavoy District, *Banya Ta Ram* Battalion in Moulmein District and Thaton Battalion in the north.[35]

In addition, the MNLA fielded two special mobile battalions established in 1987: 777 Battalion operated in the southern Ye River-Kanni area, while 111 Battalion patrolled further to the north. The final contingent of MNLA regulars were some two hundred headquarters troops, under the control of the Nai Taw Mon at Central. The NMSP also commands the uncertain loyalty of several hundred part-time 'village defence' militiamen, spread out across the liberated zones, and beyond. At any one time, 'depending on the situation', one or several of the above formations may be on the point of breaking away from the party.

Since 1971, Mon military strategy has been supervised by the Mon War Council (or Military Committee), whose Chairman and MNLA Supreme Commander is the NMSP President, Nai Shwe Kyin. Nai Taw Mon is Secretary of the War Council and senior military advisor to the NMSP Central Committee, the members of which include a number of ranking MNLA officers.

Generally, the top army leadership is younger than that of the party: several battalion commanders and other colonels are in their forties. Unlike the *Tatmadaw* – or most insurgent armies – the MNLA is reported to use child soldiers only rarely.[36] Like the KIA and a number of Shan groups though, the Mon army has recruited relatively large numbers of women. For many years, there was a regular MNLA woman's company, which saw front-line duty on a number of occasions, but was disbanded in the 1990s.

Compared with the Karen, the Mon insurgency has had relatively little recourse to 'foreign volunteers'. However, since the 1980s the occasional Western or Japanese mercenary has trained and fought alongside the MNLA. The Mon army has also received support over the years from the 'Thai Mon' community, members of which donated three surface-to-air missiles in the late 1980s.

Desmond Ball reports that, at least until the mid-1990s, the MNLA, KNLA and CPB People's Army "maintained very extensive SIGINT (signals intelligence) activities throughout southern Burma from Moulmein down to Maw Daung Pass."[37] The Signals Intercept Section, under MNLA intelligence chief, Colonel Nai Kao Rot,[38] was staffed by ten-to-fifteen male and female operatives. The MNLA conducted regular SIGINT training workshops throughout the 1980s and '90s, and its Signals Section maintained a limited crypto-analysis capability, providing two communications experts to each battalion.[39]

Most MNLA radio equipment was purchased in Thailand, either on the open market, or through contacts in the Thai military with access to 'surplus' stocks. Some sets and training were also provided by the KNU[40] and Koumintang (KMT). According to Ball, throughout the 1980s and '90s, MNLA intercepts of Burma Army radio traffic "gave a detailed picture of the *Tatmadaw* order of battle . . . their locations and movements . . . operational plans and objectives . . . tactical movements and reinforcement activity. All this intelligence was extremely useful to the insurgents; it was used to plan counter-actions, to provide warning for evacuation . . . and to organise ambushes."[41] (At the beginning of the 1997 Burma Army offensives against the KNU, MNLA intelligence in Sangkhlaburi kept the Mon refugee authorities, and this author, informed about the movements of *Tatmadaw* columns in Ye and Kya-In Seik Gyi.[42])

In 1990 MNLA troop strength stood at an all-time high of 3–4,000 men. Together with events 'inside' Burma between 1988–90, another contributory factor in this expansion was the relative unity of the Mon insurgent leadership. However, by the mid-1990s, MNLA numbers had fallen again to no more than 2,000 men. This decrease was both a result of the insurgents' loss of territory and revenue, and a symptom of declining idealism and waning commitment.

CHAPTER TWELVE

The Mon Refugees and the Border Relief Programme

For many years, Burma's refugees were the largely forgotten victims of an obscure war. Until the late 1990s, the plight of hundreds of thousands of civilians, forced from their lands by the Burma Army's brutal counter-insurgency programme, went largely unnoticed by the international community. In the long decades following independence, Burma's insurgents bore the brunt of *Tatmadaw* offensives, whilst at the same time providing what little protection and support was available to the people in whose name they fought.

The control of civilian populations has long been a major concern to all sides in the civil war, and the situation of the beleaguered inhabitants of the liberated zones and refugee settlements along Burma's borders has been central to the history of the ethnic insurgencies. As well as their undoubted role as havens of protection, the refugee camps have been used as a base for retired and recuperating combatants and their families, as a pool of recruits to the insurgents' cause – and also sometimes as a source of supplies. In recent years the NMSP, KNU and other organisations have found in the refugees a source of legitimacy. Control of the camp populations has been central to these groups' claims to represent sizeable constituencies among their communities. Like their counterparts elsewhere in Southeast Asia, Mon, Karen and Karenni insurgents have, through the refugee camps under their partial control, come to rely on foreign aid. It is a moot point whether or not this has strengthened the ethnic nationalist struggle in hte long-term.

The refugee camps along the Thailand-Burma border have played an important role in the generation and transmission of ethnic identity. For the NMSP, being Mon has definite political connotations: it is not enough to be ethnically Mon, yet subject to the assimilationist Burmese state. The ethnic nationalist agenda demands the (re-)creation of Monland, independent of Burman-dominated 'Myanmar'. To this end, the Mon National Schools in the refugee camps – and beyond – have consciously

178

projected a distinct ethno-national identity, enthusiastically participating in the propagation of Mon history and the celebration of Mon National Day and other holidays.

Although studies indicate that the majority of Mon refugees identified themselves as such before fleeing to the border, it is often only on arrival in the camps that they have been exposed to sustained ethnic nationalist rhetoric – and been identified both by the NMSP and the *Tatmadaw* as insurgent supporters. The refugees themselves have had little say in such developments. It would be a distortion to state that they – or the much larger population of Internally Displaced Persons (IDPs) inside Burma – all whole-heartedly support the insurgent cause. Nevertheless, many thousands of these people have 'voted with their feet': having fled the *Tatmadaw's* well-documented abuses, they have sought refuge in the rebel-controlled liberated zones and refugee settlements, rather than the government's relocation sites.

The insurgents' obviously still enjoy a degree of support. Together with fear of the *Tatmadaw*, another factor influencing villagers' flight to the difficult and dangerous border areas is the assistance of international NGOs which, since the early 1980s, have sustained an ever-growing refugee population, which might otherwise have perished or fallen into the clutches of their persecutors.

While the wider international community has enjoyed the luxury of distance and humanitarian compassion, neighbouring countries' responses to the Burmese refugee crisis have been determined primarily by national security considerations. In the case of Thailand, asylum policy has been strongly influenced by the experience of hosting more than a million Indochinese refugees between 1975–97 – a period during which victims of the 'Third Indochinese War' often served as pawns in the Cold War (and post-Cold War) regional power struggle.

Thailand is not a signatory to the 1951 Convention Relating to the Status of Refugees, or its 1967 Protocol, and the authorities still describe those fleeing the civil war in Burma as 'temporarily displaced people', rather than refugees. However, since the early 1980s, the Royal Thai Government has granted these people temporary refuge (informed observers suspect that the kingdom may eventually endorse the primary refugee protection instruments). Meanwhile, the international community has been quietly assisting the Burmese refugees, through private aid agencies and local NGOs. It was not until April 1992 – eight years after the first regular Karen refugee camps were established – that United Nations High Commissioner for Refugees (UNHCR) staff undertook their first trip to the Thailand-Burma border. Until 1998, the role of UNHCR Bangkok was mostly limited to irregular 'long distance monitoring' of the refugees. This lack of an international presence along the border added an extra – and unusual – burden of responsibility to the tasks of the NGOs working there.

The phenomena of Burmese refugees in Thailand is not new: displaced people have been seeking refuge in the kingdom for hundreds of years. The seventeenth century inhabitants of Martaban called the Siamese monarch a "the haven of the Mon race"[43] and many subsequent generations have found asylum in Thailand, often going on to enrich the host country with their skills and culture. The causes of migration have varied, and have included the desire for new land and improved economic opportunities, as well as flight from war and oppression. It is only in the modern period that these population movements have been characterised as 'refugee' situations.

Pre-nineteenth century Thai and Burman kings had been keen to attract subjects to their emergent states, which were characterised by low population density. The taking of captives to be resettled as chattels in the conqueror's lands was a major feature of the Burman-Thai-Mon, when manpower was at a premium in determining the power and status of the precolonial Southeast Asian *mandala*. The opposite is now the case: a major tenet of Thai policy today is the discouragement of refugee and migrant inflows.

Over the last twenty years, increasingly large numbers of Burmese people have entered Thailand, in search of work and an end to the grinding poverty in their homeland. It is often difficult to separate such 'economic migrants' from 'genuine refugees'. It is perhaps more realistic to think of a continuum, between people hoping to find a better life abroad – and send money back to their families in Burma – and those fleeing the devastation of direct warfare. Oppression, slavery and dispossession, the desire for new land and new opportunities – the causes of migration have not changed, but the mode of reception has.

The Indochinese Refugees

Thailand's involvement in Indochinese politics stretches back nearly a thousand years, to the hey-day of Khmer power at Angkor. More recently, the kingdom's relations with her troubled eastern neighbours have been determined primarily by fears of Vietnamese expansion. Thai troops fought alongside Americans and others in the Vietnam War, during which Thailand hosted thousands of US airmen, who conducted bombing raids against the kingdom's neighbours to the north and east.

From the outset, the Thai and other regional governments were wary of hosting refugees from the subsequent 'Third Indochinese War', as some three million people fled their homes following the communist victories in Laos, Cambodia and Vietnam. Thai policy towards the Burmese refugees has been shaped by the experience of hosting a cumulative total, since 1975, of 600,000 Cambodian and 350,000 Lao refugees – in camps along the kingdom's north and eastern borders – plus nearly 120,000 'boat people' and 40,000 other Vietnamese, in the south and the east.[44] For two decades, the Lao refugee settlements were administered by the Royal Thai

Government and UNHCR, whilst on the Cambodian border after 1979 UN agencies fed up to 400,000 'displaced persons', under the control of various Khmer factions.[45]

Although, with the exception of the Cambodian border caseload, most of these people were accepted as *de facto* refugees, they were clearly not welcome in Thailand, and on a number of occasions the authorities were responsible for refugee push-backs by land and sea.[46] Nevertheless, they were not without utility to Thai security policy.

With the US smarting from defeat in Vietnam, Thai and American agents began to exploit their contacts with anti-communist ethnic Hmong and other armed groups in Laos, and with the notorious, ultra-leftist – but crucially, anti-Vietnamese – *Khmer Rouge*. The Hmong and Khmer insurgents enlisted recruits in the refugee camps along the Lao and Cambodia borders and diverted supplies to the war effort.[47] Their Western and Chinese backers appeared only too happy to see the anti-Vietnamese opposition prosper.

An important – if unspoken – goal of Thai foreign and security policy throughout this period was the promotion of low-level conflict in Burma, Laos and Cambodia, keeping these potential rivals weak and divided, while preventing communist insurgents in Burma from linking-up with those in Thailand and Indochina. The displaced populations along the borders provided convenient buffer populations between Thailand and her traditional enemies, while the military chaos that prevailed next-door provided a ready market for Royal Thai Army munitions.

Since the 1950s, the US military had supplied the Royal Thai Army with large amounts of arms and training, and from 1978 tonnes of American and Chinese-supplied weaponry were routed through Thailand to the *Khmer Rouge*-dominated Cambodian resistance. Significant quantities found their way onto the black market, for re-sale on the Burmese and other borders. A booming two-way trade developed: weapons and other supplies were sold or given by Thai military officers to their clients among the insurgent forces in Burma, Cambodia and Laos; logs, precious stones and narcotics came out of these countries, to pay for the guns. A number of prominent Thai fortunes were made during this period. Among the insurgent groups, the times favoured the emergence of tough leaders with good Thai connections.

Although, during the Cold War era, a series of right-wing Thai governments were staunch allies and clients of the United States, by the mid-1970s the Royal Thai Government was nevertheless beginning to disengage from the American bloc, and pursue a closer relationship with the Association of Southeast Asian Nations (ASEAN).

From the outset, the huge UNHCR-administered refugee camps were perceived as a burden, and instance of international interference in Thailand's affairs. The Thai authorities were therefore relieved when the Indochinese exodus came to a halt in the mid-1980s, and the Lao-Hmong,

Cambodian and Vietnamese refugees were either resettled in third countries or repatriated.[48] By this time however, a new refugee crisis had emerged in the west. Thai policy-makers were determined not to see the Burmese refugee situation become internationalised along the lines of the Indochinese.

The Burmese Refugees and the 'Four Cuts'

Since the late-1960s, the civil war in Burma has been characterised by a counter-insurgency policy known as the 'Four Cuts' (*Pya Ley Pya* in Burmese). This strategy borrows elements from the pacification of upper Burma following the Third Anglo-Burmese War, from British practice in the Boer War and 1960s Malaya, and from the US military's 'strategic hamlets' programme in Vietnam. Under the Four Cuts policy, *Tatmadaw* units issue orders to villages in 'black' (rebel-held) and 'brown' (contested) areas, to relocate to government-controlled ('white') areas, usually with very little warning.

Villagers' erstwhile homes are designated 'free-fire zones'. The policy has at times amounted to a form of ethnic cleansing, as vast areas of the Burmese countryside have been depopulated, and civilians subjected to a range of human rights abuses.[49] The strategy is aimed at undermining the insurgents, by targeting their support base. There are *four* cuts, designed to undermine the rebels' supply of recruits, and to cut off their access to intelligence, food and finances (the undeclared fifth cut is said to be the insurgents' decapitation). The idea is, as a Burmese proverb has it, 'to drain the sea, in order to kill the fish'.

Since the 1980s, the *Tatmadaw* has implemented the Four Cuts in combination with a massively increased nation-wide use of forced labour. In July 1998 an International Labour Organisation (ILO) Commission of Inquiry reported that the government and military "treat the civilian population as an unlimited pool of unpaid forced labourers and servants at their disposal." The report went on to describe "a saga of untold misery and suffering, oppression and exploitation of large sections of the population", including large numbers of women, children and the elderly. Workers were usually not provided with food, and rarely received any payment or medical treatment. Those perceived by their guards as "unwilling, slow, or unable to comply with a demand for forced labour" were subject to "physical abuse, beatings, torture, rape and murder." Only those villagers able to pay off local *Tatmadaw* commanders could avoid extensive periods of forced labour and forced portering.[50]

As the *Tatmadaw* stepped-up its campaign against ethnic minority populations in rural areas in the 1970s, Burma became 'home' to large numbers of IDPs. The February 2000 preamble to the 1998 UN *Guiding Principles on Internal Displacement* estimates that internal displacement world-wide "affects over twenty million people[51] (who) suffer from severe deprivation, hardship and discrimination."[52] The Norwegian Refugee Council's Global IDP Database calculates that a minimum of 600,000 people have been forced to flee their homes in eastern Burma alone.[53] Other researchers have suggested that Burma's total IDP population may number as many as two million people.[54] Credible local research suggested that at least 700,000 IDPs were either living in hiding, or in forced relocation sites, in areas adjacent to the Thailand-Burma border in 2002.[55]

Those who choose not to enter relocation sites must flee their villages, and live in hiding in the jungle. The *Tatmadaw* launches regular patrols, aimed at seeking out these non-compliant IDPs, and destroying their temporary shelters and rice supplies. Those villagers who do move to the government's 'new villages' often face acute shortages of food and medicines, and are subject to a range of human rights abuses, including extortion and forced labour. The situation of Burma's relocations sites has generally been under-reported, in comparison with the overall IDP situation (which itself has not received the attention its seriousness merits).

Types of relocation site include large 'relocation centres', the residents of which have been forced to move from several outlying villages, to one central *Tatmadaw*-controlled location, often situated along a car road. Residents sometimes retain limited food stocks and access to farmland, although they are usually liable to various 'rice taxes', and subject to extensive bouts of forced labour. There are also smaller, pre-existing villages, living under an imposed contract, which states that they may stay-put *if* no fighting occurs nearby. Although these 'peace villages' have not been relocated in their entirety, outlying houses are usually forced to move onto confiscated land in the village centre. Residents of 'peace villages' are also often called upon to do forced labour, but usually have some opportunity to tend their farms.

The third main category of relocation sites are those controlled by non-state parties, such as the United Wa State Army (UWSA). Between 1999-2002, the Wa authorities forcibly relocated at least 125,000 people from northern Shan State to the UWSA's Southern Command area, 400 Km to the south, on the Thailand border. Tens of thousands of original Shan and Lahu inhabitants were themselves displaced in the process.

While insurgent armies still controlled large areas of the countryside, IDPs could often re-settle in the liberated zones. In the 1990s though, this became an increasingly insecure option. The fighting had previously tended to follow a cyclic, seasonal pattern: during the December-May dry season, the Burma Army would launch attacks against rebel positions, spreading terror in the 'free fire zones'. Villagers meanwhile, would often hide in the forests and hills, waiting for the 'invading' soldiers to withdraw at the beginning of the rainy season, allowing villagers to re-occupy their land and attempt to re-build their communities. However, in the 1980s the

Tatmadaw began to intensify the war against the insurgents along the border, capturing their bases, then digging-in for the rains. As more and more people became displaced, they found their backs to Thailand.

Refugee Camps on the Thailand-Burma Border

Karen refugees had been fleeing to Thailand since the 1970s, but it was not until 1984 that the first regular Karen camps were established in Tak Province, opposite the KNU's embattled Kaw Moo Rah stronghold.[56] The Thai authorities refused to recognise these people as refugees and dissuaded a complacent UNHCR from exercising its protection mandate. Instead, in February 1984 the Ministry of the Interior (MOI), the most powerful bureau in the Royal Thai Government, "invited Non Government Organisations working with Indochinese refugees in Thailand to provide emergency assistance to around 9,000 Karen refugees. . . . Thailand was prepared to accept these people temporarily on humanitarian grounds."[57]

The Karen refugees were assisted by those NGOs already working on the Lao and Cambodian borders. Sensitive to local politics and respectful of the refugees' culture, these private charitable organisations were also less likely to publicly challenge Thai policy. In response to the Royal Thai Government's invitation, a small group of international, non-evangelical Christian agencies established the loosely-structured Consortium of Christian Agencies (CCA), with the aim of supplying food and other essential relief items. Meanwhile, Medecins Sans Frontieres (MSF) and two other French agencies attended to the refugees' most basic medical needs.

Unlike the Indochinese caseloads, many Karen refugees fled with their community structures more-or-less intact. The areas of Burma immediately adjacent to the new settlements in Thailand were still mostly controlled by the KNU and other insurgents, so the refugees' security was not at first a major issue. It seemed most efficient therefore, to deal with these people through the refugee committees established by the KNU. This approach suited the Thai authorities' desire for a low-key solution to the crisis – one that would meet the refugees' basic humanitarian needs, while costing Thailand little. The Royal Thai Government wished to avoid provoking Rangoon, while at the same time elements in the army and security agencies continued surreptitiously to support the KNU. The NGOs meanwhile, did not wish to impose alien structures upon the refugees, hoping to avoid encouraging 'aid dependency'. From the outset therefore, the CCA and other agencies worked through the insurgent-nominated refugee committees.

In the late 1980s a number of non-religious NGOs joined the CCA, and in April 1991 the consortium was reorganised, as the Burmese Border Consortium (BBC). The principal BBC donors were ecumenical Christian agencies and Western governments, with the Swedes and European Union playing important roles from the outset.[58] Most of the BBC member-agencies were registered with the Thai authorities under the aegis of the Committee for Co-ordination of Services to Displaced Persons in Thailand (CCSDPT), which had been established in September 1975 to co-ordinate the activities of NGOs working with the Indochinese refugees. The monthly CCSDPT meetings in Bangkok, which were attended by UNHCR and several of the Bangkok embassies, served as an information sharing forum and locus of the Thailand-Burma border NGO scene.

As well as the officially-registered NGOs, by the 1990s a number of small, unofficial groups had emerged, some of which consisted of only one or two foreign volunteers. Members of the Burma-NGO community in Thailand fell into two broad camps: those with a specific interest in Burma, many of whom had little or no training in the fields of relief and development, and those professionals who worked for international agencies with a sectoral specialisation, but sometimes little interest in Burma issues *per se*. The CCA/BBC field staff were at first draw largely from the former community. There were few Thais in either group.

In 1984 most observers had assumed that the crisis would be short-lived and the Karen would soon be able to return to Burma. However, this was not to be the case, and throughout the 1980s and '90s the NGOs – and in particular the BBC – provided aid via indigenous refugee committees, which were in effect the humanitarian wings of insurgent organisations. Whilst this policy certainly empowered the refugee leadership, the concerns of the majority of refugees remained largely unheard. In retrospect, it was probably a mistake to rely so heavily on the refugee committees, without providing the training necessary for them to become more responsive to and representative of their clients' needs. Furthermore, in establishing such close relations with the Christian KNU elite, the NGOs inadvertently contributed to a growing factionalism among the Karen population along the border, and reinforced the polarisation between the Burmese government and opposition forces.

By 1989, when the first Karenni camps were established in Mae Hong Son Province, the Burmese refugee caseload had risen to 22,751 people, and the annual BBC budget at twenty-two million Baht (nearly one million dollars).[59] The Karen and Karenni refugee authorities administered a dozen-or-so camps, with a laid-back paternalism that sat well with the NGOs' low-profile mandate. For the refugees, the camps were a safe haven from the civil war in Burma. If those families with no members 'in the revolution' were occasionally asked to act as porters or pay tax to the insurgents, then few questions were asked. Until the late 1980s, the situation on the border suited most of these different players' agendas. Over the next few years though, all this would change.

The Mon National Relief Committee, the NGOs and the Mon Refugees

In early 1984, at the same time as the first Karen refugees began to settle in the kingdom, some 5,000 Mon refugees also fled to Thailand, after a *Tatmadaw* attack on an NMSP base 25 Km west of Three Pagodas Pass. Included among these people were villagers who had already been internally displaced at least once within Burma, before fleeing to the relative security of the NMSP-controlled liberated zones.

This was not the first time that Mon refugees had crossed into Thailand. During previous *Tatmadaw* offensives against insurgent positions around the pass, Mon and other civilians had fled to Songk'lier village, not far from NMSP Central at Nam Khok. However, these influxes had generally been short-lived, and the refugees had returned to Burma before the onset of the rainy season. However, the 1984 offensive against the pass was more intensive than usual and it seemed that the refugees might be forced to remain in Thailand for longer than before.

The NMSP therefore established a Mon National Relief Committee (MNRC), to seek assistance for, and help to organise, the refugees. Its Chairman, Nai Wieng Chet, contacted those NGOs already helping the Karen refugees around Mae Sot and elsewhere in Tak Province. The Catholic Office for Emergency Refugee Relief (COERR) agreed to supply the Mon with rice and other foodstuffs, while MSF France and Aide Medicale Internationale (AMI – another French NGO) provided medical assistance. Within two months however, the Royal Thai First Army (Ninth Division), which was responsible for the border between Kanchanaburi and Prachuab Kiri Kahn Provinces, had ordered the refugees to return to Burma. By the start of the rainy season, the last refugees had re-crossed the border, and the Ninth Division had established its credentials as one of the least refugee-friendly units in the Royal Thai Army.

Soon after this episode, a well-regarded AMI health workers' training was established at Three Pagodas Pass, which continued to turn out medics until the fall of the pass, in 1990. According to the MNRC, the next major influx of Mon refugees occurred in 1987, when the *Tatmadaw* attacked and burnt down parts of the settlement at the pass, following which "about 7,000 refugees stayed in temporary shelters at Songk'lier village for nearly one month. They received assistance from COERR and MSF, especially foods, clothing, and medicines.... MNRC set up operations in the Three Pagoda Pass area and they provided community reconstruction assistance to the new arrivals."[60] Again, within a month or so, these people were repatriated by the Ninth Division.

It was not until the fall of Three Pagodas Pass, in February 1990, that refugees from NMSP-controlled areas established what would prove to be longer-term settlements around Sangkhlaburi. As well as 'ordinary villagers', the refugee population from the pass included nationalist cadres and old soldiers, as well as members of the ABSDF and other armed groups. Unlike on previous occasions, these people could not just be repatriated, with the *Tatmadaw* now in control of the pass, and more than one NGO in the vicinity, to monitor the Thai response.

As the 1990 influx was obviously a substantial caseload, the BBC agreed to take over responsibility for food supplies in the Sangkhlaburi area, from the less well-funded COERR. In March 1990 the consortium started to ship rice, iodised salt, prawn paste (*ngapi*), blankets and mosquito nets to the Mon refugees. These supplies were distributed by the MNRC and camp authorities. By this time, some 30,000 Karen and Karenni refugees were already being fed by the BBC in camps further to the north, and the annual BBC budget stood at thirty-four million Baht ($1.3 million).[61]

By December 1990, the BBC, MSF and AMI were assisting 10,374 Mon refugees in seven small, temporary camps in Thailand. At least as many people again remained displaced inside Burma, but these were mostly beyond the reach of the relief programme. By the end of the year, the NMSP had re-organised the MNRC under the Chairmanship of Nai Tin Aung, a wily politician with excellent English language skills and smooth demeanour. The MNRC structure was based on that of the Karen Refugee Committee (KRC), with day-to-day responsibilities being under-taken by the General Secretary, and the Chairman in a guiding, policy-making role.

The Mon refugee administration, while arguably more efficient, was no more democratic than the Karen. Undoubtedly though, the MNRC staff worked hard on behalf of the refugees, often at some personal risk to themselves. Between 1990–96, they were involved in a series of fraught negotiations regarding the sites of, and conditions in, the Mon refugee camps. Situated between the competing agendas of the Thai military and civil authorities, the Burmese government and army, the NMSP, and the NGOs, MNRC officers had to strike balances between conflicting interests, whilst all the time looking out for the refugees' best interests.

Between 1991–93, the Ninth Division ordered a series of Mon refugee camp relocations and consolidations, one of the first of which was conducted in August 1991, when 2,000 refugees from Day Bung camp, near Three Pagodas Pass, were forced to move to Grung Gan, near Loh Loe. Given only a few day's notice, the refugees had to pack up the few belongings with which they had fled their homes, and trudge for a day through the mud and pouring rain to the new site. On each subsequent occasion, the refugees were forced to move at short notice, often through difficult terrain. The Thai objective seems to have been threefold: to exert pressure on the refugees (the civilian base of the NMSP), to ensure that the Mon did not become accustomed to life in Thailand, and to re-locate them away from strategic border trading passes.

187

Meanwhile, by the end of 1993, AMI had handed over full responsibility for health and sanitation at the Mon refugee camps to MSF, the largest of the half-dozen medical agencies on the border. Based in Sangkhlaburi since 1991, the multi-national MSF team worked more closely with the MNRC and the Mon National Health Committee (MNHC) than their colleagues in Mae Sot did with the KRC and the KNU Health Department. The MSF-sponsored wood and bamboo hospitals were generally the largest and most well-constructed buildings in each camp, and the although MSF undertook little in the way of sustained training with the Mon medics, the NMSP was happy enough with the relationship.

By the end of 1993, the BBC was feeding 72,366 refugees, of whom 10,346 were resident in two 'consolidated' Mon camps: Loh Loe, with a population of more than 7,000, was the largest Burmese refugee camp in Thailand; fourteen Km to the west, Pa Yaw ('border') refugee camp was located on a hillside right on the border with Burma. There were also some 1,500 Mon refugees (or IDPs) living at three sites in NMSP Mergui District, across the border and further to the south.[62]

However, these populations represented only a minority of displaced people. Exact figures are not available, but there were at least as many 'Burmese Mon' living – and often working – illegally in Thailand, as there were in the camps. Furthermore, there were still thousands of Mon IDPs on the Burma side of the border, living in the forest and trying their best to avoid *Tatmadaw* patrols. In 1998 the Burma Ethnic Research Group (BERG) estimated the proportion of Karen refugees to other displaced people from Kaw Thoo Lei as 1:4 (91,000 refugees, to approximately 400,000 IDPs in Burma and illegal migrants in Thailand).[63] Similar calculations led to an estimated Mon displaced population of 50,000 people (including 10,000 refugees) – a figure arrived at independently by Mon refugee authorities and human rights groups in 1998.[64]

Despite the uncertainty of life in the refugee settlements, between 1990–95 Mon refugee numbers remained fairly stable, at around 10,000 people. However, when the first systematic survey of the refugee population was undertaken in 1995, it was discovered that only forty-one per cent of Mon refugees had been at the border for more than a year.[65] Many new arrivals stayed for only a few weeks or months in the camps, before moving on to seek employment in Thailand's black economy, often through the agency of Thai labour brokers with connections to the Sangkhlaburi police.

These regular departures from the camps were roughly matched by the number of new arrivals. Every dry season, more refugee families would arrive from 'inside', often bringing stories of terrible deprivation and abuse. Many more families, especially those of the elderly or infirm, remained in their villages, hoping that somehow conditions would improve.

In late 1994 the MNRC established an Emergency Relief and Development Programme (ERDP), designed to assess the needs of Mon

IDPs. The ERDP received funding from a range of international donors and was modelled on the Karen Office for Relief and Development (KORD), established in 1993. It was however, more closely connected to the main refugee programme than the KORD cross-border relief operation was to the KRC. As well as distributing short-term emergency assistance to thousands of Mon villagers, ERDP personnel were instrumental in communicating the plight of the Mon IDPs to the outside world.

Meanwhile, as the civil war dragged on, refugees from the events of 1988–90 began to arrive in Bangkok. In May 1989 a new NGO alliance had been established, to assist the 'students' on the border (rather than in the Thai capital). The Burma Co-ordinating Group (BCG) was formed in part due to the reluctance of some BBC member-agencies to support non-civilian groups, such as the ABSDF. However, large numbers of students and others were becoming disillusioned with or exhausted by life on the border, and started heading for Bangkok (an often perilous journey, which involved dodging, or paying-off, numerous Thai check-points). Many of these people were eventually accepted by UNHCR as 'persons of concern' – i.e. *de facto* refugees. On receipt of a small allowance from UNHCR, some returned to the border, to share these funds with their colleagues in the fight against the SLORC.

By 1992, the Thai authorities had become alarmed at the number of 'students' at large in Bangkok, many of whom were very obviously still involved in military and political agitation along the border. The MOI drew up plans to designate a 'Safe Camp' for these 1,500-odd 'persons of concern', and the following year a special camp was opened at Maneeloy, in Ratchaburi Province. The Thai authorities soon began to insist that Burmese student refugees at large in Thailand move to Maneeloy, on pain of arrest.

Although over the next few year a number of Mon, Karen and other non-Burman people passed through the over-crowded Safe Camp, there developed a widespread resentment among the ethnic minority groups, that Burman refugees were receiving preferential treatment in terms of asylum options and opportunities to resettle overseas. Unlike those who could prove that they had been directly involved in urban-based opposition to the government, the vast majority of displaced Burmese had no access to international recognition or protection. The UN refugee agency referred to these people as 'border cases', and it was considered sufficient that they had access to the shelter and precarious security of the NGO-supplied 'displaced persons camps' along the border. However, even before the security situation in the Karen and Karenni camps began to deteriorate badly in the late 1990s, there were categories of refugees who found no refuge along the border.

For decades, economic migrants from Shan State had been arriving in Thailand to seek work in the kingdom's expanding agricultural sector and black economy. The ethnic similarity between the Shan and their northern Thai cousins had generally allowed these people to blend-in among their hosts. However, in 1996 a new wave of Shan refugees began to arrive along the border in Mae Hong Son Province, fleeing large scale relocations and gross abuses in their homeland. Due to the Thai (and American) authorities' desire not to be seen as complicit in the narcotics trade in Shan State, and to the fact that the Shan, Lahu, Lisu and Akha villagers lacked coherent political representation, these refugees were not allowed to settle in camps, but had to disperse among the villages and towns of northern Thailand. A new, largely invisible refugee emergency began to develop in the shadow of the 'official' crisis.

Refugee Camp Conditions

As much as was possible, the BBC and other NGOs attempted to keep 'aid dependency' on the Thailand-Burma border to a minimum. At least until the late 1990s, the Burmese refugee camps were characterised by a degree of autonomy, self-reliance and local participation in the relief process unusual in other refugee situations.

The presence of a Mon refugee population on the Thailand-Burma border since 1990 testified more to a 'push factor' in Burma than to any 'pull factor' generated by the refugee settlements. Although day-to-day life in the camps, and the distribution of relief supplies, was governed by MNRC-appointed camp and section leaders, the NMSP lacked the ability to coerce refugees' continued presence in these settlements.

The Mon camps were though, very much within the NMSP sphere of influence. At times the refugees provided the insurgents with food but, due in part to the BBC's low staffing levels, the extent to which relief supplies left the camps was not effectively monitored. However, the refugees' generally acceptable nutritional status would seem to indicate that the amount of 'wastage' was not great.

The refugees, and especially those with no family members in the NMSP, also served as an occasional a pool of 'volunteer labour'. Apologists point out that there is only a subtle distinction between refugees repairing a road used to transport humanitarian supplies to a refugee camp, and their being asked to dig a bunker protecting the camp from attack. Furthermore – and as was the case in the Cambodian border camps – it has generally been impossible for donors to distinguish among camp residents between combatants and non-combatants.

Until 1995 at least, visitors often remarked how different the Burmese camps were to the huge refugee settlements on Thailand's northern and eastern borders, in the 1970s and '80s. The camps on the Thailand-Burma border retained much of the atmosphere of the villages from which the refugees had fled – although the bamboo and leaf-thatch houses were generally more densely concentrated than in villages on the Burma side of the border. Life in the camps was far from ideal of course, but for tens of thousands of villagers it was the least unattractive of a poor set of options.

Camp populations in the mid-1990s varied from two hundred to seven thousand people. All the refugee settlements were within a few kilometres either side of the ill-defined border, but while the longest-established Karen camps in the Mae Sot area were easily accessible by road, the Karenni and northern Karen settlements along the Salween River were more isolated, as were the Karen and Mon camps along the southern stretch of the border.

A particular feature of the Mon camps was the annual mad scramble of the rainy season stockpile. Supplies through to November or December had to be sent in by April-May before the onset of the rains, when the roads were cut-off by mudslides and the rising level of the Kao Laem (Sangkhlaburi) reservoir. Delivering the stockpile was a major undertaking: at the best of times, the 'roads' to the camps were little more than mud tracks through the steep, forested hills. In such circumstances, and with only a limited number of four, six and ten-wheel drive vehicles able or willing to make the journey, even small delays could have major implications for the refugees' food security.

Since 1992–93, each shipment of supplies to the refugees had required the completion of a multitude of forms, as the Thai authorities attempted to assert control over the growing refugee crisis. The Ninth Division in particular, exploited the situation to the full, often delaying the issue of necessary permits in order to put pressure on the NMSP, via the refugees.

A further complicating factor in the Sangkhlaburi area was the Immigration Detention Centre (IDC) system. In line with Thai immigration law, illegal aliens arrested in the kingdom usually received a short term in the crowded Bangkok or local IDC, before being deported. In 1994 the Bangkok and Kanchanaburi IDCs started to conduct weekly deportations to the new Mon camp at Halochanee (see below). Every week, hundreds of deportees were trucked-in by the authorities, unloaded and marched seven Km up the steep hillside, over the border and down into the camp.[66]

The deportees came from all over Burma, and sometimes included people from Cambodia, Bangladesh, and even Nepal. Dealing with these vulnerable peoples' needs took up a disproportionate amount of time, but between them the BBC, MNRC and Kwai River Christian Hospital (KRCH) staff, together with the local Thai Karen Christian community, did the best they could.

Demographics and Livelihood, Education and Identity

The first systematic studies of the Burmese refugee caseload were undertaken in 1995–96. The primary objectives of the perhaps rather belated CCSDPT 'Education Survey' were to assess the current state of education and training in the camps, and examine the refugees' needs in the context of possible repatriation to Burma.

The two-part 'Education Survey' was carried out by teams of young teachers, under the auspices of the Mon, Karen and Karenni refugee committees, co-ordinated by BBC field staff and the CCSDPT Education Working Group. It was directed by Dr Philip Guest, a demographer at Mahidol University in Thailand.[67] The survey found the refugee population to be composed mostly of young families. Very few of the refugees were older than fifty-five, and more than ninety per cent came from rural backgrounds. Before coming out to the border, most Mon camp residents had been subsistence rice farmers. Approximately fifteen per cent of Mon refugees were identified as NMSP members or their families – i.e. the majority were not 'party people', but villagers.

Most refugees supplemented their relief supplies by foraging for vegetables in the forest, while some camp residents made a useful supplementary income by selling bamboo stalks and shoots to local Thai traders. Many families had one or more members working in the Sangkhlaburi area, usually as day labourers, or as porters employed by Mon, Thai and Burmese merchants trading between Mon State and Thailand. However, during the 1990s, as the refugee camps were relocated to increasingly isolated areas, and Thailand introduced tough new immigration policies, opportunities for this kind employment decreased.

With such a young demographic profile in the camps, schooling was a major priority. When interviewed in 1995, the great majority of Mon refugees mentioned the importance of education in expanding their children's opportunities.

The NMSP education system linked the refugees with the population of the liberated zones and the body of Mon nationalism. As in other Burmese communities, teachers enjoy great respect among the Mon, not least because the role of educator has traditionally been associated with the *sangha*. The NMSP attempted to capitalise on this fact, by using education as a means to inculcate a 'national spirit' among the refugees.

The MNEC ran a primary school in every refugee camp, as well as a high school in the vicinity of Central.[68] Like most other buildings in the refugee camps and liberated zones, these schools were made of bamboo walls and leaf-thatch (or sometimes zinc sheet) roofing. Most classes, particularly at the lower levels, were overcrowded and relied heavily on rote-learning techniques, which have characterised monastic education in Burma for centuries. Due to a shortage of teachers and limited opportunities for teacher training, levels of enrolment in Mon refugee schools were low, and drop-out levels high.[69]

In 1992 the MNEC began to address the problem of outmoded teaching techniques, by organising the first of an annual series of six week Summer

Teacher Training Seminars at Central. With financial support from the NGOs, since 1996 the MNEC has also conducted regular teacher training workshops, and a number of Mon teachers have attended and taught on programmes organised by the NCUB's National Health and Education Committee (NHEC). By the late 1990s, a new generation of young teachers and educationalists were moving the Mon National School system towards new, more student-centred models of learning.

Although training initiatives for adults were generally limited to a literate, male elite, the MWO did impressive work in the field of Mon literacy, publishing an occasional Mon language journal. Furthermore, a number of women from the refugee camps and 'inside' Burma participated in MWO-organised handicraft projects, community development programmes and empowerment workshops.

Such educational initiatives obviously furthered the nationalist cause: NMSP leaders – many of whose children are in fact educated 'inside' Burma or in Thailand – understood the symbolic importance of an indigenous school system. Here was something the revolution could offer the people – a concrete advertisement for the NMSP. In providing an important service to its people, the party maintained a presence on the ground and was seen to pursue a readily-understood agenda.

Given the traditional importance of education in Mon culture, it is not surprising that the party organised a school system soon after establishing itself at Three Pagodas Pass in the mid-1960s. The first Mon National Schools were established in 1972–73, and by the mid-1990s the NMSP was running a high school, several middle schools and nearly one hundred primary schools – plus more than one-hundred-and-fifty 'mixed' schools (government-run schools, in which Mon was taught after school hours, and unofficially).

The Mon National Schools offered Mon language teaching in all subjects at primary level, except for foreign languages (English and Burmese). In the middle schools, history was taught in Mon and the other subjects in Burmese, while the medium of high school instruction was usually Burmese.[70] In part, this was due to the NMSP's inability to recruit sufficient numbers of Mon-speaking teachers. Furthermore, and despite the Textbook Committees' efforts to replace them with Mon language equivalents, many schoolbooks were of necessity those used in the state system. Nevertheless, the Mon National School curriculum was 'purged' of the latter's Burmanisation of history and culture.[71]

The Human Rights Foundation of Monland (HRFM), a Thailand-based group that has not always toed the NMSP line, has observed that the state and NMSP education systems' objectives "are opposite. The government education system aims to implement government's protracted assimilationist policy by pushing the non-Burman ethnic students to learn and speak Burmese.... The main objectives of the Mon education system are to preserve and promote Mon literature ... Mon culture and history, to not forget the Mon identity."[72]

Ironically, the Burma Army has played a part in this. Mon villagers have routinely been persecuted *because* of their ethnicity, and as a result many have had little choice but to turn to the insurgents. It is a truism of cultural studies that differentiation reinforces identity. Despite the government's avowal that a separate Mon ethnic and national identity is redundant, it has by its oppression of the Mon people ensured that – at least among the displaced populations along the border – the notion of a distinct Mon identity lives on. If nothing else, the refugees' flight and subsequent dependence on the NMSP is likely to have reinforced their public identification with Mon ethnicity.[73]

CHAPTER THIRTEEN

Constructive Engagement
and the Gas Pipelines

As they lost control of the liberated zones during the 1980s and '90s, the Mon, Karen and Karenni insurgents became increasingly dependent on the refugee camps in Thailand, and the continued good will of the Thai military and security establishments. As the extent of rebel-controlled territory shrank and the number of black market trade gates along the border became fewer each year, the rebels' finances came under pressure. By the end of the 1980s, logging operations had replaced the cross-border trade in contraband as many insurgent groups' prime source of funding. Meanwhile, increased opium production and heroin trafficking continued to finance a number of armed ethnic groups along the Chinese border and in the Golden Triangle.

The late 1980s and early '90s saw radical changes in the relationships between Thailand and the Burmese government and insurgents. Behind the new Thai (and ASEAN) policy of Constructive Engagement with Rangoon lay powerful political, security and – above all – economic interests. Following its suppression of the 1988 democracy uprising and 1990 election results, Burma's Western and Japanese donors had withdrawn all development assistance to the SLORC. The Burmese economy was crumbling, and the regime in desperate need of foreign exchange. Meanwhile, the economies of Burma's Southeast Asian neighbours were booming and capital in the region was looking for new markets.

The growth of a closer relationship between the Thai military-political establishment and the Burmese junta was based on natural resource extraction and the prospect of developing new investments in Burma. The most important and controversial of these projects was the development of the Yadana and Yetagun natural gasfields in the Gulf of Martaban, and the construction of two gas pipelines linking these to Thailand. The largest infrastructure project ever undertaken in Burma, the Yadana pipeline alone would eventually provide Rangoon with more than $200 million a year in foreign exchange. First though, the gas pipeline area would have to be 'pacified'.

The Southeast Asian Détente:
ASEAN and Constructive Engagement

At an historic meeting at Bandung in Indonesia, in April 1955, U Nu's Burma had become a founder member of the Non-Aligned Movement (NAM) of newly-independent nations. Situated between the Indian and Chinese spheres of influence, in the 1950s Burma had seemed set to play an active role on the world stage, as symbolised by the appointment in 1962 of the Burmese diplomat, U Thant, as Secretary General of the UN. However, by the early 1970s, under General Ne Win, the country had become a by-word for international isolation.

In 1979 Burma withdrew from the NAM, in part because Ne Win felt that Cuba and other 'Third World' countries were attempting to move the organisation away from China and into the Soviet camp. Under U Nu, in the late 1950s and '60s, Burma had enjoyed cordial relations with the USSR. However, in the years following the 1967 anti-Chinese riots in Rangoon (which occurred at the height of the Cultural Revolution), Ne Win moved Burma deeper into international isolation. This process was reinforced in the 1970s by China's large-scale support for the CPB, and Western governments backing of U Nu's PDP. However, by the 1980s, diplomatic relations had come full circle, as the BSPP regime (and later the SLORC) began to cultivate post-Mao China.

Despite some misgivings on the part of India, twelve years later the SLORC re-joined the NAM, signalling Rangoon's desire to re-engage with the international community. Following the 1988 coup, the SLORC announced its intention of jettisoning Ne Win's Burmese Way to Socialism and twenty-five years of state economic planning. Burma would be opened-up to private enterprise and foreign investment. The generals hoped to replace lost overseas development assistance with an ASEAN-style economic boom, and for a few years it seemed that Burma might even one day achieve Southeast Asian 'tiger economy' status.

With the end of the 'communist threat' in Southeast Asia in the late 1980s, US and Thai Cold War strategic interests had given way to geo-commercial considerations. The need to contain the growing power of China – which seemed intent on extending its influence into South and Southeast Asia, via Burma – was still of paramount concern but, by 1995, Thai relations with Rangoon had come full circle. On the surface at least, centuries of antipathy between the two great Theravada Buddhist nations had given way to an unprecedented fraternalism.

This was somewhat ironic, as in the 1990s Thailand seemed at last to be shaking-off the tradition of government by cyclic military coup. The Thai economy was enjoying record GDP growth rates and Bangkok had become a regional financial hub. A bi-product of this rapid growth was the import of migrant workers from poorer countries in the region: Thai businesses needed workers to fill the dirty and dangerous jobs that Thai citizens were no longer willing to do. The country's capitalists also needed to expand their markets. They turned to Thailand's impoverished, war-torn neighbours: Cambodia, Laos and Burma. In 1989 the prime minister, (retired) Maj-General Chatchai Choonhaven, characterised the kingdom's new regional policy as 'turning battlefields into marketplaces'.

Relations with Thailand's neighbours had long been the domain of the Thai military. In the 1970s and '80s a number of Thai and Burmese officers had trained together in the USA, and these soldier-politicians often had as much in common with each other as they did with civilians at home. Although, as a nation, the Thais have never forgotten the Burmese sacking of Ayuthaiya, the Royal Thai Army cannot be accused of letting national stereotypes interfere with the pursuit of profitable relations with Burma.

According to a 1994 Human Rights Watch/Asia report on the Mon refugees, Thai foreign policy, "like so many others in the region, was driven by 'commercial diplomacy'."[74] Whilst other ASEAN nations too, such as Indonesia, Malaysia and Singapore, helped bring the pariah SLORC regime 'in from the cold', powerful Thai interests hoped also to profit from the new policy of 'constructive engagement'. First coined in 1991, the phrase came to mean drawing the Burmese military government into dialogue with the international community, via trade links. The concept emerged in Kuala Lumpur, at a meeting between ASEAN foreign ministers and their Western 'dialogue partners'. The latter criticised ASEAN for its failure to press for changes in Burma. In reply, the ASEAN secretariat sketched a policy of Constructive Engagement with Rangoon. The idea was that by 'engaging' with the junta, other countries could effect a liberalisation of Burma's economic and political regime. The theory was more heavy on carrot than stick, and the process whereby these changes were supposed to occur was not clear.

Since its inception in 1967, ASEAN had always been conceived of as a grouping of all ten Southeast Asian nations. However, until the end of the Cold War, it had operated as a pro-Western, anti-communist (or at least, anti-Vietnamese) bloc. Therefore, when in 1995 Vietnam joined Brunei, Indonesia, Malaysia, the Philippines, Thailand and Singapore, as the seventh member of ASEAN, it seemed to many that a new order was emerging in the region. From this point on, for Burma, Laos and Cambodia, ASEAN membership was a matter of 'when', not 'if'.

Since 1994, Burmese ministers had attended various ASEAN meetings, and in July 1995 the SLORC acceded to the grouping's Treaty of Amity and Co-operation. In November 1996 ASEAN announced that Burma, Laos and Cambodia would be invited to join simultaneously. The only pre-conditions were technical, rather than ethical or political: ASEAN would maintain its tradition of non-interference in member states' internal affairs.

The majority of ASEAN governments' human and civil rights records fell below the standards imposed on them by the international community.[75] They did not therefore, wish to set precedents for outside scrutiny, by themselves engaging with candidate-members on these issues. Whilst not all ASEAN members were convinced it made good diplomatic sense to embrace the unpredictable and widely-criticised SLORC regime, the majority – including Malaysia and Singapore, whose companies played a leading role in opening up the Burmese economy in the 1990s – were determined to welcome Burma into the regional fold.

Burma and Laos eventually joined ASEAN in June 1997, on the thirtieth anniversary of the bloc's formation. However, following Hun Sen's violent coup that month, Cambodia's membership bid was suspended. This was a potentially significant development, representing a first, tentative step away form ASEAN's long-standing policy of non- intervention member states' domestic affairs.[76] Meanwhile, having seemingly been legitimised by its entry into the regional grouping, the SLORC renewed its efforts to 'develop' Burma.

Border Area Development?
The Ye-Tavoy Railway and the Gas Pipelines

In May 1989 the SLORC initiated a new Border Areas Development Programme, ostensibly aimed at improving conditions in the ethnic minority borderlands.[77] However, the opposition claimed that the programme was in fact designed to consolidate military control over the rural population.

By the end of the decade, infrastructure development in Burma remained decades behind Thailand. Nevertheless, several businessmen in the region had plans for Burma, and stood to make large amounts of money, so long as the insurgent groups along the border did not interfere with the 'development' of their homelands. Among other projects in lower Burma, the SLORC was eager to up-grade the road from Three Pagodas Pass, northwest along the route of the old 'death railway' to Thanbyuzayat, Moulmein and Rangoon.[78] However, the largest infrastructure developments in Mon State and Tenasserim Division were the Yadana and Yetagun gas pipelines, and the Ye- Tavoy Railway.

The 160 Km Ye-Tavoy railway was built to link the underdeveloped, but resource-rich, Tenasserim Division to lower Mon State. For most of its distance, the railway ran parallel to the Ye-Tavoy motor road, the maintenance of which had for many years relied on local villagers' forced labour. With the start of work on the railway in 1993, the human rights situation in Mon State and upper Tenasserim Division went from bad to worse, as increased demands for labour were added to the burdens of arbitrary taxation, forced relocation and the *Tatmadaw's* use of press-ganged porters. Human rights workers calculate that, in the mid-1990s, 300,000 labourers each year did some form of unpaid work on the railway.[79] One result was the gradual emptying of Mon and Karen villages along its route. As the demand for forced labour intensified, those families least able to provide workers, or pay off the authorities, fled to the jungle. Many continued on to the Mon refugee camps on the border.

The Ye-Tavoy railway was however, less important strategically than the gas pipelines that crossed its route. Following two years of discussions, in July 1992 the Burmese and Thai governments' state energy enterprises signed contracts with a consortium of Western oil companies, under which Thailand agreed to buy natural gas from the Yadana ('treasure') gas-field in the Gulf of Martaban.[80] By this time, extra *Tatmadaw* battalions had already moved into the pipeline area and begun enlisting local villagers to work unpaid on the construction of barracks and other installations. In September 1994 the Burmese and Thai governments finalised arrangements for the purchase of the gas, and the following year construction of the 666 Km pipeline got underway.

The billion dollar project was financed by a consortium led by TOTAL of France (the implementing company), and including the American oil company UNOCAL, the state-owned Petroleum Authority of Thailand (PTT) and Myanmar Oil and Gas Enterprise (MOGE, with a fifteen per cent holding). The Electricity Generating Authority of Thailand (EGAT) was contracted to 'take or pay' the consortium for the gas, and Rangoon eventually stood to earn \$2–400 million per year from the project, making the pipeline Burma's most important source of foreign currency.[81]

Coming ashore at Kambauk, just south of the Tenasserim Division-Mon State boundary, the Yadana pipeline ran east for forty Km to Baan E-Thaung, on the Thai border.[82] In the 1970s and '80s E-Thaung had been an important KNU base, before falling to the *Tatmadaw* in December 1991, during the on-going pipeline negotiations. In early 1992 two Karen-Tavoyan and Burmese student refugee camps had been established on the Thai side of the border opposite E-Thaung, but the Ninth Division considered these a threat to the pipeline's security, and in April 1993 burnt them down. Given three minutes warning, the refugees were forced to relocate to the abandoned and windswept tin mines in the Ten Aw See hills, above E-Thaung, where they continued to receive rice from the BBC

The last twenty-three Km of the pipeline route through Burma ran through heavily forested hills, containing a dozen-or-so mostly Karen villages. From E-Thaung and the border, the pipeline headed southeast for nine Km through an important watershed forest, home to several endangered species (including wild elephants, tigers and a species of bat unique to the area), before turning south towards the power station in Ratchaburi Province.

In the mid-1990s several Thai NGOs and community organisations launched a vigorous campaign against the pipeline, pointing out that

Thailand did not even need the over-priced Burmese gas.[83] Nevertheless, in 1997 the Royal Thai Government announced that, despite a deeply flawed Environmental Impact Assessment, construction of the pipeline would be completed by the end of 1998. In fact, technical and financial delays on the Thai side meant that, by the time the project was fully operational, it was more than a year behind schedule.

The history of the $700 million Yetagun ('waterfall') natural gas project is a little more obscure. Burma's MOGE, Nippon Oil of Japan, Malaysia's Petronas and Premier Oil of the UK (which in 1997 bought-out the American oil giant, Texaco) had been involved in negotiations since the early 1990s. However, it was only in the middle of the decade that details emerged of plans to develop the Yetagun natural gas field, to the south of the Yadana field in the Gulf of Martaban. By 1998–99, it had become clear that a second gas pipeline would be constructed from the Yetagun field to Kambauk, and from there to E-Thaung where the two pipelines would be joined. Work on the second gas pipeline was scheduled for completion in November 1999, with the gas to start pumping by mid-2000. By this time, the companies hoped that the turbines in Ratchaburi would be ready.

Unsurprisingly, the pipeline projects were characterised by widespread human rights abuses. Reports began to emerge in 1992 that the *Tatmadaw* had relocated several Karen villages in the vicinity of the pipeline corridor. From around this time, people in the area began to experience a significant rise in demands for forced labour, working on projects directly related to the pipeline, or indirectly linked to security operations in the area, such as the Ye-Tavoy railway and nearby motor road.[84] Other abuses included forced portering, the extortion of illegal 'pipeline taxes' and the arrest, torture and killing of suspected rebel sympathisers. Within a few years, dozens of previously self-sufficient farming and fishing villages had been wholly or partly depopulated, and several thousand people deprived of their lands and income.[85] It seems highly improbable that no oil company employees were aware of such activities, undertaken by their partners and bodyguards.

The pipeline area was divided into 'inner' and 'outer' security zones. In the 'outer security zone', on the periphery of the pipeline corridor, the *Tatmadaw* was charged with security duties, and road-building and maintenance responsibilities directly related to the pipeline. It is these activities, rather than the showcase projects in the closely-guarded 'inner zone' (where most oil company staff worked), which were characterised by the most severe human rights abuses.

Allegations regarding these abuses formed the basis of two related lawsuits bought against UNOCAL, on behalf of a number of refugees from the pipeline area, in a Los Angeles court in late 1996. The oil companies denied complicity and focused instead on their investment of tens of thousands of dollars in local schools, clinics and other development projects in the pipeline area. However, several small-scale livelihood projects, sponsored by UNOCAL and TOTAL, failed, and the limited number of short-term local jobs offered by the oil companies pushed up inflation, without achieving any sustainable economic benefits.[86] The companies countered that many local workers had received payment, but critics argued that these were merely token efforts, and that in any case a significant percentage of such assistance was later 're-claimed' by the *Tatmadaw*. The author has interviewed several refugees who were forced to work unpaid on pipeline-related projects, and others whose payments received from 'the foreigners' were stolen soon afterwards.

In February 1999 reports emerged in the Thai press that the oil companies had made payments directly to *Tatmadaw* units involved in counter-insurgency operations in the pipeline area, and were thus directly implicated in security-related abuses.[87] The companies were also keen to support the planned Myinmoletkat Nature Reserve, a huge 'bio-diversity sphere' in the Tenasserim region, below the pipeline area. Human and environmental rights groups feared that creation of this proposed wildlife sanctuary might involve the removal of human settlements in the area, effectively creating an extensive security zone.[88]

Before such ambitious plans could be implemented, the pipeline area had to be fully 'pacified'. In the early 1990s the forests north of E-Thaung were still patrolled by the MNLA's Tavoy Battalion, while KNLA Fourth Brigade (Tenth Battalion) operated to the south of the pipeline corridor. According to the KNU, whilst in 1990 there had been only two, by 1996 there were more than ten *Tatmadaw* battalions stationed between Kambauk and E-Thaung.[89] Mon sources claim that, by 1999, the number of battalions in the pipeline area had risen to twenty-five.[90] Inevitably, the militarisation of this once quiet backwater brought suffering to the local population, and provoked a sometimes violent response.

In March 1995 five TOTAL employees were reportedly killed during an attack on the pipeline.[91] Further incidents occurred in early 1996, in retaliation for which local *Tatmadaw* units reportedly tortured and executed nine villagers,[92] and in May 1998 ten Burmese soldiers were killed near the pipeline, in clashes with the KNU.[93] This was the first time that KNLA regulars had been involved in such attacks, the earlier incidents apparently being carried out by autonomous local Karen militia. In fact, sabotage attempts against the pipelines occurred less frequently than might have been expected, had the insurgents been seriously determined to disrupt the projects. At least in part, this was due to the fact that in 1996 American diplomatic personnel in Bangkok had secretly warned the KNU that any attack on an American company (i.e. UNOCAL) would result in US denunciation of KNU 'terrorism', and the withdrawal of American funding for the refugee relief programme.

Logging, Mining and Border Business

The development of the Yadana and Yetagun gasfields in the long-neglected Tenasserim Division symbolised a new opening-up of Burma's previously insular economy. Since the late 1980s, the insurgents' finances too had undergone a transformation.

As government forces secured a string of bases along the border, the rebels' control of the black market trade had further decreased. As a result, the Thai National Security Council (NSC) and military establishment began to reassess their covert support for the insurgents, and to seek improved relations with Rangoon, under the ASEAN policy of Constructive Engagement. The new environment was epitomised by the rise of the soldier-businessman-politician, sometime Royal Thai Army Commander-in-Chief and Armed Forces Supreme Commander, General Chavolit Yongchaiyud. In December 1988 General Chavolit had become the first foreign leader to visit Burma since the SLORC coup that September.[94] He and his entourage were rewarded with several lucrative, cut-price logging concessions in the border areas, the income from which helped to fund more than one Thai election campaign.

According to the World Resources Institute, between December 1988 and late 1989 the SLORC sold forty-two logging concessions, covering an area of 18,800 square Km, to Thai firms with high-level Thai military and/or government patrons. The estimated $112 million generated by these deals made a considerable contribution to maintaining the SLORC's grip on power.[95] A number of exclusive fishing concessions were also sold, as a consequence of which scores of predominantly ethnic Mon and Tavoyan villages on the Gulf of Martaban were barred from their traditional waters, or found their catches greatly reduced.

In a parallel development, following a series of disastrous floods caused by deforestation, in January 1989 the government announced a complete ban on logging in Thailand. The new ruling put Burmese timber at a premium, at a time when the SLORC was in desperate need of foreign currency, and had just sold logging rights to one of the most powerful men in Thailand.

A number of the new timber concessions were located in rebel-held areas. The insurgents had little choice but to comply with Thai demands for access to the rich teak and other hardwood stands under their control. In compensation the NMSP, KNU, KNPP and other groups were able to extract a cut in the business from their Thai 'partners', which in the Mon area included the Sia Hook and Chao Phya-Irrawaddy logging companies. In desperate need of cash, and seeing the profits to be made from logging, the rebels soon began to offer their own concessions and negotiate local side-deals with well-connected timber merchants.[96]

The economics of the civil war have sometimes been confusing. Since the 1940s, the insurgents have on occasion purchased ammunition from local

Tatmadaw units, and the conflict has long been characterised by incidents of economic co-operation across the front-line. Local arrangements between Thai soldiers-cum-businessmen, *Tatmadaw* field commanders and insurgent officers have sometimes led to bizarre partnerships in natural resource exploitation. Indeed, under the 1988–89 logging deals, it was not unknown for timber felled by Thai companies in insurgent-controlled territory to be inspected and cleared for export by Burmese state officials.

A number of insurgent officers made personal fortunes in the 1990s, and income from logging also went some way towards replenishing ethnic nationalist treasuries, as well as ensuring them a degree of continued influence in powerful Thai circles. However, the long-term effects of the logging boom were catastrophic. According to conditions attached to the SLORC concessions, Thai companies operating in rebel-controlled territory were required to monitor insurgent activities and construct strategically important logging roads in the liberated zones.[97] As well as the severe ecological damage caused by widespread deforestation, the new roads opened up previously inaccessible areas to the *Tatmadaw*.

In an effort to protect some of the remaining forested areas under its control, in the late 1980s the NMSP established forest reserves behind Three Pagodas Pass and in the Ye River watershed. The party soon came under pressure from Thai logging companies to open up these protected areas. A compromise could not be negotiated, and at the end of the 1991 dry season an MNLA (or possibly ABSDF) unit attacked two Sia Hook logging trucks, that were removing felled trees from the area without Mon – but with SLORC – permission. *Sia* Hook was furious, and vowed revenge.

In November 1991 three senior NMSP leaders were invited to 'peace talks' with the logging tycoon's representatives and interested Thai authorities in Sangkhlaburi. The meeting was a set-up: the Mon leaders were arrested and spent the next six months in the Immigration Detention Centre (IDC). This humiliating incident made it clear whose interests would prevail in the struggle for power and money along the border.

In 1992 the SLORC earned as much as $200 million from timber concessions. Nevertheless, in July that year Rangoon announced that no new logging licences would be issued.[98] The government was apparently embarrassed by adverse publicity attached to extensive deforestation along the Thailand-Burma border, and dismayed at Thai companies' rapacious exploitation of Burma's natural resources. The new restrictions were routinely dodged by well-connected Thai businessmen, but rebel finances were badly hit by the ban. Furthermore, as the amount of territory they controlled continued to decline with each dry season's fighting, the insurgents had increasingly fewer natural resources to exploit, and thus less bargaining power.

Another sector from which the rebels, and particularly the KNU, had long derived some income was mining. Like the logging business, mining operations were undertaken by privately-owned companies, which paid the rebel administrations a license fee. These small outfits were often controlled by the children or spouses of senior insurgent officers. They sold their lead, tin or wolfram to big Thai and Korean mining companies, which processed and marketed the minerals and, together with the Mon and Karen middle-men, made the big profits. The miners themselves remained poor, their small shanty towns lacking even rudimentary health or education facilities.

The Karen have traditionally been reluctant to disturb the earth spirits by digging deep in the ground, and even in KNU-controlled areas many mine workers were Mon.[99] Similarly, in Cambodia between the 1970s and mid-90s, large number of Mon migrants worked in gem mines controlled by the *Khmer Rouge* and other armed groups.

Back in Burma meanwhile, with the end of the Cold War and the decline in cross-border trade, Thai military and commercial interests had few reasons to continue supporting the losing side in Burma's civil war. By 1993–94, the MNLA was no longer able to patrol along the pipeline corridor, and had lost access to a number of villages along the coast between Kambauk and Tavoy, from which the Mon army had previously gathered taxes and launched hit-and-run guerrilla operations. As the *Tatmadaw* systematically re-located Mon and Karen communities in the vicinity of the gas pipelines and elsewhere, the MNLA found it increasingly difficult to move around and live off the land.

About half of the MNLA's remaining two thousand troops still operated in long-distance columns, the remainder being deployed along the border, particularly in the Ye River valley and environs. This area extended from NMSP Tavoy District headquarters, opposite Pa Yaw refugee camp (some 50 Km north of E-Thaung), to the front-line near Three Pagodas Pass (another 60 Km to the north). The apex of a triangle was formed by the front-line positions around Hanni and Kanni villages, half way up the Ye River. A new NMSP/MNLA Central had been established in 1993 at the foot of this triangle, in the Ye River watershed.

Further to the north and west, in NMSP Moulmein and Thaton Districts, were several more MNLA positions, defended by two battalions of about two hundred troops each. There were also some two-to-three hundred Mon troops at two main strongholds in the southern Mergui District. However, these forces' loyalty to Central was not unconditional.

CHAPTER FOURTEEN

The 1994 Halochanee Crisis

By 1993, the NMSP was coming under increasing pressure from the Thai security establishment to agree a ceasefire with the SLORC, thus clearing the way for the exploitation of gas deposits and other natural resources in the Mon homelands. This pressure came in a number of forms, including restrictions on the movement and activities of NMSP personnel in Thailand, continued harassment of the refugees and Mon illegal immigrants in the kingdom, and a general tightening of security measures along the border.

In late 1993 the MNRC opened a new camp, called Bee Ree, near NMSP Central in the Ye River headwaters. The following year, the Thai authorities ordered the Loh Loe refugees to be repatriated, either to Bee Ree or Halochanee, another new camp right on the border, and only two hour's walk from the *Tatmadaw* garrison at Three Pagodas Pass. Just four months later, the Burma Army attacked Halochanee and the refugees fled back into Thailand. Despite an international outcry, by August the Thai authorities had again forcibly expelled them.

The 1994 'Halochanee crisis' taught the NMSP and MNRC the limits of international protection, while the NGOs and representatives of the international community were put on notice that the Thai authorities would countenance no challenge to their Burma policy. Under such circumstances, the future for the refugees looked bleak.

Talks About Talks

As pressure increased on the Thai side of the border, the *Tatmadaw* stepped-up its military and political campaign against the NMSP and allies. When the powerful Military Intelligence chief and SLORC Secretary One (and Chairman of the Work Committee for the Development of Border Areas and Ethnic Minorities), Khin Nyunt, visited Mon State in November 1993, he announced that he wished to extend the government's ceasefire package to the NMSP.

205

Lt-General Khin Nyunt had been head of the Directorate of Defence Services Intelligence (DDSI) since 1984, the year after his predecessor was purged from Ne Win's inner circle; to some observers, Khin Nyunt was the still-powerful Ne Win's heir-apparent. The DDSI, which provided most Military Intelligence Service personnel, operated under Lt-Colonel (later Maj-General) Kyaw Win, who together with Lt-Colonel Kyaw Thein of the Office of Strategic Studies (OSS, established in 1994), acted as Khin Nyunt's representative in dealings with the insurgents.[100]

Khin Nyunt's offer of talks was conveyed to the NMSP by the Kachin businessman Khun Myat, a key figure in mediating the 1993–94 KIO-SLORC ceasefire, who was later also involved in talks with the KNU (see below). In November 1993 the NMSP Central Committee voted to commence formal negotiations with the government.

The NMSP delegates met the SLORC in Moulmein in late December 1993, at the start of the military campaigning season. As the two sides began negotiations, reports reached the Mon team that *Tatmadaw* columns had begun moving down the Ye river towards the MNLA 777 Battalion base at Hanni. The message was clear: agree a ceasefire, or prepare to face a new offensive.

The first round of 'talks about talks' ended on 3rd January 1994, with both sides agreeing to report back to their superiors and resume negotiations in March.[101] In February the NMSP Central Committee met to discuss ceasefire strategy. The leadership drew-up a 'Fourteen-Point Plan', outlining the issues they wished to raise with the government. Following the DAB agenda, these included demands for a nation-wide ceasefire, the release of political prisoners (including Daw Aung San Suu Kyi) and the holding of tripartite talks between the SLORC, the ethnic nationalists and the NLD. At this stage, a majority on the Central Committee was still opposed to any agreement with the SLORC other than a full political settlement. The Mon had not fought for nearly fifty years, only to accept a ceasefire that merely recognised the military *status quo*, without addressing the issues that had caused the them to take up arms in the first place.

During the second round of discussions, in Moulmein that March, the SLORC negotiators reminded the NMSP that a political settlement was out of the question and that only discussion of a military ceasefire was on the agenda. This stance, which recalled Ne Win's position in the abortive 1963 peace talks, was consistent with the SLORC' line in the other ceasefires of the late 1980s and early '90s. Beyond a certain amount of ill-defined development assistance, all other arrangements regarding Burma's ethnic groups were to be decided by the National Convention in Rangoon, which had been inaugurated in January 1993 to draft a new state constitution (but to which no Mon representatives had been invited).[102]

Having been disappointed on the political front, the NMSP made little progress in military negotiations. The party demanded the right to station troops in fifty-four zones, most of which were currently patrolled by the MNLA, but less than half of which were in any real sense controlled by the insurgents. The Burma Army Southeast Command was prepared to countenance a continued MNLA presence in only twelve of these fifty-four map reference points.[103]

After a further round of talks in late June and early July, the negotiations broke down. The sticking point with the Mon was what was to later prove the main obstacle to a KNU ceasefire: the SLORC would not accept any discussion of political issues. The only thing on offer was permission for the NMSP to continue in occupation of the same limited amount of territory in Mon State that they had rejected in March. The NMSP leadership considered the extent of the proposed 'ceasefire zones' inadequate. However, as the MNLA was weaker than the KIA and ex-communist armed groups, the NMSP had less bargaining power.

As NMSP Deputy Foreign Minister Nai Pe Thein Za put it to James Fahn of *The Nation*, the SLORC message was simple: "take it or leave it."[104] With their rear supply lines under pressure and civilian dependants under threat of repatriation, the Mon insurgents were faced with a limited set of options.

Thai Policy, UNHCR and the Move to Halochanee

There had been eight Mon refugee camps in 1992, but by the end of 1993 there were only four. Camp moves were usually initiated by the Ninth Division, then endorsed by the MOI in Bangkok. The MNRC and the NGOs had little say in such matters.

In January 1993 the Ninth Division proposed closing Loh Loe refugee camp and sending the refugees back to Burma.[105] Although, on this occasion, the MNRC was able to lobby for a suspension of this move, it was clear that the Thai authorities would continue to press for a Mon refugee repatriation. By harassing their civilian support base in the refugee settlements, the Royal Thai Army and Thai National Security Council (NSC) hoped to pressurise the NMSP into adopting policies friendly to Thai strategic interests – which in practice often meant private commercial concerns.

Until the early 1990s, it had been easy for the NMSP and KNU elites to travel in Thailand and gain access to the outside world. However, from around the time of the fall of Three Pagodas Pass, it became increasingly difficult for the Burmese opposition to operate freely in Thailand. In 1994 the Thai authorities closed down the NMSP office in Bangkok, and although it was still possible for insurgent personnel to travel with passes issued by Thai intelligence agents, the tenor of Thai policy had changed.

Meanwhile in early 1994, the Bangladeshi government – with the co-operation of an uneasy UNHCR – was in the process of repatriating more than a quarter million Muslim *Rohingya* refugees who had fled Burma in 1991–92, following a more than usually brutal wave of *Tatmadaw* persecution in Rakhine State.[106] In Thailand, the authorities had still not invited UNHCR to assist or effectively monitor the Burmese refugee caseload. The Thai government wished to avoid a repeat of the huge refugee in-flows from Cambodia and Laos in the 1970s and '80s. The cash-strapped UN agency meanwhile, seemed unwilling to get involved along the Thailand-Burma border, perhaps out of fear of jeopardising the on-going *Rohingya* repatriation.[107]

Although, since 1992, UNHCR staff had made a few visits to the camps, in general the Bangkok office of the High Commissioner relied on the NGOs to monitor the situation along the border. In response to BBC Chairman Jack Dunford's enquiries, in February 1994 UNHCR finally accepted that "the Myanmar ethnic minority populations in settlements along the Thai/Myanmar border ... would be considered as prima facie refugees within the mandate of UNHCR."[108] Nevertheless, the BBC, MSF and other humanitarian agencies continued to look after the refugees' food and medical needs, and there was little concern about the lack of a recognised international presence along the border.

Until the mid-1990s, attention remained focussed on the supply of assistance to the refugees, rather than their protection – although Jack Dunford urged UNHCR to get more involved on a number of occasions.[109] However, some within the NGO community were quietly opposed to the agency taking on a larger role. Internationalisation of the situation would inevitably further distance the refugees from decisions affecting their daily lives, and from the liberated zones in Burma. Where possible, the NGOs sought to empower these displaced communities. However, in practice they usually worked through local elites, and were not well-placed to stop either the Thai or insurgent authorities using the refugees to their own ends.

This is not to suggest however, that the Mon nationalists abused their power over the refugees. While the NMSP took advantage of opportunities to attract international support and recognition, the party was aware that too close an association with the refugees could be counter-productive, for both parties.

Therefore in early 1994, in a timely move to de-politicise the MNRC, Nai Tin Aung was replaced as chairman by the tough-talking monk, Phra Wongsa Pala, Secretary of Wat Prok in Bangkok. The change in MNRC leadership reinforced the committees' relationship with Thailand, while distancing the refugees from the party.

Since the 1980s, Phra Wongsa had played an important intermediary role, between different factions within the nationalist community. In recent years, his monastery had sheltered large numbers of displaced Mon and other Burmese refugees in the Thai capital. His arrival at the helm of the MNRC signalled the influence of the *sangha* within the Mon nationalist movement and allowed Nai Tin Aung to resume his political career. The latter became NMSP foreign spokesman, and from 1994 was increasingly involved in the ceasefire negotiations.

By 1994, there were some 9,000 Mon refugees living in two camps in the Sangkhlaburi area, plus more than 2,000 IDPs receiving NGO assistance on the Burma side of the border, in NMSP Tavoy and Mergui Districts (the latter group's rice was supplied by COERR). In October the Ninth Division again ordered the refugees at Loh Loe to relocate, this time to a new site at Halochanee, where the boundaries of Mon and Karen States meet, six Km south of Three Pagodas Pass, and four Km from the old NMSP headquarters at Nam Khok. Thai military sources reminded UNHCR and the NGOs that Loh Loe had always been a temporary camp,[110] and blamed the refugees for deforestation in the surrounding National Park. The refugees countered that the trees around Loe Loh had been cut down several years before their arrival, and protested that they were being made scapegoats for Thailand's lax forestry protection regime.

In late 1993 several dozen displaced Mon families, living illegally in the area, were forcibly re-settled at Halochanee and, by March 1994, 5,000 Loh Loe residents had made the 35 Km journey by truck and foot to the new camp. By the end of April, the move was complete. Some 2,000 of the original 7,402 Loh Loe refugees had moved west to Pa Yaw and the remaining few hundred had gone to the new camp at Bee Ree, on the Burma side of the border (see below). A small number of refugees were 'lost' during the move, choosing to join relatives in Sangkhlaburi and elsewhere.

Prior to the move, General Charan Kullavanijaya, Secretary-General of the Thai National Security Council (NSC), had given guarantees that international NGOs would be allowed continued access to the refugees. According to the NSC and Royal Thai Army, Halochanee was 'on the border'. However, the NMSP and MNRC were adamant that the site was in Burma. Although the UNHCR Representative in Bangkok did not feel able to protest the move to Halochanee as a case of *refoulement* (non-voluntary repatriation), the agency did privately express its concern to the Royal Thai Government. The Thai authorities assured UNHCR that, in the event of attack, the refugees would be allowed to move "further into Thai territory".[111]

The move to Halochanee was the latest and most drastic in a series of forced camp relocations. Since the early 1990s, it had become clear that Thai policy involved moving the Mon refugees in stages up to – and eventually back across – the border. Respecting Thailand's right to situate refugee camps wherever they deemed most appropriate within the kingdom's borders, neither the representatives of the international community in Bangkok, nor the official NGOs, had felt able to protest camp moves, whilst these occurred within Thailand. As it was apparently situated right 'on' the border, Halochanee was a moot case.

By the start of the 1994 rainy season, Pa Yaw refugee camp, fifty Km west of Sangkhlaburi, was the only Mon refugee settlement still definitely located in Thailand. Bee Ree meanwhile, was very much in Burma.

Since the start of the 1993–94 dry season, several hundred displaced Mon villagers, many of whom had fled forced labour on the Ye-Tavoy railway, had begun to congregate in the Ye River ('Bee Ree') watershed area. *Dacoits* (bandits) had previously operated along the river, but when the NMSP moved its headquarters to the area the security situation stabilised, and the party found it useful to settle a civilian population in the vicinity of Central.

Between 1992–94, the Thai military and Border Patrol Police destroyed a number of small, Mon and Lao 'squatter' villages, in the officially protected forest opposite Central, between the border and Loh Loe. Having cleared this area, the authorities were unwilling to allow the new arrivals at Bee Ree to enter, and set up a camp in, Thailand. Therefore, in early 1994 they persuaded the MNRC to announce the creation of a new camp at Bee Ree. The most isolated and inaccessible of all the refugee settlements on the Thailand-Burma border, Bee Ree was also the camp furthest inside rebel-held Burma. As the Ninth Division and MOI were for the time-being prepared to allow cross-border NGO assistance to the new settlement, the BBC and MSF agreed to include Bee Ree in the refugee caseload.[112]

The Attack on Halochanee

The 1994 dry season had again seen fighting between the *Tatmadaw* and MNLA, in Tavoy and Moulmein Districts. Despite the Thai authorities' security guarantee, the refugees at Halochanee lived in fear of attack. Three months after their arrival from Loh Loe, at the start of the rainy season, their worst fears were realised.[113]

Early on the morning of 21st July, a one hundred-strong column from *Tatmadaw's* 62nd Battalion entered Baleh Donephai, the westernmost section of Halochanee, and home to five hundred refugees and a few dozen NMSP personnel. One month previously, two Burmese soldiers had been discovered in Baleh Donephai at night, lurking in the vicinity of an NMSP forestry officer's house. The Mon gentleman had opened fire on the intruders, killing one of them. Two Burma Army issue G2 rifles were recovered the next morning, abandoned nearby. It was ostensibly these that the *Tatmadaw* had come to retrieve.

The 62nd Battalion was rotating out of Three Pagodas Pass, and should have been heading back to the garrison at Ye, 50 Km to the west. However, its officers had decided to make a detour, reclaim the lost rifles and create a little havoc. By eleven AM the Burmese troops had rounded up fifty refugees, whom they proceeded to drive before them as a 'human shield', as they advanced up the narrow wooded valley towards the main section of the camp, two Km to the east. The intruders were met in the forest, half way to 'Halochanee proper', by a small detachment of the local MNLA Moulmein Battalion, which had a base behind Halochanee. A fire-fight broke out and a Burmese soldier was killed, following which the *Tatmadaw* retreated to Baleh Donephai.

In retaliation for the attack on their column, the Burmese soldiers set fire to the middle section of Baleh Donephai, destroying one hundred refugee houses. The intruders then departed in the direction of Ye, taking sixteen refugees with them as porter-hostages (one of these men was only released at the end of the following year, after the ceasefire). The remaining Baleh Donephai refugees were told that anyone still there when the *Tatmadaw* returned, would be killed.

Meanwhile, more than 3,000 refugees from the main part of the camp had fled over the hill into Thailand, where they sought shelter around the Border Patrol Police checkpoint at Baan Don Yang, just a few hundred yards inside Thai territory. The Baleh Donephai refugees began to arrive at the new site during the afternoon and evening. When the author visited Baleh Donephai early the next day it was eerily quiet, with the remains of a BBC rice store still smouldering.

Responses to the Attack

The next day, the Burmese Foreign Minister, U Ohn Gyaw – who was in Thailand for an ASEAN Foreign Ministers' meeting – told the world's press that Burma did not have a human rights problem, and denied reports of *Tatmadaw* attacks on ethnic minority villages. Amnesty International disagreed, and on 23rd July released a typically prompt 'Urgent Action', drawing attention to the plight of the Halochanee refugees and abductees. The following morning, the bulletin was on the desks of Bangkok embassy staff and journalists.[114] Over the following weeks, Amnesty and the MNRC issued several more widely-reported situation updates.

Within three days of the attack, the Thai authorities were already telling the refugees to return to Burma, which they refused to do. In late July the Thai prime minister, Chuan Leekpai, was met on a trip to Canada by angry demonstrators, including exiled Mon refugees and activists, who demanded fair treatment for the Halochanee refugees. Nevertheless, on 4th August, and again on the 10th, the Ninth Division ordered the refugees to return to Burma, insisting that guarantees of their safety had been obtained from the *Tatmadaw*.

On 8th August the Bangkok-based Overseas Mon Young Monks Union (OMYMU) and Overseas Mon National Students Organisation (OMNSO) held a demonstration outside the UNHCR offices in Bangkok. The UN refugee agency gave assurances that the refugees' plight had been raised with the Thai authorities. Meanwhile, the Wat Prok monks brought in extra

211

relief supplies and moral support and the OMYMU published a timely report on the *Forgotten Refugees*.[115]

The flimsy bamboo and plastic refugee shacks at 'New Halochanee' (Baan Don Yang) were huddled together behind the Border Patrol Police checkpoint, not more than a kilometre from the border hill. Despite the import of drinking water and extra food, the situation in the little shanty town was dire. The mud was terrific and it was a tribute to the work of MSF and the Mon medics that a feared outbreak of cholera never materialised. Visits that August from UNHCR and American Embassy staff also helped to boost the refugee's morale.

The refugees were adamant that they could not – and the MNRC, that they should not – return to Burma. This conviction was strengthened by news, in the first week of August, of clashes between the *Tatmadaw* and MNLA in Ye Township. Meanwhile, the rain poured down and the refugees still refused to move.

Throughout August, the NMSP leadership was gathered for meetings at Central, which during the rainy season was two day's walk from Halochanee. Unfortunately, when a senior party official did eventually visit the refugees, his off-the-cuff remarks – to the effect that Halochanee was now quite safe – served only to undermine the MNRC and refugees' position. Although some observers interpreted these unfortunate comments as indicative of the Thai military's influence over the NMSP, it is more likely that the Central Committee member in question was just poorly briefed.

His timing though, could not have been worse. A 10th August deadline to return to Burma, set by the Ninth Division, had just passed and the Thai authorities were by now refusing BBC and MSF personnel access to New Halochanee. *The Bangkok Post* quoted UNHCR's Ruprecht Von Arnim as being' "very worried about the safety of the refugees" and stating that if they were sent back "we can only fear the worst."[116]

However, the refugees' continued presence in Thailand was not without attendant dangers: after a two week hiatus at the beginning of the month, from the second week of August, IDC deportations recommenced at the temporary New Halochanee camp, stretching relief supplies to the limit and increasing the strain on an already difficult environment. Then on 13th August, during an attempted rape on a Karen IDC deportee, a drunken Thai policeman shot and seriously wounded one of the Mon refugees. There was an outcry in the Thai press, and the victim eventually received some compensation; the perpetrator was never punished.[117]

Less than a week later, on 22nd August, Lt-General Sanan Kajornklam of the Royal Thai Army Supreme Command – a veteran of refugee operations on the Cambodian border[118] – held a joint press conference at Three Pagodas Pass, with Colonel Tin Kyi, commander of the *Tatmadaw* 61st Battalion. They called for the refugees to return to Burma, and again guaranteed their safety at Halochanee. On the same day, Thai NSC agents led by the notorious businessman, 'Mr X',[119] flew by helicopter to Pa Yaw, where they threatened Nai Shwe Kyin that unless the NMSP co-operated, the party's activities in Thailand would be further curtailed.

On the last day of August, the Royal Thai Army presented the refugees with a *fait acompli*: Thai soldiers seized and blockaded the refugees' rice store, refusing to allow them access to humanitarian relief supplies.[120] Despite protests from UNHCR, whose Representative said he "would not call it a voluntary repatriation",[121] on 7th September 1994 the refugees were forced by the threat of starvation to begin returning to Halochanee. Although UNHCR continued to voice doubts as to whether Halochanee was in Thailand or Burma (i.e. as to whether or not this was technically a repatriation), Mr Von Arnim promised to press the NSC for renewed access to the site.[122]

Back to Square One; More Pre-Ceasefire Manoeuvring

As the MNRC noted, it was "on the very day that (the Thai and Burmese governments) signed the Memorandum of Understanding for exploitation of the massive natural gas in the Mon territory in Burma that the 6,000 Mon refugees were finally pushed back to their unsafe shelters in the Burmese territory by the Thai Army."[123] By 9th September, the last of the refugees were back in 'no man's land', and their temporary shelters in Thailand had been destroyed. On 6th October the first of a new wave of 1994–95 dry season refugees began to arrive at Halochanee.

A nasty footnote to the Halochanee crisis is provided by the fate of the MNRC General Secretary, Nai Mon Chan, who was abducted by Thai security agents shortly after the refugees' return. Fearing for their colleague's safety, neither the MNRC nor NMSP felt able to publicly protest his disappearance. Although he was released after two months, it was no longer safe for Nai Mon Chan to remain in Thailand, and he was forced to seek refuge overseas. This treatment of a senior refugee official sent a clear message to the MNRC and NMSP: to oppose Thai military policy along the border was to invite punishment. The Mon had been taught the limits of international protection.

As well as the MNRC, between June–September 1994 several Thailand-based NGOs had advocated on behalf of the Halochanee refugees – but to no avail. This activism did though, reinforce the Thai and Burmese authorities' perceptions of the NGOs as 'rebel supporters'.

Although Mr X began to speak against and smear the BBC among his international contacts, it still suited the Thai authorities to keep UNHCR out of the picture, and continue to rely on private relief agencies to feed the refugees. Thai policy-makers might lament the 'burden' of the refugees, but in fact the international community footed the bill and, like the NMSP and MNRC, the NGOs could ultimately be bullied into accepting Thai policy.

Although the NGOs were still primarily focused on the supply of humanitarian assistance, in 1994 *protection* became the key refugee issue – both along the border and among illegal Burmese communities in Thailand. In April Wat Prok was raided, and scores of displaced people were arrested, including a blind, handicapped Mon refugee and his family, whose case became something of a cause-celebre. A UNHCR 'person of concern', who in the mid-1980s had lost his sight and both of his arms while fighting for the MNLA, Nai Maung Kyan was detained with his family for several weeks, in the crowded and insanitary Bangkok IDC. Their plight was featured in the Thai press, which helped to ensure the family's eventual release.

The Bangkok Post also reported a new trend in the intimidation of Mon activists in Thailand: the arrest and forcible de-robing of Mon refugee monks from Burma. *The Post* agreed with a hard-hitting Human Rights Watch/Asia report published the previous year, which suggested that the renewed clamp-down on the Mon was directly related to Thai interests in securing a Mon ceasefire, thus enhancing stability in the strategically important gas pipeline area.[124]

Meanwhile inside Burma, the NMSP was coming under more pressure. In January 1995 the SLORC closed down over ninety Mon National Schools. According to observers on the ground, "as a result more than 5,000 local Mon students ... lost their access to education."[125] At the same time, the *Tatmadaw* launched a series of attacks on MNLA positions across Mon State.

During the 1995 dry season, the Kachin go-between, Khun Myat, and the Mon National Democratic Front (MNDF) MP-elect, Nai Khin Maung, helped convene a series of secret meetings in Kanchanaburi, attended by representatives of the SLORC and the NMSP. As a result of these contacts, in May 1995 the NMSP announced its willingness to pursue a new round of ceasefire negotiations with Rangoon. By this time, another NDF member-organisation, the KNPP, had succumbed to a similar package of Thai and Burmese pressure, becoming the fifteenth armed ethnic group to agree a ceasefire with the SLORC.[126]

Even before ceasefire negotiations recommenced, Mr X and representatives of the Ninth Division had met with Nai Shwe Kyin to talk about refugee repatriation, a process that had been discussed in an NMSP document the previous year.[127] The MNRC was out of the loop; the NGOs, and the highly-supportive American Embassy Refugee Affairs Section, were concerned that the Mon would be forced into accepting a refugee repatriation plan in the aftermath of any ceasefire deal, before the security implications had been properly worked-out. Meanwhile, UNHCR was trying to find a split between the positions of the MNRC and NMSP, which would justify the agency's continued inaction on behalf of the Mon refugees.

At the start of the 1995 rainy season, the author met Nai Htin, Nai Tin Aung, Nai Soe Myint, Colonel Nai Kao Rot and a small group of Mon soldiers in the jungle, near the site of the old Loh Loe refugee camp, on the way to Pa Yaw and Central. They were on their way out, by foot and on elephant back, to Sangkhlaburi; the author was walking in to Pa Yaw. On this occasion, none of the NMSP leaders seemed eager to stop and chat with the friendly aid worker, or respond to his enquiries regarding the ceasefire negotiations. However, Nai Tin Aung did let slip that the party was on its way to Moulmein.

PART FIVE

THE MON CEASEFIRE
AND SINCE

"The Mon people have supported us for more than fifty years – in fact since 1757. Their sacrifices and support have never stopped. This is the important story of Mon nationalism, not whether we are fighting or have a ceasefire."

Major-General Nai Taw Mon, Commanding Officer,
Mon National Liberation Army[1]

CHAPTER FIFTEEN

The 1995 NMSP-SLORC Ceasefire

By 1995, with the MNLA outgunned by the *Tatmadaw* and Thailand no longer willing to provide covert support or safe refuge, it was clear that only a negotiated settlement with Rangoon would allow the NMSP to retain control over its remaining liberated zones. The June 1995 ceasefire agreement brought the NMSP leadership a good deal of criticism, not least from within the wider Mon nationalist community. However, there was also a widespread understanding that, faced with a poor set of options, the party had had little choice but to agree a deal with Rangoon.

The Mon ceasefire agreement was similar to that negotiated in 1993 between the SLORC and KIO. It was though, generally less advantageous: although the NMSP was to retain control over some territory along the border, this was far less extensive than that granted to the KIO in northern Burma. The MNLA had to withdraw from positions outside the boundaries of Mon State, abandoning a number of strategically important positions to the *Tatmadaw*. In return, the NMSP was to be granted some limited 'development assistance' (which was to prove a mixed blessing). Another complicating factor was the plan to repatriate the remaining Mon refugees in Thailand, which the NMSP seemed keen to implement as quickly as possible. As the Thai authorities were past masters at refugee push-backs, the Mon refugees along the border entered 1996 fearing the worst.

Although, following the ceasefire, the NMSP was obliged to withdraw from the Democratic Alliance of Burma (DAB), many cadres retained an oppositionist mindset. Indeed, beyond the senior leadership, it was difficult to find party members who were positively enthusiastic about the agreement. The majority seemed resigned to its inevitability; a significant minority rejected it outright.

A damaging split in the Mon ranks eventually occurred in late 1996. However, tight manoeuvring around the time of the ceasefire ensured that divisions among the Mon nationalists did not have the same devastating effect on the NMSP as similar splits had the previous year, within the KNU.

In late 1994 religious and political differences within the Karen ranks had led to a disastrous fragmentation, and the loss of the previously impregnable Mannerplaw headquarters.

The fall of Mannerplaw removed any last doubts about which way the civil war in Burma was going. This was more than just another set-back for the Karen insurgents. Mannerplaw was the headquarters of the National Democratic Front (NDF), DAB and National Council of the Union of Burma (NCUB) alliances, as well as the KNU. The capital of Kaw Thoo Lei, this small town on the Moei River had been the symbolic heart of armed ethnic resistance to Rangoon.

The Fall of Mannerplaw

On 28th April 1992, just a few days after Senior General Than Shwe replaced the unstable Saw Maung as SLORC Chairman, the government announced a unilateral ceasefire in the all-out offensive against the KNU. Over the previous four months, during the 'Battle of Sleeping Dog Mountain', the Karen forces had suffered greatly, but the *Tatmadaw* had been unable to overrun Mannerplaw.

Despite the SLORC's 'ceasefire', throughout 1992–94 the Burma Army continued to wage a 'low intensity' war against the Karen. Nevertheless, in the Mannerplaw area this was a period of relative stability, during which the KNU attempted to re-group.[2] At the same time, the Karen leadership entertained exploratory overtures from government intermediaries, who hoped to persuade General Bo Mya to lead his followers into 'the legal fold'. However, most of the KNU's remaining DAB allies were opposed to entering into negotiations which did not recognise the legitimacy of those – predominantly Burman-led – parties that had emerged between 1988–90. The SLORC refused to talk with the DAB or 'political' groups, such as the All Burma Students Democratic Front (ABSDF), but would only negotiate with individual ethnic nationalist organisations.

After two years of deadlock, armed opposition politics on the Thailand-Burma border underwent a massive upheaval when the KNU suffered the most damaging split in its forty-eight year history. The repercussions of this largely self-inflicted disaster are still felt to this day.

Throughout 1992–94, there had been a number of seemingly minor religious conflicts in the Mannerplaw area, arising from years of neglect of the Buddhist Karen majority by the Christian KNU elite. Although in most outlying districts religious tolerance was the norm, some of General Bo Mya's closest associates in the headquarters area actively discriminated against their non-Christian subalterns. The underlying tensions caused by such behaviour, together with strains generated by the decades-long civil war and a growing resentment in non-elite circles of the KNU leadership's apparent corruption and lack of political vision, came to a head in late 1994.[3]

On 1st December a company of (Buddhist) Karen National Defence Organisation (KNDO) soldiers moved, without orders, from their positions near the front-line at Sleeping Dog Mountain, towards the monastery at Thoo Mweh Hta. Situated on the Burma side of the border, at the confluence of the Salween and Moei Rivers, over the previous few years, Thoo Mweh Hta had grown into an important Buddhist centre, under the patronage of U Thuzana, an ambitious Karen monk from 'inside' Burma. Although located in KNU territory, the monastery shared little of the culture of Mannerplaw, and was in practice largely free of outside control.

Whether U Thuzana's followers had connived with the KNDO men, or merely responded to their spontaneous desertion, has never been fully clarified. Soon however, events took on their own momentum. The day after their arrival, the disaffected troops held a meeting in the monastery compound. Together with a group of radical Karen monks, they aired complaints about religious persecution and poor leadership within the KNU. Over the next few days, more disaffected, battle-hardened troops abandoned their positions and moved towards the monastery. Clearly, this was a serious development, which required a prompt response from the KNU leadership in nearby Mannerplaw.

However, General Bo Mya and colleagues failed to deal with the situation effectively, dismissing events at Thoo Mweh Hta as merely a local disturbance. Elements of the KNU leadership have been in denial over the issue of Christian-Buddhist tensions ever since. By the end of December, the rebels had established the Democratic Kayin Buddhist Organisation (DKBO) and Army (DKBA),[4] creating a major split in the Karen insurgent ranks. From the outset, the DKBA received military and logistical support from local *Tatmadaw* units, and government agents among the Karen *sangha* probably played a role from the early stages of the rebellion. However, the emergence of the DKBA, at a time of great crisis in the Karen nationalist movement, was a result of genuine grievances within the Buddhist community, combined with poor political skills at the top of the KNU.

Aided by their DKBA allies' intimate knowledge of the terrain, by the end of January the *Tatmadaw* had overrun Mannerplaw, and a new wave of 10,000 Karen refugees had fled into Thailand. In March 1995 Kaw Moo Rah, the KNU's last major stronghold north of Mae Sot, fell to a sustained and massive onslaught. The KNU remnants retreated north into the Papun hills and south to KNLA Sixth Brigade, in lower Karen State. Life in the Karen insurgency would never be the same again.

Mon Unity and the June 1995 Ceasefire

The Burmese political scene is notorious for its factionalism and ethnic strife, and the *Tatmadaw* has claimed to be the only institution willing or able to maintain a unitary state amid the chaos. The military government has certainly been more successful than the opposition in preventing the emergence of damaging splits within its own ranks. Indeed, the unity of the *Tatmadaw* has been a decisive factor in the state's ability, since the early 1950s, to reassert control over large areas of Burma, fighting a civil war on several fronts. In contrast, the disunity of different communist and non-communist armed opposition groups had, by the 1980s, allowed Rangoon to gain a decisive upper hand in the civil war. It was only in the late 1980s, following the collapse of the CPB, that the insurgents managed to form a reasonably effective coalition. However, by then the international climate had changed dramatically, and it was already too late to achieve victory in the civil war.

The issue of unity has long been of central concern to the Mon nationalists. The formation of the Mon People's Front (MPF) in 1952 demonstrated the importance attached by Nai Shwe Kyin and colleagues to presenting a single, united front. In 1988, when the DAB alliance was established, the NMSP had only recently recovered from a series of damaging splits. Party leaders were keen to put such episodes behind them, but in the mid-1990s the memory of disunity was still fresh.

By 1995, the MNLA was weaker than at any time since the 1970s. Front-line units were running low on ammunition, and for financial and political reasons headquarters was finding it difficult to replenish supplies on the Thai black market. Furthermore, the Mon army was not noted for the effectiveness of its command structure: particularly in outlying areas, where logging operations and smuggling had a direct effect on the local balance of power, troops were as likely to be loyal to individual commanders, as to Central. Warlordism has been perennial in Burma; whenever and wherever the centre cannot hold, local armed groups have tended to break away from the main insurgent armies and – sometimes with *Tatmadaw* encouragement – set up in business on their own. Above all else, it was the emergence of such splinter groups that the Mon leadership most feared in the run-up to the ceasefire.

The issue of Mon unity was at the forefront of a special Congress of Mon National Affairs, held at Central in May 1995. Attended by representatives of both the Thai and Burmese Mon communities, including members of the Mon National Democratic Front (MNDF), the aim of the congress was to discuss NMSP ceasefire strategy and the future of the struggle for Monland. A number of delegates, including several from inside Burma, urged the NMSP to continue with the armed struggle, as even a symbolic resistance to the SLORC was preferable to 'capitulation'. However, the majority advocated negotiation of a ceasefire, arguing that only an end to the fighting could prevent further military reversals, and allow the NMSP to re-organise and re-establish a presence in government-controlled areas. In general, the Thai Mon did not support this position; even a majority of the

Thailand-based Mon monks wanted to see the NMSP continue the war. However, shortly before the congress opened, the NMSP Central Committee had in fact voted – although with reservations, and not unanimously – to pursue an agreement with the SLORC. As is often the case in Burmese politics, the big decisions were taken in private by a small group of leaders, before being endorsed in a more public forum.

After some further meetings conducted via go-betweens in Kanchanaburi, a fourth NMSP delegation departed for Moulmein in early June 1995, and met with the *Tatmadaw* and Military Intelligence between 2nd and 6th June. Mr X and the Thai National Security Council (NSC) arranged air transport. The NMSP delegation was empowered by the Central Committee to negotiate a full ceasefire with the SLORC. Party Vice-President Nai Htin led a negotiating team which included party General Secretary Nai Rot Sah, MNLA Chief-of-Staff Nai Aung Naing, NMSP Foreign Minister Nai Tin Aung, the party's influential Thaton District Governor, Nai Soe Myint, and the delegation's secretary (and MNLA intelligence chief), Colonel Nai Kao Rot. Observers deemed it significant that, despite pressure from the SLORC and Mr X, Nai Shwe Kyin was not a member of the Mon ceasefire team. Although the ageing NMSP President claimed that ill-health prevented him from attending the negotiations, rumours persisted that he was far from enthusiastic about the prospective ceasefire, considering it at best an unavoidable temporary move.

The senior *Tatmadaw* officer at the talks was Burma Army Southeast Regional Commander, Maj-General Ket Sein, who oversaw the mechanics of the settlement. Ket Sein had joined the *Tatmadaw* after taking part in an abortive student uprising following the 1962 coup, and was considered to be on the 'liberal' wing of the SLORC (as a regional army commander, he was automatically a member of the junta). From the outset of the talks, it was obvious that Khin Nyunt's Military Intelligence Service, represented by Lt-Colonel Kyaw Win, had not moved from its previous position, insisting that negotiations must centre on troop positions, with some general discussion regarding future development schemes. As political matters were not on the agenda, and each side was already well-appraised of the other's position, the talks moved swiftly to a conclusion.

Like the KIO truce, the NMSP-SLORC ceasefire was a 'gentleman's agreement' only: no treaty or memorandum was signed. It was a couple of days before the 29th June ceasefire agreement was featured in the state-controlled media. Myanmar TV footage showed the Mon leaders looking smart in traditional *longyis* and white jackets, while Khin Nyunt and the SLORC looked sinister in olive green.[5] The TV voice-over left it unclear exactly what Nai Htin had said in his speech but, in a statement issued on 7th July, the Burmese Embassy in Bangkok stated that the NMSP had agreed to a peace deal, after realising "the true attitude of the government."

The NMSP had 'returned to the legal fold'. However, unlike a number of ex-communist armed ethnic groups, such as the Myanmar National Solidarity Party (MNSP) – also known as the United Wa State Party (UWSP), the political wing of the United Wa State Army (UWSA) – the NMSP was not withdrawn from the SLORC's 'List of Unlawful Associations'.[6]

Having met to endorse the agreement, on 13th July 1995 the party Central Committee issued the following *Statement on the Ceasefire between the State Law and Order Restoration Council and the New Mon State Party*:

It is almost half a century that Mon resistance movement has gone through for freedom enjoying full rights of self-determination. In so doing, Mons prefer to solve their desired aspirations by peaceful means. But successive governments' denial and oppressive actions left them with no other alternative than to take up arms which has lasted more than 47 years. Though the armed resistance had borne some fruits in their favour, painful sacrifices in lives and property had also been paid by them.

The trend of the world events in the past few years have changed and gathered momentum in such a way that political problems are solved by peaceful negotiation rather than by arm conflict. The New Mon State Party also believes that political problems could successfully be solved by political means through dialogues.

Deep contemplation by the Mon leadership of the current situation was made after initiative for ceasefire was called for by the State Law and Order Restoration Council. With a view to unify the Mon populace and to further develop the fruits of armed resistance, acceptance of dialogue with representatives of the SLORC was made.

After negotiating for four times an amicable agreement was reached resulting in ceasefire ceremony on 29 June, 1995. This truce is just merely a military ceasefire. An arduous task to find satisfactory political solution is still in abeyance. During period of this ceasefire, the NMSP armed forces will retain their arms while carrying on its miscellaneous tasks as situation permits. On the other hand, work beneficial to the party as well as to general public would be carried out widely in consultation with the SLORC. For development for Mon areas, in some cases, joint-ventures between the party and the SLORC would be practised, while in the other case, it would be done between the party and the private sector. Endeavours would be made as much as feasible to boost up Mon national movement.

Thus, after abandoning the method of violent struggle, the method of peaceful negotiation will be followed for our national movement. The

NMSP will carry on with the trend of current political tidal waves of changes. With full endurance and without surrendering our arms, we will solidify the unity of the Mons and hereby declare to struggle with determination together with the peoples of other ethnic nationalities for restoration of peace, democracy and human rights in the country, in accordance with the programme laid for Mon freedom.[7]

In an unfortunate piece of timing, just as the Mon ceasefire was being finalised, the Karenni National Progressive Party (KNPP) ceasefire broke down. The only one of the post-1988 ceasefires not to have held, the three month long KNPP-SLORC agreement ended in mutual recrimination: the SLORC accused Karenni leaders of acting in bad faith, while the KNPP blamed the resumption of fighting on local *Tatmadaw* commanders' military opportunism. Insiders suggested that the renewal of hostilities was mainly due to differences between the SLORC and Karenni leadership regarding post-ceasefire logging deals. Within a few weeks of the outbreak of fighting, the KNPP had lost most of its remaining territory along the border and the Karenni Army had been forced to re-organise into small guerrilla units.

The resumption of fighting in Karenni State fuelled speculation that the Mon ceasefire might prove equally short-lived. The NMSP Central Committee was determined that this should not be the case, and promptly issued a statement regretting the collapse of the SLORC-KNPP ceasefire.[8]

Military Arrangements

Basically, the Mon accepted the same package as the Kachin and other ceasefire groups before them. However, the NMSP was militarily less significant than the KIO, and the amount of territory granted to the Mon reflected this.

As proposed by the SLORC the previous year, the MNLA would continue to station troops in twelve 'permanent' ceasefire positions in Mon State, each of which consisted of a specific map point, five Km in diameter. The northernmost of these 'permanent' positions was situated in NMSP Thaton District, near Kya-In Seik-Kyi; four more were in Moulmein District, including one near Halochanee; the remaining seven were grouped around Central and along the Ye River, west of the refugee settlements at Bee Ree. In addition to the 'permanent' positions, eight more 'temporary' ceasefire positions were recognised, including two each in NMSP Mergui and Tavoy Districts. Crucially, the NMSP agreed to vacate these bases by the end of the year.

In theory, MNLA troops could only move between different ceasefire positions after consultation with the Burma Army Southeast Command. Liaison offices were established for this purpose at Three Pagodas Pass,

Mudon, Ye and Moulmein, and a few months later the NMSP opened offices in Rangoon and Thanbyuzayat. In practice, the party had been granted one contiguous, roughly triangular block of land on either side of the Ye River, plus a couple of isolated outposts to the north and – temporarily – the south. The agreement meant that, by 1996, the MNLA should have no troops south of Central. This was significant: it meant that Mon forces were to be contained within the boundaries of Mon State, as defined in the 1974 constitution. Furthermore, withdrawal from Tavoy District (south of Central, opposite Pa Yaw refugee camp) would effectively deny Mon forces access to the Yadana and Yetagun gas pipelines, which were scheduled to converge at the border, just a few hour's walk south of NMSP Tavoy District headquarters. The Mon ceasefire would ensure a degree of stability in the pipeline area, allowing the SLORC and oil companies to reinforce road links to this strategically important zone, under the guise of 'local development'

A key element in the SLORC ceasefire agreements was the insurgents' retention of their arms. At the time of the ceasefire, the NMSP claimed a membership of 7,860 people, with an arsenal of 8,346 weapons. These figures may have reflected the total number of party members and their arms, but the actual number of MNLA troops in 1995 was not more than 2,500 men, including local militia and reserves. Although the government media reported that Mon arms had been 'exchanged for peace', the MNLA did not in fact hand over any weapons.

Prior to the ceasefire, a number of small, predominantly ethnic Burman opposition groups had operated out of Tavoy District, under NMSP patronage. Most had been with the Mon at Three Pagodas Pass and were members of the DAB. As the district was now designated a 'temporary' ceasefire position, the presence of these unreconstructed opposition groups posed something of an embarrassment to the NMSP. From now on, the National League for Democracy [Liberated Area] (NLD[LA]), Democratic Party for a New Society (DPNS), People's Defence Force (PDF), Arakan Liberation Party (ALP) and Mergui-Davoy United Front (MDUF)[9] would have to keep a very low profile – and certainly would not be allowed to launch operations against the *Tatmadaw* from bases in Mon-controlled territory. Of these organisations, only the PDF[10] and the MDUF[11] had significant armed contingents – of approximately sixty and 4–500 men respectively. By the end of 1997, all of these groups, with the exception of some 2–300 MDUF family members, had vacated the NMSP ceasefire zones.

After some intense lobbying of the *Tatmadaw* Southeast Command, and Khin Nyunt's Office of Strategic Studies (OSS), at the end of 1995 the SLORC agreed to extend the deadline for vacating the strategically important Mergui and Tavoy District 'temporary' ceasefire positions, until December 1996. Nai Aung Naing and Nai Tin Aung, the NMSP negotiators, had won a respite, but those who opposed the ceasefire were dismayed at the extent of the party's concessions.

Further Aspects of the Ceasefire Agreement

The NMSP was offered certain incentives to sweeten the agreement. Within a few weeks, the party had established a commercial wing, the Rehmonya International Company, with offices in Rangoon and Moulmein. Rehmonya International was granted an import-export license, together with permission to transport goods and passengers on various routes, including between Three Pagodas Pass and Thanbyuzayat. Mon businessmen with NMSP contacts also set up a regular boat service between Singapore, Penang and Moulmein. Following the ceasefire, Nai Shwe Kyin's only son, who had previously worked as a government irrigation engineer, joined the Rehmonya International board, of which his father was chairman, and the ex-Thaton governor, Nai Soe Myint, managing director. The MNDF MP-elect, Nai Khin Maung, also had interests in Rehmonya International and other companies.

However, enthusiastic early talk of ambitious development schemes in Mon State, including a proposed hydro-power project, proved unfounded. Within a few months, several post-ceasefire business deals had begun to go wrong. If the NMSP leadership expected to receive special treatment from the state authorities, they were perhaps naïve. In some cases, what had been offered to Rehmonya International as 'exclusive contracts' (i.e. monopolies), proved to be only standard operating licenses, subject to competition. Inexperienced in business, the Rehmonya directors were often outwitted by 'devious' competitors and, by the end of 1995, cadres on the border were already lamenting their leaders' lack of business acumen.

Critics have accused the 'ceasefire groups' of being motivated primarily by commercial considerations. Whilst this may have been true of the ex-CPB groups in Shan State, in the case of the NMSP, the ceasefire led to a deterioration in party finances. In particular, revenues from the taxation of trade, and of Mon and Karen villages in the vicinity of MNLA bases, were affected.

In exchange for no longer raising local taxes, which Rangoon regarded as its prerogative, the ceasefire agreement provided the NMSP with two million Kyat ($13–15,000 at 1995 rates) per month, as well as 30,000 Kg of (poor quality) rice – enough to feed about 1,800 people. In addition, the party was given authority to issue travel passes to NMSP personnel, or to sell them to villagers and traders who wished to travel across the ceasefire line, to or from government-controlled areas (a form of 'indirect' taxation). Observers questioned whether the NMSP was wise to accept this dependence on the government. Some accused the party of having become a SLORC client.

The fundamentals of the ceasefire have generally been honoured by both parties. Many aspects of the truce though, have proved a mixed blessing. For example, although the government's pledge to develop the infra-structure of Mon State resulted in the construction of several new roads and bridges, many of these were built using forced labour, and/or partly financed through extra local taxation (see below). Furthermore, the completion of such projects opened up previously inaccessible areas to regular *Tatmadaw* patrols, thus compromising the remaining MNLA base areas. Most depressingly, within a few months, human rights monitors were again reporting serious abuses perpetrated against Mon villagers. Whilst the ceasefire agreement may have brought the fighting to an end, the *Tatmadaw* in Mon State continued to behave like an occupying army.

Language and Culture, Human Rights and Refugees

One anticipated benefit of the ceasefire that did eventually materialise – although not for another four years – related to the use of Mon language scriptures by the *sangha*. As noted above, language, history and religion, and thus education, are key elements in the construction of Mon national identity. Under the Ne Win and SLORC regimes, Mon monks had been forced to study and take religious examinations in Burmese and Pali, rather than the ancient Mon language. Despite intensive NMSP lobbying during and after the ceasefire negotiations, this situation was to continue until the end of the decade before it was resolved.[12]

During talks that took place on the afternoon of 29th June, following the ceasefire ceremony, Khin Nyunt is reported to have promised that Mon State would be "developed within three years."[13] Presumably he was talking about infrastructure, rather than human development. Certainly the SLORC Secretary One was not keen to allow the Mon nationalists to consolidate the progress they had made, under the most difficult of circumstances, in the field of education. He refused a request for Mon language and literature to be taught in state schools, although he did agree to these subjects being covered outside of school hours (in 'mixed' schools), and in the NMSP's own Mon National Schools.[14]

Consequently, in 1995–96 the party opened a number of new schools across Mon State, for which the NMSP's widely-respected Education Secretary managed to attract funding from foreign donors. However, the SLORC did not meet its commitment to build more state schools and hospitals.[15] Following the ceasefire, ten million Kyat in Japanese Overseas Development Assistance had been earmarked for building a Mon high school, which was to be constructed at Hanni, an MNLA permanent ceasefire position on the Ye River. However, over the following year, it became clear that there were strings attached. The school – and a strategically important access road – would have to be built by SLORC contractors, using *Tatmadaw* security, under the aegis of the Border Areas Development Programme. It would also have to follow the SLORC syllabus.

The NMSP rejected this package, suspecting it was designed to bring the remaining Mon liberated zones, and bodies of Mon national identity, under central government control.[16] The new school that was never built became a symbol of ceasefire: although the fighting had stopped, neither side seemed willing or able to overcome decades (centuries even) of distrust, and move on to a new, more constructive relationship.

Japanese Overseas Development Assistance to the SLORC had been resumed in August 1995, in response to the release from house arrest of Daw Aung San Suu Kyi, who was 'freed' (her movements remained severely restricted) on 10th July 1995, just two weeks after the NMSP-SLORC ceasefire was finalised. On 23rd July the NMSP issued a statement welcoming "her release with profound gladness", deeming "it to be a process of promotion to countrywide peace."[17] Although it could hardly take credit for securing the NLD leader's freedom, the NMSP leadership obviously hoped that this would herald a breakthrough in the search for a negotiated settlement to the crisis in Burma. It was though, to prove a false dawn.

In the climate of repression that characterised Burma in the late 1990s, the NMSP remained wary of contact with foreign governments or inter-government agencies in Rangoon, such as UNHCR or the International Committee of the Red Cross (ICRC). It was not until the ceasefire entered its fifth year, that the party began to cultivate these potential sources of development assistance (see below). Meanwhile, the population of lower Burma continued to suffer. The situation of the Mon IDPs and refugees was particularly tenuous.

Although, during the ceasefire negotiations, Generals Khin Nyunt and Ket Sein had been unwilling to discuss the refugee issue, they had been informed by Nai Tin Aung of the NMSP's plans for refugee repatriation and rehabilitation, as discussed by Nai Shwe Kyin and agents of the Thai NSC in early 1995. Perhaps hoping to encourage any repatriation process, Khin Nyunt is reported to have agreed to ease the amount of forced labour demanded of villagers in Mon State, over the following dry season. Beyond this quickly-broken promise, the government negotiators refused to address any issues of human and political rights, that had motivated the Mon and other ethnic insurgencies since the earliest years.

Within weeks of the ceasefire, the Thai NSC was again pushing for repatriation of the Mon refugees. The 3,900 people at Halochanee, as well as the 1,535 at Bee Ree and 1,200-odd in Mergui District, were already back in Burma. It was now proposed that the 2,500 people at Pa Yaw be moved across the border to Tavoy District, as quickly as possible. The district was already home to some three hundred NMSP and MNLA personnel, and several hundred MDUF family members and other IDPs.

The Mon refugees repeatedly proclaimed their distrust of the ceasefire and fear of returning to Burma.[18] The prospect of moving Pa Yaw residents across the border, to a 'temporary' ceasefire zone, that was due to be handed over to the SLORC at the end of the year, filled the NGOs and MNRC with trepidation. Furthermore, with a KNU ceasefire possibly in the offing, the fate of the 10,000 Mon refugees might set a precedent for the 80,000-plus Karen and Karenni refugees along the border.

By the end of 1995, Thailand was temporary home to 75,554 Karen refugees, living in twenty-three camps.[19] Until quite recently, for most residents, life in these settlements had been quite bearable. However, on 23rd February 1995 DKBA troops had ambushed a convoy of Karen refugees moving down the Thai side of the border, opposite Mannerplaw. They killed three people, including a Thai truck driver.

Through 1995, the situation in the Karen camps became increasingly unstable, as the DKBA and their *Tatmadaw* allies launched several more attacks against the refugees, apparently with the aim of driving them back to Burma, thus undermining the KNU's civilian support base along the porous border. With the Royal Thai Army apparently unable to protect the refugees, the already demoralised Karen nationalist movement was in dire straits.

Meanwhile, secret KNU-SLORC talks were apparently making some progress. In December 1995, and three times in 1996, KNU delegations travelled to Moulmein and Rangoon, where they met with Colonels Kyaw Thein and Kyaw Win of the OSS and Directorate of Defence Services Intelligence (DDSI). For a while, it seemed that the symbolically important, although militarily much weakened, KNU might join the NMSP and KIO in the 'legal fold'. However, General Bo Mya was still unwilling to accept the standard SLORC ceasefire package. The KNU demanded a nation-wide ceasefire, the release of political prisoners and substantive political dialogue. Unsurprisingly, Rangoon was unwilling to compromise. The deadlock persisted, and the Thai security establishment began to step-up its pressure on the KNU.

Nai Shwe Kyin and the Ceasefire

Only after details of the ceasefire agreement had been discussed by the NMSP Central Committee, did Nai Shwe Kyin travel to Rangoon, for the first time since the early 1960s. The 'return to the legal fold' of such a well-known politician was a boost to Khin Nyunt and the 'ceasefire movement'. Nai Shwe Kyin's decision, in June 1995, to send Nai Htin in his stead, to attend the final round of ceasefire negotiations, had been interpreted by many observers as a demonstration of his less than whole-hearted support for the agreement. While this may then have been the case, the NMSP President's position had changed considerably over the following months.

230

Having been persuaded, by Mr X, that he should take up Rangoon's offer of a VIP reception in his homeland, in July and August 1995 Nai Shwe Kyin visited more than a dozen government-controlled villages in Mon State, where he addressed communities amongst which the NMSP had previously been able to organise only with great difficulty. The tour dramatically illustrated the veteran leader's standing among his people, and videos of it constituted must-see viewing in Sangkhlaburi.

The cable TV business on 'Mon side' was run by a Thai Mon businessman and politician, with links to the NMSP. This semi-legal, local network usually featured a mixture of pirated Asian satellite channels and Burmese video dramas. Shortly after the ceasefire though, it broadcast an unusual double bill: 'Beyond Rangoon' – Martin Borman's tedious but well-intentioned account of the 1988 democracy uprising – followed by footage of Nai Shwe Kyin's triumphal tour of Mon State.

The basic format was the same each in each village: a lengthy motorcade of trucks and saloon cars would pull into town, to be greeted by streets lined with cheering villagers dressed in traditional Mon costume. Later the NMSP worthies, village elders and the *Tatmadaw* contingent would visit the local monastery, where there would be speeches in praise of the ceasefire, and on the prospects for future development. Despite years of oppression and black propaganda against the NMSP, the people's respect for Nai Shwe Kyin and colleagues was obvious. The video footage was shaky and not always in focus. However, the author has spoken to several people who attended such events and is satisfied that the enthusiasm was genuine. However, it is also true that these 'triumphs' were stage-managed, and that over the preceding days local headmen had collected 'donations' to pay for the festivities and gifts for the visiting dignitaries.

The author met Nai Shwe Kyin in Bangkok, on his return from this historic visit. When we had last talked, in late March at his house near Pa Yaw, he had seen the ceasefire as a "last resort." Now though, less than six months later, Nai Shwe Kyin was far more optimistic. Although understandably tired, he was soon extolling the benefits of the ceasefire and the exceptional concessions granted to the NMSP. Had his head been turned by the respect paid to him by the SLORC top-brass, or had the eighty-two year old Mon leader reassessed the situation, and determined to make the best the agreement? Its success would determine his political legacy, and place in Mon history.

CHAPTER SIXTEEN

The 1996 Mon Refugee Repatriation

In July 1996, a year and a month after the ceasefire, *The Nation* reported a "senior NMSP leader" (probably Nai Rot Sah) confirming that the agreement had come about primarily due to pressure from the Thai military. The interviewee was anxious to contradict any suggestion that the Mon nationalists might view the post-ceasefire situation in a positive light. He pointed out that human rights were still being regularly abused across Mon State, and in particular denied that Nai Shwe Kyin was enthusiastic about future prospects: the NMSP President hoped for the best, "but is prepared for the worst."[20]

Following the ceasefire, the government had begun to up-grade road and bridge links to and within Mon State. In most cases, these infrastructure developments were carried out using forced labour and/or by raising local taxes. Such projects certainly aided the *Tatmadaw*, which gained improved access to previously inaccessible areas. Whether local people also benefited is unclear. The majority of the Mon State population are rice farmers. Obliged to sell their surplus to the government, they had little to gain from better access to markets.

By the end of 1995, many within the Mon nationalist community were already expressing their dissatisfaction with the ceasefire. As was the case during the protracted negotiation process, in the post-ceasefire era the NMSP leadership placed considerable importance on maintaining a show of unity. However, by 1996 it was clear to most observers that the party and the wider movement were still divided along pro- and anti- ceasefire lines.

Having agreed to a cessation of hostilities, the NMSP leadership had no clear vision of the party's future role. Many of those who supported the agreement saw no option, other than to pursue a new, closer relationship with the military government; others remained sympathetic to the opposition, and proposed an open alliance with Daw Aung San Suu Kyi and the NLD. Meanwhile, effort was devoted to exploiting the economic opportunities open to the NMSP and its Rehmonya International Company.

Those within the nationalist movement who opposed the ceasefire, and distrusted any form of engagement with the SLORC, were highly suspicious of such commercial activities, which they regarded as opportunistic, and invitations to corruption.

It was in the context of such debates, that a new Mon 'umbrella group' emerged. The Mon Unity League (MUL) went on to play an important role in Mon politics, acting as a link between the NMSP, Burmese and Mon groups in Thailand and overseas, and the growing international campaign for democratic change in Burma.

Following the ceasefire, the Thai security establishment continued to exert pressure on the NMSP and MNRC. In late 1995 Nai Shwe Kyin was persuaded to endorse a Mon refugee repatriation plan, although the refugees themselves clearly did not want to return to Burma, before security guarantees had been put in place. The MNRC and the NGOs applied to UNHCR for support in lobbying the Thai authorities, to at least postpone the repatriation. However, the UN refugee agency proved unable to protect the Mon refugees, excusing its inaction by pointing to policy differences between the NMSP and MNRC.

Therefore, during the 1996 dry season, the last Mon refugees in Thailand were moved back to Burma, while those who had already been repatriated, or had never been allowed access to the kingdom, prepared to start growing some of their own food supplies. However, it would be several years before the Mon refugees could hope to achieve even limited self-sufficiency in food production. In the meantime, they would continue to depend on the cross-border supply of humanitarian assistance, and thus on the Thai authorities' good will.

Human Rights in the Post-Ceasefire Phase

By early 1996, increasing numbers of NMSP members in the ceasefire zones along the border, as well as exiled Mon nationalists in Thailand and overseas, were voicing concern over the direction of party policy. Critics of the ceasefire complained that Mon villagers' rights continued to be abused, and asked whether the party was really engaged on the political front, or if low-level co-operation with the Burmese military authorities was just a smokescreen for inactivity. If it was to continue to inspire the nationalist community, either NMSP strategy would have to change or the advantages of the ceasefire would have to be more clearly communicated.

As a result of the ceasefire, travel in much of Mon State had become easier, as the number of military checkpoints was reduced. However, the agreement had had few other positive effects on the lives of Mon villagers in Burma. Indeed, since the ceasefire, the *Tatmadaw* had been able to operate with impunity in areas of Ye, Yebyu and Tavoy Townships to which it had previously had only limited access. For example, at the end of the 1995 rainy season the MNLA's Moulmein Battalion began to withdraw from positions in western Ye Township, following which *Tatmadaw* units moved in. The newcomers were soon making demands for cash, forced labour and porters, well in excess of those previously requisitioned by the Mon troops.[21]

According to the Mon Information Service, "after the signing of the NMSP-SLORC ceasefire agreement, such serious human rights abuses as summary and arbitrary killings of Mon villagers ... have come to a halt in Mon State", but "other traditional types of human rights abuses – such as forced labour including forced porterage, extortion including portering taxes etc. – have all remained in place as usual" and "force labour and extortion (had) relatively even increased."[22]

Throughout 1996, refugees from 'inside' continued to arrive at the border, even as repatriation operations were getting underway. The refugees' stories shared similar elements: on average, unless they could pay off the authorities, families in Mon State were required to contribute one or two people, for an average of two weeks forced labour per month. In some areas, entire villages were forced to work unpaid on the Ye-Tavoy railway and other projects, often for months at a time. Furthermore, villagers were in constant danger of being abducted by the army, to be used as porters or unpaid servants at the local *Tatmadaw* garrison.

Another burden was the 'rice quota' system, which since the 1960s had been used to feed government employees and the *Tatmadaw*, and to earn foreign currency for the regime. Under this nation-wide policy, a remnant of the Burmese Way to Socialism, the authorities annually purchased a set amount of rice from each farm, at considerably below the market rate. According to some estimates, since 1994, when the government announced a new drive to increase rice exports, the state has appropriated a much as twenty-five per cent of the rice crop.[23] Numerous reports have confirmed the Mon Information Service's finding that "any rice farmers who cannot sell paddy fully to SLORC are normally subjected to arrest", and sometimes to "torture and other serious ill-treatment."[24] The Mon refugees were already identified by the *Tatmadaw* as rebel sympathisers, and thus had good treason to fear return to Burma.

'Forced Repatriation' or 'Spontaneous Resettlement'?

The Thai position regarding the Mon refugees was spelled-out at a meeting in Sangkhlaburi, in November 1995. The meeting was attended by Mr X and officers of the Ninth Division, and by Nai Shwe Kyin and members of the MNRC. Mr X criticised the young MNRC workers for their public criticism of Thai policy, and informed them that the Pa Yaw refugees would be moved to the Burma side of the border in the new year, regardless of any protests. As in previous years, a rainy season stockpile of supplies could be delivered to the refugees, but beyond this they were on their own. All NGO assistance would be cut-off from 30th April 1996.

The MNRC and refugees looked to UNHCR for protection. Debate focussed on the degree of 'voluntariness' that might characterise any refugee repatriation. The United Nations refugee agency's own 1996 *Voluntary Repatriation Handbook* notes that the concept of "voluntary repatriation" is based on the absence of any "well-founded fear of persecution" (a key element in the definition of refugee status, in the 1951 Convention Relating to the Status of Refugees). It goes on to conclude that, before endorsing any repatriation, "UNHCR should be convinced that the positive pull-factors in the country of origin are an overriding element in the refugees' decision to return." Ironically, these guidelines were published just as the Mon refugees were being sent back to Burma – to a situation in which they clearly had a very "well-founded fear of persecution."[25]

Later that year, the Jesuit Refugee Service (JRS) – a BBC member-agency – released an independent report, documenting the Mon refugees well-founded fear of returning to Burma. The 1995 ceasefire agreement was too fragile and unstable to allow for their repatriation in conditions of security. Even in the 'permanent' NMSP-controlled zones, fighting could resume at any time (as had happened the previous year in Karenni State), and in the 'temporary' ceasefire zones, such as NMSP Tavoy District (opposite Pa Yaw), the arrival of the *Tatmadaw* was expected imminently.[26]

Although plans were afoot to return the Pa Yaw refugees to Burma as soon as possible, and against their will, UNHCR refused to become involved, either as an advocate or critic of repatriation. The UN refugee agency was in a difficult position, having no legal means of intervention (other than under 'customary international law'). However, the agency could have been more open in its disapproval of the Mon refugee repatriation, as it clearly contravened many of UNHCR's own guidelines. Certainly, one UNHCR official's characterisation – during a CCSDPT co-ordination meeting – of the proposed repatriation as "spontaneous", was pushing the envelope of definition too far.

During the 1994 Halochanee crisis, the NMSP leadership had learnt that they could not rely on the international community for protection, and that opposition to Thai security policy was likely to have the most serious consequences, both for the party and for individual members and their families. Although the NMSP might accept a repatriation package, the refugees themselves had a right to expect that the UNHCR would act in their best interests. They clearly did not want to return to Burma, and stated so on more than one occasion, to UNHCR officers visiting Pa Yaw and Halochanee.

Despite some discrete lobbying on behalf of the Mon refugees by the American Embassy's Refugee Affairs Section, in early 1996 UNHCR Bangkok advised Geneva that the NMSP had accepted a refugee repatriation package, and only the MNRC did not endorse the arrangement. This assessment, which exploited Mon weakness and hinted at self-interest within the MNRC, was obviously self-serving. The supposed 'split' between the NMSP and the MNRC was used as a pretext to limit the agency's involvement in a complex and messy situation.

During the second half of 1996, UNHCR officers made several trips to Rangoon, to discuss the refugee situation on Burma's eastern and western borders. The agency feared that a rift with the SLORC might disrupt the on-going $50 million repatriation of *Rohingya* refugees in Bangladesh, to Rakhine (Arakan) State in southwest Burma.[27] The 'refugee professionals' at UNHCR needed to find a compromise formula, to provide them with some cover regarding their responsibilities to the Mon, whilst protecting the relationship with Rangoon. Eventually, after the operation was all-but complete, Geneva announced that the agency would monitor the Mon refugee repatriation up to, but not *across* the Thailand-Burma border.

The implications of this inactivity were far-reaching, as is illustrated by a statement released by the Karen Refugee Committee (KRC) in November 1995, just a few weeks before the Mon repatriation got under way. According to the KRC, "some observers ... see repatriation of the Mon refugees as establishing a precedent which may at some future time be applied to the more than 70,000 Karen refugees ... The KRC wishes to re-iterate its belief that it is in the best interests of the refugees that they should return to Burma, but it believes that the return must be voluntary and it must be to a situation of safety."[28] Clearly, UNHCR failed to protect or effectively advocate on behalf of the Mon refugees. Fortunately, by the time Karen refugee repatriation became a distinct possibility, the UN had been prodded into taking a more active role along the border.[29]

Ultimately, it was clear that the Thai authorities would call the shots. According to the Royal Thai Government, now that the fighting was over, the displaced Mon could return home. The well-documented fact of on-going human rights abuses in Mon State was not sufficient reason for them to be granted continued asylum in Thailand. Therefore in late 1995, having persuaded Nai Shwe Kyin to endorse his plans, Mr X started to put together a detailed repatriation package. Although the BBC was kept informed, the MNRC and the refugees were not consulted.

The Mon Refugee Camps and the Resettlement-Repatriation Plan

At the end of 1995 the Mon refugee population stood at 10,852 people, living in four camps. The largest of these, Halochanee, was (depending on the time of year and the state of the road) between forty-five minutes and three hour's drive northwest from Sangkhlaburi. Bee Ree and Pa Yaw, further to the south, were only accessible by road between December and

June, and then only to four or special ten-wheel drive vehicles. Depending on the state of the road and the skill of the driver, the trip to Bee Ree took between four and eight hours. The old logging and mining road to Pa Yaw initially followed the route to Bee Ree, but after the last Border Patrol Police checkpoint at Loh Loe the track ran up into the border hills, due west of Sangkhlaburi.

The 3,900 refugees at Halochanee, who included about 400 displaced Karen, lived spread out along a narrow valley, two hour's walk south of the *Tatmadaw* garrison at Three Pagodas Pass. The eastern end of the valley opened out into a landscape of streams and rolling hills. This was where the smaller, Baleh Donephai section of the camp – scene of the 1994 Burma Army incursion – was located. It was anticipated that a number of families would move here from Halochanee proper, as part of the relocation process.

To reach the next camp by foot involved a very long, hard day's walk southwest from Halochanee, to the Ye River (Bee Ree) watershed hills. At the beginning of 1996, Bee Ree had a population of 1,535 people, at two sites about twelve Km inside Burma. The Bee Ree area was mountainous and in 1995 still heavily forested. By January 1996, several Bee Ree families had already started to clear the hillside in order to plant rice. Others derived some income from harvesting bamboo and rattan in the forest, which they floated down-river for sale in Ye.

'Central' was situated on a tributary of the Ye River, three Km south of the refugee settlements. The bamboo and plank lodgings and offices of the Mon leadership were modest, in comparison with the teak mansions of the former KNU headquarters at Mannerplaw, a fact partly explained by the isolation and frequent re-location of the Mon HQ. Spread out along the riverbank in the middle of the forest, Central was beautiful, even by the picturesque standards of Mannerplaw. On sunny days, the light fell through the branches of hundreds of huge trees, left standing to provide cover from air attack. However, during the rainy season, when the river often burst its banks, it was near-impossible to make one's way from one end of headquarters to the other. At this time of year, the few remaining vehicles, which had not headed out to Thailand for the duration of the rains, were covered in plastic sheeting, as the long road over the steep hills was unusable between June–January.

Another six hour's walk south, through the forest from Central, was NMSP Tavoy District. Just over the border, on the eastern face of a steep and windy hillside, was Pa Yaw refugee camp. At the end of 1995 the camp had an official population 4,170, which included about eight hundred people living across the border in NMSP Tavoy District, in three sites spread out along a narrow river at the bottom of the border hill. The District Headquarters itself was seventeen Km southwest of the bottom of the hill, and was the epicentre of the MNLA temporary ceasefire position.

A further four hundred Km to the south was the last of the Mon refugee settlements. Mergui District, site of two more temporary ceasefire positions, was located opposite Thailand's Prachuab Kiri Kahn Province, and had a reported population in 1995 of 1,247 people. The District was isolated from Central, both geographically and politically. Income from logging, and the taxation of fishing vessels along the seacoast, had enabled the local MNLA Battalion to build up quite an arsenal, and maintain good relations with local Ninth Division commanders.

Technically, only the Pa Yaw refugees were to be repatriated in 1996. In the case of the Halochanee, Bee Ree and Mergui District refugees (or IDPs), the term 'resettlement' was more accurate. However, such terminology ignored the fact that many of these people had already been repatriated to Burma, and were 'internal refugees' within their own country.

In December 1995 the NMSP established a Development Committee, which together with the MNRC would handle all aspects of the impending repatriation-resettlement operation. District sub-committees were established to co-ordinate activities at each of the proposed resettlement zones. In addition to the pre-existing refugee camps at Halochanee and Bee Ree, these included three new sites in NMSP Moulmein District, behind and to the north of Halochanee (including Palaung Japan, near the old NMSP HQ at Nam Khok), three on the Ye River near Bee Ree, four in NMSP Tavoy District and two in Mergui District.

The initial NMSP resettlement plan called for the bulk of the refugees to move from the densely populated camps along the border, further into the NMSP-controlled ceasefire zones. The resettled refugees would be encouraged to clear farms and cultivate rice and other crops, in order eventually to become independent of humanitarian assistance. House plots would be allotted by ballot and the quota of farm land in the resettlement zones was set a generous ten acres per family (about three times what the average household would be able to clear and plant before the coming rains). However, little thought was given as to how the returnees and their farms would be integrated into the fragile local economy and ecology. The resettlement plan lacked strategic vision, betraying the haste and pressure under which it was conceived. Although the aim of promoting refugee self-sufficiency was admirable, it was not properly thought through.

To garner data upon which to base NGO assistance, between November–December 1995, the MNRC, BBC and MSF carried out a joint assessment of the proposed resettlement sites. The survey team visited each of the Mon refugee settlements and talked with camp leaders and residents, including teachers and medics, and to local NMSP and MNLA personnel. The refugees were well-informed regarding the limited options available to them. Most of those at Pa Yaw considered their immanent repatriation inevitable, and many had already staked-out plots of land across the border. However, at all of the 'town hall' meetings conducted by the survey team, the refuges expressed strong reservations about their future security, ceasefire or no ceasefire. They would rise to the challenge of resettlement, but would continue for some time to need outside assistance. As well as on-going food, medical and other basic humanitarian supplies, they would also need tools, seeds and plenty of good luck.

The Halochanee refugees were already in Burma. Although the NMSP encouraged more families to move down to Baleh Donephai, most would stay put near the border, in or to be able to flee quickly into Thailand, in case of attack. Furthermore, many of those at Halochanee continued to derive some income from the cross-border trade which passed through the camp, either working as porters for local Thai, Mon and Burmese merchants, or by selling cakes and cola to the traders and loggers. Some refugees with family members in nearby Sangkhlaburi, went to join them.

At Bee Ree, half of the refugees would resettle at Naung Perng, a few Km west of the main camp, on the banks of the Ye River.[30] This was the most promising of the Mon resettlement zones: in the heart of the NMSP liberated zone, the Ye River valley enjoyed better security than the other sites, and there was plenty of land to accommodate resettlement.

Whereas at Halochanee it was space, in Tavoy District the refugees' main problem was security: this was a temporary ceasefire zone only, and it was expected that, within a year, the *Tatmadaw* would occupy the area. There was also the need to move *en masse* from the old camp at Pa Yaw, then build houses, a hospital, a school, wells and a rice store at the new site. It seemed unlikely that the Pa Yaw-Tavoy District refugees would be able to undertake much in the way of agricultural activities in 1996.

Mon Unity; Implementing the Plan

In January 1996, with implementation just getting under way, the NMSP Central Committee decided to reduce the number and size of the resettlement sites. The revised plan required the refugees to settle in areas closer to the border, and further from the 'ceasefire front-line'. Primarily a security measure, this new policy effectively maintained the old distinction between (repatriated) refugees, and the IDP and other populations further inside the Mon liberated zones. The new plan reflected the state of NMSP-SLORC relations – stalemate, characterised by lack of trust and a failure to co-operate in the promised development of Mon State. It also meant that there would be less agricultural land available to the returnees.

In early 1996, as the Pa Yaw repatriation was getting under way, the NMSP held its Fourth Congress. Amid considerable debate, and with substantial reservations, the gathering endorsed the ceasefire, but could agree on little else. One striking feature of the Fourth Congress, was the requirement that senior leaders swear an oath before members of the *sangha*, to behave with integrity and not use their positions to seek personal gain. Obviously, there was a perception at large that the party leadership could not always be trusted.

In March 1996, following the NMSP congress, a second Congress of Mon National Affairs was held, in Tavoy District. This meeting voted to establish a new 'umbrella group', drawing together fourteen different Mon nationalist organisations from Thailand and Burma. Formation of a pan-Mon league had been mooted since at least 1993, and was discussed at length at the previous year's Congress of Mon National Affairs. The new Mon Unity League (MUL) vowed to strengthen Mon solidarity, to work "for the betterment of the Mon people" and "to restore Monland."[31]

The NMSP was the largest and most important of the leagues' member-organisations, some of which consisted of only a few dozen people. The party's paramount position was recognised in the appointment of the NMSP Joint General Secretary, Nai Hongsa, as the first MUL President. This was a great encouragement to many younger Mon nationalists, for whom the progressive Nai Hongsa was something of a figurehead.

Since its inception, the post of MUL General Secretary has been held by Nai Sunthorn Sriparngern. A sometime businessman and ex-NMSP member, in the late 1980s and '90s he emerged as an important figure in and historian of the nationalist community. (In 1974 Nai Sunthorn's elder brother, Nai Kyan Sein, an NMSP activist, was ambushed by the *Tatmadaw* near Mudon, following which he was executed and his head displayed on a spike in Mudon cemetery. This grisly incident persuaded Nai Sunthorn to flee to Thailand, where he was adopted by Captain Anond. Nai Sunthorn's famous uncle, U Tissa, the Abbot of Kyaik Soi Mon in Rangoon, was a guest at ceremonies marking Daw Aung San Suu Kyi's wedding, and at the funeral of her mother.)[32]

The MUL emerged in the context of sometimes heated arguments, between the NMSP leadership and anti-ceasefire factions within the party and wider Mon community. Rather than risk a damaging public split, the Mon nationalists agreed to disagree – and carried on doing so through three more Congresses of Mon National Affairs. These pan-Mon gatherings were jointly hosted by the MUL and the NMSP. However, as they were actually held in NMSP-controlled territory, some hard-line, anti-ceasefire activists declined to attend. Nevertheless, in recognising the NMSP as the primary political representative of the Mon people, the 1995 Mon Congress of Mon National Affairs had created the space within which the MUL could present the views of the wider nationalist community. Whilst acknowledging the leading role of the NMSP, the MUL (which never endorsed the ceasefire) was free to criticise party policy. This arrangement prevented a major fracturing of the nationalist community, at a crucial juncture. For the refugees however, such political considerations were of less importance than issues of food and physical security.

From the outset, the MNRC and the NGOs had considered 30th April an impossible deadline by which to finish stock-piling the Mon camps. With the help of lobbying by the American and other embassies in Bangkok, the deadline was extended until the start of rainy season, and supplies until the end of the year were successfully transported into the camps before the roads went down in mid-June. By this time, nearly a thousand new refugees from the Ye-Tavoy railway had arrived in Tavoy District. The great majority were Mon, although there were also a few Karen, Burmans and Pa-O. It was clear that, despite the assurances made at the time of the ceasefire, the kind of systematic human rights abuses from which the refugees had fled were continuing more-or-less unabated across much of Tenasserim Division and Mon State.

The author visited Pa Yaw and Tavoy District with two EU diplomats (representing the BBC's largest donor) on 26th March 1996, the day after the last refugees moved back to Burma. When we were about an hour's drive from the camp, a helicopter flew overhead, in the direction of Pa Yaw; half-an-hour later, it returned in the opposite direction. When we arrived at Pa Yaw, a number of houses were in flames and the leaf-thatch roofs of many others had already burnt out. An old man who had remained at the site, waiting for his family to come back and help him make the steep climb up and over the border hill, told us that ten men and a woman in Thai military uniform had alighted from the helicopter and set fire to the middle section of the camp. The message to the refugees could hardly have been more clear: get out of Thailand – and stay out.

By the end of the year, the first phase of the resettlement-repatriation operation was complete. In a follow-up survey of the returnees, the total northern Mon refugee population was recorded as 9,269 people, including 2,921 new arrivals in 1996; the Mergui District population was reported as 2,483.[33] Not more than one-in-three refugee families had managed to grow crops during the 1996 rainy season.[34] Of these, the great majority could not cover more than half of their needs.

Rice was cultivated using 'slash and burn' (swidden) techniques. Most of the refugees had experience of working irrigated rice, but the resettlement sites were too hilly for this type of cultivation to be effective. Furthermore, the security situation was not stable enough to encourage the degree of physical investment necessary for large-scale, sustainable agricultural development. The provision of humanitarian assistance to the refugees had previously contributed to the preservation of forests along the Thailand-Burma border. One consequence of the Mon refugee resettlement operation was the gradual deforestation of a number of environmentally sensitive areas, as the refugees began to clear the jungle in order to grow rice and other cash and subsistence crops.

By the end of 1996, the Mon refugees were still largely dependant on humanitarian assistance from Thailand. The situation in the resettlement-repatriation zones was stable, but the people were isolated and fearful. This state of affairs was not helped by a severe malaria epidemic in Bee Ree and Tavoy District during the 1996 rainy season.[35]

As noted above, the NMSP had no detailed plans for the resettlement zones, other than generally to encourage the refugees' agricultural activities. According to party leaders, the ceasefire was too unstable to allow for implementation of a strategic development plan. It would first be necessary to make progress on the political front. For nearly fifty years, the Mon nationalists had been fighting to hold on to territory, without seriously addressing the developmental needs of the populations under their control. For the time being at least, the war was over. However, the NMSP seemed unable to begin a post-ceasefire phase of the struggle – one of much-needed reconstruction and rehabilitation.

There were some exceptions: throughout the 1990s, the Mon National Education Committee (MNEC) was active in a number of fields and, despite some setbacks, offered a model for community development along the border. The Mon National School system was the pride of the nationalist movement, and an important symbol of the NMSP's commitment to a programme of Mon cultural revival. The party's Agriculture Department also conducted training and other NGO-sponsored activities, although these were of variable quality.

More valuable, were the efforts of the Mon Women's Organisation (MWO). Under the auspices of the NMSP Education Department, the MWO conducted a series of Mon literacy campaigns in the refugee-resettlement sites, as well as further inside Burma, including, after 1996, in government-controlled areas.[36] With financial and technical assistance from two Thailand-based NGOs, the MWO also ran a series of weaving and needlecraft workshops, and organised trainings for its one hundred-strong core membership, as well as for women in the camps and beyond. Even the recently-formed MUL initiated a community health and small-scale agriculture project in the Ye River area in 1996, demonstrating that non-NMSP groups could implement programmes in the ceasefire zones.

In January 1997 the MNRC formally asked the NGOs to continue their assistance to the Mon returnees for another year, and strongly hinted that this request was likely to be repeated in 1998. Sympathetic lobbying by the US and EU missions in Bangkok, combined with BBC Director Jack Dunford's behind-the-scenes diplomacy, succeeded in persuading the Royal Thai Government to allow continued cross-border assistance, at least through the 1997 dry season.

Hoping to encourage the resettled refugees to meet some of their own food requirements, but recognising that the security situation in Tavoy District was too unstable for this to be realistic, the BBC agreed to support Bee Ree and Halochanee at eighty per cent of needs, and the Tavoy District returnees at one hundred per cent.[37] Furthermore, MSF would also continue to work with the Mon refugees, with support for hospitals and dispensaries, and vaccination and other public health campaigns. The Mon refugees were though, still highly vulnerable. So were thousands of IDPs, some of whom continued to receive some short-term assistance from the MNRC's Emergency Relief and Development Programme (ERDP), and the Mon National Health Committee's Mobile Medical Teams.

CHAPTER SEVENTEEN

The 1997 Burma Army Offensives

For the majority of Mon refugees, 1997 was marked by increased efforts to begin meeting their own food needs, either by means of agriculture, trade or wage labour. However, the security situation in the Mon ceasefire zones was far from stable. In Tavoy District in particular, the NMSP was challenged by the emergence of armed anti-ceasefire factions. Meanwhile, further to the south in Mergui District, the strains of the ceasefire were also proving too much for the party to control. In late 1996, a combination of strategic and economic self-interest led independent-minded local military commanders to form the breakaway Mon Army Mergui District (MAMD), the most significant non-NMSP Mon armed group since the 1980s.

The centre of a weakened NMSP could no longer hold, and warlordism again threatened to overwhelm the movement. There were also disagreements among those who remained loyal to the NMSP, most notably over whether the party should associate itself with the SLORC, the NLD and/or the rump DAB-NCUB alliance. As tensions continued to mount, it seemed that the 1995 ceasefire agreement might break down completely. One reason why this did not happen was the terrible example of the 1997 *Tatmadaw* offensives against the last KNU strongholds in southeast Burma. This massive assault on the remaining Karen rebel-held positions followed the armed ethnic opposition's defiant Mae Tha Raw Hta Conference, held in KNLA Sixth Brigade that January, immediately after General Bo Mya had rejected the government's ceasefire overtures. The overwhelming force unleashed against the Karen – professional insurgents and ordinary villagers alike – sent a clear message to the Mon and other groups: failure to toe the SLORC line would not be tolerated.

Throughout 1997, the *Tatmadaw* continued to clash with KNU units in Karen and Mon States and the wilds of Tenasserim Division. The NMSP could not prevent Karen troops moving through its zones particularly in the vicinity of the Ye and Zami Rivers (behind Bee Ree and Halochanee), and in some cases MNLA officers probably lent some assistance to their old allies.

Meanwhile, *Tatmadaw* patrols regularly operated right up against the Mon ceasefire positions.

The 1997 dry season also saw a major *Tatmadaw* offensive against the MAMD and their ABSDF allies in the south. After a series of pitched battles in April and May, the *Tatmadaw* overran the MAMD stronghold at Chaung Chee and the breakaway Mon faction was forced to surrender. For a while, it seemed that the Mergui District leaders might have won concessions from the government, and achieved their objective of maintaining control over the strategically important area. However, it soon became clear that, as per the 1995 ceasefire arrangements, the district had reverted to Burmese military control. Remnants of the MAMD forces formed a new armed group and vowed to carry on the fight against Rangoon. As so often in the war, it was those caught in the middle – the refugees – who suffered most from the conflict.

Security Issues in the Mon Ceasefire Zones

In mid-1996 MNRC personnel joined representatives of the KNU, the Karen Refugee Committee (KRC) and other groups at a workshop in Bangkok, held to discuss responses to any proposed repatriation of the Karen and Karenni refugees. The meeting focused on the issue of protection, in the light of the Mon experience, and the importance of demonstrating that return to Burma was not a safe option for the Karen refugees, who continued to suffer attacks on their camps by the Democratic Kayin Buddhist Army (DKBA).

Meanwhile, thousands of Mon refugees were facing their first rainy season back in Burma. By mid-1996, the MNLA had withdrawn from all but two of the eight temporary positions agreed the previous year, and in many places the departing Mon forces had been replaced by *Tatmadaw* battalions and SLORC administrative control. However, the twelve permanent and two temporary ceasefire zones remained under NMSP control. The MNLA's Thaton Battalion still maintained two-to-three hundred troops in the vicinity of Kawbein and Kya-In, behind Moulmein in central Mon State (bordering on KNLA Sixth Brigade to the east), where the NMSP controlled twenty-plus villages. Further to the south, were two of the four permanent ceasefire positions in NMSP Moulmein District, at In Quoit (the District HQ, near Kya-In) and Pong Katar, on the Three Pagodas Pass-Thanbyuzayat road (again, overlapping with KNLA Sixth Brigade).

Thirty Km further to the south was Halochanee, the nearest of the Mon refugee camps to the ceasefire front-line. There was an MNLA base and permanent ceasefire position between Baleh Donephai and Halochanee proper, and another MNLA outpost at Palaung Japan, near the old NMSP HQ at Nam Khok. The fourth Moulmein District permanent ceasefire position was located further to the west, in the thickly-forested hills north of Ye.

During 1996–97, *Tatmadaw* columns visited the Baleh Donephai every three-to-six months, on their way to and from the garrison town of Ye. On each occasion the MNLA was informed in advance, via the Three Pagodas Pass ceasefire liaison office. Despite the bad memories of July 1994, these incursions occurred by-and-large without incident. Meanwhile, weekly Immigration Detention Centre (IDC) deportations continued to complicate the situation at Halochanee.

The most secure of the resettlement sites, at Bee Ree, was guarded by seven permanent ceasefire positions. This was the heart of the Mon ceasefire zone, where troops from Headquarters and Number 777 Battalions guarded the NMSP and MNLA leadership at Central. The KNLA also still patrolled to the northwest, around Hammom village.

At the end of 1996 the MNLA still maintained about two hundred troops in Tavoy District, one of the two temporary ceasefire zones from which they had yet to withdraw. Nearly 2,000 Pa Yaw refugees had been repatriated to the district earlier in the year, and with the advent of the dry season the security situation was tense. It was not clear whether the SLORC would enforce the 1996 deadline for vacating Tavoy and Mergui Districts – a deadline that had already been extended for a year. It was also uncertain whether MNLA withdrawal would be followed by *Tatmadaw* occupation, and whether the repatriated Pa Yaw refugees would be able or willing to stay put. There were rumours of discontent among units of the Tavoy Battalion, and in outlying villages, but for the time being these were muted due to the proximity of Central, and the astute leadership of the NMSP District Governor, Nai Myin Htut. Meanwhile, in Mergui District, Mon unity had begun to come unstuck, with local MNLA officers openly challenging Central's order to abandon their hard-won positions.

The first armed Mon faction to break the ceasefire was the Hongsa Command, led by that colourful figure, General Yap (the sometime KMT advisor to the NMSP). After the fall of Three Pagodas Pass, General Yap and his small band of supporters had withdrawn to Bangkok and a secluded farm near Sai Yok, in lower Kanchanaburi province. By the mid-1990s, the KMT had ceased to be a force in Burma and there seemed to be little reason for General Yap to be further involved in Mon politics. However, the old warrior resurfaced briefly in 1995–96, to oppose the NMSP-SLORC ceasefire.

In mid-1995 General Yap and associates established the Hongsa Command, which at the height of its influence numbered perhaps fifty men. This was basically a paid, anti-ceasefire pocket army, which for the next eighteen months was active along the border between Tavoy District and E-Thaung, where the gas pipelines were to enter Thailand. Towards the end of the 1995 rainy season, the Hongsa Command was involved in a series of clashes with the Thai Border Patrol Police, in which at least one Thai policeman was killed. There were also a handful of fire-fights with the

246

MNLA. In response, the Thai authorities arrested General Yap's key aides in Bangkok and Kanchanaburi, effectively ending the activities of the Hongsa Command.

The following year another, more persistent anti-ceasefire faction emerged in Tavoy District. Drawn from disgruntled former MNLA troops, the 'Nai Soe Aung Group' operated in the forest to the south and west of the district headquarters. In late 1996 its epinomomynous leader, who hailed from the rebellious Mergui District, was overthrown and replaced by two of his lieutenants. Throughout 1996–97, the re-formed 'Nai Soe Aung Group' continued to clash regularly with both *Tatmadaw* units and regular MNLA troops. Particularly worrying to the mainstream NMSP, was the degree of support it enjoyed among villagers and returnees in Tavoy District.

Despite such alarms, for the majority of Mon refugees, the key issues in 1996–97 were still fear of *Tatmadaw* incursion and concern over food security. About 2,000 returnees left the camps during 1996, including more than a thousand from Tavoy District. Rather than return to Burma, most chose to re-enter Thailand as illegal immigrants. Although this development undermined the Thai authorities' attempts to remove the Mon from their territory, the 1996 repatriation had been primarily a symbolic act, and the fact remained that there were no Mon refugee camps on Thai soil. Those who left the resettlement sites were replaced by a roughly equal number of new arrivals from 'inside', as the human rights situation in lower Burma had improved only marginally since the ceasefire.

In 1995 the majority of Mon nationalists had been willing to give the agreement the benefit of the doubt. However, by late 1996, the pressure to withdraw from Tavoy and Mergui Districts, and the overall lack of benefits the ceasefire had brought the NMSP, led to an escalation of tensions within the nationalist movement. Most senior NMSP leaders advocated remaining within the 'legal fold', in order to continue operating inside SLORC-controlled Burma and to avoid resumption of a war the party was bound to lose. However, many of the younger generation, and those on the periphery of the party apparatus, were becoming increasingly restive.

When in October 1996 the order came from Central for a phased withdrawal from Mergui District, a number of NMSP cadres relocated north to Sangkhlaburi. However, the bulk of the 300-strong MNLA force refused to move, and their officers proceeded to unceremoniously expel the recently-installed Mergui Battalion commander, the ex-MNLA intelligence chief, Colonel Nai Kao Rot. One of the architects of the June 1995 ceasefire agreement, and an ally of the MNLA Chief-of-Staff, Brig-General Nai Aung Naing, Nai Kao Rot had been considered a 'safe pair of hands'. His posting to the south had demonstrated the leadership's concern that the Mergui Battalion might attempt to regain the independence from Central it had enjoyed before 1990. His untimely departure from the district proved these fears to have been well-founded.

On 6th November 1996 the hard-liners announced the formation of the Mon Army Mergui District (MAMD, also known as the Mon Army of the Front Line).[38] Under the command of Colonel Nai Ong Suik Heang (previously Mergui Battalion Second-in-Command) and Major Nai Ba Sein, the MAMD was a formidable force of 250–300 troops, seemingly well-equipped to defend its territory against allcomers. Mergui District was of some strategic importance, as the Mon troops had access to the Maw Daung Pass fifty Km to the north, an historic overland link between Thailand and the Tenasserim seaboard.

The MAMD was opposed to any territory being handed over to the *Tatmadaw*, stating that it would "reunite with the NMSP... the day when the NMSP withdraw the agreement of ceasefire with the SLORC."[39] Ten days later, on 17th November, the Burma Army launched a new offensive against the Mon rebels in the south.

At the prompting of Thai security agents, the NMSP offered to mediate between the *Tatmadaw* and the new group, while at the same time hastening to reassure the SLORC that the split was genuine, and that the Mon nationalists were not pursuing a double game. The *Tatmadaw* failed to make significant advances against the well-armed MAMD, and towards the end of November the fighting in the south died down. By this time, several hundred refugees had fled to MAMD-controlled territory, as the *Tatmadaw* had forcibly relocated up to sixteen villages around the garrison town of Lenya.

The emergence of the MAMD constituted a more significant challenge to the NMSP than had the Hongsa Command or the 'Nai Soe Aung Group', neither of which seriously threatened the *status quo*. Ultimately, all three factions represented local vested interests, moving to maintain control over lucrative concessions and the 'taxation' of villagers, merchants and shipping off the Tenasserim seaboard.

Such a scenario was hardly unique in Burmese politics. In periods when the centre – be it rebel headquarters or the state – has been unable to extend its authority over peripheral areas, local strong-men have tended to accrue power to themselves, establishing nascent power bases. This phenomena, perennial since before the colonial era, may be characterised as 'warlordism'. In parts of northern Burma during the British period, and across much of the country in the decades since independence, local armed groups patrolled the 'no-man's land', and in many cases controlled quite substantial slices of territory.

These pocket armies often operated under the patronage of 'mainstream' insurgent groups, like the NMSP and KNU. Indeed, they were frequently incorporated into the loosely-integrated insurgent forces.[40] However, since the 1980s, armed opposition to Rangoon has grown increasingly weak and fragmented, and many of these small groups have switched allegiance, to operate independently, or under unofficial license from *Tatmadaw* commanders in the field.

The Politics of a Post-Insurgent Organisation

Following the ceasefire, powerful interests within the NMSP, including Nai Shwe Kyin, continued to press for closer relations with the SLORC. Others included Nai Soe Myint, the Managing Director of Rehmonya International and head of the NMSP Development Commission in Moulmein, who had been replaced by Nai Kao Rot as NMSP Thaton District Governor, following the latter's ousting from Mergui District. Nai Soe Myint remained enthusiastic about the prospects for economic and infrastructure development in Mon State.

By far the largest such projects were the Yadana and Yetagun gas pipelines. In September 1994 the NMSP Deputy Foreign Spokesman, Nai Pe Thein Za, told *The Nation* that the party might be prepared to attack the pipelines, as a last resort.[41] Since his departure from the NMSP, following the ceasefire, this threat has not been repeated. In general, and especially since 1995, the NMSP had preferred to keep a low profile regarding the pipelines, an approach which helped fuel rumours of oil company agents having reached a 'private agreement' with elements of the Mon leadership.

In August 1996 Nai Shwe Kyin spoke at a SLORC news conference, endorsing the Yadana project and talking about the "slowly improving" human rights situation in Mon State, since the ceasefire.[42] In an interview with *The Nation* later that year, the NMSP President was quoted as saying that "although abuses continue (in the pipeline area), they are slowly stopping."[43]

This position, which lent some credibility to the government and oil companies' claims regarding the benefits of foreign investment in Burma, had not been endorsed by the NMSP Central Committee,[44] which voted to officially rebuked the veteran party President for his words. Likewise, a number of overseas Mon organisations issued protest statements. Among the rump DAB-NCUB alliance along the Thailand-Burma border, Nai Shwe Kyin's comments were taken as further proof that the Mon leader had 'sold out'.

Observers began to talk of an open split within the Mon nationalist ranks. Indeed, throughout 1996–97 the NMSP sent out confusing signals regarding the party's relationship with the SLORC. Disappointed with the lack of political or economic progress since 1995, in late 1996 a majority on the party Central Committee endorsed a 'go slow' policy on joint ventures with the government, such as the Ye-Hanni road and school project. This approach was exemplified by the new plan to resettle the refugees only in those border areas under full NMSP control, rather than further inside the ceasefire zones, as had been originally intended.

In early 1997 the NMSP Central Committee voted to oppose construction of an all-weather toll road between Three Pagodas Pass and Thanbyuzayat, even though a Memorandum Of Understanding had been signed the previous September, by the SLORC, the NMSP and Power P Company, a Thai contractor with links to senior Royal Thai Army officers. Nevertheless, Nai Aung Naing, Nai Soe Myint and the pro-business wing of the NMSP continued to pursue negotiations with their Thai partners. In a well-timed swipe at the pro-engagement elements, it was only after Power P had gone into liquidation, in the second half of 1997, that the Central Committee gave permission for the road construction to go ahead.[45]

During this period, the NMSP's relationship with the NLD was equally controversial and complex. In general, the Mon leadership was wary of too close an association with Daw Aung San Suu Kyi and the democracy movement, both out of fear of the junta and because of a deep-seated suspicion of the predominantly Burman NLD leadership. Although individual NMSP members maintained low-level contacts with the NLD, the leaderships' trepidation drew criticism from Mon nationalists overseas. Many of these were heartened by a re-newel of contacts between the MNDF and the NLD in the late 1990s.[46]

More consistent than its dealings with Rangoon, were the NMSP's relationships with other 'ceasefire groups', and in particular the KIO. Since the 1994 ceasefire, the KIO had kept in touch with its erstwhile allies in the NDF and DAB, often leading the way among the ex-insurgent ceasefire groups. Having 'returned to the legal fold', the Kachin leadership continued to value inter-ethnic unity, and to push for a political settlement to the conflict in Burma. In this, they enjoyed a degree of support from 'their' people that the NMSP and other armed groups could not always rely on.

Meanwhile, along the border, NMSP personnel surreptitiously kept in touch with the KNU, which still operated out of territory adjacent to the Mon ceasefire zones. The multi-track attempt to maintain relations with the government, the NLD and the insurgents, demanded a degree of diplomacy and stealthy manoeuvring which the NMSP would find it difficult to sustain.

The Last Stand of Kaw Thoo Lei;
Another Halochanee Crisis

Two years after the fall of Mannerplaw, the ageing KNU leadership was still in denial over the causes of the DKBA rebellion. Largely devoid of ideological rigour and weakened by numerous *Tatmadaw* offensives and decades of inefficient administration, the KNU leadership had grown dangerously out-of-touch and the Karen nationalist movement was in deep crisis. Nevertheless, most observers were surprised by how rapidly the KNLA collapsed in 1997.

On-and-off over the previous eighteen months, a series of 'talks about talks' had been held in Thailand between representatives of the KNU and the government. Among the go-betweens had been Karen churchmen and

250

academics, as well as the Kachin, Khun Myat, who had helped to broker the KIO and NMSP ceasefires. However, little substantial progress was made.

In mid-1995 KNU Headquarters had been relocated to Htee Ker Pler village, in the north of KNLA Sixth Brigade, opposite Um-Phang District in Thailand. The following year, the KNU held its first congress since the fall of Mannerplaw. It was convened at Mae Tha Raw Hta, forty-five Km southwest of the new HQ, in the stronghold of the newly-promoted KNU Vice-Chairman (and NDF Chairman) Saw Shwe Saing, previously commander of Sixth Brigade. Marked by high expectations, this gathering ultimately achieved little, beyond a cosmetic restructuring of the KNU and a belated reassessment of KNLA guerrilla strategy.

Later in 1996, the KNU sent out invitations to an Ethnic Nationalities' Conference, also to be held at Mae Tha Raw Hta, convened to review insurgent strategy. In the last week of December 1996, three NMSP representatives set off for Mae Tha Raw Hta from Sangkhlaburi. On the bumpy truck ride north through Thung Yai forest, Nai Hongsa, who had previously been NMSP representative on the NDF ethnic alliance, must have wondered what his erstwhile allies hoped to achieve at Mae Tha Raw Hta. He was keen to see a new common strategy emerge, embracing both the 'ceasefire groups' and those still fighting the regime.

The conference, which was funded by international donors, got under way in late January. The resulting 'Mae Tha Raw Hta Declaration' was signed by Nai Hongsa, but two Kachin observers, who had been present during the talks' the early stages, had already left by the time the statement was drafted. They were therefore not pleased to see the KIO's name added to the list of organisations endorsing the declaration. This statement rejected any compromise with the SLORC, and reiterated several key DAB-NCUB policies, such as the call for a nation-wide ceasefire and tripartite negotiations between the government, NLD and ethnic groups. According to Nai Shwe Kyin and other sources, Nai Hongsa's backing for the declaration was a rogue act, unauthorised by the party Central Committee. It did though, provoke admiration for the NMSP Joint General Secretary and MUL President, among Mon activists along the border and overseas.

The Burmese and Thai military authorities were deeply displeased at the Mon delegates' support for the Mae Tha Raw Hta Declaration. In retaliation for Nai Hongsa's apparently unauthorised endorsement, within a few weeks the *Tatmadaw* Chief-of-Staff, General Maung Aye, had personally abrogated a joint SLORC-NMSP-Thai logging concession behind Halochanee (operated by the Chiang Mai-based Htoo Company). In an attempt to placate Rangoon, Nai Hongsa was quickly demoted from the NMSP's powerful Central Executive Committee. However, he retained much of his influence, and in late 1998 was quietly re-instated.[47]

The fallout from Mae Tha Raw Hta may have put the NMSP under pressure, but this was as nothing compared to the consequences for the

KNU. The declaration helped to re-enforce the position of Bo Mya's hard-line 'old guard'; it also strengthened the resolve of hawks within the *Tatmadaw*, who wanted to punish the 'uncooperative' Karen. Whatever its intended purpose, the Mae Tha Raw Hta Conference presaged a massive and devastating offensive against the last militarily and politically significant armed opposition group still at war with Rangoon.

Starting on 5th February 1997, an estimated 35,000 Burma Army troops were deployed on two broad fronts, against a KNLA and allied force one tenth as strong.[48] In the south, the *Tatmadaw* met little organised resistance, and proceeded rapidly down the Tenasserim River to KNLA Fourth Brigade HQ at Htee Kee, which fell on the 26th February. By the end of March, Karen nationalist forces had been driven from nearly all their bases in the Tenasserim Division, and were reduced to launching hit-and-run guerrilla attacks from the jungle.

Meanwhile, in Sixth Brigade, Htee Ker Pler had fallen on 13th February. Four days later, two hundred-plus soldiers under the command of KNLA Lt-Colonel Thu Mu Hei had surrendered, in a prearranged deal with the *Tatmadaw* – an act of treachery which severely undermined Karen defensive capacity. The KNU's strategy had been to hold the Burma Army, but only for long enough to allow civilians to evacuate. The KNLA would then abandon fixed positions, to harass the enemy guerrilla-style. However, even this limited battle plan proved untenable and, as the KNLA and allies were overwhelmed, large numbers of civilians found themselves trapped behind advancing *Tatmadaw* columns.

According to Human Rights Watch/Asia, the 1997 Burma Army offensives were characterised by the wide-spread use of press-ganged porters, and the rape and murder of scores of villagers.[49] The Human Rights Foundation of Monland has estimated that not less than 30,000 porters were forced to carry munitions for the *Tatmadaw* during the 1997 offensives, most of whom were either Mon or Karen.[50] Furthermore, a number of long-established Mon and Karen villages around Kya-In Seik-Kyi, in the Ye-Yebyu area, and along the Tenasserim and Mae Kah Rivers (in the vicinity of the recently-gazetteered Myinmoletkat Nature Reserve) were forcibly relocated and/or de-populated as a result of the offensive.[51]

By May, the official Burmese refugee population in Thailand had risen from 101,000 (in January) to 115,000.[52] However, these figures under-estimate the extent of the refugee crisis, as continued cross-border attacks, camp relocations and the Thai military's policy of forced repatriation meant that many refugees had limited access to the refugee camps.[53]

On at least two occasions in February 1997, Sia Hook logging company vehicles were used by the Ninth Division to forcibly repatriate Karen civilians. The company's trucks were also used to transport *Tatmadaw* units through KNLA Fourth Brigade. *Sia* Hook, and his associates in the Burmese and Thai armies, expected to profit from the post-offensive 'economic

252

development' of areas previously controlled by the insurgents. One project standing to benefit from the 1997 dry season offensives in Tenasserim Division was the construction of a highway between Tavoy – where construction of a deep-sea port was in the planning stage – and the Thai border at Bong Htee (or possibly Htee Kee), near Kanchanaburi.[54]

For many within the Mon nationalist movement, the 1997 Burma Army offensives confirmed the inevitability of the NMSP-SLORC ceasefire. Whatever the disadvantages of the agreement, a return to fighting would result in the NMSP being rapidly dislodged from its remaining strongholds and, like the KNU and the KNPP, forced to wage a desperate hit-and-run guerrilla war in the jungle. The SLORC's reaction to the Mae Tha Raw Hta Declaration had shown the danger of the NMSP's dual-track approach to Rangoon. Although the party remained in discreet contact with the NLD and KIO, and to a lesser extent with the remaining insurgent groups along the Thailand-Burma border, for a year following the 1997 offensives, the NMSP leadership kept a low political profile.

In March 1997 the Burma Army Southeast Command requested that the MNLA withdraw from the Pong Katar permanent ceasefire position, and allow the *Tatmadaw* to conduct operations against KNLA units in the area, on the Three Pagodas Pass road 40–50 Km northwest of Halochanee. The Karen Refugee Committee (KRC) feared that the *Tatmadaw* might be planning to target some 2,000 Karen refugees, who had fled the offensive and congregated at Htee Wah Doh village, five km behind Halochanee. Denied access to Thailand by the Ninth Division, these displaced villagers had begun to construct temporary shelters on the edge of the Mon ceasefire zone.[55]

The NMSP leadership honourably refused the Southeast Command's request. Nevertheless, as the 1997 rainy season took hold across southeast Burma, the *Tatmadaw* undertook the systematic relocation of some 10,000 Mon and Karen villagers in the Kya-In Seik-Kyi area. The forced relocations, often accompanied by serious human rights abuses, were primarily aimed at pushing the KNLA remnants further to the south, to the Mon State border. However, the *Tatmadaw* was only partially successful, and by the end of the year Karen guerrilla units were still active over large parts of southern Sixth Brigade.

Meanwhile, further to the south, by late 1997 most of the Pa Yaw returnees in Tavoy District had been forced to abandoned the resettlement sites, to build temporary bamboo shelters in the border foothills. The NMSP Tavoy District headquarters also moved to a secure position on the hillside, although the MNLA continued to maintain a skeleton presence near the old HQ. After months of uncertainty, the *Tatmadaw* finally entered the recently-vacated temporary ceasefire zone in mid-July. Three days later, the column withdrew, to a position two hour's walk from the westernmost resettlement site. It seemed that, although the SLORC intended to enforce the conditions of the ceasefire agreement, for the time being at least, the NMSP would be allowed to keep a low-profile presence in Tavoy District.

During the 1996–77 dry season, there had been further clashes between the MNLA and anti-ceasefire Mon forces in Tavoy District. In one daring attack, members of the 'Nai Soe Aung Group' crept up through the jungle to Central and attempted to loot an arms cache. They were driven out by loyal MNLA troops, with heavy casualties to the Nai Soe Aung Group. Over the following weeks, a number of these beleaguered rebels were reported to have succumbed to malaria and/or MNLA patrols.

There were also alarms further to the north, in Moulmein District. In June 1994 the *Tatmadaw* had attacked Halochanee from the rear. On 10th March 1997 they marched straight down the border from Three Pagodas Pass. By early morning, more than one hundred Burmese troops were camped out at the entrance to the camp, on the escape route into Thailand. By coming down the border, the *Tatmadaw* had cut the 6,000-plus Mon and Karen refugees' access to Thailand, thus avoiding a repeat of the 1994 exodus. A Burmese officer informed the refugees that the *Tatmadaw* was here to ascertain the position of the border. The Mon ceasefire liaison office at Three Pagodas Pass had not been notified of the visit and the local MNLA was taken by surprise.

Overnight on the 10th March, the MNLA infiltrated the camp and set up a mortar position near the hospital. Meanwhile, the NMSP made a formal complaint regarding the incursion, to the Burma Army Southeast Command at Moulmein. After five days of mounting tension, on the morning of 14th March, several Ninth Division officers arrived from Kanchanaburi, and met with the *Tatmadaw* to demarcate the border at Halochanee. Later that day, twenty refugee houses, which were apparently situated on the Thai side of the border, were bulldozed into the ground, following which the Burmese and Thai soldiers withdrew.

Dissidents in the South:
the Mon Army Mergui District and Allies

At the beginning of 1997, the MAMD controlled perhaps ten of the thirty or forty villages east of the *Tatmadaw* garrison town of Lenya, in the heart of Tenasserim Division. The nearly three hundred MAMD troops were allied with the one hundred-strong southernmost battalion of the ABSDF Students' Army. Based to the north of the Mon base at Huay Pak, the 8-8-88 Battalion's tough 'student soldiers' were natural allies with the anti-ceasefire Mon faction, in their continued armed struggle against the SLORC. A small group of KNU-allied All Burma Muslim Union (ABMU) soldiers operating further to the north were perhaps less-likely fellow insurgents, but were nonetheless committed to the defence of their villages.[56]

254

By March 1997, the liberated zone between Huay Pak and the other main MAMD base at Chaung Chee Pass, 50 Km to the south, constituted the last substantial rebel bastion on the southern stretch of the border. It was therefore only a matter of time before the *Tatmadaw* launched a major offensive in the south.

In mid-April a column of 1,000 Burma Army troops set out from Maw Daung, towards Huay Pak. The mediation attempts of NMSP go-betweens had bought some time but, having dealt a decisive blow to the KNU further to the north, the Burma Army Southeast Command now decided that the time was right to move decisively against the MAMD.

On 18th April the *Tatmadaw* overran the northernmost insurgent position, the ABMU base at Muh Gaw Paw. About 150 refugees fled to Thailand, where the authorities' response to their plight set the pattern for the lower Tenasserim region. The local Border Patrol Police granted the villagers temporary shelter, but soldiers of the Ninth Division immediately began exerting pressure on them to return to Burma.

Following the fall of Muh Gaw Paw, the *Tatmadaw* force split into two columns, each with a compliment of some 500 press-ganged porters. On 22nd April the main ABSDF base fell, and for several days there was heavy fighting around Huay Pak. Despite superior *Tatmadaw* numbers, the outcome of the battle was inconclusive and the Burma Army failed to take the well-fortified base. Therefore, the bulk of the attacking force headed south, to besiege the other main MAMD stronghold, at Chaung Chee. With most of the MAMD leaders and the bulk of their forces at Huay Pak, Chaung Chee fell on 27th April. Aware that they could not defend the village for long against a sustained Mon counter-attack, the *Tatmadaw* withdrew the same day.

The resumption of fighting in the south had put the mainstream NMSP under re-renewed pressure. Those who opposed the ceasefire saw this as an opportunity to resume the armed conflict, and many within the nationalist movement were disappointed not to see the NMSP intervene on behalf of the MAMD. The widely-respected MNRC Chairman, Phra Wongsa Pala, who was not known for his support of the ceasefire, used his position as a senior monk to gain access both to the southern hard-liners and the more pragmatic leaders at Central. The MNRC was thus able to liaise between the two sides, while at the same time securing from the BBC and MSF some humanitarian support for those displaced by the fighting.

The *Tatmadaw* offensive had doubled the number of IDPs in Mergui District. From a recorded 1,247 refugees at the end of the 1996 rainy season, by the end of the following April the total had risen to nearly 3,000.[57] On 24th April, 792 of these people crossed into Thailand as refugees.[58] They were crowded into a small, insanitary site near the border, in Bang Saphan District, from where the sound of intermittent shelling at Chaung Chee was clearly audible. On the same day 300 refugees from

Huay Pak tried to enter Thailand, but were denied access to the Kingdom by the Ninth Division.

The fighting continued throughout May, as the refugees huddled in their temporary shelters, dependant on the MNRC and the NGOs, and always fearful of repatriation by the Thai military. In the middle of the month, *Tatmadaw* reinforcements arrived, and a column was re-deployed from Chaug Chee, to attack the KNLA Number Twelve Special Battalion further to the south. During a let-up in the fighting, in mid-May, the MAMD leadership met with NMSP representatives in Huay Pak. It seemed that a negotiated settlement to the three-way MAMD-NMSP-SLORC conflict might be possible.

On the morning of 24th May 1997 the MAMD announced that it had agreed a ceasefire with the government. The move surprised most observers, including the Mon monks, who until the last minute had been seeking a formula whereby the MAMD could reunite with the NMSP, whilst maintaining some presence in Mergui District. Over the next few days, it emerged that a group of senior MAMD officers, led by the intelligence chief, U Ko Ko Aung, had struck a deal with the *Tatmadaw*. The local Mon commanders could retain powerful positions, if they arranged for the refugees to return, and let the *Tatmadaw* into Mergui District.

Ten days later, *The Bangkok Post* reported that 300 MAMD troops had surrendered, handing over 1,700 items of arms and ammunition to the *Tatmadaw* (an indication of how well-equipped the faction had been).[59] This was a classic example of SLORC ceasefire strategy, which had the added advantage of splitting the Mon nationalist movement. Hard-liners denounced the MAMD 'surrender', as did the ABSDF.

Within days, nearly half the MAMD troops had deserted, indicating that – as in the surrender organised by the KNLA's Saw Thu Mu Hei, earlier in the year – insurgent soldiers on the ground had probably not been warned before the 'ceasefire' was announced. Some MAMD troops joined the refugees at Bang Saphan; most escaped into the forest, to await developments. Meanwhile, the ABSDF remnants began to move up the border to the KNLA's Eleventh Battalion area, where they re-grouped alongside the beleaguered Karen guerrillas.

The Southern Mon Refugees and the Demise of the MAMD

On 29th May, five days after their 'return to the legal fold', a group of MAMD leaders met with the refugees at Bang Saphan, where they asked 'their' people to return to Burma, promising six month's rice supply to any who did so. There was a catch: the *Tatmadaw* had established a base in Chaung Chee and would not depart until after the refugees had returned. This was a cue for the Ninth Division to step up the pressure on the refugees, whose living conditions were by now beginning to deteriorate. Three days later, on 1st June, at a formal ceremony on Chaung Chee parade ground, Colonel Nai Ong Suik Heang and U Ko Ko Aung of the MAMD formally handed over their weapons and control of the district to the Burma Army Coastal Strategic Commander, Brig-General Sit Maung.

Since mid-May, about three hundred Bang Saphan refugees had already drifted back to the Chaung Chee area. These people were rounded up by the MAMD and *Tatmadaw*, and returned to the border, where on 6th June they rejoined the four hundred-plus people remaining at Bang Saphan. In a nasty piece of political circus, the refugees were then re-(or re-re)patriated *en masse* to Chaung Chee. A representative of UNHCR Bangkok, which up to this point had shown little interest in the southern Mon refugees, came down to 'monitor' this operation, which was later broadcast on a Thai TV (by an army-owned station).

Presumably, the Thai military hoped to improve its tarnished image with this 'voluntary' repatriation. The presence of UNHCR seemed to endorse practices that went against many of the agency's guidelines. Over the previous few days, their leaders had signed documents, stating that the refugees wanted to return to Burma. However, they had done this under duress, and the day before the repatriation thirty-to-forty families had expressed, to relief workers, their strong desire not to return to Chaung Chee. However, following another visit from Ninth Division officers, none of these people were prepared to voice their concerns to the UNHCR official. As a Thai national, he was too closely identified with the state.

As feared, the situation of the returnees was far from satisfactory. A handful of MAMD commanders and their families lived well enough in the Chaung Chee-Huay Pak area, and Nai Ong Suik Heang and Nai Ba Sein were even allowed to set up a cattle trading business. However, the SLORC provided the returnees with only one week's supply of rice, rather than the promised six month's. Furthermore, from the outset villagers were forced to work on projects for both the MAMD and the *Tatmadaw*.[60]

Therefore, few observers were surprised when in July four hundred Chaung Chee villagers again fled to Bang Saphan. This time, the Thai authorities were better prepared: the refugees were not allowed to congregate in one location, but were forced to disperse. The UNHCR official visited the area again on 18th July, but as soon as he left, the Border Patrol Police started rounding-up refugees. Many escaped the clamp-down; some returned to Burma, while others continued to receive shelter from the sympathetic local Thai community, in the rubber and fruit plantations of Bang Saphan.

On 16th November 1997, a few days after the first anniversary of its formation, the MAMD split into two factions. The majority of MAMD soldiers were unhappy with the cosy nature of MAMD-SLORC relations, and the increasing local incidence of forced labour and involuntary local conscription into the *Tatmadaw*. Mon soldiers in Huay Pak rebelled, and re-joined about fifty of their colleagues who had left in the immediate aftermath of the ceasefire. Soon, yet another Mon armed faction had been established.

The Ramanya Restoration Army (RRA, also known as the Monland Return Army) was opposed to the MAMD, but not necessarily pro-NMSP. The new group originally numbered about one hundred armed men, under the command of an ex-MNLA platoon commander, Captain Nai Sein Hla (or *Kya Min*: 'Tiger King'). The RRA soon began to launch guerrilla attacks against the *Tatmadaw* and dwindling MAMD forces, which responded by burning villages deemed sympathetic to the rebels.

Inevitably, a new wave of several hundred refugees fled to Thailand. On 21st November the Ninth Division organised the transport of sixty of these people to Halochanee refugee camp – a further act of *refoulement* that was not challenged by UNHCR. The remaining refugees were forced either to disperse and seek shelter in the local plantations, or return to Burma.[61] Over the next two years, the southern Mon refugees crossed and re-crossed the border several times, often being forcibly repatriated by the Ninth Division.[62] These repeatedly displaced people continued to receive occasional assistance from the BBC, which channelled aid through the new Ramanya Human Rights Committee (RHRC).

Led by an ex-monk from Ye, the RHRC operated under the patronage of Phra Wongsa Pala and the MNRC. As the name suggests though, it was more closely associated with the RRA than the NMSP. By mid-1998, not more than sixty RRA soldiers were still actively fighting the *Tatmadaw* and rump MAMD. Having no permanent base from which to launch operations, the group faced a difficult future.

Meanwhile, their usefulness to the *Tatmadaw* having expired, during the 1998 rainy season, the MAMD leaders found themselves squeezed out of cattle business in Mergui District. With their rice rations cut, the remaining MAMD troops began to disappear into Thailand, join the RRA, or depart to seek their fortunes elsewhere in Burma.

CHAPTER EIGHTEEN

Burma, Thailand, ASEAN and the International Community

Throughout the late 1990s, the political deadlock in Rangoon wore on. In general, this stalemate suited the SLORC, and its successor-regime, the State Peace and Development Council (SPDC), better than it did the opposition.

Meanwhile the cultural and economic decline of Burma continued apace. In a back-handed tribute to the continuing influence of the student movement, for much of the decade the universities remained closed. In fact, for periods in the second half of the 1990s, the teacher training colleges run by the KNU and the KIO in the border areas were the only functioning centres of tertiary education in the country.

Due in part to an effective lobbying campaign by the opposition in exile and its supporters, the Burmese economy was further weakened in the early 1990s by the imposition of partial US and EU sanctions, the consequences of which were compounded by a dearth of foreign investment in the aftermath of the 1997 'Asian financial crisis'. Meanwhile, Burma continued to exploit and be exploited by the relationship with China, playing-off the emergent Asian superpower against her Southeast Asian neighbours. Nevertheless, by 1999 it was becoming apparent that support for the regime within ASEAN, and in Thailand in particular, was by no means unconditional.

Developments in Rangoon

Following its seizure of power in 1988, the SLORC had promised to open the economy to private and foreign investment. Despite such discontinuities with the Burmese Way to Socialism, seasoned observers continued to discerned Ne Win's influence, behind the scenes.

In December 1991 the ageing dictator is reported to have gathered General Saw Maung and other SLORC leaders at his lakeside residence in Rangoon, and scolded their failure to win over the hearts and minds of the people.[63] Following this dressing-down, and a subsequent nervous break-down – during which he reputedly claimed to be an avatar of king Anawratha – in April 1992 General Saw Maung was replaced by his deputy, General Than Shwe. The new SLORC Chairman lifted some aspects of martial law (declared in 1988) and ordered the release of more than one hundred political prisoners.[64]

Another new development occurred in January 1993, the year after the MNDF was outlawed. A National Constitutional Convention was established in Rangoon, composed of about one hundred MPs-elect from 1990, together with a much larger number of delegates hand-picked by the military. Having originally pledged to relinquish power to the victors of the 1990 election, the SLORC now proposed that the elected lawmakers participate in its constitution-drafting process.

The draft constitution would offer 'self administered zones' – after the Chinese model – to the Kokang, Wa and other ethnic groups.[65] Generally, these were the more powerful ex-CPB organisations, which had been the first to agree ceasefires with Rangoon. However, it soon became obvious that any government elected under the new charter would continue to be dominated by serving and retired army officers, and probably also by members the Union Solidarity and Development Association (USDA), a mass organisation established by the SLORC in September 1993, along the lines of the pro-military Golkar party in Indonesia.[66] By end of the decade, the USDA had a membership of some fifteen million people, many of whom had been more-or-less coerced into joining. Its objectives included upholding the regime's 'Three National Causes' and the 'promotion of national pride.' Other government-organised 'NGOs' (GONGOs) included the economically influential War Veterans Organisation, the Myanmar Red Cross and the Myanmar Maternal and Child Welfare Association. Beyond this highly circumscribed sector, 'civil society' and the operation of independent political parties, such as the NLD, were severely restricted, as was the population's freedom of expression and association, and access to information and independent media.

Unsurprisingly, the draft National Constitution endorsed the leading political role of the military. It also contained residency and other measures specifically designed to exclude Daw Aung San Suu Kyi from office. Realising that the NLD could make little headway in such a biased forum, within a few months of her release from house arrest in July 1995, Aung San Suu Kyi withdrew the league from the convention.

For a while in mid-1995, it had seemed that dialogue between the NLD and the government might be possible. However, Daw Aung San Suu Kyi's release was to prove a false dawn. Over the following months, the Nobel laureate provoked the SLORC, by initiating a series of impromptu Sunday morning rallies outside the gates of her compound, on Rangoon's University Avenue. She talked to the crowd, which on some days numbered as many as three thousand people, on the political situation in Burma and the nature of democracy. Videos of these speeches were viewed clandestinely across the country, helping to keep the flame of resistance alive. In speaking directly to her people, the NLD leader by-passed the state-controlled media and demonstrated her readiness to take on the SLORC, whilst inspiring people across Burma and the world. She also knowingly antagonised the generals.

In the context of Burmese politics, where status and public standing are of huge importance, Daw Aung San Suu Kyi's open criticism of the regime made it difficult for moderate elements within the *Tatmadaw* to argue for compromise. The government held most of the cards, and if the NLD was not prepared to respect and defer to the leading role of the army, then the regime would 'Crush All Destructive Elements' (a policy spelled-out on billboards across Burma).

Military Intelligence agents finally brought the gatherings outside Daw Aung San Suu Kyi's compound to an end, in September 1996. In October, an NLD conference was broken-up by the authorities, and five hundred party members were arrested. The following month, a group of USDA thugs attacked Daw Aung San Suu Kyi's vehicle, pelting her with stones. Although 'the lady' emerged with only minor injuries, the incident sent a stark message to the people: if even Daw Suu was not safe, then no one was.

Following a wave of more-or-less forced resignations in the second half of 1998 and 1999, by the end of the decade the NLD was unable to function effectively beyond the leadership circle in Rangoon. The NLD leaders were nearly all members of the urban, Burman political class, and beyond the obvious popularity of Daw Aung San Suu Kyi, the party had limited natural appeal to non-elite (and non-Burman) groups in Burma. However, the NLD did make some attempts to embrace a wider constituency. As noted above, prior to her arrest in 1989, Daw Aung San Suu Kyi had been keen to develop ties with MNDF and other ethnic minority politicians. She also made overtures to the Karen, and following her release from house arrest visited the famous Thamanya *Sayadaw*, at his monastery near the Karen State capital of Pa'an. She later donned Karen national costume to appear in a video address marking Karen National Day, in January 1997. This speech was recorded around the same time as the release of the 'Mae Tha Raw Hta Declaration', which called on the SLORC to initiate tripartite dialogue with the NLD and the ethnic groups. Rather belatedly, the NLD seems to have realised that the insurgents were making many of the same demands as the above-ground opposition, supporting Daw Aung San Suu Kyi against the SLORC.

Meanwhile, by the end of the 1990s, Burma's students – traditionally the most radical sector of society – had again become restive. Universities and other institutes of higher education were closed in 1988, re-opened after the 1990 election and then closed again in December 1991, after students in

Rangoon took to the streets to celebrate the announcement that Daw Aung San Suu Kyi had been awarded the Nobel Peace Prize.[67]

The government allowed the universities to resume teaching in the mid-1990s, but following a series of small student demonstrations in downtown Rangoon in December 1996, all but the medical and military schools were once more closed. The universities only began to re-open again in late 1999, by which time it was calculated that just four per cent of Burma's national budget was spent on education, whilst over thirty-one per cent went to the 400,000-strong *Tatmadaw*.[68] When undergraduate teaching did resume, there was often such a back-log of students in the system that syllabi for entire years were compressed into a few month's study. Furthermore, in an effort to prevent the re-emergence of campus radicalism, many bachelor's degree courses were taught by 'distance education', with students confined to Government Technical Colleges (such as that at Moulmein) and other out-of-the way sites.[69]

The education system was obviously in deep crisis. With the exception of the children of the military-business elite – many of whom were educated abroad – a 'lost generation' had been denied the opportunity to complete their education, whilst for millions of children in the countryside, even the most basic schooling was either unavailable or unaffordable.[70]

In an effort to distract attention from such negative developments, in November 1997 the SLORC was disbanded and replaced by the State Peace and Development Council (SPDC). Two particularly corrupt generals were dismissed, but otherwise the change was largely cosmetic. A number of regional *Tatmadaw* commanders were 'promoted' to the SPDC in Rangoon, including Maj-General Ket Sein, the Burma Army Southeastern Commander at the time of the 1995 NMSP-SLORC ceasefire, who became Minister for Health.

The military continued to dominate the executive, judiciary and legislature. Generals Than Shwe, Maung Aye and Khin Nyunt still held all the top jobs, and policy continued to be determined by a paranoid, short-term security agenda.

Foreign Relations, Foreign Investment, Drugs and the 1997 Financial Crisis

By the mid-1990s Burma's relations with her neighbours were generally warmer than at any time since the early 1960s. The on-going repatriation of *Rohingya* refugees from Bangladesh, and the conduct of joint Indian Army-*Tatmadaw* counter-insurgency operations along the Burma-India border, had seen relations with Burma's two western neighbours improve substantially since 1988, when the Indian government had been a strong supporter of the NLD. The prospect of Burma being driven further into the orbit of China had persuaded Indian politicians and military men to befriend the SLORC, despite the misgivings of Indian Defence Minister George Fernandes, who in 1998 accused China of installing surveillance systems in Burmese Bay of Bengal islands.

China's interest in Burma was most obviously expressed in terms of trade, the volume of which had gradually increased since the early 1980s. By 1989, annual bilateral trade had reached two billion dollars (twice the figure for 1987) and China had begun to undercut Thailand's influence on the Burmese bazaar economy.[71] Since 1991, the *Tatmadaw* is calculated to have spent some $1.5 billion on Chinese armaments, including F7 jet fighters, tanks, armoured personnel carriers, naval patrol vessels, small arms and ammunition.[72] Many of these purchases were financed by soft loans.

Although, since 1997, trade relations between Rangoon and Beijing have cooled somewhat, Burma remains very much within China's sphere of influence, with Beijing as one of Rangoon's few international allies. The porous nature of the China-Burma border, and the economic power of the Chinese, have resulted, in Mandalay and other parts of northern Burma, in Chinese influence and immigrants beginning to displace Burmese.

Moving further east, (ex-)communist and other rebels had long controlled the mountainous and inaccessible Laos border, where the narcotics trade is monopolised by warlords with high-level connections in China, Laos, Thailand and Burma. In February 1991 the Lao prime minister became the first foreign head of state to visit Burma since 1988, signalling a new strategic alliance between the two one-party regimes, both of which aspired to ASEAN membership.

Before 1997, Thailand was the only ASEAN nation to share a land border with Burma. The Thai economy dwarfed the Burmese and, as was the case across much of the region, in the 1980s and '90s money politics had come to dominate Thai affairs of state. The need to check corruption was given by the Royal Thai Army Commander-in-Chief, General Suchinda Kraprayoon, as a primary justification for the military coup of 23rd February 1991, which installed the National Peace Keeping Council (NPKC) in power.

The 1991 coup took most observers by surprise, as Thailand had in recent years attained a degree of prosperity and stability, that was judged to preclude any new seizure of power by the military. However, the kingdom had a tradition of elite rotation by means of cyclic military intervention, and the 1991 coup ultimately represented only a spasm in Thailand's political development. The new regime soon moved to reassure foreign and domestic opinion, and the jittery nerves of investors. On 2nd March the NPKC appointed as prime minister a scion of the Mon aristocracy, Anand Panyarachun, a respected businessman and diplomat. Ironically, Khun Anand proved to be among the most popular, competent and honest of recent Thai prime ministers.

Although the economy continued to boom, opposition to the NPKC regime was kept up by students, NGOs and academics, a vigorous free press, and (behind the scenes) by big business. New elections were eventually held in March 1992, following which the pro-military majority in the new parliament nominated the unelected military strong-man, General Suchinda, as prime minister. It seemed for a few weeks that Suchinda, who before the poll had promised not to assume the premiership, might succeed in usurping power on at least a semi-constitutional basis. However, in April and May hundreds of thousands of ordinary people came out onto the streets of Bangkok, in a series of demonstrations which recalled the student-led mass rallies of October 1973 (which brought down a previous military dictatorship). As in Rangoon in 1988, the presence among the crowds of office workers and business people indicated that the middle classes were not prepared to let the military rule the country unopposed.

During the February 1991 coup, radio and TV stations had broadcast martial music and a couple of tanks had appeared at strategic points in Bangkok, but the shops had stayed open and life had gone on much as usual. The events of the following year did not go so smoothly. The showdown came in late May, when troops of the Thai Army First Army opened fire on tens of thousands of demonstrators in Ratchadamri Avenue, not far from the Grand Palace. At least thirty-eight unarmed people were killed, the bodies of several victims reportedly being removed by army personnel, in an attempt to hide evidence of the massacre.[73]

Unlike its counterpart in Burma four years previously, the Thai military was unable to maintain its grip on power, in the aftermath of the killings. Since the 1970s, Thai citizens had acquired a raft of liberties unobtainable in Burma, and Thai society had developed a degree of civility and openness that made the more extreme forms of authoritarian rule unworkable. Following the intervention of His Majesty the King, on 24th May 1992 General Suchinda was forced to resign in disgrace, after only six weeks as prime minister. After a second brief interregnum led by Anand Panyar-achun, a new government was elected in September.

The first Chuan administration lasted until mid-1995. It was followed by the short-lived and corrupt governments of Banharn Silpa-archa, and the ex-Royal Thai Army chief and Armed Forces Supreme Commander, General Chavolit Yongchaiyud. By the time Chuan and the Democrats returned to power in September 1997, Thailand and the region were in the throes of a major financial crisis, triggered by a collapse in the value of the Thai Baht. Three months previously, in June 1997, Burma and Laos had joined Vietnam as the newest, poorest members of ASEAN (see below).

Following the withdrawal of virtually all Western and Japanese relief and development assistance in 1988–89, the SLORC had come to rely on private capital for its foreign exchange needs. Under the 'open-door' economic policy of 1990–98, Burma received more than two-and-a-half billion dollars of direct investment from companies in more than twenty countries, including Singapore, Thailand and other ASEAN members, as well the United Kingdom and other European nations.[74]

Although manufacturing, banking and other sectors received some investment, the extraction of non-renewable natural resources (timber, fish, oil and gas), together with hotels and tourism, took the lion's share of funding. Despite these inputs, the regime ran up an increasingly serious balance of payments deficit, which by 1995 stood at more than $500 million. The following year, the failure of the SLORC's 'Visit Myanmar Year' promotion hit projected earnings hard, contributing to a lack of confidence in the country's medium-term economic prospects. Then regional financial meltdown struck.

The 'Asian financial crisis' reduced the amount of investment capital available in the region, and helped to accelerate Burma's decades-long decline into poverty. In mid-1997 six Thai banks had had offices in Rangoon; by 1999 all but one had pulled out, and the balance of payments deficit stood at nearly $1.4 billion.[75] Furthermore, delayed payments to the Yadana pipeline consortium further undermined investor confidence.

The Yadana gas pipeline had been completed in August 1998. However, it was more than a year later before special turbines for the Ratchaburi power plant were installed. In the meantime, the Petroleum Authority of Thailand (PTT) was unable to fulfil its contractual obligation to take delivery of the gas, and the state-owned energy company had to negotiate re-scheduled payments to the pipeline consortium. The Yetagun pipeline was completed in early 2000, and gas started pumping in June that year. By this time, a Los Angeles District Court had accepted jurisdiction in the lawsuit brought on behalf of a group of Karen refugees against UNOCAL, a key member of the Yadana consortium. Although the case was dismissed on technical grounds in September 2000, US-based activists and lawyers continued their campaign against UNOCAL's links with the SPDC (and with the Taleban in Afghanistan), and one year later the California Superior Court ordered the case to proceed.

Other Burmese mega-projects under consideration in Thailand included a series of proposed dams on the Salween River and its tributaries, along the border with Karenni and Shan States. Due in part to rampant logging during the 1970s and '80s, throughout the 1990s Thailand experienced increasingly severe dry season water shortages. In January 1999 the Royal Thai Government commissioned an inquiry into the proposed dams, which would divert water to the Thai agricultural and industrial sectors, as well as generating electricity.[76] Such infrastructure projects promised big contracts for well-connected Thai and international construction companies, as well as the opportunity to cut down valuable timber reserves in the vicinity of the proposed dams. However, as in the pipeline area, local villagers were identified by the *Tatmadaw* as rebel sympathisers, and stood to loose everything from the 'development 'of their homelands.

Meanwhile, the SPDC had more immediate concerns. By mid-1999, inflation in Rangoon was running at close to fifty per cent[77] and foreign investment had slumped to a paltry $29.5 million.[78] By August 2000, the value of the Kyat had fallen to 390 to the US Dollar, although officially the two currencies remained pegged at the ludicrous ratio of 6.5:1. This grossly-distorted official exchange rate was criticised in a November 1999 draft World Bank report, which concluded that economic recovery would require fundamental economic and political reforms.[79]

Despite the much-publicise announcements of the early SLORC years, since 1988 only limited economic restructuring had been carried out, and the state sector continued to suffer serious macro-economic problems. Meanwhile, the rural population continued to struggle for survival, while attempting to cope with interminable demands for forced labour and taxes.

Nevertheless, until mid-1998 Burma's still relatively isolated economy had weathered the Asian financial storm somewhat better than its neighbours. Decades of protectionist, *derigiste* fiscal practice had insulated the country from the worst ravages of globalisation. In 1998–99 though, the economy began to deteriorate rapidly; by mid-2001, the Kyat was being traded on the Rangoon black market at over seven hundred to the dollar. However, state finances did not collapse entirely, as some observers had predicated.

Since the 1960s, the country's current account had been underpinned by a huge 'black market' cash economy. Unofficial sources of foreign exchange included the diminishing funds remitted by migrant workers in Thailand and elsewhere, the legal and illegal export of timber, gems and jade, and the hundreds of millions of dollars generated by the drugs trade.

In 1998 the US State Department estimated the value of Burma's informal economy, including narcotics exports, to be equal to all legal exports combined.[80] Following the SLORC's ceasefire agreements with trafficking groups in northern Burma, opium cultivation had increased rapidly, and by 1999 accounted for nearly ninety per cent of total production in Southeast Asia. According to the American State Department, in 1999 Burma continued to be "the world's largest source of illicit opium and heroin."[81] Although, in 1997 and '98, cultivation had declined by an impressive twenty-six per cent, the 1998 harvest still yielded a massive 1,750 metric tons of opium. In 2001 the heroin business was still in full swing, and had been joined in the hills of north-east Burma by a massive increase in amphetamine-type stimulant production.[82]

Although the KIO had made successful efforts at drug eradication in its territory,[83] the announcement by some Wa and Kokang leaders that their areas would become opium-free zones by 2005 enjoyed limited international credibility. The State Department concluded that the United Wa State Army

(UWSA), the Myanmar National Democratic Alliance Army (MNDAA), the Shan State Army – East (SSA – East), the Mongko Defence Army (MDA) and other groups based along the Chinese border, were little more than narco-trafficking organisations, which had been encouraged by the government to establish money-laundering operations across Burma. Although there was no evidence linking the SLORC leadership directly to the business, it was obvious that *Tatmadaw* commanders were implicated in the narcotics trade, at the very least as recipients of bribes from the drugs cartels. While the US government's attitude helped to further isolate the SPDC regime and its clients among the ceasefire groups, this position failed to recognise the genuine desire of many Wa and Shan leaders to work towards the elimination of drugs production.

Meanwhile, economies across the region were in crisis, and the resulting social fallout exposed hundreds of thousands of vulnerable young people to a new generation of cheap amphetamines being aggressively marketed by Burmese and Thai drug dealers. Another consequence of the financial crash of 1997 was a contraction of the jobs market across Southeast Asia, which affected Burmese migrant workers in Thailand and Malaysia, who tended to be concentrated in the fishing, sweat shop and agricultural sectors. Many had fled their homeland not only to seek their fortunes abroad, but because life in rural Burma had become impossible to bear, and they could find no other way of feeding their families. The Thai and Malay governments declared that they would no longer tolerate the presence of these illegal immigrants.

By 1998, there were probably still nearly 100,000 illegal or semi-legal Mon workers in Thailand,[84] out of an estimated migrant labour population in the kingdom of 1.3 million people.[85] By April, deportations to Halochanee through the IDC system had risen to approximately 2,000 people per month.[86]

In mid-1998, Thai-Burmese relations were in a state of flux. The Chuan administration had overseen the promotion of a new generation Royal Thai Army commanders, most of whom were committed to disengage the army from politics. Unlike in neighbouring Burma, the Thai political class seemed to have gained the upper hand in their long power struggle with the military.

Prime minister Chuan attempted to put relations with Burma, Laos and Cambodia on a more professional footing. Although the Thai military and various shady intelligence agencies continued to exercise considerable influence on the ground, after 1998 the role of the Thai NSC was re-defined, as one of co-ordination and policy development, rather than direct implementation.[87] In principal, this meant a decline in the influence of well-connected power-brokers, such as Mr X.

In mid-1998 the Thai Foreign Minister, Surin Pitsuwan, and his assistant, the well-known liberal, MR Sukhumband Paribatra, began to elaborate a tentative new policy of 'flexible' (or even 'critical') – as opposed to 'constructive' – ASEAN engagement with Burma.[88] This semantic shift was reflected in similar language used by members of the new Estrada government in the Philippines, if not by other ASEAN member-states.

While hardly a return to the old policies of the 1950s–80s, the tentative elaboration of new a new relationship with Burma did represent a cooling of the Thailand's relationship with the SPDC. Although the Thai authorities remained anxious to co-operate on specific issues, such as drug control and border demarcation, there was less sympathy, under the second Chuan administration, for Burma's military rulers than there had been under some previous Royal Thai Governments.

However, the new tone of government-military relations in Thailand did not necessarily mean that the kingdom's Burma policy would be transformed. In March 1999 Senior General Than Shwe became the first Burmese head of state to visit Thailand since the Ne Win era. As well as being granted an audience with the His Majesty the King, Than Shwe visited an crop-substitution project near Chiang Mai, and agreed to establish a joint anti-drugs forum with Thailand and Laos. The Chuan administration hoped that Constructive Engagement might bear fruit in the field narcotics suppression at least, by drawing the notoriously paranoid SPDC regime into a working partnership. However, heroin and amphetamines continued to flow out of Burma into China and Thailand, and the benefits of engagement remained mostly limited to the commercial sector.

Thai-Burmese relations came under the spotlight again in early October 1999, when five armed student activists stormed the Burmese Embassy in Bangkok, holding some eighty people captive for twenty-five hours, before exchanging their hostages for safe transport to the Thailand-Burma border, at Ratchaburi.[89] In the aftermath of these events, the authorities further restricted the movements of Burmese opposition figures and refugees in Thailand.

Meanwhile, Burma's membership of ASEAN continued to dog the regional grouping's relations with the West, at a time when international financial institutions were underwriting economic rescue packages across East Asia, in the aftermath of the 1997 crisis. Throughout 1998–99, a series of planned EU-ASEAN meetings had to be postponed, because of the Europeans' distaste at sharing a forum with the SPDC. An ASEAN-EU meeting was eventually held, in Bangkok in May 1999, with Burma and Laos limited to observer roles.

The 1997 financial crisis had undermined the credibility of ruling elites across Southeast Asia, presenting opportunities to those who challenged the authoritarian politics of 'Asian Values'. In May 1998, following months of unrest across the vast nation, President Soeharto of Indonesia was forced to resign. Although the Indonesian army continued to exert considerable influence, the fact remained that a combination of 'people's power' and ethnic revolt had brought down a regime once considered a model by Burma's military rulers. In the June 1999 elections that followed the fall of Soeharto, opposition parties made major inroads into the hold on power of the army-sponsored Golkar party. Then in September, a referendum in East Timor returned a massive vote in favour of independence from Jakarta.

For the first time in the modern era, a Southeast Asian ethnic nationalist movement was on the verge of achieving independence. Timorese resistance leaders expressed solidarity with the democracy movement in Burma, and frustration with the lack of ASEAN support for self-determinism across the region. Meanwhile in Jakarta, with the military in disgrace and progressive forces ascendant, Indonesia's electoral college selected a Muslim leader and sometime social critic, Abdurrahman Wahid, as the country's president. Megawatti Sukarnoputri, who like Daw Aung San Suu Kyi was a daughter of her nation's independence leader, became vice-president. In 2001 she succeeded 'Gus Dor' as president.

Throughout the region, the 'consensus politics' of the 1990s were beginning to break down. In Malaysia, the less militaristic but no more democratic Mahatir regime managed to hold on to power, but only at the expense of alienating many of those on whom the government had been relying to implement its ambitious modernisation plans. With the old military and money-dominated elites in Thailand coming under pressure, from a new generation of technocrats and professional politicians, it seemed that the regional balance of power might be shifting.

However, the SPDC still had powerful friends in ASEAN. In addition to the governments of Malaysia and Singapore, these included Vietnam and Laos, as well as Cambodia, which was eventually admitted into the grouping in April 1999. Dominated by Hun Sen's Cambodian People's Party (CPP), the Phnom Penh government, like those in Vientiane and Rangoon, had survived various Thai attempts to undermine it, and was battle-hardened in a way the Burmese generals could relate to.

The International Response and Western Sanctions

As the SDPC maintained its grip on power in Burma, far away in Europe another despotic regime became the focus of an international political and military campaign, launched against it in the name of humanitarian principles. Burma had often been compared with Yugoslavia, a similarly troubled and ethnically mixed state. The relationship between Serbia and Kosovo in particular, reflected aspects of the situation in Burma. The chauvinistic Milosevic regime's occupation of the Kosovar homeland – which was also an ancient crucible of Serbian national identity – and the subsequent wave of ethnic cleansing, recalled the *Tatmadaw's* actions in the ethnic minority lands of Burma. Likewise, the Serbian authorities' insistence on their right to crush separatist revolt in defence of the integrity of the state, recalled statements made on similar themes by the leaders of the BSPP, SLORC and SPDC regimes in Burma. Whilst NATO justified its actions in Kosovo as an attempt to prevent ethnic cleansing, similar phenomena had been a fact of life in Burma for decades.[90]

Increased international awareness of (and indeed, the creation of) human rights issues in the late twentieth century, and the growth of support among electorates in Europe and North America for sanctions against repressive regimes, led Western governments to adopt a variety of interventionist approaches to the crises Burma. Particularly after 1991, when the UN General Assembly first expressed its outright condemnation of the SLORC, Western governments acted to shun Burma diplomatically, if not always commercially.

By the end of the decade, the annual UNGA resolution condemning the Burmese military government's appalling human rights record had become something of a ritual, if necessary, reminder of the dire situation in the country. The October 1999 resolution, regarded as the strongest ever, was based on a particularly hard-hitting report by the UN Commission on Human Rights (UNCHR) Special Rapporteur on Myanmar, Judge Rajsoomer Lallah. The 1999 resolution deplored the widespread practice of extra-judicial and arbitrary arrest, torture and execution of members of the democratic opposition and ethnic minority groups, criticised the severe restrictions placed on freedom of expression, denounced the abuse of women and children, the arbitrary seizure of land and property and the destruction of crops, and noted the regime's systematic use of forced relocation and forced labour. The November 2001 resolution likewise condemned the SPDC's human rights record, while noting that some limited progress had been made on the political front.[91]

In August 1998 an International Labour Organisation (ILO) Commission of Inquiry had found the SPDC guilty of employing forced labour on a nation-wide scale. As the government was still deploying some 800,000 unpaid labourers across the country, in June 1999 the ILO all-but suspend Burma's membership.[92] One year later, the UN agency voted to introduce unprecedented (if unspecified) sanctions against Burma.[93] In response, in late October 2000 the SPDC announced that it had banned the use of forced labour in Burma, and issued directives to this effect to front-line military commanders. Although the 2000–01 dry season saw somewhat fewer villagers compelled to work unpaid for the *Tatmadaw*, or on state infrastructure projects, incidents of forced labour still occurred across the country, including in Mon State.[94]

In June 2001 the SPDC agreed to receive a four-member ILO High Level Team, which visited the country in September–October, in order to assess whether the incidence of forced labour had abated. Led by Sir Ninian Stephen, who had been a judge in the International Tribunals for the former Yugoslavia and Rwanda, the ILO team found that, despite the new regulations in force, and notwithstanding some marginal improvements, forced labour was still a fact of life across most of Burma.[95] Following the ILO inspection, Mon sources continued to report regular incidences of forced labour, particularly in relation to the construction or up-grading of country roads.[96]

Meanwhile, as the UN Secretary General's Special Envoy to Burma attempted to engage the junta in dialogue,[97] Western governments had begun to exert more direct pressure on the regime. In May 1997 the Clinton administration issued a ban on American companies initiating new investments in Burma. Although UNOCAL's participation in the Yadana natural gas pipeline project was not affected, the Burmese opposition took heart.[98] The State Department's 1999 and 2000 human rights report again heavily criticised the SPDC regime, ensuring that Burma continued to receive far more international attention than it had prior to the events of 1988–90. By mid-2000, US sanctions were in their fourth year, and the Americans were funding the Burmese opposition overseas to the tune of more than seven million dollars annually. The SPDC took note, accusing its opponents of being in the pay of foreign powers, bent on undermining Burma' independence.

In 1996 the EU had initiated an aid and arms embargo against the regime, revoked Burma's preferential term of trade, and imposed a travel ban on senior members of the *Tatmadaw* and government. Three years later, EU sanctions were extended to include further export restrictions, and a freeze on junta members' assets. By contrast, in 1994–95 the Japanese government recommenced limited development assistance (and debt relief) to Burma. Although levels remained well below those prior to 1988, Tokyo was keen to resume substantial aid to Rangoon.

Seeking to break the political deadlock in Burma, in 2000 the Australian government organised two human rights awareness workshops in Rangoon, which were attended by selected military and government personnel. Although severely criticised in opposition circles, such training was essential if the regime was ever to change its complexion.

Burma's Development Impasse and the SPDC Development Model

Clearly, any sustainable, long-term solution to the problems of Burma will have to involve a substantial realignment of national politics. Despite the paranoid assertions of the regime, it seems unlikely that outsiders could implement such transitions. If and when it comes, the initiative for change will originate with the Burmese people themselves.

However, foreigners can influence conditions in the country. To this end, Western approaches to Burma have not relied entirely on the stick: on several occasions in the 1990s, carrots were dangled before the SLORC-

SPDC regime. Of these, the most widely-reported was an initiative developed at a high-level diplomatic meeting held in October 1998, at Chilston Park in Kent, in southern England. The 'Chilston Park initiative' proposed that the World Bank offer Burma $1 billion in development assistance, in exchange for the SPDC and NLD establishing some common ground, and entering into substantial dialogue. Although it was soon condemned and the new Burmese Foreign Minister, U Win Aung (previously ambassador to London), the proposed incentive package added further urgency to the on-going debate as to whether and how inter-governmental and non-government organisations should approach Burma.

The controversy had first emerged in the early 1990s. Prior to 1988, under Ne Win's isolationist Burmese Way to Socialism, few international agencies had had a presence in Burma. Following the events of 1988–90, nearly all Western agencies had left the country, while ethnic minority refugees along the Thailand-Burma border continued to receive international aid. This assistance was mostly funded by US and European governments and church groups, which tended to reinforce perceptions within the military government that Burma's ethnic insurgents – and their civilian support base along the border – were part of a western 'neo-colonial' conspiracy.

Against this backdrop, between 1991–93 MSF (Netherlands) and World Vision (UK) became the first international NGOs to establish official programmes in Burma.[99] By 1995, thirteen more NGOs had opened offices in Rangoon, and although some later left, or were denied the opportunity to implement their programmes, by 1999, the number of Western charitable agencies in Burma had risen to sixteen.[100] Many of these NGOs were focussed on the population's worsening health status, and in particular on the deepening HIV/AIDS crisis, the seriousness of which the government for many years refused to acknowledge.[101]

In mid-2001, MSF (France) set up a malaria project in Mudon township,[102] and by the end of the year a number of previously Thailand-based NGOs were considering establishing operations inside Burma. The majority of these were medical agencies; they certainly did not include organisations such as the BBC, which remained opposed to the implementation of relief programmes in border areas, via Rangoon.

Overseas and Thailand-based opposition activists, and their sponsors in the western NGO community, argued that even if church and other groups operating inside Burma could assist rural IDPs, they could do so only with the approval of the SPDC (or at least local Military Intelligence), and in the vicinity of relocation sites. This would effectively be to endorse the government's forced relocation ('Four Cuts') programme. Those involved in such activities might point to the clear humanitarian needs of accessible populations as their justification. Furthermore, the establishment of relief networks and largely independent associations was an important first step in developing capacity and autonomy at the community level – a prerequisite for the development of a civil society, that might one day emerge to fill the power and social vacuum in Burma.[103]

From the outset, many development professionals in Burma were alert to the importance of working with local people, to re-build skills bases that had been undermined by thirty years of military misrule. However, the effective implementation of programmes was often undermined by a shortage of trained Burmese personnel,[104] as well as by heavy-handed Military Intelligence surveillance and the difficulty of accessing the most deprived communities in Burma.

Ultimately, foreign NGOs were unable to address the structural inequality and oppression characteristic of military-ruled Burma. However, several did work with Burmese counterparts to analyse and begin to negotiate some of these issues at the local level. Nevertheless, critics argued that the presence of foreign agencies served to legitimise the government and its policies. For example, in providing water and sanitation services to forcibly relocated communities in Rangoon 'satellite towns', NGOs might be accused of doing the regime's dirty work. Some observers questioned whether, given their inability to challenge the structural roots of Burma's many problems, well-intentioned Western NGOs should be engaged in applying 'band aid' solutions to the crises. In contrast, those working inside the country considered the nurture of community networks an essential prerequisite of social and political progress.

By 2002, the refugees along the Thailand-Burma border had been receiving international aid for eighteen years. In many areas, the need for assistance 'inside' was at least as great as that on the border, but while the government might be willing to see international agencies establish a presence in Rangoon, access to the most needy – such as displaced populations in ethnic minority areas – was still very difficult.[105] While it was often possible for small, well-designed NGO programmes to work with such communities, the ability of large-scale inter-governmental organisations to implement effective work remained questionable. Critics suggested that, without effective monitoring and the genuine participation of local people, such programmes had little chance of success. Although, since the early 1990s, UN bodies had been required to implement projects in partnership with local people, it was by no means clear whether initiatives such as the United Nations Drug Control Programme (UNDCP)'s five year, multi-million dollar 'integrated rural development project' in the southern Wa sub-state, really benefited local people or contributed to sustainable development.

Such concerns were highlighted in 1996, when Daw Aung San Suu Kyi stated that NGOs should only work in Burma after consulting with the NLD.[106] Three years later, in June 1999, a conference on NGO Strategy for the Democratisation of Burma, in South Korea, formulated a dual-track approach, under which some agencies might take a 'hard-line' position, campaigning against the regime from outside Burma, whilst others adopted a 'softer' mode, in order to be able to work inside the country.

As noted however, by no means all foreign NGOs in Burma toed the SPDC line. After several years of careful groundwork, by 2002, a few agencies had developed programmes working with minority groups in sensitive parts of northern, eastern and southern Burma. The Kachin Baptist Convention (KBC) and other indigenous NGOs had established programmes across large parts of northern Burma. In partnership with such groups, some international NGOs established officially sanctioned programmes in the Kachin and other states where the government's ceasefire strategy had been most successful.

However, Seng Raw, a Kachin community worker, has written of her frustration that:

> no major government or international agency has yet come forward to support (conflict resolution and progress towards political transition). As a result many ethnic groups feel extremely disappointed that in general foreign governments are not responding to the progress of these ceasefire or indeed even understand their significance or context. Rather, it seems that certain sectors of the international community have the fixed idea that none of the country's deep problems, including ethnic minority issues, can be addressed until there is an over-arching political solution based upon developments in Rangoon.

> In contrast, the ceasefire groups believe ... that simply concentrating on the political stalemate in Rangoon and waiting for political settlements to come about ... is simply not sufficient to bring about the scale of changes that are needed ... Thus, in our view, assistance should be extended for economic and infrastructure development.[107]

The small amount of aid received by the Kachin from the Japanese and German embassies in Rangoon, in the mid-to-late 1990s, was viewed as symbolically important by the KIO. So too were Memorandums of Understanding granted by the SLORC in 1994 to the TEAR Foundation of Australia and World Concern,[108] allowing them to work in Kachin State. Negotiated by the Reverend Saboi Jum, a key player in the KIO-SLORC ceasefire process, these agreements represented advances in the ability of elites within Burma's ethnic populations to access international support.[109] However, as noted above by Seng Raw, levels of international aid to Burma's ethnic minority areas remained negligible. Nevertheless, following the opening of the Reverend Saboi Jum's 'Shalom Peace Centre' in Myitkyina, in December 2001, observers and participants expected the processes of development – and political transition – in Kachin State to continue, if at an uneven pace.

In contrast to the KIO, in the late 1990s the NMSP was generally wary of initiating contacts with representatives of the international community. In late 1998 the International Committee of the Red Cross (ICRC) had resumed its activities in Burma, after a break of three years, caused by the government's unwillingness to grant access to the country's notorious jails. On several occasions between 1999–2001, ICRC teams visited Karen IDPs in the war-zone along the Thailand-Burma border. By early 2002 ICRC personnel had met with more than 30,000 prisoners in twenty-five Burmese jails, including over one thousand 'security detainees', and the agency had opened offices in Kentung, Pa'an and Moulmein.

In late 1998 ICRC personnel had contacted the NMSP in Rangoon and Moulmein, to explore the possibility of visiting the repatriated Mon refugees and other displaced people in the ceasefire zones. The Red Cross wanted to undertake a needs analysis, including a pilot project to help disabled war victims. In the last week of May 1999, an ICRC team travelled to Moulmein, where they met with Nai Shwe Kyin, before travelling on to Ye. Here they attempted to contact the local NMSP, in order to travel on to Halochanee and Bee Ree. However, the ICRC team was turned back by Military Intelligence officers, who cited the unseasonably early rains, together with security concerns, as reasons why the trip had to be postponed.[110] Despite such frustrations, the ICRC mission persevered, and eventually established a health and sanitation programme in Mudon Township.

The NMSP was initially wary of the ICRC, fearing that to co-operate with the Red Cross would be to invite accompanying government penetration into the NMSP-controlled zones. However, unlike the High Commissioner for Refugees (UNHCR) and other UN agencies, the ICRC was able to demonstrate to the NMSP – both at the central level and locally – that it could operate independently of the SPDC. Since late 1999, a high level of trust has developed between the NMSP and ICRC personnel in Burma and Thailand.

With one or two such exceptions however, the party tended to keep a low international profile. Nevertheless, in the new millennium this strategy came under review, with the NMSP adopting a more pro-active role vis-à-vis the government and international community.[111]

However, efforts to improve human and infrastructure resources continued to be frustrated by the state's 'development model'. When allocating funds for road or bridge projects, the SLORC-SPDC generally provided only thirty-to-fifty per cent of costs. Of these monies, a proportion would 'disappear' into the pockets of government and military officers associated with the project. In order to complete work on time, these same local authorities – who were usually *Tatmadaw* officers, and thus beyond public account – had to collect money from local people, in the form of special 'taxes'. Adding insult to injury, villagers were often forced to work unpaid on such infrastructure projects, or to pay for labourers to work in their stead.[112]

PART SIX

THE SHELDRAKE
AND THE PEACOCK

"The lions ... would restore the crest of the Golden-drake which caused the lord peacock, national symbol of the Burmans, to take flight and hide in bamboo groves."

Astrological prediction of the sage, U Kyaw Hla, cited in NMSP, 'When Will the Civil War in Burma Be Over?' (1988)[1]

CHAPTER NINETEEN

Legacies

By the eve of the millennium, the struggle to "restore the crest of the Golden-drake" had reached a turning point. Following the 1995 NMSP-SLORC ceasefire, the Mon nationalists faced new challenges. If the *hamsa* was to rise like a phoenix from the ashes of the civil war, the movement would have to adapt to the changing realities of modern Burma.

Despite occasional predictions of its imminent breakdown, and the brief rebellion of the Mon Army Mergui District (MAMD) faction in 1996–97, the ceasefire had proved quite durable – at least until late 2001. However, the agreement had not resolved the underlying issues, which for nearly fifty years had fuelled the Mon insurgency. Many within the nationalist community considered the ceasefire merely expedient, at best. Although anti-ceasefire elements had been chastened by the 1997 *Tatmadaw* offensives against the KNU, and disappointed by the outcome of the MAMD adventure, armed Mon resistance to the military government continued to flare up from time-to-time on the edges of the NMSP-controlled ceasefire zones. Furthermore, significant numbers of Mon nationalists in Thailand and overseas maintained their outright opposition to the SPDC regime, making common cause with the wider Burmese opposition along the border and in exile.

Given such a complex scenario, it is convenient to divide the Mon nationalist movement in the late 1990s into half-a-dozen camps. In reality of course, membership of particular blocs was fluid, and allegiances sometimes changed.

Among the more high-profile of these six sectors, was the collection of small activist organisations established by Mon exiles in North America, Australia and Europe. Other sectors of the nationalist community were based in Thailand and Burma – the traditional Mon homelands. These included Mon citizens of Thailand, whose families had in most cases been settled in the kingdom for several generations. The majority of 'Thai Mon' probably had little or interest in the nationalist cause. However, a significant minority were committed to reviving the Mon cultural and linguistic heritage, and a small number remained actively engaged in the struggle for Monland.

A third sector was more closely identified with Burma, though still largely dependent on Thailand (and on overseas benefactors). In many ways the most radical and heterogeneous of the various strands of Mon nationalism, the half-dozen or so activist organisations in Thailand had historically been associated with the pre-ceasefire NMSP. However, by the late 1990s some of these groups had assumed the characteristics of indigenous NGOs or pressure groups, and following the ceasefire they often operated independently of the NMSP line.

In terms of human and material resources, the NMSP remained the most powerful player in Mon politics. The product of decades of armed struggle, with a presence 'inside' Burma and along both sides of the border, it was against the NMSP that most other sectors of the nationalist community defined themselves. In practice, many non-NMSP groups were obliged to operate within the party's sphere of influence. These included the Mon Unity League (MUL), an important Thailand-based 'umbrella' organisation.

The NMSP itself was not monolithic, but contained a number of factions, as well as semi-autonomous administrative units, like the Mon National Education Committee (MNEC), the Mon National Health Committee (MNHC), the Mon Women's Organisation (MWO) and the Mon National Relief Committee (the MNRC – later MRDC – which technically was not part of the NMSP). To the ageing NMSP leadership, the ceasefire had not been without its successes. These included an end to the fighting, a degree of political (if not legal) recognition for the party, the emergence of new business opportunities for the Mon elite, the opportunity to expand the NMSP education system and the party's presence in government-controlled areas, and the completion of a number of infrastructure projects in lower Burma. However, any marginal improvements in the human rights situation in Mon State since 1995, or of the cultural and political development of the Mon people, had been achieved in the teeth of government intransigence. Many cadres worried that the NMSP was in danger of being side-lined in the post-ceasefire era. However, they generally saw no option but to continue working within 'the legal fold', whilst attempting to link up with other ceasefire groups and, where possible, the NLD.

The fifth sector in this rough classification of Mon nationalist camps consists of those who actively opposed the ceasefire. Many critics had gone into exile overseas, and by late 1997 the MAMD had effectively ceased to operate. However, between 1997–99 a hardcore group of about fifty ex-MNLA soldiers continued to launch occasional guerrilla attacks against the *Tatmadaw* in Mergui District, while further to the north, in Ye and Yebyu Township (NMSP Tavoy District), a new 'Mon Armed Group' emerged in 1998, led by ex-MNLA Captain Nai Hlaing. At the end of the 2001 rainy season, this breakaway faction was joined by another group of disaffected Mon army veterans, led by a senior MNLA Colonel, Nai Pan Nyunt. Unlike the Mergui District rebels, this new anti-ceasefire faction – the Hongsawatoi Restoration Party (HRP) – with more than three hundred men under arms, posed a serious threat to the stability of the ceasefire.

The final sector in the Mon nationalist equation was the MNDF, an independent political party which was outlawed by the SLORC in 1992, but still remained active. With the legitimacy of its five MPs-elect, the MNDF rivalled the NMSP for leadership of the nationalist community. In the late 1990s the front adopted a dynamic approach to the minefield of Burmese politics, drawing down the full repressive force of the military regime.

One further, potentially very powerful, unifying force cut across the different strata of Mon communities in Burma and Thailand, and through the various sectors of the nationalist movement. The Mon *sangha*, a distinct entity within the wider (state-controlled), Burmese monkhood, had since time immemorial played a key role in Mon cultural and political life. In the 1990s Mon monks were particularly active in the fields of education, and refugee relief and resettlement. As they had for centuries, many people still looked to the *sangha* for the leadership and development of the community.

Meanwhile, by the year 2000 the Mon refugees had been back in Burma for four years. The Mon refugee authorities continued to remind observers that the returnees had not returned home, and that the "resettlement sites are similar to the previous refugee camps in Thailand."[2] The repatriated refugees were still partly dependent on (reduced) humanitarian assistance from international NGOs, as were a large number of NMSP personnel in the ceasefire zones. For how much longer would these people be eligible for international assistance?

For as long as the human rights and political situation in Burma remained in deep crisis, it was unlikely that those displaced along the border would be willing or able to return to their villages. Protection was the key issue. Any lasting solution to the plight of refugees would also have to take account of the millions of Internally Displaced Persons (IDPs) in Burma, and address the reasons for their displacement.

◄◆►

Part Six is divided into two sections, organised thematically, rather than strictly chronologically. Chapter Nineteen brings the situation of the various Mon communities in Thailand, Burma and elsewhere up to date, and outlines developments in the recent history of the KNU and other 'unreconstructed' opposition groups. Chapter Twenty examines the relationship between the Mon nationalists, the ceasefire groups, the NLD and the government, before returning briefly to some of the issues raised in Part One.

Overseas Mon Groups

Following the epoch-making events of 1988–90, a new generation of activists joined the struggle for justice and democracy in Monland and Burma. Many of these newcomers eventually united with the older generation of nationalists, making careers in the NMSP. Others became disheartened by the turn of events along the border, and frustrated by the direction of NMSP policy. Hundreds of these young people sought to continue the struggle from overseas, while at the same time recommencing their interrupted studies. Many departed for the West via the UNHCR-MOI Safe Camp at Maneeloy, in Ratchaburi Province.

Following the October 1999 Burmese Embassy siege, in which two 'Safe Camp' residents had participated, the always tense situation at Maneeloy became increasingly oppressive. During disturbances in late October 1999, two Mon students (or according to some accounts, one Mon and a Tavoyan) were set upon by Burman students, in a dispute which escalated into an ugly confrontation between some twenty Mon, and up to one hundred Burman and Karen students. The latter bound and beat the Mon, accused them of being spies, and burned down their huts and schoolroom. According to Mon sources, the Burmans were upset by the 'divisive' pursuit of a Mon literature and cultural programme in the Safe Camp.

Following a series of violent incidents along the border in 1999–2000 (see below), the Thai National Security Council ordered the Safe Camp to close at the end of 2001. Its residents were all either either resettled in third countries, or moved to Tham Hin Karen refugee camp (also in Ratchaburi).[3]

By the mid-1990s, Mon nationalist groups had been established in Australia, Canada and the United States – the three main countries of permanent asylum for Burmese refugees. Most of these organisations tended to down-play the issue of Mon independence, preferring instead to support a federalist agenda, and work for Mon rights in the context of the nation-wide democracy movement. They maintained close contact with each other and their compatriots in Thailand, as well as with other Burmese expatriate organisations. The new technologies of email and the internet were instrumental in the overseas opposition's ability to network and publicise the plight of Burma. By the end of the decade, the Australia Mon Association (AMA), Mon Community of Canada (MCC) and Monland Restoration Council (MRC) were publishing regular bulletins on the situation in Burma, and had all established websites, as had the Mon students in Australia.[4]

In 1999 the Vancouver provincial government officially recognised the nearly one hundred Mon residents of Canada as an ethnic community, and their association was re-organised as the Mon Community of Canada.[5] With state funding, the MCC flourished, holding a well-attended Sixth AGM in Vancouver, on New Year's Day 2001.

Meanwhile, in November 2000 in the United States, members of the Monland Restoration Council (MRC)[6] had purchased two buildings, to serve as a Mon Buddhist temple in Fort Wayne, Indiana. The following month, the MRC held its Seventh Conference at the new headquarters. Some sixty delegates, including Mon monks, discussed the prospects for democratic change in Burma, and made plans for the celebration of the forthcoming Mon National Day.[7]

Like their colleagues in Thailand and Burma, the overseas Mon groups put great emphasis on the celebration of national holidays. On 10th February 2001 the MCC invited five hundred guests to 54th anniversary Mon National Day celebrations, held in Calgary, Toronto and Vancouver. At approximately the same time, four hundred people attended similar festivities organised by the MRC in Fort Wayne, and over three hundred people celebrated National Day with the Australia Mon Association (AMA). These festivities were attended by Mon and other Burmese expatriates, as well as by a number of Canadian, American and Australian students, academics and politicians. Mon and Burmese songs and dances were performed, speeches were made and the guests enjoyed feasts of traditional food. The Overseas Mon Association [New Zealand] (OMA [NZ]), established in August 2000, also observed the anniversary, as did the Mons in Finland and elsewhere.

To mark the 54th National Day, a coalition of overseas Mon groups issued a joint communiqué, recalling the glorious Mon heritage and the more recent history of the nationalist movement, and calling on the international community to persuade the SPDC to recognise and respect Mon human, cultural and political rights.[8] As well as those in Australasia and North America, the sponsors of this statement included Mon organisations based closer to home, in Southeast Asia. These groups worked among Mon migrant labour communities, which although numerically larger, tended to be less well-organised or politically active than those in the West. Nevertheless, by 1999 a Mon expatriate's welfare group, the Overseas Mon Workers' Organisation (OMWO), had established branches in Thailand, Malaysia, Singapore and Japan. One of the OMWO's first chairmen was Nai Sunthorn Sriparngern, later the founder General Secretary of the MUL.[9]

Mon Groups in Thailand

The MUL had been formed at the second Congress of Mon National Affairs, nine months after the June 1995 ceasefire. The league's busy secretariat maintained contacts with and between its constituent member-groups, in Thailand and Burma, while staying in touch with Mon organisations in the West (none of which were official MUL members). With Working Groups devoted to Justice and Human Rights, Relief,

Culture and Women's Affairs, the MUL was a major player in Mon politics.

An important condition of the ceasefire agreement was the proscription of contacts between the NMSP and foreign third parties. Therefore, between 1995–99 the MUL was the NMSP's preferred conduit for international contact. Although there was little love for the ceasefire among many of the league's non-NMSP members, there was a general understanding that the strategic choices open to the party in 1995 had been limited. Although the MUL was not beyond criticism of the NMSP and the ceasefire, it was in general supportive.

In 1998 the NMSP Joint General Secretary, Nai Hongsa, completed his two year term as the league's first president. He continued to serve as MUL Vice-President, together with Nai Khun Leal (a Mon agriculturist, medic and politician), but was succeeded as president by the Thai Mon, Nai Pisanh Paladsingha, a journalist and author,[10] film maker and director of the Mon Information Service (MIS). In February 1999 Nai Pisanh organised Mon National Day festivities at Wat Bangyaphrek in Samut Sakorn Province (where the author attended National Day celebrations on 28th February 2002). Attended by nearly one thousand people, – many of whom were migrant workers and most of whom wore Mon costume – the celebrations commenced with a salute of the Thai and Mon national flags, and assembled Mon elders. The speeches were followed by a Mon luncheon, accompanied by traditional and revolutionary music.

To coincide with the event, the MUL issued a statement recalling the glories of the Mon heritage, and the sacrifices incurred in the long struggle for Monland. The communiqué noted that, although the NMSP had 'returned to the legal fold', the party had gained little from the ceasefire. However, "we, the younger generations of the Mon, would not blame our leaders in the past, since they had founded our national freedom movement and had been struggling in the jungle for ... forty years."[11] The statement struck a balance between respect for the sacrifices and limited achievements of the NMSP, and a strong commitment to maintaining the political struggle. Other Thailand-based Mon groups, most of which were MUL members, were sometimes less tolerant of the old guard.

Whether or not they were recognised as refugees – and most were not – many non-NMSP activists who stayed on in Thailand after the ceasefire could only return to Burma under conditions of personal danger. Nevertheless, members of the Mon Information Service (MIS) – incorporating the Committee to Publicise the People's Struggle in Monland (CPPSM) – the Human Rights Foundation of Monland (HRFM), the Independent Mon News Agency (IMNA) and the Kao Wao News Agency,[12] continued to monitor events on both sides of the Thailand-Burma border, as did the Mon refugee authorities. These groups, which sometimes received funding from the same donor agencies, published reports and newsletters in English,

Burmese, Mon and Thai. The busy editor of the HRFM's monthly journal, *The Mon Forum*, was for a time also a correspondent for the Norwegian government-sponsored radio station, the Democratic Voice of Burma (DVB).[13]

Other Mon publications in Thailand included the Mon language periodicals, *Bop Htaw* ('Golden Sheldrake'), *Snong Tine* ('Northern Star') and *Khit Poey* ('Our Times'), and English and Mon language *Mon Students Bulletins*, issued every few months by the Overseas Mon National Students Organisation (OMNSO). The NMSP also published a Mon and Burmese language *NMSP Journal*, about twice a year.

In the mid-1990s members of the Mon community in Bangkok produced occasional issues of the Thai language *Kao San Mon* newsletter, and the Thai Ramon Association (TRA) published a regular newsletter in Thai and Mon. Although, due to lack of resources, not all of these publications appeared regularly, Mon was clearly not a 'dying language', and the Mon students and monks, in particular, were keen to see that it continued to flourish.

The OMNSO, which was founded by '1988 generation' Mon students, had by the late 1990s established branches in Australia and North America. It often co-ordinated its activities, such as demonstrations in front of the Burmese Embassy in Bangkok, with the Wat Prok-based Overseas Mon Young Monks Union (OMYMU), which also published an occasional English and Mon language magazine.[14] The OMYMU had been established in Bangkok on 15th February 1990, four days after the fall of Three Pagodas Pass. Its founders were a small group of radical young *Ramanya Nikaya* sect monks, most of whom had fled Burma in 1988. Other members of the Mon *sangha* in Thailand were also active in the nationalist and pro-democracy movements.[15] However, their ability to organise effectively was restricted both by their religious observances and by the attentions of the Thai police, who did not always discriminate between monks and other illegal Burmese in Bangkok.

Organisations such as the OMYMU, OMNSO, HRFM, MIS,[16] IMNA and MUL, and their contemporaries, such as the Karen Students Network Group (KSNG) and Shan Herald Agency for News (SHAN), represented one of the more dynamic strands within Burmese ethnic nationalism in the late 1990s. Several such groups counted less than a dozen active members; only a few were characterised by the factionalism seemingly endemic to Burmese politics. In general, they adopted 'flat', participative decision-making and working practices, reflecting their understanding of democratic forms of political organisation. At the same time, groups such as the IMNA and SHAN began to modernise their out-put, and move from the documentation and dissemination of (sadly, voluminous) reports on human rights violations, towards a more-news based approach. Complementing and contrasting the in-depth reports and analysis still provided by the

HRFM's *Mon Forum*, their stories were driven more by a narrative of events, and intended for a wider audience, including the international press.

An NMSP-affiliated Mon Youth Progressive Organisation (MYPO) – with a seventeen member Central Committee, including seven women – was established in Sangkhlaburi on 18th November 2001. According to *Kao Wao*, when "asked to express their views on their organization and its purpose, the newly elected EC members agree that MYPO will not only be working at forging solidarity among the Mons but to reach out in cooperation to network with other ethnic youths, democratic forces and the international community as well."[17]

The emergence of such progressive organisations as the HRFM, IMNA, MUL and MYPO represented a generally positive development, in an otherwise rather bleak political scene. These groups occupied space vacated by mainstream ethnic insurgents. With the declining influence of the NMSP and KNU, these youthful organisations represented a new model of political and human rights work. As a result, all those engaged in the struggle for ethnic rights and self-determination in Burma (including the NMSP and KNU 'old guard') were obliged to acknowledge the importance of human rights and democracy – not just as distant goals but as on-going processes. The NMSP and other armed organisations were challenged to reassess their own records, and examine the degree to which their strategy and practices incorporated such principals.[18] The NMSP's history of reasonably open political debate should have meant that these issues could begin to be addressed. In general however, the mechanisms for doing so were lacking and they were left to gather momentum at lower leadership levels, and among young cadres and the wider nationalist community.

Meanwhile, the Thai Mon and Karen communities continued to lend some assistance to their cousins from Burma. The most substantial of the Thai Mon groups was the TRA, an officially-registered cultural organisation, established in the late 1960s. With well-appointed offices in Bangkok and a membership of several thousand, including monks and academics, the TRA represented the 'respectable', apolitical face of Mon revival in Thailand. Other, more politically adventurous Thai Mon groups, included the Mon Youth Community (MYC), established in 1977,[19] and the Mon Literature Promotion Organisation (MLPO), led by the MNRC Chairman and secretary of Wat Prok, Phra Wongsa Pala.

In his description of the Thai Mon community on Koh Kret, Donald Wilson relates a prophesy: "On the northeastern side of the island, immediately recognisable from passing vessels, is a leaning white pagoda, called Chedi Songmon. Legend has it that when this *chedi* eventually collapses – and it tilts more each year due to a combination of subsidence and annual flooding – the Mons of Koh Kret will be able to return to their homeland."[20] It is questionable whether the Mons of Thailand really aspire to life in severely underdeveloped Burma, a country which for the majority is little more than a folk memory. However, since the 1940s, many members of the Thai Mon community – including people in political, military and intelligence circles – have supported the struggle for Monland.

Mon communities in Thailand have experienced something of a cultural mini-renaissance since the early 1990s, accompanied by a modest revival in Mon studies.[21] With an increased awareness of their historical legacy, community leaders on Koh Kret, in Ratchaburi and elsewhere have initiated literacy projects, and sought to preserve and refresh the Mon cultural heritage.

Such initiatives gained impetus following the promulgation, during the second Chuan Leekpai administration, of a new Thai constitution. Introduced in 1997, Article 46 of the charter recognised the Mon as a 'traditional community', with a legitimate interest in conserving their customs, arts and culture, and with rights to participate in the management, preservation and exploitation of local resources and the environment. As part of a national survey, a team of academics and NGO workers was established to investigate Mon human and community rights, and elicit a greater degree of Mon participation in the Thai political process. The team's two Mon members hoped to extend the survey's remit, to include those denied legal status in the kingdom, such as the majority of residents of 'Mon side' in Sangkhlaburi. It was also hoped to investigate issues effecting the refugees, such as the Yadana gas pipeline. Although these ambitious proposals probably fell beyond the survey's remit, the project received a major boost when one of the chief architects of the new constitution, the widely-respected Thai Mon statesman, Anand Panyarachun, gave it his backing during a visit to Sangkhlaburi in November 1999.[22]

Such developments reflected the important role played by the Thai NGO and academic communities in the struggle for democracy and rights in Burma. The extent of unofficial Thai support for the Mon nationalist cause was demonstrated in early 1999, when a group of one hundred Thai activists and academics, including several Mon citizens, accompanied MUL President Nai Pisanh on a trip to the NMSP bases at Kanni (on the Ye River) and Halochanee, where they joined the refugees in celebrating Mon National Day.

Despite such cross-border excursions, Mon nationalists in Thailand and overseas have generally observed events in Burma from a distance. The experience of exile has tended to encourage the adoption of uncompromising, hard-line positions. For those engaged on the ground however, the conflict of principle and practicality has been more immediate.

Post-Ceasefire Quandaries:
Ideology, Strategy and Development

Since the collapse of the Communist Party of Burma (CPB), and the rash of ceasefires across Kachin and Shan states in the late 1980s and early '90s, many of the ex-insurgent groups in the north had come to resemble private – rather than revolutionary – armies. While elite politics in Rangoon remained deadlocked, their leaders showed little interest in challenging the SPDC, preferring instead to concentrate on 'economic development'. In lower Burma too, the importance of ideology was in decline.

Like the KNU in the 1970s, and rebel movements across the world in the post-Cold War era, in the 1990s the NMSP abandoned much of its left-wing baggage, whether Soviet or Chinese-inspired. The process of political re-alignment had begun with reunification in 1987, and had accelerated during the late 1980s and '90s, as the party was exposed to a new wave of non-communist democracy activists from the cities. Although the party remained constitutionally committed to 'national liberation', it evinced limited interest in outlining the social or political characteristics of the proposed Mon Democratic Republic. The ethnic nationalist agenda was defined more by what it opposed – Burman chauvinism and centralised military rule – than any positive programme.

Having accepted the protracted failure of armed revolt, the NMSP and other ceasefire groups urgently needed to redefine themselves, and what they stood for as post-insurgent organisations. Otherwise, they risked becoming increasingly marginalised. The survival of the ethnic nationalist cause was at stake: if the NMSP failed to offer strong leadership, and formulate a clear and popular strategic vision, then its membership would fragment, or drift into inactivity. According to one well-placed source, between 1995–99 the NMSP lost half of its active members. Another half-decade of stagnation might see the party wither on the vine.

Fifty years of factional civil war, and the continued cohesion of the *Tatmadaw*, had taught the armed opposition that unity was essential. However, even more important in the long-term was the need to cultivate ethnic constituencies 'inside' Burma. If the nationalist programme was to have any meaning, the Mon population in Burma (and in Thailand?) would have to identify themselves as Mon, and subscribe to a unifying political vision. (Nai Shwe Kyin has often told the author that, should the NMSP ever gain significant power in Burma, large numbers of assimilated Mon would re-discover their 'true identity' and flock to the nationalist cause.)

Many of the NMSP's ill-defined wartime goals were inapplicable to the post-ceasefire era. How could the insurgents' territorial claims be squared with the facts of the ceasefire? If not by armed liberation, then how was the party to work for Mon self-determination and national development? And what of the relationship between the NMSP and the democracy movement in Burma, and the need for democratisation and change within the party itself? Unfortunately, the Mon and other ceasefire groups had only limited political space within which to formulate and discuss such issues. The government meanwhile, had developed a much clearer raft of strategies for the post-ceasefire era. One broad policy theme to emerge in the 1990s emphasised the 'development' of previously neglected ethnic minority areas.

Although bitterly opposed by many within the party, a number of senior NMSP leaders endorsed the government's agenda of beating swords into ploughshares. This strategy was symbolised by the presence in April 1999 of Lt-General Khin Nyunt and various *Tatmadaw* commanders and government officials, as well as a visiting Japanese parliamentary delegation, at a series of large-scale celebrations of the tenth anniversary of the first wave of SLORC ceasefires, in northern Burma. The festivities, which were covered extensively in the state media, provided a showcase for projects under the government's Border Areas Development Programme.

These included agricultural schemes and the construction of hydro-power dams, factories, schools and hospitals (but not necessarily the provision of books or medicines). Among the programme's most dramatic results were the construction of new roads and bridges, which opened-up previously inaccessible regions to trade – and to the *Tatmadaw*. A number of the northern ceasefire groups, with their significant financial resources and control over extensive territory, rivalled government agencies in the development of towns and villages under their control. For example, leaders of the 20–25,000-strong United Wa State Army (UWSA) oversaw construction of an extensive road network around the old CPB headquarters at Pangsang, building large numbers of brick houses, a hotel, and a casino; from the late 1990s, leaders of the UWSA Southern Command developed the town of Mon Yawn, near Tachilek, the construction of which was reportedly financed by drugs money.[23]

Of the ex-Democratic Alliance of Burma (DAB) groups, the Kachin Independence Organisation (KIO) again led the way, with the renovation of a dilapidated sugar mill at Nam Ti, donated by the SLORC at the time of the ceasefire. However, the mill did not make a profit, and although the government constructed a number of roads and bridges in Kachin State, such projects often used forced labour (although probably on a lesser scale than before the ceasefire).

There were also significant infrastructure projects in government-controlled parts of Mon State. In particular, the construction of two bridges crossing the Ataran and Gaing Rivers, north of Moulmein, opened up the route to Pa'an, reducing the journey time to the Karen State capital from several hours to a little over ninety minutes. Another new bridge was constructed over the Salween River south of Pa'an, facilitating travel to the ancient Mon capital of Thaton (now a small town on the border of Mon and Karen States). In May 1999 yet another new, 1000-foot bridge was officially opened, crossing the Hlaingbwe River southeast of Pa'an. In March 2000 construction began on Burma's longest bridge, a road and rail link between Moulmein and Martaban.[24]

However, the road network in Mon and Karen States was still in a sorry state. The main road from Pegu to Martaban was dotted with potholes and, away from the main routes, many tracks were unusable during the rainy season. Unlike the situation in the north, where new roads had facilitated a growth in trade between Burma and China, in the late 1990s commerce between Burma and Thailand stagnated. Goods which had once passed through Karen and Mon States now bypassed the border, often travelling by ship, directly to and from Malaysia or Singapore. The major beneficiary of the new infrastructure developments was probably the *Tatmadaw*, which used the improved road and bridge network to move troops around more easily. Local people meanwhile, were often forced to work unpaid on these projects[25] – many of which involved the confiscation of village land[26] – and to contribute their time and money to the upkeep of village schools and health centres.

Such institutionalised abuse characterised even the smallest-scale projects, including some of those involving the NMSP. In order to participate in the 'development' process, the party needed money, and although it mostly eschewed direct co-operation with the government, the NMSP was not beyond accepting state funds to carry out local road-building projects. In fact, between 1998–2001, the party's Regional Development Committee (RDC) in Moulmein proposed a number of road and bridge projects to Khin Nyunt and the Border Areas Development Programme, several of which received support in Kyat or in kind.

In general, these projects were designed to link government-controlled towns and road networks to areas on the periphery of NMSP-controlled territory. For example, starting in 1999–2000, the party used a combination of its own and Border Areas Development Programme resources to construct a new fourteen-and-a-half mile tarmac road, that would eventually connect Kawbein with the party's Thaton District headquarters. As this area was already exposed to government and *Tatmadaw* penetration, the NMSP and RDC felt that making it more accessible did not involve any appreciably enhanced security risk. However, more remote areas – such a Central and the Ye River valley – were jealously guarded: despite government invitations to initiate 'development projects' in these zones, the NMSP continued to exclude its primary base areas from state intervention.

As the monies received to implement local infrastructure development projects were usually inadequate to the task, the NMSP was in danger of falling into the same abusive practices as the SPDC, and alienating the very people it was pledged to liberate. Nevertheless, party coffers needed replenishing, and elements within the RDC and Rehmonya International continued to pursue a policy of 'constructive engagement' with the SPDC.

At the end of the 1998 rainy season, senior NMSP officers, acting on behalf of the company, had been involved in another survey of the Three Pagodas Pass-Thanbyuzayat road, which they proposed to upgrade to an all-weather toll-way. The route would link up with the road from Thanbyuzayat to Moulmein and Rangoon, and perhaps eventually with a port facility on the Mon State seaboard, which Rehmonya International (or the Hongsawatoi Company, another NMSP-controlled business) hoped to have a hand in building, and which might handle regional and even inter-continental trade.

The Kanchanaburi Chamber of Commerce was reportedly prepared to underwrite the project, in a bid to secure access to Burmese and international markets and raw materials. However, by 2001 the NMSP had still not found a replacement for the Power P Company, its Thai partner which, despite high-level Thai military contacts, had gone out of business in late 1997. Although Daewoo of South Korea had surveyed the proposed route in 1997–98, the giant corporation had pulled-out of the project, citing understandable security concerns.

At the end of the 2000 dry season the SPDC lent the NMSP one hundred million Kyat (c. $28,000) towards completion of the project.[27] Although this sum was less than would be required to pay for both equipment hire and labourers' wages, by September, the up-graded road had reached Zeehtitpin village, about 15–20 Km from Thanbyuzayat. Sections of the road passed through areas of KNLA Sixth Brigade that had fallen to the Burma Army in 1997. Since then, the KNLA had kept-up sporadic guerrilla activity in the area, and the *Tatmadaw* had implemented a campaign of forced labour and village relocation.[28]

Although Nai Shwe Kyin had asked the KNU not to interfere with the project, pushing a new road through the middle of this long-disputed territory was bound to re-open old wounds and rivalries. Whilst no doubt suiting Rangoon's policy of 'divide and rule', any resumption of the old Mon-Karen conflict would represent a major setback to inter-ethnic relations. A majority on the NMSP Central Committee therefore remained opposed to the project. Nevertheless, Rehmonya International seemed determined to push ahead, if necessary with only limited outside support or investment.[29] Few observers were therefore surprised when the KNLA began to step up operations in the vicinity of the road, culminating in an attack on a construction team in late March 2001, which left a dozen *Tatmadaw*-men and engineers dead.

Meanwhile, the government continued to expand its presence in rural districts previously contested with the NMSP. For example, in 1999 in northern Ye Township, the SPDC began to renovate an old Japanese air base, in an area once patrolled by the MNLA's Number 777 and Moulmein Battalions. Villagers' lands were confiscated, as the *Tatmadaw* extended its control over previously semi-autonomous areas. During the 2001 dry season, the Southeast Command established a new battalion headquarters on confiscated land near Kwan Pier, on the Ye River, just a few Km from the 'ceasefire front line'.[30] In total, in 2001, about 1000 acres of land were reportedly confiscated from Mon civilians in northern and eastern Ye Township. Many of these people subsequently fled to Bee Ree.

The NMSP seemed powerless to prevent such developments. According to *The Mon Forum*, "the Mon army is blocked at (the) border area and they have lost contact with their own people from the villages."[31] Trouble was building up for the future stability of the ceasefire zones.

Armed Mon Groups on the Border

Between April–May 1998, the NMSP War Council held a Special Military Conference at Kanni, on the Ye River. The meeting concentrated on internal organisation, re-structuring the MNLA under two Strategic Commands: the Northern (Moulmein) Command, under Nai Kao Rot, and the Southern (Ye) Command, under Nai Win Aung (later, Nai Pan Nyunt). However, NMSP – and *Tatmadaw* – commanders were aware that the Burma Army had the capacity to wipe out the last MNLA strongholds. The MNRC has calculated that, between 1995–98, more than fifteen new *Tatmadaw* battalions were moved into Ye and Yebyu Townships, making the consequences of any resumption of fighting in the Mon heartland potentially devastating.[32]

By mid-2001, six years after the ceasefire, MNLA troop strength stood at about 1,500 men, of whom a proportion were on standby in the ceasefire zones and their home villages. The MNLA fielded 150–200 troops in the northern Thaton District, where the KNLA continued to clash sporadically with the *Tatmadaw* and DKBA. Another three hundred Mon troops were stationed at two main bases in Moulmein District, while the bulk of the MNLA forces – some eight hundred men – were spread out between Central and Kanni, with another one hundred or so in Tavoy District. There were also some one thousand local militia, most of whom answered to commanders whose loyalty to Central was never beyond question.

Although the Mon army had retained its weapons in 1995, ammunition was often in short supply, especially for larger calibre weapons, such as mortars. Although munitions were still available in Thailand – and Burma[33] – the NMSP was short of funds and had fewer sympathetic contacts in Thai military circles than in the 'good old days'.

In mid-1999 NMSP membership stood at 600 active cadres, plus about 200 'candidate members'. These included about thirty women, most of whom were medics or teachers. There were a further 1,500 'NMSP associates', who worked with, but chose not (or were not chosen) to join the party, and at least as many dependant family members, plus as many as 1,000 MNLA regulars who were not party members.[34] These figures represented a slight drop in membership since the ceasefire. However, not all those regarded by the party as active members were involved full-time with the nationalist cause. Insiders consider active party membership to have declined sharply since 1995. Many of those who left the NMSP and

MNLA returned quietly to civilian life. However, some chose to throw in their lot with alternative Mon organisations.

Since the 1940s, the effectiveness of the Mon armed forces had been hampered by factionalism, and throughout the post-ceasefire period pockets of armed resistance continued to undermine security, and the authority of the NMSP, in the border regions. Although, by mid-1998, the MAMD had effectively disbanded, some of its leaders continued to co-operate with the *Tatmadaw* in running Mergui district. Meanwhile, a group of about fifty Ramanya Restoration Army (RRA) soldiers, under the command of ex-MNLA Captain Nai Sein Hla, had regrouped in the forest south of Chaung Chee.

Well-armed and supplied with modern communications equipment, in late 1998 and '99 the RRA launched a series of hit-and-run attacks against *Tatmadaw* patrols in the area. In response, the Burma Army Coastal Strategic Commander, Brig-General Sit Maung, is reported in 1999 to have considered re-arming the MAMD, as a proxy army to fight against the RRA. Although the predicated intra-Mon fighting in Mergui District failed to materialise, Mon refugees continued to enter Thailand on a regular basis. More often than not, they were soon repatriated by local units of the Ninth Division.

On 12th January 2000 the Cambodian authorities in Battambang arrested two Mon arms dealers with connections to the RRA, one of whom was its commanding colonel. They had been engaged in purchasing arms and ammunition, to top-up the southern rebels' stockpile. They were released by the Cambodian authorities, after serving three month sentences on immigration charges (neither was in possession of valid travel documents). In an interesting turn of events, the two were repatriated to the Thailand-Burma border with the assistance of UNHCR.

In December 1999 the humanitarian wing of the RRA, the Ramanya Human Rights Committee (RHRC), which had been working under the patronage of the MNRC, was cut off by the mainstream Mon refugee authorities. Phra Wongsa and his colleagues felt unable to continue supporting a group so obviously opposed to the ceasefire. Following the MNRC-RHRC split, the BBC gave the latter three month's rice supply, but could not extend further assistance, because of the near impossibility of monitoring the dispersed and highly mobile southern Mon refugee population.

Meanwhile, further to the north, in Tavoy District, the NMSP continued to be troubled by the 'Nai Soe Aung Group'. In early 1998 the increasing incidence of banditry on the road between Moulmein and Tavoy led the *Tatmadaw* Southeast Command to request the MNLA to 'police' the area. The Tavoy Battalion therefore continued to patrol parts of the one remaining 'temporary' ceasefire zone, on licence from the Burma Army. Several members of the 'Nai Soe Aung Group' are reported to have surrendered to the NMSP in the first half of 1998, and it seemed for a while that a degree of stability had returned to Tavoy District.

However, by the end of the year, a new anti-ceasefire faction had emerged in the area. According to NMSP-affiliated sources, "this group has no name but is led by ... former Mon soldiers.... They are named as a robber group by Burmese Army... They have no political aim, but are a militia group protecting their local villagers from the looting of Burmese soldiers. They also collected tax from the sea."[35] Led by an ex-MNLA Captain, Nai Hlaing, the core of the new group consisted of about three dozen Mon soldiers, disappointed with the NMSP's inability to protect Mon villagers from abuse by the *Tatmadaw*, and frustrated by a lack of post-ceasefire financial opportunities.

The new splinter group exploited the opportunities presented by a limited MNLA presence in areas around Yebyu, which had never been fully penetrated by the *Tatmadaw*. The new Mon National Defence Army (MNDA)[36] was usually referred to rather disparagingly by NMSP sources, as a – rather than *the* – 'Mon Armed Group'. Indeed, it was a while before the faction established a formal command structure. In May–June 1998 this new, fifty-strong unit received supplies from the KNU, and began to sprang a series of ambushes on Burma Army patrols in Ye and Yebyu Townships, in the vicinity of the hyper-sensitive gas pipeline corridor. In retaliation, the *Tatmadaw* stepped-up its mistreatment of Mon civilians in the area, and a number of cases of torture, extortion and rape were reported.[37] In addition, the *Tatmadaw* re-commenced the forced relocation of Mon, Karen and Tavoyan villages in the Ye-Yebyu area,[38] and closed down a number of local Mon National Schools.[39]

By mid-1998, Central was growing increasingly concerned about the security situation on its doorstep. The party leadership worried that clashes between the 'Mon Armed Group' and the *Tatmadaw* might destabilise the ceasefire, especially as the splinter group seemed to enjoy some support among local villagers, who shared Nai Hlaing and colleagues' disappointment over the lack of positive developments, and the continuation of land confiscation and other human rights abuses, since the ceasefire.

In March and April the following year, the MNDA (or 'Mon Armed Group') began launching occasional sorties against the MNLA. Both sides suffered casualties, and the NMSP welcomed the early start of the 1999 rainy season, and a lull in the Tavoy rebels' activities.

Although the spectres of disunity and warlordism were disturbing enough, the activities of the MNDA and its predecessors still lacked the significance of the MAMD adventure. The Tavoy District dissidents were less numerous or well-organised than the MAMD, and it was anyway much easier for loyal MNLA forces to intervene so close to Central. Nevertheless, the fact of continuing Mon armed resistance to Rangoon undermined the NMSP's claim to solely represent the Mon community in the border areas.

Since 1995, the NMSP had been embarrassed by the obvious fact that, despite promises made at the time, the ceasefire had not eliminated human rights abuses against the Mon civilian population. In fact, following the emergence of the MNDA in the Ye-Yebyu area, the *Tatmadaw* introduced a full-blown Four Cuts operation, displacing several hundreds families.

However, in the permanent ceasefire zones the situation in 1999 was somewhat more stable, although what the future might hold for these isolated areas was still far from clear. The strategic importance of the NMSP-controlled 'ceasefire zones' was not equivalent to that of the 'liberated zones' during the period of armed insurgency. If the ceasefire was to have any real meaning, beyond the party's ability to remain in control of a slither of land along the border, then the struggle for self-determination and development would have to be carried to the Mon community 'inside' Burma. The NMSP no longer had the debatable luxury of merely criticising the military government from its strongholds along the border. It now shared responsibility for the success of the ceasefire process. However, the government was by far the stronger of the two parties to the agreement, and often provoked and worked to undermine the Mon nationalists.

For example, reports emerged during the 2000 rainy season of the Burma Army Southeast Command having established armed 'anti-insurgency groups' in Mon villages across Ye Township. In a development reminiscent of the *Ka Kwe Ye* (KKY) militia programme of the late 1960s and '70s, village tracts were given responsibility for housing and feeding the new groups (which unlike the old KKY militias, came under direct *Tatmadaw* control). The 'anti-insurgency groups' were to be deployed in the campaign against the KNU and MNDA, raising the spectre of Mon villagers being set against Mon rebels.[40]

The KNU and Allied Groups

Since 1995, and especially following the 1997 Mae Tha Raw Hta crisis, official NMSP contact with the KNU-dominated DAB and National Council of the Union of Burma (NCUB) alliances had been kept to a minimum. Nevertheless, informal relations were maintained, and in February 1999 a Mon delegation from the border travelled to Bangkok, to celebrate Shan National Day. A few weeks latter, Mon representatives participated with Karen, Karenni, Shan and other youth groups in an ethnic affairs seminar, held in Sangkhlaburi. Given the physical proximity of the Mon and Karen communities, continued contacts were inevitable. Such on-going relations, between members of the ceasefire groups and those still at war with Rangoon, reflected the complex nature of Burmese ethnic politics.

By the time of the 1997 *Tatmadaw* offensives, the KNU – together with the Shan States Army – South (SSA – South)[41] – also known as the Shan United Revolutionary Army (SURA)[42] – was the last major insurgent group not to have agreed a ceasefire with Rangoon. Since 1997, the KNU-DAB-NCUB leadership had been largely confined to Thailand, where their activities were closely monitored by the Thai security services. Nevertheless, KNLA units continued to operate in the Fourth, Fifth, Sixth and Seventh Brigade areas along the border, often patrolling close to the Mon ceasefire zones. The KNU posted regular battle reports on the internet, detailing military engagements in these and the other brigade areas, further inside Burma (First through Third Brigades), where die-hard Karen guerrillas carried on the armed struggle against Rangoon. In retaliation for such stubborn resistance, the *Tatmadaw* continued its campaign against the civilian victims of the civil war.

Following the dictates of the KNU president and martyr, Saw Ba U Gyi, the Karen insurgents vowed never to surrender. Over the years, General Bo Mya had purged many of his opponents in the KNU, and his hard-line faction continued to demand that the SPDC meet a series of tough conditions, before ceasefire negotiations could recommence. This position owed much to pride, principle and the weight of history: for the KNU to accede to the type of ceasefire accepted by the NMSP and KIO, was regarded by General Bo Mya as an admission of defeat, and a betrayal of the revolution.[43] Of course, the KNU's uncompromising stance also served to reinforce the position of the 'old guard', who had built their careers on armed resistance to Rangoon.

A ceasefire at the time of the KIO-SLORC agreement, in 1993, might have secured KNU control over a considerable amount of territory in southeast Burma. However, by 2002, the Karen insurgents had little left to bargain with. They might be better-off hanging-on in Thailand and along the border, in the hope that changes inside Burma would eventually relieve their situation. According to this perspective, the KNU's symbolic resistance retained more value than any temporary benefits that might be derived from a truce with Rangoon.

Certainly, this was the position of most of the KNU's allies. The KNU might eventually agree terms with Rangoon and 'return to the legal fold'. However, the various Burman-dominated groups along the border were struggling to achieve political objectives for the country *as a whole*, rather than achieve concessions on behalf of a particular ethnic group. Nothing less than the military government's complete overthrow would be sufficient for many of their members to return home. Thus, the All Burma Students Democratic Front (ABSDF),[44] and many other DAB-NCUB member-groups[45] had a strong interest in encouraging General Bo Mya to maintain his uncompromising stance, and continue the war.

Meanwhile, further divisions had occurred within the Karen ranks. By the end of 1999, at least six ex-KNU factions had 'exchanged arms for peace' with Rangoon. These included the Democratic Kayin Buddhist Army (DKBA), which by this time could field nearly as many troops as the KNLA.

Another disaffected Karen splinter group was 'God's Army' (or 'The Soldiers of the Holy Mountain'). In a fateful episode, which set the tone in the new millennium for Thai-Karen relations along the southern half of the border, in early January 2000 one or more 'God's Army' members joined a group of Burman student dissidents in occupying a Thai hospital near Ratchaburi. After a tense twenty-two hour stand-off, Thai special forces moved in, freed the more than two hundred hostages, and executed ten guerrillas on the spot.[46] Over the following days, questions were raised in the Thai and international press regarding the summary nature of Thai justice, and attention was drawn to the extent of the Ninth Division's military and economic co-operation with the *Tatmadaw*.[47] Ultimately though, the incident served to undermine public sympathy in Thailand for the Karen.

Less than a week after the hospital siege, the KNU attempted to reassert its leadership of the Karen nationalist movement, by announcing the election of a new Chairman, Saw Ba Thin. Having held the position of KNU General Secretary since the 1980s, Ba Thin was a close ally of Bo Mya. The General himself was retained as KNU Vice-Chairman, with overall responsibility for military strategy. Despite such continuities, the change in leadership, together with the promotion of a younger generation of second rank leaders, encouraged some observers to predict a revival in the KNU's fortunes. In the short term however, the situation along the border remained dire, and a stream of disillusioned cadres continued to leave the KNU, often to seek asylum in third countries.

Meanwhile, several other groups maintained a fitful armed opposition to the *Tatmadaw* and military government. Among these were the Ramanya Restoration Army (RRA), whose camp in the forest south of Chaung Chee was attacked by Burma Army troops in pursuit of 'God's Army' remnants, in early February 2000.[48] Following this assault – and the arrest of its leaders – the RRA became largely inactive. Many of its members sought refuge in Prachuab and Bangkok, where they formed a Monland Independence Organisation (MIO), under the leadership of Nai Parana, an old associate of Nai Pagomon and the National Mon Democratic Organisation (NMDO).[49]

Other die-hard insurgent groups in southeast Burma included the dwindling forces of the ex-CPB Mergui-Tavoy United Front (MDUF),[50] the Karenni National Progressive Party (KNPP), whose ceasefire had broken down in 1995, and the SSA – South. Several other rebel groups continued to operate in Shan State, while Chin, Rakhine and other insurgent forces still launched occasional sorties from bases along the borders with India and Bangladesh. The most important of these latter groups were two small National Democratic Front (NDF) member-organisations, the Chin National Front (CNF) and the Arakan Liberation Party (ALP).

In June 1999 the ALP, CNF, KNPP, KNU and SSA – South announced the formation of a new anti-Rangoon military alliance. Although none of these groups were able to exert sustained military pressure against the *Tatmadaw*, the remaining insurgent armies could probably maintain current levels of guerrilla activity for several years, especially while they still had some friends in Thai military circles (see below). The insurgents – and particularly the KNU – still possessed considerable symbolic importance. The fact of on-going ethnic rebellion demonstrated that armed opposition to Rangoon was not entirely at an end and that, somewhere in the jungles of Kaw Thoo Lei, the dream of a free Karen state lived on.

Food, Security, Human Rights and Displacement

In July 1998 Lt-General Khin Nyunt informed the ceasefire groups that, from the end of the year, they would no longer be provided by the government with rice rations. This would seem to confirm two phenomena: that, following the terrible floods of 1997,[51] food was becoming increasingly scarce, and that a combination of state mismanagement and regional economic collapse had engendered a crisis in state finances.

Following an appeal to Khin Nyunt, the NMSP in fact continued to receive two million Kyat (c.$5–6,000) per month from the SPDC, with which the party bought rice on the open market. To many observers, the party's continued receipt of government payments indicated an unhealthily dependant relationship with its erstwhile enemy. To others, it merely underlined the parlous state of NMSP finances in the post-ceasefire era.

In July 1998 the government also announced that *Tatmadaw* battalions would have to start growing some of their own food. As a result, in the second half of the year the Burma Army began to implement a nation-wide programme of land appropriation. In Thaton Township alone, some 20,000 acres of arable land were reportedly seized.[52] Furthermore, in early 1999 the authorities significantly increased the 'paddy quota' in Mon State, under which farmers were forced to sell rice to the government at well below the market rate;[53] in 2000 and 2001, farmers and rubber plantation owners were again forced to sell produce to the state at artificially low prices.[54]

As had been the case with many of the heralded economic reforms of the late 1980s and early '90s, by the end of 1998, plans announced the previous year to open up Burma's rice economy to private capital and expertise had been quietly abandoned. The SPDC could not afford to deregulate the rural command economy: the rice quota was needed to feed military and government personnel, and the acquisition of large amounts of cheap paddy was a key element in the regimes' planned export drive. As a consequence of the government's continued interference, the price of rice continued to rise steeply in 1999, while the situation of Burma's farmers further deteriorated.[55]

In October 1999 the Asian Human Rights Commission (AHRC)'s 'People's Tribunal on Food Scarcity and Militarization in Myanmar' concluded that Burma faced nation-wide food shortages, as a direct result of government policy.[56] Citing evidence from Mon State, the AHRC concluded that "even without insurgency, rural people face local military rule and hunger."[57]

Nevertheless, security in parts of Mon State had improved, and in many places there were fewer checkpoints on the roads. For the residents of the ceasefire zones, one of the most tangible benefits of the agreement was the opportunity to travel inside Burma, and visit relatives sometimes not seen for many years. However, for ordinary villagers there were still perils attached to such journeys: the danger of being victimised as a rebel sympathiser may have been reduced, but the possibility of being taken as a *Tatmadaw* porter was still very real. Furthermore, hundreds of thousands of ethnic minority Burmese citizens still had no state identity card, without which they were unable to buy bus or train tickets, or vote in any future election.[58]

The worst *Tatmadaw* abuses may have been curbed, but the underlying human rights situation was still grave. The most serious abuses were often linked to infrastructure projects, such as the construction of the Ye-Tavoy railway. On 26th March 1998, SPDC Secretary Two, Lt-General Tin Oo, presided over an opening ceremony for the newly-completed line. On pain of a 200 Kyat fine, thousands of villagers were forced to attend the ceremony, at which Tin Oo praised the *Tatmadaw's* contribution to the project. However, according to the MNRC "he did not mention about any participation of local inhabitants who were constantly forced to work in the construction."[59] As Mon observers had correctly predicted at the start of the year, erosion during the 1998 rainy season soon led to a resumption of forced labour on the project, as gangs of workers were taken from local villages to shore-up the embankment. The same pattern repeated itself the following year, when Mon and other villagers were again conscripted to re-build the railway following subsidence caused by heavy rains.[60]

In late 2000 reports began to emerge regarding plans to build a new gas pipeline between Kambauk and Pa'an Township, in Karen State, where an existing cement factory was to be up-graded (the 'retired opium warlord' Khun Sa, the *Tatmadaw* and a Japanese company were reported to be among the investors in this project). In preparation for the construction of this off-shoot from the main Yadana pipeline, Mon and Karen village lands along the more than 400 Km route were confiscated, without compensation.[61] Among a host of human rights complaints, the issue of land rights was becoming one of increasing concern to Mon nationalists and villagers alike.

In June 2001 Amnesty International issued a report stating that, "Myanmar's ethnic minorities, comprising one third of the population, continue to suffer disproportionately from a wide range of human rights violations.... Shan, Karenni, Mon and Karen civilians are targeted for punishment by the SPDC because of their ethnicity and presumed support for armed groups ... the vast majority of these people, who bear the brunt of the armed conflict, are subsistence rice farmers."[62] Despair and frustration at such abuses, which the NMSP seemed powerless to prevent, was a factor in the popularity of the MNDA (or 'Mon Armed Group'). The continued spiral of rebellion and counter-insurgency inevitably led to further displacement in the countryside.

In 1998 the Burma Ethnic Research Group (BERG) calculated that, in the 1990s, half a million (or thirty per cent) of the population of Kaw Thoo Lei had been displaced.[63] The MNRC estimated the number of IDPs in Mon State at about 40,000 people, including at least 20,000 Mon, Karen and Tavoyans in the Ye-Yebyu area, perhaps another 15–20,000 in the vicinity of Kya-In Seik-Kyi and Three Pagodas Pass, and at least 5,000 displaced around Moulmein and other urban centres.[64] Mon human rights workers presented these findings to the UN Commission on Human Rights (UNCHR)'s Special Rapporteur on Myanmar, Judge Rajsoomer Lallah, at a meeting in Kanchanaburi on 18th November 1998.

Internal displacement was a phenomena that obviously required further research, and from 1998 the BBC and other NGOs in Thailand began to focus more on the plight of Burma's one million-plus IDPs. Meanwhile, the MNRC's Emergency Relief and Development Programme (ERDP) continued to provide limited assistance to the Mon IDPs.

A 1999 survey of Burmese migrant workers along the border found that Mon villagers were still coming "in large numbers to Thailand, (suggesting) that the end of insurgency (had) little effect on the status of communities" still subject to "forced labour, heavy corruption, taxation, impoverishment, and theft or confiscation of property, livestock and land."[65] Those who did not enter the refugee camps were among the most vulnerable groups in Thailand, living under constant threat of repatriation.[66] Although many longer-established Mon migrant workers possessed some form of Thai identity document, they too were subject to the vagaries of immigration policy.

In the late 1990s the Burmese Mon community in Thailand had few friends in high places. Throughout the decade however, *Loong Phoor Oktama*, Abbot of Wat Wanka in Sangkhlaburi, continued to offer some protection and patronage to the roughly 5,000 people living on the 'Mon side' of town. As the venerable abbot became increasingly frail though, and spent longer and more frequent periods in Bangkok, there was a growing apprehension as to how much longer he would be able to help his people. With its golden pagoda and views towards the rolling hills of Mon State, the picturesque west bank at Sangkhla was ripe for exploitation. Many locals suspected that, in the absence of their patron, powerful Thai interests might step in to exploit the area.[67]

However, in the meantime *Loong Phoor* Oktama remained a powerful voice for the Mon in Thailand. His high standing in Thai society was illustrated on 8th December 1999, four days after His Majesty the King's birthday, when the venerable monk presided together with members of the Thai royal family at a Mon-style Buddhist ceremony at Thammasat University Hall in Bangkok (situated near the old site of the Mon palace guards' quarters).

Refugees, Protection and Humanitarian Assistance

In late 1997 the MNRC announced the formation of two new resettlement sites, at Ying Ye on the Ye River, and Chan Toih, between Bee Ree and Halochanee. The latter had originally been one of the proposed Halochanee resettlement sites, before the resettlement-repatriation operation was scaled-back in early 1996. The fact that they were again willing to settle people in these front-line positions indicated that, despite the tumultuous events of 1997, the Mon authorities felt a little more secure than they had in 1995–96. This perception was reinforced at the end of 1998, when the MNRC announced the formation of another new settlement at Suwanaphon, west of Bee Ree, where fifty families of new arrivals set about clearing land from the forest.[68]

Meanwhile, a little further to the south, off-duty soldiers from the nearby Burma Army outpost sometimes visited the Tavoy District 'temporary' ceasefire zone, to buy vegetables and other supplies. However, the *Tatmadaw* did not return *en masse*.

Between 1998–2001, the BBC, and its supporters among the diplomatic community in Bangkok, persuaded the Ministry of the Interior (MOI) to continue to allow humanitarian assistance (including MSF medicines) through to the Mon resettlement sites. In 1998 BBC supplies to the Mon refugees were calculated at sixty-five per cent of needs for Halochanee, eighty per cent for Bee Ree and ninety per cent for Tavoy District. The shortfall was designed to provide the refugees with an incentive to move towards self-sufficiency. In 1999, 2000 and 2001 the BBC again agreed to support the Mon refugees, at fifty per cent (and later, thirty-three per cent) of calculated needs.[69]

Under pressure from the Ninth Division, the NMSP and MNRC decided in 1998 to send all refugee supplies through Halochanee camp, and transport rice onwards from here to Bee Ree and Tavoy District. This decision involved the NMSP, MNRC, BBC and the refugees in the construction of nearly fifty Km of new road over the forested mountains between Halochanee and Bee Ree.[70] However, the logistical problems involved in transporting perishable food over this route led BBC to purchase all 1999–2001 supplies for Tavoy District, and fifty per cent of those for Bee Ree, in the vicinity of Ye. To get permission to ship such large quantities of rice up-river to the camps, NMSP and MNRC personnel had to negotiate with Burmese Military Intelligence in Moulmein, rather than with the Thai authorities in Sangkhlaburi – a switch in focus that neatly symbolised the post-ceasefire scenario.

In August 1998 the MNRC reported that, due to nearby *Tatmadaw* activity against the KNU, several families from Halochanee were forced to abandon their farms, in areas close to the ceasefire front-line. The Thai authorities in Sangkhlaburi later drove another fifty-four families off farms along the border near Palaung Japan, claiming that they were encroaching on Thai territory.[71] To further complicate matters, in September 1998 local government officials at Three Pagodas Pass started to issue land registration documents to some Mon villagers at Paluang Japan. This move, which greatly angered Maj-General Sanchai Ratchawan, the influential Ninth Division Second-in-Command,[72] seems to have been designed to sow confusion regarding the position of the oft-disputed border in this strategically important area. Once again, Mon civilians were being used as a buffer population, between Burma and Thailand.

Since the mid-1990s, the prospect of Three Pagodas Pass re-gaining its prominence as a lucrative trade route had been at the forefront of Thai, Burmese and Mon strategic planning. In an attempt to secure some of the action, in early 1999 the NMSP began to encourage displaced Mon in the Sangkhlaburi area to resettle along the route of a proposed new border road, to be built by the Thai authorities between Halochanee (Don Yang) and the pass. The NMSP too, was still willing to use displaced people to forward its agenda.

Meanwhile, the MNDA (or 'Mon Armed Group') remained active in Tavoy District, launching occasional raids on *Tatmadaw* outposts and patrols. In February 2000, with several Burma Army units rotated out of the area to fight Karen insurgents in south and central Tenasserim Division, the MNDA held its own National Day celebrations at Paupingwin village, in Yebyu Township.[73] In retaliation for this act of defiance, the *Tatmadaw* once again stepped-up its intimidation and harassment of the local population. According to the Human Rights Foundation of Monland (HRFM), approximately one thousand people were forcibly expelled from Paupingwin village in May 2000, taking the total number of new IDPs in Ye and Yebyu township over the dry season to about 5,000 people.[74] Further MNDA-*Tatmadaw* clashes were reported during the following rainy season, and throughout the 2001 dry season. Inevitably, these led to a further round of intimidation and reprisals against villagers, further confiscation of lands, and the arrival of more displaced people in NMSP-controlled parts of Ye Township. Thus new arrivals had continued to arrive throughout 1999–2001.

Not more than fifteen-to-twenty per cent of families would harvest a rice crop at the end of 2001. Of these, few could supply more than twenty per cent of their annual needs.[75] These figures represented a decrease in rice production of more than twenty-five per cent since 1998. This reduction was partly explained by the precarious nature of the security situation, and in part by the devastating effects of early rains (and later, severe flooding) in 1999 and 2000.

The Bee Ree refugees in particular, continued to grow rice, in the expectation that supplies from the BBC would not last forever. Deforestation had escalated to an alarming extent in the ecologically important Ye River watershed, where the fragile soil would soon be exhausted. Indeed, the decline in rice yields was in part explained by decreasing soil fertility, as well as by floods, and the increasing incidence of pests (rats, wild pigs and insects).[76]

Meanwhile, some residents of the resettlement sites had prospered. Several hundred families at Halochanee and Bee Ree received electricity from privately-run generators. Many households had begun to plant cash crops, such as fruit, rubber, cashew and betel nut trees, all of which attracted a better price at market than did rice (which in any case was still being supplied by the BBC). With indebtedness becoming a problem in the resettlement zones, the ability to raise additional income was important to most families. However, the most needy were often the least able to take advantage of the limited opportunities available, and malnutrition remained a problem among the more vulnerable sectors of the refugee population.[77]

Although efforts had been made to increase the amount of rice grown in the resettlement zones, geographical and security considerations allowed for only a limited agricultural expansion. The Mon returnees were attempting to make the best of a poor set of circumstances, but it was clear that the neither the NMSP nor the MNRC had a clear vision for the future of the resettlement sites. Although the MNRC helped to establish refugee community organisations and develop farmers' co-operatives, work towards an integrated approach to development sites progressed slowly. For both the refugees and their leaders, everything depended on the situation 'inside'. While Burma remained in crisis, the issue of displacement would remain unresolved.

According to the Mon authorities, in November 2001 the Mon refugee population stood at 13,604 people, living in three main resettlement zones.[78] By this time, the total refugee caseload along the border (excluding the 'Safe Area' and displaced people not resident in the camps) stood at 137,691 people, including the Mon, plus 104,355 Karen and 20,037 Karenni refugees.[79] Meanwhile, several thousand Chin and other refugees from Burma still languished in India, while thousands of *Rohingya* refugees remained in Bangladesh, despite government efforts to expel them.[80] However, only along the Thailand border had a substantial Burma-focussed NGO community been allowed to develop.

January 1999 had marked the fifteenth anniversary of the arrival in Thailand of the first long-term Karen refugees, and March that year was the fifteenth birthday of the BBC, the most important NGO on the border. What had started as a low-key, low-budget operation, not expected to exist for more than few years, had grown into a major international relief agency. The projected BBC budget for 2002 was 562 million Thai Baht (c. $12.75 million, depending on the exchange rate); the number of field staff along the border had grown from two in 1994 (when the author joined the BBC), to four in 1997 (when he left), to ten in 2002, plus nine more staff in Bangkok.[81] The long-serving BBC Director, Jack Dunford, was created a Member of the British Empire (MBE) in the New Year 2001 honours list, in recognition of his services to the refugees.

In the early days, the primary requirements in BBC personnel had been sensitivity to the refugees' culture, and some awareness of the complex military and political environment along the border. However, by the late 1990s the paramount concerns were maintaining good relations with the Thai authorities, and satisfying new donor requirements for monitoring and accountability. Until the early-to-mid 1990s, relations with the Thai authorities had been a secondary consideration, as BBC Bangkok had handled national-level liaison, while the Mon, Karen and Karenni refugee committees managed many aspects of the relief operation on the ground. By 1999 however, all this had changed, as the refugees' freedom of movement and their representatives' ability to operate in Thailand was restricted. Meanwhile, the BBC had undergone a cultural evolution: a new professionalism and detachment from border politics had replaced the original, clubby enthusiasm of the early days.

While it had been providing limited cross-border assistance to IDPs since the mid-1990s, the BBC's core business remained the supply of refugee camps in Thailand. Since 1997, the basic ration of rice, salt and fish paste had been supplemented for all Karen and Karenni refugees, by the addition of yellow beans and cooking oil. Fuel and building materials were also provided, now that there were a smaller number of much larger, 'consolidated' refugee settlements, making a bigger impact on local eco-systems. By the end of 2001, Mae La Karen refugee camp had a population of 40,503. As Jack Dunford had put it in July 1999, the closely-controlled environment in the camps was "eroding the refugees' sense of self-sufficiency and making them increasingly aid dependent."[82]

From the perspective of 'aid dependency' at least, the Mon refugees were not so badly off. They could still collect firewood and forage in the vicinity of the resettlement sites. Although, like many of the refugees in Thailand, they lived in fear of *Tatmadaw* incursions, they did not suffer the added burden of harassment by their Thai 'protectors'. However, some observers questioned whether the Mon refugees were still eligible for humanitarian assistance, especially as the NMSP continued to receive rice payments from the SPDC.

By the start of 2000, the last batch of Mon refugees had been back on 'Burma side' for more than three years. These people still had a 'well-founded fear of persecution', and thus might be considered refugees, were it not for their presence within Burma, rather than a neighbouring country. Nevertheless, the BBC donors were entitled to wonder for how much longer the Mon returnees would continue to require refugee relief supplies. Was their plight really any different to that of hundreds of thousands of other poor and oppressed ethnic minority villagers in the border areas? Could the situation in the Mon resettlement zones still be characterised as a refugee emergency?

To the MNRC, the answer was clear: the refugees would require assistance for as long as the political and human rights situation in Burma prevented their return home. Meanwhile, the MNRC would continue to encourage moves towards limited self-sufficiency and local development in the resettlement sites.

Having worked with two Thailand-based NGOs to train Mon community workers over the previous year, the MNRC re-launched itself for the year 2000, as the Mon Relief and Development Committee (MRDC). At the same time, the ERDP was re-organised as the Relief Programme for IDPs (RPI). The MRDC entered the new millennium determined to move towards a more pro-active, developmental approach.[83] However, the immediate humanitarian crisis continued to demand attention. The first report of the new MRDC, in January 2000, claimed that, since mid-November 1999, between one and two thousand Mon and Karen villagers from Kya-In Seik-Kyi Township had fled to the NMSP-controlled ceasefire zones. Of these, about six hundred (including four hundred Karen) had settled at Halochanee-Htee Wah Doh.[84] By the end of the year, several hundred more villagers from this area had been displaced, as the *Tatmadaw* moved against Karen *and* Mon insurgents operating on the edge of the NMSP 'ceasefire zone' (see below).[85]

Throughout 1996–2001, the MNRC had issued a series of statements, reminding UNHCR and the international community that the issue of returnee and IDP protection had yet to be addressed. The Bangkok and Geneva offices of UNHCR indicated that the Mon authorities should apply to the agency's Rangoon office for assistance. However, UNHCR Rangoon proved unable to carry out even the most basic monitoring of the Mon returnees, and in mid-1997 failed in its attempts to establish a field office in Moulmein.[86]

Since 1996, international attention had focused primarily on the plight of the Karen and Karenni (but not the 100,000-plus Shan) refugees. Would the Mon refugee repatriation prove a precedent for the Karen – in the event of a KNU ceasefire, or even without one? The situation of the Karen refugees was complicated by their identification as enemies not just by the *Tatmadaw*, but by factions among their own people. By 1998, the number of incursions into Thailand by the DKBA and their Burma Army allies had risen to more than one hundred and fifty and at least seventy refugees and local Thai and Thai-Karen villagers had been killed.[87] (Since then, DKBA activity had largely been confined to Burma, at least until new incursions on to Thai soil occurred in May 2000).

Ethnic minority refugees from Burma were clearly not safe in Thailand. Therefore, in November 1997, the new Chuan Leekpai government announced that UNHCR would be invited to play a greater role in protecting the Burmese refugees. Following a period of intensive behind-the-scenes lobbying, in July 1998 the Thai authorities and UNHCR issued conflicting versions of an agreement under which the agency would become more closely involved with the refugees.[88] It seemed that UNHCR would assume an expanded role in the remaining refugee camps in Thailand, but it was not clear whether these would in practice remain open to new arrivals.[89] Also unresolved, were the Royal Thai Government and UNHCRs' roles in registering and screening refugees. It did seem though, that the UN agency had been coaxed into accepting a greater protection role along the border. However, the BBC would continue to supply and administer the camps, together with the KRC (which in 1998 initiated a major – if belated – restructuring and training programme).

By early 1999, UNHCR had established offices in Kanchanaburi, Mae Sot and Mae Hong Son, and was ready to begin playing a more active role along the border. Refugee leaders and NGO workers however, remained suspicious of the agency and its tendency to promote repatriation as a solution to refugee crises the world over. Some of these concerns were addressed by the out-going UN High Commissioner for Refugees, Sadako Ogata, in November 2000. Following a visit to Tham Hin – the over-crowded Karen refugee camp near Kanchanaburi, where many families from KNU Fourth Brigade lived – Ms Ogata stated that conditions deplorable. Importantly, she also insisted that any future Karen refugee repatriation must depend on substantial political change in Burma. She also confirmed that UNHCR was still interested in establishing a presence in Mon State.[90]

Language, Education and Culture

February 21st 1997 marked the golden jubilee of Mon National Day. To the outrage of the nationalist community, just hours before the onset of fiftieth anniversary celebrations planned in towns and villages across Mon State, Military Intelligence officials stepped-in to ban the proceedings.[91] Two years after the ceasefire, the authorities obviously still regarded Mon nationalist sentiment as a threat. The Mon cause retained its potency, despite more than two centuries of repression.

A Human Rights Foundation of Monland (HRFM) statement, issued to commemorate the following year's National Day, described how:

At the same time, the SLORC has also attempted to stop the Mon Education System adopted by the NMSP and the local community. In every dry season from the beginning of March to the end of April, the Mon community leaders including Buddhist monks and university students arranged for the dry season literacy training to teach the Mon language to children and adults.... Since 1996, the authorities changed the tactics in suppressing the literacy training. While the community leaders were running the training, the authorities also came in and conducted another training such as the Buddhist Cultural Training, in the town and villager levels to divide the students and attempt to weaken the Mon literacy training.[92]

These claims were particularly disturbing in their allusion to the use of Buddhism as a divisive force. Religious strife was unlikely to have the same devastating effects among the Mon community as it had in recent years among the Karen, but this was still a worrying development.

Although, in late 1990, *sangha* members in Mandalay had organised a short-lived boycott of alms from *Tatmadaw* personnel,[93] the monkhood was generally reluctant to engage in politics. It was therefore, all the more significant, when in early December 1999 the abbot of the famous Kha Khat Waing monastery in Pegu wrote an open letter to Khin Nyunt, calling for compromise and an end to the political stalemate. *Sayadaw* U Zawti Pahla's letter called for the emergence of a broker to promote dialogue between the opposition and government, and extended the good offices of the *sangha* in this role.[94] Later the same month, a respected *Sayadaw* from Mandalay published a series of lectures on a similar theme, addressed to political leaders on both sides of the divide in Burma. The SPDC's low-key response to these rare instances of public criticism illustrated the regime's reluctance to provoke the *sangha*. Like the Christian churches, the monkhood was one of the few institutions in Burma not directly controlled by the military. Through the Mon *sangha* in particular, ran deep channels of national culture.

According to Christian Bauer, the transmission and survival of the Mon language has depended primarily on the maintenance of wide-spread literacy.[95] During the classical and colonial eras, the *sangha* provided a religious-orientated Mon language education, directed at young males (who unlike girls could reside in monasteries). Anthony D. Smith observes that "in societies where formal systems of education were lacking or deficient, temples and their votaries and ministrants assumed a pivotal role in ensuring the perpetuation of ethnic lore and ritual, and in elaborating and interpreting the collective myths and symbols and memories which provided the axis for identification."[96] Since the late 1930s, cultural organisations such as the All Ramanya Mon Association (ARMA) and its successor, the Mon Literature and Culture Committee (MLCC), as well as more overtly political groups, such as the NMSP and its predecessors, have joined the *sangha* as providers of Mon language education.

Although, since 1962, such efforts have often fallen-foul of the state authorities, in the late 1980s the Mon politician (and future MNDF MP-elect), Nai Thaung Shein, established a branch of the MLCC in Moulmein. Together with the Mon Youth Organisation (MYO), the MLCC was soon active among Mon students at Moulmein University, initiating a number of cultural projects. It maintained branches at Rangoon, Moulmein and Yezin (Pyinmana) universities. As well as producing post-cards, t-shirts and posters etc., the MLCC published a Mon, Burmese and English language yearbook, *U-Chan Hongsa* ('Hongsa Garden'), featuring articles on social, cultural and historical matters.

However, until 1995, the Mon monks and students' ability to implement literacy and cultural programmes among the wider population was limited. As a consequence of the NMSP-SLORC ceasefire though, a degree of political space emerged, within which such efforts flourished.

Based at the Nai Chit Thaung Hall in Rangoon (the headquarters of the dormant ARMA), the MLCC drew its membership from the Mon *sangha* and intelligentsia. Together with the Association for Summer Mon Literature and Buddhist Teaching, in April–May 1996 university students from the MLCC conducted a major literacy drive, in which approximately 25,000 schoolchildren attended Mon language and Buddhism classes in more than one hundred monasteries across Mon State and in Rangoon, Karen State and Tenasserim Division.[97] Most of the trainees, who included more than a thousand girls, were state primary school pupils, who would otherwise have had no formal schooling in their native tongue. By 1998, the number of trainees had risen to nearly 34,000; in 2000, 46,435 children attended these classes (sixty per cent were girls).[98]

The annual Summer Language Training had become a key focus of efforts to preserve and rejuvenate the Mon heritage. Crucially, the literacy drive was carried out by monks, students and other grass roots activists, rather than NMSP cadres, and was thus not identified as an immediate threat by the government. Although, in May 2000, the authorities ordered the Summer Language Trainings in Moulmein to be terminated, they were again successfully implemented in other townships across lower Burma that year, and again in 2001.

Meanwhile, the NMSP continued to develop its own education network. To many observers, the party's ability since 1995 to deliver an expanded education system was one of few concrete achievements of the post-ceasefire era. By the late 1990s, the party had replicated the Mon People's Front (MPF)'s success in the late 1950s, establishing schools in both the liberated zones and government-controlled areas across lower Burma. The NMSP however, had achieved this goal without state (but with foreign NGO) assistance.

Over the 1995–96 (May–February) academic year, the MNEC had administered 283 schools. Of these, 177 were 'mixed' institutions, and 106 NMSP Mon National Schools (including eight in the refugee settlements). The Mon schools – at least at the primary level, which most children attended – were mostly run by and for local communities. By defining many of these schools as 'mixed' institutions (where Mon classes were officially taught outside of school hours), the NMSP was able to maintain its education system, even in areas where local *Tatmadaw* commanders sought to repress party schools.

The state education sector, with its relatively high fees and restrictions on the use of Mon language, was less popular, in many villages, than the NMSP school system. Large numbers of parents seemed to prefer a distinctly Mon education for their children, if for no other reason than that such lessons were easier for native speakers to follow. No other ethnic nationalist organisation in Burma ran such an extensive education network (the KIO's schools, for example, were mostly restricted to the Kachin ceasefire zones, with few institutions operating in government-controlled areas).

As a condition of the ceasefire, the NMSP was no longer able to collect taxes, with which to fund its education and other services. Therefore, like the refugee relief operation, the Mon National School system was largely dependent on foreign donors. These paid for most buildings, teaching materials and textbooks, teacher training programmes, and teachers' salaries and rice allowances. While the NMSP remained unable (or unwilling) substantially to fund the Mon National Schools, and local villagers could only be expected to support a portion of the costs involved, the system was inherently unsustainable.[99]

Although it was generally recognised that the ceasefire would not survive a wholesale suppression of the Mon National Schools, in 1996 and '97 the authorities in Mudon and Thanbyuzayat Townships initiated an intermittent clamp-down on Mon language and culture, culminating in the above-mentioned suppression of National Day celebrations. Several dozen 'mixed' schools were forced to close and, despite NMSP protests, Mon language use was further restricted in many of the others.[100]

In 1998 things got worse. The SPDC had issued a directive in June, prohibiting the work of independent schools in Chin State. Then, in a letter to Nai Shwe Kyin, dated 1st July, the commander of Military Intelligence Group Five, based in Moulmein, ordered all Mon National Schools to close, effectively curtailing the education of six-to-ten thousand children.[101] Explanations for the clamp-down focused on the regime's displeasure at the NMSP's calls for political reform and dialogue with the NLD (see below).

In late July 1998, at a hastily-arranged meeting in Moulmein, between representatives of the Burma Army Southeast Command, the NMSP and the *sangha*, the number of Mon National Schools forced to close was reduced to only two. Although the use of Mon in state schools was still to be outlawed, the MNEC was able to continue with its ambitious teaching and teacher-training programmes. However, the authorities proscribed the establishment of Mon National Schools within a four-to-ten Km distance of any state school.[102]

The political atmosphere across lower Burma remained tense, and the hard-working MNEC staff were not surprised when in November an order came from the Southeast Command, banning Mon classes in eighteen schools in Kawkareik Township, in Karen State. Headmasters and village headman were warned that they risked a seven year jail term if they violated this directive.[103]

Despite such setbacks, by the end of 1998, a total of 332 schools in Burma were teaching Mon. These included 144 Mon National and 188 'mixed' schools, an increase, since 1995, of 38 National and 11 'mixed' institutions.[104] Over the 1999–2000 school year, the MNEC opened another eleven schools, bringing the total to 343 (including 150 National) schools, teaching 46,202 students.[105] In 2001 the MNEC opened a second high school at Thaungbauk, south of the In-Quoit permanent ceasefire position, near Kawbein (Thaton District). By this time, there were 148 Mon National Schools and 217 'mixed' schools, in nine townships (plus the resettlement sites), teaching 51,050 pupils, approximately seventy per cent of whom lived in government-controlled areas.[106] Illustrating an important aspect of the post-ceasefire educational environment, a handful of graduates of the Mon National High Schools had the opportunity to continue their studies at state further education colleges. Others attended a two year post-tenth standard course at Nye Sah, near Central.[107]

There were 917 teachers in the Mon school system (including a few dozen ethnic Burmans and Karens), many of whom were members of the Mon Women's Organisation (MWO). In 1998 members of the MWO, which ran two nursery schools in Burma, had been unable to attend a Burmese Women's Forum in Chiang Mai. The following year, the MWO was the only local group not represented at a series of women's rights workshops, organised by a Thailand-based NGO in the Sangkhlaburi area. In both cases, the NMSP had been anxious not to offend the government, by sending delegates to events organised by the un-reconstructed opposition. The party leadership feared a repetition of the Mae Tha Raw Hta debacle. In response to such restrictions, in 1999 an independent Mon Women's Human Rights Group (MWHRG) was established, by ex-MSF medics and MWO members in Sangkhlaburi.

Rather than in Thailand, in the late 1990s MWO officers had begun to develop potentially fruitful contacts with Kachin and other indigenous NGOs in Burma. The MNEC and MWO cautiously expanded their programmes beyond the geographically limited NMSP-controlled ceasefire zones, and into the Mon heartland. Significantly, by 1999 the Mon

Textbook Committee was printing materials in Moulmein, rather than Bangkok.

Meanwhile, the government was extending its influence into the farthest corners of Monland. By 1999, there were several hundred government-run schools across Mon State, including fifty-four high schools, where "emphasis (was) given to inculcating students with a sense of patriotism, Union spirit and preserving national culture."[108] However, two months into the 1999–2000 academic year, enrolments in the state education system were reportedly down twelve per cent, as large numbers of Mon parents could not afford to send their children to SPDC schools.[109]

In mid-1999, Nai Shwe Kyin combined the related themes of language and religion, to win a symbolically important concession from the government. Popularly regarded among Mon communities in Burma as one of the most positive developments of the post-ceasefire era, this breakthrough had been a long time coming. Mon monks, whose predecessors had played such an important role in propagating Buddhism, would once again be allowed to take most written examinations in their own language, a privilege withdrawn by the Ne Win regime in the early 1980s. In recognition of his services to religion, in July 1999 Nai Shwe Kyin was invited to preside over the opening of a conference of the Mon *sangha* at Kyaikmaraw, the beautiful monastery near Moulmein, founded by the great Mon Queen, Shinsawbu, in the fifteenth century.

In 1999 the SPDC allowed Mon communities across lower Burma to celebrate National Day. Senior NMSP leaders played a leading role in organising the festivities, although the MNDF leadership was prevented from taking part. However, celebration of Mon National Day 2000 was again suppressed by the authorities across much of lower Burma, leading many to question whether any substantial progress had been achieved since 1995.[110] Since the ceasefire, government policy had been marked by inconsistency, sometimes restricting even the most apolitical expressions of Mon identity, while on other occasions seeming to allow a degree of politico-cultural freedom.

On 10th February 2001, National Day festivities were again held throughout the Mon lands. The NMSP held a ceremony near Central, and in each of its three remaining districts, and Mon communities in government-controlled areas organised similar events. A sprightly-looking Nai Shwe Kyin attended an indoor event in Rangoon. However, the main celebrations planned by the Rangoon Mon community were cancelled at the last moment by the authorities (who insisted that ethnic national day festivities should only be celebrated in the respective groups' home states), as was the Summer Language Training in the capital.[111] Mon National Day 2002 was celebrated in Burma under similar circumstances.

The Legacy of Nai Shwe Kyin

The NMSP President's health has been the subject of speculation for many years. In 1989 the SLORC described him as "old and feeble ... undergoing medical treatment in Bangkok."[112]

When – having not seen him for three years – the author met Nai Shwe Kyin in Moulmein, in August 1999, the veteran politician was kind enough to spend the best part of two days talking about Mon history and politics. He was suffering from liver problems, and still mourning the death, the previous week of his wife, Daw Tint, but was mentally alert, able to walk unaided, and even to prostrate himself before a visiting Mon abbot. By November 2001, Nai Shwe Kyin was noticeably more feeble, but still alert and mobile. However, he was no longer actively concerned with day-to-day party business, and generally delegated chairmanship of Central and Executive Committee meetings to his deputy, Nai Htin.

In March 2002 Nai Shwe Kyin was eighty-nine (less than three years younger than Ne Win). Following his return from forty-four years in the jungle, he chose to reside in Moulmein, where in 1999 a large compound was built for him near the university. Due to his frailty, since 1996 the party President has rarely re-visited the inaccessible NMSP ceasefire zones along the border.

Nai Shwe Kyin's obvious successor as leader of the party he founded is Nai Htin, who is nearly eighty. The NMSP Vice-President has worked his way into the senior leader's position, maintaining and developing good relations with most constituencies within the party, including the younger cadres. However, some observers doubt whether Nai Htin has the charisma and political strength to hold the party together, or to rejuvenate it in the long-term. Balancing the pro- and anti-ceasefire factions, managing tensions between the generations, and controlling multiple patronage and power networks within the party required a skilful political operator. Certainly, if men such as Nai Taw Mon, Nai Rot Sah or Nai Hongsa aspired to the top job, they would have to strike a deal with Nai Aung Naing and the MNLA. In the meantime, Nai Shwe Kyin would remain an indispensable figurehead, but the NMSP would be far from united.

Some observers accused Nai Shwe Kyin of inconsistency, or worse. He occasionally featured on state TV, and in *The New Light of Myanmar* (as well as in several exhibits at the Defence Services Museum in Rangoon) – a symbol of the ethnic rebel groups' 'return to the legal fold'.[113] Naturally, such appearances were unpopular in many quarters.

A particularly damaging indiscretion occurred on Mon National Day 1998, when Nai Shwe Kyin gave an interview to the Thai language *Bangkok Phuchatkan* newspaper. Breaking with the NMSP's previous pro-sanctions position, he called for more foreign investment in Mon State and Burma.[114] After making clear his support for the National Convention

312

(in which the Mon had not been invited to participate), the NMSP President stated that "politically speaking we have stopped fighting the government." He reportedly proposed Lee Kwan Yew's Singapore and Soeharto's Indonesia as desirable models for Burma's development, before apparently going on to accuse the KNU of oppressing the Karen people, and Daw Aung San Suu Kyi of being a CIA agent. He said that "Aung San Suu Kyi wants democracy and human rights while the Mon want national liberation and self determination." It seems that the Mon leader was making a not-very-subtle distinction between the predominantly Burman pro-democracy movement and the ethnic nationalists' autonomy-seeking agenda.

There was a predictably angry response to Nai Shwe Kyin's comments, which were soon posted on the internet. The outcry in the Mon nationalist community, and wider Burmese opposition circles, was perhaps out of proportion to the somewhat off-the-cuff nature of the interview, but illustrated the degree of frustration felt by those who regarded the ceasefire groups as profiting from the unhappy situation in Burma. On 6th March 1998, after a full day's debate at the fourth Congress of Mon National Affairs, the MUL issued a statement condemning Nai Shwe Kyin's views, and commenting on the high degree of disunity within the NMSP. If they had not done so before, from this point on, many party leader began to harbour serious doubts about the MUL's loyalty.

Following the *Phuchatkan* interview, some began to suspect that Nai Shwe Kyin's political and diplomatic skills were in decline. A few months after its publication, party General Secretary Nai Rot Sah is said to have prevented the NMSP President attending a meeting with British Embassy staff in Rangoon. Apparently, Nai Rot Sah feared that Nai Shwe Kyin might offend the British diplomats' strongly pro-Aung San Suu Kyi sentiments.

Some months later, on the third anniversary of the June 1995 ceasefire, Nai Shwe Kyin made another, somewhat less enthusiastic statement regarding the political situation in Burma (see below). Although this speech was less widely publicised than the *Phuchatkan* interview, it did go some way towards redressing the balance between co-operation with and opposition to the government.

International Contacts and Mon Unity

As noted in Part Five, when the International Committee of the Red Cross (ICRC) attempted to contact the NMSP and visit the Mon 'liberated zones' in 1999, the move was (initially) blocked by Military Intelligence agents. It is significant that this initiative had come from the ICRC, rather than the NMSP. In 1995 the NMSP had been instructed by the SLORC that any contact with third parties, including inter-government agencies and NGOs, should be made through the state. Whether due to fear or apathy, for the next four years the NMSP proved either unable or unwilling to contact international partners via Rangoon or Moulmein. This luke-warm approach to the development of contacts, which contrasted with the KIO's cultivation of foreign embassies and NGOs, was only reassessed in late 1999 (see below).

In the meantime, one relationship that the NMSP did cultivate, via membership of the MUL, was with the Unrepresented Nations and Peoples' Organisation (UNPO). A kind of 'alternative UN', which lobbied in international fora on behalf of marginalised ethnic groups, the UNPO was founded in 1991 under the patronage of the Dalai Lama. Mon, Karenni, Naga and Shan organisations from Burma were among the UNPO's more than fifty members, several of which – including the SSA – South and KNPP – sent observers to the September 1999 independence referendum in East Timor. As a result of this historic vote, a territory represented in the UNPO was, for the first time outside of the ex-Soviet bloc, set on the road to independence.

Especially after the 1997 Mae Tha Raw Hta Conference, the NMSP was wary of being too closely associated with opposition groups in Thailand and overseas. Thus the party leadership chose to be represented abroad by the MUL. The NMSP's unwillingness to upset the SPDC was to result in another potentially serious spilt within the Mon nationalist community.

All through the MAMD and other crises of the post-ceasefire era, the NMSP had retained the grudging loyalty of most Mon activists in Thailand. Although it seemed, at times, that the party's partners in the MUL might desert the mainstream nationalist camp, in the end it was the NMSP which pulled out of the Mon alliance. Matters came to a head in early 1999, following an MUL representative's participation in hearings on Burma, at the UN Commission on Human Rights (UNCHR). The hearings once again condemned the SPDC's human rights record,[115] as did those held in April 2000 and April 2001.

The NMSP Vice-President, Nai Htin, wrote to the MUL in March 1999, to withdraw the party from the league. Some observers saw this move as a direct consequence of the MUL's involvement in the UNCHR hearings. However, the decision had in fact been taken by the party's Central Committee two months earlier. The NMSP leadership had become increasingly annoyed at the MUL's propensity to issue statements vehemently criticising the SLORC-SPDC, ceasefire and – by implication – the party itself. This tendency had been particularly marked since Nai Hongsa's replacement as MUL President, in 1998.

For the NMSP, the final straw had come that October, following a meeting at Central between NMSP and MUL leaders, who agreed that the league would refrain from issuing public statements, unless its twenty-one member Central Committee agreed unanimously to do so. The NMSP had three members on this body, in effect giving the party a veto. However, on

12th October a statement was issued in support of the NLD and its struggle to convene the 1990 parliament (see below). Although the statement was attributed to a new United Mon Patriotic Forces [Overseas] (UMPF[O]) – consisting of fifteen Mon nationalist organisations from Thailand, Japan, Malaysia, Singapore, North America, Australia and Europe – the NMSP leadership was not amused, and suspected the hand of Nai Sunthorn. Membership of the MUL had become a liability, and the NMSP felt obliged to distance itself from the league, if for no other reason than to satisfy the SPDC that it was not openly consorting with the opposition.

Nevertheless, regular Congresses (or Seminars) of Mon National Affairs continued to be held in the ceasefire zones along the border. Following the Fifth NMSP Congress and subsequent February 2000 Mon National Day celebrations (see below), a fifth Seminar of Mon National Affairs was held at Baleh Donephai. Nai Hongsa acted as congress chairman, and Nai Shwe Kyin made the opening speech, which dwelt on the twin themes of Mon unity and the deed to complete a Mon State constitution.

The seminar later resolved to continue participating in the NCUB's constitution-drafting process. To this end, Nai Saik Lon presented a draft constitution of the Republic of the Union of Goldenland, which emphasised constituent states' rights to self-determination, the protection of minorities, the insidious nature and effects of 'Burmanisation', and the importance of conducting a proper census in Burma, upon which to base future constitutional arrangements.

The theme of Mon solidarity was reinforced the following year, at an International Conference of Mon National Affairs, held between 5th and 7th February 2001. The gathering, which was attended by about sixty representatives from Burma, Thailand, the US, Australia and Canada, was funded by foreign donors and organised by the MUL, which used the occasion to convene its Third Congress. The Congress elected Nai Damrong Pungbangkadee as the MUL's new Chairman, and Nai Khun Leal as Vice-Chairman; Nai Sunthorn retained his positions as General Secretary, and the MRDC's Phra Wongsa Pala[116] became MUL treasurer.[117] The league again called for tripartite solutions to Burma's myriad cultural, social, ethnic and political problems, adding that "the MUL supports the MNDF and the NMSP to speak for the Mon in such dialogue."[118]

CHAPTER TWENTY

Politics in Transition?

In the post-ceasefire era, the ex-insurgent groups found themselves in legal limbo. Although no longer at war with Rangoon, these organisations were still technically illegal. The vision of the late KIO chairman, Brang Seng, had been only partially realised. The ceasefire groups had come in from the cold, and could now envisage participation in mainstream national politics. The government seemed keen for some armed organisations to participate in the National Constitutional Convention, which was attended by a number of ex-CPB and other groups from northern Burma, but not by the KIO – which excused itself from this discredited forum – or the NMSP, which made a virtue of not being invited. At the same time as the SPDC encouraged the ceasefire groups to engage in processes controlled by the state, the military authorities were determined to suppress any independent political initiatives on the part of the erstwhile insurgents.

The NMSP's options on the eve of the millennium appeared threefold. The party could abandon 'the legal fold' and go back to war. Such a thorough-going rejection of the ceasefire process would silence those who accused the NMSP of having capitulated to Rangoon. It was eventually adopted by a significant number of Mon veterans, who had grown frustrated at the slow rate of progress in the post-ceasefire era. Such developments put the party – and the whole ceasefire process in lower Burma – under considerable strain.

In the short term, quite large numbers of new recruits (re-)joined the anti-ceasefire factions, which went back to doing what it knew best: waging guerrilla war. However, if the mainstream NMSP was to resume the armed struggle, this would almost inevitably lead to military defeat, a further deterioration of the human rights situation in Mon State, and another acute phase in the refugee crisis along the border. After nearly fifty years of civil war, Burma's insurgencies had seemingly reached a dead-end, and new strategies were required.

A second option for the NMSP was to deal directly with the government, accepting the *status quo* and striking the deals necessary to keep the party going as a viable concern. For the present at least, the NMSP would retain control of the ceasefire zones, with dispensation to carry out limited cultural, educational, organisational and business activities. In return, the party was expected to steer clear of national politics, and especially of Daw Aung San Suu Kyi and the democracy movement. To many within the NMSP and the wider nationalist community, it was debatable whether the politics of survival and piecemeal economic development – sometimes combined with individual enrichment – were legitimate strategies. Nevertheless, and despite some inconsistencies, between 1995–98 the NMSP adopted a course of non-confrontation with the regime.

In the second half of 1998 however, party policy began shifting towards a more oppositionist relationship with Rangoon. Between 1998–2001, the NMSP was in general more vocal in its discourse with the government and diplomats (such as UN Special Rapporteurs and Envoys). However, by late 2001 the party faced renewed internal crises, as elements split from the NMSP to resume the armed struggle.

The post-1998 shift in policy and rhetoric, towards a more adversarial engagement with the SPDC, illustrated the third alternative open to the NMSP. This involved working towards fundamental change in Burma, in more-or-less open alliance with the democracy movement. In theory, this had long been DAB policy. In practice however, the insurgents had often paid little more than lip service to the concept of democracy. On more than one occasion since 1995, Nai Shwe Kyin had publicly questioned the degree to which it was possible, or even desirable, to establish an effective understanding with the NLD. Others among the Mon nationalist community, and in particular the MNDF's MPs-elect, pursued relations with the democracy movement more enthusiastically.

The MNDF leaders' attempts to renew their alliance with Daw Aung San Suu Kyi and the NLD came to fruition during the tense months marking the eighth anniversary of the May 1990 election, and the tenth anniversary of the August–September 1988 democracy uprising. A new coalition began to emerge during the 1998 rainy season, around the issue of convening the 1990 parliament. As well as the MNDF and other parties elected in 1990, the fledgling NLD-led alliance apparently included four ceasefire groups, among them the NMSP. By September, it seemed that the opposition might yet achieve a breakthrough.

However, the NMSP and other parties were not prepared for the government backlash with followed the exposure of their support for the NLD. They found themselves co-opted into supporting an agenda formulated by a well-intentioned, predominantly Burman elite, without being properly consulted. As at Panglong in 1947, and more recently in relations with the Communist Party of Burma (CPB), the support of ethnic minority parties was being taken for granted. Meanwhile, the SPDC deployed a timely combination of coercion and bribery, to break up this potentially powerful threat to military rule. In the face of pressure from Military Intelligence agents, the NMSP and other groups backed-down. The MNDF was crushed and its leaders imprisoned; the NMSP escaped a similar fate only by quickly distancing itself from the NLD.

This was a classic example of 'divide and rule'. However, the events of 1998 had shown the potential for a new form of coalition politics, and a possible new relationship between the ethnic nationalists and the Burmese political class. Within a year, signs were emerging that the NMSP was no longer content to toe the SPDC line. Nai Shwe Kyin and colleagues seemed at last to be preparing to challenge the government in the political arena.

The NMSP and the Ceasefire Groups

As Burma entered the new millennium, the NMSP ceasefire was in its fifth year, the KIO ceasefire its sixth, and those of some ex-CPB groups were eleven years old. Although these agreements had led to a significant nation-wide reduction in armed conflict, and even to marginal improvements in the human rights situation in some parts of rural Burma, these were not peace settlements. The ceasefires did not grow out of, or result in, an improved understanding or appreciation – by either side – of the other's point of view.

Of course, the nature of the ceasefire groups, and their relations with Rangoon, were not uniform. While many of the ex-CPB organisations had shed most vestiges of political credibility, a number of ex-DAB member-groups still retained a fair degree of nationalist legitimacy.

It was unclear for how much longer the ceasefire arrangements would continue to hold. During their negotiation, Khin Nyunt had insisted that the SLORC could only discuss military arrangements, not politics. As a provisional, 'caretaker' government, the SLORC had no authority to grant political concessions. Ironically, having come to power by means of a bloody coup, and having subsequently denied the results of a free election, the regime was concerned to observe certain legal and constitutional distinctions.

When, in November 1997, the SLORC was replaced by the similarly-constituted SPDC, some observers thought that the ceasefire agreements might come up for review. Many doubted whether the ceasefires would out-last their architect, Khin Nyunt. Should the Military Intelligence chief loose out in his power struggle with the powerful army boss, General Maung Aye, then the ceasefires he had negotiated – which represented part of his power-base – could easily break down.

Whatever the outcome of manoeuvring within the junta, it seemed only a matter of time before the seemingly never-ending Constitutional Convention was concluded, and the government finally addressed the political role of the armed ethnic groups. At this point, the ex-insurgent groups might either be re-defined as part of the state security establishment (perhaps as local militia, or instructed to give up their arms. The latter possibility would test the ceasefires to the limit: according to most Mon sources, the MNLA would not accept disarmament.

Meanwhile, under the notorious article 17/1 of the 1908 Unlawful Associations Act, the NMSP and other ceasefire groups remained technically illegal. Nevertheless, the party's Rehmonya International Company had opened offices in Moulmein and Rangoon, where the company's golden sheldrake logo was displayed proudly on signboards outside. However, business inside was not booming.

The party made somewhat more progress in its relations with other ceasefire groups. In early 1998 Nai Shwe Kyin and Nai Rot Sah were among the guests at the well-attended fifth anniversary celebrations of the KIO-SLORC ceasefire, held in the Kachin State capital of Myitkyina. On 29th June, the third anniversary of the NMSP-SLORC ceasefire was celebrated in Moulmein. The event was attended by the new KIO Chairman, General Zau Mai, who before Brang Seng's death, in 1994, had been Kachin Independence Army (KIA) commander. In his speech to the gathering, Zaw Mai explained that the Kachin ceasefire had now entered its "third stage". An initial "confidence building stage", between 1993–95, had been followed by a second stage of partially successful, but under-funded, "development programmes." Zau Mai suggested that the NMSP was currently engaged in this difficult second stage. The KIO however, had recently entered a third stage, which involved cultivating relations with both the SPDC and representatives of other ethnic groups.[119]

From within the 'legal fold', the KIO was attempting to construct a "political agreement", between the military regime and its erstwhile battlefield opponents.[120] At the same time, the KIO continued to pursue local development programmes, including two major refugee resettlement projects along the Chinese border, and a number of deals with influential businessmen in Kachin State.

If successful, the KIO approach would constitute a highly significant breakthrough: it had been the lack of a political aspect to the ceasefire agreements, and the refusal of the government to negotiate with the ethnic groups *en masse*, that had led the KNU and others to reject the ceasefire process. If the KIO-led coalition was able to engage the SPDC on substantive issues, this might result in the first genuine dialogue between the ethnic nationalists and the government since the 1950s.

However, such a daring strategy required the utmost caution. Only if the government did not perceive the proposed alliance of ceasefire groups as a direct challenge to its rule, might dialogue materialise. The KIO plan therefore envisaged separate, parallel negotiations between the ceasefire groups and the SPDC, and between the NLD and the regime (which in some respects is what transpired – see below). Although the Kachin recognised the NLD's centrality to any future national political settlement, what Zau Mai proposed was not the old DAB-NCUB line of tripartite talks between the military, the ethnic groups and the NLD. Rather, the KIO hoped to initiate a dialogue between the government and the ceasefire groups collectively, to be followed by some kind of three-way national agreement, including the NLD.

In his speech of welcome to the 1998 Mon ceasefire celebrations, Nai Shwe Kyin adopted a similar 'softly, softly' approach. According to the NMSP President, the party had accepted the ceasefire primarily because of the need for national reconciliation. It was important that "mutual trust is established through the exchange of opinions and discussion rather than ignoring and leaving problems untouched."[121] However, Nai Shwe Kyin went on to complain that in the three years since the ceasefire, little progress had in fact been made. He ended his address by suggesting that the host of problems facing the country must be solved by negotiation. A "forgive and forget policy" was the best way for all sides to work towards democracy and development in Burma.

In reality, the NMSP faced a more limited set of options than the KIO. With fewer financial resources and a smaller army than the KIA, UWSA and other big ceasefire groups, the party naturally wielded less influence. Furthermore, the KIO (though not the UWSA) may have enjoyed a greater degree of contact with, and support from, its ethnic constituency than did the NMSP.

Nevertheless, the 1994 KIO ceasefire was by no means universally popular within the Kachin community. As were the Mon exiles, members of the Kachin diaspora in Europe and North America were often critical of KIO leaders' engagement with Rangoon. More significantly, like their counterparts in the NMSP, many rank-and-file KIO members, and villagers, were becoming increasingly dissatisfied with the ceasefire agreement, and the perceived distance of their leaders – some of whom were accused of having enriched themselves since 1994.

These concerns came to a head on 24th February 2001, when General Zau Mai was replaced as KIO Chairman by his deputy, Brig-General Lamung Tu Jai.[122] In mid-February a group of thirty-forty disgruntled KIA officers had demanded that the sixty-five year old Zau Mai resign. In response, Zau Mai announced that he would retire in June or July, due to ill health. However, this was not acceptable to the Young Turks, and on 20th February they repeated their demands at a stormy protest meeting held at KIO headquarters in Pajau, on the Chinese border. Soon after, Zau Mai agreed to step-down.

Although stories of a 'KIO coup' seem to have over-dramatised the situation, Zau Mai's departure hardly constituted a regular hand-over of power, as it was accompanied by debate so heated that KIA security forces had to be put on alert. Following his resignation, the ex-Chairman was said to be resting with his family. Meanwhile, the new leadership set about explaining their actions by reference to the need for democratic reform within the KIO. There were also suggestions that the erstwhile leadership had become too close to the SPDC, both politically and in business. However, the new KIO leadership was also rumoured to be close to influential business interests in Myitkyina and elsewhere.

This was a central dilemma of the ceasefire groups: if they did not prosper financially, they were unlikely to remain significant politically. However, given the relationship between power and money in Burma, economic progress was largely dependant on developing closer relations with the *Tatmadaw* and government – relations which could expose ethnic nationalist politicians to accusations of betrayal.

The NMSP faced similar dilemmas to the KIO regarding engagement with Rangoon, but from a less secure base. Since 1995, the party had generally failed to excite the Mon political imagination. Having 'returned to the legal fold', the NMSP no longer represented even token armed resistance to Rangoon (a role which was enthusiastically taken up by other Mon groups). The party was in danger of failing to connect with either its own people or the SPDC.

The occasional public appearance by NMSP leaders, praising the gas pipeline and other projects through faint criticism, was no doubt of some publicity value to the government, as had been the Mon refugee repatriation. Nevertheless, the NMSP's utility to the generals in Rangoon was fairly limited. Nai Shwe Kyin and other senior leaders did though, enjoy relatively warm relations with individual SPDC leaders, and in particular with Secretary One, Khin Nyunt, who sent his trusted deputy, Colonel Kyaw Thein, to the fourth anniversary ceasefire celebrations, held at the Moulmein Hotel on 29th June 1999. Also in attendance were the head of MI5 and the new *Tatmadaw* Southeast Commander, Maj-General Myint Aung (who retired on health grounds in October 2000 and was replaced by the Coastal Strategic Commander, Brig-General Sit Maung[123]). Representatives of both the intelligence wing and the regular army also sent representatives to the funeral of Nai Shwe Kyin's wife, Daw Tin, the following month.

Many within the nationalist movement, including Nai Hlaing's Mon National Defence Army (MNDA) and other restive elements in the jungle, questioned the appropriateness of such contacts. Meanwhile, the regime encouraged the ceasefire groups to concentrate on economic activities. However, the successes of the Rehmonya International and Hongsawatoi Companies were inconsistent. Attempts to make money out of sugar mills, salt production and a bus company all foundered, due to a lack of entrepreneurial experience, combined with the tough economic climate of Burma in the late 1990s.[124] However, Rehmonya International did profit from that old standby, commercial logging – and also from a fishing concession in the Andaman sea. Although this latter deal turned sour when the Mon attempted to exceed their quota, it was later resurrected, and provided some income for the party.[125]

Throughout the late 1990s, NMSP pragmatists in Moulmein and elsewhere 'inside' Burma continued to try and accommodate and engage with the regime. They were often criticised by hard-liners in the ceasefire zones along the border, who had never been reconciled to the ceasefire. A party congress, planned for late 1997, had to be abandoned, as it was felt not to be conducive to unity.

Meanwhile, the NMSP Central Executive Committee maintained a low political profile, and endeavouring to keep the government at a distance. In late 1998 Nai Soe Myint, a leading proponent of greater political and economic co-operation with the SDPC, was moved to the post of NMSP Education Minister. Hardly in line with his qualifications and experience, this transfer was designed to remove the wily ex-governor of Thaton District from the orbit of Rangoon.

The NLD, the Ceasefire Groups and the MNDF

The 1997 admission of Burma into ASEAN had underlined and reinforced the SPDC's control over the country. Large parts of rural Burma that were now under direct *Tatmadaw* subjugation had never previously been occupied by any government in Rangoon, including the British and Japanese. However, the SPDC still faced obstacles to its total domination of the country. Chief among these was the stubborn and principled opposition of Daw Aung San Suu Kyi and the NLD, whose struggle provoked widespread admiration, both at home and abroad. While the NLD party machine was all-but paralysed, its general secretary's moral authority was enhanced by her refusal to engage with the regime.

Meanwhile, whatever the outcome of the power-struggle in Rangoon, the *Tatmadaw* was not likely to disappear. In fact, it continued to expand, towards a planned troop strength of half a million men.[126] Although the NLD promised political participation and representation for all ethnic groups, any new government that might emerge would still have to deal with the army and its security-based agenda. In particular, the generally conservative regional *Tatmadaw* commanders, who had been co-opted onto the SPDC in 1997, were unlikely to take a positive view of challenges to their vested interests and local power. Political change would not necessarily translate into improvements in the troubled countryside. In fact, any political upheaval was likely to involve further violence and suffering. Ethnic support for the NLD and the democracy movement was thus tempered by the reality of a powerful military regime, that dominated national and provincial politics, ruthlessly punishing any sign of dissent.

Burma's ethnic nationalist leaders tended to adopt a long-term view, informed by the experience of decades of resistance to Rangoon. Although the urban-based democracy movement might offer the best prospect for change, the leaders of the NMSP, KIO and other ceasefire groups had to take into account the considerable risk attached to siding openly with the opposition. Any such alliance would be certain to invite the displeasure of the *Tatmadaw*. However, cultivation of too close an association with the SLORC-SPDC regime, was to risk being left high-and-dry in the event of a major sea-change in Burmese politics.

As members of the urban, predominantly Burman, political elite, NLD (and SPDC) leaders were members of a different political class to the veteran ethnic minority leaders. (Daw Aung San Suu Kyi was the daughter of the *Tatmadaw's* first Commander-in-Chief, while the NLD Chairman, U Aung Shwe, was a retired Burma Army Brigadier, who had played a key role during the 1958 ceasefire negotiations;[127] Vice-Chairman U Tin Oo was once Ne Win's defence minister.) It is therefore not surprising that differences existed between the centre and periphery, especially at the level of political culture.

To some long-term political players in the ethnic nationalist camp, it made more sense to cultivate relations with the people in power – with whom the ceasefires had been negotiated – than it did court the NLD. However, prior to the ceasefires, the NMSP, KIO and other ex-DAB members had, in principle, been fighting for democracy, and might thus be expected to share elements of a common philosophy with the NLD. However, the UWSA, and other ex-CPB groups in northern Burma, had little historical reason to forge an alliance with the democracy movement. Although many of their leaders still distrusted the Burman-dominated government, and some even remained committed to ethnic-nationalist principles, since the late 1980s, the ex-CPB groups had shed most vestiges of ideology. It seemed unlikely that they would be in the forefront of moves to challenge the political deadlock, at least while their ceasefire arrangements remained so profitable.

There was however, another ethnic constituency more amenable to the NLD's overtures. The MNDF, the Shan Nationalities League for Democracy (SNLD), and other ethnic parties whose candidates had been elected in 1990, had as much in common with the NLD as with the insurgents.

There were, of course, longstanding personal connections between individual NMSP and MNDF leaders. Nais Shwe Kyin, Tun Thein and Ngwe Thein had worked together in the MPF and other Mon insurgent organisations in the 1940s and '50s, and the urban-based (underground) and rural (insurgent) wings of the nationalist movement had maintained ties throughout the 1960s–90s. Similarly, members of the SNLD and various Shan rebel groups had worked closely together for many years.

Nevertheless, the above-ground political parties had developed under very different circumstances to the insurgent organisations. With a clear interest in focusing attention on the results of the 1990 election, and a history of party political organisation, the MNDF was a natural ally of the NLD.

Like the NLD, since 1990 the MNDF had suffered severe repression. The front had been outlawed in 1992, and all five of its MPs-elect had at one time or another been detained by the authorities. Nevertheless, the MP-elect for Kyaikmaraw, Nai Khin Maung, had played a key role during the 1994–95 ceasefire negotiations, and was an important businessman in Moulmein.

As a consequence of the somewhat more relaxed political atmosphere in Mon State following the ceasefire, between 1996–98 the MNDF gained a degree of space within which to manoeuvre. Cautiously at first, its leaders began to explore new approaches to the 'ethnic' and 'democratic' questions in Burma.

The Struggle for Ethnic Support

Despite pressure from Western governments and the UN, three years after Daw Aung San Suu Kyi's release from house arrest, the long hoped-for political breakthrough in Burma had still not materialised. Therefore, in mid-1998 the NLD adopted a new, more confrontational strategy.

In May 1998 the NLD called on the government to recognise the results of the 1990 election. In June the veteran MNDF leader and MP-elect, Nai Tun Thein, together with members of Shan, Rakhine and Chin political parties elected in 1990, wrote to the SPDC, demanding recognition of the election results and the transfer of power to the '1990 parliament'.[128] The following month, Daw Aung San Suu Kyi and the NLD began to step-up their campaign of defiance against the regime.

Three times during the 1998 rainy season, the NLD General Secretary attempted to travel outside Rangoon, to visit party cells in Bassein and elsewhere in lower Burma. On each occasion, her vehicle was stopped and prohibited from continuing further. The third such aborted trip ended with Daw Aung San Suu Kyi stranded on a bridge in the middle-of-nowhere, while Burma-watchers the world over awaited the results of this bizarre stand-off. After ten days, the small NLD party was forced to return to the capital, having effectively publicised both the lack of freedom in Burma, and the opposition's inability to carry out even the most basic activities.

Two years later, in the middle of the 2000 rainy season, Daw Aung San Suu Kyi and colleagues spent another nine days stuck on the roadside south of Rangoon, barred by the SPDC from proceeding further. A few days after that, having first returned to Rangoon, the NLD General Secretary and a small group of supporters spent several forlorn hours at Rangoon railway station, having been prevented from taking a train to upper Burma.

Following this second incident, Daw Aung San Suu Kyi was effectively placed under house again.

Meanwhile, NMSP-SPDC relations had soured further. Officers of the Burma Army Southeast Command repeated accusations that the Mon were aiding KNU remnants in the forests between Three Pagodas Pass and Ye, and as noted above, in mid-1998 a number of Mon National Schools were temporarily ordered to close. Such developments fuelled growing dissatisfaction within the nationalist community. Both Thailand-based activists and MNDF members were unhappy with Nai Shwe Kyin's apparent closeness to the SPDC. In late July 1998 three MNDF leaders, including Vice-Chairman Nai Ngwe Thein, wrote to the NMSP Central Committee, condemning the party's co-operation with the government and urging it to support the NLD.

Together with his widely-respected colleague Nai Tun Thein, Nai Ngwe Thein was regarded as Nai Shwe Kyin's most serious rival for leadership of the Mon nationalist community in Burma. (In many respects their relationship mirrored the rivalries between Nai Shwe Kyin and Nai Aung Htun, and his follower, Nai Non Lar, in the 1950–60s and '80s.) Nai Ngwe Thein had been close to Daw Aung San Suu Kyi, prior to her arrest in 1989, and hoped to re-new the NLD-United Nationalities League for Democracy (UNLD) alliance of 1988–90 (see below).

His secret letter to the NMSP Central Committee precipitated a crisis. The NMSP leadership was damned if it did, and damned if it didn't. Support for the NLD would invite the wrath of the SPDC; inaction would provoke criticism from rank-and-file party members, and the wider nationalist and opposition communities. No doubt peeved by the MNDF leaders' suggestion that the NMSP should urgently address its poor standing in the community, the party leadership decided to respond decisively.

On 18th August the Central Executive Committee issued a policy document, officially marked "for NMSP members only", but in fact intended for wider distribution. Noting that "the whole country greatly desires democratic rights", and that "all ethnic nationalities in Burma demand human rights ... and greater self-autonomy", the document went on to state that these issues had not been addressed by the ceasefire agreements. Continued unrest and nation-wide instability were therefore inevitable, unless the government recognised the results of the 1990 election, and initiated a substantial dialogue with the NLD. The NMSP called on the SPDC "to solve political problems by political means."[129]

Within a month, the statement had been posted on the internet, presumably by opposition activists. Its publication was highly significant, especially when taken together with a letter to Khin Nyunt, which had been leaked earlier, in which the party apparently objected to the regime's use of the expression 'exchanging arms for peace', in reference to the ceasefire agreement.[130] Three years after the ceasefire, the NMSP seemed at last to be taking-on the SPDC and openly backing the NLD. However, the NMSP had not been the first ceasefire group to issue such a declaration.

One week before the NMSP statement was issued, on 11th August 1998, the Karenni State Nationalities Liberation Front (KSNLF, also known as the Karenni State Nationalities People's Liberation Force), the Kayan New Land Party (KNLP) and the Shan State Nationalities Liberation Organisation (SSNLO) – all ceasefire groups – had issued a joint declaration in support of the NLD, urging the SPDC to convene the 1990 parliament. Their statement, which also called for tripartite dialogue between the ethnic groups, the NLD and the government, marked the first occasion, since the Mae Tha Raw Hta Declaration, that any ceasefire group had publicly challenged the regime.

On 15th September, a month after the first batch of statements supporting the NLD were released, the SSA – South issued its own unequivocal declaration, calling for tripartite dialogue and the transfer of power to MPs elected in 1990. Later the same week, the KNU and CNF issued similar statements. In the meantime, NLD and ethnic nationalist politicians in Rangoon had been working on a new strategy.

In early September the NLD announced that its MPs-elect would unilaterally convene the 1990 parliament. Despite the arrest that month of some nine hundred NLD members, including 200 elected lawmakers, on 16th September the NLD established a ten member Committee Representing the People's Parliament (CRPP). The following day, the CRPP declared that all laws passed by the SLORC-SPDC, since May 1990, would be considered illegal, unless endorsed by the newly-formed 'emergency parliament'. This body included MPs-elect from the MNDF, SNLD, Arakan League for Democracy (ALD) and Zomi (Chin) National Congress (ZNC). Furthermore, the 'emergency parliament' announced that it would work in close association with the NMSP and two other ceasefire groups, the Shan State Nationalities Liberation Organisation (SSNLO) and Karenni State Nationalities Liberation Front (KSNLF), which had earlier issued statements in support of the NLD and CRPP.[131]

The SPDC was furious, and the NMSP, MNDF and other parties allied with the CRPP came under immediate pressure to recant. In retaliation for the party's support for the 'emergency parliament', by the end of the month, the government had suspended most NMSP logging and fishing concessions.

By this time, Nai Ngwe Thein and all five of MNDF MPs-elect (including Chairman Nai Tun Thein, then aged eighty) had been detained, together with other Mon figures in Rangoon and Moulmein.[132] During the crackdown, Military Intelligence agents came across drafts of the MNDF letter to the NMSP, calling on the party to support the NLD. The discovery of such documents reinforced government convictions that the Mon and other ceasefire groups were not to be trusted.

Meanwhile, NMSP General Secretary Nai Rot Sah had been called to Rangoon, together with representatives of five other ceasefire groups, including the KIO and UWSA (neither of which had released pro-CRPP statements). The ceasefire groups were angrily warned of the dire consequences of supporting the NLD, and instructed to publicly distance themselves from the 'emergency parliament'. An SPDC agent was also despatched to northern Burma, to reprimand and warn the other Karenni and Shan State groups.[133] The regime's strong-arm tactics proved effective. Over the next two weeks, a series of armed groups released statements condemning the attempt to convene parliament and 'destabilise the country'.

These statements, which were almost immediately posted on the internet, were aimed as much at the international community, as they were at a domestic audience. Among those groups to support the government at this time, were the DKBA and two other ex-KNU factions, as well as a number of ex-CPB organisations, most of which were implicated in drug trafficking activities. However, the UWSA refrained from comment and, for a while, the KIO too remained neutral.

In mid-September, fifteen *Tatmadaw* officers were reportedly arrested, for having made contact with members of the opposition in Rangoon and elsewhere. Among those detained was a Navy Lt-Colonel, who was apparently picked-up after meeting with an MNDF MP-elect in Moulmein.

To drive home the anti-NLD message, from late September the state-controlled Union Solidarity Development Association (USDA) began organising a series of mass rallies in other towns and cities across Burma. Crowds of up to 30,000 people were persuaded to listen to speakers denounce the NLD and its 'foreign sponsors'.

On 28th September, following a period of sustained pressure from the SPDC, the NMSP Central Committee issued a second statement regarding the "national democratic parliament and movement." The party declared that convening parliament was the sole responsibility of the government, and criticised "violent demonstrations and illegal actions that do not benefit the whole nation". The party announced that it would continue its endeavours to develop Mon State, and "keep its promises" to the government, under the 1995 ceasefire agreement. The statement went on to add, almost as an afterthought, that the NMSP did not support the NLD.[134]

To the disappointment of most activists, the NMSP had been forced to climb down. While the earlier statement in support of the NLD had been drafted without consulting Nai Shwe Kyin, the second declaration (of 28th September) was composed as a direct result of his intervention. Senior NMSP leaders are reported to have admitted as much, during a protracted meeting with the MUL at Central, in the first week of October. Rather confusingly, the NMSP officials are said to have declared, during this meeting, that the party would continue to secretly support the NLD.

Clearly, the NMSP remained divided over both strategy and fundamental goals.

Under pressure from Rangoon, in early October the KIO Central Committee issued a statement criticising the NLD for unilaterally convening parliament and endangering the union.[135] Significantly however, both the NMSP and KIO explained their opposition to the CRPP in legalistic terms: the stipulations of the ceasefire agreements constrained them from supporting the 'emergency parliament'. The Mon and Kachin statements contained little of the virulent language characteristic of several other ceasefire groups' denunciations. Whilst the NMSP and KIO publicly distanced themselves from the NLD and CRPP, they avoided personal condemnation of Daw Aung San Suu Kyi.

On 3rd October *The New Light of Myanmar* reported that a government delegation, led by Khin Nyunt, had met with Nai Shwe Kyin, Nai Rot Sah and colleagues to discuss various "transport and development issues."[136] The NMSP was apparently to be rewarded for its renewed loyalty. The MNDF was not treated so leniently.

On 9th October 1998 the front's seventy-five year old Vice-Chairman, the veteran politician Nai Ngwe Thein, was formally charged under the 1950 Emergency Provision Act, as were two MNDF MPs-elect, the medical doctors Min Soe Lin (aged forty-one) and Kyi Win (aged forty-five). Citing Nai Ngwe Thein and colleagues' letter of July 1998, which scolded the NMSP for its cosy relations with the SPDC, the authorities accused the MNDF leaders of undermining state security.[137]

It is unfair to suggest that MNDF leaders were jailed for their criticism of the NMSP old guard. However, the fact that no NMSP members were arrested in late 1998, led to the circulation of some nasty accusations. Certainly, there was no love lost between Nai Shwe Kyin and his old rival, Nai Ngwe Thein. Within the MNDF leadership, only the eighty-one year old Nai Tun Thein was sufficiently close to the NMSP President to act as an intermediary between the two wings of the nationalist movement. However, the MNDF Chairman and MP-elect continued to be held for 'talks', as a 'guest of the government' in Rangoon, together with several hundred other members of the opposition.

A fourth MNDF MP-elect, Nai Thaung Shein, observed the direction of events, and made a dramatic flight into exile in Thailand, in December 1998. Having spent a few weeks in Chiang Mai, in early 1999 Nai Thaung Sein travelled down to Sangkhlaburi, where he held discussions with the NMSP and MUL.

Meanwhile, on 11th December 1998, Nai Ngwe Thein, Dr Min Soe Lin and Dr Kyi Win were convicted of attempting to derail the Mon ceasefire, disrupting state security and possessing correspondence and other documents linking them to opposition groups in Rangoon and overseas. During the trial, their wives were forced to testify against the MNDF leaders.[138] Each was sentenced to seven years with hard labour, in Moulmein's colonial-era jail. Thaung Shein's son was also jailed for seven years, accused of aiding his father's escape and having illegal contact with foreigners and opposition groups in Thailand.[139]

Subsequently, Nai Thaung Shein briefly entered the *sangha*, reversing the usual order of filial piety (according to which sons become monks in order to make merit for their parents), in order to make merit for his jailed son. A few months later, in June 1999, he held a series of meetings with the NCGUB 'government in exile' which, as an elected MP, he was entitled to join. Rather than doing so however, in mid-1999 Nai Thaung Shein established the Overseas Mon National Democratic Front (OMNDF, or Mon National Democratic Front [Liberated Area]), to represent the MNDF cause in exile. At around the same time, the Mon lexicographer, Nai Tun Way, helped to found a branch of the OMNDF in Australia. In January 2001 another branch was established among Mon workers in Malaysia.

Nai Khin Maung was the only MNDF MP-elect not to be persecuted in late 1998. He had kept his head down throughout the year, and furthermore enjoyed warmer relations with Khin Nyunt's Military Intelligence circle than the other MNDF leaders. Other than for electoral purposes, he was not particularly close to the more politically adventurous Nai Ngwe Thein, but was loosely allied with Nai Soe Myint, and the pro-business, pro-ceasefire wing of the NMSP.

By the end of 1998, with most of its leaders in detention and its network inside Burma in disarray, the MNDF was virtually moribund. In January and February the following year, the SPDC kept up the pressure on those who had dared to oppose it, by convicting several hundred of the democracy activists arrested in 1998, including a number of MPs-elect. The MNDF suffered a further blow on 2nd July 1999, with the death of Central Committee member Nai Bala, who had contracted TB whilst serving a twenty-five year jail term (during which he had reportedly been severely tortured).

Another consequence of this renewed repression in Burma was that Nai Tun Thein was unable to publish his recently-completed, Burmese language *Mon Political History*. Fortunately, MUL General Secretary Nai Sunthorn, himself an accomplished author, was able to arrange for publication of this important essay in Thailand. A detailed and balanced account of the Mon nationalist movement between 1945–62, written by one of the key players, Nai Tun Thein's book made a major contribution to Mon and Burmese political studies.[140]

Dictatorship, Dialogue and Development

On 27th March 1999 (Armed Forces Day in Burma), the SPDC top brass were preoccupied by elaborate ceremonies in celebration of a substantial renovation of the Shwedagon Pagoda, the first major repairs to the venerable structure since 1970.[141] To much fanfare and extensive coverage in the state media, a sacred and richly-decorated umbrella (*htidaw*) was hoisted atop the pagoda.

The specially-invited audience included a number of opposition politicians, some of whom had been released for the occasion from government 'guest houses'. However, neither the top NLD leaders, nor the NMSP, were not present. Five days later, part of the Shwedagon was damaged in a suspected arson attack – a bad omen for the state sponsors of the restoration, who had intended their patronage to generate significant stores of merit, and thus reinforce perceptions of their legitimacy.

In general however, throughout 1999–2001, events went the regime's way. The SPDC continued to deploy a security-based strategy, reliant on heavy-handed political repression. The *Tatmadaw*, which for fifty years had fought to preserve the unity of the state, was determined not yield an inch to the demands of what was presented, in the government-controlled media, as a foreign-backed conspiracy, bent on subverting the Union. The SPDC and NLD had become so estranged, that it was difficult to see from which direction change might emerge. Locked into a cycle of mutual antagonism and recrimination, neither side seemed prepared to make concessions.

Although the party machine had been largely dismantled, NLD leaders in Rangoon continued to regularly criticise the regime, although some league members would have preferred a less confrontational approach. Between March–May 1999, a group of about twenty NLD MPs-elect distanced themselves from this hard-line strategy, calling for accommodation with the SPDC, and an end to the cycle of defiance and repression. Daw Aung San Suu Kyi expelled several of the rebels from the NLD, vowing to maintain her principled and uncompromising stance.

Despite NLD leaders' bold statements, the occasional student demonstration, and sporadic outbursts of sometimes racial or religiously-inspired unrest in the provinces (including a particularly virulent spate of anti-Muslim violence in July–November 2001), the government did not seem to be in imminent danger of collapse. Although the international Burma campaign promoted protests marking the numerologically and historically resonant date of 9th September 1999, the anticipated uprising failed to materialise, which served further to reinforce perceptions of the regime's total control.

Meanwhile, the SPDC, and in particular the Khin Nyunt faction, continued to bolster its support, by co-opting ethnic minority leaders into the government camp. In November 1999 Foreign Minister U Win Aung told *Time* magazine that "the programme of democracy will be secondary" to that of national security. Only when the ethnic groups' quiescence could be guaranteed would the SPDC be willing to countenance political reform.[142]

History was repeating itself. As minority leaders had been persuaded to accept the reality of General Aung San's soon-to-be independent Burma, at Panglong in February 1947, so the SPDC sought to cajole ethnic nationalist leaders into supporting its version of the military-dominated union. Although the government offered little in the way of political progress, in the short-term at least, it was a more powerful patron than the opposition. The regime sought to buy the armed ethnic groups' loyalty, by means of various 'development' programmes and economic concessions, which often amounted to little more than licenses to extract natural resources. As well as the negative long-term environmental and economic consequences of such short-term policies, the government was storing up political trouble for the future.

Although the state-sponsored construction of roads and bridges in rural areas was regarded by some as a positive development, critics accused the NMSP and other ceasefire groups of looking for a short-cut to development, and pointed to the danger of playing Rangoon's game. Although, since 1996, the widely-perceived need for Mon unity had prevented the emergence of another outright split within the NMSP, in 1999 differences between pro-business pragmatists 'inside' Burma, and the anti-government faction along the border, became increasingly serious. At the same time, and notwithstanding the party's achievements in the field of education, the Mon community in Burma and overseas was finding the NMSP increasingly less relevant to its concerns.

The party leadership's failure to develop contacts with the international community was regarded by many as reflecting a lack of political vision, or courage. Nai Shwe Kyin went some way towards addressing this concern, when on 25th October 1999 he met with the UN Secretary General's Special Envoy to Burma, Alvaro de Soto. They met at a government-convened meeting in Rangoon, together with other ethnic minority leaders, including Nai Tun Thein, who had recently been released from his sojourn in a state 'guest house'. Nai Shwe Kyin spoke on behalf of both the NMSP and KIO, indicating the Mon and Kachin nationalists' continued commitment to some form of joint representation, as well as the degree of respect in which he personally was held. Sources indicate that Nai Shwe Kyin acquitted himself with distinction, asking the UN envoy to press the government for the release of political prisoners, and for tripartite talks to be held at the earliest opportunity. This was a far cry from some of his previous comments on the NLD. Whether it represented a shift in NMSP policy – and a reassertion of Nai Shwe Kyin's support for the democracy movement – or merely highlighted the ageing Mon leader's lack of consistency, was a moot point.

Khin Nyunt apparently tended towards the latter interpretation, regarding Nai Shwe Kyin's comments as an example of the NMSP's inability to hold a consistent political line. Once again however, the MNDF was treated more harshly. On 3rd November 1999, a week after meeting with de Soto, Nai Tun Thein was re-arrested, together with a Chin leader who had also attended talks.

A few weeks later, between 14th November and 2nd December, the NMSP held its much-delayed Fifth Congress, near Central. This was the first such gathering since early 1996. In a development that reinforced the tenor of Nai Shwe Kyin's recent comments, rank-and-file delegates voted for an overhaul of the Central Committee, instructing it to adopt a more critical policy towards the SPDC. Nai Soe Myint, who the previous year had been transferred to the semi-inactive post of Education Minister, was voted off the Central Committee, as were Nai Chan Toih and other pro-ceasefire cadres. The ex-Tavoy District Governor, Nai Myin Htut, who was regarded as a calm and clear thinker, and was popular with the troops, joined the seven man Central Executive Committee. Progressive NMSP members were disappointed by the failure of any women to be elected to the Central Committee, although the MWO General Secretary came close.

For better or for worse, the NMSP would enter the new millennium with a mandate to push the government on a number of issues, and perhaps re-gain some of political momentum lost in recent years. The new direction of NMSP policy was made clear the following February, on the 53rd anniversary of Mon National Day, when Nai Rot Sah made a robust speech calling for tripartite dialogue to solve Burma's social and political problems.[143]

Twice that month, the NLD spelled-out its position regarding the ethnic nationalists. In a video address released on 2nd February 2000, Daw Aung San Suu Kyi noted that a "ceasefire is not peace. Unless there's a settlement of peace made through political means, there will always be a danger that violence will break out again."[144] Ten days later, in a speech commemorating Union Day (12th February, the 53rd anniversary of the Panglong Agreement), U Lwin, an NLD Central Executive Committee member, stated that:

> in our democratic struggle, the slogan we have been using until now is democracy is priority, and after democracy, we can address the requirements of states and divisions. We believe that after we achieve democracy we will be able to discuss our needs among ourselves. As a person, an ethnic Mon, and a patriotic revolutionary, I absolutely believe this slogan.[145]

Unlike the government, which proposed dealing with the 'ethnic question' – however inadequately – before addressing issues of political reform, the NLD would concentrate on national politics first, and ethnic issues later. Such priorities were hardly likely to encourage the ceasefire groups.

However, other national politicians were prepared to go further in their advocacy of ethnic rights. One such was the Arakanese, U Aye Tha Aung of the ALD, who was secretary of the CRPP and chairman of its Committee for Ethnic Nationalities Affairs. The regime considered U Aye Tha Aung too dangerous to remain at liberty. The SPDC justified his arrest, on 24th April 2000, by reference to U Aye Tha Aung's supposed links to "outlawed armed groups operating along the Thai-Myanmar border."[146] Two months later, he was sentenced to twenty-one years in jail.

U Aye Tha Aung had been a key player in the United Nationalities League for Democracy (UNLD), established in 1989 to fight the 1990 general election as a broad pan-ethnic front. Together with Nai Ngwe Thein and others, he had worked on building bridges between the NLD and ethnic minority parties. His arrest coincided with publication of a statement announcing the formation of a United Nationalities League for Democracy [Liberated Area] (UNLD [LA]), on the Thailand-Burma border.[147]

The UNLD [LA] was derived from the original UNLD alliance, which had stood for "a genuine union based on equality and the full right to self-determination and to ensure that the struggle for the right of self-determination should be integrated with the struggle for democracy (which) must be based on equality among the ethnic peoples including Burmans." As these aspirations had been thwarted by the government, the UNLD [LA] was preparing to go on the political offensive. Although, to some observers, the new league was merely another exile group, waging a probably hopeless campaign against Rangoon, the UNLD [LA] counted a number of credible ethnic nationalist leaders among its sponsors. These included the Shan nationalist and scholar, Dr Chao-Tzang Yawnghwe, the Chin, Dr Lian Satchong, the well-known Kachin, Maran La Raw, and the Mons, Nai Thaung Shein, Nai Tun Way and Nai Pe Thein Za (who was NMSP Deputy Foreign Minister, prior to the ceasefire).

At a meeting held on the border between 16th and 19th January 2001, the UNLD [LA] selected the Shan MP-elect, Khun Markoban, as its honorary Chairman. In a seminar on 30th August 2001 the UNLD [LA] joined eight remaining ethnic insurgent groups and ceasefire groups in forming the Ethnic Nationalities Solidarity and Co-operation Committee (ENSCC), chaired by the new KNU President, Saw Ba Thin.[148]

The UNLD [LA] also maintained contacts with the UNLD 'inside' Burma, and thus shared in its legitimacy, derived from the election of sixty-five candidates in May 1990. Like most border-based opposition groups, the UNLD [LA] and ENSCC called for tripartite dialogue and a new 'Panglong Initiative'. Interestingly, they proposed working with the ceasefire groups, as well as the NDF alliance.[149] Certainly, if they were to be more than just talking shops, the two alliances would have to reach out beyond the limited constituency of border politics.

Meanwhile in Rangoon, the year 2001 seemed to present new opportunities for political progress. In late January, news emerged that Daw Aung San Suu Kyi had been engaged in secret talks with Khin Nyunt, and his assistant Kyaw Win, since the previous October. The talks had apparently been facilitated by the new UN Special Envoy to Burma, the

Malaysian diplomat, Razali Ismail, who announced their existence to the world. Although few details of the negotiations were released, it seemed that a combination of international pressure and domestic stagnation had led the SPDC to resume tentative negotiations with NLD.

In an interesting secondary development, on 27th January a KIO spokesman went on record, in an interview with the DVB opposition radio station, welcoming the re-newel of dialogue between the government and NLD. He hoped that the ceasefire groups would soon be involved in the discussions, which might develop into substantive talks. The DVB reported that the NMSP also supported the talks, but was wary of issuing a public statement to this effect.[150]

Once again, developments in Rangoon appeared to be setting the ethnic nationalist agenda. A visiting EU delegation to Burma declared that the dialogue process offered the best prospect for change since 1990. While this may have been the case, they also represented a potential threat to the ethnic nationalists. While the Burman-urban political class remained divided between pro- and anti-democracy camps, the minorities remained of some use as allies to both the government and opposition, and might negotiate from positions of relative strength. However, ethnic nationalist politicians remembered previous instances of Burman duplicity, and feared the consequences of any deal struck in Rangoon, without their participation. The issue was finely balanced. Most ethnic nationalists were convinced of Daw Aung San Suu Kyi's personal integrity, and reassured by assurances that she would not betray the NLD-UNLD alliance. However, if the SPDC and NLD were to agree a common position, without consulting the minority groups, then the latter might again find themselves marginalised and overlooked as decisions regarding Burma's future were made in the capital.

Such considerations informed the decision by six ceasefire groups to send a letter to Khin Nyunt on 1st March 2001, calling for wider participation in the talks, and drawing attention to the ethnic dimension of the political crisis. This move was initiated by the NMSP; the KIO leadership was still recovering and re-organising following the previous month's 'coup'.[151]

The NMSP's Nai Rot Sah, together with leaders of the other six groups – all of which had initially backed the formation of the CRPP in 1998 – were summoned to a televised meeting with Khin Nyunt in Rangoon. As in September 1998, they were warned not to destabilise the political situation. Secretary One told the ethnic nationalists that talks with Aung San Suu Kyi would only make substantial progress if confrontation was avoided. If the ethnic minorities wanted to make their views know, they could talk *individually* (but not as a bloc) to Khin Nyunt and the Office of Strategic Studies (OSS). The negotiations in Rangoon were to remain a bilateral process, for the present at least. Khin Nyunt repeated this message on a visit to Kachin State in early April, where he met with the new KIO Chairman, Lamung Tu Jai.[152]

Meanwhile, Senior General Than Shwe had used the occasion of his keynote speech on Armed Forces Day (27th March) to raise the prospect of political transition.[153] In early April, the new UN Human Rights Rapporteur on Burma, Paulo Sergio Pinheiro, was finally allowed to visit the country. In May, UN Envoy Razali Ismail visited Thailand, where he held talks with the government, and members of his staff met with opposition groups based in the kingdom. Razali stressed the need for a tripartite element to the Rangoon talks, incorporating the views of ethnic groups – a position which generated a degree of trust among the ethnic nationalists.[154]

However, by the time Razali returned to Burma again, in early June, the political atmosphere was less optimistic. Although the NLD had been allowed re-open some offices, several NLD and UNLD (but no MNDF) political prisoners had been released, and the government-controlled media had reigned-in its personal denigration of Daw Aung San Suu Kyi, the contents of the talks were still being kept under wraps, and informed opinion had it that the negotiations were making little progress. Many observers suspected that the SPDC was merely playing for time, while hoping to improve its international standing.

The political situation in early-mid 2001 must be considered in the context of covert manoeuvring within the *Tatmadaw* leadership to, succeed the ailing General Than Shwe, and also in light of developments along the Thailand-Burma border. The election of the multi-millionaire businessman, Thaksin Shinawatra, as Thai Prime Minister in January 2001, and his appointment of Chavolit Yongchaiyud as Minister of Defence, led some to predict that Thailand's Burma policy might revert to the cosy 'golf course diplomacy' of the 1990s. However, the first half of 2001 actually marked a serious deterioration in relations between the two countries.

In February 2001, fighting in Shan State between the *Tatmadaw* and SSA – South spilled over into Thailand, when the Burma Army occupied a position just inside Chiang Rai Province, in order to attack the Shan rebels. Subsequent shelling of Tachilek and Mae Sai caused the death of at least two Thai civilians, leading some observers to predict the immanent outbreak of hostilities between the two ASEAN neighbours.[155] Burma-watchers even detected a reactivation of the old Thai security policy, of using border-based insurgents as a buffer against the 'traditional' Burmese enemy. According to well-informed sources, the SSA – South's efforts to destroy drugs factories and disrupt trafficking routes inside Burma were being supported with Thai military intelligence and munitions. Units of the KNU also began to receive military supplies from Thailand during this time – again apparently in a bid by Thai security agencies to curb the flow of drugs across the border.

With further fighting along the border between the *Tatmadaw* and SSA – South (and the KNU) in April and May, Thai-Burmese relations suffered further set-backs. *The New Light of Myanmar* criticised the Thai Third Army (and its US military advisors) for supporting the SSA – South, demanded that Thai forces withdraw from disputed territory along the border (much of which had previously been controlled by the insurgents), lambasted the Thai government's 'hypocritical' attitude towards drugs, and promoted the notion that Burma's history is more glorious than Thailand's.

By the next time Razali Ismail visited Burma, in late August 2001, the Thaksin regime had succeeded in calming relations with the SPDC, on the surface at least. Razali again met with the SPDC and NLD, as well as with local and foreign businessmen, diplomats, and Mon, Karen, Chin, Shan and Rakhine representatives.

When he visited Burma for the sixth time, in late November, he was said to be "'optimistic' that the talks would lead to national reconciliation." However, ethnic minority politicians remained concerned that the UN Special Envoy had been unable to facilitate their participation in the dialogue process. Khun Tun Oo of the SNLD told a press conference that Razali had promised to try and speed the process up: "He meant that bipartite talks (between the military junta and NLD) will grow into tripartite talks with the inclusion of ethnic groups, and he asked us if we were prepared for it, if we have reached a common ground for it. We told him we must be allowed to meet freely without any discrimination, pressure and restriction. Only then will we reach common ground."[156] Meanwhile, MNDF Chairman Nai Tun Thein asked Razali to put pressure on the SPDC to free more political prisoners, including "ethnic politicians", and to allow "major ethnic political parties to function freely."[157]

The move towards a united front by Burma's ethnic nationalists was reinforced by a joint declaration, issued by seven ceasefire groups, including the NMSP and – for the first time – the KIO, on Union Day (12th February) 2002, the 55th anniversary of the Panglong Agreement. The statement called for solidarity, equality and democracy in Burma. However, by this time, demands within the Mon nationalist movement for real political progress had reached an acute stage. As the 2001 rainy season drew to a close, new fissures emerged within the NMSP, which put the ceasefire under unprecedented strains.

Mon Nationalism at the Crossroads

By the second half of 2001, Nai Hlaing's MNDA had grown in strength to well over one hundred men, most of whom were experienced MNLA veterans. The NMSP might refer to it as just another 'Mon Armed Group' but, with KNU support, the MNDA was challenging the authority of the party – and the SPDC – across swathes of Ye and Yebyu Townships. This activity of course, invited reprisals from the *Tatmadaw*.

Like some of their 'counterparts' in the NMSP and MNLA, some elements within the Burma Army Southeast Command were quite satisfied with these developments. Since the ceasefire, the *Tatmadaw* had seen its influence in Mon State curtailed by Khin Nyunt's Military Intelligence-OSS network (members of which had negotiated the agreement). Like many (ex-)insurgent groups, the *Tatmadaw* found it easier to deal with the certainties of wartime, than the vagaries of (relative) peace. A return to armed conflict would empower 'hard-line' officers on all sides.

The security situation in the Mon heartland deteriorated further on 9th September 2001, when a veteran NMSP Central Committee member, Colonel Nai Pan Nyunt, split from the party, taking 150 troops with him. Previously an MNLA Special Battalion commander, Nai Pan Nyunt had been appointed MNLA Southern Strategic Commander, after the death of Nai Win Aung. Thus, the majority of Nai Hlaing's troops had at some time been under his command, and it was only a matter of time before Nai Pan Nyunt made common cause with the MNDA. Throughout September–November, Nai Pan Nyunt's group maintained positions in the northern part of Ye Township, on the edge of the 'ceasefire zones', harassing the *Tatmadaw*, while negotiating with the NMSP, Nai Hlaing and the KNU (KNLA Sixth Brigade).

Meanwhile, both anti-ceasefire factions grew in strength, to the alarm of the weakened NMSP-MNLA leadership. Now that the war in Monland had seemingly recommenced, new recruits began to arrive in the jungle, and old veterans returned to arms, as disbanded Mon soldiers working in Thailand started to slip back across the border, to re-join their old comrades in the armed struggle.

On 14th September Nai Pan Nyunt issued a public letter to senior Mon monks, in which he claimed to lead one hundred and fifty-three soldiers, and outlined his reasons for breaking the ceasefire. Written in Mon, in an educated and articulate style, Nai Pan Nyunt's letter claimed that his primary reason for defecting from the party was its leaders' inability to prevent the confiscation of Mon lands. (In particular, he was incensed by the Burma Army Southeast Command's moves to confiscate land and restrict NMSP activity in villages previously under his control. Furthermore, Nai Pan Nyunt accused the MNLA leadership of oppressing Mon villagers and regular soldiers alike, and of allowing the *Tatmadaw* to deploy large numbers of troops close to 'ceasefire front line'.[158]

On 31st October the NMSP issued counter-accusations, claiming that Nai Pan Nyunt had sold weapons to unspecified third parties, and had misused party funds. The NMSP stated that it would welcome Nai Pan Nyunt's return to the NMSP fold, and extended a deadline for him to do so, until the end of 2001. In the meantime, members of his group were instructed not to enter NMSP-controlled territory, or "interrupt the administration of NMSP."[159] Nevertheless, troops on both (not always clearly-defined) sides reportedly clashed in the Ye and other areas during November.[160]

Thus far, in most respects, the mechanics of the split had reflected those of previous schisms within the NMSP. However, in the past, the parties could have agreed to disagree, and gone on to operate in different areas, and hope to eventually re-unite. The fact of the ceasefire though, made the situation far more grave. The emergence of another anti-ceasefire faction, so close to 'Central', threatened the basis of the NMSP's truce with the SPDC. If the situation escalated, more units might defect from the MNLA, and the NMSP could come under pressure to allow the *Tatmadaw* access to the 'permanent ceasefire zones', in order to pursue the rebels. In this case, chaos could ensue, and party leaders might be forced to flee to Thailand, or Ye – and beyond. Alternatively, the party might be forced by events to return to the armed struggle, despite its policy of maintaining the ceasefire. In this scenario, Nai Shwe Kyin and others would presumably be stranded in Moulmein, while the rump MNLA would take to the jungle. Of course, many party activists, including several Central Committee members, were not unhappy to see this situation develop. They sensed opportunities for the NMSP to throw-off the much-resented ceasefire agreement, and return to a policy of outright, armed opposition to the SPDC.

While Nai Pan Nyunt's main operations base remained some distance from the border, the Thai military had less influence over his group than they did over the mainstream NMSP. The same was true also for Mon nationalist groups in Sangkhlaburi and Bangkok, some members of which strongly supported Nai Pan Nyunt's actions. On 24th November the MUL Central Executive Committee, meeting in Sangkhlaburi, issued a statement calling on the two Mon factions not to "waste money and blood from our people between each Mon armed group." The MUL also offered to mediate between the two sides.[161]

In response to the party leadership's accusations of corruption, Nai Pan Nyunt is reported to have admitted collecting about two million Kyat from areas under his control, as instructed by the NMSP (but outlawed under the 1995 ceasefire agreement). Rather than remitting the money to 'Central', he claimed to have spent it locally, on his troops and villagers' welfare.

By the end of November, Nai Rot Sah and Nai Hongsa (and members of the *sangha*) had had several meetings with Nai Pan Nyunt, but been unable to persuade him to return to the party. However, they had worked-out a short-lived 'gentleman's agreement', whereby Nai Pan Nyunt's men would not intrude into the NMSP's ceasefire zones. Like Nai Hlaing's MNDA, the new faction would operate out of areas patrolled by the KNLA. It is therefore not surprising that local Karen commanders decided not to follow instructions, apparently issued by Sixth Brigade headquarters, which had been persuaded by the NMSP not to co-operate with Nai Pan Nyunt or the MNDA, at least until the current situation resolved itself.

On 29th November 2001[162] Nai Pan Nyunt's faction united with the MNDA, to form a new Hongsawatoi Restoration Party (HRP) – with a nineteen man Central Committee – and associated Monland Restoration Army (MRA), fielding about 300 troops.[163] The new force began collecting 'taxes' on the road and in villages near Three Pagodas Pass,[164] and was soon recruiting in the area, laying landmines (as was the MNLA) and threatening uncooperative villages. The MRA reportedly ambushed and killed a *Tatmadaw* colonel; inevitably, the *Tatmadaw* responded by stepping-up its operations against the Mon rebels and their Karen allies. The Independent Mon News Agency reports that on 16th November the SPDC declared 'martial law' in sectors east of the Moulmein-Tavoy motor road. Villagers were reportedly ordered not to visit plantations or farms in the area.[165]

Having earlier rounded-up porters from local villages,[166] and Moulmein jail (many of whom later absconded), on 21st November 2001 the Burma Army 62nd Battalion (together with the 106th) launched one of its occasional attacks on Htee Wah Doh-Halochanee. This was the same *Tatmadaw* formation that had burnt down a section of Halochanee in July 1994. Its latest action was aimed at flushing-out KNLA and MRA forces operating with increasing frequency in the vicinity of the Karen IDP settlement at Htee Wah Doh. It constituted another serious escalation of hostilities, on the very edge of the Mon ceasefire zone.[167]

The stakes were raised further the following month, when a two hundred man *Tatmadaw* column pursued Nai Pan Nyunt's men into the Baleh Donephai and Chei Deik permanent ceasefire zones, behind Halochanee. The invaders did not withdraw for several days, by which time the NMSP leaders at 'Central' were said to be both anxious and furious.

Meanwhile, as a result of the attack on Halochanee, about one thousand Karen fled to Halochanee (and local Thai Karen villages), where the Mon authorities and the NGOs did their best to accommodate the new arrivals. A week later, on 27th November, the 62nd Battalion returned to Htee Wah Doh and burnt down sections of the village. *Tatmadaw* officers warned that they would not tolerate any further settlement at Htee Wah Doh, which left the Karen IDPs little choice but to gather and remain in Halochanee. Meanwhile, the NMSP and MRDC had received assurances from the *Tatmadaw* and SPDC at Three Pagodas Pass that, although Htee Wah Doh was now 'out of bounds' – and could no longer be considered part of the ceasefire zone – the newly arrived Karen refugees could stay for the time being at Baleh Donephai (the westernmost section of Halochanee). The NGOs and MRDC felt the most appropriate response was to allow them into Don Yang Karen refugee camp, just across the border in Thailand. However, as the Ninth Division refused to allow them entry into the kingdom, many of the beleagured Htee Wah Doh folk began to move north and east, into KNLA Sixth Brigade (as did a number of families associated with the HRP).

Meanwhile, Nai Pan Nyunt was to be seen in the vicinity of Sangkhlaburi, deep in negotiations with the MUL and NMSP (and Thai authorities). Having been expelled by the MNLA from the main NMSP-controlled 'ceasefire zones', and then chased out of adjacent territory by the *Tatmadaw*, many of his men found themselves trapped on the border, lying-low in friendly villages. Others continued to operate further inside Burma, with the bulk of the MRA force, which had grown to about seven hundred men (half of them armed), plus dependents. With several MNLA-MRA (and *Tatmadaw*-MRA) clashes reported between January-March 2002, the future of the Mon ceasefire remained highly precarious.

◄◄►►

A number of issues were raised in Part One, regarding the nature of the Mon nationalist movement and other parties to the civil war in Burma. Is the diverse and sometimes poorly-articulated ethnic nationalist agenda a reasonable response to the current situation in Burma? Representing a constituency of perhaps one-and-a-half million people, most of whom live close to the political and economic centre, do Mon leaders have any choice but to envisage a future within the (federal?) union? If not by outright secession, how best might progress be achieved – through co-operation with the military government, or with the opposition, or via a combination of approaches?

Any conclusions are likely to depend upon where one stands on the big issues of Burmese politics. Questions of strategy are perhaps best approached through an examination of the nationalists' key aims, which returns us to the first question. The Mon nationalist community is not homogenous: different sectors have pursued sometimes divergent goals. Furthermore, Mon nationalism is in transition; debate is rigorous and sometimes involves criticism of the errors of the past.

Key to the on-going realignment of Mon and Burmese politics, is the fundamental issue of whether ethnic rights and self-determination are equivalent to human rights and democracy. If so, then whatever the frustrations and dangers along the way, alliance with the NLD would seem to offer the NMSP and MNDF a better chance of progress, than accommodation with Burma's deeply-tarnished military rulers.

In a state as bitterly divided as Burma, community leaders and politicians are presented with a stark choice: whether to support the *status quo*, or make a stand for change. Pursuit of the latter is a high risk strategy, but might answer those who question the contemporary relevance of the NMSP and other ethnic nationalist organisations. Alliance with the forces of progress might also encourage the ageing NMSP leadership to adopt more democratic decision-making processes.

Although the party has never controlled more than a fraction of the Mon people's ancestral lands, before 1995 it did represent an alternative centre of power to Rangoon. However, since the ceasefire, the NMSP has struggled to maintain its legitimacy. This issue is related to the preservation and consolidation of Mon ethnic identity in the twenty-first century. Hard-won recent progress in the fields of education and community development bode well for the future. Regardless of the fate of particular organisations, many thousands of individuals remain committed to interrelated versions of the Mon cause, and even larger numbers identify with the Mon language, culture, religion and historical legacy. Whether they continue to identify with the NMSP or MNDF will depend on how these parties meet the challenges before them.

Are armed ethnic groups in contemporary Burma an anachronism? In the long decades following independence and the outbreak of civil war, insurgency became an institutionalised, self-perpetuating phenomena. As government and rebel leaderships ossified in the 1960s and '70s, the revolution became a way of life for many, and the idealism and commitment of the early years often succumbed to incipient 'warlordism'.[168] Power, patronage, prestige and loyalty came to be based on individuals, rather than institutions, with an often minimal distinction between public and private assets. Although many leaders and organisations continued to struggle for national liberation, the 'liberated zones' came to resemble tributary mini-states, based on the control of human and natural resources.

Age-old networks of power underlie the dynamics of modern Burma. Rooted in the precolonial past, these patterns of kinship – and kingship – derive from Buddhist (and ultimately Hindu-Brahmin) paradigms.[169]

Michael Gravers observes that "it is of crucial importance to the (government) to be able to balance the patron-client system and the open economy. This intricate balance may determine the fate of the regime."[170] Michael Aung-Thwin notes that:

> the contest in Burma today is, first, primarily an elite struggle for the 'throne' (i.e. power) in which both sides have harnessed the masses for support. It closely resembles traditional patterns in Burmese history, where 'rebellions' were conflicts between elites ... fighting for the crown ... the contest is a personal, elitist struggle for power that has been shaped both by the continuity of traditional structures and the introduction of modern ideologies.[171]

Political culture shapes – but does not determine – many aspects of modern Burmese politics. Historical symbols of power are manipulated to modern political ends, while traditional concepts influence the parameters of contemporary practice.

It is a bitter irony of the civil war in Burma – and of armed liberation struggles the world over – that groups seeking to free their people from injustice and oppression have, in many cases, come to rely on authoritarian methods. Democracy as a process has often been viewed as an expendable luxury. However, since 1988, a new generation has emerged in Burma, to join the struggle for ethnic rights with that for justice and democracy in the golden land.

Notes

Prelims – Tables

1 This table excludes a number of small local militia, many of which are breakaway factions of larger armed groups, and whose status is often unclear.
2 "A handful of other small, armed groups also exist in name. Most are affiliated to the Democratic Alliance of Burma; only the Burman majority All Burma Students Democratic Front has any real organisation inside Burma": Martin Smith, *Burma: Insurgency and the Politics of Ethnicity* (Zed Books 1999; second edition), Chart Three.
3 US Dollar-Thai Baht conversion rates remained steady at 25:1, until the onset of the 1997 financial crisis, since when the rate has averaged about 44:1.
4 Occasionally between 1984, when the Mon National Relief Committee (MNRC) was established, and 1990, when the Burmese Border Consortium (BBC) assumed responsibility for the bulk of Mon food supplies, the Mon refugees were assisted by the Catholic Office for Emergency Refugee Relief (COERR); see Part Four.

Part One – The Mon in Burma (and Thailand)

1 Emmanuel Guillon, *The Mons: A Civilisation in Southeast Asia* (The Siam Society 1999), p. XI.
2 Arend Lijphart proposes that 'consociational democracy' may help to achieve political stability in plural societies like Burma (characterised by cleavages along religious, ethnic, ideological or regional lines). The main elements of 'consociational democracy' are rule by 'grand coalition', the provision of minority vetoes, proportional representation in government and civil service, and segmental autonomy, or federalism. A key characteristic in Lijphart's scheme is the co-operation of segmental elites: Arend Lijphart, *Democracy in Plural Societies: A Comparative Exploration* (Yale University Press 1977).
3 Anthony D. Smith highlights the important role played by religion, and in particular of priesthoods, in maintaining ethnic identity among dispossessed and minority peoples (the Mon *ethnie* may be characterised as vertical-lateral, rather than dynastic): Anthony D. Smith, *The Ethnic Origin of Nations* (Blackwell 1988), p. 109 & 119.

4 Rather unkindly, Benedict Anderson observes that "it is always the ruling classes ... that long mourn the empires": Benedict Anderson, *Imagined Communities: Reflections on the Origin and Spread of Nationalism* (Verso 1991; revised edition), p. 111.

5 E.J Hobsbawm, *Nations and Nationalism Since 1780: Programme, Myth, Reality* (Cambridge University Press 1990; second edition), p. 78.

6 The civil war in Burma has given rise to a somewhat artificial distinction between the 'liberated zones' in the border areas and government-controlled territory further 'inside' Burma, where the bulk of the population lives.

7 Mikael Gravers warns against the essentialist fallacy: "nationalism cannot be analysed *per se*", but only described in its specific historical manifestations: Mikael Gravers, *Nationalism as Political Paranoia in Burma: An Essay on the Historical Practice of Power* (Curzon 1999), p. 112.

8 C.F. Keyes notes that "in ancient times, the region (of mainland Southeast Asia) was known as 'the golden country' (the Indian *Suvannaphumi*) ... or the 'golden chersonese'." These Indian expressions were taken up by the earliest European visitors to Burma: C.F. Keyes, *The Golden Peninsula: Culture and Adaptation in Mainland Southeast Asia* (University of Hawai'i Press 1995; reprint edition), p. 1; see also Part Two.

9 Office of the Superintendent, Government Printing, *Report on the Census of British Burma* August 1872 (Rangoon 1875), p. 26.

10 In 1992 the government catalogued "135 ethnic groups or national races." Such pronouncements are contentious, and must be viewed in the context of the regime's strategy of 'divide and rule' vis-à-vis the minority groups. This figure does though, help to indicate the complexity of the 'ethnic question' in Burma: Gravers (1999), p. 109 & 130.

11 'Tai' refers to the ethnic group in general (including the Shan, or *Tai Yai*), 'Thai' to the Siamese in Thailand.

12 Members of the same trunk, but a different branch, of the Austro-Asiatic language group, the Palaung and Wa share a long history with the Mon-Khmer, either as distant 'cousins' or as subject peoples. Although Buddhism is widespread in the rugged hills of Shan State, many Palaungs, and the majority of Was, are animists (a minority have converted to Christianity).

13 Burma Ethnic Research Group, *Forgotten Victims of a Hidden War: Internally Displaced Karen in Burma* (Chiang Mai 1998).

14 Since the foundation of the first Mon kingdoms, the locations of coasts, rivers and human settlements have often shifted. Thaton was once a port, but is now located some ten miles from the sea; the largely un-excavated remains of the original settlement are situated a few miles from the present day town.

15 Other important agricultural products include sesame, ground nuts, pulses, jute, tobacco and sugarcane, plus livestock of various kinds.

16 The Thailand-Burma border stretches from the 'Golden Triangle' congruence of Burma, Laos and Thailand in the north, to Ranong (Victoria Point) in the south.

17 Gravers (1999), p. 2.

18 NMSP, *NBC News Interview* (1967; reprinted 1985), p. 1.

19 Bertil Lintner, *Outrage: Burma's Struggle for Democracy* (White Lotus 1990), p. 134. On 21st August in Moulmein, forty-seven protestors were shot dead in front of the library, precipitating wide-spread looting and the occupation by protestors of much of the city: *Ibid.* pp. 154–55. On 22nd, fifty-eight monks and students were reportedly killed by the *Tatmadaw*, whilst attempting to seize the customs offices: Smith (1999), p. 5.

20 Lintner (1990), p. 158.

21 *Ibid.* p. 88.

22 *Burma Debate* (Open Society Institute, Summer 1998).

23 More than 350,000 (47%) of whom are Karen: Chiang Mai University, Tribal Research Centre, Data Analysis Department (November 1996).

24 See C.F. Keyes (ed.), *Ethnic Adaptation and Identity: The Karen on the Thai Frontier With Burma* (Institute for the Study of Human Issues, Philadelphia 1979), pp. 16–20.

25 For the sake of clarity and convenience, throughout this book Christian Era notation is used (i.e. BC/AD). It should be noted that the Mon and other peoples of Southeast Asia traditionally reckon time according to the Buddhist Era.

26 For a survey of precolonial Mon history, see Part Two.

27 The distinction between various strata of Mon settlement in Thailand is based on linguistic analysis and upon Thai, Mon and Burmese historical records and traditions. The author is indebted to Emmanuel Guillon, Mathias Jenny and Nai Pisarn Boonpook for their explanations of this complex subject.

28 See Part Six.

29 Christian Bauer, in G. Wijeyewardene (ed.), *Ethnic Groups Across Boundaries in Mainland Southeast Asia* (Institute of Southeast Asia Studies, Singapore 1996).

30 Victor B. Lieberman, *Ethnic Politics in Nineteenth Century Burma* (Modern Asian Studies Vol. 12/3, pp. 455–82; 1978), and Bauer, in Wijeyewardene (1996).

31 Previously known (in Mon) as Sam Khok.

32 Previously known (in Mon) as Pak Lat, and founded by king Mongkut (Rama IV) in 1814: Guillon (1999), p. 208.

33 Including a large community of Mon and other Burmese workers at Maharchai, many of whom received temporary ID cards in 2001, under the Royal Thai Government's alien worker registration scheme.

34 For references to these last two populations, see Michael Smithies (ed.), *The Mons: Collected Articles from The Journal of the Siam Society* (Bangkok 1986), p. 33 & 60.

35 The ancestors of the small Mon population at Nakhon Pathom – the old capital of Dvaravati – were transported here from lower Burma in the mid-nineteenth century, in order to help re-build the famous Phra Pathom *chedi* with its special 'Mon-style' bricks.

36 Bauer, in Wijeyewardene (1996).

37 The Mon in Chumpon are reported to have moved there from Ratchaburi in the 1950s: *ibid.*

38 As well as more recent migrants, the Mon community in Singapore includes descendants of trading enclaves established during the pre-colonial era: Emmanuel Guillon, interview (June 2001).

39 Christian Bauer, *A Guide to Mon Studies* (Monash Centre of SEA Studies 1984), pp. 3–4, and Dr S-M- *The Mon Language: an Endangered Species* (unpublished mss 1999).

40 Nai Pan Hla, *The Significant Role of the Mon Language and Culture in Southeast Asia: Part One* (Monograph, Institute for the Study of Languages and Cultures of Asia and Africa Tokyo University of Foreign Studies 1992), p. 36, and see pp. 37–45 & 90–92

41 Bauer, in Wijeyewardene (1996).

42 Between them, the Pwo and S'ghaw branches of the family account for more than eighty per cent of the Karen population.

43 The majority of Muslims in Mon State live in Moulmein and a number of large villages to the south of the state capital.

44 Ministry of Home and Religious Affairs, Government of the Union of Myanmar, *Kayah State 1983 Population Census* (Rangoon 1987).

45 Office of the Superintendent, Government Printing (1872; 1875); see also Part Two.

46 For example the 1891 census (the first to classify according to race) recorded a Mon population of 63,935 in Pegu District: Office of the Superintendent, Government Printing *Government of India Census of 1891, Imperial Series Volume IX – Burma Report* (Rangoon 1892), p. 185. The 1901 census recorded significant Mon populations across the delta and lower Burma, of which only a fraction spoke the language: Pegu – 44,645 Mon, including 1,854 speakers; Hanthawaddy – 32,726 Mon, 216 speakers; Maubin – 25,116 Mon, 260 speakers; Bassein – 4,730 Mon, none of whom spoke the language; Henzada – 1,463 Mon, no speakers: Office of the Superintendent, Government Printing, *District Gazetteers*, multiple volumes (Rangoon 1906–07). By 1911, the Mon population of Bassein had declined to 2,871, and by 1931 to 508 (out of 571,043 people). However, "no account was taken (in compiling these figures) of the strain of Mon blood that must exist in many of those ... regarded as Burmese": Maung Maung Gyi, *Report of the Revision Settlement of the Bassein District, Season 1935–39* (Rangoon 1941), pp. 12–13. Martin Smith notes that in Henzada, in the heart of the delta, in 1856 half the population were Mon, but that by 1911 only 1,224 Mon resident were recorded (of whom 399 could speak the language and just a handful write it): Smith (1999), p. 43; see also Office of the Superintendent, Government Printing, *District Gazetteers*, multiple volumes (Rangoon 1915), pp. 29–30.

47 Frank Lebar, Gerald Hickey and John Musgrave, *Ethnic Groups of Mainland Southeast Asia* (Human Relations Area Files Press, New Haven 1967), p. 95. The 1891 census likewise recorded 315,749 of Burma's 466,324-strong Mon population as living in Amherst District: Office of the Superintendent, Government Printing (1892), p. 185. See Guillon (1999), p. 210, for a breakdown of the population of Amherst between 1901–31.

48 In a 1999 essay on 'The Mon Language: an Endangered Species', a prominent Mon scholar expressed the concern that within two generations these scattered migrants will have forgotten their Mon roots: Dr S-M- (1999).

49 During *Tatmadaw* operations against Mon insurgents in the Mergui region in 1997, the majority of villagers fleeing to the border were in fact Karen and ethnic Thais, whose ancestors had been subjects of Ayuthaiya; see Parts Two and Five.

50 The preamble to the 1953 Burmese census stated that "in this country ... it has been practised all along to classify the race of a person according to the language spoken.": Office of the Superintendent, Government Printing, *Union of Burma First Stage Census – 1953* (Rangoon 1957). In fact, this practice was instituted by the British in 1891.

51 Martin Smith, *Paradise Lost? The Suppression of Environmental Rights and Freedom of Expression in Burma* (1994), p. 17.

52 *The Mon Forum* (August 1998).

53 This estimate seems to be confirmed by recent (1993) government data: Bauer, in Wijeyewardene (1996), and in *Thai-Yunan Project Newsletter* (Australian National University June 1993).

54 Ministry of Home and Religious Affairs, Government of the Union of Myanmar, *Mon State 1983 Population Census* (Rangoon 1987); 28.15 per

cent were urban dwellers; 92.2 per cent were Buddhist, 6 per cent Muslim and 0.5 per cent Christian.

55 Burma Ethnic Research Group (1998). In November 1999 a draft World Bank report estimated the 1998 population of Mon State at 2,391,000 people, out of a total population of 47.25 million.

56 In 1984, a year after the government census was completed, Mon sources in Burma estimated the total population of Mon State at 3,174,400 people, of whom 1,567,930 could speak Mon and 655,370 could read and write the language. The great majority of Mon speakers were concentrated in the central and southern parts of the state: of 980,000 people in Ye Township, 740,000 reportedly could speak Mon and 610,000 were literate. Released by the Thailand-based Mon Literature Promotion Organisation/Committee (MLPO) in 1984, the accuracy of these findings is uncertain.

57 Speech delivered by Nai Non Lar, on the fortieth anniversary of Mon Revolution Day (9–8–87); see also NMSP (1967; 1985).

58 Lebar et al (1967). This was almost unchanged from the 1911 census, which had recorded 320,629 Mon, of whom not more than half spoke the language: Robert Halliday, *The Talaings* (Government Printing Office, Rangoon 1917; reprinted Orchid Press, Bangkok 1999, with an introduction by Michael Smithies), p. 1. The 1881 census had recorded 154,553 "pure" Mon and 177,939 "mixed" Mon-Burmans. Thus over a period of forty years, while the population of Burma increased, the number of Mons apparently remained static. Interestingly, the 1891 census had recorded a population of 466,324 Mon (including 226,304 Mon speakers), an increase of forty-six per cent over the figure for 1881. This may be explained by the demise of the Burman monarchy in 1886 and subsequent decline of fears associated with being identified as Mon: Office of the Superintendent, Government Printing (1892), pp. 148–49 & 166–67 & 185.

59 The 1872 census, which had recorded 181,602 Mons in lower Burma, acknowledged that mixed-race Mon-Burmans were usually recorded as ethnic Burman: Office of the Superintendent, Government Printing (1872; 1875), p. 30.

60 An example is given by Nai Sunthorn Sriparngern, General Secretary of the Mon Unity League (MUL): "there are several small villages along the sea coast between Moulmein and Amherst (Kyaikammi), namely Kadongbaw, Balauk, Nyaung-Wain, Wekali and Kamar-Okk, and all these villagers speak Burmese. My grand father told me that his grand father ... told him that they came from Irrawaddy delta by boats... They are Mon descendants" (personal correspondence: June 1999).

61 Bauer (1984), p. 2, and Nai Pan Hla (1992), p. 3.

62 See Part Two.

63 Smithies (1986), p. 1, and Nai Pan Hla (1992), p. 3. The S'ghaw Karen refer to the Mon as *Der Ler*, which is probably a variant of *Talaing*.

64 Sir Arthur P. Phayre, *History of Burma: Including Burma Proper, Pegu, Taungu, Tenasserim, and Arakan. From the Earliest Time to the End of the War With British India* (London 1883; reprinted Orchid Press, Bangkok 1998), p. 28.

65 Nai Tun Thein, *Mon Political History* (Mon Unity League, Bangkok 1999; translated from the Burmese by Poo C-, Bellay Htoo and S-S-), p. 11.

66 NMSP (1967; 1985), p. 1.

67 Co-ordinating Committee for Services to Displaced People in Thailand, *Educational Assessment of Mon and Karenni Refugee Camps on the Thai/ Burmese Border* ('The Education Survey'; Bangkok 1995).

68 Since the mid-1990s, Mon monks and their followers have been constructing
the world's largest reclining Buddha image, at Yadana Daung, between
Kyaikmaraw and Mudon. Financed largely by voluntary subscription, the 160
meter long figure should be complete by 2003.

69 The 1911 census recorded a figure of 1,911 Mon Christians: Halliday (1917;
1999), p. 93.

70 There are Mon Baptist communities in Mudon, Moulmein, Thanbyuzayat and
Ye Townships of Mon State, and at Insein, near Rangoon. Until 1996, there was
a small Mon and Karen Baptist community at Pa Yaw refugee camp.

71 Halliday (1917; 1999), p. 94 & pp. 101–04 & 147–60 ('A *Kalok* Dance'); see
also Smithies (1986), p. 44, and Guillon (1999), pp. 45–50, and Melford E.
Spiro, *Burmese Supernaturalism* (Prentice-Hall 1978).

72 The evocative title of a recent nationalist account of Mon history – Mon Unity
League, *The Mon: A People Without a Country* (Bangkok 1997; re-printed
1999) – echoes a phrase in Halliday, *The Talaings* (1917; 1999), p. 17.

73 See Halliday's 1922 article, in Smithies (1986), pp. 21–28.

74 D.F. Raikes, *The Mon: Their Music and Dance* (Siam Society 1957), pp. 15–19.
Over the past half-century, with the rise of the Thai middle class and
commercialisation of the cremation business, Mon music has replaced Thai at
funerals in Bangkok and central Thailand. According to Deborah Wong, "late
twentieth century Thais are likely to include a *piiphaat Mon* ensemble in a
funeral ritual because it speaks sadness, status, and fun": Deborah Wong, *Mon
Music For Thai Deaths: Ethnicity and Status in Thai Urban Funerals* (Asian
Folklore Studies, Vol. LVII [No. 1] pp. 99–130; 1998), p. 125.

75 Guillon (1999), p. 8.

76 Smithies (1986), p. 54.

77 According to Smithies, "all Mons have a tortoise tradition. If they see a tortoise
and do not want it, or can avoid it, they can say 'It stinks' and pass on. But if
they catch a tortoise or cannot avoid one, they must on no account let it go, and
must take it to the house, cook it and eat it ... after having first offered the head
and feet ... to the house ghosts.... If however a tortoise is released the Mon
ghosts are considered to have been offended... Two exceptions are observed. A
very large tortoise must not be eaten; it is old, and like an old person and so
must be placed in the temple. A tortoise with letters carved in its underside ... is
considered a protected tortoise since the characters are carved on tortoises
raised in the temple: likewise it must be released in the temple": *ibid.*; see also
Halliday (1917; 1999), pp. 105–07, and Guillon (1999), p. 23.

78 According to one respondent, belief in these taboos has undergone a revival in
recent years in some villages in Ye Township.

79 According to Smithies, "these concern snakes, chickens and pigs. Members of a
household observe the taboo of the male household head", under which for
example "snake families may not kill or eat snakes. Chicken families may not
sell or give chickens (though they may raise them, eat them, and kill them)":
Smithies (1986), pp. 55–56.

80 Foster, in Smithies (1986), p. 76.

81 Another distinctively Mon set of rituals revolve around fish (which in the Pegu
marriage ritual were presented and sacrificed to the 'Buffalo mother of Pegu'):
Benedicte Brac de la Perriere, *La Bufflesse de Pegou: un Exemple D'Incorporation de Rituel dans le Culte Birman* (Bulletin de L'Ecole Francaise D'Extreme-
Orient No. 82, pp. 287–299; 1995); see also Part Two.

82 Guillon Emmanuel, *History of the Mons* (Siam Society lecture, 18-2-99);
parenthesis added.

83 The author has met many Mon-Karen and Mon-Burman couples in Thailand and Burma – e.g. the case of a young Burman man who married a Mon woman, joined the NMSP, and for several years was a leading member of the party's Agriculture Department – even going so far as to adopt the Mon honorific 'Nai'. On two occasions in the 1990s, French *Medicins Sans Frontieres* (MSF) medics working with Mon refugees in Sangkhlaburi fell in love with and married their Mon counterparts. For a disturbing account of Mon-Karen intermarriage, see Part Three.

84 Smithies (1986), p. 40.

85 Foster, in Smithies (1986), p. 65.

86 For a discussion of the physical anthropology and physiognomy of the Mon, see Guillon (1999), p. 16.

87 Halliday (1917; 1999), p. 18.

88 *Ibid.* p. 17. Haswell, an earlier missionary, was of the same opinion.

89 In unguarded moments, even the more liberal and progressive NMSP cadres can be rather patronising in their attitudes to other, historically 'less developed' peoples. According to one senior party leader, an important aspect of historical research and education is to ensure that future generations do not forget "the genetic superiority of the Mon" (1995 interview).

90 H.L. Shorto, *A Dictionary of the Mon Inscriptions From the Sixth to the Sixteenth Centuries* (Oxford University Press 1971), p. ix.

91 Guillon (1999), p. 10.

92 *Ibid.* p. 59, and the 'Introduction' to Shorto (1971).

93 Vadhana Purakasikara, *The Characteristics of Thai Words of Mon Origin* (Tech Promotion and Advertising, Bangkok 1998; Thai language); this study includes Thai words of Pali origin as borrowings from Mon.

94 Bauer, in Wijeyewardene (1996).

95 Purakasikara (1998).

96 Shorto (1971), pp. xxviii–xxxiii.

97 See Part Two.

98 Robert Halliday, *A Mon-English Dictionary* (The Siam Society 1922; Ministry of Union Culture, Government of the Union of Burma 1955) and Guillon (1999), p. 20. Nai Shwe Kyin mentions a fourth 'Mon' dialect: *Mon Du*, or Mon Karen (presumably Pwo): Nai Tun Thein (1999), Appendix One.

99 However, according to a recent study, the differences between Thai and Burmese Mon dialects are nearly sufficient for them to be classified as separate languages: F.E. Huffman, *Burmese Mon, Thai Mon and Nyah Kur: a Synchronic Comparison* (Mon-Khmer Studies, Vols XVI–XVII pp. 31–84; 1987), p. 56.

100 Halliday, in Smithies (1986), pp. 15–16.

101 NMSP (1967; 1985), p. 12 (no source is provided for this claim).

102 Nai Tun Thein (1999), p. 11.

103 Office of the Superintendent, Government Printing (1892), pp. 166–67.

104 Interview (August 1999).

105 J.M. Haswell, *Grammatical Notes and Vocabulary of the Peguan Language* (American Missionary Press, Rangoon 1874).

106 See Bauer, in Wijeyewardene (1996).

107 Bauer, in Wijeyewardene (1996). In the 1980s such magazines often had print runs of up to 5,000 copies: Bauer (1984), p. 22. Obviously, widespread censorship in Burma has limited the range of themes available to authors: Anna J. Allott, *Inked Over, Ripped Out: Burmese Storytellers and the Censors* (Silkworm Books 1994).

108 Three Mon theatres are registered with the state Theatre Council in Moulmein: Mon Htaw Kyaing, Ong Kyaw San, Mon Chit So. There are many other small theatre troupes in the villages.

109 Bauer, in Wijeyewardene (1996).

110 CCSDPT 'Education Survey' (1995), pp. 12–15; for more on refugee demographics, see Part Four.

111 Among the author's acquaintances, a number are fluent in more than two languages – e.g. Burmese, Karen and Thai. Of course, these people do not constitute a representative sample, but are members of a relatively well-educated elite. However, among the Burman and Thai communities along the border this range of language mastery is far less common. It seems that more Karen speak Mon, than Mon speak Karen, perhaps reflecting the unequal historical relationship between the two peoples; see Part Two.

112 Nai Pan Hla (1992), p. 44.

113 Dr S-M- (1999). Of course, this 'accessibility' has also been a factor in the Mon culture's historically influential role.

114 Donald Wilson, *The Contented Mons of Koh Kret* (Crescent Press Agency 1997).

115 Foster, in Smithies (1986), p. 75.

116 *Ibid.* p. 77.

117 *Ibid.* p. 79.

118 *Ibid.* D.F. Raikes' 1957 essay drew a similarly gloomy conclusion: Raikes (1957), pp. 13–14.

119 Smithies later edited a collection of articles on the Mon, taken from *The Journal of the Siam Society*: Smithies (1986).

120 *Ibid.* p. 34.

121 *Ibid.* p. 58.

122 Wao Kao News Agency reports that "Geeta Mon, a popular Mon band, performed at Wat Kumphar of Maharchai temple festival this week for three nights from November 28–30, attracted thousands of fans. The Mon people have longed for this kind of excitement, which has been missed for many years back home. Leading Mon celebrity star, Hongsar Marn, Jeol Marn, and Chem Hongsar attracted the lively crowd during the concert which was accompanied by traditional dances performed by migrant Mon girls during the fund raising event for this annual festival at Maharchai, thirty km west from Bangkok": *Kao Wao 3* (3–12–01).

123 Nai Pan Hla (1992), p. 36.

124 Huffman (1987), p. 58.

125 Wong (1998), p. 116.

126 Khun Anand's ancestors were Mon aristocrats who settled in Baan Pong-Photharam during the mid-nineteenth century. Another well-known 'Thai Mon' is the respected academic Dr. Sued Gajaseni, President of the Thai Ramon Association (TRA). Dr Sued is a descendant of Phraya Choei, an eighteenth century Peguan general, whose family went on to become scions of the Thai aristocracy; see Part Two.

127 For example, Field Marshal Phibun Songkhram, twice military dictator of Thailand and in the 1950s a patron of the Mon insurgents, was a Mon from Nonthaburi province; see Part Three.

128 Robert H. Taylor, *The State in Burma* (Hurst 1987), p. 286. See also Taylor's *Perceptions of Ethnicity in the Politics of Burma* (*Southeast Asian Journal of Social Science* Vol. 10, No. 1; 1982).

129 For an interesting (although in the case of Burma, limited) discussion of this issue, see Benedict Anderson, *The Spectre of Comparisons: Nationalism, Southeast Asia and the World* (Verso 1998), pp. 318–30.

130 To argue that ethnic identity must rest on an unchanging 'essential nature', shared by all Karens, is to commit the 'essentialist fallacy'.

131 For an incisive analysis of these issues (including Chatterjee's critique of Anderson's 'imagined community'), see Mikael Gravers, *The Karen Making of a Nation*, in Stein Tonnesson and Hans Antlov (eds) *Asian Forms of the Nation* (Curzon 1996), pp. 265–69.

132 *Kaw Thoo Lei* may be translated as either 'the land burned black' (by 'slash-and-burn' farming, or by warfare), 'the pure land' or 'the land of the *thoo lei* plant' (i.e. 'flowerland').

133 Lieberman (1978), p. 480.

134 *Ibid.*

135 *Ibid.* p. 472; see Part Two.

136 Michael A. Aung-Thwin, *Myth and History in the Historiography of Early Burma: Paradigms, Primary Sources, and Prejudices* (Ohio University Centre for International Studies 1998), p. 147.

137 Mikael Gravers too warns against adopting ethnicity as the sole criterion of identity, arguing that religion (or cosmology) is at least as important: Gravers (1999), pp. 19–20 & 35.

138 Taylor (1987), p. 24.

139 See Part Two.

140 Dr S-M- (1999).

141 Guillon (1999), pp. 170–71.

142 Halliday (1917; 1999), p. 86.

143 Guillon (1999), pp. 170–71.

144 Like the Shwedagon, the Shwemawdaw Pagoda is reputed to house hair relics of the Buddha.

145 The original Mon name for Sule Pagoda in downtown Rangoon is *Kyaik Kyiew Ley*, the 'resting pagoda' (so called because the Buddha's hair relic is said to have rested in a pavilion here, on its way to be interred at the Shwedagon; see Part Two).

146 Office of the Superintendent, Government Printing (1872; 1875), p. 28.

147 *Ibid.* p. 30.

148 Guillon (1999), p. 213. Interestingly, during a meeting with the NMSP in 1996, SLORC-SPDC Secretary One, Lt-General Khin Nyunt, is reported to have declared his own Mon ancestry, before calling for the Mon to unite with the Burmans. According to Nai Shwe Kyin, Khin Nyunt's mother was a Mon from Kyauk Tan, in the Irrawaddy Delta: interview (August 1999).

149 An extract is quoted in Gravers (1996), p. 240.

150 A similar reproach may be levelled at scholars who criticise the ethnic nationalist position, whilst failing to recognise this as a response to the 'Burmanisation' of the state.

151 Interview (August 1999); other sources for this incident include the Bangkok magazine *Feature* (Vol. 90; 8-8-92).

152 Gustaaf Houtman, *Mental Culture in Burmese Crisis Politics: Aung San Suu Kyi and the National League For Democracy* (Monograph 33, Institute for the Study of Languages and Cultures of Asia and Africa Tokyo University of Foreign Studies 1999), pp. 142–47.

153 Gravers (1996), p. 240.

154 These include a large bell from the Shwemawdaw Pagoda at Pegu, cast and inscribed in the Mon language in 1755, two years before the fall of the last Mon kingdom. Looted by the British during the Second Anglo-Burmese War, the bell was only returned in 1957, two hundred years after the fall of Pegu. Among the most striking items in the museum are two golden betel nut containers in the shape of the mythical *hamsa* (golden sheldrake). One of these gorgeous objects has an amber beak and forehead, the other (which is featured on the five Kyat Burmese stamp) is studded with semi-precious green gems. Other important Mon items in the collection include a number of characteristic glazed plaques from Pagan.

155 Similarly, most visitors to the National Museum in Bangkok will not realise that the numerous and extraordinarily beautiful 'Dvaravati' sculptures on display are in fact Mon.

156 An earlier example from academia is provided by Nai Sunthorn Sriparngern: "*Mon Myanmar Sarpay Paung-Ku* (*The Connection of Mon and Burmese Literature*) by Dr. Min Tin Mon, Dean of Rangoon University, was not allowed even (to be presented to) a seminar on ethnic culture which was held on 23rd July 1983 at Rangoon University": personal correspondence (February 1999).

157 Similarly at Pagan, to the dismay of Burmese and foreign experts, the authorities have acquiesced in the often shoddy and historically inaccurate 'reconstruction' of Burma's cultural heritage.

158 The inscriptions indicate the various regions of the kingdom from which these logs were sent as tribute. Interestingly, the posts sent from the Mon lands are the only ones the language of their donors, rather than Burmese. This fact would seem to confirm that, following the fall of Hongsawaddy, the Mon culture still retained a high status.

159 *The New Light of Myanmar* (20-9-99).

160 The 'first Myanmar dynasty': eleventh-to-thirteenth century Pagan; the second: the Toungoo dynasty, founded by kings Tabinshwehti and Bayinnaung; the third: Alaungphaya's Konbaung Dynasty, dating from the mid-eighteenth century; the fourth: independent Burma, culminating in the military oligarchy established by Ne Win 1962 (by some reckonings, Aung San and U Nus' independent Burma constitutes the fourth dynasty, and Ne Win's and successor regimes the fifth); see *The New Light Of Myanmar* (14-12-99), which contains an attack on Houtman's critique of 'Myanmafication'.

161 In March 1999 human rights groups reported that the *Tatmadaw* Northeast Command had ordered Shan language notice boards removed from villages across the state. Such attacks recall the authorities' destruction of the Kentung Palace, an historic and beautiful symbol of Shan identity, dynamited in 1991 and replaced with a luxury hotel. For further examples of the Burmanisation of Shan culture, see Christina Fink, *Living Silence: Burma Under Military Rule* (Zed Books 2001), p. 226.

162 Overseas Mon Young Monks Union, *Mon: the Forgotten Refugees* (Bangkok August 1994).

163 D.R. SarDesai, *Southeast Asia: Past and Present* (Westview 1994; third edition), p. 135.

164 *Ibid.* p. 135. This definition reflects that formulated by UNESCO in 1990.

165 Hobsbawm (1992), p. 10.

166 See for example, Nai Tun Thein (1999), Appendix One – 1951 statement by Nai Shwe Kyin's Mon Freedom League (MFL).

167 Gravers (1999), p. 145.

168 Government attitudes are summarised in a 1998 report by the Burma Ethnic Research Group (BERG): "the Burmese approach to the ethnic question has been to aggressively embrace an assimilationist agenda, a refusal to grant any real autonomy to ethnic minorities in outlying regions, and a heavy reliance on military force to contain opposing impulses": Burma Ethnic Research Group (1998), p. 21.

169 Like Nai Chit Thaung, Nai Pan Hla began his career as a chemist and later joined the All Ramanya Mon Association (ARMA); see Part Two. Among his other contributions to Mon language and culture, Nai Pan Hla has donated prizes to the winners of a recently inaugurated Mon language essay writing competition.

170 H.L. Shorto, *A Dictionary of Modern Spoken Mon* (Oxford University Press 1962), p. XIV.

171 A Mon-Burmese-Pali-English dictionary was published in Ye in 1965. The first (and so far, only) volume of Nai Tun Way's Mon-Burmese dictionary was published in Rangoon in 1977; his *Modern English-Mon Dictionary* was published in Bangkok in 1997; *The Modern Mon-English Dictionary* was published in Bangkok in 2001. On the historic relationship between dictionary compilation and the emergence of nationalism, see Anderson (1991), pp. 67–75.

172 Mon National Education Committee report (2001).

173 Bauer, in Wijeyewardene (1996); the MLCC continued publishing Mon language texts into the 1980s: Bauer (1984), p. 22.

174 For further details of the Summer Language Training campaign, see Part Six.

175 Dr S-M- (1999).

176 "Among siblings, there were conflicts when one joined an ethnic-based organisation and another joined a broader organisation. Nai Panna talked about how upset he was in 1988 when his brother joined the ABSDF instead of the NMSP. Nai Panna's brother . . . felt that the best way forward was to work for democracy first. More than ten years later, they still do not see eye to eye": Fink (2001), p. 118.

177 Similarly, in 1947 a Shan National Day was established, to be celebrated annually on 7th February.

178 During a recent visit to a Mon monastery in Bangkok, the author came across a group of monks and novices avidly watching a video of the 1999 Mon National Day celebrations in the Mon State capital.

179 On the suppression of Mon National Day celebrations in 1997 (the fiftieth anniversary) and 2000, see Part Six.

180 See Part Six.

181 Statements issued the following year by the MUL in Thailand, and by the Mon National Day Celebration Committees in Australia, Canada and the United States, made many of the same points, as did a 1999 letter sent by a coalition of overseas Mon organisations to UN Secretary General Koffi Anan (19–11–99).

182 Because travel in rural Burma can be very difficult in August, at the height of the rainy season, the NMSP often re-schedules Revolution Day festivities to a more convenient date – e.g. in 1998 the main celebrations were held on December 27th, at Nye Sah on the Ye River near 'Central'.

183 See Part Three.

184 In 1996, the year after the ceasefire, an especially impressive MNLA Day celebration was held at Nye Sah, where about 800 Mon soldiers took part in a military parade. Since the ceasefire, MNLA troop numbers had been in decline

and this turnout represented more than a third of the total armed forces available to the NMSP at the time. (Several of the young men on parade were in fact students, medics and other civilians reserves.)

185 According to Guillon, this "is sometimes regarded as a literary text rather than properly historical, sometimes as a handbook of military strategy, but, for the learned Mon people, mainly a book of their national history": Guillon (Siam Society lecture, 18–2–99).

186 This text, composed in 1776, is an account of the life of the Buddha, the foundation of the Shwedagon Pagoda and the history of Pegu: Venerable Acwo, *History of Kings* (1776; *Journal of the Burma Research Society* Vol. XIII pp. 1–67; translated by Robert Halliday 1923); see Part Two.

187 *Ahan songkran* – *songkran* food, consisting of rice floating in iced water, plus dried fish – is recognised in Thailand as a distinctively Mon dish. For a description of 'Thai Mon' *songkran* at Phra Padaeng, see *The Bangkok Post* (30–4–97) and Foster, in Smithies (1986), p. 69, where the traditional Mon holiday game of *sabaa* is described.

188 On Thai royalty and the *Maha Yen* sect, see Part Two.

189 See Part Four.

190 In fact the red and white check 'Burmese Mon' *longyi* is an innovation of the 1950s and '60s; the more colourful 'Thai Mon' sarong, with its large squares of blue, pink and yellow silk, is of older pedigree.

191 NMSP statement (13–7–95).

192 See Part Six.

Part Two – Classical Mon Civilisation and the Colonial Period

1 Quoted in Guillon (1999), p. 180.

2 *Ibid.* p. 52 & 214.

3 Gravers (1999), p. 145.

4 Keyes (1995), p. vi.

5 Gravers (1999), p. 122.

6 CCSDPT 'Education Survey' (1995) and Guillon (1999), pp. 39–40.

7 For detailed accounts of Mon studies in the West, see Bauer (1984) and Guillon (1999), Appendix Three. For recent publications in Burma and Thailand, see Bauer's Bibliography in Robert Halliday, *The Mons of Burma and Thailand: Volume One – The Talaings* (White Lotus, Bangkok 2000 – ed. and with a Foreword and photographs by Christian Bauer).

8 C.O. Blagden and G.H. Luce, *Certaine Words of Pegu Language* (*Journal of the Burma Research Society* Vol. XXX, II pp. 371–375; 1940).

9 Guillon (1999), Appendix Three.

10 A second, expanded edition was edited in 1901 by the Rev. E.O. Stevens, whose own 'Vocabulary' had been published in 1896.

11 John S. Furnivall, *The Fashioning of Leviathan: The Beginnings of British Rule in Burma* (*Journal of the Burma Research Society* Vol. XXIX, II 1939; reprinted Occasional Paper, Department of Anthropology, Australian National University 1991), p. 102.

12 Aung-Thwin (1998), p. 65 & pp. 146–47.

13 More recently, the Siam Society has been in the forefront of research into the Mon in Thailand and Burma. In 1999 the society published Dr Guillon's *The Mons: A Civilization in Southeast Asia*, the most important treatment of Mon history since Luce.

14 Robert Halliday, *The Talaings* (1917; 1999) *op. cit.*, and *The Mons of Burma and Thailand: Volume One – The Talaings; Volume Two – Selected Articles* (White Lotus, Bangkok 2000 – ed. with a Foreword and photographs by Christian Bauer).

15 Shorto (1962), p. XIV.

16 Bauer (1984), p. 12.

17 C.O. Blagden, *Mon Inscriptions*, in U Mya, Charles Duroiselle et al (ed.), *Epigraphia Birmania* (Superintendent Government Printing and Stationary, Rangoon 1923–1960; multiple volumes).

18 Professor Luce's 'crimes' may have included his patronage of the proto-nationalist All Ramanya Mon Association (ARMA); it has also been suggested that Luce earned Ne Win's animosity in the 1930s, when he apparently expelled the future dictator from a student hostel: *The Irrawaddy* (August 2000).

19 Shorto (1962).

20 Shorto (1971). Reflecting the comparative spirit of the age, during Shorto's 1971–84 tenure, the Mon professorship at SOAS was re-defined as a Mon-Khmer seat; see also Bauer (1984), p. 8.

21 See for example, George Coedes, *The Indianised States of Southeast Asia* (East-West Centre Press, Honolulu 1968; ed. Walter Vella, translated by Susan Brown Cowing).

22 Guillon (1999), p. 82.

23 The Burman kings sat on a 'peacock throne', and the symbol of a peacock was used by anti-British resistance forces in the 1880s, and has been an icon of the student movement since the 1930s: Gravers (1999), p. 9, and Liddell, in Burma Centre Netherlands and Transnational Institute (eds), *Strengthening Civil Society: Possibilities and Dilemmas for International NGOs* (Silkworm Books 1999), p. 68.

24 Itself known in classical Mon as the *bup, bip, buip* or *bap*: Shorto (1971), p. 406.

25 Boonsong Lekagul and Philip D. Round, *A Guide to the Birds of Thailand* (Saha Karn Bhaet 1991).

26 Nai Shwe Kyin recalls, as a boy of five, seeing one of a pair of ruddy sheldrakes shot by hunters on the Irrawaddy River near Prome. The remaining fowl, mourning its partner's death so keenly that it failed to flee the scene, was dispatched soon afterwards. What symbolic importance should be attached to this anecdote?

27 Acwo (1923), p. 48, and Nai Pan Hla (1992), p. 50.

28 For a novelistic account of the legend of the two sheldrakes, see 'P. Nop', *Tangay: The Setting Sun of Ramanya* (Song Sayam 1997; translated by Eveline Willi); see also Guillon (1999), pp. 170–71.

29 The use of yellow or golden figures against a red background is widespread on Burmese flags and emblems, particularly among opposition groups – e.g. the yellow star/red background of the NLD flag and the golden 'fighting peacock' on a red background of the ABSDF standard.

30 Guillon (1999), p. 24.

31 Foster questions whether the statue of a sheldrake erected upon a pole – which is characteristic of certain Khmer monasteries, as well as those of the Mon – does in fact indicate a pagoda's Mon origins: Foster, in Smithies (1986), p. 78.

32 Phayre (1883; 1998), p. 26.

33 For the classic Mon version of the legend (and a colourfully detailed history of Rangoon, from the earliest times until the 1930s), see B.R. Pearn, *A History of Rangoon* (Corporation of Rangoon 1939).

34 Another statue recalling the legend is found at Wat Yai Nakom Chum in Ratchaburi Province, Thailand. Although the Mon origins of Wat Yai Nakom Chum are much earlier, the image – which is flanked by white plaster-clad reproductions of the Shwedagon – was built in the mid-1930s.

35 Guillon (1999), p. 41.

36 *Ibid.* p. 34.

37 One of the earliest Chinese references to Burma mentions the native practice of brewing 'toddy wine' from palm juice. This delicious and potent beverage, which begins to sour within twenty-four hours of fermentation, is still a staple of rural communities: Guillon (1999), pp. 70–71.

38 Founded at Wat Chana Songkhram in Bangkok, in November 2001, the CRMCH is led by Dr. Sued Gajaseni, President of Thai Ramon Association (TRA),and advised by Dr Emmanuel Guillon and Nai Pisarn Boonpook. It has begun to investigate and care for palm leaf manuscripts from a number of sources, including those discovered during a 2000 Royal Thai Government (Education Department) Survey of Thai monasteries: *Kao Wao 3* (3–12–01).

39 Mon sources claim that in the late 1950s eleven buffalo carts of important Mon language manuscripts from across lower Burma were interred, on prime minister U Nu's instructions, beneath the newly-constructed Kaba Aye Pagoda in Rangoon.

40 Guillon (1999), p. 76.

41 *Ibid.* p. 72. In recent years, Burmese archaeologists have undertaken some excavations at Thaton and other sites in lower Burma.

42 Guillon (Siam Society lecture, 18–2–99).

43 Nai Pan Hla (1992), p. 6. The China theory was favoured in a manifesto issued by Nai Shwe Kyin, shortly after his release from jail in December 1951. This statement goes on to give a sketchy, and not always very accurate, overview of the highlights of Mon history: Nai Tun Thein (1999), Appendix One. (Nai Tun Thein also follows Nai Pan Hla's theory of Mon origins.)

44 Which Nai Pan Hla suggests may originally have been situated nearer the Sittaung River: Nai Pan Hla (1992), p. 46 & 51.

45 Acwo (1922), p. 47.

46 Nai Pan Hla (1992), pp. 54–55.

47 *Ibid.* pp. 60–65.

48 In recent years the 'proto-Malay' hypothesis has been challenged: Keyes (1995), p. 16.

49 Hall suggests that proto-Mon peoples may have occupied the area since the early bronze age (circa 3,000 BC): D.G.E. Hall, *A History of South-East Asia* (Macmillan 1981; fourth edition), p. 182.

50 For the classic account of *The Indianised States of Southeast Asia* (i.e. the Mon, Khmer, Funanese and Cham), see Coedes (1968).

51 Shorto (1971), p. xxviii and Guillon (1999), Appendix Two.

52 Guillon (1999), p. 33.

53 Emmanuel Guillon, *Champa* (in *Dictionary of Art* Vol. VI; Macmillan 1996), pp. 417–18.

54 It was only in the early 1900s that historians realised that the Dvaravati civilisation *was* in fact Mon: Guillon (1999), Appendix Three.

55 Guillon (1999), pp. 100–101 and Nai Pan Hla (1992), p. 27. The Lawa may have possessed more advanced social institutions than their common designation of 'hilltribe' suggests; indeed, Camadevi may even have been a Lawa princess, adopted by the Mon ruler of Lopburi: Georges Condominas, *From Lawa to Mon, From Saa' to Thai: Historical and Anthropological Aspects of*

Southeast Asian Social Spaces (Occasional Paper, Department of Anthropology, Australian National University 1990; translated by Stephanie Anderson et al), pp. 10–18.

56 David K. Wyatt, *Thailand: A Short History* (Yale University Press 1984), p. 31
57 *Ibid.* p. 79 & 159.
58 Guillon (1999), p. 154.
59 *Ibid.* p. 8 & 30.
60 *Ibid.* pp. 91–92.
61 Nai Pan Hla (1992).
62 *Ibid.* pp. 58–60.
63 See Emmanuel Guillon and Nai Pan Hla, *A Mon Copper Plate in the National Library, Bangkok* (*Journal of the Burma Research Society* Vol. LV; 1972).
64 Hall (1981), p. 22, and Keyes (1995), p. 66.
65 Hall (1981), p. 243.
66 Keyes (1995), pp. 259–269.
67 Guillon (1999), p. 32 & 56.
68 Maurice Collis, *Siamese White* (Faber and Faber 1936; reprinted DD Books 1986), Keyes (1995), p. 65, and Guillon (1999), p. 67.
69 Guillon (1999), pp. 187–89.
70 *Ibid.* pp. 186–87.The extent of these early trade networks is demonstrated by the discovery at U-Thong of a third century AD Roman silver coin, and by the unearthing at Pong Tuk (near Baan Pong, in Ratchaburi) of what may be a Roman bronze lamp: Nai Pan Hla (1992), p. 24.
71 *Ibid.* p. 74.
72 Taylor (1987), p. 14.
73 Gravers (1999), p. 20.
74 Theodore Stern, *Ariya and the Golden Book: A Millenarian Buddhist Sect Among the Karen* (The Journal of Asian Studies Vol. 27/2 pp. 297–328; 1968), p. 300; see also Guillon (1999), p. 54.
75 Keyes (1995), p. 73 & pp. 260–61.
76 Guillon (1999), p. 54.
77 Keyes (1995), p. 92.
78 Acwo (1923), p. 57.
79 Keyes (1995), p. 142.
80 Spiro (1978), p. 133, and see Keyes (1995), p. 72.
81 Brac de la Perriere (1995), and personal correspondence (September 2000); see also below.
82 Gravers (1999), p. 19.
83 Such 'tribal' structures have sometimes characterised the social and political modalities within and between the Mon, Karen and other ethnic insurgent groups in the modern era. Insurgent field officers owe their positions to the patronage of headquarters and are often expected to repay the leadership with loyalty, as well as kick-backs derived from the taxation of local economic activity. For their part, field commanders are often left to their own devices in governing and raising income in 'their' areas. In recent years, the Mon and other ethnic nationalist movements have had to contend with a contradiction between their message of democracy and national liberation, and a patriarchal tradition; see Parts Three, Four and Six.
84 Anderson (1991), p. 19.
85 Thongchai Winichakul, *Maps and the Formation of the Geo-Body of Siam*, in Tonnesson and Antlov (1996), pp. 73–74; this chapter is an abridged version of Thongchai's acclaimed 1994 study, *Siam Mapped*.

86 According to Lieberman, "the greater the sway of Pegu, the greater the potential number of 'Mons'": Lieberman (1978), p. 458.

87 Martin Stuart-Fox, *A History of Laos* (Cambridge University Press 1997), p. 7.

88 Guillon (1999), pp. 155–170. In the fourteenth century however, Pegu was a vassal of Martaban (see below).

89 Western interpretations of the precolonial 'cosmic polity' originated with Robert von Heine-Geldern's work in the 1930–50s, and were developed by Georges Condominas, Oliver Wolters and others in the 1970–80s. However, recent scholarship has cautioned against over-reliance on such hierarchical concepts, which tend to legitimise elite hegemony at the expense of 'marginal' groups.

90 Guillon (1999), p. 5.

91 Keyes (1979), Chapter Two, and Ronald D. Renard, *Kariang: History of Karen-T'ai Relations From the Beginning to 1923* (University of Hawaii 1980; unpublished PhD thesis).

92 The eighteenth century Mon chronicler, the monk of Acwo, refers to the Chin, Karen and Wa as 'ruder peoples' (whose property rights should nevertheless be respected): Acwo (1923), p. 66.

93 For a rosy account of precolonial Mon-Karen relations, see Nai Tun Thein (1999), Appendix One (1951 statement by Nai Shwe Kyin).

94 Stern (1968), pp. 299–300.

95 Guillon (1999), p. 78.

96 Keyes (1995), p. 19.

97 Stern (1968) and Keyes (1995), p. 54.

98 SarDesai (1994), p. 76.

99 Guillon (1999), p. 113.

100 *Ibid.* pp. 111–13.

101 C.f. the confusion of fact and mystification uncovered in Michael Aung-Thwin's analysis of 'Myth and History in the Historiography of Early Burma' (with the obvious difference that the legends associated with Anawratha were the creation of indigenous, rather than colonial, myth-makers): Aung-Thwin (1998).

102 Smith speculates that the Pa-O migration may in fact have occurred in the eighteenth century and that the Pa-O may be identified with the mysterious 'Gwe' Karen, who briefly emerged onto the historical stage as allies of the Mon (see below): Smith (1999), p. 33 & 460.

103 G.H. Luce, *Mons of the Pagan Dynasty* (Rangoon University 1950), p. 7; see also Luce's pupil, Nai Pan Hla (1992), p. 31.

104 Following her release from house arrest in 1995, Daw Aung San Suu Kyi had cause to reflect upon the Mon king's imprisonment at Pagan, and his apparent grace and dignity in confinement: Aung San Suu Kyi, *Letters from Burma* (Penguin 1997), pp. 7–8.

105 Hall (1981), p. 158, and Keyes (1995), p. 71.

106 Guillon (1999), p. 113.

107 For descriptions of the art, monuments and history of 'Mon Pagan', see *ibid.* pp. 114–39, and G.H. Luce et al, *Early Pagan, Old Burma* (Antibus Asiae and Institute of Fine Arts, New York University 1969 [vol. 1] & 1970 [Vols 2 & 3]).

108 Guillon (1999), p. 139.

109 Other plaques portray images of the *hamsa*: Emmanuel Guillon, *L'Armee de Mara: Au Pied de L'Ananda (Pagan-Birminie)* (Editions Recherche sur les Civilisations 1985).

110 Guillon (1999), p. 53.
111 Remnants of the ancient Pyu people may also have played a part here.
112 Guillon (1999), p. 145.
113 Hall (1981), p. 188.
114 Wyatt (1984), p. 72
115 Brac de la Perriere (1995)
116 Luce (1950), p. 8
117 Guillon (1999), p. 127.
118 Hall (1981), pp. 162–63, and Keyes (1995), p. 72.
119 Guillon (1999), p. 149.
120 Luce attributed this transition to an invasion from Sri Lanka. However, Michael Aung-Thwin concludes that such an interpretation is probably unsound: Aung-Thwin (1998), p. 26.
121 Keyes (1995), p. 80, and Guillon (1999), p. 150.
122 Keyes (1995), p. 81, Guillon (1999), pp. 150–52, and Aung-Thwin (1998), p. 29.
123 Keyes (1995), p. 262.
124 Predominantly Hindu, pre-Islamic Cham art may have been influenced by Mon Pagan: Guillon (1996), p. 419 & 426.
125 Michael Aung-Thwin concludes that "there is no evidence, certainly no conclusive evidence" that Pagan itself was ever captured or sacked by the Mongols, or that the Pagan dynasty ended with these invasion (as most previous scholars had assumed): Aung-Thwin (1998), p. 65.
126 Keyes (1995), p. 74, and Guillon (1999), 145.
127 Lieberman (1978), p. 459.
128 The Mon word for 'city' or 'state' (*dun*) can also be translated as 'house', denoting a feudal or clan bond between sovereign and subjects: Guillon (Siam Society lecture, 18–2–99).
129 Guillon (1999), p. 157.
130 For the traditional Mon account of these events, see Acwo (1923), pp. 51–52.
131 Guillon (1999), p. 157.
132 Wyatt (1984), p. 59.
133 Keyes (1995), p. 75.
134 *Ibid.* p. 76.
135 According to Hall (1981), p. 188.
136 Keyes (1995), pp. 75–76.
137 Guillon (1999), p. 102 & pp. 108–10.
138 *Ibid.* p. 140.
139 Wyatt (1984), p. 47.
140 *Ibid.* pp. 48–49.
141 Hall (1981), p. 180.
142 Acwo (1923), p. 52.
143 Hall (1981), p. 180.
144 Guillon (1999), pp. 165–68.
145 Acwo (1923), p. 52. The practice of renovating and 'improving' religious monuments, in order to promote social cohesion and legitimise the ruling authorities, has persisted into the modern era; see Part Six.
146 Some of Queen Victoria's Mon subjects apparently considered the empress a reincarnation of Queen Shinsawbu: Guillon (1999), pp. 169–70,
147 Guillon (1999), p. 160.
148 *Ibid.* p. 173.
149 Acwo (1923), p. 56.

150 Guillon (1999), p. 173.
151 Donald M. Stadtner, *King Dhammaceti's Pegu* (*Orientations* February 1990).
152 *Ibid*. C.f. king Mongkut's reforms in nineteenth century Siam, which were likewise inspired by Mon-Sinnhalese practices (see below).
153 Based on a Sinnhalese model, the original Maha Kalyani Sima was a prototype for hundreds of similar ordination halls constructed over the following centuries: Guillon (1999), p. 175, and Nai Pan Hla (1992), pp. 76–84. The Maha Kalyani Sima was rather speculatively re-built in 1954 by Burma's pious prime minister, U Nu.
154 Hall (1981), p. 180, and Guillon (1999), pp. 166–68.
155 Dorothy Woodman, *The Making of Burma* (The Cresset Press 1962), p. 11. Woodman goes on to mention the sixteenth century visit to Pegu of the Venetian merchant-adventurer, Caesar Frederick. He noted "the King's passion for elephants, above all for a white elephant, and the royal pastime of elephant hunting": *ibid*. p. 19.
156 Phayre (1883; 1998), p. 159.
157 Guillon (1999), pp. 181–82.
158 Acwo (1923), pp. 56–5.
159 Hall (1981), p. 288, and Guillon (1999), p. 183.
160 Phayre (1883; 1998), p. 98.
161 Guillon (1999), p. 183.
162 See Lieberman (1978) and the same author's *Burmese Administrative Cycles: Anarchy and Conquest, c.1580–1760* (Princeton University Press 1984).
163 Guillon (1999), p. 189.
164 *Ibid*. p. 190.
165 *Ibid*. p. 189.
166 Nai Tun Thein (1999), p. 6.
167 Wyatt (1984), p. 93.
168 *Ibid*. p. 95.
169 *Ibid*. p. 101.
170 *Ibid*. pp. 102–03.
171 In 1680, on his way to France, the younger brother was shipwrecked and marooned for several months near the Cape of Good Hope: *Ibid*. p. 113.
172 Paul Ambroise Bigandet, *An Outline of the History of the Catholic Burmese Mission From the Year 1720 to 1887* (Hanthawaddy Press, Rangoon 1887; reprinted White Orchid, Bangkok 1996), p. 6. Phayre offers an alternative translation: "it is a lamentable spectacle to see the ruins of temples and noble edifices, the ways and fields full of skulls and bones of wretched Peguans killed and famished, and cast into the river in such numbers that the multitude of carkasses prohibiteth the way and passage of any ship": Phayre (1883; 1998), p. 271.
173 Blagden and Luce (1940).
174 Guillon (1999), p. 195.
175 Bigandet (1887; 1996), pp. 6–7.
176 C.f. the adventures of his near contemporary, the Englishman, Samuel White of Mergui (see below).
177 Halliday (1917; 1999), p. 93, Hall (1981), p. 398, and Guillon (1999), p. 195.
178 Guillon (1999), p. 196.
179 Hall (1981), pp. 399–401.
180 *Ibid*. p. 401.
181 *Ibid*. p. 385 & 403, and Guillon (1999), p. 196.
182 Woodman (1962), pp. 27–29.

183 Hall (1981), p. 407.

184 Stern (1968) and Gravers (1999).

185 The 'Gwe' may have been a Karen tribe, such as the Pa-O, or possibly the ancestors of the Lahu, or the Wa, or even a Shan group, as Hall and the Mon chronicler, the monk of Acwo, suggest. See Nigel J. Brailey, *A Re-investigation of the Gwe of Eighteenth Century Burma* (*Journal of Southeast Asian History* Vol.1/2 pp. 33–47; 1970) – characterised by Gravers as "highly speculative" – and Lieberman (1978), who suggests that the *Smin Daw* may have claimed to be half-Gwe and half-Burman princeling, and therefore not ethnically Mon at all (c.f. the 'Burman' king Alaungphaya, who was from Arakan). Martin Smith offers a simpler explanation, derived from interviews with modern Mon sources: *Gwe* may be a Mon term for 'ally': Smith (1999), p. 33.

186 Hall (1981), p. 408, and Guillon (1999), p. 199.

187 Lieberman (1978), p. 466.

188 Acwo (1923), p. 63.

189 Lieberman (1978), p. 467.

190 *Ibid.*

191 Bigandet (1887; 1996), p. 16.

192 Hall (1981), p. 409,and Guillon (1999), p. 199.

193 *Ibid.* and Bigandet (1887; 1996), pp. 14–16.

194 Guillon (1999), p. 199.

195 Hall (1981), p. 479.

196 Wyatt (1984), p. 130.

197 *Ibid.*

198 In the seventeenth century, the monopolistic Company had vied for control over the strategically important Negrais point with 'interlopers' under the command of the singular Englishman, Samuel White, the king of Siam's commercial and military commander at Mergui (and sometime pirate): Collis (1936; 1986).

199 Guillon (1999), p. 204.

200 *Ibid.* pp. 198–200.

201 Hall (1981), p. 410 & 426, and Guillon (1999), p. 200–202.

202 Lieberman (1978), p. 473.

203 Bigandet (1887; 1996), p. 18.

204 Phayre (1883; 1998), p. 168, and Woodman (1962), pp. 36–37.

205 Bigandet (1887; 1996), p. 18, Hall (1981), pp. 427–30, and Guillon (1999), p. 203.

206 Phayre (1883; 1998), p. 163.

207 See Halliday (1917; 1999), Brailey (1970), Hall (1981), Lieberman (1987) and Guillon (1999); for the classic Mon version of these events, see Acwo (1923), pp. 63–65.

208 Acwo (1923), p. 65.

209 Guillon (1999), p. 203.

210 Nai Tun Thein (1999), p. 7.

211 Lieberman (1978), pp. 472–74, and Thant Myint-U, *The Making of Modern Burma* (Cambridge University Press 2001), pp. 90–91.

212 Lieberman (1978). p. 476.

213 Thant Myint-U (2001), p. 94.

214 Guillon (1999), Appendix Two.

215 Brailey (1970).

216 Acwo (1923), p. 65.

217 Hall (1981), p. 434.

218 *Ibid.*
219 Guillon and Nai Pan Hla (1972) identify at least six major waves of Mon migration to Ayuthaiya-Siam between the sixteenth and nineteenth centuries. As is still the case today, the principal escape routes from Burma were from Mandalay to Lamphun and Chiang Mai in the north, via the Three Pagodas Pass half-way up the Thailand-Burma border, and via Tavoy to Kanburi and Prachuab Kiri Kahn in the south.
220 Karen villages were already well-established across large parts of northern and western Siam and the new migrants were encouraged to settle near them, in places such as Three Pagodas Pass and Si Sawat, in the Kwai River watershed. In the late eighteenth century, a Karen leader was made *Nai Amphur* (District Chief: lowest rung of the Thai administrative aristocracy) of Si Sawat and was charged with defence and intelligence gathering duties along the border: Renard (1980), pp. 71–72, and Maria Hovemyr, *A Bruised Reed Shall Not Break ... A History of the 16th District of the Church of Christ in Thailand* (Office of History, Church of Christ in Thailand 1997), pp. 1–4; see also Part Three.
221 Raikes (1957), p. 12.
222 Guillon (1999), p. 205.
223 Stern mentions that this uprising was lead by a fisherman, "who drew a following on the strength of the prophesy that a man of his calling would deliver the Peguans": Stern (1968), p. 302.
224 Guillon (1999), pp. 206–07.
225 Wyatt (1984), p. 152.
226 Halliday, in Smithies (1986), p. 11, and Guillon (1999), p. 208.
227 A later king, Chulalongkorn (Rama V), also drafted Mon seamen into his navy.
228 Foster, in Smithies (1986), p. 67.
229 Guillon (1999), p. 208.
230 *Ibid.* p. 208.
231 Guillon and Pan Hla (1972), p. 9.
232 Wilson (1997).
233 Halliday (1917; 1999), p. 17.
234 Reproduced in *The Nation* (13–12–99).
235 Mon music was used at the funerals of kings Rama III and IV: Wong (1998), p. 117.
236 Halliday (1917; 1999), p. 44.
237 Bauer, in Wijeyewardene (1996).
238 Nai Pan Hla (1992), p. 22.
239 For details of the *Thammayut* reforms, see HRH Prince Dhani Nivat, *A History of Buddhism in Siam* (The Siam Society 1965), pp. 30–36, and Foster, in Smithies (1986), p. 67.
240 Guillon (1999), p. 211. In 1993 the small community of Mon monks in Sri Lanka formed a Mon Buddhist Students' Association of Sri Lanka (MBSASL).
241 Wilson (1997). According to Wilson, the *pakhoma* – the characteristic Thai peasant sarong, made of lightly woven cotton, with a distinctive chequered pattern – is of Mon origin.
242 Lieberman (1978)
243 See, for example, Foster, in Smithies (1986), p. 75.
244 Keyes (1995), p. 146.
245 Foster, in Smithies (1986), p. 61.
246 Collis (1936; 1986); SarDesai (1994), pp. 60–62, and Woodman (1962), p. 26.

247 Fifteen thousand British troops died during the war, most of them from disease: A.T.O. Stewart, *The Pagoda War: Lord Dufferin and the Fall of the Kingdom of Ava 1885–6* (Faber and Faber 1972), p. 38; see also Woodman (1962), p. 80, and Thant Myint-U (2001).

248 Woodman (1962), p. 751; this license to revolt followed a similar address to the Arakanese, the previous year: *ibid.* p. 69.

249 Mon Unity League (1997; 1999), pp. 3–4.

250 See Part Three.

251 Hall (1981), p. 490.

252 Halliday, in Smithies (1986), p. 11.

253 Guillon (1999), p. 208.

254 *Ibid.* p. 208.

255 Taylor (1987), p. 155; see also Woodman (1962), p. 163. In contrast, at a key juncture in the Second Anglo-Burmese War, Karen guides led the British forces into Rangoon: Hall (1981), p. 639.

256 This account is taken from Nai Pan Hla's *Thu-tay-tana Sar-pay Myar* (or 'Combination of Researches'); unofficial translation.

257 Taylor (1987), p. 153.

258 Nai Pan Hla, *Thu-tay-tana Sar-pay Myar*, p. 157. According to Furnivall, Maung Zat's followers numbered 10,000: Furnivall (1991), p. 174.

259 *Thai-Yunan Project Newsletter* (June 1990).

260 Office of the Superintendent, Government Printing (1915), p. 24, and Furnivall (1991), p. 174.

261 *Ibid.* p. 64 and pp. 103–08.

262 Office of the Superintendent, Government Printing (1915), p. 43.

263 Furnivall (1991), p. 105.

264 *Ibid.* p. 106.

265 Office of the Superintendent, Government Printing (1915), pp. 67–68.

266 *Ibid.* p. 43.

267 Furnivall (1991), p. 108.

268 Stern (1968), p. 302.

269 Gravers (1999), p. 105, citing the *Journal of the Royal Asiatic Society of Bengal* (1845).

270 Stewart (1972), p. 44, and Thant Myint-U (2001).

271 Taylor (1987), p. 160.

272 'Report on the Census of British Burma', Government Press (1872; 1875), p. 11.

273 Taylor (1987), p. 154.

274 Woodman (1962), p. 100. From 1826–34, the British governed Tenasserim from Penang Island, off the Malay peninsula.

275 Smith (1999), p. 42.

276 Michael Aung-Thwin, *The British 'Pacification' of Burma: Order Without Meaning* (*Journal of the Southeast Asian Studies* Vol. XVI, II 1985; pp. 245–61).

277 Thant Myint-U (2001), pp. 207–240.

278 Keyes (1995), p. 96.

279 On integrative/exclusive patterns of nation-building in Indonesia and Vietnam, see Anderson (1991), pp. 114–19.

280 Chao-Tzang Yawnghwe, a Shan nationalist and scholar, goes so far as to state that, "under the British, there was no 'Burma'." According to this reading of history, the British cannot be accused of dividing Burma. Rather, the division between Burma Proper and the Frontier Areas constituted a recognition of the

political independence of these areas in the pre-colonial era: Chao-Tzang Yawnghwe, *Burma and National Reconciliation: Ethnic Conflict and State-Society Dysfunction* (Vancouver 29–4–2001), p. 3.

281 Thant Myint-U (2001), p. 253.

282 Taylor (1987), pp. 66–67.

283 A marble plaque in the southeast corner of the First Baptist Church in Moulmein (built in 1827) lists the names of missionaries, including 'the father of Mon studies', Robert Halliday, and his wife.

284 Guillon (1999), Appendix Three, and Hovemyr (1997), pp. 1–2.

285 *The Mon Forum* (August 1998).

286 Guillon (1999), p. 212.

287 *Ibid*. Appendix Three.

288 C.O. Blagden, *The Chronicles of Pegu: A Text in the Mon Language* (*Journal of the Royal Asiatic Society*; April 1907).

289 *District Gazetteer: Amherst District*; quoted by Bauer, in Wijeyewardene (1996).

290 Bauer (1984), p. 8 & 14.

291 *Ibid*. p. 8.

292 Lebar et al (1967), p. 96, and Guillon (1999), p. 209.

293 Nai Pan Hla, *Thu-tay-tana Sar-pay Myar*. This text describes Maung Thaw Lay's successful attempt in 1852 to prevent British troops, who had just entered Rangoon, from looting the Shwedagon Pagoda.

294 Furnivall mentions the desire of many 'Burmese Mon' migrants in Siam to return to Burma in the 1830s: Furnivall (1991), p. 144. NMSP President Nai Shwe Kyin's parents returned from Siam to British Burma in the late nineteenth century: interview (August 1999).

295 Taylor (1987), pp. 66–67.

296 Keyes (1995), p. 97, and Taylor (1987).

297 Dr S-M- (1999).

298 Thant Myint-U (2001), pp. 253–54.

299 Smith (1999), pp. 60–80.

300 Taylor (1987), p. 164.

301 *Ibid*. pp. 169–70 (characteristically, Taylor neglects to mention U Chit Hlaing's ethnicity).

302 *Ibid*.

303 *Ibid*.

304 Nai Tun Thein (1999), p. 9.

305 Taylor (1987), p. 67 & 74.

306 Nai Tun Thein (1999), p. 61. By great good omen, Emmanuel Guillon too was born on 6th August 1939.

307 Other founder-members included Vice-Chairman, U Ba Thaw (who in 1940 became Chairman, due to U Kyan's ill health), General Secretary U Dwe (a monk from Pegu) and U Ba Thein (the assembly member for Ye and House Secretary for Finance and Taxation): Nai Tun Thein (1999), pp. 10–11.

308 On the career of Aung San, see Aung San Suu Kyi, *Aung San of Burma* (Kiscadale 1991; second edition). The young idealists of the *Dohbama Asiayone* developed their political ideas in the face of constant harassment by the authorities (i.e. the predominantly Karen and Indian-staffed police and army), at a time when the foundations of Buddhist-Burman identity were felt to be under threat.

309 Nai Tun Thein (1999), p. 9.

310 Smith (1999), p. 59.

311 On the careers of the 'Thirty Comrades', see Bertil Lintner, *Bertil Burma in Revolt: Opium and Insurgency Since 1948* (Westview 1994), Appendix Four.
312 Taylor (1987), p. 226.
313 Nai Tun Thein (1999), p. 12, 17 & 24.
314 *Ibid.* p. 11.
315 Taylor (1987), p. 284.
316 *Ibid.* p. 285.

Part Three – Independence and Civil War

1 NMSP (1967; 1985).
2 Gravers (1999), p. 129.
3 Both Nai Ngwe Thein and Nai Tun Thein later served as ARMA Honorary Secretaries: Nai Tun Thein (1999), p. 13.
4 Bauer, in Wijeyewardene (1996). In 1939, the year of the ARMA's foundation, U Chit Thaung had published a Mon language general science textbook.
5 Nai Po Cho was the nephew of Dr Sholu (1837–1929), an American-educated Mon doctor (and another Christian), who spent some time on diplomatic missions to the still-independent court of lower Burma in the 1860s, before opening a private clinic and orphanage in Moulmein.
6 Sometimes known as the Mon National League.
7 Nai Tun Thein (1999), pp. 14–16.
8 *Ibid.* p. 14.
9 Annex 'A', Minutes of the Third Meeting of the Karen Affairs Sub-Committee – Regional Autonomy Inquiry Commission, Rangoon (November 1948); quoted in Renard (1980), pp. 23–24.
10 Nai Tun Thein (1999), pp. 15–16.
11 Taylor (1987), p. 234.
12 Taylor (1987), p. 286; Mikael Gravers' analysis of Aung San's conception of the state bears out this supposition: Gravers (1999), p. 42.
13 In October Nai Ba Lwin, Nai Hla Maung and other Mon leaders attended another Karen Congress, in Moulmein: Nai Tun Thein (1999), p. 26.
14 Taylor (1987), p. 227.
15 *Ibid.*
16 Thein Lwin, *Education in Burma (1945–1999)* (manuscript 10-7-99), pp. 13–14.
17 These were Nai Ba Lwin, Nai Mon U Ya, Nai Hla Maung, Nai Tha Hnin, Mon Sein Tun and Mon Ngwe Gaing.
18 Nai Shwe Kyin has described a number of incidents in which local authorities and militias in Mudon, Paung and Moulmein Townships intimidated Mon citizens, preventing them from voting: interview (August 1999).
19 Nai Tun Thein (1999), p. 18.
20 Nai Shwe Kyin, *Resume of Nai Shwe Kyin* (1994; revised 1999); Nai Tun Thein's account of the election agrees in most essentials with Nai Shwe Kyin's. He provides details of the Mons' seven demands, which included the provision of special Mon-dominated constituencies, and the creation of a state-controlled Mon armed force: Nai Tun Thein (1999), p. 20.
21 Nai Shwe Kyin (1999). There are some inconsistencies between Nai Shwe Kyin and Nai Tun Theins' accounts of these hectic months. Both agree though, that the MFL was established prior to the Mon Affairs Organisation (MAO) and Mon United Front (MUF); see below.

22 Nai Ngwe Thein had been close to Aung San during the war, and was a member of the BIA.
23 Nai Tun Thein (1999), p. 21.
24 Nai Shwe Kyin: interview (August 1999).
25 The wartime MYO had been re-established at Rangoon University in 1946: Nai Tun Thein (1999), p. 22.
26 *Ibid.*
27 *Ibid.* p. 23.
28 Smith (1999), p. 109.
29 Nai Tun Thein (1999), p. 27.
30 Nai Shwe Kyin (1999).
31 Nai Tun Thein (1999), pp. 27–29.
32 *Ibid.*
33 In July 1953 the agreement was published as part of a 'Joint Statement of the Executive Council of the Mon Peoples' Front and the Executive Council of the Kawthoolei Governing Body': Nai Tun Thein (1999), Appendix Three. The language of this memorandum bears some examination: having first stated that "the common urge for greater self-expression in our two peoples resolved itself into a common determination to acquire Independent Sovereign States", it goes on to outline a common platform: "1. That the achievement of Sovereign Independence was to be a 'joint effort' within Constitutional Means; 2.That ... if driven to it, the Mon people and the Karen people will without hesitation and in a united effort lay down their lives for the fulfilment of their common objective; 3. That no separate agreement, whatsoever, was to be signed by either the Mon people or the Karen people without the knowledge and consent of the other; 4. That in this common avowed purpose, all shall enjoy equal rights and privileges"; see also NMSP (1967; 1985), p. 10.
34 Nai Shwe Kyin (1999).
35 On 26th August: Lintner (1994), p. 9; MUF President Nai Hla Maung was also detained.
36 Nai Shwe Kyin (1999).
37 Nai Tun Thein (1999), p. 31.
38 *Ibid.* p. 29.
39 Smith (1999), p. 112.
40 Nai Tun Thein (1999), pp. 29–30.
41 *Ibid.* p. 31.
42 Government of the Union of Burma, *Burma and the Insurrections* (Rangoon September 1949), p. 26. Such a commission was provided for under the 1947 constitution: Smith (1999), p. 114.
43 Nai Tun Thein (1999), p. 32.
44 Nai Po Cho had been obliged to release a statement distancing the rump UMA from the occupation of Moulmein: *ibid.* pp. 31–32.
45 Nai Shwe Kyin (1999); see also the 'Joint Statement of the Executive Council of the Mon Peoples' Front and the Executive Council of the Kawthoolei Governing Body' (July 1953): Nai Tun Thein (1999), pp. 35–37, and Appendix Three.
46 Nai Tun Thein (1999), pp. 35–37.
47 Government of the Union of Burma (1949) and the 'Joint Statement' of July 1953.
48 Government of the Union of Burma (1949), pp. 27–30.
49 Nai Tun Thein (1999), Appendix Two.
50 Nai Shwe Kyin: interview (August 1999).
51 The MNDO was outlawed in August 1948: Lang (2002), p. 50.
52 Nai Tun Thein (1999), p. 38.

53 Who, upon his death in battle the following year, was replaced as MNDO Thaton area commander by his lieutenant, Bo Tint: *ibid.*

54 *Ibid.* p. 33.

55 Nai Shwe Kyin (1999); Nai Tun Thein confirms these facts, including the assassination (but not the date) of Nai San Thu: Nai Tun Thein (1999), p. 37.

56 Lintner (1994), p. 343.

57 Smith (1999), p. 140.

58 *Ibid.* p. 153. Nai Tun Thein reports that from the outset the KMT in lower Burma dealt in opium, which was distributed through the large Chinese community in Moulmein: Nai Tun Thein (1999), p. 44.

59 *Ibid.* p. 39.

60 Eye-witness interviewed by the author, plus Woman's American Baptist Foreign Mission Society, *Faithful Unto Death* (New York 1950).

61 *Ibid.* pp. 5–6.

62 Personal correspondence (June 2000).

63 *Ibid.* p. 39.

64 Smith (1999), p. 142.

65 Wyatt mentions the existence of a Burmese Mon separatist organisation in Bangkok in 1947: Wyatt (1984), p. 264.

66 Nai Tun Thein (1999), p. 39–40, and Sunthorn Sriparngern, *Eight Years in Monland* (Mon Unity League 1999; Thai language).

67 See Part Six.

68 Nai Tun Thein (1999), p. 42.

69 Nai Shwe Kyin (1999).

70 Nai Tun Thein (1999), Appendix One.

71 *Ibid.* p. 43.

72 MPF Executive Council Declaration: *ibid.* Appendix Two.

73 Nai Shwe Kyin (1999).

74 Interestingly, in the early 1960s this 'fundamentalist' sect was adopted by General Ne Win, who patronised it throughout his years in power. Originating in the town in central Burma of that name, the *Shwegyin* sect was founded during the reign of king Mindon Min, in 1856. Well-known adherents today include U Vinaya, the influential *Sayadaw* Thamanya, and his disciple, U Thuzana, patron of the Democratic Karen Buddhist Army (DKBA): Gravers (1999) p. 61 & pp. 95–97; see also Fink (2001), pp. 220–22, Thant Myint-U (2001), p. 151, and Part Five.

75 Nai Shwe Kyin (1999); see also the Declaration of the Executive Council of the MPF: Nai Tun Thein (1999), Appendix Two.

76 Nai Tun Thein (1999), pp. 44–45.

77 'Joint Statement of the Executive Council of the Mon Peoples' Front and the Executive Council of the Kawthoolei Governing Body' (July 1953): *ibid.* Appendix Three.

78 *Ibid.* pp. 45–46.

79 Ministry of Information, Government of the Union of Myanmar, *Burma Communist Party's Conspiracy to Take Over State Power* (Rangoon 8-9-89), p. 68, and Ministry of Information, Government of the Union of Myanmar, *The Conspiracy of Treasonous Minions Within the Myanmar Naing-Ngan and Traitorous Cohorts Abroad* (Rangoon 9-9-89 & 23-10-89), p. 71-72.

80 KMT leaders promised to continue working on behalf of the Mon and Karen nationalists – "a promise that was never more heard of", according to Nai Tun Thein: (1999), p. 46. However, Francis Yap and other KMT officers did maintain support for the KNU and NMSP; see below.

81 Nai Shwe Kyin (1999).
82 For example, in 1950 ARMA Chairman U Chit Thaung presided over a meeting of the Rangoon University Mon Society, at which Professor Gordon Luce presented a paper on 'Mons of the Pagan Dynasty': Luce (1950).
83 Nai Tun Thein (1999), pp. 49–50.
84 In 1957 a similarly-constituted Mon military academy was established by the MPF: *Ibid.* p. 46 & pp. 49–50.
85 *Ibid.* pp. 46–48
86 *Ibid.* p. 49.
87 Saw Moo Reh's Karenni National Progressive Party (KNPP) soon joined the front. The KNPP was however, regarded as 'politically backward': *Ibid.* Appendix Four.
88 Smith (1999), pp. 171–73
89 Nai Tun Thein (1999), Appendix Four.
90 However, the independent-minded KNU Thaton Battalion, which was to surrender in 1964, still refused to allow the MPF to organise in areas under its control: Smith (1999), pp. 172–73
91 Nai Tun Thein (1999), pp. 52–53.
92 *Ibid.*
93 Smith (1999), pp. 168–69; see also NMSP, *Report on Activities of the New Mon State Party* (1994).
94 See below and Part Four.
95 The following month, Sarit Thanarat launched a successful military coup in Thailand.
96 Nai Tun Thein (1999), pp. 54–56.
97 *Ibid.*
98 *Boak Dern Mon Tamoit* (in Mon); *Mon Pyi Thait Partee* (in Burmese).
99 Smith (1999), p. 185.
100 Nai Aung Htun continued as MPF Chairman, with Nai Tun Thein as General Secretary: Nai Tun Thein (1999), p. 57.
101 Nai Tun Thein dates this relocation project to the late 1940s: Nai Tun Thein (1999), p. 15.
102 Guillon (1999), p. 213. In August 1960 U Nu's commitment to create a Mon State was re-confirmed in a parliamentary statement: Nai Tun Thein (1999), p. 66.
103 *Ibid.* pp. 60–63, and Appendix Six.
104 *Ibid.* pp. 66–67.
105 *Ibid.* pp. 68–69, and Appendices Seven and Eight.
106 *Ibid.* p. 70.
107 *The Mon Forum* (August 1998).
108 Nai Pe Thein Za, a Mon Youth Organisation (MYO) activist and later NMSP deputy foreign minister, was also arrested at this time, and spent seven years in jail: Smith (1999), pp. 207–212.
109 *Ibid.* p. 211.
110 Thein Lwin (1999), pp. 9–10.
111 Nai Tun Thein (1999), p. 14.
112 Taylor (1987), p. 302. The BSPP considered Taylor a sympathetic commentator: Smith (1999), p. 199.
113 In 1981 seventy-two per cent of the BSPP Central Committee were ethnic Burmans; among the remainder nine were Mon, one Mon-Burman and one Mon-Shan: Taylor (1987), p. 320.
114 Bauer, in Wijeyewardene (1996).

115 Taylor (1987), p. 334.

116 Raja, in Wijeyewardene (1996).

117 Smith (1999), pp. 294–95.

118 *Ibid.* p. 281.

119 The decline of the CPT came about as an indirect result of Vietnam's 1978 invasion of Cambodia, followed by the outbreak of hostilities between Vietnam and China. The pro-*Khmer Rouge* CPT loyally supported the Chinese line and opposed the Vietnamese. Therefore, after 1978 CPT cadres were denied assistance from Vietnam or her client states, neighbouring Laos and Cambodia (which bordered on Thailand). At the same time, Deng Xiaoping's China, which sought closer relations with Thailand and other anti-Vietnamese Southeast Asian nations, began to withdraw support from the communist insurgencies in Burma and Thailand. In 1979 the Thai dictator, Kriangsak Chomanon, announced an amnesty for all CPT members. This offer was taken up by large numbers of activists, including many of the students who had gone underground in the early and mid-1970s. (Royal Thai Army Commander-in-Chief, later Supreme Commander, and later still prime minister, General Chavolit Yongchaiyud, also gained credit for his role in defeating the Thai communist insurgency.)

120 *Ibid.* p. 306.

121 Martin Smith mentions the presence of ethnic Mon CPT members in Tak in the early 1980s: Smith (1999), p. 299.

122 According to the usual method of insurgent strategy – derived from Mao's theory of 'people's war' – guerilla forces extract support and other resources from the rural population, which in turn invites retaliation from state forces, directed against villagers (the 'sea' in which the 'fish' swim).

123 See Part Four.

124 Gravers (1999), p. 145.

125 Smith (1999), p. 145.

126 Biographical details from Nai Shwe Kyin (1999).

127 Martin Smith has pointed out that the Thai Baht, rather than the highly unstable Burmese Kyat, remains to this day the preferred currency in the liberated zones along the Thailand-Burma border, and that the extent to which settlements in eastern Burma are in the orbit of Rangoon or Bangkok can be assessed by checking which currency is most readily accepted: Smith, in Peter Carey (ed.), *Burma: the Challenge of Change in a Divided Society* (Macmillan 1997)

128 Nai Shwe Kyin (1999).

129 On such occasions, Than Aung took the Mon name, Nai San Meit: Smith (1999), p. 269.

130 *Ibid.* pp. 273–280; see also Part Four.

131 *Ibid.* p. 288.

132 *Ibid.* p. 280.

133 Desmond Ball, *Burma's Military Secrets: Signals Intelligence (SIGINT) from the Second World War to Civil War and Cyber Warfare* (White Lotus 1998), p. 113.

134 Smith (1999), pp. 288–90.

135 *Ibid.* p. 222.

136 *Dop Panan Daleh Phu Kun Gakao Mon* (in Mon); *Mon Ahmyo Tuar Lut Myout Ye Tatmadaw* (in Burmese).

137 This, and the accounts of MNLA history in Part Four, are based on interviews with Nai Shwe Kyin, Nai Taw Mon, Nai Aung Naing and others, conducted between 1994–2001.

138 Smith (1999), p. 35.
139 Taylor (1987), p. 305. The veteran Mon politician, Nai Po Cho, who worked with Ne Win on the formation of the new state, lobbied unsuccessfully for Pegu to be included in its territory.
140 According to a well-researched article in *Focus*, a Bangkok news magazine (January 1982).
141 *Focus* (January 1982). Although some locally-grown *ganja* also found its way into Thailand, the large-scale trade in opium and its derivatives was largely confined to the Golden Triangle and northern Burma.
142 Quoted in Smith (1999), p. 25.
143 The party's inaugural 'General Congress' had been held in 1971.
144 'Clarification of Current Situation in the New Mon State Party – Clarification Statement Number One' (17–4–81), issued by Nai Shwe Kyin.
145 *Focus* (January 1982).
146 SarDesai (1994), p. 298.
147 'Clarification of Current Situation in the New Mon State Party – Clarification Statement Number One' (17–4–81).
148 *Ibid.*
149 *Ibid.*
150 'Clarification of Current Situation in the New Mon State Party – Clarification Statement Number Two' (3–7–81).
151 *Ibid.*
152 See, for example, Chamlong Thongdee, *Three Pagodas Pass* (Political Leaders Magazine 1997; Thai language).
153 *Mon National University Charter* (1984).
154 Among the administrative staff were a Mon language instructor from the Royal Thai Army, and Nai Pisarn Boonpook of Koh Kret: Mon National University, *1994–1996 Catalog* (1996), p. 30.
155 *Ibid.* p. 1.
156 In February 2001 the Mon Unity League (MUL), of which Dr Chamlong was a member, discussed re-establishing the MNU; see Part Six.
157 For example, NMSP (1967; 1985).
158 *Focus* (January 1982) and Smith (1999), p. 395.
159 See Part Four.
160 Ball (1998), p. 134.
161 Nai Shwe Kyin (1999). Although undoubtedly loyal to Bo Mya, Shwe Saing apparently maintained some contacts with the CPT in the 1970s (like Nai Shwe Kyin).
162 NMSP (1994).
163 Nai Shwe Kyin (1999).
164 Smith (1999), p. 359.
165 *Ibid.* p. 388.
166 MNLA sources and Ball (1998), p. 97.
167 'Joint Statement of the Executive Council of the Mon Peoples' Front and the Executive Council of the Kawthoolei Governing Body': Nai Tun Thein (1999), Appendix Three; see also NMSP (1967; 1985), p. 10.
168 Submissions to the September 1948 Regional Autonomy Inquiry Commission: Nai Tun Thein (1999); see also NMSP (1967; 1985), p. 10, and Gravers (1996), pp. 258–59.
169 'Statement Depicting Unjust Fatal Warlike Atrocities Committed by the Karen National Union Over the New Mon State Party and the Mon People' (28–7–88).
170 *Ibid.*

171 'Statement of KNU Central Standing Committee on Armed Conflict Between KNU and NMSP' (27-7-88).
172 KNLA sources claim that only twenty-eight Karen soldiers were killed; the NMSP says that the number was closer to one hundred.
173 The KNPP declined to join the DAB, as the Karenni leaders distrusted the alliance's federal agenda and did not wish to be distracted from the longstanding KNPP policy of reviving the Karenni states' historic independence.
174 Smith (1999), p. 410.
175 After leaving the PDP, U Nu had gone into exile in India, before returning to Burma under a 1980 government amnesty. He was replaced as leader of the re-named Peoples Patriotic Party (PPP) by Bo Let Ya, one of the legendary 'Thirty Comrades'. However, the PPP never regained the momentum of the early 1970s.
176 Smith (1999), pp. 405-6.
177 Christian P. Scherrer, *Burma: Ethnonationalist Revolution and Civil War Since 1948 – the Authentic Voice of Ethnonationalists, Insurgents and the Democratic Opposition* (Institute for Research on Ethnicity and Conflict Resolution 1997), p. 166 (interview with Nai Shwe Kyin).
178 See Part Four.
179 See Part Five.
180 Smith (1999), pp. 405-06.
181 But, see Part Six.
182 For details of the SLORC ceasefires, see Smith (1999).
183 *Ibid.* p. 315.
184 *Ibid.* p. 408.
185 A recent novel, *Tangay: the Setting Sun of Ramanya*, includes a dramatisation of these events: Nop (1997).
186 According to Christian Goodden, after taking possession of the three pagodas (situated on the Thai side of the border) the *Tatmadaw* men gave them a fresh coat of paint: Christian Goodden, *Three Pagodas: A Journey Down the Thai-Burmese Border* (Jungle Books 1996), pp. 269-70.
187 Government Press Release (19-2-90).
188 See Part Four.
189 The main thrust of this briefing, and a related publication, was to persuade local and foreign journalists that the CPB was behind the Burmese democracy movement. In passing, the SLORC identified Nai Shwe Kyin, Nai Pan Tha and other Mon leaders as long-term communist sympathisers: Ministry of Information (8-9-89), pp. 53-54.
190 This practice may derive from memories of the long-haired Mon warriors of the precolonial era. Karen insurgents at Kaw Moo Rah and elsewhere have been known to swear a similar vow, which should not be confused with the traditions of the Karen *Telekhon* cultists.
191 See Lian H. Sakhong's profile of the UNLD, in *Burma Debate* (Summer/Fall 2001).
192 Daw Aung San Suu Kyi was detained from 1989 until 1995. In 1991 she was awarded the Nobel Peace Prize, underlining her status as the most famous prisoner of conscience in the world during the 1990s.
193 Nai Thaung Shein was leader of the MNDF youth wing, the Mon Democracy Youth (MDY), established in 1990.
194 Among the unsuccessful MNDF candidates was the lexicographer Nai Tun Way, an ex-high school teacher from Rangoon, who stood in Bilu Kyun constituency and was later compelled to flee Burma.

195 The Kyaikmaraw MP-elect, Nai Khin Maung, was also detained for a time: *The Mon Forum* (October 1998).

196 Hovemyr (1997), p. 59.

197 The principal logging company concerned was owned by the tycoon, *Sia* Hook, who donated a covered market to the town he helped create.

198 Bauer, in Wijeyewardene (1996).

199 Donald M. Stadtner, *King Dhammaceti's Pegu* (*Orientations* February 1990).

200 Three Pagoda Pass and Wat Wiwaikarm reportedly received a combined total of 50,417 tourist visits in 1999: *The Bangkok Post* (18-6-00).

201 Many of the 20,000 ethnic Hmong residents of Wat Tham Krabok were previously allies of the USA and Thailand in the war against the communist *Pathet Lao*. For two decades after the 1975 communist victory in Laos, the community at Wat Tham Krabok continued to be closely associated with US and Thai-backed covert operations in their homeland. In the 1980s the temple became famous for the success of its drugs rehabilitation programme.

202 Keyes (1979), p. 51, Renard (1980), pp. 81-82, and Halliday, in Smithies (1986), pp. 11-15.

203 Renard (1980), p. 73.

204 An ancient Karen settlement, the remains of which are to be found near the village of that name, in the forest eight Km northeast of Sangkhlaburi.

205 Another ancient Karen village, further to the east.

206 Renard (1980), p. vi.

207 *The Bangkok Post* (21-8-2000).

208 The 1997 Thai constitution may yet address this issue (see Part Six). In the meantime, the Karen of Thung Yai continue to be harassed by the Thai military authorities, who seem determined to evict them from the forest.

209 Hovemyr (1997), pp. 49-50 & p. 59.

210 The presence of Burmese Border Consortium (BBC) and Medecins Sans Frontieres (MSF) staff in the area dates from the fall of Three Pagodas Pass; see Parts Four and Five.

211 See Part Four.

212 According Nai Sunthorn Sriparngern, "there is a similar cave (hiding Japanese war gold) in Mon State called Mount Sameinblai. In 1995 when NMSP entered ceasefire agreement with SLORC, Khin Nyunt whispered to Nai Rot Sa that he wanted to dig the cave. 'But I have no idea (where it is)' said Nai Rot Sa": personal communication (August 2000).

213 Renard (1980), p. 67.

214 *Ibid.* p. 87.

215 Interview (January 1999).

216 Re-organised in 2000 as the Mon Relief and Development Committee (MRDC); see Part Six.

217 For an interesting glimpse of Burmese opposition forces in Sangkhlaburi in the late 1960s, see Hovemyr (1997), p. 26.

Part Four – Revolutionaries, Warlords and Refugees

1 Aung San Suu Kyi, *The Voice of Hope: Conversations With Alan Clements* (Penguin 1997), p. 72.

2 Keyes (1995), p. 23.

3 Taylor (1987), p. 159.

4 Nai Shwe Kyin (1999).

5 The PDF brought eleven MPs-elect out to the border, including NCGUB prime minister, Dr Sein Win (a cousin of Daw Aung San Suu Kyi). The number might have been higher, had Mannerplaw not precipitously announced the NCGUB's formation, thereby tipping-off the SLORC, which was able to prevent the departure of further dissident lawmakers.

6 Other reasons given for the reduction in NMSP support for the ABSDF include a story that Nai Tin Aung, the party's influential refugee and foreign affairs commissioner, was angry with a student leader who planned to elope with one of his four daughters. If there is some truth to this, it is also true that Nai Tin Aung did not have the authority to act alone on such a matter: other NMSP leaders must also have been ill-disposed towards the often troublesome students.

7 Smith, in Burma Centre Netherlands and Transnational Institute (1999), p. 26.

8 Kachin Independence Organisation (1995). By this time, another group, the breakaway Kayan National Guard (KNG) from Karenni State, had also agreed a truce with Rangoon: Smith (1999), pp. 444–46.

9 Smith, in Burma Centre Netherlands and Transnational Institute (1999), p. 32.

10 Kachin Independence Organisation, *Kachin Resettlement Report* (1995).

11 The majority of returnees were settled at two main sites near the Chinese border. According to the KIO, "there is no official repatriation programme per se, rather ... these [resettlement] areas are already existing towns and villages which are in the process of being upgraded. Others were villages destroyed and abandoned during the civil war and must be re-established": KIO (1995), p. 2.

12 See Smith, in Burma Centre Netherlands and Transnational Institute (1999), p. 27.

13 See Part Five.

14 Quoted by Silverstein, in Carey (1997).

15 Lintner (1994), p. 384.

16 Smith (1999), pp. 445–46.

17 Lintner (1994), p. 385.

18 New Mon State Party, *Answer to Questionnaire on Mon Freedom Movement* (Mon National University 1985), p. 4.

19 See Smith (1999), pp. 262–68.

20 *Fundamental Political Policy and Fundamental Constitution of Administration* (Department of Party Procedure 15–12–94; Mon language document), p. 27.

21 Smith (1999), p. 286.

22 In 1976 the KIO and CPB, having previously been battlefield enemies, signed an agreement committing them to joint-struggle against "imperialism, feudal-landlordism and bureaucratic -capitalism": *ibid*. p. 331.

23 NMSP (1967; 1985), p. 1.

24 NMSP (15–12–94), pp. 43–44.

25 *Ibid.* p. 30.

26 On a possible new (ethnic nationalist) Mon State constitution, see Part Six.

27 Smith (1999), pp. 389–401.

28 In comparison, between 1974–91 neither the KNU nor KIO held a full congress: Smith (1999), p. 392.

29 See Part Five.

30 See Part Six.

31 The NMSP administration is divided into three main spheres – party affairs, administration and military: Lang (2002), p. 51. Each sector is directed by two of the six less senior CEC members.

32 See Part Six.

33 Mergui District is situated between KNLA Fourth Brigade's Eleventh (to the north) and Twelfth (to the south) Battalions.

34 Taylor (1987), p. 77. Taylor uses 1985 government figures to calculate that ten per cent of townships (between 1.3 and 3.5 million people, or between four and somewhat less than ten per cent of the population) were "not under the state's hegemony." Although he does take account of the incomplete nature of government staffing in the 'grey' and 'back' areas, the lower limit of this range probably underestimates the proportion of the country not controlled by the government in the mid-1980s.

35 Ball (1998), pp. 151–52, and MNLA sources.

36 Images Asia, *No Childhood At All: Child Soldiers in Burma* (Chiang Mai 1997)

37 Ball (1998), p. 151.

38 In 1996, when Nai Kao Rot became MNLA Mergui Battalion Commander, he was succeeded as MNLA Intelligence chief by Captain Nai Bagow Nedo.

39 Ball (1998), pp. 151–52.

40 Ball (1998), p. 152.

41 *Ibid.* p. 127.

42 See Part Five.

43 Quoted by Halliday, in Smithies (1986), p. 10.

44 W. Courtland Robinson, *Terms of Refuge: The Indochinese Exodus and the International Response* (Zed Books 1998), Appendix One.

45 *Ibid.* pp. 73–74.

46 *Ibid.* pp. 45–50 & p. 182.

47 *Ibid.* p. 74 (re. Cambodia) & 111 (re. Laos).

48 Less than 100,000 Lao were repatriated, but following the October 1991 Paris Peace Agreement, over 350,000 Cambodians returned home: *Ibid.* p. 240.

49 For a horrific catalogue of well-documented incidents, see Mon Information Service, Forced Labour on the Ye-Tavoy Railway Construction (Bangkok 1996), and Abuses Against Peasant Farmers in Burma: Emphasis on Mon State, Karen State and Tenasserim Division (Bangkok 1998), and Atrocities Against Mon, Karen and Tavoyan Villagers in Southern Burma (Bangkok 1999); see also Amnesty International reports, including Myanmar – Human Rights Violations Against Ethnic Minorities (August 1996; ASA 16/38/96), and Myanmar – Human Rights Under Attack (July 1997; ASA 16/02/97).

50 International Labour Organisation, Commission of Enquiry (1998). Two months after publication of the ILO report, its findings were corroborated by the US Government Department of Labor. The SLORC and SPDC have sought to justify the use of forced labour by referring to traditional practices of Buddhist merit-making, such as the donation of voluntary labour to civic and religious projects. Certainly corve (tax-in-kind) labour was an integral part of the precolonial state, and during the British period 'pacification' was often followed by the development of labour-intensive infrastructure projects. However, Buddhism is voluntary in nature, and the British usually rewarded their workers.

51 United Nations Office for the Co-ordination of Humanitarian Affairs, *Guiding Principles on Internal Displacement* (Geneva and New York 2000), Foreword. The Guiding Principles were presented to the United Nations Commission on Human Rights (UNCHR) in March 1998. See also, United Nations High Commissioner for Refugees, *Refugees and Others of Concern to UNHCR – 1999 Statistical Overview* (Geneva 2000), Table I.1.

52 *Ibid.* Introductory Note, by Francis Deng.

53 Global IDP Database <http://www.idpproject.org>.

54 For various estimates, see Burma Ethnic Research Group (1998), p. 16.

55 Various confidential sources (2002).

56 Htoo Wah Loo, Pwe Baw Lu and the dozen-or-so other KNU 'secret villages' established in Thailand in the 1970s and '80s cannot properly be regarded as refugee settlements.

57 Burmese Border Consortium, Programme Report (Bangkok August 2000), p. 32. It was only in 1991 that the Ministry of the Interior (MOI) issued formal, written approval for the relief operation. This mandate restricted assistance to food and medicines, although in 1998 MOI granted permission for a limited expansion of education programmes in the refugee camps.

58 *Ibid.*

59 BBC (August 1998).

60 Personal communication (1998).

61 BBC (August 2000).

62 BBC Programme Reports (1989 and 1994). Unlike the other camps along the border, Mergui District was always supplied by the Catholic Office for Emergency Refugee Relief (COERR), rather than the BBC.

63 Burma Ethnic Research Group (1998).

64 See Part Five.

65 CCSDPT 'Education Survey' (1995).

66 For a critical appraisal of the IDC system, see Amnesty International, *Thailand – Burmese and Other Asylum-Seekers at Risk* (September 1994; ASA 39/02/94).

67 CCSDPT (1995), and CCSDPT, *Educational Assessment of Karen Refugee Camps on the Thai/Burmese Border* (Bangkok 1996).

68 In 1996, following the ceasefire, this institution (established in 1993) was relocated from Pa Yaw to Nye Sah (Bee Ree), inside Burma. The location of the high school has generally followed that of the NMSP leaders' families; see Part Six.

69 CCSDPT 'Education Survey' (1995).

70 Thein Lwin, *The Teaching of Ethnic Language and the Role of Education in the Context of Mon Ethnic Nationality in Burma – Initial Report of the First Phase of the Study on the Thai-Burma Border (November 1999–February 2000)* (3-3-2000).

71 The Mon National Schools tend to overcompensate for the 'Burmanisation' of the state system, emphasising the glorious history of the Mon, while down-playing the Burmans' historical achievements: *ibid.*

72 For a thorough, academic-oriented account of the Mon and Burmese refugees, see Hazel J. Long, *Fear and Sanctuary: Burmese Refugees in Thailand* (Cornell Southeast Asia Program 2002).

73 *The Mon Forum* (August 1998).

74 Human Rights Watch/Asia, *The Mon: Persecuted in Burma, Forced Back from Thailand* (C614; December 1994).

75 In a number of essays and speeches, Daw Aung San Suu Kyi has discussed the universality of human rights, and the applicability of such 'Western' notions to Asian societies. Arguing from a profound knowledge of Burmese politics, culture and religion, she has demonstrated that such concepts are inherent to Buddhist ethics; see Aung San Suu Kyi (ed. Michael Arris), *Freedom From Fear* (Penguin 1991) and Aung San Suu Kyi (1997).

76 Another consequence of the disturbances in Cambodia was the flight of some 65,000 refugees to Thailand, most of whom were repatriated within a year: Robinson (1998), p. 279 & 284.

77 Ministry of Border Areas and National Races Development, Government of the Union of Myanmar, *Measures Taken For Development of Border Areas and National Races (1989–1992)* (Rangoon 1992).

78 See Part Six.

79 Human Rights Watch/Asia (1994), and Jesuit Refugee Service, *Compassion and Collusion: the Mon Repatriation and the Illusion of Choice* (Bangkok 1996), and *The Mon Forum* (January and July 1998).

80 Earth Rights International, *Total Denial Continues: Earth Rights Abuses Along the Yadana and Yetagun Pipelines in Burma* (Bangkok, Massachusetts and Seattle 2000), p. 22.

81 *The Bangkok Post* (5-9-96) and Earth Rights International (2000), pp. 160–61.

82 Human Rights Watch/Asia (1994). By the end of 1995 the Ten Aw See camps had again been relocated by the Thai military, and forced back across the border to KNU-controlled territory a few hours walk to the south.

83 Earth Rights International (2000), pp. 160–64.

84 *The Mon Forum* (March 1999) and Earth Rights International (2000).

85 Human Rights Watch/Asia (1994), and *The Mon Forum* (March and May 1999), and Earth Rights International (2000), pp. 112–14.

86 *Ibid.* pp. 127–35.

87 *The Bangkok Post* (14-2-99). Earth Rights International (ERI), an environmental and human rights NGO, has used cables from the American Embassy in Rangoon to demonstrate that TOTAL and UNOCAL did indeed establish a direct financial relationship with the *Tatmadaw*: ERI (2000), pp. 62–63 & 72–81.

88 World Resources Institute, *Logging Burma's Frontier Forests: Resources and the Regime* (1998), p. 8.

89 Karen National Union, Information Department, *Conditions in the Gas Pipeline Area* (1996).

90 *The Mon Forum* (March 1999).

91 Earth Rights International (2000), p. 40.

92 Mon Unity League (1997; 1999).

93 Earth Rights International (2000), p. 40.

94 Another key foreign supporter was the government of Singapore, which in October 1988 sent arms shipments to the new SLORC regime, which was still in the process of 'mopping up' resistance.

95 World Resources Institute (1998).

96 Martin Smith records that, under the Chavolit logging deals, the insurgents received 5,000 Thai Baht per ton for premium teak, and the SLORC 20,000 Baht: Smith (1999), p. 409. In a 1993 interview, Nai Shwe Kyin had put the NMSP cut as low as 1,500 Baht per ton for teak, and 600 Baht for other hardwoods: Scherrer (1997), pp. 67–68.

97 World Resources Institute (1998).

98 *Ibid.*

99 In the early and mid-1990s the author visited a number of lead and tin mines in KNLA Fourth and Sixth Brigades and adjacent parts of Thailand, where the miners were mostly Mon and Burman. 'Jonathan Falla' reports the presence of Mon miners in KNLA Fourth Brigade in the 1980s: Jonathan Falla, *True Love and Bartholomew: Rebels on the Burmese Border* (Cambridge University Press 1991), p. 356.

100 Ball (1998) pp. 61–65 & 70–80, and Smith (1999), p. 424.

101 NMSP (1994).

102 See Part Five.

103 *The Nation* (7-9-94).

104 *Ibid.*

105 *Thai-Yunan Project Newsletter* (March 1994).

106 Human Rights Watch/Asia, *The Rohingya Muslims: Ending a Cycle of Exodus?* (C8089; September 1996), and *Burma/Bangladesh – Burmese Refugees in Bangladesh: Still No Durable Solution* (C1203; May 2000).
107 For a critical analysis of Thai asylum policy and the role of UNHCR, see Human Rights Watch/Asia, *Burma/Thailand – Unwanted and Unprotected: Burmese refugees in Thailand* (C1006; October 1998).
108 Letter to Jack Dunford from Karola Paul, Acting UNHCR Representative in Thailand (22–2–94).
109 Personal communication (June 2000).
110 Letter to Jack Dunford, from Karola Paul (22–2–94).
111 *Ibid.*
112 A precedent for sending relief supplies across the border from Sangkhlaburi had been established in 1992, when a mixed Karen-Muslim settlement was founded inside Burma following a *Tatmadaw* offensive against KNLA Sixth Brigade. This and other Sixth Brigade refugee camps continued to be supplied from Sangkhla until 1997.
113 Sources for the 'Halochanee crisis': BBC Programme and (unpublished) field Reports (1994), Overseas Mon Young Monks Union (1994), Human Rights Watch/Asia (1994), and Mon National Relief Committee, *Mon Refugees: Hunger for Protection in 1994* (Bangkok 1994), plus eyewitness accounts and subsequent interviews.
114 *The Nation* (9–9–94).
115 Overseas Mon Young Monks Union (1994).
116 *The Bangkok Post* (10–8–99).
117 *The Bangkok Post* (20–8–99).
118 Robinson (1998), p. 85.
119 To the annoyance of regular staffers, the NSC Secretary-General, Charan Kullavanijaya, relied heavily on unofficial advisors. Chief among these was 'Mr X', a sometime arms dealer from an influential Thai-Chinese family, with contacts in the CIA. Mr X was intimately involved in pressurising the NMSP, and later the KNU, to agree a ceasefire with Rangoon. He was said to have stakes in a number of business ventures expected to profit from the pacification of lower Burma; see *Thai-Yunan Project Newsletter* (March 1994).
120 *The Nation* (7–9–94).
121 *The Nation* (9–9–94).
122 *Ibid.*
123 MNRC (1994); the actual number of refugees at New Halochanee was closer to four thousand people.
124 *The Bangkok Post* (23–4–95); Human Rights Watch/Asia (1994).
125 *The Mon Forum* (August 1998).
126 Smith (1999), p. 446.
127 NMSP (1994).

Part Five – The Mon Ceasefire and Since

1 Interview (August 1999).
2 Between September 1992 and January 1994, the author lived in, and taught English at, the Karen Teacher Training College in Pwe Baw Lu, a KNU-controlled village in Thailand, opposite Mannerplaw.
3 The following account is derived from confidential sources, plus Smith (1999), pp. 446–50.

4 *Kayin* is the Burmese exonym for the Karen. Observers found it suspicious that an avowedly nationalistic Karen organisation should adopt a Burmese name.

5 To the dismay of many activists, the 1996 NMSP calendar featured photographs of the SLORC and Mon leaders gathered at this historic occasion. Interestingly, the 1997 and subsequent calendars returned to more militaristic themes, depicting parading MNLA troops and senior officers. (The front of the 1999 NMSP calendar featured a young Nai Shwe Kyin, dashingly clad in *longyi* and fatigues, with a pistol in his belt.)

6 On the legal status of the MNSP, see Yan Nyein Aye, *Endeavours of the Myanmar Armed Forces Government for National Reconciliation* (U Aung Zaw, publisher 4–1–2000), p. 18.

7 NMSP statement (13-7-95).

8 NMSP statement (23-7-95).

9 Previously known as the Democratic Patriotic Army (DPA) – and before that, the CPB Southern Command – the MDUF was re-named in 1995, with the intention of emphasising its members' Tavoyan (or *Dawei*) ethnic identity. C.f. the ex-CPB groups in northern Burma, which in the late 1980s moved from the armed 'political' (communist) to the 'ethnic' insurgent camp.

10 Following the death from malaria of Colonel Sein Mya, in December 1993, the PDF had continued to undertake guerrilla activities behind enemy lines, while developing a capacity for human rights information collecting. In the late 1990s the last two dozen PDF fighters moved their base of operations to the Kya-In Seik-Kyi area.

11 In the mid-to-late 1990s the MDUF operated in two zones, in western Tavoy District and further to the south, in Mergui District.

12 See Part Six.

13 *The Mon Forum* (April 1999); the editor of *The Mon Forum* was present during the negotiations, in a different capacity.

14 *The Mon Forum* (July 1998).

15 Lacking teachers, books or government support, many of those state schools established in Wa and Kokang ceasefire zones, under the Border Areas Development Programme, were not a good advertisement for the programme.

16 *The Mon Forum* (August 1998).

17 NMSP statement (23-7-98).

18 Human Rights Watch/Asia (1994 and 1998) and Jesuit Refugee Service (1996).

19 BBC Programme Reports (1995).

20 *The Nation* (2-7-96).

21 *The Mon Forum* (November 1999).

22 Mon Information Service (1998), p. 9.

23 *Ibid.*

24 *Ibid.* p. 11. If a farmer is unable to fulfil his quota, he is forced to buy rice on the open market, then sell it back to the authorities – at about half the price. A 1997 Mon Information Service study of six Mon villages in Yebyu Township found that only 12.5 per cent of households were left with enough rice to feed the whole family, once the 'paddy tax' and various other payments had been made: *ibid.* pp. 24–26. Another scourge of the rural farmer is the forcible introduction of double – or even treble – cropping, often without regard to the appropriateness of this method to local conditions: *The Mon Forum* (March and November 1998; July and September 1999) and *Burma Issues* (October 1998); see also Part Six.

25 United Nations High Commissioner for Refugees, *Handbook Voluntary Repatriation: International Protection* (Geneva 1996), p. 11. These guidelines were drawn up in the context of UNHCR becoming increasingly involved in

refugee repatriation the world over: Human Rights Watch/Asia (1998). As Courtland Robinson notes, "when UNHCR won a second Nobel Prize, primarily for its work with Vietnamese boat people, voluntary repatriation was still not of great importance ... By the 1990s, however, repatriation was a growth industry (which) accounted for fifteen-twenty per cent of UNHCR expenditures in the 1990s, against less than five per cent in the 1970s and 1980s": Robinson (1998), p. 278.

26 The JRS report noted the importance of "ensuring that the returnees have been given the freedom and information to intelligently choose to return.... That they will enjoy protection, assistance, and international monitoring as they begin new lives": Jesuit Refugee Service (1996).

27 This huge sum included extensive 'integration and rehabilitation' elements. The *Rohingya* repatriation been criticised as less than voluntary in nature, and for effectively endorsing aspects of the government's forced labour campaign in Rakhine State: Human Rights Watch/Asia (1996).

28 Karen Refugee Committee statement (19–11–95).

29 See Part Six.

30 The new village at Naung Perng ('Throne of the Palace') may be located near the site of a precolonial Mon settlement: villagers have reported coming across the remains of ancient fortifications deep in the forest.

31 Mon Unity League (1997; 1999), p. 21–22.

32 Nai Sunthorn's *Eight Years in Monland* recounts the story of his adopted father, Royal Thai Navy Captain Anond Puntrikapha. After playing a leading role in the unsuccessful 'Manhattan Coup' of 1948, Captain Anond fled to Burma, where for a while he enjoyed the protection of then-*Tatmadaw* Commander-in-Chief, General Ne Win. Following this sojourn, he joined forces with the Mon People's Front (MPF),and when the front 'surrendered' in 1958, Captain Anond returned to Thailand: Nai Sunthorn Sriparngern (1999).

33 Figures for Mergui District were unverified, as it was not considered safe for outside observers to visit the area.

34 At Halochanee and Bee Ree, nearly forty per cent of refugee families had grown some rice, but at Tavoy District only seventeen per cent had done so.

35 Of the four strains of malaria, two – *plasmodium falsciparum* (PF) and *plasmodium vivax* (PV), both of which can be fatal – are endemic along the Thailand-Burma border. In 1990s, the world's most virile and drug-resistant strains of PF were found along the border.

36 Following the ceasefire, the Mon National Health Committee (MNHC) was also able to expand its activities (especially mobile medical tames) into government-controlled areas.

37 BBC (December 1997).

38 MAMD Statement (6–11–97).

39 *Ibid.*

40 Numerous examples among the Karen include Saw Da Bleh's militia in northern Tenasserim Division, and various groups in KNLA Sixth Brigade; on 'God's Army' in Fourth Brigade, see Part Six.

41 *The Nation* (7–9–94).

42 *The Nation* (3–10–96).

43 *Ibid.*

44 However, the following year in *The Bangkok Post*, party General Secretary Nai Rot Sah too praised the Yadana project, promising that the NMSP would not disrupt its completion (somewhat contradictorily, he went on to criticise the policy of Constructive Engagement): *The Bangkok Post* (25–2–97).

45 See Part Six.

46 See Part Six.

47 Having first received guarantees of his security, in April 1999 Nai Hongsa was persuaded to visit government-controlled Burma, for the first time since joining the insurgency in 1968.

48 In early 1997, the KNLA could field 4–5,000 troops, including about 1,000 in Sixth Brigade and perhaps another 1,000 (maximum) in Fourth Brigade. In addition, the KNU was able to call on as many as 1,000 thinly-spread KNDO militiamen, and small numbers of allied Peoples Patriotic Party (PPP), All Burma Muslim Union (ABMU) and All Burma Students Democratic Front (ABSDF) soldiers.

49 Human Rights Watch/Asia, *Burma/Thailand – No Safety in Burma, No Sanctuary in Thailand* (C906; July 1997).

50 *The Mon Forum* (January and March 1998).

51 *Ibid.*

52 BBC (December 1997).

53 Human Right Watch/Asia (1997 and 1998).

54 *The Bangkok Post* (18-6–2000).

55 Htee Wah Doh had been home to less than 500 villagers before the start of the offensive. By May 1997, there were 2,100 IDPs at the site, which was administered as a Karen refugee camp, by KRC Sangkhlaburi.

56 The ex-CPB Mergui-Davoy United Front (MDUF) had also previously operated in northwest Mergui District, but by 1997 had moved its forces further north, to the KNLA Eleventh Battalion (Fourth Brigade) area. Throughout 1996–99, Burmese state media reported the surrender of small groups of these communist remnants.

57 MNRC Report (April 1997).

58 This group included 100–150 Karen and Tavoyan refugees. Large numbers of ethnic Burmans and Thais were also displaced by the fighting – the latter being descendants of the pre-1792 Siamese population of Tenasserim Division. Having initially taken shelter with the Mon, the Thais soon moved on into Thailand.

59 *The Bangkok Post* (3-7–97).

60 *The Mon Forum* (January 1999).

61 *The Mon Forum* (January 1998).

62 In April 1998 the Thai authorities are reported to have forcibly repatriated two hundred Mon residents of Bang Saphan, most of whom had been living in the area for twenty years or more: *The Mon Forum* (June 1998).

63 Lintner (1994) p. 381.

64 Zunetta Liddell, in Burma Centre Netherlands and Transnational Institute (1999), pp. 62–64.

65 Martin Smith, in *Ibid.* p. 40.

66 David Steinberg, in *Ibid.* pp. 11–12.

67 By this time, the Academy for the Development of National Groups, established in 1965 to facilitate the and identification with the state (Burmanisation?) of ethnic minority cadres, had been up-graded to university status: Smith (1999), p. 441.

68 US Government, Department of State, *Country Commercial Guide Financial Year 1999: Burma* (1998), Chapter Two.

69 While many Rangoon Institute of Technology (RIT) students were taught at Moulmein Government Technical College, numerous Moulmein University undergraduates were shipped-out to a site near Mudon.

70 See Fink (2001), pp. 91–93 & 174–192.

71 Smith (1999), p. 361.

72 Lintner (1994), p. 380.

73 Rumours persist that these bodies were secretly buried in the spacious grounds of the Ninth Division headquarters, near Kanchanaburi. First Army personnel had done well out of the coup, Ninth Division officers gaining a more-or-less free hand in directing affairs along 'their' stretch of the Thailand-Burma border.

74 This was less than half the amount pledged: (draft) World Bank report (November 1999), Appendix Table 9.2.

75 Economist Intelligence Unit, *Myanmar Economy: ASEAN's Black Sheep* (18–4–2000).

76 *The Nation* (14–3–99).

77 US Government (1998), Chapter Two.

78 Economist Intelligence Unit (18–4–2000).

79 (Draft) World Bank report (November 1999).

80 "Narcotics has a major impact on Burma's balance of trade and maybe its leading export in monetary terms": US Government (1998), Chapter Two.

81 Bureau for International Narcotics and Law Enforcement Affairs, US Government Department of State – *International Strategy Report* (Washington DC, March 1999); quoted in *Burma Debate* (Spring 1999), pp. 5–12.

82 According to Ronald Renard, in the mid-1990s, Burma was producing 1,500–800 tons of opium per year, of which about 340 were exported (as heroin): Ronald Renard, *The Burmese Connection: Illegal Drugs and the Making of the Golden Triangle* (United Nations University and UN Research Institute for Social Development/Lynne Rienner 1996), pp. 100–03.

83 *Ibid*. p. 74.

84 Martin Smith, *Ethnic Groups in Burma* (Anti-Slavery International 1994), p. 51. This figure includes at least ten thousand Mon living in the Sangkhlaburi and Thong Pah Pohm districts of Kanchanaburi Province.

85 In June 1998 the Royal Thai Government estimated the total number of migrant workers in Thailand at 1.3 million, of whom less than half a million were legally registered. According to a Ministry of Foreign Affairs spokesman, about 700,000 of these people came from Burma: *The Bangkok Post* (11–6–98).

86 *The Mon Forum* (April 1998). In November 1999 the Thai authorities launched a concerted new crack-down on illegal immigrants in the border areas, during which several thousand migrant workers were forcibly repatriated.

87 *The Nation* (23–12–98).

88 *The Nation* (8–6–98).

89 The Nation (1 & 10–10–99).

90 A further similarity between Kosovo and Burma is illustrated by a strategic dilemma faced by the guerrillas of the Kosovo Liberation Army (KLA) in the first half of 1999 – one which has long confronted the KNLA and other rebel armies in Burma. Should insurgent forces be deployed in order to defend IDPs, the victims of ethnic cleansing (and in many cases the rebels' friends and family members) or should the insurgents adopt a mobile, guerrilla strategy, giving up the defence of vulnerable, fixed positions, and leaving civilian populations to fend for themselves? In the case of the KNU, the latter option was only adopted as a last recourse, after the fall of their last strongholds (and access to many cross-border black market routes) in 1997. The KLA was saved from such a drawn-out denouement by NATO intervention in Kosovo.

91 See Part Six.
92 All eight of the ASEAN member-states present in Geneva voted against Burma's suspension from the ILO: *The Nation* (25-6-99).
93 In a significant departure from the ASEAN policy of 'non-interference', Royal Thai Government delegates to the ILO were the only regional government representatives not to oppose the resolution making sanctions inevitable: *The Nation* (16-6-2000).
94 For example, according to Mon sources, in December 2000 the *Tatmadaw's* Light Infantry Battalion 299 forcibly conscripted porters to carry supplies and munitions along the sixty mile Thanbyuzayat -Three Pagodas Pass road. The NMSP complained to the Burma Army Southeast Command that this and other incidents violated the new labour regulations, but to no avail: *The Mon Forum* (December 2000).
95 International Labour Organisation, *Developments Concerning the Question of the Observance of the Government of the Union of Myanmar of the Forced Labour Convention, 1930 (No. 29): Report of the High-Level Team* (Geneva November 2001).
96 Independent Mon News Agency (8-11-01).
97 See Part Six.
98 In the late 1990s a number of US state and metropolitan administrations initiated selective purchasing laws, refusing contracts to companies doing business in Burma. Although, under pressure from the World Trade Organisation, the US Appeals Court eventually declared these statutes illegal, they helped to increase the pressure on Rangoon and persuade a number of American firms withdrew from Burma.
99 For a well-informed analysis of the issues under discussion here, see David Tegenfeldt (World Vision Burma Representative), *International Non-Governmental Organizations in Burma*, in Robert H. Taylor (ed.), *Burma: Political Economy Under Military Rule* (Hurst 2001).
100 Smith, in Burma Centre Netherlands and Transnational Institute (1999), p. 52.
101 Chris Beyrer, *War in the Blood: Sex, Politics and AIDS in Southeast Asia* (Zed Books 1998), pp. 36-52 & 140-146.
102 During the 2001 rainy season, a serious malaria epidemic ravaged southern Mon State, claiming several hundred lives.
103 In December 2001 the International Crisis Group reported that civil society in Burma was chronically repressed and under-developed, and should be supported. Only then could this sector take the lead in political transition in Burma: International Crisis Group, *Myanmar: Civil Society Too Weak to Effect Change* (Bangkok/Brussels, 6-12-01).
104 Smith, in Burma Centre Netherlands and Transnational Institute (1999), p. 52.
105 In *Responding to Myanmar's Silent Emergency*, in Carey (1997), Rolf C. Carriere (UNICEF representative in Burma from 1989-92) outlines the case for international humanitarian assistance to tackle the 'silent emergency' in Burma. Carriere outlines the crises in health and nutrition, water and sanitation, education, child and human development. He criticises the "new conditionality" that has lead many donors to embargo aid to Burma since 1988, and makes a well-argued case for re-instating foreign assistance to Burma. However, he underestimates the difficulty of implementing large-scale programmes in such a way as to actually reach – let alone empower – those communities most in need of assistance.
106 Marc Purcell, in Burma Centre Netherlands and Transnational Institute (1999), p. 92.

107 Seng Raw, *Views From Myanmar: An Ethnic Minority Perspective*, in Taylor (2001), pp. 161–62; parenthetic synopsis added.
108 World Concern also received permission to undertake a pilot community health programme in the four northern townships of Mon State – i.e. those areas least under the influence of the NMSP.
109 See Marc Purcell, in Burma Centre Netherlands and Transnational Institute (1999), p. 91.
110 According to Mon sources, the 'local Red Cross personnel' that the ICRC team met in Ye were in fact Military Intelligence agents, dressed in Red Cross apparel.
111 See Part Six.
112 For example, in 1998 families in Moulmein Township were forced to pay between 1,500–2,000 Kyat each towards the cost of building a bridge across the Ataran River, although the project was supposedly funded under the Border Areas Development Programme. In mid-1999 the Ye Township authorities built a hospital at Kyaung Ywa village, on the edge of the NMSP liberated zone, which was partly funded by the direct taxation of local villagers: *The Mon Forum* (April 1999).

Part Six – The Sheldrake and the Peacock

1 NMSP, *When Will the Civil War in Burma Be Over?* (1988). The original interpretation of this prophesy identifies 'the lions' with the allied forces returning to Burma at the end of the Second World War; alternatively, the emblem of the MNLA is a golden lion rampant.
2 MNRC Report (October 1998).
3 *The Nation* (27-10-99 & 26-4-2000). The Mon monks in Bangkok were credited with influencing the Finish government's decision in 2000 to accept one hundred Maneeloy residents (including more than a dozen Mon) for resettlement. However, three hundred residents remained in the 'Safe Area' in December 2001, including 70 Mon, many of whose future was highly uncertain.
4 Selected Mon Websites:
Australia Mon Association <http://www.geocities.com/CapitolHill/Congress/7408>
Mon Community of Canada <http://www.geocities.com/Athens/Column/8582>
Mon Culture and Literature Survival Project <http://www.monland.org>
Mon Forum <http:/www.monforum.cjb.net>
Mon Information Homepage (University of Albany, includes Mon hypertext grammar) <http://cscmosaic.albany.edu/~gb661>
Monland Restoration Council <http://www.monlandnet.org>
Mon Unity League (established in late 1999 by the MCC, on behalf of the MUL) http://www. geocities.com/Athens/Bridge/1256
Other Websites:
Amnesty International <http://www.amnesty.org>
Free Burma Coalition (information and links to opposition and other websites) <http://www.freeburma.org>
Human Rights Watch <http://www.hrw.org>
Karen Website <http://www.karen.org>
Myanmars Net (information and links to government, commercial and opposition websites) <http://www.myanmars.net>
Open Society Institute, Burma Project (information and links) <http://www.soros.org/burma>

Unrepresented Nations and Peoples' Organisation
<http://www.unpo.org>

5 The MCC incorporated, rather than succeeded, the Mon Canadian Association (MCA), which had been founded in 1995, and in 1998 had changed its name to the Mon National Organisation of Canada (MNOC).

6 The MRC was established in 1993, and originally known as the Independent (i.e. non-NMSP) Mon Council of Burma (IMCB).

7 In March 2000 the MRC had become embroiled in a public spat with the Burmese opposition in Fort Wayne, where many expatriates lived. The MRC accused Burman activists of co-opting the Mon, without adequate prior consultation: MRC Statement (9–3–2000).

8 'The Declaration of the Worldwide Mon Community on the 54th Anniversary of Mon National Day' (10–2–2001).

9 In the late 1990s Nai Sunthorn and representatives of the overseas Mon community engaged in a debate over the role of opposition groups in exile. Conducted primarily by email (mailing-list), the argument centred on whether it was better to establish and maintain Mon culture in foreign lands, or if the exiles' energies should focus more on the situation in Burma: monnet@yahoogroups.com.

10 See for example, Pisanh Paladsingha, *The Mon People* (Than Bua Kaeo 2000; Thai language).

11 MUL statement (1–2–99).

12 Established in mid-2001 by the Bangkok Mon, *Kao Wao* collected information from a variety of Mon sources in Burma and Thailand, and posted well-crafted information updates to the monnet mailing-list and elsewhere.

13 Together with the BBC World Service and the Voice of America, the DVB provided many people inside Burma with their only reliable news about the country.

14 The first edition of the *Mon Young Monks Magazine* included an article (*Democracy is the Name of the Game*), penned anonymously by Nai Shwe Kyin: Overseas Mon Young Monks Union, *Buddhist Way to Democracy: Mon Young Monks Magazine* (Bangkok April 1992).

15 In mid-1999 a small group of young Mon monks in Bangkok, recently arrived from Burma, chose to form a new Mon Young Monks Democratic Action Group (MYMDAG), rather than join the OMYMU.

16 Following the retirement of its co-director in 1999, the MIS-CPPSM became more-or-less dormant.

17 *Kao Wao 2* (22–11–01).

18 In December 2001 the International Crisis Group noted that "even organisations outside the regime's direct control tend to replicate the hierarchical organisational structures and lack of tolerance for dissent which characterise state-controlled organisations": International Crisis Group (6–12–01).

19 From October 2000, the MYC was chaired by Ms Armphai Markhamarn, a retired schoolteacher from Baan Pong.

20 Wilson (1997).

21 See Guillon (1999) and Bauer's Foreword to Halliday (2000).

22 *The Bangkok Post* (16–11–99).

23 Between 1999–2001, at least one hundred thousand Wa and other villagers from the north of the UWSA-controlled 'Wa Special Region 2' were transported to Mong Yawn and other sites in the South of UWSA territory, often against their will. Several thousand people died in the process, although the UWSA did provide some rice assistance to the new arrivals. The Wa authorities' intentions seem to have been to irradiate poppy cultivation in the north, to bring out-lying

populations more firmly under the party's control, to establish a strong presence on the Thailand border (both for the UWSA itself and for its Chinese backers), to outflank and displace Shan groups in the area, and to facilitate the supply of heroin and amphetamines-type stimulants to Thailand. The SPDC's interests in allowing the project to go ahead probably include provoking a further deterioration in Wa-Shan relations, splitting the UWSA, and unsettling the Thai state. UNDCP Rangoon has denied any involvement in the relocation project: interview (7–11–01).

24 *The New Light of Myanmar* (21–3–00)

25 For details of forced labour on various 'development projects' *since* the SPDC's order to halt such activities in October 2000, see *The Mon Forum* (May 2001).

26 E.g. a new irrigation dam constructed in Paung Township, in 2001, involved the forcible relocation of three Mon villages: *The Mon Forum* (April 2001).

27 Yan Nyein Aye (4–1–2000), p. 80.

28 MNRC (April 1999) and *The Mon Forum* (January 1998).

29 At the end of the 2000 rainy season, Myanmar Unique Diesel (a company with close links to the influential Kanbawza Bank) emerged as a potential new partner in the development of the Three Pagodas Pass-Thanbyuzayat road; the NMSP's old ally-nemesis, *Sia* Hook, and other Chinese associates were reportedly also involved in the project.

30 *The Mon Forum* (April 2001).

31 *The Mon Forum* (October 1999); see also MUL statement (1–6–2000).

32 MNRC (September 1998).

33 The NMSP was apparently still able to purchase arms from corrupt *Tatmadaw* officers: according to Karen reports, in May 2000 a captain from Burma Army Battalion 881 sold M79 grenades and assorted cartridges to the NMSP at Three Pagodas Pass: *Kwe Klu* (KNU-affiliated Karen language journal; 10–7–00).

34 Figures supplied by NMSP Joint General Secretary, Nai Hongsa (August 1999).

35 Confidential communication (December 1998); see also *The Mon Forum* (July and November 1998) and Mon Information Service (February 1999).

36 Also known as the Mon National Watch Army.

37 *The Mon Forum* (June, July and November 1998).

38 Mon Information Service (February 1999) and *The Mon Forum* (March 1999).

39 *The Mon Forum* (January and April 1999); see also below.

40 See *The Mon Forum* (September 2000), and Amnesty International, *Myanmar – Ethnic Minorities: Targets of Repression* (June 2001; ASA 16/014/2001).

41 Not to be confused with the Shan *State* Army East (SSA – East), a ceasefire group.

42 In January 1996 the SURA split from the mainstream Mong Tai Army (MTA), when in a surprise move its leader, the notorious 'opium warlord' Khun Sa, defected to Rangoon. A number of commanders from central and southern Shan State vowed to continue the armed struggle, and throughout 1996–2001 the SSA – South remained active, and pursued an anti-drugs policy. In retaliation, the *Tatmadaw* implemented a particularly brutal Four Cuts campaign against the civilian population, and tens of thousands of people fled to Thailand.

43 Smith (1999), pp. 448–49.

44 In 1997 the much-weakened ABSDF had made a virtue of necessity, more-or-less abandoning the armed struggle in favour of a campaign of political defiance. In the year 2000, most of the front's leaders, including Dr Naing Aung and Moe Thi Zun, resigned.

45 However, from its foundation in May 1999, National Reconciliation Programme (NRP) organised a series of seminars, training programmes and political campaigns, addressing the issues of peace and reconciliation, across ethnic lines.

46 Led by twelve year old twin boys, who were credited by their followers with the possession of supernatural powers, 'God's Army' had emerged in the aftermath of the 1997 *Tatmadaw* offensive in KNLA Fourth Brigade. Following the collapse of the mainstream Karen insurgent forces along the Tenasserim River, this millennial Christian group enjoyed some early military success against the *Tatmadaw*, thus cementing the twins' legend. By October 1999, the group numbered about one hundred and fifty armed followers. That month, the students who had occupied the Burmese embassy in Bangkok sought refuge with 'God's Army', thus provoking the *Tatmadaw* into concentrating its fire on their Kamarplaw base, in the forest on the Thailand border, near Suan Phung. Angered by the embassy siege (and hoping to dislodge 'God's Army' in order to exploit local hardwood stands), in early January 2000 the Ninth Division started to shell the Karen rebel village, killing a number of fighters and civilian followers. Denied refuge in Thailand, on 24th January ten desperados from Kamarplaw occupied the Ratchaburi Hospital. They demanded an end to Thai military shelling of their camp and medical treatment for their colleagues and villagers: *The Nation* and *The Bangkok Post* (25/31-1-2000). Crucially, the Thai military identified the hostage-takers as 'God's Army' members, thus turning sections of Thai popular opinion against the Karen, and justifying the Ninth Division's actions against Kamarplaw. However, subsequent information released by the Thai authorities revealed that 'God's Army' members had played only a small part in the siege, which was conducted by the 'Vigorous Burmese Student Warriors'.

47 *The Nation* (25-1-2000) – editorial.

48 After spending another desperate year in the jungle, the following January the twins surrendered to the Thai authorities, together with a small band of followers. Illustrating their ambiguous standing, Johnny and Luther Htoo were granted an audience with the outgoing Thai prime minister, Chuan Leekpai: *The Nation* (16-1-01). They were later offered asylum in the USA.

49 Nai Pagomon 'returned to the legal fold', and retirement in Rangoon, in early 2002.

50 During the second half of 1996 and early '97, the MDUF had attempted to negotiate a ceasefire with Military Intelligence Group Five in Moulmein. A meeting was arranged for September 1997, but the thirty-two member MDUF delegation was ambushed near Yebyu by a regular Burma Army unit. All but two of the MDUF team were reportedly tied to trees and beaten to death. (This incident recalls a 1983 *Tatmadaw* ambush on the CPB's southern leadership near Tavoy, during which more than twenty party officials and family members were killed.) Tavoyan sources report that MI5 later contacted the MDUF to 'apologise' for the *Tatmadaw*'s actions, which seem to have arisen out of a power struggle between Khin Nyunt's intelligence wing and front line military commanders. The government has since insisted that the MDUF does not represent an ethnic group (i.e. Tavoyans) but rather is a 'political' (i.e. ex-CPB) origination and as such faces the same bleak options as the ABSDF: surrender or be destroyed.

51 The 1997 floods affected "nine of Burma's fourteen states, inundating hundreds of thousands of paddy fields ... The United States Department of Agriculture reported that in the first 10 months of fiscal 1997/1998 rice exports declined from an average level of 300,000 tons per year in the mid-1990s to a mere 15,000 tons": *The Bangkok Post* (5-4-98). In August and September 1999 extensive flooding again occurred across much of Mon State. In Ye Township alone, some 200 households were made homeless, while as many as 60,000

people along the Gaing River in Moulmein Township and Karen State were affected: *The Mon Forum* and MNRC (August 1999).

52 *Burma Issues* (September 1998). On one army plantation alone, during the 1998 rainy season as many as 700 villagers were forced to work on what had once been their own land: MNRC (November 1998). For further details of land confiscated by the *Tatmadaw*, see Mon Information Service (1998).

53 In Mudon Township in 1998–99 farmers were reportedly forced to sell 800,000 baskets of paddy to government agents: *The Mon Forum* (June–November 1998 and June 1999). In August 1999 the author interviewed farmers in central Mon State, who were forced to sell around sixteen baskets of paddy per acre to government officials, at a rate of 400 Kyat per basket (about half the market rate). Failure to do so could result in a three year jail sentence. Alternatively, compliance with the government's demands could bankrupt poorer farmers, forcing them off of their land. The amount of rice villagers were required to sell at a discount was not adjusted even after the severe floods of August 1999: *The Mon Forum* (September 1999).

54 *The Mon Forum* (July 2000 & April 2001) and Amnesty International (June 2001).

55 As 'Nyah Phay Thwet' noted with bitter irony, "while the government is dependent on rice-production, rice is being burned in ethnic areas as part of the Army's ongoing 'four-cuts' programme": Burma Issues (March 1999).

56 Report reproduced in *Burma Debate* (Fall 1999).

57 *Ibid.*

58 Liddell (in Burma Centre Netherlands and Transnational Institute (1999), p. 64. According to some reports, in October 2001 the Ministry of Immigration and Population issued a directive stating that members of ceasefire groups living in Rangoon and Mandalay would be eligible for identification cards. It is expected that members – and clients – of Wa and Kokang groups in particular would benefit from this development: *The Irrawaddy* (November 2001).

59 Since mid-1996, the SLORC had "started to use soldiers in building the railway construction with payment. At the same time, the local civilians were still forced to provide free labour in the construction": MNRC (September 1998).

60 *The Mon Forum* (August 1999).

61 *The Mon Forum* (November 2000 & May 2001).

62 Amnesty International (June 2001). Such abuses were not limited to the countryside: during the 1998 dry season, one hundred residents of Moulmein were reportedly taken each day to work unpaid on the construction of an exclusive army golf course, built on confiscated land: *The Mon Forum* (April 1998), plus eyewitness accounts.

63 Burma Ethnic Research Group (1998).

64 MNRC (September 1998).

65 *Burma Debate* (Fall 1999).

66 In April 2000, for example, thirty Mon refugee families living illegally around Thong Pah Pohm were repatriated to NMSP Tavoy District: Mon Relief and Development Committee (April 2000).

67 A number of houses on 'Mon side' were burnt down during the 1999 dry season. Although arson was suspected, a local Thai businessman was allowed to construct a small hotel on the now conveniently empty site. Similar incidents occurred the following year.

68 MNRC (December 1998).

69 BBC Programme Reports (1998–2001).

70 MNRC (January–April 1998).

71 MNRC (August and October 1998).

72 *The Bangkok Post* (16–10–98). Maj-General Sanchai was promoted to Ninth Division Commander in 1999; he died in a helicopter crash on 25th February 2000: *The Nation* (26–2–00).

73 *The Mon Forum* (May 2000).

74 Mon Relief and Development Committee (April and May 2000).

75 Over the 2001 rainy season, nineteen per cent of families at Halochanee (including Htee Wah Doh), forty per cent of those at Bee Ree and twenty-three per cent in Tavoy District had cultivated rice farms: Mon Relief and Development Committee (November 2001).

76 *Ibid*.

77 Between January–June 2000, under-fives at Halochanee suffered the highest rates of malnutrition among the refugees along the border (2.62 per cent moderate and 0.17 per cent severe malnutrition): BBC (August 2000). It should be noted however, that these figures compared favourably with the standards of rural Burma: the most malnourished refugees tended to be new arrivals.

78 6,742 people at Halochanee (including the Karen from Htee Wah Doh – see below), 3,484 at Bee Ree and 3,378 in Tavoy District: Mon Relief and Development Committee (November 2001). The BBC's slightly more conservative, and probably more accurate, figures put the population of Halochanee at 6,437 (including 800 Karen): BBC (November 2001).

79 BBC (November 2001).

80 Over the 2000 dry season, more new arrivals from Arakan State had arrived in Bangladesh, further swelling the *Rohingya* refugee caseload and complicating UNHCR's controversial repatriation programme: Human Rights Watch/Asia (2000).

81 BBC (February 2002).

82 BBC (July 1999).

83 MNRC (December 1999); for details of community development training and implementation, see MRDC (June 2000 and February 2001).

84 MRDC (January 2000).

85 MRDC (November 2000).

86 Burma Ethnic Research Group (1998), p. 47.

87 Images Asia, *A Question of Security* (Chiang Mai 1998). In 1997 an anti-KNPP group, with links to the *Tatmadaw*, began launching attacks on Karenni refugee camps in Thailand.

88 BBC Programme Report (1998).

89 BBC Programme Report (1999).

90 *The Nation* (17 & 18–10–00). In August 1998 UNHCR Bangkok officials had met with MNRC and local KRC personnel, in Sangkhlaburi. They later visited the Karen refugee camp at Baan Don Yang (the site to which Mon refugees had fled in July 1994), but did not go to Halochanee.

91 Among those responsible for organising the aborted celebrations was the MNDF General Secretary and MP-elect, Dr Min Soe Lin, who was briefly detained by the authorities the following November: *The Mon Forum* (October 1998).

92 HRFM statement (9–2–98).

93 Fink (2001), p. 71.

94 *The BurmaNet News* (7–12–99); electronic newspaper <www.burmanet.org>

95 Bauer, in Wijeyewardene (1996).

96 Anthony D. Smith (1988), p. 157.

97 *The Mon Forum* (October 1998).

98 Mon Language Literacy Training Course report (2000).

 99 At the time of writing, it was not clear whether donors would continue to support the NMSP school system.
100 *The Mon Forum* (August 1998).
101 *Ibid.*
102 *The Mon Forum* (July 1998 and January 1999).
103 *The Mon Forum* (January 1999). The ban on Mon language teaching in Kawkareik was re-enforced at the end of the rainy season: *The Mon Forum* (October 2000).
104 MNEC report (1999).
105 Thein Lwin (2000).
106 Of these 365 schools, 109 were located in Tavoy District, 133 in Thaton District, 108 in Moulmein District and 15 in the resettlement sites: MNEC report (2001).
107 Another benefit of the ceasefire – at least for the individuals concerned – was that a number of Mon students who had had their studies interrupted between 1988–92 were able to return to college or university, and complete a truncated education.
108 SPDC 'Information Sheet No. B-1156', posted to <soc.culture.burma> usegroup (21–11–99).
109 *The Mon Forum* (September 1999).
110 *The Mon Forum* (February 2000).
111 *The Mon Forum* (April 2001).
112 Ministry of Information (9–9–89), p. 131
113 For example, *The New Light of Myanmar* (1–11–2000): report on the NMSP President meeting with Generals Khin Nyunt, Ket Sein, Kyaw Win and others, at a government guest house in Rangoon.
114 *Interview With Mon Leader* (16–2–98; translated from the Thai). The 1999 addendum to Nai Shwe Kyin's *Resume* also disparages the value of sanctions and criticises the NLD for lobbying in their favour: Nai Shwe Kyin (1999), p. 5.
115 In July 1998 an MUL representative had attended the UN Working Group on Indigenous Populations, in Geneva: MUL Statement (28–7–98). In August 1998 a representative of the Monland Restoration Council (MRC) attended the First International Conference on the Right to Self-determination and the United Nations, in Geneva.
116 Phra Wongsa left the *sangha* in early 2001, and the new Nai Wamsa was married on 14th December, in Sangkhlaburi.
117 MUL member-organisations (and number of representatives on Central Committee), February 2001: Thai-Mon Youth Community (7); Mon Youth Association (3); All Mon Youth Organisation (3); Mon Literature Promotion Association (3); Mon Women Rights Organisation (3); Mon Youth Organisation, Sangkhlaburi (3); Mon Literature and Culture Committee (3); Committee for Dry Season Mon Literacy Training (3); Mon Information Service (3); Human Rights Foundation of Monland (3); Mon National Democratic Front, Australia (3); individual representatives (8): MUL Report on International Conference on Mon National Affairs (15–2–01).
118 MUL General Statement (15–2–01).
119 Seng Raw, in Taylor (2000), p. 163.
120 Among those ceasefire groups in loose alliance with the KIO were the Kachin Democratic Army (KDA) – the breakaway KIA Fourth Brigade, which observers expected eventually to re-unite with the KIO – the Paluang Sate Liberation Party (PSLP) and three ex-CPB groups: the United Wa State Army (UWSA), the Mongko Region Defence Force and the National Democratic Army (NDA); the latter two groups included many ethnic Kachins in their ranks.

121 Quoted by Seng Raw, in Taylor (2000), p. 163.

122 KIO Central Committee Announcement (26–2–01).

123 Maj-General Sit Maung died, together with SPDC Secretary Two, Lt-General Tin Oo, on 19th February 2001, when their helicopter crashed into the Salween River, killing at least fourteen *Tatmadaw* men. This. Tin Oo had been close to the SPDC Vice-Chairman, General Maung Aye – the man regarded as Khin Nyunt's main rival within the junta (and General Than Shwe's most likely successor).

124 Not long after the ceasefire, Rehmonya International had been granted a banking license, but this was withdrawn following the 1997 'Asian financial crisis'.

125 Since the mid-late 1990s, fishing fleets owned by Mon businessmen – some of whom may be associated with the NMSP – have played a key role in smuggling narcotics and amphetamine-type stimulants overseas from Moulmein, under contract from cartels in northeast Burma and elsewhere.

126 In the mid-1990s, the *Tatmadaw* had numbered about 350,000 men: Andrew Selth, *Transforming the Tatmadaw* (Cambridge Papers on Strategy and Defence No. 113, 1996).

127 Smith (1999), p. 169.

128 *The Mon Forum* (January 1999).

129 NMSP statement (18–8–98).

130 *The BurmaNet News* (25/27–9–98).

131 *The Mon Forum* (October 1998).

132 The MNDF leaders were arrested on 6th and 7th September: *ibid.*

133 *The BurmaNet News* (25/27–9–98).

134 NMSP statement (28–9–98).

135 KIO statement (11–10–99).

136 *The New Light of Myanmar* (3–10–98).

137 *The Mon Forum* (October 1998 and January 1999).

138 *The Mon Forum* (January 1999).

139 Nai Ngwe Thein is diabetic, and his colleague, Dr Min Soe Lin, suffers from hypertension; both have experienced serious health complications in jail: Overseas Mon Young Monks Union, *La Gam Bop Paw* (Issue I, Bangkok February 2000; English and Mon language).

140 Nai Tun Thein's other publications (mostly written under his pen-name, Nai Thaw Sun) include *A History of Hongsawatoi* (in Mon), *The Mon Kingdom of Thaton, Pada and Hongsawaddy* (in Burmese), and a number of Mon grammars and dictionaries.

141 On the same day, Daw Aung San Suu Kyi's husband, the respected British Tibetan scholar, Dr Michael Arris, passed away, on his 53rd birthday.

142 Quoted in *The Nation* (18–11–99).

143 NMSP statement (20–2–2000).

144 *The BurmaNet News* (2–2–2000).

145 *The BurmaNet News* (12/13–2–2000).

146 Government 'Information Sheet': *The BurmaNet News* (29/30–4–2000).

147 The UNLD [LA] was actually founded in February 1998: 'Announcement For Holding of UNLD [LA] Inaugural Congress' (24–4–2000).

148 The ENSCC Way on initiative of the NRP: ENSCC, *The New Panglong Initiative: Re-building the Union of Burma* (2002).

149 'Announcement For Holding of UNLD [LA] Inaugural Congress' (24–4–2000).

150 Democratic Voice of Burma, Oslo: *The BurmaNet News* (30–01–01). On 30th January leaders of the Shan Nationalities League for Democracy (SNLD)

and other groups met with a visiting EU delegation to Burma, to whom they expressed similar hopes regarding the future participation of 'ethnic' parties in the NLD-SPDC talks: *The BurmaNet News* (31-01-01).

151 A week later, a major NCUB-NCGUB meeting likewise welcomed news of the NLD-SPDC talks, and called for their contents to be made public, and for the rapid introduction into the negotiations of a tripartite element, to include the remaining insurgent groups: *The Bangkok Post* (9-3-01).

152 *The Nation* (21-4-01).

153 *The New Light of Myanmar* (28-3-01).

154 *The Nation* (7-4-01).

155 *The Nation* (18-2-01).

156 In 2001 the Humanitarian Dialogue Centre in Rangoon was mandated by the UN Special Envoy to assess the responses of ethnic minority parties (including both ceasefire and no-ceasefire groups) to the dialogue process.

157 *Reuters*, Rangoon (28-11-01).

158 Confidential source.

159 Independent Mon News Agency (4-11-01).

160 *Kao Wao 2* (22-11-01).

161 MUL Statement (24-11-01).

162 On 7th November the DVB opposition radio station reported that Nai Pan Nyunt's men had taken part, together with the KNU, in fighting with the *Tatmadaw*, in the vicinity of the gas pipeline. If this was the case, then Nai Pan Nyunt must already have joined forces with the MNDA, which patrolled close to the pipeline corridor.

163 Hongsawatoi Restoration Party Declaration No. 2/2001.

164 *Kao Wao 3* (3-12-01).

165 Independent Mon News Agency (5-12-01).

166 According to *Kao Wao*, "the troops conscripted local villagers to carry their ammunition and food at Chaung Zone village which is located west from Three Pagodas Pass border town ... The local village was in turmoil with people fleeing in panic, because the army forces people to be conscripted into portering. When the villagers flee and hide away from the village, the village headmen is forced at gunpoint to find 15 villagers to serve the army": *Kao Wao 2* (22-11-01).

167 Account based on BBC reports, and the Independent Mon News Agency, *Kao Wao*, *The Mon Forum* and MRDC.

168 Martin Smith suggests that the existence of structural similarities between armed opposition and government forces helps to explain the phenomena of insurgent leaders agreeing ceasefires with counterpart warlords in the *Tatmadaw*: Smith, in Burma Centre Netherlands and Transnational Institute (1999), p. 48.

169 On the contemporary influence of traditional Burmese political and religious concepts, see Gravers (1999), Houtman (1999), and also Chris Cusano's article in *Burma Issues* (March 1999); see also Benedict Anderson's influential analysis of *The Idea of Power in Javanese Culture*, and the necessity of understanding traditional concepts, in order to transform them: Benedict Anderson, *Language and Power: Exploring Political Cultures in Indonesia* (Ithaca: Cornell University Press 1990), pp. 72-77.

170 Gravers (1999), p. 124.

171 Aung-Thwin (1998), pp. 158-59.

Key Dates in Mon History

Date	Thailand	Burma
5th Cent. BC–5th Cent. AD	Mon-Khmer people settle across mainland Southeast Asia; separation of proto-Mon from Mon-Khmer language group	
3rd Cent. BC		Indian Buddhist king Asoka's mission to Burma (traditional)
Early Centuries AD		Mon displace Pyu in central Burma, establish city states in lower Burma (early capital at Thaton)
6th Century AD	Earliest inscriptions and remains of Mon settlements in Menam basin	
7th–9th Centuries	Flourishing Dvaravati culture	
Early 9th Century	Foundation of Haripunjaya (by Queen Camadevi of Lopburi)	
825		Foundation of Pegu (traditional)
1057		Anawratha of Pagan makes war on Thaton, captures Mon king Manuha and Buddhist monks and scriptures, transporting them to Pagan (traditional)
c. 1050–1180		'Mon Pagan' – profound Mon influence in fields of religion, law and architecture
Mid-late 12th century	Reformation of Haripunjaya	
13th Century	Theravada Buddhist revival across Southeast Asia, emanating from Sri Lanka, via Pagan and the Mon	

Date	Thailand	Burma
1283	King Rama Khamhaeng of Sukhothai; extension of Tai influence	
1287		Mongol forces invade upper Burma; King Wareru re-establishes Mon dynasty in lower Burma
1292	Fall of Haripunjaya; foundation of La Na	
1369		Following Thai incursions, Bannya U re-establishes capital of Hongsawaddy at Pegu
1393		King Rajadhirat reigns at Pegu
15th Century	Theravada Buddhist revival in mainland Southeast Asia, emanating from Sri Lanka, via Pegu	
1453		Queen Shinsawbu reigns at Pegu
1470		King Rajaddapti (Dhammaceti) reigns at Pegu
1539 & 1541		Pegu and Martaban fall to king Tabinshwehti; extensive massacres
1550		*Smin Daw* Rebellion in lower Burma; crushed by king Bayinnaung
1595	First recorded mass exodus from Pegu to Ayuthaiya	
1599		Arakanese invasion; lower Burma laid waste
1613		De Brito and Bannya Dalas' rebellion crushed by king Aneukpetlun; refugees flee to Ayuthaiya
1628 & 1661		Mon rebellions crushed; refugees flee to Ayuthaiya
1740		Second *Smin Daw* uprising; Mon power restored at Pegu
1747		Bannya Dala replaces *Smin Daw* in palace coup
1752–1753		With French and Portuguese help, Mon army captures – then loses – Ava; Burman forces resurgent under king Alaungphaya
1756–1757		Fall of Syriam and Pegu; extensive massacres; refugees flee to Ayuthaiya
1758–1815		Repeated, unsuccessful Mon rebellions in lower Burma

Date	Thailand	Burma
1767	Ayuthaiya sacked by Burman army	
1824–1826		First Anglo-Burmese War; British annexation of Tenasserim and Arakan
1838		Mon uprising in lower Burma
Mid-late 19th Century	Renewed Mon influence on Thai court and *sangha*	
1852		Second Anglo-Burmese War; annexation of Pegu and lower Burma
1886		Third Anglo-Burmese War; annexation of Mandalay and upper Burma
6–8–1939		Foundation of All Ramanya Mon Association (Rangoon)
December 1941	'Thirty Comrades' swear oath at Wat Prok, Bangkok; foundation of Burma Independence Army	Japanese 'liberation' of Burma; Ba Maw regime established

Date	Event (Burma)
9–11–45	Following reformation of ARMA, foundation of United Mon Association – first overtly political Mon organisation of modern era (UMA expelled from ARMA in early 1947)
5–2–47	Foundation of Karen National Union
February 1947	'Conference of the Nationalities' at Panglong, Shan State
9–4–47	Six independent Mon politicians defeated in elections to Constituent Assembly
19–7–47	Assassination of Aung San and cabinet colleagues
August 1947	Foundation of Mon Freedom League, following government rejection of Mon 'Seven Point Demand'
Late 1947	Foundation of Mon United Front at Mon National Conference in Mudon; decision to achieve Mon national self-determination by any means necessary
4–1–48	Burmese Independence; U Nu prime minister
March 1948	Foundation of Mon National Defence Organisation – first armed Mon group of modern era
20–7–48	Mon rebels seize weapons from Zarthabyin police station, raise Mon flag and initiate armed conflict

Date	Event (Burma)
August 1948	Mon-Karen 'Four Point Agreement' (Moulmein); Mon leaders arrested
30 & 31–8–48	Karen and Mon forces occupy Thaton and Moulmein
September 1948	Insurgents withdraw from Moulmein; formation of Enquiry Commission for Regional Autonomy (interim report February 1949)
January 1949	KNU rebels occupy Insein, supported by MNDO troops; withdraw after three months of constant bombardment
April 1950 & 12–8–50	Deaths of MUF Chairman Nai Tha Hnin and KNU Chairman Saw Ba U Gyi
19–2–52	Foundation of Mon People's Solidarity Group, forerunner to Mon People's Front (established 1955)
1956	MPF joins Democratic Nationalities United Front
12–7–58	Mon People's Front agrees ceasefire with Rangoon
20–7–58	Foundation of New Mon State Party
Sept. 1958– April 1960	First Ne Win administration
1959	NMSP joins CPB-sponsored National Democratic United Front
1960–62	Mon Ministers in last U Nu administration; preparations for creation of Mon and Arakan States
2–3–62	Ne Win coup d'etat; Mon and other politicians imprisoned
1965	NMSP headquarters established under KNU patronage near Three Pagodas Pass
12–5–70	NMSP-KNU-U Nu alliance (Bangkok)
August 1971	NMSP inaugural General Congress; formation of Mon National Liberation Army
1972	Mon National Relief Party contingent joins MNLA, which throughout 1970s is dogged by splits
March 1974	New Burmese constitution; Mon State created
December 1974	Disturbances at U Thant's funeral in Rangoon; more dissidents join insurgents in border areas
October 1980 –January 1981	NMSP Congress at Three Pagodas Pass; party splits into two factions, led by Nai Non Lar and Nai Shwe Kyin
June 1982	Nai Non Lar's 'official' NMSP joins National Democratic Front
1984 dry season	Following attack on Three Pagodas Pass, Mon refugees flee to Thailand; foundation of Mon National Relief Committee
12–8–84	Mon National University established (Bangkok)
9–12–87	NMSP re-unified; Nai Shwe Kyin President, Non Lar Vice-President
23–7–88– 18–8–88	Mon-Karen 'civil war' at Three Pagodas Pass; democracy uprising in Rangoon, followed by State Law and Order Restoration Council coup and massacres
14–9–88	Foundation of National League for Democracy

Date	Event (Burma)
17–10–88	Foundation of Mon National Democratic Front
18–11–88	Foundation of Democratic Alliance of Burma
March & April 1989	Mutinies break out within Communist Party of Burma; formation of new ethnic armies in northern Burma, five of which agree ceasefires with the SLORC
11–2–90	Fall of Three Pagodas Pass; Mon refugees flee to Thailand; MNLA detachment sent south to establish control over Mergui District; Mon refugees assisted by MNRC, Burmese Border Consortium and Medecins Sans Frontieres
22–3–90	Joint MNLA-ABSDF force launches disastrous attack on Ye town
27–5–90	General election: NLD wins 392 seats; 65 United Nationalities League for Democracy candidates elected, including 5 from MNDF; SLORC refuses to had over power
18–12–90	Foundation of Democratic Front of Burma (later National Council of the Union of Burma) and National Coalition Government of the Union of Burma
1990–94	'Consolidation' of Mon refugee camps
(23–2–91)	(National Peace Keeping Council installed by military coup in Thailand; first of two administrations led by prime minister Anand Panyarachun; Thailand returned to civilian rule under Chuan Leekpai in September 1992)
November 1991	Following a dispute over logging concessions, Thai authorities arrest and incarcerate three senior NMSP leaders in Sangkhlaburi
2–3–92	MNDF outlawed; leaders arrested
1993 dry season	Construction work begins on Ye-Tavoy railway, characterised by massive use of forced labour
December 1993	NMSP enters into ceasefire negotiations with SLORC
January–April 1994	Thai authorities move Loh Loe refugees to Pa Yaw and Halochanee camps; MNRC establishes new Bee Ree camp in Burma
February 1994	SLORC-Kachin Independence Organisation ceasefire finalised in Myitkyina
March 1994	Second round of NMSP-SLORC ceasefire negotiations; government side rejects Mon 'Fourteen Point Plan'
June–July 1994	Third round of NMSP-SLORC ceasefire negotiations; talks break down over demarcation of ceasefire zones
21–7–94	*Tatmadaw* attack on Halochanee; refugees flee to Thailand
September 1994	Halochanee refugees forcibly repatriated; Thai state energy corporation agrees to purchase natural gas from Yadana field in Gulf of Martaban (construction of gas pipeline completed between 1997–98)
Dec 1994–Feb 1995	Formation of Democratic Kayin Buddhist Army; fall of Mannerplaw; DKBA launches attacks on Karen refugees

Date	Event (Burma)
March 1995	Karenni National Progressive Party agrees ceasefire with SLORC (breaks down in July)
March–April 1995	Further NMSP-SLORC 'talks about talks'
29-6-95	Following a Congress of Mon National Affairs at 'Central' (May 1995), NMSP delegation agrees ceasefire with SLORC (Moulmein)
July–Dec 1995	General Francis Yap's anti-ceasefire Hongsa Command active in Tavoy District
Sept 1995–June 1996	MNLA troops withdraw from 'temporary' ceasefire positions in western Mon State
Dec 1995–June 1996	Thai authorities repatriate last Mon refugees at Pa Yaw (March '96); NMSP, MNRC and NGOs resettle some Halochanee, Bee Ree and Tavoy District refugees; new refugees continue to arrive at the border, citing on-going *Tatmadaw* abuses
March 1996	Formation of Mon Unity League at Second Congress of Mon National Affairs
April–May 1996	Annual Mon literacy trainings initiated across lower Burma; despite setbacks, NMSP undertakes expansion of Mon National School system
From Mid-1996	Anti-ceasefire 'Nai Soe Aung Group' active in Tavoy District
6-11-96	Formation of anti-ceasefire Mon Army Mergui District
January 1997	Ethnic Nationalities' Conference held at Mae Tha Raw Hta; NMSP representative signs 'Mae Tha Raw Hta Declaration'
February–March 1997	Major *Tatmadaw* offensive against KNU Fourth and Sixth Brigades; refugees flee to Thailand; many are forcibly repatriated,
April–May 1997	*Tatmadaw* offensive against MAMD and ABSDF positions in Tenasserim Division; refugees flee to Thailand
24-5-97	MAMD surrenders; refugees subsequently repatriated
June 1997	Burma and Laos join ASEAN regional grouping ('Asian financial crisis' mid-1997 to 1999)
16-11-97	Formation of anti-MAMD Ramanya Restoration Army; over the next two years refugees regularly flee to, and are repatriated from, Thailand; occasionally assisted by Ramanya Human Rights Committee and BBC
From Mid-1996	Anti-ceasefire Mon National Defence Army ('Mon Armed Group') active in Tavoy District
June 1998	MNDF Chairman and MP-elect Nai Tun Thein and other ethnic leaders write to SPDC, demanding recognition of 1990 election results
July 1988	MNDF Vice-Chairman Nai Ngwe Thein writes to NMSP, calling on party to distance itself from SPDC and support NLD
11-8-98	Three Karenni and Shan ceasefire groups call on SPDC to convene 1990 parliament

Date	Event (Burma)
18–8–98	NMSP circulates statement calling on SPDC to convene 1990 parliament; similar statements from other groups follow
16/17–9–98	NLD establishes Committee Representing the People's Parliament; announces support of several ethnic political parties and ceasefire groups, including MNDF and NMSP, following which several hundred MPs-elect and others are arrested
28–9–98	NMSP obliged to recant and issue statement condemning moves to convene 1990 parliament
11–12–98	Nai Ngwe Thein and MNDF MPs-elect Dr Min Soe Lin and Dr Kyi Win sentenced to seven year jail terms (Nai Tun Thein under house arrest); MP-elect Nai Thaung Shein flees to Thailand
March 1999	NMSP withdraws from MUL
May 1999	ICRC team meets NMSP, visits Ye, but is blocked from travelling to Mon ceasefire zones (later, good NMSP-ICRC relations develop)
(Sept Oct 1999)	(East Timor votes for independence; Indonesian army and local militias create havoc; Australian-led UN peacekeeping mission oversees move to independence)
25–10–99	Nai Shwe Kyin and Nai Tun Thein meet in Rangoon with UN Secretary General's Special Envoy to Burma; Nai Shwe Kyin calls for political reform and tripartite dialogue
3–11–99	Nai Tun Thein re-arrested
November 1999	Delegates at NMSP Fifth Congress vote pro-ceasefire elements off party Central Committee
October 2000	Daw Aung San Suu Kyi and Lt-Gen. Khin Nyunt enter into secret talks in Rangoon, aimed at breaking the political deadlock
2001	SPDC relesases some NLD (but not MNDF) political prisoners, and allows the league to re-open some offices
February 2001	Fighting between the *Tatmadaw* and Shan State Army – South spills over into Thailand, destabilises Burmese-Thai relations
27–3–01	Senior General Than Shwe marks Armed Forces Day by raising the prospect of political transition in Burma
9–9–01	MNLA Colonel Nai Pan Nyunt takes 150 men back to war; joins MNDA in opposing *Tatmadaw* (and MNLA) in Ye-Yebyu area
November 2001	UN Special Envoy Razali visits Burma for the sixth time; NLD-SPDC talks said to be progressing, but ethnic minority politicians still have no participation in dialogue process
29–11–01	Nai Pan Nyunt and colleagues form Hongsawatoi Restoration Party and Monland Restoration Army. Clashes with *Tatmadaw* and MLNA ensue.

Bibliography

Books, Theses, Manuscripts and Articles

Venerable Acwo, *History of Kings* (1776; *Journal of the Burma Research Society* Vol. XIII pp. 1-67; translated by Robert Halliday 1923)

Anna J. Allott, *Inked Over, Ripped Out: Burmese Storytellers and the Censors* (Silkworm Books 1994)

Benedict Anderson, *Language and Power: Exploring Political Cultures in Indonesia* (Ithaca: Cornell University Press 1990)

Benedict Anderson, *Imagined Communities: Reflections on the Origin and Spread of Nationalism* (Verso 1991; revised edition)

Benedict Anderson, *The Spectre of Comparisons: Nationalism, Southeast Asia and the World* (Verso 1998)

Aung San Suu Kyi, *Aung San of Burma* (Kiscadale 1991; second edition)

Aung San Suu Kyi (ed. Michael Arris), *Freedom From Fear* (Penguin 1991)

Aung San Suu Kyi, *Letters from Burma* (Penguin 1997)

Aung San Suu Kyi, *The Voice of Hope: Conversations With Alan Clements* (Penguin 1997)

Michael Aung-Thwin, *The British 'Pacification' of Burma: Order Without Meaning* (*Journal of the Southeast Asian Studies* Vol. XVI, II 1985; pp. 245-61)

Michael Aung-Thwin, *Myth and History in the Historiography of Early Burma: Paradigms, Primary Sources, and Prejudices* (Ohio University Centre for International Studies 1998)

Desmond Ball, *Burma's Military Secrets: Signals Intelligence (SIGINT) from the Second World War to Civil War and Cyber Warfare* (White Lotus 1998)

Christian Bauer, *A Guide to Mon Studies* (Monash Centre of SEA Studies 1984)

Chris Beyrer, *War in the Blood: Sex, Politics and AIDS in Southeast Asia* (Zed Books 1998)

Paul Ambroise Bigandet, *An Outline of the History of the Catholic Burmese Mission From the Year 1720 to 1887* (Hanthawaddy Press, Rangoon 1887; reprinted White Orchid, Bangkok 1996)

C. O. Blagden, *The Chronicles of Pegu: A Text in the Mon Language* (*Journal of the Royal Asiatic Society*; April 1907)

C.O. Blagden and G.H. Luce, *Certaine Words of Pegu Language* (*Journal of the Burma Research Society* Vol. XXX, II pp. 371-375; 1940)

Bibliography

C.O. Blagden, *Mon Inscriptions*, in U Mya, Charles Duroiselle et al (ed.), *Epigraphia Birmania* (Superintendent Government Printing and Stationary, Rangoon 1923-1960; multiple volumes).

Boonsong Lekagul and Philip D. Round, *A Guide to the Birds of Thailand* (Saha Karn Bhaet 1991)

Benedicte Brac de la Perriere, *La Bufflesse de Pegou: un Exemple D'Incorporation de Rituel dans le Culte Birman* (*Bulletin de L'Ecole Francaise D'Extreme-Orient* No. 82, pp. 287-299; 1995)

Nigel J. Brailey, *A Re-investigation of the Gwe of Eighteenth Century Burma* (*Journal of Southeast Asian History* Vol.1/2 pp. 33-47; 1970)

Burma Centre Netherlands and Transnational Institute (eds), *Strengthening Civil Society: Possibilities and Dilemmas for International NGOs* (Silkworm Books 1999)

Peter Carey (ed.), *Burma: the Challenge of Change in a Divided Society* (Macmillan 1997)

Chamlong Thongdee, *Three Pagodas Pass* (Political Leaders Magazine 1997; Thai language)

Chao-Tzang Yawnghwe, *Burma and National Reconciliation: Ethnic Conflict and State-Society Dysfunction* (Vancouver 29-4-2001)

George Coedes, *The Indianised States of Southeast Asia* (East-West Centre Press, Honolulu 1968; ed. Walter Vella, translated by Susan Brown Cowing)

Maurice Collis, *Siamese White* (Faber and Faber 1936; reprinted DD Books 1986)

Georges Condominas, *From Lawa to Mon, From Saa' to Thai: Historical and Anthropological Aspects of Southeast Asian Social Spaces* (Occasional Paper, Department of Anthropology, Australian National University 1990; translated by Stephanie Anderson et al)

HRH Prince Dhani Nivat, *A History of Buddhism in Siam* (The Siam Society 1965)

Economist Intelligence Unit, *Myanmar Economy: ASEAN's Black Sheep* (18-4-2000)

Jonathan Falla, *True Love and Bartholomew: Rebels on the Burmese Border* (Cambridge University Press 1991)

Christina Fink, *Living Silence: Burma Under Military Rule* (Zed Books 2001)

John S. Furnivall, *The Fashioning of Leviathan: The Beginnings of British Rule in Burma* (*Journal of the Burma Research Society* Vol. XXIX, II 1939

Christian Goodden, *Three Pagodas: A Journey Down the Thai-Burmese Border* (Jungle Books 1996)

Mikael Gravers, *Nationalism as Political Paranoia in Burma: An Essay on the Historical Practice of Power* (Curzon 1999)

Emmanuel Guillon, *L'Armee de Mara: Au Pied de L'Ananda (Pagan-Birminie)* (Editions Recherche sur les Civilisations 1985)

Emmanuel Guillon, *Champa* (in *Dictionary of Art* Vol. VI; Macmillan 1996)

Emmanuel Guillon, *History of the Mons* (Siam Society lecture, 18-2-99)

Emmanuel Guillon, *The Mons: A Civilisation in Southeast Asia* (The Siam Society 1999)

Emmanuel Guillon and Nai Pan Hla, *A Mon Copper Plate in the National Library, Bangkok* (*Journal of the Burma Research Society* Vol. LV; 1972)

D.G.E. Hall, *A History of South-East Asia* (Macmillan 1981; fourth edition)

Robert Halliday, *The Talaings* (Government Printing Office, Rangoon 1917; reprinted Orchid Press, Bangkok 1999, with an introduction by Michael Smithies)

Robert Halliday, *The Mons of Burma and Thailand: Volume One - The Talaings & Volume Two - Selected Articles* (White Lotus, Bangkok 2000 - ed. and with a Foreword and photographs by Christian Bauer)

Bibliography

Robert Halliday, *A Mon-English Dictionary* (The Siam Society 1922; Ministry of Union Culture, Government of the Union of Burma 1955)

J.M. Haswell, *Grammatical Notes and Vocabulary of the Peguan Language* (American Missionary Press, Rangoon 1874)

E.J. Hobsbawm, *Nations and Nationalism Since 1780: Programme, Myth, Reality* (Cambridge University Press 1990; second edition)

Gustaaf Houtman, *Mental Culture in Burmese Crisis Politics: Aung San Suu Kyi and the National League For Democracy* (Monograph 33, Institute for the Study of Languages and Cultures of Asia and Africa Tokyo University of Foreign Studies 1999)

Maria Hovemyr, *A Bruised Reed Shall Not Break A History of the 16th District of the Church of Christ in Thailand* (Office of History, Church of Christ in Thailand 1997)

F.E. Huffman, *Burmese Mon, Thai Mon and Nyah Kur: A Synchronic Comparison* (Mon-Khmer Studies, Vols XVI-XVII pp. 31-84; 1987)

C.F. Keyes (ed.), *Ethnic Adaptation and Identity: The Karen on the Thai Frontier With Burma* (Institute for the Study of Human Issues, Philadelphia 1979)

C.F. Keyes, *The Golden Peninsula: Culture and Adaptation in Mainland Southeast Asia* (University of Hawai'i Press 1995; reprint edition)

Hazel J. Lang, *Fear and Sanctuary: Burmese Refugees in Thailand* (Cornell Southeast Asia Program 2002)

Frank Lebar, Gerald Hickey and John Musgrave, *Ethnic Groups of Mainland Southeast Asia* (Human Relations Area Files Press, New Haven 1967)

Victor B. Lieberman, *Ethnic Politics in Nineteenth Century Burma* (Modern Asian Studies Vol. 12/3, pp. 455-82; 1978)

Victor B. Lieberman, *Burmese Administrative Cycles: Anarchy and Conquest, c.1580-1760* (Princeton University Press 1984)

Arend Lijphart, *Democracy in Plural Societies: A Comparative Exploration* (Yale University Press 1977)

Bertil Lintner, *Outrage: Burma's Struggle for Democracy* (White Lotus 1990)

Bertil Lintner, *Bertil Burma in Revolt: Opium and Insurgency Since 1948* (Westview 1994)

G.H. Luce, *Mons of the Pagan Dynasty* (Rangoon University 1950)

G.H. Luce et al, *Early Pagan, Old Burma* (Antibus Asiae and Institute of Fine Arts, New York University 1969 [Vol. 1] & 1970 [Vols 2 & 3])

Maung Maung Gyi, *Report of the Revision Settlement of the Bassein District, Season 1935-39* (Rangoon 1941)

Mon Unity League, *The Mon: A People Without a Country* (Bangkok 1997; reprinted 1999)

P. Nop, *Tangay: The Setting Sun of Ramanya* (Song Sayam 1997; translated by Eveline Willi)

Nai Pan Hla, *The Significant Role of the Mon Language and Culture in Southeast Asia: Part One* (Monograph, Institute for the Study of Languages and Cultures of Asia and Africa Tokyo University of Foreign Studies 1992)

Nai Pan Hla, *Thu-tay-tana Sar-pay Myar* ('Combination of Researches'); unofficial translation

B.R. Pearn, *A History of Rangoon* (Corporation of Rangoon 1939)

Sir Arthur P. Phayre, *History of Burma: Including Burma Proper, Pegu, Taungu, Tenasserim, and Arakan. From the Earliest Time to the End of the War With British India* (London 1883; reprinted Orchid Press, Bangkok 1998)

D.F. Raikes, *The Mon: Their Music and Dance* (Siam Society 1957)

Ronald D. Renard, *Kariang: History of Karen-T'ai Relations From the Beginning to 1923* (University of Hawaii 1980; PhD thesis)

Ronald Renard, *The Burmese Connection: Illegal Drugs and the Making of the Golden Triangle* (United Nations University and UN Research Institute for Social Development/ Lynne Rienner 1996)

W. Courtland Robinson, *Terms of Refuge: The Indochinese Exodus and the International Response* (Zed Books 1998)

D.R. SarDesai, *Southeast Asia: Past and Present* (Westview 1994; third edition), p.135

Christian P. Scherrer, *Burma: Ethnonationalist Revolution and Civil War Since 1948: The Authentic Voice of Ethnonationalists, Insurgents and the Democratic Opposition* (Institute for Research on Ethnicity and Conflict Resolution 1997)

Andrew Selth, *Transforming the Tatmadaw* (Cambridge Papers on Strategy and Defence No. 113, 1996)

H.L. Shorto, *A Dictionary of Modern Spoken Mon* (Oxford University Press 1962)

H.L. Shorto, *A Dictionary of the Mon Inscriptions From the Sixth to the Sixteenth Centuries* (Oxford University Press 1971)

Anthony D. Smith, *The Ethnic Origin of Nations* (Blackwell 1988)

Martin Smith, *Ethnic Groups in Burma* (Anti-Slavery International 1994)

Martin Smith, *Burma: Insurgency and the Politics of Ethnicity* (Zed Books 1999; second edition)

Michael Smithies (ed.), *The Mons: Collected Articles from The Journal of the Siam Society* (Bangkok 1986)

Melford E Spiro, *Burmese Supernaturalism* (Prentice-Hall 1978)

Donald M. Stadtner, *King Dhammaceti's Pegu* (*Orientations* February 1990)

Sunthorn Sriparngern, *Eight Years in Monland* (Mon Unity League 1999; Thai language)

Theodore Stern, *Ariya and the Golden Book: A Millenarian Buddhist Sect Among the Karen* (The Journal of Asian Studies Vol. 27/2 pp. 297-328; 1968)

A.T.O. Stewart, *The Pagoda War: Lord Dufferin and the Fall of the Kingdom of Ava 1885-6* (Faber and Faber 1972)

Martin Stuart-Fox, *A History of Laos* (Cambridge University Press 1997)

Robert H. Taylor, *Perceptions of Ethnicity in the Politics of Burma* (*Southeast Asian Journal of Social Science* Vol. 10, No. 1; 1982)

Robert H. Taylor, *The State in Burma* (Hurst 1987)

Robert H. Taylor (ed.), *Burma: Political Economy Under Military Rule* (Hurst 2001)

Thant Myint-U, *The Making of Modern Burma* (Cambridge University Press 2001)

Thongchai Winichakul, *Maps and the Formation of the Geo-Body of Siam*, in Tonnesson and Antlov (1996)

Stein Tonnesson and Hans Antlov (eds) *Asian Forms of the Nation* (Curzon 1996)

Nai Tun Thein, *Mon Political History* (Mon Unity League, Bangkok 1999; translated from the Burmese by Poo C-, Bellay Htoo and S-S-)

Nai Tun Thein (Nai Thaw Sun), *A History of Hongsawatoi* (Mon language), *The Mon Kingdom of Thaton, Pada and Hongsawaddy* (Burmese language)

Vadhana Purakasikara, *The Characteristics of Thai Words of Mon Origin* (Tech Promotion and Advertising, Bangkok 1998; Thai language)

G. Wijeyewardene (ed.), *Ethnic Groups Across Boundaries in Mainland Southeast Asia* (Institute of Southeast Asia Studies, Singapore 1996)

Donald Wilson, *The Contented Mons of Koh Kret* (Crescent Press Agency 1997)

Dorothy Woodman, *The Making of Burma* (The Cresset Press 1962)

Deborah Wong, *Mon Music For Thai Deaths: Ethnicity and Status in Thai Urban Funerals* (Asian Folklore Studies, Vol. LVII [No. 1] pp. 99-130; 1998)

David K. Wyatt, *Thailand: A Short History* (Yale University Press 1984)
Yan Nyein Aye, *Endeavours of the Myanmar Armed Forces Government for National Reconciliation* (U Aung Zaw, publisher 4-1-2000)

Government Publications

Government of the Union of Burma, *Burma and the Insurrections* (Rangoon September 1949)
Ministry of Border Areas and National Races Development, Government of the Union of Myanmar, *Measures Taken For Development of Border Areas and National Races (1989-1992)* (Rangoon 1992)
Ministry of Home and Religious Affairs, Government of the Union of Myanmar, *Kayah State 1983 Population Census* (Rangoon 1987)
Ministry of Home and Religious Affairs, Government of the Union of Myanmar, *Mon State 1983 Population Census* (Rangoon 1987)
Ministry of Information, Government of the Union of Myanmar, *Burma Communist Party's Conspiracy to Take Over State Power* (Rangoon 8-9-89)
Ministry of Information, Government of the Union of Myanmar, *The Conspiracy of Treasonous Minions Within the Myanmar Naing-Ngan and Traitorous Cohorts Abroad* (Rangoon 9-9-89 & 23-10-89)
Office of the Superintendent, Government Printing, *Report on the Census of British Burma* August 1872 (Rangoon 1875)
Office of the Superintendent, Government Printing, *Government of India Census of 1891, Imperial Series Volume IX - Burma Report* (Rangoon 1892)
Office of the Superintendent, Government Printing, *District Gazetteers*, multiple volumes (Rangoon 1915)
Office of the Superintendent, Government Printing, *Union of Burma First Stage Census - 1953* (Rangoon 1957)
US Government, Department of State, *Country Commercial Guide Financial Year 1999: Burma* (1998)
US Government Department of State, Bureau for International Narcotics and Law Enforcement Affairs, *International Strategy Report* (Washington DC, March 1999)

Reports, Manuscripts and Grey Literature (including United Nations documents)

[For statements and press releases, see main text.]

Amnesty International, *Thailand: Burmese and Other Asylum-Seekers at Risk* (September 1994; ASA 39/02/94)
Amnesty International, *Myanmar: Human Rights Violations Against Ethnic Minorities* (August 1996; ASA 16/38/96)
Amnesty International, *Myanmar: Human Rights Under Attack* (July 1997; ASA 16/02/97)
Burmese Border Consortium, *Programme Reports (passim)*
Burma Ethnic Research Group, *Forgotten Victims of a Hidden War: Internally Displaced Karen in Burma* (Chiang Mai 1998)
Co-ordinating Committee for Services to Displaced People in Thailand, *Educational Assessment of Mon and Karenni Refugee Camps on the Thai/ Burmese Border* ('The Education Survey'; Bangkok 1995)

Co-ordinating Committee for Services to Displaced People in Thailand, *Educational Assessment of Karen Refugee Camps on the Thai/ Burmese Border* (Bangkok 1996)

Earth Rights International, *Total Denial Continues: Earth Rights Abuses Along the Yadana and Yetagun Pipelines in Burma*

Human Rights Watch/ Asia, *The Mon: Persecuted in Burma, Forced Back from Thailand* (C614; December 1994)

Human Rights Watch/ Asia, *The Rohingya Muslims: Ending a Cycle of Exodus?* (C8089; September 1996)

Human Rights Watch/ Asia, *Burma/ Thailand: No Safety in Burma, No Sanctuary in Thailand* (C906; July 1997)

Human Rights Watch/ Asia, *Burma/ Thailand: Unwanted and Unprotected - Burmese Refugees in Thailand* (C1006; October 1998)

Human Rights Watch/ Asia, *Burma/ Bangladesh: Burmese Refugees in Bangladesh - Still No Durable Solution* (C1203; May 2000)

Images Asia, *No Childhood At All: Child Soldiers in Burma* (Chiang Mai 1997)

Images Asia, *A Question of Security* (Chiang Mai 1998)

International Crisis Group, *Myanmar: Civil Society Too Weak to Effect Change* (Bangkok/Brussels, 6-12-01)

International Labour Organisation, Commission of Enquiry, *Forced Labour in Myanmar (Burma)* (Geneva 1998)

International Labour Organisation, *Developments Concerning the Question of the Observance of the Government of the Union of Myanmar of the Forced Labour Convention, 1930 (No. 29): Report of the High-Level Team* (Geneva November 2001)

Jesuit Refugee Service, *Compassion and Collusion: the Mon Repatriation and the Illusion of Choice* (Bangkok 1996)

Kachin Independence Organisation, *Kachin Resettlement Report* (1995)

Karen National Union, Information Department, *Conditions in the Gas Pipeline Area* (1996)

Mon Information Service, *Forced Labour on the Ye-Tavoy Railway Construction* (Bangkok 1996)

Mon Information Service, *Abuses Against Peasant Farmers in Burma: Emphasis on Mon State, Karen State and Tenasserim Division* (Bangkok 1998)

Mon Information Service, *Atrocities Against Mon, Karen and Tavoyan Villagers in Southern Burma* (Bangkok 1999)

Mon Language Literacy Training Course report (2000)

Mon National Education Committee report (2000)

Mon National Relief Committee, *Mon Refugees: Hunger for Protection in 1994* (Bangkok 1994)

Mon National Relief Committee, *Reports (passim)*

Mon National University, *Mon National University Charter* (1984)

Mon National University, *1994-1996 Catalog* (1996)

Mon Relief and Development Committee, *Reports (passim)*

New Mon State Party, *Answer to Questionnaire on Mon Freedom Movement* (Mon National University 1985)

New Mon State Party, *When Will the Civil War in Burma Be Over?* (1988)

New Mon State Party, *Fundamental Political Policy and Fundamental Constitution of Administration* (Department of Party Procedure 15-12-94; Mon language)

New Mon State Party, *Report on Activities of the New Mon State Party* (1994)

Overseas Mon Young Monks Union, *Buddhist Way to Democracy: Mon Young Monks Magazine* (Bangkok April 1992)

Overseas Mon Young Monks Union, *Mon: the Forgotten Refugees* (Bangkok August 1994)

Overseas Mon Young Monks Union, *La Gam Bop Paw* (Bangkok February 2000)

Dr S-M- *The Mon Language: an Endangered Species* (unpublished mss 1999)

Nai Shwe Kyin *Resume of Nai Shwe Kyin* (1994; revised 1999)

Martin Smith, *Paradise Lost? The Suppression of Environmental Rights and Freedom of Expression in Burma* (1994)

Thein Lwin, *Education in Burma (1945-1999)* (manuscript 10-7-99)

Thein Lwin, *The Teaching of Ethnic Language and the Role of Education in the Context of Mon Ethnic Nationality in Burma - Initial Report of the First Phase of the Study on the Thai-Burma Border (November 1999-February 2000)* (manuscript 3-3-2000)

United Nations High Commissioner for Refugees, *Handbook Voluntary Repatriation: International Protection* (Geneva 1996)

United Nations High Commissioner for Refugees, *Refugees and Others of Concern to UNHCR - 1999 Statistical Overview* (Geneva 2000)

United Nations Office for the Co-ordination of Humanitarian Affairs, *Guiding Principles on Internal Displacement* (Geneva and New York 2000)

Woman's American Baptist Foreign Mission Society, *Faithful Unto Death* (New York 1950)

World Resources Institute, Logging Burma's Frontier Forests: Resources and the Regime (1998)

Journals, Periodicals and News Media Quoted

[For statements and press releases, see main text.]

Bangkok Phuchatkan (Thai language newspaper)

The Bangkok Post (English language newspaper)

Burma Debate (English language journal, USA)

Burma Issues (English language newsletter/ journal, Bangkok)

The BurmaNet News (electronic newspaper www.burmanet.org)

Focus (English language magazine)

Independent Mon News Agency (English language e-news service)

Information Sheet (posted by SPDC to <soc.culture.burma> usegroup)

The Irrawaddy (English language magazine, Chiang Mai)

Kao Wao News Agency (English language e-newsletter)

Kwe Klu (KNU-affiliated, Karen language journal)

The Nation (English language newspaper, Bangkok)

The New Light of Myanmar(English and Burmese language government-controlled newspaper, Rangoon)

The Mon Forum (English language)

NBC News (news agency)

Thai-Yunan Project Newsletter (Australian National University)

Also consulted

Bop Htaw ('Golden Sheldrake', Mon language)

Kao San Mon (Thai language)

Khit Poey ('Our Times', Mon language)

Mon Students Bulletin (Overseas Mon National Students Organisation, Mon language)

New Mon State Party Journal (Mon and Burmese language)

Snong Tine ('Northern Star', Mon language)

Thai Ramon Association Newsletter (Thai and Mon language)

Internet Resources

Selected Mon Websites
Australia Mon Association
<http://www.geocities.com/CapitolHill/Congress/7408>
Mon Community of Canada
<http://www.geocities.com/Athens/Column/8582>
Mon Culture and Literature Survival Project
<http://www.monland.org>
The Mon Forum
<http:/www.monforum.cjb.net>
Mon Information Homepage (University of Albany, includes Mon hypertext
    grammar)
<http://cscmosaic.albany.edu/~gb661>
Monland Restoration Council
<http://www.monlandnet.org>
Mon Unity League
http://www. geocities.com/Athens/Bridge/1256

Other Websites
Amnesty International
<http://www.amnesty.org>
Free Burma Coalition (information and links to opposition and other websites)
<http://www.freeburma.org>
Global IDP Database
<http://www.idpproject.org>.
Human Rights Watch
<http://www.hrw.org>
Karen Website
<http://www.karen.org>
Myanmars Net (information and links to government, commercial and opposition
    websites)
http://www.myanmars.net
Open Society Institute, Burma Project (information and links)
http://www.soros.org/burma
Unrepresented Nations and Peoples' Organisation
<http://www.unpo.org>

Index

[Page numbers in *italics* refer to entries in the notes.]